HANDBOOK OF
FORENSIC DRUG ANALYSIS

HANDBOOK OF FORENSIC DRUG ANALYSIS

Editor:
Frederick P. Smith, Ph.D.

With contributions by:
Sotiris A. Athanaselis, Ph.D.
Maciej J. Bogusz, M.D., Dr. Sc.
John T. Cody, Ph.D., D-FTCB
John Hugel
David A. Kidwell
David C. Lankin, Ph.D.
John Mario
John A. Meyers
Robert B. Palmer, Ph.D., DABAT
Charles Tindall, Ph.D., DABC
Jane S.-C. Tsai, Ph.D., FACB

Series Editor:
Jay A. Siegel

ELSEVIER
ACADEMIC
PRESS

Amsterdam • Boston • Heidelberg • London • New York • Oxford
Paris • San Diego • San Francisco • Singapore • Sydney • Tokyo

Acquisitions Editor	Mark Listewnik
Project Manager	Sarah Hajduk
Associate Acquisitions Editor	Jennifer Soucy
Developmental Editor	Pamela Chester
Marketing Manager	Christian Nolin
Cover Design	Dick Hannus
Composition	SNP Best-Set
Printer	The Maple-Vail Book Manufacturing Group

Elsevier Academic Press

30 Corporate Drive, Suite 400, Burlington, MA 01803, USA
525 B Street, Suite 1900, San Diego, California 92101-4495, USA
84 Theobald's Road, London WC1X 8RR, UK

Library of Congress Cataloging-in-Publication Data
APPLICATION SUBMITTED

British Library Cataloguing in Publication Data
A catalogue record for this book is available from the British Library

ISBN: 0-12-650641-8

For all information on all Elsevier/Academic Press publications
visit our Web site at www.academicpressbooks.com or www.books.Elsevier.com.

Transferred to Digital Printing 2009

CONTENTS

FOREWORD

A glance at the publications list of most large publishers indicates that books on the subject of forensic science are flourishing. A recent search of the books for sale on the topic of drug and pharmaceutical analysis at *Amazon.com* had 303 entries! Why, then, do the editors of this *Handbook of Forensic Drug Analysis* believe that another entry in this field is needed? The reason is that there is a gap in the available works on drug analysis: a comprehensive, detailed, up-to-date work aimed at drug chemists and other scientists who need to analyze abused drugs. Many books discuss drug analysis and even present a few methods in some detail, but there is no volume that covers all of the important methods of analysis on the most commonly abused drugs in a comprehensive way.

There are literally hundreds of drugs that are commonly abused, and many of these are legally sanctioned by many countries. In the United States, the Uniform Drug Control Act covers many of the most common illicit drugs. But if one looks at what drugs show up in forensic drug laboratories day after day all over the world, one finds really only a handful of common ones. The *Handbook of Forensic Drug Analysis* covers these few, most important illicit drugs. They include marijuana, cocaine, the major opiates, the common hallucinogens, and amphetamines. Beyond these drugs, the *Handbook* also explores the subject of clandestine laboratories, which are becoming an epidemic in the United States, especially methamphetamine labs. Detailed methods for handling and analyzing the drugs and other materials seized from these labs are presented. There is also a major chapter on immunoassay technologies applied to illicit drugs. Very few works on drug analysis even mention immunoassay methods, let alone describe them in detail, yet they are widely used in workplace drug testing and drug screenings.

The *Handbook of Forensic Drug Analysis* is not meant for the casual reader interested in gaining an overview of illicit drugs. This book is for the serious scientist who needs to have the latest comprehensive information on the analysis of the most common illicit drugs.

The editor of this volume is Dr. Frederick P. Smith at the University of New Haven, West Haven, Connecticut. Dr. Smith has spent his career in research, publishing, and teaching in the area of forensic drug chemistry and is recognized as one of the most qualified U.S. scientists in the field. He has assembled a veritable who's who of experts in this field to contribute their special insights and knowledge about controlled substances. Readers and users of this handbook will find the most current and comprehensive information available on the subject of the analysis of illicit drugs.

Jay Siegel
Director, Forensic and Investigative Sciences Program
Indiana University, Purdue University, Indianapolis
Indianapolis, Indiana

PREFACE

Forensic drug analysts and toxicologists utilize methods and techniques that continue to develop rapidly. To this end, forensic scientists need comprehensive information concerning drug analysis. Many have found it difficult to find in-depth information on drug analysis in one place. Although the field is constantly changing, this book attempts to compile current information on the analysis of illicit drugs, condensed and distilled to provide analytical applications appropriate to diverse needs, in hopes of making this information readily accessible. Of particular value throughout are the authors' comments concerning the relative value of the analytical methods for each of the drug classes. I hope this will be useful not only to forensic drug analysts and toxicologists but also to advanced students of forensic science, attorneys involved in drug analysis litigation, scientists working in methods research and development, technicians employed in drug-testing laboratories, and others whose work requires substantive penetration of complex drug analysis problems.

While many different drugs are subject to abuse, cannabis, hallucinogens, cocaine, opioids, and amphetamines comprise the common drugs-of-abuse classes. These drugs vary widely in origin, from plant material to semisynthetic plant derivatives to purely synthetic drugs. Due to the distinct chemical properties of these drugs, the analytical methods presented in this book provide not only immediately useful solutions to forensic practitioners but also models for future drug analysis problems as the field evolves. The prevalence of illicit-drug use in today's society ensures the analysis of these substances a permanent place in modern forensic laboratories.

In addition to the major emphasis on methods available for the analysis of the major categories of misused drugs, the rapid growth of methamphetamine synthesis warrants special consideration. Low-cost methods include color (or spot) tests, thin-layer chromatography (TLC), spray visualization methods, and microcrystal tests. Traditional instrumental methods, such as gas chromatography (GC), GC/mass spectrometry (GC/MS), infrared (IR) spectroscopy, and ultraviolet (UV) spectroscopy, comprise moderate-cost instrumental techniques that often require extraction and, with GC, derivatization. Both low-cost and higher-cost methods of analysis are addressed. The explosive growth in clandestine drug laboratories worldwide, particularly involving methamphetamine, warrants the extensive consideration given this topic in a separate chapter (Chapter 8). This is designed to assist law enforcement and forensic drug analysts in the numerous challenges they face dealing with illicit-drug manufacture. Immunoassay (IA) methods can be applied to solid dosage analysis of controlled substances easily, without extensive extraction and purification. For this reason, forensic toxicologists find these methods indispensable for analyzing biological specimens for abused drugs.

Chapter 2 provides a concise review of immunoassay technology for drugs-of-abuse testing. Starting with historical and theoretical background information, this chapter explains clearly each immunoassay class: radioimmunoassay (RIA), enzyme immunoassay (EIA), enzyme multiplied immunoassay technique (EMIT), enzyme-linked immunosorbent technique (ELISA), fluorescent polarization immunoassay (FPIA), and kinetic interaction of microparticles in solution (KIMS). Onsite (point-of-collection) immunoassays are described next. The final section summarizes the important subject of performance characteristics used for evaluation and quality management.

Chapter 3 is an extensively referenced treatise that provides the scientific underpinning for the history, extraction, derivatization, and determination of cannabinoids. The authors have crime laboratory, academic, and industry expertise with cannabis. Their chapter contains a thorough evaluation of the background and analysis of cannabis and related materials. They begin with a useful discussion of why law enforcement officers perform qualitative field tests, how laboratory personnel analyze cannabis, and how the courts interpret analytical results. In their review of field and laboratory testing they compare current field tests for plant material, resin, and liquid cannabis products. Their comprehensive literature review shows how various authors have evaluated laboratory tests to identify cannabis with forensically acceptable certainty using combinations of wet chemical, microscopic, chromatographic, and spectroscopic methods. In addition, they discuss trace cannabis residues on drug-use paraphernalia. The authors cover botanical features, both macroscopic and microscopic. Likewise, the array of cannabinoids specific to cannabis preparations are described in the context of their identification by TLC, liquid chromatography (LC), and GC/MS. Test methods are described in detail, with appropriate cautions concerning the strengths and limitations of analytical results. The chapter includes the recommendations for cannabis identification made by professional organizations, including the United Nations Drug Control Program (UNDCP), the Scientific Working Group for Seized Drug

Analysis (SWGDRUG), the International Association of Official Analytical Chemists (AOAC), and the American Board of Criminalists (ABC), as well as those of senior scientists of national laboratory systems in the United States, Britain, Australia, and Holland. As an additional investigative tool, the authors show how "profiling" cannabinoids could assist law enforcement with tactical intelligence. Specific cannabinoid immunoassays occupy an entire section, where they are compared and evaluated. Separately, DNA typing of cannabis is described as a novel, nonchromatographic approach. While unusually broad in scope, this chapter provides the depth requisite to understanding diverse results from cannabis analyses.

Chapter 4, on hallucinogens, provides a different and very useful approach to forensic drug analysis. The authors explain the theory and practical application of major instruments, including IR, Fourier transform infrared (FTIR), mass spectrometry, and nuclear magnetic resonance (NMR). While each instrument has special applications to hallucinogens (lysergic acid diethylamine/LSD, tryptamines, phencyclidine/PCP, and phenylalkylamines/MDMA), the authors' approach assists the forensic analyst with helpful background for the use of these instrumental methods with other drugs. Generous use of spectra and related figures clearly illustrate the techniques.

Chapter 5 reviews the forensic analysis of cocaine. Because cocaine abuse prevalence transcends economic boundaries, the authors present a range of analytical approaches. The authors explain simple, low-cost, noninstrumental techniques (i.e., microcrystal tests, spot tests, and thin-layer chromatography). Photomicrographs of the crystal tests provide useful illustrations not readily available elsewhere. Cocaine-related immunoassays are compared and evaluated. A wide range of instrumental techniques are described, including several less commonly employed in a forensic setting as well as those that find wide application, such as gas chromatography with nitrogen-phosphorous detection (GC-NPD), high-performance liquid chromatography (HPLC), capillary zone electrophoresis (CZE), ion mobility mass spectrometry (IMS), GC/MS, tandem mass spectrometry (MS/MS), IR and Fourier transform infrared spectroscopy (FTIR), Raman infrared spectroscopy, and NMR. The meaningful evaluations presented explain the strengths and limitations of these tests, thereby enhancing the forensic utility of this chapter.

Chapter 6, on opioids analysis, draws on the author's expertise to shed valuable insights on the interpretation of results, including subtleties such as monoacetyl morphine (6-MAM) measurements. First, preliminary tests include those suitable for field tests on the street drugs themselves (color tests and immunologically based tests) and individuals who may have consumed them (onsite tests). Concerning other initial or presumptive tests, the screening test section presents various opiate-specific immunoassays, common adulterants, and countermeasures laboratories use to defeat adulteration and sample tampering. Particularly useful is the practical information devoted to specimen extraction, glucuronide separation, derivatization, and analysis (routinely by GC/MS). The text addresses efforts to discern opiates consumed inadvertently from foodstuffs such as poppy seed cake. Because the practice of heroin smoking has increased, the inclusion of pyrolysis product research had increased relevance. Specific analytical treatment is given to each major biological fluid (urine, blood, and alternative matrices). The authors discuss therapeutic uses of numerous opioids, including codeine-related drugs, buprenorphine, methadone, tramadol, keto-opioids, fentanyl-related drugs, ketobemidone, butorphanol, and dextromethorphan. Finally, the text critiques methods for comparing (or "profiling") illicit heroin samples.

Chapter 7, on the analysis of amphetamines, reviews the common analytical methods in forensic laboratory and onsite testing. These include immunoassays (both instrumental and onsite) and TLC. The text addresses matrix issues inherent in saliva, hair, sweat, and meconium analyses, with attention to environmental exposure. Because chiral considerations impact forensic interpretations of amphetamines analyses, the author cites numerous references to illustrate approaches taken to separate and quantify amphetamine-class enantiomers. The author highlights the potential of underutilized methods, such as LC and LC/MS. While not widely used in routine practice, their future applicability is evidenced by the research references for these methods as well as for polarimetry and capillary electrophoresis (CE). The author applies "profiling" methods to both biological specimens and solid dosage material. An interesting consideration with amphetamine is whether prescription medications may be metabolized to amphetamine, a subject well researched in this chapter.

Finally, Chapter 8 looks to the future while elucidating a rapidly expanding forensic drug problem: clandestine drug laboratories. Methamphetamine laboratories in particular have proliferated recently due to simple synthesis methods readily available over the Internet. This chapter provides broad coverage of clandestine drug laboratories, including many other illicit-drug syntheses. These include opioids (i.e., conversion of morphine to heroin), sedatives, nonmethamphetamine stimulants (MDMA), and hallucinogens (LSD, DMT, etc.). Syntheses and yields described should help investigators predict laboratory production capacity. The discussion of chemical hazards (e.g., explosives, vapors, acids, caustic bases, liquid/solid spills, and compressed gas cylinders resulting in fires, explosions, severe burns, and potentially lethal toxic exposures) and tactical hazards (e.g., "booby traps") will assist those charged with the dangerous work of clandestine-lab investigation. Finally, the necessary work of environmental impact and cleanup is described. This chapter is designed not only to meet the current needs of forensic drug chemists and investigators who assist law enforcement of clandestine drug laboratory operations, but also as a model for addressing future illicit-drug-lab operations.

I thank the fine team of experts who authored the chapters. Their writing benefits from many years of professional accomplishments and exceptional work in the field of forensic applications involving controlled substances analysis. As editor of this volume, I appreciate their painstaking and diligent efforts to produce insightful treatises. Many thanks are due to the series editor, Jay Siegel, who recognized the importance of this effort and whose constructive comments, creativity, and determination helped mold its direction and completion. I recognize and thank profusely Mark Listewnik, Acquisitions Editor at Academic Press. His vision, technical grasp, guidance, patience, and personal congeniality are truly exceptional. With equally high esteem, I acknowledge Elsevier Science & Technology Books Project Manager, Sarah Hajduk, for her understanding of the complex scientific issues, thoroughness, tact, diplomacy, and undaunted dedication to task completion. Ultimately it is my hope that this book will ameliorate the tasks of those who improve and implement forensic drug analysis methods, to whom it is dedicated.

Frederick P. Smith
University of New Haven, West Haven, Connecticut

Sotiris A. Athanaselis, Ph.D., received his BS in pharmacy from the University of Athens, Greece, in 1981. In 1982 he started to work as a scientific associate at the Department of Forensic Medicine and Toxicology, where today he holds the position of associate professor. He received his Ph.D. in toxicology in 1986 from the School of Pharmacy of the University of Athens after serving for 21 months in the Greek army. He has taught students of pharmacy, toxicology, and medical forensic toxicology. In addition, he is employed as a supervising forensic toxicologist by the laboratory of the Department of Forensic Medicine and Toxicology, developing methodology for the detection of drugs and chemicals in biological samples and performing routine toxicological analyses on biological samples as well as on seized materials, evidence, or paraphernalia that concern forensic or clinical poisoning cases. He has received specialized training on the detection of alcohol and drugs of abuse by the United Nations Drug Control Program, the United States Federal Bureau of Investigation, the Society of Forensic Toxicologists, and the Naval Research Laboratory. He has published more than 30 papers in international scientific journals and more than 50 in Greek scientific journals. He has also made numerous scientific presentations at international and domestic professional conferences.

Maciej J. Bogusz, MD, DSc, studied medicine at Copernicus University School of Medicine in Krakow and qualified as a physician in 1963. He then joined the Institute of Forensic Research in Krakow, eventually serving as head of the Biochemical Laboratory before moving on to the Department of Clinical Toxicology at the University School of Medicine in Krakow. He received his doctorate in 1976 for his work on the usefulness of enzymatic tests in clinical toxicology. After emigrating to Germany in 1986, he held posts in Heidelberg and Aachen, as assistant professor and professor of toxicology, respectively. Since 2000 he has been employed in the Department of Pathology and Laboratory Medicine, King Faisal Specialist Hospital and Research Centre, as a consultant toxicologist. Dr. Bogusz is an expert in the pharmacology and toxicology of illicit drugs and their active metabolites. His work on the application of modern analytical methods (particularly liquid chromatography/mass spectrometry) in clinical and forensic toxicology has made him an internationally recognized expert in this area. He also studies the toxicological danger of herbal remedies. His numerous publications include work on enzymological diagnostics in clinical toxicology, acute alcohol poisoning, the applicability of capillary gas chromatography to systematic toxicological analysis, and the forensic-toxicological study of illicit drugs. He is the editor of *Forensic Science. Handbook of Analytical Separations, Vol.2*, published by Elsevier in 2000.

John T. Cody, Ph.D., D-FTCB, is Director of the Biomedical Science Division of the Interservice Physician Assistant Program at Ft. Sam Houston, Texas, where he directs the teaching of basic science courses and teaches pathology. He received a BA from Iowa Wesleyan College and the MS and Ph.D. degrees from the University of Iowa. His doctoral research was in the area of enzyme mechanisms. Dr. Cody became involved in forensic toxicology when assigned to the Air Force Drug-Testing Laboratory, where he filled a number of different positions and provided affidavits and declarations and testified in numerous federal and military courts. Since that time, Dr. Cody has served as a consultant in forensic toxicology to federal, state, and local government agencies and private industry. He has also previously served as consultant to the U.S. Air Force Surgeon General for Drug Testing. Dr. Cody is board certified by the Forensic Toxicologist Certification Board (D-FTCB) and currently serves as president of that organization. He also serves as chairman of the forensic drug toxicology examination committee. Dr. Cody has given a variety of presentations at professional meetings and published numerous articles and book chapters on forensic toxicology topics. He has served on the American Academy of Forensic Science (AAFS) and NCCLS committees that developed standards for GC/MS analysis. His current areas of research interest include the metabolism of amphetamine and related compounds and LSD. He is a fellow of the AAFS (toxicology) and an active member of the Society of Forensic Toxicologists. He also currently serves as an inspector for the National Laboratory Certification Program. Dr. Cody is an adjunct associate professor in the Division of Physician Assistant Studies at the University of Nebraska Medical School and is on the faculty of the Graduate School of Biomedical Sciences at the University of Texas Health Sciences Center at San Antonio, where he has directed the research of several graduate students in toxicology. He was awarded the Lucas Research Award by the Lucas Foundation for research in forensic toxicology, and several of his students have been awarded the Educational Research Award for their work by the Society of Forensic Toxicologists.

John Hugel has been analyzing suspected illicit-drug exhibits and investigating clandestine laboratories for over 28 years. He graduated in 1974 with a BSc with a specialization in chemistry from the University of Toronto. He began working with Health Canada in June of that year. After 6 months analyzing pharmaceuticals to determine compliance with legislation, he transferred to the Drug Analysis Service, where he is employed to this day. Over the course of his career with the Drug Analysis Service, he has analyzed over 10,000 suspected illicit-drug exhibits and provided assistance in the investigation of about 100 clandestine laboratories. Because of his experience, John is regarded as one of the most knowledgeable persons in the investigation of clandestine laboratories in Canada. His willingness to share his knowledge has led him to spend a significant portion of his time as a guest lecturer at the Canadian Police College in Ottawa, Canada. John has published several articles in the journal of the Canadian Society of Forensic Sciences, *Microgram*, and the *Journal of the Clandestine Laboratory Investigating Chemists Association*. He has served on the executive committee of the Clandestine Laboratory Investigating Chemists Association in several capacities, including the position of president in 2002. John regularly presents at the annual meeting of this chemists' group. He is a member of the team that produced the Drug Yield Calculator—a computer program to calculate illicit-drug yields given an amount of precursor and a known reaction. John is a member of the Canadian Society for Chemistry and the Canadian Society of Forensic Sciences, and he is a chartered chemist in the Province of Ontario.

David A. Kidwell, Ph.D., received his B.S. in chemistry from the University of North Carolina at Greensboro in 1978, *Magna cum laude*. He received his Ph.D. in 1982 from the Massachusetts Institute of Technology in organic chemistry applying Mass Spectrometry, NMR, and HPLC to the structural analysis of organic biomolecules. From there, he received an NRC-NRL Post Doctoral Associateship at the Naval Research Laboratory (NRL) in the area of Secondary Ion Mass Spectrometry, applying this technology to the detection of drugs of abuse. Since 1984, he has been working at NRL developing better screening tests, better immunoassays, and novel confirmation tests for drugs of abuse in the diverse matrices of saliva, urine, hair, and sweat. Dr. Kidwell was one of the first to propose new mechanisms by which drugs of abuse bind to hair, observe bias in hair testing, and point out the inadequacies of decontamination procedures to remove inadvertent environmental contamination. He is a court certified expert on hair testing for drugs of abuse, a field in which he is well known. He is also known for his work on determining drug use by sweat testing, where like in hair analysis, environmental contamination can play a role in generating false positives. More recently, his work has centered on comparing the detection efficiency of hair, urine, saliva, and sweat, development of remote monitors for drugs of abuse and alcohol, and field assays for drugs on surfaces and in saliva. He has published over 60 technical papers and book chapters, made a number of presentations, and holds thirteen patents.

David C. Lankin earned his Ph.D. at the University of Cincinnati in 1972 (Hans Zimmer). Following a 2-year postdoctoral stint at the University of New Orleans (Gary W. Griffin/photochemistry), he joined Borg-Warner Chemicals. During that time, he was involved in research in organophosphorous chemistry and developing NMR capability for the Borg-Warner Research Center in Des Plaines, Illinois. In 1985 he joined the Physical Methodology Department of G.D. Searle (now Pharmacia Corporation), where he is currently principal research scientist and supervisor of the NMR laboratory. He has coauthored more than 50 papers in the field of organic chemistry, with recent emphasis on the structural applications of NMR.

John Mario holds a MS degree in forensic science (1979) from John Jay College of Criminal Justice in New York City as well as an MA degree in philosophy from the University of Connecticut. In 1981 he joined the Suffolk County Criminalistics Laboratory, where his responsibilities included seized-drug analysis and crime scene processing. He currently supervises the drug chemistry section of the laboratory. In addition to lab activities, he teaches forensic science and chemistry at Suffolk County Community College. Jack has published in the area of forensic professional codes of ethics and has served as a Core Committee member of the Scientific Working Group for Seized Drug Analysis (SWGDRUG) since 1998.

John A. Meyers received a BS degree in chemistry from the American University (Washington, D.C.) in 1969. He joined the Bureau of Narcotics and Dangerous Drugs (BNDD) Chicago laboratory in 1970. In 1973, BNDD was merged with and became a part of the Drug Enforcement Administration (DEA). In 1989 John became a senior forensic chemist for the DEA, with a specialty area of NMR. He has worked with NMR since 1976. He has coauthored four papers relating to forensic NRM use. He has presented several papers related to forensic drug analysis in general and forensic NMR analysis. He is involved with the evaluation and selection of new instruments for the laboratory system.

Robert B. Palmer Ph.D., DABAT received a BS degree in chemistry from the University of Idaho in 1990. He then completed both MS and Ph.D. degrees in organic medicinal chemistry at the University of Washington in 1991 and 1994, respectively. For 2 years following, he worked as an National Institute on Drug Abuse postdoctoral fellow at the University of Washington Health Sciences Center. In 1996, he accepted a position as assistant professor of medicinal chemistry and toxicology at the University of New Mexico Health Sciences Center. In 2000, Dr. Palmer relocated to Colorado and continued his training by completing a fellowship in clinical toxicology in 2002 through the Rocky Mountain Poison and Drug Center in Denver. He is currently board certified in clinical toxicology and continues to work as a staff toxicologist and researcher at the Rocky Mountain Poison Center. Dr. Palmer is also a frequent lecturer on a variety of toxicologic and chemical issues, including clandestine laboratories. His current research focuses primarily on venom–antivenom studies, safety of nonprescription analgesics, and the chemistry and toxicology of illicit-drug synthesis.

Frederick P. Smith, Ph.D., is a full professor in forensic science at the University of New Haven. He studied at New York University and Antioch College, where he earned his baccalaureate degree in biology (1974). He went on to study forensic science at the University of Pittsburgh, earning an MS degree in forensic chemistry (1976) and a Ph.D. in analytical chemistry (1978). His dissertation topic involved the detection of drugs in blood stains, saliva, saliva stains, semen stains, sweat stains, and hair. In 1979 Dr. Smith joined the faculty of the University of Alabama at Birmingham as an assistant professor, designing the undergraduate and graduate curricula in forensic science. He was granted tenure as an associate professor 3 years later. He served as the first director of the forensic science program and held the rank of full professor in the Department of Justice Sciences and the Department of Chemistry. Additional appointments include a summer research faculty at the U.S. Naval Research Laboratory in Washington, D.C., and scientific director of AccuTox, a National Laboratory Certification Program-accredited forensic urine drug-testing laboratory. Dr. Smith is the recipient of awards and honors, including the Fulbright Research Scholar Award, the University of Alabama at Birmingham's Excellence in Teaching Award, and the U.S. Naval Research Laboratory's Alan Berman Research Publications Award. His research has been cited in the major print, electronic, and television media, including the *New York Times, Wall Street Journal,* CNN, CBS, ABC, and NBC. He has been invited to speak domestically and abroad. An elected fellow in the American Academy of Forensic Sciences, Dr. Smith has authored or coauthored more than 100 book chapters, reports, and articles in professional journals. Dr. Smith has served as an expert witness regularly since 1982. He has assisted law enforcement and independent clients, examining forensic evidence in more than 5000 cases and testifying more than 100 times in civil and criminal cases located in 15 different states involving federal, military, and state courts.

Charles Tindall, Ph.D., holds a BA in chemistry from the College of Wooster (1964) and an MS and Ph.D. in organic chemistry from The Ohio State University (1967, 1970). After completing a postdoctoral fellowship at the Nucleic Acid Research Institute, he joined the Forensic Science Bureau of the New Jersey State Police, where he served for 26 years as a forensic scientist, laboratory administrator, and, finally, the chief forensic scientist. He is currently the director of the forensic science program at Metropolitan State College of Denver. He is a diplomate of the American Board of Criminalistics and was formerly a fellow in drug analysis. He is currently a member of the Scientific Working Group on Seized-Drug Analysis and a member of the Forensic Science Education Program Accreditation Commission. He is a fellow in the criminalistics section of the American Academy of Forensic Sciences. Dr. Tindall has published or presented papers on breath testing of alcohol and on the use of GC-IR for drug analysis.

Jane S.-C. Tsai, Ph.D., FACB, received a BS degree in Medical Technology from National Taiwan University College of Medicine, where she received the Duke Foundation Scholarship. Upon graduation in 1978, she joined the Department of Experimental Diagnostics (Clinical Pathology) at the NTU Hospital. She worked on two research projects at NTU, first on medicinal herbs, and then on natural toxicants in the artesian well water of arseniasis endemic areas. Her MS research was in environmental virology at the University of Southern Mississippi. She received her Ph.D. degree in 1985 from the former Department of Microbiology, Biochemistry, and Molecular and Cell Biology at The Pennsylvania State University. Her doctoral and post-doctoral research projects were in the interdisciplinary fields of biological response modifiers (cytokines, lymphokines, and various growth factors and receptors), especially in tumor promotion/inhibition, protein chemistry, cellular mechanisms, and assay development. She then joined the Department of Veterinary Sciences at Penn State, where she studied host immunity and developed new assays for detecting Mycobacterium infections. In 1989, she joined the Michigan Cancer Foundation where her research areas included cancer immunology, immune-endocrine interaction, gene expression, and immuno- and gene-therapy. She joined Roche Diagnostics in 1993 and has served as a Director of Research and Development since 1998. Her job functions have included leading and managing the R&D groups in rare reagents, immunoassay development, new technology exploration, and instrument applications. She has coauthored over 100 scientific abstracts and articles in various fields and holds several patents related to drug testing. She is a Fellow of the National Academy of Clinical Biochemistry. In addition, she completed several executive business/management programs and holds a Graduate Certificate in Healthcare Information Systems from New Jersey Institute of Technology.

CHAPTER 1

OVERVIEW OF FORENSIC DRUG ANALYSIS

Frederick P. Smith

University of New Haven, West Haven, Connecticut

Contents

The scientific and legal validity of drug evidence analyses must be defensible to be effective. This requires application of the proper legal statutes, knowledge of the relevant pharmacological properties, and selection of the optimal analytical approach. In addition, chain of custody dictates that evidence integrity be protected by acceptable collection, packaging, documentation, and storage. Occasionally, controlled-substance seizures contain other, associated evidence that serves to link it to specific people or places. Other factors affecting drug evidence reliability are the testing laboratory's capabilities and accreditation. As if to complicate matters, the analyst must decide not only *how to test* but also *how many samples* to test from bulk drug seizures. This chapter focuses on these and related drug analysis issues not covered elsewhere in this volume.

1.1 DRUG CLASSIFICATIONS

Legal authorities require scientific identification of many medications and banned drugs to enforce laws. Legal statutes for drug offenses vary among various local, state, and national jurisdictions. For example, penalties for the possession of *Cannabis* range from as small as a fine to as severe as the death penalty. Some medicinal drugs may be used only with a physician's prescription, while others are freely available "over the counter" (OTC). Occasionally street drugs are concealed in OTC drugs. Likewise, sometimes OTC drugs are marketed to resemble controlled substances. Forensic chemists must distinguish these and identify those materials that violate laws.

Most countries regulate the possession of drugs by imposing sanctions in proportion to the potential hazard to the individual and to society in general. In the United States, controlled substances are categorized into five schedules. In Schedule I, those with the highest potential for abuse and no prescribed medical use result in the most severe sanctions. Penalties apply to individuals who possess, consume, manufacture, cultivate, or distribute any controlled substance in a manner inconsistent with the law. Drugs in Schedules II through V may be prescribed when deemed appropriate, and punishments for improper use generally decrease with the higher schedules.

Drugs may be classified by pharmacological categories. *Depressants*, such as barbiturates, glutethimide, chloral hydrate, methyprolon, and ethanol, have sedative/hypnotic properties that lead to anesthesia, coma, and death with increased dosage. *Stimulants* induce euphoria, a sense of well-being, increased mental activity, and anorexia in some cases. This class includes amphetamines, cocaine, caffeine, and phenmetrazine. *Analgesics* relieve pain. They may be narcotic and nonnarcotic and may be strongly addictive, mildly addictive, or not addictive. *Psychomimetics* create the perception of objects, sounds, smells, or sensations with no basis in reality. They include marijuana, LSD, and other hallucinogens. *Cardiovascular drugs*, such as diuretics and digoxin, as well as *gastrointestinal drugs*, like antiacids, may be less frequently abused. *Chemotherapeutic agents* include antibiotics, and they may be misused more often than abused. This book does not include a focus on drugs that are less frequently encountered in a forensic setting, although the methods described are certainly applicable to their analysis.

In performing literature searches, the same drug may be described under different names. For example, the trade name (Seconal), the generic name (secobarbital), the chemical name (5-allyl, 5-secpentyl barbituric acid), and the street name ("red devils") are all used in different contexts. In the case of chemical classification, names follow a prescribed order of precedence, depending on which functional groups are present, starting with onium, acid, acid halide, amide, imide, amidine, aldehyde, nitrile, isocyanide, ketone/quinone, alcohol, phenol, thiol, amine, imine, ether, sulfide, sulfoxide, and sulfone. The *Physician's Desk Reference* cross-indexes drugs by their different names.

1.2 COLLECTION OF EVIDENCE IN DRUG CASES (DOCUMENTATION, SAFETY, PACKAGING, CUSTODY)

Drugs and drug-related evidence require safe handling, proper packaging, and appropriate documentation (including chain of custody), from collection

OVERVIEW OF FORENSIC DRUG ANALYSIS 3

through forensic analysis and presentation in court. Safe handling includes such precautions as gloved hands and dust masks, when appropriate, to minimize health hazards, as well as full chemical protection suits when potentially lethal toxins are handled, as with clandestine drug laboratories (see Chapter 8). Disposable body suits and shoe covers protect the handler from "tracking" contamination to his or her work or home environment. In addition, personnel wear protective clothing and take other measures to prevent extraneous materials/contamination from being deposited inadvertently during scene investigation. Depending on the drug quantity, various sizes of envelopes, cans, bags, and boxes normally serve as packaging materials, unless large amounts are involved. In some cases (i.e., *Cannabis*), high moisture content dictates air-drying and/or paper packaging to reduce mold formation. In other instances, clear polyethylene bags benefit from the security of heat sealing. Furthermore, transparent packaging allows visual examination in court without breaking the custody seal. Other evidence, such as fingerprints on drug-related paraphernalia (i.e., plastic bags, containers, and pipes), could be destroyed by improper handling prior to laboratory examination. Of particular evidentiary value is drug-related trace evidence (hairs, fibers, dust, etc.), which can provide crucial links between evidence, suspects, victims, weapons, and crime scenes. To a greater specificity, torn or broken fragments (paper, plastic, metal, glass, etc., that may form a physical match/jigsaw fit) and DNA in hair root cells or saliva deposited on smoking materials can associate items to a common origin in a unique, individualizing manner. Though further details on their forensic analysis are beyond the scope of this book, proper collection and packaging of these diverse items will maximize evidence preservation while minimizing potential contamination. To be most effective, each evidence type requires specialized handling and packaging procedures specific to its potential contamination and degradation. *Custody* means within the immediate field of view of the responsible official or locked in secure storage with very limited access. As a matter of custody, in addition to documentation, the presence of one or more witnesses during drug evidence collection may protect officers from allegations of handling drugs improperly. Whenever feasible, it is useful to photograph drug-seizure evidence. This verifies the circumstances of the drug bust, approximate drug quantity, and other investigational aspects. Once drugs are packaged, tamper-evident tape is used to seal polyethylene evidence envelopes as well as other packaging materials, which improves security. The person performing the packaging signs and dates across and overlapping the boundaries of the evidence tape.

Chain-of-custody documentation includes the following: the signature of the person who has custody of the drug evidence, his (or her) purpose for handling it, any changes made in the evidence, the date the evidence was received, the date transferred, to whom, and why. What constitutes a minimum signature varies, but for evidence purposes anything less than the signatory's first initial and surname is usually considered insufficient. Appropriate legal procedures for handling drug evidence include transfer to a locked cabinet for secure storage, photographic documentation, transport to laboratory for testing, weight determination, screening test, confirmation test, and transport to court for presentation as evidence. Evidence may be changed by testing, particularly if sample testing is destructive. This should be documented with reference to the quantity removed and destroyed. Whenever evidence is not within the immediate field of view of the person who has documented his or her custody on the forensic chain-of-custody document, that evidence should be in a locked cabinet. The locked cabinet should have strictly limited access, preferably secure access, limited to the person who placed it there.

1.3 LABORATORY CAPABILITIES AND ACCREDITATION

Forensic drug analysis may rely upon various tests, including spot tests, TLC, HPLC, CE, fluorimetry, IR, GC, GC/MS, immunoassay, and a combination of these. Consensus on the superiority of one method over another is difficult to obtain. For example, Manfred R. Möller once suggested that it would be easier to get two forensic drug analysts to share the same toothbrush than to share the same method of analysis.

Laboratory accreditation implements guidelines to provide quality and standardized results. Accreditation is more easily accomplished when several laboratories are performing the same basic tasks, as with routine drug analysis. Accreditation programs examine both the specific procedure being followed and the general procedure for unknowns. Occasionally in forensic cases, the drug identity or other question to be answered may be unusual enough that only general scientific principles can be evaluated for its detection rather than a set procedure. Certainly, no accreditation program could reasonably include blind proficiency testing for every conceivable drug that might be submitted for analysis.

In the United States the acceptance of forensic testimony has recently experienced rapid revision, which impacts forensic drug analysis (Tagliaro et al., 1998). Expanded from the 1923 "Frye standard" that the scientific methodology be generally accepted, *U.S. Federal Rules of Evidence*, the 1993 U.S. Supreme Court ruling in *Daubert v. Merrill Dow Pharmaceuticals, Inc.* (and subsequent refinements) state that courts should consider at least four aspects before admitting expert testimony. *Scientific* is defined as something founded in valid methods and procedures of sciences based on scientifically valid principles. Evidentiary reliability is based on scientific validity. The four are (1) whether the drug analysis technique or method has been tested (i.e., reputable scientific journal articles, adequate controls used accurately, etc.); (2) whether it has a known error rate (i.e., determined through blind proficiency testing, where known drug specimens are submitted to practicing forensic laboratories as if they were actual evidence); (3) whether the drug analysis technique or method has passed peer review scrutiny (without which courts should be skeptical); and (4) whether it is generally accepted by the scientific community. (Laboratory accreditation of drug analysis in particular facilitates many of these requirements, helping courts to make decisions about drug-testing results.)

Laboratory accreditation for drug analysis encompasses external oversight of laboratory operations, including whether the laboratory facilities are adequate, whether the laboratory personnel have the appropriate background (expertise and experience) and opportunities for continuing education to perform drug analysis tasks satisfactorily, whether the laboratory has a quality control program and the degree to which this program strives to achieve excellence, how the laboratory performs on drug analysis proficiency tests, how the laboratory complies with established standards as determined by laboratory inspections, and other factors that affect the reliability and accuracy of testing and reporting done by the laboratory. An example of specific requirements for urine drug testing may be used as a guide.

1.3.1 LABORATORY FACILITIES

Forensic drug analysis laboratories require safe, secure, and uncontaminated work areas containing the proper reagents and instrumentation. An unsafe forensic laboratory not only jeopardizes the health and safety of workers, but also risks the compromise of drug evidence. Security extends from normal working hours to whenever the laboratory is closed. Visitors (including all service personnel) must be documented and escorted at all times to protect the integrity of drug testing and the chain of custody. Scientific personnel should have access restricted to only those specific areas that their work requires. After-hours security should deter and detect any unauthorized entry to the laboratory. A convenient method of restricting access and recording entry is by the use of key cards connected to a central computer system for logging. Unnecessary clutter can be unsafe, and contamination must be minimized and assessed periodically to learn its potential to affect results. Finally, a laboratory cannot meet modern analytical expectations without the proper instrumentation, maintained and in good working order for drug analysis.

1.3.2 LABORATORY PERSONNEL

The quality of forensic drug analysis work rests on good personnel. The expertise and experience of laboratory personnel require opportunities for continuing education to remain current in forensic drug analysis tasks that may be assigned. Accrediting organizations may require academic degrees for positions such as laboratory director (graduate degree) and certifying scientist (master's or bachelor's degree in chemistry or forensic science, for example). Accreditation organization guidelines for educational attainment may underestimate the value of on-the-job experience. Not all requirements of accreditation need be imposed simultaneously. Accreditation of a laboratory must proceed slowly to allow personnel time for educational improvements and to obtain qualified personnel to avoid disruption of laboratory services. When new accreditation agencies are forming, often current personnel who do not meet the new, more stringent requirements may be "grandfathered," granting them a special exception for a certain time. The work skills of drug analysis laboratory personnel may be brought to acceptable standards and/or improved first by probationary training periods of up to 3 years; in-service continuing educational programs conducted within the laboratory itself; scientific seminars about drug analysis, conferences, symposia, and meetings; and part-time completion of degree programs.

1.3.3 QUALITY CONTROL PROGRAM

A drug analysis laboratory's quality control program indicates the extent to which excellence is a priority. One gauge may be the percentage of quality control samples per drug analysis (frequently 10% in urine drug-testing programs). Where applicable, standards and controls (from different sources) analyzed within established tolerances add confidence to identification and quantification, as do equipment calibration records (how often, how thorough, and what steps are taken when outside of established tolerances) and maintenance records. Written standard operating procedures are necessary in order to reduce subjectivity and to provide objective analysis and interpretation of results. Because reliability of drug analysis decreases near the limit of detection (LOD), it is important to define what method(s) are used to measure the LOD and the limit of quantification (LOQ). In forensic drug analysis, experimentally determined LOD and LOQ use signal-to-noise ratios of $3:1$ and $10:1$, respectively, measured with serial dilutions in the matrix of concern, while statistically determined LOD and LOQ rely on quantification of a series of blank samples (usually at least 10), calculation of the mean and standard deviation(s), applying the formulas LOD = mean + $3s$ and LOQ = mean + $10s$. Although more difficult when analyzing unique substances, written procedures that detail the approach and specific criteria for the analysis of novel drugs provide useful guidance to analysts and crucial insight to those tasked with evaluating a laboratory's performance. An approach to developing procedures for detecting unusual drugs should consist at a minimum of searching the literature for relevant literature references, obtaining standard compounds, placement of reference compounds in a matrix similar to the specimen matrix, and analyzing with standard procedures, all before analysis of the questioned specimen. A fallback approach would be to contact and transfer the specimen to a laboratory better equipped to perform the needed drug analysis.

1.3.4 PROFICIENCY TEST PERFORMANCE

Proficiency tests (PTs) measure drug-testing laboratory performance by submitting specimens containing specific drugs known only to the submitting agency. Open PTs are known to the laboratory to be PT samples, although the specific materials and/or their concentration are unknown. Blind PTs are submitted like any other sample from a client so that the forensic laboratory does not recognize them as PTs. The quality of the PT program depends on the rigor of the PT challenge. For example, where cutoff concentrations are mandated by statute, as in workplace drug testing, PT samples containing 75% and 125% of the cutoff would be more appropriate than ones containing 25% and 250% because the expectation is to distinguish concentrations at ±20% around the cutoff. Similarly, PTs containing known interferences or metabolites, normally present in real specimens, represent more rigorous challenges. The frequency of PTs may vary from daily to yearly, depending on accreditation requirements and the sample volume of the laboratory. Certain failures in the PT program can cause a laboratory to lose accreditation. For example, an accrediting organization may partially withdraw a laboratory's accreditation for incorrectly quantifying a given percentage of specimens; however, laboratories can lose accreditation for reporting a single false-positive result (such as reporting a drug as present that is not present).

1.3.5 LABORATORY INSPECTIONS

Drug analysis laboratories in an accreditation program should be inspected at least annually by an outside panel of experts knowledgeable in forensic drug analysis. The inspection process should have several objective criteria, such as: (1) examining recent drug analyses and checking for compliance with their own standard operations procedure (SOP). (2) Does the SOP reflect established standards and current regulations? (3) Where failure of the laboratory in previous proficiency testing programs has occurred, have specific steps been implemented to correct the deficiencies and are these steps adequate? The inspectors should provide a written report of the results of their inspection. Laboratory personnel should be at least familiar with how drug analyses that they are performing compare to drug analyses by other groups in the world. This can be accomplished by having the laboratory director or members attend national and local conferences and, to a lesser extent, review the professional literature. Also, it is helpful to hold periodic staff meetings where discussions of drug analysis problems are held, each person's tasks are reviewed, and the staff reviews specific literature and discusses that literature. Such a scheme allows the staff to remain current with drug-testing technology and to become aware of how their role in a multistep process may impact the subsequent steps.

1.3.6 STANDARDS

Compliance with established drug-testing standards is determined by any other factors that affect the reliability and accuracy of testing and reporting done by the laboratory. For example, the paperwork trail includes identification of samples, custody, documentation of exceptions (such as a custody seal that was broken, quality control that was not right, what the submitting authority was told before testing, whether the samples were appropriately stored, etc.).

1.3.6.1 Presence of Retest Criteria

One example of retest criteria, in the case of urine drug testing, is the presence of the drug on retesting of the sample (above the LOD) rather than its presence above the cutoff. Is there an explanation for why a sample fails to meet normal criteria when it is retested? For example, benzoylecgonine degrades to ecgonine if the urine is basic, and ecgonine is not normally detected.

1.3.6.2 Checking of Sample Integrity

Are checks for adulteration routinely performed? If not, does the capability exist to conduct such tests if requested? Was the chain-of-custody documentation intact? Were discrepancies present (such as broken seals, a submission form that says it contained a liquid when it actually contained a powder, inappropriate signatures on custody documents)? Were all samples present? Positive samples and all evidence should be saved and stored appropriately for a set period of time, in accordance with the laboratory SOP. Evidence is usually kept for 1 year or more, and notification is normally made to the submitting organization before routine discarding of samples. Are negative drug-testing samples normally discarded or returned soon after testing?

A number of problems arise in establishing a good accreditation system for forensic laboratories. Unlike urine testing for drugs of abuse, drug testing in general is more varied; samples have a history and are frequently part of a larger body of evidence. This makes blind proficiency testing difficult because the examiner would likely know that a sample being submitted was a test sample rather than a case specimen. Frequently, law enforcement would not have the funds or knowledge to submit samples to evaluate a laboratory.

Accreditation of drug-testing laboratories is an expensive undertaking. Smaller laboratories, associated with police units, or private laboratories may not have the resources to become accredited. Accreditation may force consolidation of forensic drug testing into state or regional laboratories. This has the advantage of concentrating resources and allowing modernization, with the distinct disadvantage of loss of local control and possibly greater turnaround times. The loss of private laboratories could increase costs for private litigants and defendants. One possible solution would be for public laboratories to do private testing for a fee. This builds confidence in the public that the government is doing a good job but opens it to criticism by unscrupulous private individuals. Participation in national round-robin drug tests, possibly sponsored by accreditation agencies or national standards agencies, could be an interim solution to full accreditation. Such participation would build confidence that a laboratory performed satisfactorily and make the transition to full accreditation easier or provide tiers of accreditation for forensic laboratories. A list of accrediting organizations and their addresses is given in Table 1.1.

DEFINITION OF TERMS

Accuracy: How closely the laboratory result agrees with an accepted or true value. Philosophically there exists a "right answer" in terms of analytical quantitation. Where no right answer is known, there is a striving for precision rather than accuracy. Often accepted values are not known but are determined by sending duplicate samples to a number of laboratories performing similar work and then averaging the results. This procedure results in a standardization of values but may give results in gross error because of new scientific knowledge that has accumulated. For example, many vitamin standardizations are based on bioassays tied to international units rather than to chemical purity because various forms of the vitamins produce the same

Table 1.1

Accreditation and information organizations

Organization	Contact Information	Comments
ILAC: International Laboratory Accreditation Cooperation	http://www.ilac.org/	Many worldwide contacts for accreditative Country-specific contacts
ISO: International Organization for Standardization	http://www.iso.ch/	Promulgates international laboratory accreditation standard ISO 17025. ISO 17025 is a generic standard for laboratories performing tests and calibrations.
CAP: College of American Pathologists	College of American Pathologists 325 Waukegan Road Northfield, IL 60093 (800) 323-4040 (847) 832-7000 http://www.cap.org/	Web site contains laboratory accreditation checklists and manual. CAP provides proficiency samples in several areas. Four separate accreditation programs: the Laboratory Accreditation Program (LAP), for all clinical laboratories, the Forensic Urine Drug Testing (FUDT) accreditation program, the Athletic Drug Testing Program (ADT), and the Reproductive Laboratory Program (RLAP), directed jointly with the American Society of Reproductive Medicine (ASRM).
ASCLD: American Society of Crime Laboratory Directors	ASCLD, c/o NFSTC, SPJC Allstate Center 3200 34th Street South St. Petersburg, FL 33711 (727) 549-6067 Fax: (727) 549-6070 http://www.ascld.org	Certification program
ABFT: American Board of Forensic Toxicology, Inc.	ABFT P.O. Box 669 Colorado Springs, CO 80901-0669 (719) 636-1100 Fax: (719) 636-1993 http://www.abft.org/ http://www.abft.org/	Certification program
USP: U.S. Pharmacopeia	U.S. Pharmacopeia 12601 Twinbrook Parkway Rockville, MD 20852 (800) 822-8772 (301) 881-0666 (international) http://www.usp.org/	Provides standard reference materials and analysis procedures for pure substances

Table 1.1

continued

Organization	Contact Information	Comments
SAMHSA: Substance Abuse and Mental Health Services Administration	http://www.health.org/	Workplace drug testing and guidelines. Also sets cutoff and procedures for regulated drug testing. Guidelines may be downloaded at http://www.health.org/GDLNS-94.htm
NIDA: National Institute on Drug Abuse	http://www.nida.nih.gov/	Provides many low-cost or free publications dealing with drug use and drug testing
NIST: National Institute of Standards and Technology	NIST100 Bureau Drive Gaithersburg, MD 20899-0001 (301) 975-NIST http://www.nist.gov/ NVLAP: (301) 975 4016 Fax: (301) 926-2884 nvlap@nist.gov http://www.ts.nist.gov/nvlap	Provides standards and some testing technical documents. Manages NVLAP—National Voluntary Laboratory Accreditation Program. However, the accreditation fields are mainly in consumer products rather than areas of forensic interest.
AFIP: Armed Forces Institute of Pathology	(202) 782-2100 http://www.afip.org/	Certifies and inspects Department of Defense laboratories
AOAC: Association of Official Analytical Chemists	AOAC International 481 North Frederick Avenue, Suite 500 Gaithersburg, MD 20877-2417 (800) 379-2622 (301) 924-7077 Fax: (301) 924-7089 aoac@aoac.org http://www.aoac.org/	

physiological effect. Other examples may be in immunoassays where the results depend on antibody specificity and the metabolites in the sample and their individual cross-reactivity. These are easy to verify with spiked samples of pure compounds but can give widely varying results with real samples due to metabolites. For many drugs of abuse, the metabolites are not stable in solution, and degradation products occur in real samples. The best solution may be to pool samples from real users and then send them to reference laboratories to obtain an accepted value.

Blind PT (proficiency testing): Samples submitted by the agency that uses the laboratory services and that are known entities. For example, for urine testing, both certified negative urine and urine containing known quantities of drugs should be submitted in the same containers as patients' samples. Blind PT samples also may be submitted by the laboratory's own quality control/quality assurance department for larger facilities. The identification number for blind PT samples must be an identifier not in use in the general population. For example, the Department of Defense submits blind PT urine sample with Social Security numbers that have yet to be issued. Making up numbers runs the risk of falsely identifying an individual.

CLIA: Clinical Laboratories Improvement Act of 1988.

CV (coefficient of variation): Another name for standard deviation. This should be calculated from the nonbiased formula $CV = S.D./mean \times 100\%$.

REFERENCE

Tagliaro, F., Smith, F.P., Tedeschi, L., Castagna, F., Dobosz, M., Boschi, I., and Pascali, V. (1998). Toxicological and forensic bioscience applications of advanced chromatographic and electromigration methods. In *Advanced Chromatographic and Electromigration Methods in Biosciences* (ed. Z. Deyl, F. Tagliaro, and E. Tesarova). Elsevier, Amsterdam, pp. 918–961.

CHAPTER 2

IMMUNOASSAY TECHNOLOGIES FOR DRUGS-OF-ABUSE TESTING

Jane S.-C. Tsai
Roche Diagnostics, Indianapolis, Indiana

Contents

2.1 INTRODUCTION

The application of immunoassays as the "initial tests" to screen for drugs of abuse in urine specimens is well established and regularly practiced. Immunoassays have also been adapted as initial tests for the presence of drugs or drug metabolites in various biological fluids and forensic matrices. Generally speaking, immunoassays refer to analytical systems that rely on specific antigen–antibody reactions for detecting analyte(s) of interest in a variety of sample matrices. Diverse immunoassay principles have been applied to develop techniques for drug monitoring and analysis. For drugs-of-abuse testing, immunoassays serve as "an economic and efficient screening tool to eliminate negative specimens from further consideration" and "to identify the class of drugs that requires the second step confirmatory test."

Worldwide, a number of government agencies, professional organizations, and forensic or clinical societies have established regulations or developed guidelines for substance abuse management, including the scientific, technical, and procedural guidelines for initial drug screening and confirmation analysis. The types of drugs and specimens tested and the practical utility of immunoas-

Handbook of Forensic Drug Analysis
Frederick P. Smith, Editor

says can vary among different drug analysis fields and disciplines. The "standard menu" of immunoassays has mainly been designed to meet the guidelines mandated by the Substance Abuse and Mental Health Services Administration (SAMHSA). In recent years, SAMHSA has been working on the revision of the guidelines. The next version will contain several major changes but the principle of using immunoassays for initial drug testing will remain unchanged. Current SAMHSA *Mandatory Guidelines* (59 FR 29908, 1994 and 63 FR 63483, 1998) state that the initial test "shall use an immunoassay which meets the requirements of the Food and Drug Administration (FDA) for commercial distribution." The *Mandatory Guidelines* permit multiple initial tests (i.e., rescreening) to be performed utilizing different immunoassays for the same drug or drug class under the stipulation that "all tests meet all Guideline cutoffs and quality control requirements." A sample containing drugs below the cutoff will be reported as negative on the screen. For the specimen identified as positive in the initial test, a confirmatory test that "uses a different chemical principle" is then employed to identify and quantify the presence of a specific drug or metabolite in the "presumptive positive" specimen.

The College of American Pathologists (CAP) offers proficiency testing (Surveys) in all clinical medicine specialties, including Toxicology Surveys. The CAP Forensic Urine Drug Testing (FUDT) laboratory accreditation program does not specify cutoffs but requires that laboratories identify the drug/metabolites tested for, as well as the threshold concentration for each whenever appropriate. The joint *Forensic Toxicology Laboratory Guidelines* established by the Society of Forensic Toxicologists and American Academy of Forensic Sciences (SOFT/AAFS) do not include forensic urine drug testing in the scope, but do specify minimal requirements for laboratories to perform immunoassays. A second immunoassay may be used to "augment the initial screen" prior to confirmation but cannot be used to confirm another immunoassay. Voluntary accreditation for forensic laboratories are also offered by the American Society of Crime Laboratory Directors/Laboratory Accreditation Board (ASCLD/LAB) and the American Board of Forensic Toxicologists (ABFT).

The discussions of immunoassay utility and evaluations for specific drug classes will be reviewed as appropriate in this book in their respective chapters. This chapter aims to provide an overview of the fundamental principles and to serve as a general reference for the commonly used immunoassay technologies for drug screening. The evolution of the development and commercialization of these technologies will be briefly reviewed. Although the commercial immunoassays are referred to directly with their product names in this chapter, their brand names are usually trademarked and identified with a sign^{TM} or a registered sign®. The performance characteristics and quality management of immunoassays will also be discussed. However, due to the vast and ever-expanding number of evaluations and publications in the drug-testing fields, this review and the references cited are not intended to be inclusive.

2.1.1 IMMUNOASSAY OVERVIEW

Immunoassays utilize the specific molecular recognition of antibody–antigen binding interactions to detect and quantify substances that are present in minute amounts in complex biological materials. The antigen and antibody binding pair is a form of ligand and receptor binding pair. Fundamentally, most immunoassays depend upon the labeling of either the ligand (such as a drug analog) or the receptor molecule (such as an anti-drug antibody) to monitor and measure the interactions of the binding pair. Most immunological techniques are categorized and named after the technology used for "labeling." The term label describes any substance that can be chemically attached to an antigen or antibody to convey a measurable property as required for the specific immunoassay.

The labels selected for the designated assay format ideally are capable of sensitive detection and are free from interference by common matrices. The types of labels that can afford the requisite sensitivity include radioisotopes, enzymes, fluorescence, (electro)chemiluminescence, or phosphorescence molecules and microparticles. Depending on the design of each immunoassay methodology, the labeled reagent and its binding partner as well as the reaction modulators are prepared in predefined, optimized, stabilized, and buffered reagent formulations. To carry out an immunoassay, the testing specimen is mixed with the designated reagents according to specific protocols and conditions developed for each of the immunoassay techniques.

Immunoassays for small molecules are based on the principle of a competitive immunoassay. Free drugs in the specimen compete with drug-derivative reagent for binding to a predetermined amount of antibody. These small-molecular-weight compounds are haptens that can react with a specific antibody but cannot induce the formation of antibodies unless bound to an antigenic carrier molecule. The key success factors for the development of a competitive immunoassay include the innovative design and synthesis of two haptens, namely, a hapten for "immunogen" and a hapten for drug derivative. The immunogen is designed for eliciting the production and selection of antibody with desired reactivity characteristics when used to immunize suitable host animals. The "activated drug derivative" contains an appropriate molecular linker that can be attached to a carrier or a labeling molecule. The drug derivative is structurally related to, and immunologically similar to, the drug molecules of interest. Thus the drug-derivative reagent can successfully compete with the free drugs for binding to the limited amount of antibody.

The signal changes associated with the binding to form a labeled "antibody and drug-derivative immune complex" can be measured in a "qualitative" or "semiquantitative" mode. The qualitative mode is employed to identify the presence or absence of an analyte relative to a cutoff value, so the amount of drugs and metabolites detected in any given sample cannot be estimated from the immunoassay. Semiquantitative determinations are conducted by comparing the signal value of the unknown sample to the calibration curve. Questions were raised regarding the use of immunoassays as a quantitative tool (Baselt, 1989; Haver et al., 1991). Indeed drug immunoassays are considered "semiquantitative" in nature because the assay result reflects the summative contribution of all compounds in a sample that can compete for binding to the antibody and is usually not a definitive measurement of the intended analyte.

There are two types of competitive immunoassays, homogeneous and heterogeneous, depending on whether or not extra steps are used to separate the complex of "antibody bound" from the "free" drug derivative in the reaction mixture. The heterogeneous immunoassays require washing or centrifugation to remove the unbound labels, and these physical separation steps can increase the signal-to-noise ratio by decreasing background generated from the free labels and potential sample matrix effects. Thus the heterogeneous assays can more readily achieve lower detection limits for drug screening. In contrast, the homogeneous assays are based on the modulation of the label property by the immuno-reaction and hence can be carried out in one reaction mixture in the original reaction container. Homogeneous immunoassays can be more readily adapted to large-volume processing and automation. Once samples are aliquoted and loaded, a typical high-throughput analyzer can screen hundreds of samples per hour with minimal operator intervention. Automation increases test throughput, lowers testing cost, decreases intra-assay variability, and reduces analyst error liability.

Sophisticated laboratory automation instruments have greatly contributed to efficient tests for both clinical and drug-testing laboratories (Bonini et al., 1992; J. Smith et al., 1993; Palmer et al., 1995; Costongs et al., 1995; Chan, 1996; Domke et al., 2000). Drugs-of-abuse testing can be performed with dedicated analyzers or as part of a test menu of large analyzers. For most instrument-based immunoassays, the order and timing of sample pipetting and reagents mixing can be controlled by instrument operating parameters. The resulting change of the signal generated by the modulating labels is monitored and mathematically related to the drug concentration in the specimen by the analyzers.

2.2 RADIOIMMUNOASSAY (RIA)

Radioimmunoassay (RIA) was first described by Yalow and Berson in 1959. Dr. Yalow received the 1977 Nobel Prize in Physiology and Medicine for her contribution to the development of RIA of peptide hormones. The first RIA that could detect and quantify an abused drug, morphine, was published by investigators from Roche Molecular Institute (Nutley, NJ) and Washington University (St. Louis, MO) (Spector and Parker, 1970). Numerous RIA tests have since been developed or evaluated for drug analysis in a variety of biological fluids and forensic matrices, especially in urine, blood, serum, plasma, oral fluid, fingernails, hair, and meconium (e.g., Teale et al., 1974; Gross et al., 1974; Mule et al., 1975; Bergman et al., 1981; Hanson et al., 1983; Baselt, 1984; Jones et al., 1984a, 1984b; R.N. Smith, 1988; Ostrea et al., 1989; Moody et al., 1992; Armbruster et al., 1993a, 1993b; Ward et al., 1994; Mieczkowski, 1995; Collison et al., 1998; Lemos et al., 1999; Spiehler, 2000).

RIA is a heterogeneous immunoassay and two common methods have been applied for the separation of "free" and "antibody-bound" radiolabeled antigens: coated-tube techniques and second antibody precipitation. The "coat-a-count" technique utilizes a precoated primary antibody in the reaction tube to allow for the removal of unbound, labeled antigen. In the "double antibody" approach, the drug in the sample and the radiolabeled drug derivative compete for binding to the primary anti-drug antibody. The second antibody reagent (e.g., second antibody–PEG complex) is added, which can then bind the primary antibody and yield a complex that precipitates, allowing the separation from the free radiolabeled drug in the supernatant. Samples, reference standards, and controls have to be incubated for the same amount of time (e.g., 60 minutes) and centrifuged at a specified speed and time to optimize the formation of suitable pellets.

Most of the drug-testing RIAs developed in the 1970s utilized ^{3}H radiotracer. Hanson et al. (1983) compared ^{3}H-RIA and ^{125}I-RIA for cannabinoids in blood and serum with GC/MS and found that the three methods gave parallel but significantly different quantitative results. The disadvantages of ^{3}H radiotracer include the relatively low specific activities and the use of liquid scintillation counting. Most commercial RIAs utilize ^{125}I as the label, instead of ^{131}I isotope, due to its longer half-life. Because radioactivity from the precipitated complex is inversely proportional to the amount of drug in the sample, the drug concentration can be determined by comparing average counts per minute (CPM) obtained from the sample with the CPM obtained from the positive reference standard. For quantification, a dose–response curve can be established by plotting standard concentrations against the B/B_0 values, where B is net bound CPM for an experimental point and B_0 is the net bound CPM for zero dose.

Mathematical transformation of data produces a standard curve that plots logit B/B_0 against the natural log of the corresponding standard concentration. Values for unknown samples are obtained by interpolation from the standard curve. The major suppliers of RIA kits have included Diagnostics Products Corporation (DPC, Los Angeles), Roche Diagnostics (previously Nutley/ Branchburg, NJ), Immunalysis Corporation (Pomona, CA) and Research Triangle Institute (RTI, NC). The cross-reactivity profile and regression analysis of RIA kits from different times and/or manufacturers have been analyzed in a number of studies (Bergman et al., 1981; Jones et al., 1984a; Weaver et al., 1998; R.H. Liu et al., 1994; R.H. Liu, 1995; Brendler and Liu, 1997).

One of the advantages of RIA is the low detection limit for quantifying drugs in diverse biological samples while staying relatively free of matrix effects. On the other hand, the disadvantages of RIA include the handling of radioactive materials, the requirement to separate free and bound radiolabeled ligand, limited shelf life due to radioactive decay, and concerns for radioactive waste disposal. Moreover, the RIA procedures are more laborious, with higher carry-over risks, and automation has not been as efficient as with other technologies (Armbruster et al., 1993a, 1993b). One of the examples of RIA instrumentation is the MARK 5 Robotic Sampler (DPC), a flexible, open system that accommodates tubes and plates and supports customized applications with Windows-based random-access software. In addition, PerkinElmer Life Sciences (Boston, previously Packard BioSciences) offers robotic pipetting stations and automatic gamma counters.

2.3 ENZYME IMMUNOASSAY (EIA)

The utilization of enzymes as labels for antigen and antibody in immunological characterization started in the 1960s (Nakane and Pierce, 1967; Avrameas, 1968). Various formats of EIA have since been developed for a wide variety of applications. The most versatile EIA technique is the enzyme-linked immunosorbent assay (ELISA; Engvall and Perlmann, 1971, 1972). The first homogeneous EIA developed for diagnostic applications is the enzyme-multiplied immunoassay technique (EMIT) (Rubenstein et al., 1972). Later, the recombinant DNA technology facilitated the development of "diagnostic enzymes" for developing other enzyme-based homogeneous immunoassay systems, including the new enzyme for EMIT and cloned enzyme donor immunoassay (CEDIA) (Henderson et al., 1986). Enzymes have also been used as amplification means in conjunction with chemiluminescent technology to achieve immunoassays with low detection limits and a large potential dynamic range (Arakawa et al., 1981; Whitehead et al., 1983; Sharma et al. 1989; Pringle, 1993; D.J. Li et al.,

1998). A commercial drug test based on enzyme-enhanced chemiluminescence technology is the DPC (Los Angeles) IMMULITE cannabinoids assay.

2.3.1 ENZYME-MULTIPLIED IMMUNOASSAY TECHNIQUE (EMIT)

The Syva EMIT assays were developed based on the observation that certain enzymes could be inhibited by antibodies directed against specific haptens that were covalently bound to the enzymes (Rubenstein et al., 1972; Rodgers et al., 1978). Drug assays based on the EMIT principle rely on the competition of free drugs and drug derivatives that are conjugated to an enzyme for antibody binding. Antibody binding to the conjugated drug derivative results in modulated enzyme activity that is indicative of drug concentration present in the specimen. The enzyme activity can be monitored spectrophotometrically without the need for separating the bound from unbound reagent in the reaction mixture.

A number of enzymes have been used in the homogeneous EMIT assays. Initially EMIT assays utilized lysozymes and mitochondrial malate dehydrogenase (MDH) (Rubenstein et al., 1972; Rodgers et al., 1978). Curtis and Patel (1978) reviewed the basic mechanism of EMIT and discussed the specific advantages and disadvantages of this method. The original commercial kits included the Syva Emit-st assays and the Emit d.a.u. assays (Irving et al., 1984; Ellis et al., 1985). The change of the enzyme used from MDH to glucose-6-phosphate dehydrogenase (G6P-DH) simplified the assay procedure. Syva commented on the reformulation of the reagents (Gorsky, 1988). The formulations of Emit II use new drug–G6P-DH conjugates and new antibodies to improve performance (Armbruster et al., 1993a, 1994).

A simplified diagrammatic representation of the basic EMIT assay theory is depicted in Figure 2.1. When G6P-DH oxidizes the substrate G6P to glucuronolactone-6-phosphate, it also reduces the cofactor nicotinamide adenine dinucleotide (NAD) to NADH. The quantity of NADH produced can be determined by monitoring absorbance at the maximal wavelength of 340 nm. Antibody binding to drug derivative suppresses the enzymatic activity, but the suppression can be reduced by the presence of free drugs that compete for binding to a limited amount of antibody. The change of G6P-DH enzyme activity is directly related to the rate of NADH production and the change in absorbance. Therefore the concentration of the drug in the specimen is also proportional to the change in absorbance (ΔA) at 340 nm.

EMIT has the advantages of low cost, flexibility, and broad analyzer applications, although the calibration curves are relatively flat compared to other immunoassays. The EMIT d.a.u. assays consist of lyophilized reagents that

Figure 2.1

Diagrammatic*
representation of EMIT

Positive Specimen: Drugs present in the specimen (at or above the assay cutoff concentration)

Preliminary Positive Result: **Antibodies bind to free drugs; enzyme activity is not affected**

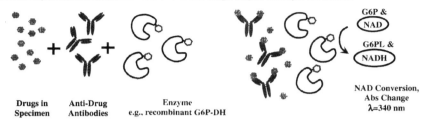

G6P &
NAD

G6PL &
NADH

NAD Conversion,
Abs Change
λ=340 nm

Drugs in   **Anti-Drug**   **Enzyme**
Specimen   **Antibodies**   e.g., recombinant G6P-DH

Negative Specimen: **No drug in the specimen (or drugs present but below the cutoff concentration)**

Negative Result: **Antibodies bind to drug derivatives and modulate (reduce) the enzyme activity**

NAD

No or Low NAD
Conversion,
No or Low Abs Change

*Not to scale - for illustration only

require reconstitution while EMIT II assays employ ready-to-use liquid reagents. Using Syva Emit reagents and a Roche Cobas Bio centrifugal analyzer, F.M. Moore and Simpson (1990) reported the development of a cost-effective assay that can test 2470 samples with a single 100-test EMIT kit while maintaining acceptable precision. Gooch et al. (1992) also described modification of the Syva Emit assay and cost reduction by reagent dilution. However, it is recommended that immunoassays be performed according to the manufacturer's instructions. In addition to urinary drug testing, EMIT assays have been applied to matrices such as blood, plasma, saliva, and meconium (Peel and Perrigo, 1981; Peel et al., 1984; Lewellen and McCurdy, 1988; Blum et al., 1989; Bogusz et al., 1990; Gjerde, 1991; Wingert et al., 1994).

Through serial acquisition and divestiture processes, Syva company is now part of Dade Behring Inc. (Deerfield, IL). In addition to Dade Behring, drugs-of-abuse assays that utilize a similar assay principle are available from a number of companies such as Beckman Coulter Synchron (Dietzen et al., 2001) and Diagnostic Reagents Inc. (Broussard and Hanson, 1997), now part of Microgenics DRI. The analyzers used for EMIT assays have included Dade Behring benchtop or dedicated drug-testing analyzers (e.g., Syra ETS, ETS PLUS, Viva, 30-R, and V-Twin) and the Dimension system, Olympus AU Chemistry-Immuno Systems (Melville, NY), Roche Cobas instrument families, and the Roche/Hitachi analyzer family (Indianapolis, IN).

2.3.2 ENZYME-LINKED IMMUNOSORBENT ASSAY (ELISA)

ELISA has become the most extensively utilized immunoassay since the technology was first developed (Engvall and Perlmann, 1971, 1972). A highly sensitive method for determining the amount of antigen or antibody by means of an enzyme-catalyzed signal change, ELISAs have been adapted to detect or quantify diverse analytes in many different sample matrices. Various ELISAs for drug testing have been developed for forensic and toxicological analyses, although many of them are esoteric tests. An array of commercial ELISA kits is available for various forensic matrices, such as urine, blood, serum, oral fluid, sweat, meconium, bile, vitreous humor, and tissue extracts (e.g., Spiehler et al., 1998; K.A. Moore et al., 1999; Huestis et al., 2000; Spiehler, 2000; Kerrigan and Phillips, 2001; Niedbala et al., 2001).

Excluding reagent preparation, reconstitution, and protocols, essentially all ELISA drug screens employ similar methodology. ELISA kits for drug testing use high-affinity "capture antibody"-coated microtitration plates together with enzyme-labeled drug derivatives. The microtiter plates used are usually in 12 × 8 well strips. An appropriate amount of sample, standard, or control is added to the corresponding well in designated replicates, followed by an enzyme conjugate. The enzyme conjugate competes with the compound in the sample for binding sites on the antibody-coated well during the incubation period. The commonly used enzyme for drug ELISA is horseradish peroxidase (HRP). The enzyme conjugate usually is in concentrated solution and needs to be freshly diluted each day. After washing the wells, substrate is added for the final color development in the presence of peroxide. The ready-to-use substrate for HRP typically consists of tetramethylbenzidine (TMB). When the color development is stopped by a diluted acid solution, the result can be measured by absorbance at 450 nm for result calculation. The amount of drug present is inversely proportional to the amount of signal produced. An optical density value greater than the relevant positive control is considered negative, whereas a value less than or equal to that of the positive control would be interpreted as a presumptive positive. The steps to add stopping agent and to read the absorbance can be omitted for visual qualitative screening. The negative control wells should have developed a medium blue color before adding stop reagent or show a bright yellow color after the reaction is stopped.

Various instrument platforms for ELISA are available with optional data-management software. The ELISA kit manufacturers can assist customers in selecting the appropriate systems tailored to their laboratory needs. For smaller labs, a manual to semiautomated system would be sufficient. For larger labs, there are fully automated two-plate analyzers, or an automated system with approximate throughput of six to seven plates per hour. Companies such as Tecan (Maennedorf, Switzerland), Tecan US Inc. (Research Triangle Park, NC), or Wampole Laboratories (Princeton, NJ) offer solutions for ELISA that include liquid handling, microtiter plate washers, readers, and semiautomatic or automatic, up to fully integrated microtiter plate processors. Various microplate instruments are also available from PerkinElmer LifeSciences (Boston, MA), Bio-Rad Laboratories (Hercules, CA), etc.

K.A. Moore et al. (1999) evaluated the use of ELISA (STC Microplate EIA) and RIA kits (DPC and Immunalysis) as a screening procedure and concluded that ELISA is an adequate alternative to RIA for screening postmortem specimens, including blood and tissue, for nine major classes of drugs. Spiehler (2000) reviewed the use of ELISA for analysis of drugs in hair. Kerrigan and Phillips (2001) compared the performance of ELISA kits from STC (now OraSure Technologies, Inc.) and Immunalysis for the detection of six common classes of drug in blood and urine. The analytical performance was determined in terms of binding characteristics, dose–response curves, limits of detection, sensitivity, intra- and interassay imprecision, lot-to-lot reproducibility, as well as the assay performance using forensic casework samples. The authors concluded that these comparative assessments indicated some key differences in analytical performance.

2.3.3 CLONED ENZYME DONOR IMMUNOASSAY (CEDIA)

CEDIA is a homogeneous EIA that was developed using enzyme fragments prepared by the genetic engineering of genes encoding the microbial enzyme β-galactosidase (Henderson et al., 1986). A simplified diagrammatic representation of the basic CEDIA assay theory is depicted in Figure 2.2. The smaller, amino-terminal polypeptide is called an enzyme donor (ED), and a large residual polypeptide is called an enzyme acceptor (EA). The ED and EA fragments are inactive but can spontaneously associate in solution in a process called complementation, forming a tetrameric enzyme that is as enzymatically active as the natural galactosidase. In the assay, antigens can be attached to the ED in such a way that "the degree of recombination is controlled by the binding of antibodies to the ED–ligand conjugate" (Khanna et al., 1989; Engel and Khanna, 1992). Drug in the specimen competes with the drug derivative–ED conjugate for antibody and thus modulates the amount of active enzyme formed. The amount of β-galactosidase created is monitored spectrophotometrically through the hydrolysis of an appropriate enzyme substrate, such as chlorophenol red-β-D-galactopyranoside (CPRG). The signal generated by enzyme substrate hydrolysis, and hence the resulting absorbance rate change, is directly proportional to the drug concentrations in the specimen.

Positive Specimen: **Drugs present in the specimens (at or above the assay cutoff concentration)**

<u>Preliminary Positive Result:</u> **Antibodies bind to free drugs; EA and ED form active enzymes**

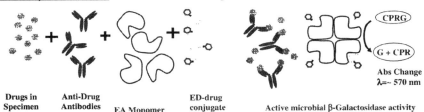

| Drugs in
Specimen | Anti-Drug
Antibodies | EA Monomer | ED-drug
conjugate | Active microbial β-Galactosidase activity |

Figure 2.2

Diagrammatic*
representation of CEDIA

Negative Specimen: **No drug in the specimen (or drugs present but below the cutoff concentration)**

<u>Negative Result:</u> **Antibodies bind to drug derivatives and inhibit the complementation of EA and ED**

*Not to scale - for illustration only

The CEDIA drugs-of-abuse assays have been evaluated in various comparative assessments with other commercial immunoassays and GC/MS (Armbruster et al., 1995; Wu et al., 1995; Fraser and Meatherall, 1996; Cody and Valtier, 1997; M.L. Smith et al., 2000; Spanbauer et al., 2001). The effects of adulterants or interfering substances were investigated in some of these evaluations. CEDIA has also been applied for drug analysis in blood specimens (Cagle et al., 1997; Iwersen-Bergmann and Schmoldt, 1999).

CEDIA technology has the advantages and the capability to develop assays with a linear calibration curve and relatively broad dynamic range by proper selection of antibody and the matched pairs of EA and ED. Because enzyme activity is greatly diminished when the fragment reassociation is blocked by antibody binding, the production of colored products exhibits a linear dose–response relationship to the drug of interest. The rate separation by CEDIA assays between the negative and cutoff calibrators is generally greater than that of the Emit II assays (Wu et al., 1995). However, CEDIA assays require reagent preparation for the reconstitution of the lyophilized reagents and have relatively limited reagent on-board stability and calibration stability.

Through serial acquisition and divestiture processes, the CEDIA business and Diagnostic Reagents Inc. (DRI) are now operated under the company name Microgenics Corporation (Fremont, CA), one of the operating subsidiaries Apogent Technologies, Inc. On the other hand, CEDIA is currently a registered trademark of Roche Diagnostics. The CEDIA assays can be run on a number of analyzers such as the Olympus AU and the Roche/Hitachi analyzer systems.

2.4 FLUORESCENCE POLARIZATION IMMUNOASSAY (FPIA)

A variety of fluorescence-based immunoassays have been developed for clinical diagnostic applications. Fluorescence polarization (FP) was first applied to the competitive immunoassay of hapten molecules by Drandliker and colleagues (1961, 1970). The application of FPIA for therapeutic drug testing (TDM) was reported by Watson et al. (1976) and McGregor et al. (1978). Colbert and colleagues published a series of polarization fluoroimmunoassays for the detection of six classes of abused drugs in urine (e.g., Colbert et al., 1984; Gooch et al., 1994). Since the 1980s, both Abbott Laboratories (Abbott Park, IL) and Roche have developed a series of FPIA-based assay kits for therapeutic drug monitoring and drugs-of-abuse testing (e.g., Jolley et al., 1981a, 1981b; Oeltgen et al., 1984; Rutledge et al., 1987; Herold and Margrey, 1987; Caplan and Levine, 1989; de Kanel et al., 1989; Schwenzer et al., 2000).

FP can be observed when fluorescent molecules, or fluorophores, are excited with plane-polarized light. When a fluorophore is irradiated with light of an excitation wavelength (e.g., 485 nm), some of the light is absorbed and re-emitted within a few nanoseconds at a longer emission wavelength (514–550 nm) in the same polarized plane. If the fluorophores are free to rotate, the polarization of the emitted light will be degraded as a result of molecular tumbling during the short time between absorption and emission of light. If vertically polarized light is used to excite the fluorophore, the emission light intensity can be monitored in both the original vertical plane and the horizontal plane. The degree to which the emission intensity moves from the vertical to the horizontal plane is related to the mobility of the fluorescently labeled molecule.

A simplified diagrammatic representation of the basic FPIA principle is depicted in Figure 2.3. A small molecule, such as a drug–fluorescein conjugate (tracer), can rotate rapidly before light emission occurs, resulting in depolarization of the emitted light relative to the excitation plane (low degree of polarization). In contrast, binding of antibody to the tracer slows down the rotation rate. Thus the polarized light absorbed is emitted with little loss of polarization (i.e., higher degree of polarization). The higher the free drug concentration in the sample, the more the free tracer and the lower the degree of polarization. Calibrators containing known amounts of drug interact with the tracer and antibody to produce a curve relating drug concentration to arbitrary "millipolarization," or mP units. The interactions of the specimen, the tracer, and the antibody under the same conditions yield mP units that can be correlated with the drug level in the specimen by making a comparison with the calibration curve.

Positive Specimen: **Drugs present in the specimen (at or above the assay cutoff concentration)**

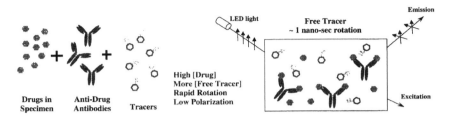

Drugs in Specimen   Anti-Drug Antibodies   Tracers

High [Drug]
More [Free Tracer]
Rapid Rotation
Low Polarization

LED light   Free Tracer ~ 1 nano-sec rotation   Emission   Excitation

Negative Specimen: **No drug in the specimen (or drugs present but below the cutoff concentration)**

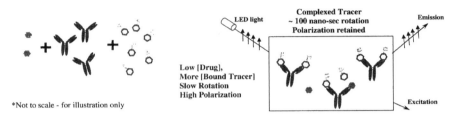

Low [Drug],
More [Bound Tracer]
Slow Rotation
High Polarization

LED light   Complexed Tracer ~ 100 nano-sec rotation Polarization retained   Emission   Excitation

*Not to scale - for illustration only

Figure 2.3

Diagrammatic* representation of FPIA

FPIA has the advantages of relatively good reagent stability, calibration stability, and good precision. The reagents are supplied as liquid reagent packs. It has been reported that vitamin B_2 and some components of the urine matrix may cause potential interference in FPIAs (Kunsman et al., 1998). In general, however, FPIA is relatively unaffected by matrices and has broad applications including the analysis of abused drugs in blood (Bogusz et al., 1990; Keller et al., 2000) and hair (Kintz et al., 1992). Lee and Lee (1989) extended FPIA application to blood, bile, and liver.

FPIA requires suitable instrumentation for measuring polarized fluorescent light, and the assays are generally more expensive. Popelka et al. (1981) described an instrument developed for quantitating FPIA that can automatically measure both polarization components and compute a polarization value corrected for background and optical bias. Abbott Laboratories first introduced the TDx batch analyzer for FPIA for TDM (Jolley et al., 1981a, 1981b). Mikkelsen and Root (1993) evaluated 11 TDM FPIA products from Roche and Abbott using the Roche Cobas FARA II random-access analyzer and Abbott TDx, respectively. The analyzers used for Abbott FPIA drugs-of-abuse assays have include TDxFLx, ADx, and the AxSYM system. AxSYM is an integrated instrument that combines continuous access, random access, and STAT processing for medium- and high-volume clinical laboratories (J. Smith et al., 1993; Costongs et. al., 1995).

Perez-Bendito et al. (1994, 1996) applied automatic kinetic methods to the direct determination of abused drugs in urine by a "stopped-flow FPIA" (SF-

FPIA). This technique provides analytical data within a few seconds by measuring the variation of polarized fluorescence with time during development of immunochemical reactions. The authors reported that detection limits and within- and between-assay precision were better than those provided by conventional FPIA technology.

2.5 KINETIC INTERACTION OF MICROPARTICLES IN SOLUTION (KIMS)

The utilization of latex microparticles for the agglutination test was first demonstrated for the detection of rheumatoid factor (Singer and Plotz, 1956; Oreskes and Singer, 1961). Hemagglutination inhibition (HI) methods were employed in the studies on heroin addiction and the detection of morphine and methadone (Adler and Liu, 1971; Catlin et al., 1973; C.T. Liu and Adler, 1973). Detection of agglutination by turbidimetry using spectrophotometry or nephelometry further extended these applications to quantitative assays (Dezelic et al., 1971; Grange et al., 1977). The technique of light-scattering spectroscopy improved the sensitivity and quantification of particle-based immunoassay (Cohen and Benedek, 1975).

Microparticle agglutination technology as explored by Roche as a technology to develop various immunoassays, including those for abused-drugs screening (Ross et al., 1975; Chiarotti et al., 1985). The commercial microparticles-based products have included the Abuscreen OnTrak immunoassay for point-of-care drug tests (Schwartz et al., 1990b; Armbruster and Krolak, 1992; Crouch et al., 1998a) and the Abuscreen ONLINE instrument-based immunoassays (Armbruster et al., 1993a, 1993b; Hailer et al., 1995; Crouch et al., 1998b; Boettcher et al., 2000). Moody and Medina (1995) applied the Abuscreen ONLINE assays to drug analysis in serum.

KIMS is a homogeneous immunoassay in which the free drugs and the microparticle-bound drug derivatives compete for binding to limited amount of antibody in solution. A simplified diagrammatic representation of the first-generation KIMS assay is depicted in Figure 2.4. The drug derivatives are conjugated to a carrier and then "labeled" with carboxyl-modified, uniform latex microparticles through covalent coupling. The microparticles in solution do not significantly block light transmission through a cuvette, so the starting absorbance is low. In the absence of the drug of interest, the drug conjugates on the surface of the microparticles bind to antibody molecules and form particle aggregates that effectively block light transmission and thus scatter transmitted light. As the aggregation reaction proceeds, the change in absorbance increases. The addition of drug-free specimen to the reagents does not interfere with lattice formation, so the absorbance will increase over a given

Positive Specimen: Drugs present in the specimen (at or above the assay cutoff concentration)

Preliminary Positive Result: Antibodies bind to free drugs; microparticle agglutination is inhibited

Figure 2.4

Diagrammatic*
representation of KIMS(I)

Drugs in Specimen	Anti-Drug Antibodies	Drug derivatives bound to microparticles	No Agglutination, No Abs change with time

Negative Specimen: No drugs in the specimen (or drugs present but below the cutoff concentration)

Negative Result: Antibodies bind to drug derivatives and initiate kinetic microparticle agglutination

*Not to scale - for illustration only

Agglutination, Abs change with time

time period. Conversely, free drug in the specimen binds to antibody and results in the inhibition of subsequent particle lattice formation. The reduction in the rate of absorbance increase is in proportion to the drug concentration.

KIMS has the advantages of stability, low cost, and relatively broad analyzer applications. Since the absorbance change of the solution is measured as a function of time while absorbance from interfering substances does not usually change with time, KIMS is relatively free from interference. The KIMS(I) technology allows for a relatively steep response plot but has a relatively smaller linear range than enzyme-based assays. A new generation of KIMS assays, called ONLINE Gen II immunoassays, has recently been developed for some of the TDM and drugs-of-abuse assays. A simplified diagrammatic representation of KIMS(II) assay is depicted in Figure 2.5. The drug derivatives are covalently conjugated to an aminodextran polymer. The binding of the soluble conjugates to antibodies that have been covalently attached to the microparticles will cause the agglutination reaction, which then leads to the increase of absorbance rate. The binding of free drug to the microparticle-bound antibody causes inhibition of the particle lattice formation. ONLINE Gen II drug-testing assays offer the advantages of ready-to-use liquid reagents, improved serum applications, and a broader measuring range. For example, the ONLINE Gen II Opiates assay (Bruton et al., 2000) can be utilized for semiquantitative measurements using six standards, from 0 to 2000 ng/mL for the 300 ng/mL cutoff, and 0 to 8000 ng/mL for the 2000 ng/mL cutoff. The ONLINE drugs-of-abuse

Positive Specimen: Drugs present in the specimen (at or above the assay cutoff concentration)

Preliminary Positive Result: Antibodies bind to free drugs; microparticle agglutination is inhibited

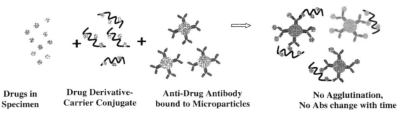

| Drugs in Specimen | Drug Derivative-Carrier Conjugate | Anti-Drug Antibody bound to Microparticles | No Agglutination, No Abs change with time |

Negative Specimen: No drugs in the specimen (or drugs present but below the cutoff concentration)

Negative Result: Antibodies bind to drug derivatives and initiate kinetic microparticle agglutination

Agglutination, Abs change with time

*Not to scale - for illustration only

assays have been evaluated in most of the comparative evaluations of major drug-testing products and GC/MS analysis (e.g., Armbruster et al., 1993a, 1995; Smith, 1993; Ferrara et al., 1994; Baker et al., 1995; Kintz et al., 1995; Huestis et al., 1994, 1995; Cody and Valtier, 1997; Smith, F.P., 1997; von Meyer et al., 1997, Domke et al., 2000; Boettcher et al., 2000; Smith, M.L. et al., 2000).

The ONLINE assays can be run using a number of instrument platforms but are most commonly run on various Roche Cobas analyzer systems, Olympus AU analyzers (Melville, NY), and the Roche/Hitachi systems, including the Modular Analytics. The Cobas INTEGRA is a random and continuous access analyzer capable of performing ion selective, absorbance, and FP assays from a single sample (Palmer et al., 1995; Passarelli and Bates, 1997). The reagents for INTEGRA are supplied in ready-to-use cassettes. The modular system has the advantages of consolidation, which leads to a reduction of the daily workflow and operational costs.

2.6 ONSITE (POINT-OF-COLLECTION) IMMUNOASSAYS

Various descriptions such as onsite, POC (point of collection or point of care), rapid, and one-step drug tests have been applied to commercial "non-instrument-based immunoassay kits" for drugs-of-abuse testing (Jenkins and Goldberger, 2002). Ideally, onsite testing is the most convenient and effective way for abused-drug screening. Realistically, the technical challenges for developing a competitive immunoassay for low concentration of small-molecular-weight drug compounds without instrument readout were higher than those for routine urinalysis dipsticks or pregnancy sandwich immunoassays. A combined two-step procedure was devised to absorb drug onto ion-exchange paper onsite before sending to laboratory for RIA or HI (Alexander, 1976; Alexander and Machiz, 1977). Early versions of dipstick papers were reported to be an unsuitable technique for drug testing (Jukofsky et al., 1981; Schwartz et al., 1989). In the 1980s, various methods of paper chromatography that utilized enzyme or radio tracer labeling were explored for convenient visual tests (Zuk et al., 1985; T.M. Li et al., 1987). With the improvement of high-flow nitrocellulose membranes, the majority of current onsite immunoassay devices utilize membrane strips as reaction media that provide vast solid-phase surfaces for immunoreactions. The resulting color signals can be read visually or with a reading instrument. The major types of "labels" used for these assays include gold sol metal nanoparticles and dyed latex microparticles.

Examples of the heterogeneous POC drug assays include the enzyme-based membrane immunoassays, such as EZ-SCREEN card test (Schwartz et al., 1990a; Jenkins et al., 1993), and ASCEND technology-based Biosite (San Diego, CA) Triage panel (Buechler et al., 1992; Wu et al., 1993). These assays require sample pipetting, solution transfer, timed incubations, and washing of the membrane. However, by allowing longer incubation of the sample and reagents in a separate compartment, the "threshold ligand–receptor assay" may improve near-cutoff differentiation. The system with sequential incubations and washing is also more forgiving of potential sample matrix effects. The Biosite Triage panel drugs-of-abuse assay has been evaluated by several laboratories (Rohrich et al., 1994; Wu et al., 1993; de la Torre et al., 1996; Peace et al., 2000). Poklis and O'Neal (1996) discussed factors that have the potential to cause false-positive results and made suggestions for prevention. Moriya and Hashimoto (1996) applied Triage tests to forensic blood samples.

An example of homogeneous POC drug immunoassays was the Abuscreen OnTrak product line, which allowed for the visual interpretation of qualitative results following a KIMS-like reaction (Schwartz et al., 1990b; Cone et al., 1991; Armbruster and Krolak, 1992; Armbruster et al., 1993a; Crouch et al., 1998a, 1998b). The assays require manual addition and mixing of sample and reagents, but the differentiation of results (visible aggregates versus smooth, milky appearance) is generally clearer than color-based reading. This classic OnTrak line was later replaced with the current Varian Inc. OnTrak TesTcup and TesTstik lines, which offer the advantages of simplicity, speed, and storage stability under broad temperature ranges (Towt et al., 1995; Crouch et al., 1998b). Additional examples of rapid, onsite devices include those from PhamaTech Inc., American Bio Medica Corporation Applied Biotech, Inc. Branan Medical

Corp., Cozart Biosciences, Princeton Biomeditech, Securetec Detection Systems, and contract manufacturers, such as Acon Labs and Syntron Biore-search, etc. Both SAMSHA and ROSITA conducted inventory studies of the devices. The markets for POC abused-drug testing devices are among the most dynamic ones in the drug-testing industry, and the number of companies and products has continued to expand and change in recent years.

In principle, the lateral-flow immunochromatographic assays are homogeneous immunoassays that can provide single or multiple results within a few minutes after a simple test start. Therefore such devices have been gaining acceptance and popularity in certain markets. In general, the "whole sample matrix" assays have some challenges of near-cutoff reading, due not only to fast reaction kinetics of "immunoassay with no measuring or timing steps," but also to the inherent variations in reading certain color intensities by human or small readers. The ready-to-use devices depend on precalibration during the manufacturing process, and hence do not have the onboard calibration flexibility of instrument-based testing. However, these assays can provide generally comparable performance with conventional immunoassays in most drug-screening settings and are useful for drug screening in the markets that demand an instant qualitative determination.

A congeries of articles have been published that report the evaluation of onsite immunoassays for screening of abused drugs (e.g., Jenkins et al., 1995; Ros et al., 1998; Crouch et al., 1998a, 1998b; Buchan et al., 1998; Wennig et al., 1998; Kintz et al., 2000; Leino et al., 2001; Gronholm and Lillsunde, 2001). In 1999, SAMHSA published a government-sponsored evaluation of 15 onsite devices that were compared to GC/MS and to the use of an instrument immunoassay (http://workplace.samhsa.gov/ResourceCenter/r409.htm). The evaluation was designed to challenge the devices on their accuracy around the cutoff. Although there are tradeoffs of sensitivity versus specificity when the majority of the samples evaluated are within ±25% of the cutoff values, the overall performance of most onsite devices was considered comparable to that of an instrument-based immunoassay. A field test sponsored by the DOT National Highway Traffic Safety Administration (NHTSA) (DOT HS 809–192, 2000) identified 30 onsite devices and rated 16 devices based on 14 criteria. From the rating results, 5 devices were selected to evaluate 800 samples in two high-prevalence counties. Moreover, Buchan et al. (1998) reported a field evaluation of onsite, multi-analyte drug-testing devices to determine their accuracy, efficiency, and cost-effectiveness as a tool for identifying impaired drivers and determining prevalence of illicit drugs in reckless drivers in a Florida county. As part of the roadsite testing assessment (ROSITA) project (www.rosita.org), Gronholm and Lillsunde (2001) evaluated the accuracy of 10 onsite testing devices. The accuracy of the devices in general was good, although there were differences in the ease of performance and interpretation of test results. Leino et al. (2001) evaluated 8 commercially available onsite drugs-of-abuse testing devices and reported that the devices differed with respect to interpretation of test results and to the ease of test performance. The authors suggested that different criteria for selecting onsite devices for either emergency laboratory in hospitals or police stations and prisons should be used. As with any immunoassay screenings, the importance to confirm any positive screening test result should always be emphasized.

2.7. PERFORMANCE CHARACTERISTICS AND QUALITY MANAGEMENT OF IMMUNOASSAYS

FDA is currently in the process of revising the guidance for industry and FDA staff regarding premarket submission and labeling recommendations for drugs-of-abuse screening tests. Likewise, immunoassays need approval from the European In vitro Diagnostic Directive (IVDD) to receive the "CE Mark".

The Department of Health and Human Services established the National Laboratory Certification Program (NLCP) that includes comprehensive performance testing and laboratory inspection programs. Essentially all guidelines developed for drugs-of-abuse testing describe the requirements and procedures of quality assurance and quality control programs. The criteria and performance of drug immunoassays for analytical diagnostic applications have been discussed in detail in relevant literature (Feinstein, 1975; Galen, 1977; Griner et al., 1981; Spiehler et al., 1988; Ferrara et al., 1994; Lawson, 1994; Scassellati, 2000). Moreover, commercial kits are subject to various clinical trials and third-party comparative assessment of diagnostic sensitivity, ($\%TP/(TP + FN)$), diagnostic specificity, ($\%TN/(TN + FP)$), and efficiency ($\%(TP + TN)/(total\ N)$), (e.g., Frings et al., 1989; Armbruster et al., 1993a, 1995; Ferrara et al., 1994; Huestis et al., 1994, 1995; Kintz et al., 1995; Wu et al., 1995; von Meyer et al., 1997; Smith-Kielland et al., 1999; Boettcher et al., 2000; M.L. Smith et al., 2000).

When comparing the evaluation results of immunoassays, it is important to take into consideration the target analyte and cutoff selections of the assays and the type and prevalence of the testing population. The "false-positive" samples usually include "unconfirmed" positives, such as samples with drugs present below the cutoff and samples containing abused or mis-used drugs not mandated for confirmatory test. In general, the respective cutoff adopted for the immunoassay for marijuana, amphetamines, and cocaine is set higher than that adopted for the GC/MS confirmation (e.g., 59 FR 29916, 1994). The CAP forensic urine drug-testing laboratory accreditation program requires that quantitative cutoff levels of the analytes be used but leaves the cutoff determinations up to the laboratory or to the intent of its clients' drug-testing programs. Internationally, many countries differ in their concerns and strategies to deal with the substance abuse problems (de la Torre et al., 1997; Wilson and Smith, 1999; Corcione et al., 1999). A survey of 269 European Union laboratories (Badia et al., 1998) indicates that screening only was a common approach of clinical laboratories, whereas screening with identification and quantification was the approach used by most forensic laboratories. Moreover, a high percentage of laboratories did not use or report cutoff. Recently, the European Workplace Drug Testing Society was founded to provide an independent forum and to ensure that workplace drug testing is performed to a defined quality standard and in a legally secured way (Verstraete and Pierce, 2001).

It is also important to recognize the variables and caveats that can influence the outcome and interpretation of immunoassay results (e.g., Baselt, 1984; Kidwell, 1992; Colbert, 1994; Wennig, 2000). The contributing variables include, but are not limited to, interindividual variations, diet, and medication, as well as analytical, statistical, and medicolegal factors. The interindividual pharmacogenetic and physiological variations ultimately affect the drug pharmacokinetics and excretion profile. Ingestion of certain known or unknown food products or medication can complicate the interpretation of drug-screening results (e.g., Maurer and Fritz, 1990; ElSohly et al., 1990; Johansen et al., 1991; ElSohly and Jones, 1995; Costantino et al., 1997; Lehmann et al., 1997; Cody and Schwarzhoff, 1993; Cody, 1996; Cody and Valtier, 2001). In addition, the importance of specimen integrity and validity is well recognized and has been addressed at both the scientific and the regulatory levels (Cody and Schwarzhoff, 1989; Schwarzhoff and Cody; 1993, Goldberger and Caplan, 1994; Cone et al., 1998; Urry et al., 1998; Wu et al., 1999; Tsai et al., 2000; Cook et al., 2000; Federal Registrar 66 FR 43876, 2001).

One of the most critical issues in interpreting immunoassay results is the understanding of cross-reactivity and potential interference of the immunoassays (Kricka, 2000). While assay specificity refers to the ability of an antibody to produce a measurable response *only* for the analyte of interest, cross-reactivity is a measurement of antibody response to substances other than the target analyte. Regardless of the rationale of selecting monoclonal or polyclonal antibodies to meet the specific assay requirement, many drug molecules have such closely related structures that the antibody cross-reactivity has to be critically evaluated in the first stage of assay design and throughout assay development. Cross-reactivity may be expressed in several ways; the most common approach is to spike a pure sample of testing substance into an analyte-free matrix to give a suitable range of concentrations, including levels above and below that of the assay cutoff. For drugs-of-abuse assays, the cross-reactivity can be calculated according to the linear regression method to determine the cross-reactant concentration that gives a response approximately equal to that of the analyte cutoff concentration.

Immunoassay specificity can be optimized by elaborate molecular design of the immunogens, derivatives, linkers and linker positions. Upon extensive screening, sophisticated tools such as Molecular Modeling and Surface Plasmon Resonance can be utilized to investigate the antibody binding characteristics and the K_{on} and K_{off} rates. Many of the wanted versus unwanted compounds can be so similar that a minute difference in structure or chirality can significantly impact the crossreactivity profile. The amphetamine structurally-related compounds exemplify the cross-reactive paradigm of abused drugs, designer drugs, herbal supplements, and prescription and over-the-counter medications. Specificity testing of the parent compound may not always predict the extent of potential cross-reactivity from its known and unknown metabolites. Moreover, cross reacting compounds can be present at much higher concentrations than the target analyte, so even minute cross-reactivity with a drug can accumulate sufficient total immunoreactivities to produce a false "presumptive positive" result.

Many effective medicines share the same essential core structure as the abused drugs. Conversely, structurally unrelated medications can have three-dimensional conformations that possess weak but sufficient binding to certain antibodies. For instance, dextromethorphine and dextrorphine can bind to phencycline (PCP) receptors *in vivo* or anti-PCP antibodies *in vitro* (Nicholson et al., 1999; Schier, 2000). Examples of the published cases include oxaprozin with benzodiazepines (Fraser and Howell, 1998), various therapeutic drugs with LSD (Ritter et al., 1997; Rohrich et al., 1998), ranitidine with methamphetamine (Dietzen et al., 2001), pholcodine, rifampicin, and ofloxacin with opiates (Maurer and Fritz, 1990; Johansen et al., 1991; de Paula et al., 1998; Meatherall and Dai, 1997), thioridazine with PCP (Long et al., 1996), diphenhydramine with PCP and propoxyphene (Levine and Smith, 1990; Schneider and Wennig, 1999), and nonsteroidal anti-inflammatory drugs with certain drug tests (Berkabile and Meyers, 1989; Rollins et al., 1990). There have been many reports of unexpected cross-reactivities in the related literature and no single technology or manufacturer was exempted from such findings. The cross-reactivity profile is one of the reasons immunoassay results across different products are comparable in the majority, but not in all, of the clinical specimens investigated. A number of pretreatment procedures can alleviate certain immunoassay crossreactivity issues. For example, glucuronidase hydrolysis can enhance the sensitivity of Benzodiazepines assays (Beck et al., 1997; Meatherall and Fraser, 1998) and periodate oxidation can improve the specificity of Amphetamines assays (Spiehler et al., 1993; Ward et al., 1994). Consequently, dedicated analyzers capable of periodate treatment can show better performance than larger, high-throughput analyzers for amphetamines screening even though the reagents *per se* are comparable. The nature of drug interference for immunoassays is different from the interference for GC/MS analysis (Wu, 1995; Ostheimer et al., 1997); however, it is equally important to recognize the potential of interference and to exercise caution while interpreting a drug-testing result.

2.8 SUMMARY

The development and advancement of sophisticated immunoassay technologies have significantly contributed to the overall efforts in deterring and detecting the abuse of illicit substances and the misuse of certain prescription medications. The efforts of numerous scientists and regulatory agencies, together with financial investment by the industry, have enabled the cost-effective and efficient screening of drugs of abuse. Substance-abuse testing has been, and continues to be, an actively published field. This chapter provided an overview of the general principle of immunoassay technologies and described the most commonly used immunoassays for drugs-of-abuse screening. Immunoassay technologies are useful tools for a preliminary analysis of drugs of abuse, providing their state-of-the-art performance characteristics, inherent limitations, and advantages are recognized. Confirmatory tests of presumptive positive specimens following the initial screening tests are important for ensuring reliability of forensic drug analysis.

REFERENCES

INTERNET

ABFT (American Board of Forensic Toxicologists); http://www.abft.org/

ASCLD/LAB (American Society of Crime Laboratory Directors/Laboratory Accreditation Board); http://www.ascld-lab.org/

CAP (College Of American Pathologists); http://www.cap.org

EWDTS (European Workplace Drug Testing Society) Laboratory Guidelines (2002). http://www.ewdts.org/guidelines.html

FDA Guidances; http://www.fda.gov/cdrh/guidance.html

NHTSA (2000). Field test of onsite drug detection devices (DOT HS 809 192); http://www.nhtsa.dot.gov/people/injury/research/pub/onsitedetection/Drug_index.htm

ROSITA (Roadside Testing Assessment) http://www.rosita.org.

SAMHSA Division of Workplace Programs; http://workplace.samhsa.gov/
    M_Level2.asp?Level1_ID=1.
SOFT / AAFS Forensic Laboratory Guidelines (2002). http://www.soft-tox.org/
    docs/Guidelines.2002.final.pdf.

Adler, F.L., and Liu, C.T. (1971). *J. Immunol.* 106, 1684–1685.
Alexander, G.J. (1976). *Clin. Toxicol.* 9, 435–446.
Alexander, G.J., and Machiz, S. (1977). *Clin. Chem.* 23, 1921–1924.
Arakawa, H., Maeda, M., Tsuji, A., and Kambegawa, A. (1981). *Steroids* 38,
    453–464.
Armbruster, D.A., and Krolak, J.M. (1992). *J. Anal. Toxicol.* 16, 172–175.
Armbruster, D.A., Schwarzhoff, R.H., Hubster, E.C., and Liserio, M.K. (1993a).
    Clin. Chem. 39, 2137–2146.
Armbruster, D.A., Schwarzhoff, R.H., Pierce, B.L., and Hubster, E.C. (1993b).
    J. Forensic Sci. 38, 1326–1341.
Armbruster, D.A., Schwarzhoff, R.H., Pierce, B.L., and Hubster, E.C. (1994). *J.
    Anal. Toxicol.* 18, 110–117.
Armbruster, D.A., Hubster, E.C., Kaufman, M.S., and Ramon, M.K. (1995). *Clin.
    Chem.* 41, 92–98.
Avrameas, S. (1968). *Bull. Soc. Chim. Biol. (Paris)* 50, 1169–1178.
Badia, R., de la Torre, R., Corcione, S., and Segura, J. (1998). *Clin. Chem.* 44,
    790–799.
Baker, D.P., Murphy, M.S., Shepp, P.F., Royo, V.R., Caldarone, M.E., Escoto, B.,
    and Salamone, S.J. (1995). *J. Forensic Sci.* 40, 108–112.
Baselt, R.C. (1984). In Advances in Analytical Toxicology, Vol. 1 (ed. R.C.
    Baselt), pp. 81–123. Biomedical Publications, Foster City, CA.
Baselt, R.C. (1989). *J. Anal. Toxicol.* 13, 1.
Beck, O., Lin, Z., Brodin, K., Borg, S., and Hjemdahl, P. (1997). *J. Anal. Toxicol.*
    21, 554–557.
Bergman, R.A., Lukaszewski, T., and Wang, S.Y. (1981). *J. Anal. Toxicol.* 5, 85–89.
Berkabile, D.R., and Meyers, A. (1989). *J. Anal. Toxicol.* 13, 63.
Blum, L.M., Klinger, R.A., and Rieders, F. (1989). *J. Anal. Toxicol.* 13, 285–288.
Boettcher, M., Haenseler, E., Hoke, C., Nichols, J., Raab, D., and Domke, I.
    (2000). *Clin. Lab.* 46, 49–52.
Bogusz, M., Aderjan, R., Schmitt, G., Nadler, E., and Neureither, B. (1990).
    Forensic Sci. Int. 48, 27–37.
Bonini, P., Ceriotti, F., Keller, F., Brauer, P., Stolz, H., Pascual, C., Garcia Beltran,
    L., Vonderschmitt, D.J., and Pei, P. (1992). *Eur. J. Clin. Chem. Clin. Biochem.*
    30, 881–899.
Brendler, J., and Liu, R.H. (1997). *Clin. Chem.* 43, 688–690.
Broussard, L.A., and Hanson, L. (1997). *Clin. Lab. Sci.* 10, 83–86.

Bruton, D.T., Cordery, R.O., Domke, I., Gandhi, S., Hon, K.L., Sheehan, M., Wagner, S., Widmann, S., and Wu, A.H. (2000). *Clin. Chem.* 46, A198.

Buchan, B.J., Walsh, J.M., and Leaverton, P.E. (1998). *J. Forensic Sci.* 43, 395–399.

Buechler, K.F., Moi, S., Noar, B., McGrath, D., Villela, J., Clancy, M., Shenhav, A., Colleymore, A., Valkirs, G., and Lee, T. (1992). *Clin. Chem.* 38, 1678–1684.

Cagle, J.C., McCurdy, H.H., Pan, Y.M., Ayton, K.J., Wall, W.H., and Solomons, E.T. (1997). *J. Anal. Toxicol.* 21, 213–217.

Caplan, Y.H., and Levine, B. (1989). *J. Anal. Toxicol.* 13, 289–292.

Catlin, D.H., Adler, F.L., and Liu, C.T. (1973). *Clin. Immunol. Immunopathol.* 1, 446–455.

Chamberlain, R.T. (1988). *Clin. Chem.* 34, 633–636.

Chan, D.W. (1996). In Immunoassay Automation: An Update Guide to Systems (ed. D.W. Chan), Academic Press, New York, pp. 1–312.

Chiarotti, M., De Giovanni, N., Carnevale, A., and Offidani, C. (1985). Clin. Chem. 31, 1087–1088.

Cody, J.T. (1996). *Forensic Sci. Int.* 80, 189–199.

Cody, J.T., and Schwarzhoff, R.H. (1989). *J. Anal. Toxicol.* 13, 277–284.

Cody, J.T., and Schwarzhoff, R. (1993). *J. Anal. Toxicol.* 17, 321–326.

Cody, J.T., and Valtier, S. (1997). *J. Anal. Toxicol.* 21, 459–464.

Cody, J.T., and Valtier, S. (2001). *J. Anal. Toxicol.* 25, 158–165.

Cohen, R.J., and Benedek, G.B. (1975). *Immunochemistry* 12, 349–351.

Colbert, D.L. (1994). *Br. J. Biomed. Sci.* 51, 136–146.

Colbert, D.L., Smith, D.S., Landon, J., and Sidki, A.M. (1984). *Clin. Chem.* 30, 1765–1769.

Collison, I.B., Spiehler, V.R., Guluzian, S., and Sedgwick, P.R. (1998) *J. Forensic Sci.* 43, 390–394.

Cone, E.J., Darwin, W.D., and Dickerson, S.L. (1991). *Clin. Chem. Newslett.* 17, 40.

Cone, E.J., Lange, R., and Darwin, W.D. (1998). *J. Anal. Toxicol.* 22, 460–473.

Cook, J.D., Caplan, Y.H., LoDico, C.P., and Bush, D.M. (2000). *J. Anal. Toxicol.* 24, 579–588.

Corcione, S., Pichini, S., Badia, R., Segura, J., and de la Torre, R. (1999). *Ther. Drug Monit.* 21, 653–660.

Costantino, A., Schwartz, R.H., and Kaplan, P. (1997). *J. Anal. Toxicol.* 21, 482–485.

Costongs, G.M., van Oers, R.J., Leerkens, B., Hermans, W., and Janson, P.C. (1995). *Eur. J. Clin. Chem. Clin. Biochem.* 33, 105–111.

Crouch, D.J., Cheever, M.L., Andrenyak, D.M., Kuntz, D.J., and Loughmiller, D.L. (1998a). *J. Forensic Sci.* 43, 35–40.

Crouch, D.J., Frank, J.F., Farrell, L.J., Karsch, H.M., and Klaunig, J.E. (1998b). *J. Anal. Toxicol.* 22, 493–502.

Curtis, E.G., and Patel, J.A. (1978). *CRC Crit. Rev. Clin. Lab. Sci.* 9, 303–320.

de Kanel, J., Dunlap, L., and Hall, T.D. (1989). *Clin. Chem.* 35, 2110–2112.

de la Torre, R., Domingo-Salvany, A., Badia, R., Gonzalez, G., McFarlane, D., San, L., and Torrens, M. (1996). *Clin. Chem.* 42, 1433–1438.

de la Torre, R., Segura, J., Williams, J., and de Zeeuw, R.A. (1997). *Ann. Clin. Biochem.* 34, 339–344.

de Paula, M, Saiz, L.C., Gonzalez-Revalderia, J., Pascual, T., Alberola, C., and Miravalles, E. (1998). *Clin. Chem. Lab. Med.* 36, 241–243.

Dezelic, G., Dezelic, N., Muic, N., and Pende, B. (1971). *Eur. J. Biochem.* 20, 553–560.

Dietzen, D.J., Ecos, K., Friedman, D., Beason, S. (2001). *J. Anal. Toxicol.* 25, 174–178.

Domke, I., Cremer, P., and Huchtemann, M. (2000). *Clin. Lab.* 46, 509–515.

Drandliker, W.B., and Feigen, G.A. (1961). *Biochim. Biophys. Res. Commun.* 5, 299–304.

Drandliker, W.B., and De Saussure, V.A. (1970). *Immunochemistry* 7, 799–828.

Ellis, G.M. Jr., Mann, M.A., Judson, B.A., Schramm, N.T., and Tashchian, A. (1985). *Clin. Pharmacol. Ther.* 38, 572–578.

ElSohly, H.N., ElSohly, M.A., and Stanford D.F. (1990). *J. Anal. Toxicol.* 14, 308–310.

ElSohly, M.A., and Jones, A.B. (1995). *J. Anal. Toxicol.* 19, 450–458.

Engel, W.D., and Khanna, P.L. (1992). *J. Immunol. Methods* 150, 99–102.

Engvall, E., and Perlmann, P. (1971). *Immunochemistry* 8, 871–874.

Engvall, E., and Perlmann, P. (1972). *J. Immunol.* 109, 129–135.

Feinstein, A.R. (1975). *Clin. Pharmacol. Ther.* 17, 104–116.

Ferrara, S.D., Tedeschi, L., Frison, G., Brusini, G., Castagna, F., Bernardelli, B., and Soregaroli, D. (1994). *J. Anal. Toxicol.* 18, 278–291.

Fraser, A.D., and Howell, P. (1998). *J. Anal. Toxicol.* 22, 50–54.

Fraser, A.D., and Meatherall, R. (1996). *J. Anal. Toxicol.* 20, 217–223.

Frings, C.S., Battaglia, D.J., and White, R.M. (1989). *Clin. Chem.* 35, 891–894.

Galen, R.S. (1977). *Arch. Pathol. Lab. Med.* 101, 561–565.

Gjerde, H. (1991). *Forensic Sci. Int.* 50, 121–124.

Goldberger, B.A., and Caplan, Y.H. (1994). *Clin. Chem.* 40, 1605–1606.

Gooch, J.C., Caldwell, R., Turner, G.J., and Colbert, D.L. (1992). *J. Immunoassay* 13, 85–96.

Gooch, J.C., Gallacher, G., Wright, J.G., Mahmood, I., Siddiqui, A., and Colbert, D.L. (1994). *Analyst* 119, 1797–1800.

Gorsky, J.E. (1988). *J. Anal. Toxicol.* 12, 300.

Grange, J., Roch, A.M., and Quash, G.A. (1977). *J. Immunol. Methods* 18, 365–375.

Griner, P.F., Mayewski, R.J., Mushlin, A.I., and Greenland, P. (1981). *Ann. Intern. Med.* 94, 557–592.

Gronholm M., and Lillsunde P. (2001). *Forensic Sci. Int.* 121, 37–46.

Gross, S.J., Soares, J.R., Wong, S.L., and Schuster, R.E. (1974). *Nature* 252, 581–582.

Hailer, M., Glienke, Y., Schwab, I.M., and von Meyer, L. (1995). *J. Anal. Toxicol.* 19, 99–103.

Hanson, V.W., Buonarati, M.H., Baselt, R.C., Wade, N.A., Yep, C., Biasotti, A.A., Reeve, V.C., Wong, A.S., and Orbanowsky, M.W. (1983). *J. Anal. Toxicol.* 7, 96–102.

Haver, V.M., Romson, J.L., and Sadrzadeh, S.M. (1991). *J. Anal. Toxicol.* 15, 98–100.

Henderson, D.R., Friedman, S.B., Harris, J.D., Manning, W.B., and Zoccoli, M.A. (1986). *Clin. Chem.* 32, 1637–1641.

Herold, D.A., and Margrey, M.H. (1987). *Clin. Chem.* 33, 955.

Huestis, M.A., Mitchell, J.M., and Cone, E.J. (1994). *Clin. Chem.* 40, 729–733.

Huestis, M.A., Mitchell, J.M., and Cone, E.J. (1995). *J. Anal. Toxicol.* 19, 443–449.

Huestis, M.A., Cone, E.J., Wong, C.J., Umbricht, A., and Preston, K.L. (2000). *J. Anal. Toxicol.* 24, 509–521.

Irving, J., Leeb, B., Foltz, R.L., Cook, C.E., Bursey, J.T., and Willette, R.E. (1984). *J. Anal. Toxicol.* 8, 192–196.

Iwersen-Bergmann, S., and Schmoldt, A. (1999). *J. Anal. Toxicol.* 23, 247–256.

Jenkins, A.J., Mills, L.C., Darwin, W.D., Huestis, M.A., Cone, E.J., and Mitchell, J.M. (1993). *J. Anal. Toxicol.* 17, 292–298.

Jenkins, A.J., Darwin, W.D., Huestis, M.A., Cone, E.J., and Mitchell, J.M. (1995). *J. Anal. Toxicol.* 19, 5–12.

Jenkins, A.J., and Goldberger, B.A., eds. (2002). On-Site Drug Testing, Humana Press, Totowa, NJ.

Johansen, M., Rasmussen, K.E., Christophersen, A.S., and Skuterud, B. (1991). *Acta Pharm. Nord.* 3, 91–94.

Jolley, M.E., Stroupe, S.D., Wang, C.H., Panas, H.N., Keegan, C.L., Schmidt, R.L., and Schwenzer, K.S. (1981a). *Clin. Chem.* 27, 1190–1197.

Jolley, M.E., Stroupe, S.D., Schwenzer, K.S., Wang, C.J., Lu-Steffes, M., Hill, H.D., Popelka, S.R., Holen, J.T., and Kelso, D.M. (1981b). *Clin. Chem.* 27, 1575–1579.

Jones, A.B., ElSohly, H.N., Arafat, E.S., and ElSohly, M.A. (1984a). *J. Anal. Toxicol.* 8, 249–251.

Jones, A.B., ElSohly, H.N., and ElSohly, M.A. (1984b). *J. Anal. Toxicol.* 8, 252–254.

Jukofsky, D., Kramer, A., and Mule, S.J. (1981). *J. Anal. Toxicol.* 5, 14–19.

Keller, T., Schneider, A., Dirnhofer, R., Jungo, R., and Meyer, W. (2000). *Med. Sci. Law* 40, 258–262.

Kerrigan, S., and Phillips, W.H. Jr. (2001). *Clin. Chem.* 47, 540–547.

Khanna, P.L., Dworschack, R.T., Manning, W.B., and Harris, J.D. (1989). *Clin. Chim. Acta* 185, 231–239.

Kidwell, D.A. (1992). *NIDA Res. Monogr.* 117, 98–120.

Kintz, P., Ludes, B., and Mangin, P. (1992). *J. Forensic Sci.* 37, 328–331.

Kintz, P., Machart, D., Jamey, C., and Mangin, P. (1995). *J. Anal. Toxicol.* 19, 304–306.

Kintz, P., Cirimele, V., and Ludes, B. (2000). *J. Anal. Toxicol.* 24, 557–561.

Kricka, L.J. (2000). *Clin. Chem.* 46, 1037–1038.

Kunsman, G.W., Levine, B., and Smith, M.L. (1998). *J. Forensic Sci.* 43, 1225–1227.

Lawson, G.M. (1994). *Clin. Chem.* 40, 1218–1219.

Lee, C.W., and Lee, H.M. (1989). *J. Anal. Toxicol.* 13, 50–56.

Lehmann, T., Sager, F., and Brenneisen, R. (1997). *J. Anal. Toxicol.* 21, 373–375.

Leino, A., Saarimies, J., Gronholm, M., and Lillsunde, P. (2001). *Scand. J. Clin. Lab. Invest.* 61, 325–331.

Lemos, N.P., Anderson, R.A., and Robertson, J.R. (1999). *J. Anal. Toxicol.* 23, 147–152.

Levine, B.S., and Smith, M.L. (1990). *Clin. Chem.* 36, 1258.

Lewellen, L.J., and McCurdy, H.H. (1988). *J. Anal. Toxicol.* 12, 260–264.

Li, D.J., Sokoll, L.J., and Chan D.W. (1998). *J. Clin. Ligand Assay* 21, 377–385.

Li, T.M., Chen, R., Leeder, S., Stiso, S.N., Sizto, N.C., Zuk, R.F., and Litman, D.J. (1987). *Anal. Biochem.* 166, 276–283.

Liu, C.T., and Adler, F.L. (1973). *J. Immunol.* 111, 472–477.

Liu, R.H. (1995). In *Handbook of Workplace Drug Testing: Evaluation of Common Immunoassay Kits for Effective Workplace Drug Testing* (eds. R.H. Liu and B.A. Goldberger). AACC Press, Washington, DC, pp. 67–129.

Liu, R.H., Edwards, C., Baugh, L.D., Weng, J.L., Fyfe, M.J., and Walia, A. (1994). *J. Anal. Toxicol.* 18, 65–70.

Long, C., Crifasi, J., and Maginn, D. (1996). *Clin. Chem.* 42, 1885–1886.

Maurer, H.H., and Fritz, C.F. (1990). *Int. J. Legal Med.* 104, 43–46.

McCurdy, H.H., Callahan, L.S., and Williams, R.D. (1989). *J. Forensic Sci.* 34, 858–870.

McGregor, A.R., Crookall-Greening, J.O., Landon, J., and Smith, D.S. (1978). *Clin. Chim. Acta* 83, 161–166.

Meatherall, R., and Dai, J. (1997). *Ther. Drug Monit.* 19, 98–99.

Meatherall, R., and Fraser, A.D. (1998). *Ther. Drug. Monit.* 20, 673–675.

Mieczkowski T. (1995). *Forensic Sci. Int.* 70, 83–91.

Mikkelsen, S.L., and Root, C.F. (1993). *Lab. Med.* 24, 729–731.

Moody, D.E., and Medina, A.M. (1995). *Clin. Chem.* 41, 1664–1665.

Moody, D.E., Rittenhouse, L.F., and Monti, K.M. (1992). *J. Anal. Toxicol.* 16, 297–301.

Moore, F.M., and Simpson, D. (1990). *Med. Lab. Sci.* 47, 85–89.

Moore, K.A., Werner, C., Zannelli, R.M., Levine, B., and Smith, M.L. (1999). *Forensic Sci. Int.* 106, 93–102.

Moriya, F., and Hashimoto, Y. (1996). *Nippon Hoigaku Zasshi* 50, 50–56.

Mule, S.J., Whitlock, E., and Jukofsky, D. (1975). *Clin. Chem.* 21, 81–86.

Nakane, P.K., and Pierce, G.B. (1967) *J. Cell Biol.* 33, 307–318.

Nicholson, K.L., Hayes, B.A., and Balster, R.L. (1999). *Psychopharmacology* 146, 49–59.

Niedbala, R.S., Kardos, K.W., Fritch, D.F., Kardos, S., Fries, T., Waga, J., Robb, J., and Cone, E.J. (2001). *J. Anal. Toxicol.* 25, 289–303.

Oeltgen, P.R., Shank, W.A. Jr., Blouin, R.A., and Clark, T. (1984). *Ther. Drug Monit.* 6, 360–367.

Oreskes, I., and Singer, J.M. (1961). *J. Immunol.* 86, 338–344.

Ostheimer, D., Cremese, M., Wu, A.H., and Hill, D.W. (1997). *J. Anal. Toxicol.* 21, 17–22.

Ostrea, E.M. Jr., Brady, M.J., Parks, P.M., Asensio, D.C., and Naluz, A. (1989). *J. Pediatr.* 115, 474–477.

Palmer, S.M., Kaufman, R.A., Salamone, S.J., Blake-Courtney, J., Bette, W., Wahl, H.P., and Furrer, F. (1995). *Clin. Chem.* 41, 1751–1760.

Passarelli, J., and Bates, M. (1997). *Am. Clin. Lab.* 16, 8–9.

Peace, M.R., Tarnai, L.D., and Poklis, A. (2000). *J. Anal. Toxicol.* 24, 589–594.

Peel, H.W., and Perrigo, B.J. (1981). *J. Anal. Toxicol.* 5, 165–167.

Peel, H.W., Perrigo, B.J., and Mikhael, N.Z. (1984). *J. Forensic Sci.* 29, 185–189.

Perez-Bendito, D., Gomez-Hens, A., and Gaikwad, A. (1994). *Clin. Chem.* 40, 1489–1493.

Perez-Bendito, D., Gomez-Hens, A., and Silva, M. (1996). *J. Pharm. Biomed. Anal.* 14, 917–930.

Poklis, A., and O'Neal, C.L. (1996). *J. Anal. Toxicol.* 20, 209–210.

Popelka, S.R., Miller, D.M., Holen, J.T., and Kelso, D.M. (1981). *Clin. Chem.* 27, 1198–1201.

Pringle, M.J. (1993). *Adv. Clin. Chem.* 30, 89–183.

Ritter, D., Cortese, C.M., Edwards, L.C., Barr, J.L., Chung, H.D., and Long, C. (1997). *Clin. Chem.* 43, 635–637.

Rodgers, R, Crowl, C.P., Eimstad, W.M., Hu, M.W., Kam, J.K., Ronald, R.C., Rowley, G.L., and Ullman E.F. (1978). *Clin. Chem.* 24, 95–100.

Rohrich, J., Schmidt, K., and Bratzke, H. (1994). *J. Anal. Toxicol.* 18, 407–14.

Rohrich, J., Zorntlein, S., Lotz, J., Becker, J., Kern, T., and Rittner, C. (1998). *J. Anal. Toxicol.* 22, 393–395.

Rollins, D.E., Jennison, T.A., and Jones, G. (1990). *Clin. Chem.* 36, 602–606.

Ros, J.J., Pelders, M.G., and Egberts, A.C. (1998). *J. Anal. Toxicol.* 22, 40–44.

Ross, R., Horwitz, C.A., Hager, H., Usategui, M., Burke, M.D., and Ward, P.C. (1975). *Clin. Chem.* 21, 139–143.

Rubenstein, K.E., Schneider, R.S., and Ullman, E.F. (1972). *Biochem. Biophys. Res. Commun.* 47, 846–851.

Rutledge, J.C., Emamian, S., and Rudy, J. (1987). *Clin. Chem.* 33, 1256–1257.

Scassellati, G. (2000). *Biochim. Clin.* 24, 493–498.

Schier, J. (2000). *J. Emerg. Med.* 18, 379–381.

Schneider, S., and Wennig, R. (1999). *J. Anal. Toxicol.* 23, 637–638.

Schwartz, R.H., Bogema, S., and Thorne, M.M. (1989). *Arch. Pathol. Lab. Med.* 113, 363–364.

Schwartz, R.H., Bogema, S., and Thorne, M.M. (1990a). *Pediatr. Emerg. Care* 6, 147–149.

Schwartz, R.H., Bogema, S., and Thorne, M.M. (1990b). *J. Pediatr.* 117, 670–672.

Schwarzhoff, R., and Cody, J.T. (1993). *J. Anal. Toxicol.* 17, 14–17.

Schwenzer, K.S., Pearlman, R., Tsilimidos, M., Salamone, S.J., Cannon, R.C., Wong, S.H., Gock, S.B., and Jentzen, J.J. (2000). *J. Anal. Toxicol.* 24, 726–732.

Sharma, J.D., Aherne, G.W., and Marks, V. (1989). *Analyst* 114, 1279–1282.

Singer, J.M., and Plotz, C.M. (1956). *Am. J. Med.* 21, 888–892.

Smith, F.P. (1993). *J. Forensic Sci.* 38, 1326–1341.

Smith, F.P., Lora-Tamayo, C., Carvajal, R., Caddy, B., and Tagliaro, F. (1997). *Ann. Clin. Biochem.* 34, 81–84.

Smith, J., Osikowicz, G., Tayi, R., Walker, D., Martin, R., and Vaught, J. (1993). *Clin. Chem.* 39, 2063–2069.

Smith, M.L., Shimomura, E.T., Summers, J., Paul, B.D., Nichols, D., Shippee, R., Jenkins, A.J., Darwin, W.D., and Cone, E.J. (2000) *J. Anal. Toxicol.* 24, 522–529.

Smith R.N. (1988). In *Radioimmunoassay of Drugs in Body Fluids in a Forensic Context* (eds. A. Maehly and R.L. Williams). Springer-Verlag, Berlin, pp. 1–89.

Smith-Kielland, A., Skuterud, B., and Morland, J. (1999). *J. Anal. Toxicol.* 23, 323–332.

Spanbauer, A.C., Casseday, S., Davoudzadeh, D., Preston, K.L., and Huestis, M.A. (2001). *J. Anal. Toxicol.* 25, 515–519.

Sokoll, L.J., and Chan, D.W. (1997). *Anal. Chem.* 69, 206R–208R.

Spector, S., and Parker, C.W. (1970). *Science* 168, 1347–1348.

Spiehler, V.R. (2000). *Forensic Sci. Int.* 107, 249–259.

Spiehler, V., Wilson, H., Pregger, K., and Harris R. (1993). *Clin. Chem.* 39, 172–173.

Spiehler, V.R., O'Donnell, C.M., and Gokhale, D.V. (1988). *Clin. Chem.* 34, 1535–1539.

Spiehler, V.R., Collison, I.B., Sedgwick, P.R., Perez, S.L., Le, S.D., and Farnin, D.A. (1998). *J. Anal. Toxicol.* 22, 573–579.

Teale, J.D., Forman, E.J., King, L.J., and Marks, V. (1974). *Lancet* 2, 553–555.

Towt, J., Tsai, S.C.J., Hernandez, M.R., Klimov, A.D., Kravec, C.V., Rouse, S.L., Subuhi, H.S., Twarowska, B., and Salamone, S.J. (1995). *J. Anal. Toxicol.* 19, 504–510.

Tsai, J.S., ElSohly, M.A., Tsai, S.F., Murphy, T.P., Twarowska, B., and Salamone, S.J. (2000). *J. Anal. Toxicol.* 24, 708–714.

Urry, F.M., Komaromy-Hiller, G., Staley, B., Crockett, D.K., Kushnir, M., Nelson G., and Struempler, R.E. (1998). *J. Anal. Toxicol.* 22, 89–95.

Verstraete, A.G., and Pierce, A. (2001). *Forensic Sci. Int.* 121, 2–6.

von Meyer, L., Hanseler, E., Lardet, G., Scholer, A., and Sieghart, W. (1997). *Eur. J. Clin. Chem. Clin. Biochem.* 35, 133–140.

Walia, A.S., and Cook, L.F. (1991). *Forensic Sci. Int.* 49, 43–56.

Ward, C., McNally, A.J., Rusyniak, D., and Salamone, S.J. (1994). *J. Forensic Sci.* 39, 1486–1496.

Watson, R.A., Landon, J., Shaw, E.J., and Smith, D.S. (1976). *Clin. Chim. Acta* 73, 51–55.

Weaver, M.L., Gan, B.K., Allen, E., Baugh, L.D., Liao, F.Y., Liu, R.H., Langner, J.G., Wennig, R., Moeller, M.R., Haguenoer, J.M., Marocchi, A., Zoppi, F., Smith, B.L., de la Torre, R., Carstensen, C.A., Goerlach-Graw, A., Schaeffler, J., and Leinberger, R. (1998). *J. Anal. Toxicol.* 22, 148–55.

Wennig, R. (2000). *Forensic Sci. Int.* 113, 323–330.

Whitehead, T.P., Thorpe, G.H., Carter, T.J.N., Groucult, C., and Kricka L.J. (1983). *Nature* 305, 158–159.

Wilson, J.F., and Smith, B.L. (1999). *Ann. Clin. Biochem.* 36, 592–600.

Wingert, W.E., Feldman, M.S., Kim, M.H., Noble, L., Hand, I., Yoon, J.J. (1994). *J. Forensic Sci.* 39, 150–158.

Wu, A.H. (1995). *Ann. Clin. Lab. Sci.* 25, 319–329.

Wu, A.H., Wong, S.S., Johnson, K.G., Callies, J., Shu, D.X., Dunn, W.E., and Wong, S.H. (1993). *J. Anal. Toxicol.* 17, 241–245.

Wu, A.H., Forte, E., Casella, G., Sun, K., Hemphill, G., Foery, R., and Schanzenbach, H. (1995). *J. Forensic Sci.* 40, 614–618.

Wu, A.H.B., Bristol, B., Sexton, K., Cassella-McLane, G., Holtman, V., and Hill, D.W. (1999). *Clin. Chem.* 45, 1051–1057.

Yalow, R.S., and Berson, S.A. (1959). *Nature* 184, 1648–1649.

Zuk, R.F., Ginsberg, V.K., Houts, T., Rabbie, J., Merrick, H., Ullman, E.F., Fischer, M.M., Sizto, C.C., Stiso, S.N., and Litman, D.J. (1985). *Clin. Chem.* 31, 1144–1150.

CHAPTER 3

CANNABIS: METHODS OF FORENSIC ANALYSIS

Charles Tindall, Jane S.-C. Tsai & John Mario
Metropolitan State College of Denver, Denver, Colorado;
Roche Diagnostics Corporation, Indianapolis, Indiana;
Suffolk County Crime Laboratory, New York

Contents

The identification of marijuana or its chemical constituents has long been one of the most often performed analyses in the forensic drug laboratory. This includes analysis of the very common botanical samples, ranging from whole plants to finely chopped vegetation, as well as preparations and extracts, such as hashish and liquid hashish. Analytical issues do not end with merely identifying such exhibits. Occasionally the scientist is asked to compare exhibits to determine if they have a common provenance or what that provenance might be. This has resulted in a considerable body of literature devoted to profiling the constituents, both organic and inorganic, of *Cannabis* specimens. Evidence of the use of *Cannabis* as a drug is also of forensic interest both in drug-screening programs and in cases in which drug-induced impairment is an issue. The focus in the analytical toxicology of *Cannabis* has been on the major metabolite 11-nor-Δ^9-tetrahydrocannabinol carboxylic acid (THC-COOH). This chapter will address each of these topics separately and will include a historical perspective and cover specific widely accepted methodologies and recent advances.

Handbook of Forensic Drug Analysis
Frederick P. Smith, Editor

3.1 QUALITATIVE SEIZED-DRUG ANALYSIS OF *CANNABIS*, HASH, AND HASH OIL: CURRENT AND HISTORICAL PERSPECTIVES

3.1.1 INTRODUCTION

Seized-drug testing is a practice involving the examination and analysis of law enforcement submissions for the presence or absence of controlled substances. The amounts submitted are usually ample enough to be visible to the naked eye. They range in size from residues often found, for example, in smoking devices to tons of material seized from large transport or storage facilities. Such samples are seized by law enforcement from those possessing, selling, manufacturing, or attempting these acts. The practice is distinguished from toxicological analysis in that it is not concerned with metabolites, nor does it typically involve extraction from physiological matrices. It differs from toxicological and environmental analysis by the larger magnitude of analyte often present for testing (typically milligrams and larger) and because, unlike these two, it is not often concerned with elemental analysis. Seized-drug testing is concerned with both qualitative and quantitative determinations. Quantitative tests are often run for investigative purposes but may also be performed to meet statutory requirements, as in the setting of criminal charges (New York State has approximately 98 controlled-substance statutes of this type) or to aid the court in sentencing (see U.S. Federal Drug Statutes). Because it occurs in a forensic context, it frequently entails presentation and defense of test results by the analyst with case responsibility in criminal court. Common techniques employed for the analysis of seized drugs include color tests; microscopy; thin-layer, gas, and high-performance liquid chromatography (TLC, GC, HPLC); mass spectrometry (MS); and ultraviolet and infrared spectroscopy (UV, IR). In keeping with good laboratory practice, a positive identification should be based on at least two positive test results from two different test methodologies made on separate aliquots of the material. The test results should be reviewed by at least two individuals who are thoroughly familiar with the testing protocol. Two very good general discussions of seized-drug analysis that include a review of federal drug schedules, test methodologies for different drugs, and sound basic principles for creating analytical protocols are found in works by Siegel (1993) and Saferstein (2001).

Cannabis, according to a report from the Drug Enforcement Administration-sponsored National Forensic Laboratory Information System (*ASCLD News*, 2001), is the most frequently identified controlled substance in forensic laboratories in the United States, at 39.68% of all submissions. Cocaine was second at 30.65%, and all others tallied were at single-digit percentages or less. These numbers were based on a sampling of 165 individual laboratories at the state and local levels. Testing for *Cannabis* typically involves identifying fresh plants or dried, crushed plant material as belonging to the genus *Cannabis* of the family Cannabinaceae. Where resins or oils of *Cannabis* are submitted, the aim is to establish that they contain constituents of *Cannabis*. Identifying any of several cannabinoids (See Figure 3.1) and remnants of the *Cannabis* plant present can accomplish this. In some jurisdictions the charge for oils and resins may be based simply on the presence of a cannabinoid like Δ^9-tetrahydro-cannabinol (THC). In modern forensic laboratories, identification of the plant material may be made from an examination of macroscopic and microscopic

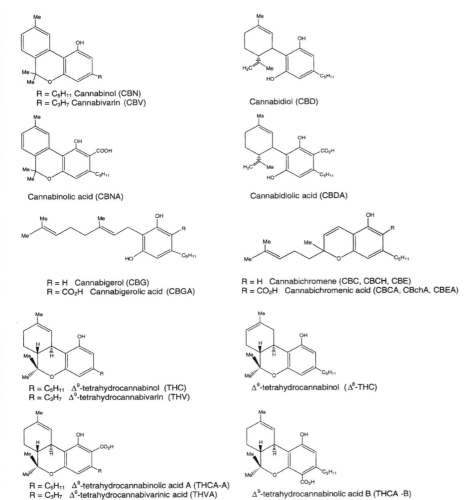

Figure 3.1
Structures of selected cannabinoids

R = C_5H_{11} Cannabinol (CBN)
R = C_3H_7 Cannabivarin (CBV)

Cannabidiol (CBD)

Cannabinolic acid (CBNA)

Cannabidiolic acid (CBDA)

R = H Cannabigerol (CBG)
R = CO_2H Cannabigerolic acid (CBGA)

R = H Cannabichromene (CBC, CBCH, CBE)
R = CO_2H Cannabichromenic acid (CBCA, CBchA, CBEA)

R = C_5H_{11} Δ^9-tetrahydrocannabinol (THC)
R = C_3H_7 Δ^9-tetrahydrocannabivarin (THV)

Δ^8-tetrahydrocannabinol (Δ^8-THC)

R = C_5H_{11} Δ^9-tetrahydrocannabinolic acid A (THCA-A)
R = C_3H_7 Δ^9-tetrahydrocannabivarinic acid (THVA)

Δ^9-tetrahydrocannabinolic acid B (THCA -B)

botanical features along with chemical tests to establish the presence of various cannabinoids.

3.1.2 REVIEW OF FIELD AND LABORATORY TESTING

3.1.2.1 Current Field Testing

At least two companies in the United States (Sirchie of Raleigh, NC, and ODV of South Paris, ME) produce kits for testing materials suspected of containing controlled substances. These are often used by law enforcement in the field to establish probable cause for an arrest. For *Cannabis*, each company manufactures two different tests, one based on the Duquenois–Levine test and the other based on the fast blue B salt test. The test reagents are dispensed in two types of containers, a plastic pouch and a plastic tube.

The tests are performed as follows (Figure 3.2). A small amount of the suspected controlled substance (as plant material, resin, or liquid) is added to the pouch or tube. The container is closed. Squeezing the outside of the container crushes ampules located within that hold reagents. These actions are done in sequence to yield various colors that are then compared to a color chart for determination of whether the presence of a controlled substance is indicated. Neutralizing reagents are provided to render the contents safe for disposal. Users are instructed on how much suspected material to use and how to read the colors and about the presumptive nature of the tests (see Figure 3.2).

Figure 3.2

Simplified testing procedure for the major drugs of abuse utilizing field test reagents

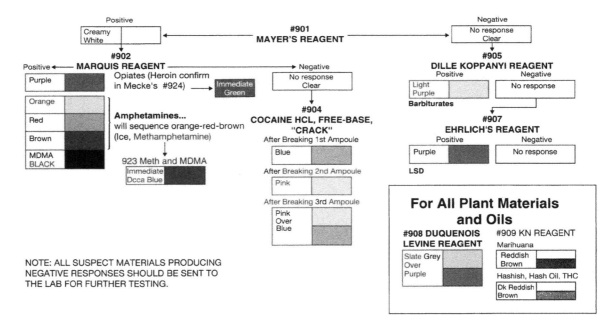

NOTE: ALL SUSPECT MATERIALS PRODUCING NEGATIVE RESPONSES SHOULD BE SENT TO THE LAB FOR FURTHER TESTING.

3.1.2.2 *Review of Laboratory Testing*

What follows is a review of much of the analytical literature from approximately the 1970s until the present regarding the testing of *Cannabis* and its constituents. The references generally fit within the seized-drug context.

3.1.2.2.1 Identification of Cannabis by Multiple Tests

Traditionally, seized-drug identification of *Cannabis* relied on various combinations of wet chemical, microscopic, chromatographic, and spectroscopic testing methods. In recent years DNA profiling techniques for identification and individualization have been described, although we know of no instance where it is being performed on a routine basis. A series of publications document a combination of techniques (usually wet chemical, microscopic, and chromatographic) for the identification of *Cannabis*. Many studies regarding seized-drug identification of *Cannabis* were published in or around the 1970s.

Thornton and Nakamura (1972) provide an extensive review of the chemistry of the phenolic constituents of the resin from the leaves and flowering tops of the marijuana plant, the chemistry of the Duquenois–Levine color test, botanical features useful for identification, along with thin-layer chromatographic and infrared absorption methods for identifying the major cannabinoid constituents. They found, based on an earlier work by Nakamura (1969), that since at least 82 species of plants from families of the subclass dicotyledon possess cystolithic hairs and despite the usefulness of other morphological features such as trichomes, a Duquenois–Levine test was necessary for confirmation of identity. They further contend that chromatographic tests are indicated where morphological features are absent. In a subsequent article (Nakamura and Thornton, 1973), the authors review, in a question-and-answer format, issues pertinent to those testing for *Cannabis*. Topics include the issue of speciation of *Cannabis*, specificity of the Duquenois test, substances yielding false positives to the analytical scheme of the Duquenois test, TLC for cannabinoids, microscopic analysis, and the potency of *Cannabis*. They conclude that no set criteria exist for the identification of *Cannabis*; some analysts rely strongly on morphological characteristics, while others stress the importance of chemical tests for cannabinoids. They add that a Duquenois–Levine test, a microscopic examination, and a TLC test may be "more than sufficient to rule out plants other than marijuana (*Cannabis*)."

A pamphlet from the former U.S. Treasury Department Bureau of Narcotics (1948) provides textual descriptions with black-and-white photos of the mature plant along with stereophotomicrographs of microscopic features, all of which can be used as "identification characteristics" for the purposes of seized-drug analysis. Fairbairn (1972) uses scanning electron micrographs to view the trichomes and glands of *Cannabis*, with emphasis on sessile glands found in abundance on the male, female, and monoecious plants studied. He notes that sessile glands provide an additional structure to be used in microscopic identification of *Cannabis*. DeForest and Morton (1972) describe a microscopic method for establishing the presence of marijuana in ash, such as from a pipe or ashtray. They show with photomicrographs how morphological structures of *Cannabis* ash differ from those of similar plant ash. This approach could be coupled with a TLC system, suggested by Kempe et al. (1972), that separates cannabinoids in charred *Cannabis*. They were able to distinguish cannabidiol, tetrahydrocannabinol, and cannabinol from residues, cinders, and paper. Hauber (1992), in an effort to avoid the hazardous waste generated by use of the Duquenois–Levine test, describes an unambiguous identification protocol that relies on the documentation of various botanical features and the running of two thin-layer systems. The systems indicate the presence of certain cannabinoids not discriminated by the Duquenois–Levine test.

3.1.2.2.2 *Identifying Botanical Features*
Seized-drug identification of *Cannabis* per se must include an examination of some of the plant's morphological characteristics as well as chemical tests to establish the presence of cannabinoids. *Cannabis* is classified, according to Nakamura (1969), as follows:

Division:	Spermatophyta (seed plants)
Class:	Angiospermae (flowering plants)
Subclass:	Dicotyledons (dicots); 31,874 species
Order:	Urticales (elms, mulberries, nettles, and hemps); 1753 species
Family:	Cannabinacea (hops and marihuana); 3 species
Genus:	*Cannabis*
Species:	*Sativa*

Morphological features may be micro- or macroscopically addressed. Since most submissions to forensic laboratories are in the form of crushed plant material, which no longer retains gross botanical features, and because most seized-drug analysts are not trained as botanists, an ability to recognize microscopic detail is critical for identification (Nakamura, 1969).

Microscopic Morphology
Some microscopic features are quite distinctive and the capacity to recognize them can be learned with moderate practice. Cystolithic trichomes and their hairs, other nonglandular trichomes, and glandular trichomes are especially useful for identification. Nakamura (1969) sampled 600 species of dicotyledons,

the botanical subclass of which *Cannabis* is a member, for those with cystolithic hairs. Many were found to possess cystolithic hairs, some with an appearance similar to *Cannabis*. He performed a Duquenois test on 80 species, with the result that many gave a positive Duqenois reaction, but none except *Cannabis* yielded a positive reaction to the Levine modification (i.e., purple color transferring to the CHCl$_3$ layer). Using a scanning electron microscope to look at *Cannabis* and other cystolith- and cystolithic hair-bearing plants, Mitosinka et al. (1972) found that the cystolithic hairs of *Cannabis* were much longer, given the broad size of their cystoliths, than they were for other plants possessing these structures. Figure 3.3 shows microscopic structures of *Cannabis*.

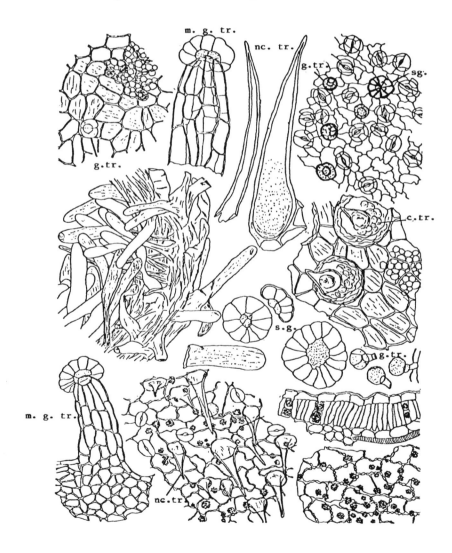

Figure 3.3

Microscopic characteristics of Cannabis g.tr. Small glanular trichomes m.g.tr. Multicellular multiseriate glanular trichomes s.g. sessile glands nc.tr. non-cystolithic trichomes c.tr. cystolithic trichomes

Microscopic detail can be viewed under a stereo- or compound light microscope. Cystoliths and their hairs are observable with a stereoscope at 10× to 25×. All of the structures shown in the Figure 3.3 sketches can be observed with a compound scope at 100× to 200×. Figures 3.3a and 3.3b are photomicrographs depicting such microscopic structures. Placing small fragments of leaf or seed husks on a microscope slide in an immersion medium facilitates observation of fine structure with the compound scope. A solution of chloral hydrate and water (5 g per 2 mL) works well as an immersion medium, particularly if the plant material is allowed to absorb the viscous liquid for a short period prior to viewing.

Macroscopic Morphology

The sketch in figure 3.4 shows some of the gross botanical features of *Cannabis*. When present, these are useful as additional evidence of identity. Characteristic features include the serrated edges of the leaves, their compound palmate structure (i.e., several leaflets arise from the same point), and the ovoid mottled appearance of the seeds. Figure 3.4a is a photomicrograph depicting *Cannabis* seeds. Identification based on gross morphology requires large portions of the plant for examination because other plants possess these structures.

3.1.2.2.3 *The Duquenois–Levine and Other Color Tests for* Cannabis

Two fast versions (less than 3 minutes to perform both) of the Duquenois–Levine and fast blue B tests are described by De Faubert Maunder (1969). Only henna, of the dozens of botanicals tested, gave a false-positive reaction. Oddly, the author describes an actual submission to his laboratory of henna mixed with *Cannabis* resin. This speedy version contrasts with how Duquenois with Negm reported the test in 1938 (Mausolf, 2001). Duquenois contends that a petroleum ether extract, evaporated to dryness, will go through a series of colors for up to an hour after adding concentrated HCl. He adds that under these circumstances, the test is specific. Fulton (1970) describes a color test using furfural for the identification of *Cannabis* resin. He claims to have been using the furfural test for *Cannabis* resin for 30 years, a fact suggesting that he found it reliable. He fails, however, to provide mention of testing other substances for indications of the test's validity. Lau-Cam and McDonnell (1978) performed a validation of the furfural test by subjecting various botanicals to it and a modified version of the test. In the same study they also tested the Duquenois reaction with various brands of coffee. They found that the furfural test is simple to implement and very sensitive. It did not yield false positives with any of the coffees tested or with teas, some of which had been reported to generate false-positive reactions to the Duquenois test. Fochtman and Winek (1971) reported some of these false positives to the Duqenois–Levine test after testing

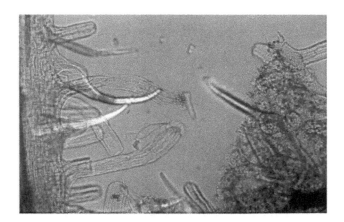

Figure 3.3a

Microscopic structures of Cannabis. *Note the cystolithic and glanular hairs. (micrograph, 100× with aqueous chloral hydrate used as mounting medium)*

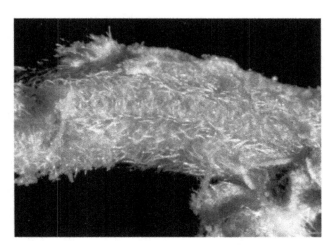

Figure 3.3b
Cystolithic hairs of Cannabis. *Note the "bear claw-like" morphology. (stereomicrograph, 25× taken with oblique light)*

Figure 3.4a

Cannabis *seeds. Note the typical ovoid shape and mottled appearance. (stereomicrograph, 7.5×, taken with oblique light)*

Figure 3.4

Macroscopic plant
morphology of Cannabis
sativa L.
1. Flowering shoot
2. Male inflorescence
3. Male flower
4. Female inflorescence
5. Female flower
6. Fruit
7. Seed

several brands of coffee. They caution that microscopic examination and color tests constitute only screening tests for *Cannabis*; a positive identification should be based on these combined with thin-layer or gas chromatography. Lau-Cam (1978) was able to eliminate the false-positive reaction of the Duquenois–Levine test to various coffees by adding 5 to 10 drops of para-dioxane to the test mixture immediately following addition of hydro-chloric acid. If only coffee is present, the colored products of the Duquenois reaction will be unstable and fade to brown within 1 minute under this procedure. The color reaction of *Cannabis*, however, will remain stable during this step, with the color being transferred to the chloroform layer during the Levine modification. El-Darawy et al. (1972) spotted thin-layer chromatographic plates with six common cannabinoids (cannabinol, cannabidiol, tetahy-drocannabinol, cannabichromene, cannabidiolic acid, and a cannabidiol isomer) and sprayed them with various visualizing reagents, including a Duquenois spray. When cinnamaldehyde was substituted for vanillin in the Duquenois spray, more of the cannabinoids responded with color reactions than reacted with vanillin. Substituting cinnamaldehyde for the aldehyde in a Duquenois and Blackie's test on hashish resin produced no appreciable improvement. Duke and Reimann (1973) compared various liquids for their efficiency in extracting Duquenois-positive cannabinoids. Alcohols, including methanol, ethanol, and propanol, were determined to be more efficient than other solvents tested. De Faubert Maunder (1974) describes an improved field test for *Cannabis* using dyes other than fast blue B, a dye suspected of posing health risks. Dyes that give similar colors to fast blue B and quick responses are fast blue BB, 1-diazo-4-benzoylamino-2,5-diethoxybenzene, and Corinth V. The testing procedure involves placing a small amount of liquefied material on filter paper, adding several reagents, and noting color changes at each step. The test can be rapidly performed. The author also comments on variables affecting the test, such as heat, different kinds of test papers, and the condition of the solvents. Hughes and Warner (1976) tested 67 compounds with a modified Duquenois–Levine test. They found that if 2 or 3 minutes is allowed to pass before adding chloroform, the selectivity of the test is greatly enhanced. They also found that only three types of coffee yield misleading test results following this procedure. In a follow-up study Jarzen (1977) observed that with a petroleum ether extract of the coffees (taken to dryness) the intense red-violet color generated with the Duquenois reagent for each brand of coffee was distinctly different than that produced with *Cannabis*. Additionally, he notes that the colors produced in the chloro-form layer decomposed with time, whereas those generated from *Cannabis* became more intense over time. Contrary to the findings of Hughes and Warner, Jarzen found that the *immediate* addition of chloroform after the purple color begins to form in the aqueous layer increases the test's discrimination between coffee and *Cannabis*. He claims that when the Duquenois–Levine test is performed by a trained investigator on dried ether extracts with chloro-form added immediately upon the appearance of a purple color in the aqueous layer, it is "a specific test for the presence of marijuana resin" and "will elimi-nate the possibility of a false-positive identification." Claims this strong for the discrimination power of the Duquenois–Levine test have not been noted elsewhere by us. Bailey (1979) reviewed three versions of the Duquenois test and their reactions to over 400 botanicals. He also looked at previous efforts to identify false positives to the Duquenois test. He observes, "There is no published report of an obviously botanical material apart from *Cannabis* that gives a positive Duquenois–Levine test." Bailey concludes that an analytical scheme of Duquenois–Levine, botanical inspection (gross or microscopic features), and a TLC system are necessary for a complete identification. He also found that of the three versions of the Duquenois reaction tested (a rapid version, a traditional version, and one employing a solid reagent of 1% metaldehyde in vanillin), the traditional version was the most discriminating for the variety of plant materials tested. A comparison of the Duquenois–Levine and the fast blue B salt test using six forms of *Cannabis* and 10 other botanicals was made by Drover and Lacienta (1980). Their studies, employing a test tube version of the fast blue B salt test (similar to that used in the commercial field test kits described earlier), revealed no false positives with fast blue B for the samples tested. Several leaf and seed samples did yield false negatives to the Duquenois–Levine test. The authors cite previous work (Fochtman and Winek, 1971; DeFaubert Maunder, 1969) stating that coffee, nutmeg, and mace do yield false positives to the Duquenois–Levine test. O'Neal et al. (2000a), using THC as the only form of *Cannabis* tested, performed a validation of the modified Duquenois–Levine test. To standardize part of the test, they referenced the reaction colors formed to the Inter-Society Color Council and the National Bureau of Standards (ISCC-BBS) and to Munsell charts. They also described the colors using common color designations. Mace, nutmeg, and tea reacted with the modified Duquenois–Levine test, but only THC generated a deep purple color.

Pitt et al. (1972) using UV/visible (VIS) spectroscopy studied the chemical mechanism of the Duquenois color test in an effort to characterize its specificity. They found that a partial resorcinol structure was necessary, but not solely sufficient, to produce the characteristic purple color. They conclude that for an identification protocol, the Duquenois test is an acceptable screening step when combined with botanical evidence. They add, however, that because of the "ubiquitousness of phenols in nature" and when botanical evidence is absent, supplementing the color test with positive chromatographic data is mandatory. Forrester (1998), using UV/VIS, IR, MS, and nuclear magnetic resonance (NMR), studied the purple dye structure of the Duquenois reaction. An aromatic substitution of Δ^9-THC with *p*-dimethylaminocinnamaldehyde was indicated. He proposes a schematic of the Duquenois product with Δ^9-THC.

3.1.2.2.4 Chromatographic Methods for Identifying Constituents (Cannabinoids) of Cannabis

Often, to complete the analytical scheme of color testing and examination of plant morphology, a chromatographic method is employed for additional evidence of the presence of *Cannabis*. Identification testing of seized hash or oils of *Cannabis* requires that the presence of various cannabinoids, many as monoterpenoids, be established. Evidence of their presence can be demonstrated with chromatographic methods such as TLC, GC, and HPLC. Most seized-drug testing for cannabinoids in *Cannabis*, its resins, and its oils typically involves only their identification.

Major cannabinoids are tetrahydrocannabinol (THC), cannabinol (CBN), and cannabidiol (CBD). Others include cannabinolic acid (CBNA), cannabidiolic acid (CBDA), cannabichromene (CBCh or CCEE), cannabichromenic acid (CBChA or CCEEA), cannabigerol (CBG), cannabigerolic acid (CBGA), cannabivarin (CBV), tetrahydrocannabinolic acid (THCA), tetrahydrocannabivarin (THV), and tetrahydrocannabivarinic acid (THVA). The isolation of Cannabisativine from the root of the *Cannabis* plant was reported by C.E. Turner et al. (1976). C.E. Turner et al. (1974) state that CBCh, though thought to be a minor component of *Cannabis*, occurs more abundantly than CND in many *Cannabis* variants. Not all cannabinoids are psychoactive, as Siniscalco Gigliano (2001) notes with CBD and CBN and as Gaoni and Mechoulam (1966) report with CBCh. However, Fonseka et al. (1976) cite evidence that CBN may elicit a slight psychoactive effect in humans. Most of the nonmajor cannabinoids occur in quantities of less than 0.01% of total cannabinoids (Siniscalco Gigliano, 2001). Studies by R.N. Smith and Vaughan (1977) revealed that methanol is the most effective solvent of the four they tested (methanol, chloroform, light petroleum, and methanol-chloroform, 9:1) for extracting cannabinoids. Both neutral and acid cannabinoid solutions are relatively stable in darkness; acidic constituents tend to decompose in sunlight. J.M. Parker et al. (1974) report that cannabinoids, particularly THC, are unstable in various solvents like $CHCL_3$. Small and Beckstead (1973a) reported that some batches of *Cannabis* studied contained no THC. J.C. Turner and Mahlberg (1984) found that variation in extraction temperature (with $CHCL_3$ at 4°C and room temperature) had no significant effect on the amount of cannabinoids extracted. They observed that the amount of cannabinoids extracted from fresh plant material with $CHCL_3$ decreased over time (1.5h to 10h); no significant difference in amount extracted for these times was demonstrated with dried plant material.

Ohlsson et al. (1971), using chromatographic and mass spectrometric methods to study fresh *Cannabis* from different parts of the world, found cannabinoids present in all parts of the plant but is more abundant in the flowering tops and the small leaves around the flowers. They also found that both male and female plants have approximately the same amounts of cannabinoids and in similar ratios. The authors cite other research in support of the latter finding. ElSohly et al. (2000), in an analysis using gas chromatography of over 35,000 *Cannabis* preparations confiscated in the United States over an 18-year period, determined that the percentages of Δ^9-THC has risen from less than 1.5% in 1980 to 4.47% in 1997. Also noted was that hashish and hash oil showed no significant potency trends and that other major cannabinoids (cannabidiol, cannabinol, and cannabichromene) showed no significant change in concentration during the period studied.

Thin-Layer Chromatography (TLC)

There are many thin-layer chromatographic systems listed in the professional literature that will separate cannabinoids. Generally they involve spotting an extract of the plant material, resin, or oil along with known cannabinoid standards on silica-coated glass plates and letting them develop in mobile phases composed of a single organic solvent or a combination of organic solvents. Early methods included partition chromatography, where plates were predeveloped, for example, in dimethylformamide, prior to development. Korte and Sieper (1964) suggest such a method using cyclohexane as the developer. Today it is probably the case that most seized-drug chemists practice adsorption chromatography. In either case, the plates are then dried and the separated cannabinoids observed in at least two ways. They can be viewed under ultraviolet light if the plates possess fluorescent agents that ascending compounds can quench or be visualized by spraying with reagents that color the separated cannabinoids. A visualizing spray used early on, fast blue B, was replaced by many practitioners with fast blue 2B because the former is thought to be carcinogenic. An alternate visualizing spray to fast blue B, a 1% methanolic solution of 2,6-dichloroquinone-4-chlorimide, was developed by Barbato (1978). He claims that it is less carcinogenic and more stable than fast blue B. TLC has the advantages for seized-drug analysis of being relatively rapid, inexpensive, and convenient to operate and interpret.

What follows is a listing of various TLC systems for separating cannabinoids.

Clarke (Moffat, 1986a) recommends two systems for separating CBN, CBD, and Δ^9-THC:

(TI) Plates of silica gel G are dipped or sprayed with a 10% solution of silver nitrate and dried. Mobile phase is toluene; plate is developed in an open tank under unsaturated conditions.

(TJ) Plates of silica gel G are sprayed with diethylamine immediately prior to use. Mobile phase is xylene/hexane/diethylamine, 25:10:1. Visualizing reagents for both TI and TJ are fast blue B or Duquenois reagent.

The *CRC Handbook of Chromatography Drugs* (Gupta, 1981) also recommends two systems for separating Δ^9-THC, Δ^8-THC, CBN, CBD, CBNA, CBDA, Δ^9-THCA, and CBChA:

(S-1) A two-dimensional system consisting of petroleum ether/diethyl ether/acetic acid, 40:10:1, in one dimension and n-heptane/diethyl ether, 80:10, for the second dimension on a silica gel G plate. Plate is sprayed with fast blue B salt in 0.1 N NaOH.

(S-2) Methanol/water, 95:5, on a silica gel plate. Cannabinoids can be visualized by spraying plates after development with a solution of sodium metal (8 g) in methanol (100 mL) and dimethyl sufoxide (8 mL) and viewing under ultraviolet light.

The United Nations (1991) Drug Control Program (UNDCP) recommends three systems for separating CBCh, CBV, CBN, THV, THC, CBD, THCN, and CBDA (the compound name that "THCN" abbreviates is not listed):

A. Petroleum ether/diethyl ether, 80:20
B. Cyclohexane/di-isopropyl ether/diethylamine, 52:40:8
C. (For cannbinoid acids) N-hexane/dioxane/methanol, 70:20:10

The UN treatise outlines minimum quantities of plant material, resin, and liquid suitable for extraction along with the advantages and liabilities of various organic solvents for extracting cannabinoids. Though not stated in the text, it is presumed that TLC plates are coated with silica gel. Plates can be visualized with a fast blue B or 2B solution and can be preserved for review purposes by a final spraying of diethylamine followed by sealing in plastic wrap. R_f values are cited for the eight cannabinoids and cannabinoid acids listed earlier.

Other TLC systems for separating cannabinoids include silica gel plates developed in petroleum ether and ether, 4:1 (Machata 1969), and a system using a mixture of pentane and ether, 88:12, described by Gaoni and Mechoulam (1971). Mechoulam (1973) notes that a 7:10 ratio of acetone/hexane on silica plates minimizes oxidative degradation of labile cannabinoids and also yields good separation. Parker and Fiske (1972), after a literature review of numerous TLC systems for separating six cannabinoids (Δ^9-THC, Δ^8-THC, CBN, CBD, CBDA, CBCh), suggest adsorption methods involving $CHCl_3$ or 1,4-dioxane as developing solvents and fast blue B as a visualizing spray.

Tewari and Sharma (1983) describe a two-dimensional TLC system that will resolve 47 *Cannabis* constituents. A 20 × 20-cm silica gel G plate was used with heptane/dichloromethane/butan-2-one, 83:5:12, as the solvent for the first dimension. After the solvent was allowed to rise 12 cm, the plate was dried, rotated 90°, run in hexane/acetone, 86:14, and sprayed with a 0.1% solution of fast blue 2B in 45% ethanol. They report that spots of the major cannabinoids, CBC, Δ^9-THC, *trans*-Δ^8-THC, and CBD, were clearly "distinct, prominent, and dense."

Gas Chromatography (GC)

Numerous qualitative methods published in the 1970s reference use of packed chromatographic columns with packings such as OV-1, OV-17, OV-225, OV-101, and SE-30 and a variety of detectors, including flame ionization (the most common at the time), MS, electron capture, and nitrogen/phosphorous detectors (Gupta, 1981). In a series of studies in the 1970s, Strömberg (1971, 1972a, 1974a, 1974b, 1976) characterized numerous (>30) minor components of hash and *Cannabis*, first with packed-column GC and later with packed-column GC/MS. Some major cannabinoids were also profiled. Packed-column GC, because of a resolution significantly lower than capillary-column GC, does not have the wide application today that it once enjoyed.

The UNDCP (1991) lists three gas liquid chromatographic systems along with operating parameters for qualitative and quantitative analysis of cannabinoids. Two involve packed columns; the third uses a 10-m OV-1 chemically bonded fused-silica capillary column. All use flame ionization detection. Mills and Roberson (1993), in a large compendium of analytical drug data, list UV, IR, Fourier-transform NMR, and MS data for Δ^8- and Δ^9-THC, CBCh, CND, CNB, CBG, cannabicyclol, and cannabispiran. The spectra were generated specifically for that publication. In a review of analytical methodology for identification and quantification of *Cannabis* products, Vollner et al. (1986) describe both a packed-column (involving derivatization) and capillary-column GC method for separating cannabinoids.

A modern seized-drug GC procedure for profiling cannabinoids utilizes a 15- to 50-m (I.D. 0.25 mm) capillary column of fused cross-linked methyl silicone (methyl siloxane, phenol siloxane, etc.). Plant material, hash, or hash oil can be prepared for injection by drying a filtered petroleum ether extract and solvating it in methanol. General GC screening parameters include starting with an injection port temperature (perhaps 250°C) and ramping up the column temperature from 110°C (at, for example, 20°C per minute) to approximately 290°C. A procedure based on these parameters should separate the three major cannabinoids: THC, CBN, and CBD. A mass selective detector can help to identify each.

The heat of GC will decarboxylize cannabinoid acids to their neutral form (Kanter et al., 1979). Cannabinoids and cannabinoid acids may be separated by using trimethylsilyl derivatives or HPLC. J.C. Turner and Mahlberg (1982) developed a method for the latter using variation in solvent pH to successfully separate neutral and acidic cannabinoids. This could be particularly useful for fresh plant material, where the amounts of cannabinoid acids are high.

3.1.3 REVIEW OF TESTING METHODOLOGIES RECOMMENDED BY STANDARDIZING ORGANIZATIONS

Two international organizations have published standards specific to seized-drug analysis and *Cannabis* in particular. They are the United Nations (UN) and the Scientific Working Group for Seized Drug Analysis (SWGDRUG). The UN treatise describes specific testing procedures to analyze for *Cannabis* in its different dosage forms. SWGDRUG has made recommendations in the form of minimum standards for drug identification. These standards apply to both *Cannabis* as plant material and its chemical constituents. Specifically, SWGDRUG recommends a minimum number and combination of tests necessary for identification of controlled substances. As important as the specifics of testing procedures is that no testing protocol is complete if not performed in an analytically sound context. Accordingly, each organization has published guidelines on good laboratory practice and/or quality assurance. The following is a review of the analytical testing standards of each organization for *Cannabis* and its constituents.

3.1.3.1 The United Nations Drug Control Program (UNDCP)

The United Nations provides technical support for many forensic laboratories worldwide under the aegis of the UNDCP. The UNDCP, based in Vienna, Austria, publishes a series of monographs describing testing methodology for various controlled substances. Included in this series is *Recommended Methods for Testing Cannabis* (United Nations, 1991). It describes various tests for the identification of *Cannabis*, as plants, as resin (hashish), and as liquid. Except for its reliance on packed-column gas liquid chromatography, the methodologies described could easily find currency in modern forensic laboratories. After a discussion of how *Cannabis* is marketed in various locations, how the resin and liquids are prepared, and a description of the macro- and microscopic botanical composition of the plant, different testing methods, including a sampling plan, are described.

3.1.3.1.1 Sampling
The UN-recommended sampling plan can be applied to a single item, multiple items, or very large aggregates. In general, it recommends that, "sampling should be undertaken to conform to the principles of analytical chemistry, as laid down, for example, in national pharmacopoeias or by such organizations

as the Association of Official Analytical Chemists. For multiple items potentially containing *Cannabis*, emphasis is placed upon visual examination of all items needed for testing."

For quantitating a cannabinoid in single-package items it recommends homogenizing the plant material by passing it through progressively finer sieves. For qualitative analysis of multiple packages, it recommends the following:

a. For 10 packages or less: sample all 10.
b. For between 10 and 100: randomly select 10 packages for sampling.
c. For more than 100 packages: "select a number of packages equal to the square root of the total number of packages rounded to the next highest integer."
d. For sampling materials containing large aggregates that cannot be broken down: random samples should be taken from at least two different parts of an item.

3.1.3.1.2 Testing

A series of microscopic, wet chemical, and instrumental tests are described in cookbook fashion for identifying *Cannabis* and its cannabinoid constituents.

Macroscopic examination is based on identifying features of the male and female plant structure such as leaf and flower morphology. Drawings of these and more are provided. There is an abundance of microscopic structures that in conjunction with chemical tests can be used to reveal the presence of *Cannabis*. These include

a. Nonglandular hairs (trichomes), which include cystoliths
b. Glandular trichomes

Two color tests are described: the fast blue B salt test and the rapid Duquenois test (Duquenois–Levine test). Instructions are provided for performing the former either in a test tube or on filter paper. Essentially, an amount the size of a match head of plant material, resin, or liquid is put together with several reagents in stepwise fashion. The appearance of colors variously indicates the presence of the cannabinoids THC, CBN, and CBD. The rapid Duquenois test requires placing a small amount of suspected material in a test tube, adding several reagents, and noting color changes. According to this source, however, the appropriate colors indicate only "a *Cannabis* product." It observes that cannabinoids are not likely to be found in the stems or seeds of the plant but are abundant in its leaves and flowers. It is stressed that these color tests are only presumptive; alternate tests are needed for confirmation of identity. Some of the reagents for both tests should be refrigerated to prevent decomposition, and fast blue BB can be substituted for fast blue B for health reasons.

The UN recommendations for TLC and GC systems were described in Section 3.1.2.2.4. The treatise ends with a description of four HPLC systems, two isocratic and two gradient, all using internal standards and UV detectors set for single-wavelength monitoring. Instructions are provided for sample preparation along with a list of the elution order of various cannabinoids and cannabinoid acids.

3.1.3.2 The Scientific Working Group for the Analysis of Seized Drugs (SWGDRUG)

Started in 1997 and sponsored by the United States Drug Enforcement Agency and the Office of National Drug Control Policy, SWGDRUG consists of a core committee of over 20 forensic scientists from around the world whose mission was to develop seized-drug analytical testing standards and to recommend them to and seek acceptance from the world forensic community. Specifically, the group's objectives were

- To specify requirements for forensic drug practitioners' knowledge, skill, and abilities
- To promote professional development of forensic drug practitioners
- To provide a means of information exchange within the forensic science community
- To promote the highest ethical standards of practitioners in all areas of forensic drug analysis
- To provide minimum standards for drug examinations and reporting
- To establish quality assurance requirements
- To seek international acceptance of SWGDRUG standards

They currently have published minimum recommendations in the areas of training and education of seized-drug analysts, quality assurance for seized-drug laboratories, and analytical protocols for drug identification. These recommendations have been adopted as standards by the American Society for Testing and Materials *International*.

The SWGDRUG recommendation for identification lists three categories of tests, categories A, B, and C, in order of decreasing discriminating power (A having the most discriminating power). The following category listing and explanatory notes are reprinted from the SWGDRUG Web site and were approved in October 2003.

3.1.3.2.1 Categories of Analytical Techniques
Table 3.1 lists categories of analytical techniques.

3.1.3.2.2 Recommended Practices
SWGDRUG recommends that laboratories adhere to the following minimum identification criteria:

- When a validated Category A technique is incorporated into an analytical scheme, then at least one other technique (from either Category A, B, or C) must be used. This combination must identify the specific drug present and must preclude a false positive identification. When sample size allows, the second technique should be applied on a separate sampling for quality assurance reasons. When sample size is limited, additional measures should be taken to assure that the results correspond to the correct sample.
- When a Category A technique is not used, then at least three different validated methods must be employed. These, in combination, must demonstrate the identity of the specific drug present and must preclude a false positive identification. Two of the three methods must be based on uncorrelated techniques from Category B. A minimum of two separate limited, additional measures should be taken to assure that the results correspond to the correct sample. All Category B techniques must have reviewable data.
- For the use of any method to be considered of value, test results must be considered "positive." While "negative" tests results provide useful information for ruling out the presence of a particular drug or drug class, these results have no value toward establishing the forensic identification of a drug.

Table 3.1

Categories of analytical techniques listed by SWGDRUG as useful for identification

Category A	Category B	Category C
Infrared spectroscopy	Capillary electrophoresis	Color tests
Mass spectrometry	Gas chromatography	Fluorescence spectroscopy
Nuclear magnetic resonance spectroscopy	Ion mobility spectrometry	Immunoassay
Raman spectroscopy	Liquid chromatography	Melting point
	Microcrystalline tests	
	Pharmaceutical identifiers	
	Thin-layer chromatography	
	Cannabis only:	
	Macroscopic Examination	
	Microscopic examination	

- In cases where hyphenated techniques are used (e.g., gas chromatography-mass spectrometry liquid chromatography-diode array ultraviolet spectroscopy), they will be considered as separate techniques provided that the results from each are used.
- *Cannabis* exhibits tend to have characteristics that are visually recognizable. Macroscopic and microscopic examinations of *Cannabis* will be considered, exceptionally, as uncorrelated techniques from Category B when observations include documented details of botanical features. Additional testing must follow the scheme outline in the first two items of this list.

  For exhibits of *Cannabis* that lack sufficient observable macroscopic and microscopic botanical detail (e.g., extracts or residues), Δ^9-tetrahydrocannabinol (THC) or other cannabinoids must be identified utilizing the principles set forth in the first two items of this list.
- Some examples of reviewable data include printed spectra, chromatograms, and photographs or photocopies of TLC plates. Contemporaneous documented peer review will suffice for microcrystalline tests and recording of detailed descriptions of morphological characteristics is sufficient for *Cannabis* (only).

Identification of *Cannabis* as plant material can be made, in the simplest way, using the two Category B macro- and microscopic examinations and a color test. Examples of the latter include a Duquenois–Levine test or a fast blue B salt test. As noted in the preceding list, resins or liquids require that Δ^9-THC be identified utilizing the principles set forth in the first two items in the list.

The recommendations stress the use of an analytical scheme consisting of multiple uncorrelated tests based on validated methods performed by competent analysts. Testing in excess of the minimums stated is not discouraged.

3.1.3.3 The International Association of Official Analytical Chemists (AOAC)

The AOAC (Cunniff, 1997) lists a Duquenois–Levine method for the identification of *cannabis* (marijuana) in drug powders. The reagent is prepared by dissolving 12 drops of acetaldehyde (fresh) and 1.0 g vanillin in 50 mL of alcohol. Approximately 100 mg of sample is extracted with 25 mL of petroleum ether, filtered into a white porcelain dish, and evaporated to dryness over a steam bath. Two milliliters of the Duquenois reagent is added to the dish and stirred to dissolve the residue. Two milliliters of HCL is then added, and the mixture is allowed to sit for 10 minutes. After noting the color, the solution is transferred to a test tube, 2 mL of $CHCL_3$ is added, and the tube is shaken. The liquids are allowed to separate. A purple color in the $CHCL_3$ layer reflects a positive test result.

3.1.4 REQUIREMENTS OF THE AMERICAN BOARD OF CRIMINALISTS' CERTIFICATION EXAMINATION REGARDING ANALYSIS OF CANNABIS

As a corollary to the topics covered relating to the seized-drug analysis of *Cannabis*, the American Board of Criminalists (ABC), a certifying body for those analyzing or examining forensic evidence, requires some mastery of these topics for applicants of their *Knowledge, Skills and Abilities Drug Analysis Specialty Examination*. In topics for review they list, under "Identification of *Cannabis*" (ABC, 2001),

A. Macroscopic and microscopic morphology
B. Duquenois–Levine test
C. Botanical characteristics of *Cannabis* (annual plant, two sexes, existence of several agronomic varieties of monospecific genera, etc.)
D. Hashish and hash oil
E. Major cannabinoid chemical components of the plant (two types of THC, other psychoactive and nonpsychoactive components)
F. TLC of cannabinoids

3.1.5 MINIMUM ANALYTICAL REQUIREMENTS OF THE NATIONAL LABORATORIES OF AUSTRALIA, ENGLAND, HOLLAND, CANADA, AND THE UNITED STATES FOR IDENTIFYING CANNABIS

An informal 2002 survey of senior scientists of the national laboratory systems in the United States, England, Australia, and Holland involved with seized-drug analysis revealed the following. Minimums of two tests are required for identification of *Cannabis*, with more being performed if there are difficulties in analysis. Canada requires four tests for plant material. For submissions that include plant material, all of the laboratories rely on microscopy as part of the analytical scheme, using either stereo or compound light scopes. All laboratories accept trace amounts of *Cannabis* for testing. With hash, hash oil, or trace amounts of material, all require at least two selections from the following approaches: a Duquenois test, microscopy, TLC, and GC/MS. England and Canada reported the occasional use of HPLC for individualizing samples of *Cannabis* to a common batch.

3.2 PROFILING—PROVENANCE

3.2.1 INTRODUCTION

In addition to identifying *Cannabis* plants and preparations or identifying the presence of THC, it has long been of interest to look at the other constituents of the plant. Analysis of the concentrations and ratios of the major constituents THC, CBN, and CBD (Doorenbos et al., 1971; Fetterman et al., 1971a, 1971b; Small et al., 1975; Small and Beckstead, 1973b; Toffoli et al., 1966) was used to explore the taxonomy of *Cannabis* and to differentiate fiber-type (low THC) from drug-type (high THC) varieties. In addition, analytical profiles, or "fingerprints," of distributions of chemical constituents of *Cannabis* preparations have been used to provide answers to two recurring questions. The first, referred to by Perillo et al. (1994) as *strategic intelligence*, addresses the country or region of origin and is important in investigating distribution. The second addresses the question of whether two or more samples have a common origin. This is referred to as *tactical intelligence* (Perillo et al., 1994). Tactical intelligence involves a sample-to-sample comparison and is of particular utility in conspiracy investigations.

3.2.2 CHROMATOGRAPHIC METHODS

3.2.2.1 History

Early attempts to address one or both of these questions utilized TLC (Chiesa et al., 1973; Fowler et al., 1979; K.D. Parker et al., 1968; Tewari and Sharma, 1983; Tewari et al., 1974). Overpressured-layer chromatography has also been used (Oroszlan et al., 1987). Gas–liquid chromatography (GLC) using packed columns offered increased resolution and discrimination (Toffoli et al., 1966; Manno et al., 1974), and combination with mass spectrometry afforded positive identification of constituents (Vree et al., 1972). Differentiation of *Cannabis* of different origins by plotting of peak areas of CBD vs. CBN plus THC was first proposed by T.W.M. Davis et al. (1963). Small et al. (1975) and Small and Beckstead (1973b) used plots of %THC vs. %CBD to assign phenotypes. As awareness of coelution of CBD and cannabichromene (CBC) grew, comparison of THC to CBD + CBC was used by some investigators (Rowan and Fairbairn, 1977). However, it became apparent that the interpretation of analytical results and the appropriate choice of analytical tools are dependent on a wide range of factors. The most important factor arises from the chemical makeup of the *Cannabis* plant itself. The major components, THC, CBN, and CBD, are absent or in low concentration in the living plant (Fetterman et al., 1971a; Kimura and Okamoto, 1970; J.C. Turner and Mahlberg, 1982), where they exist as their carboxylic acid derivatives, which can be decarboxylated for use in profiling based on the major cannabinoids (Fetterman et al., 1971a). The degree to which the precursors are decarboxylated is dependent on the time between harvest and analysis and the environmental and storage conditions to which the samples are exposed (Vollner et al., 1986). Since the heat of the injection port causes decarboxylation (Fetterman et al., 1971a), the acid constituents cannot be determined by GLC unless the samples are derivatized prior to analysis (C.E. Turner et al., 1974). In order to generate data that could be interpreted in terms of chemical strains (chemovars), samples were heated to decarboxylate the precursors and ratios, (THC + CBN)/CBD, were determined (Kimura and Okamato, 1970; Veress et al., 1990; Kanter et al., 1979). Even though cannabinoid ratios have been shown to vary with environmental factors (Coffman and Gentner, 1975; Fairbairn and Liebmann, 1974; Haney and Kutscheid, 1973; Latta and Eaton, 1975; Siniscalco Gigliano, 1984; Valle et al. 1978), sex of the plant (Siniscalco Gigliano, 1984; Ohlsson et al., 1971; Agurell, 1970), maturation (Krejčí, 1970; Hemphill et al., 1980; Latta and Eaton, 1975; J.C. Turner et al., 1977), amount of light (Mahlberg and Hemphill, 1983), part of the plant (Krejčí, 1970; Doorenbos et al., 1971; Fetterman et al., 1971a; Hemphill et al., 1980; Fairbairn and Liebmann, 1974; J.C. Turner et al., 1977), and season when collected (Latta and Eaton, 1975; Phillips et al., 1970), the bulk of the evidence indicates that the most important factor is heredity (Ohlsson et al., 1971; Siniscalco Gigliano, 2001). The interpretation of cannabinoid ratios was complicated by the inability to resolve CBN, CBC, and cannabivarin by packed-column GC (C.E. Turner and Hadley, 1973; C.E. Turner et al., 1975). The interpretation was further complicated by the observation that the ratios detected are affected by the storage and treatment of the material prior to analysis (C.E. Turner et al., 1973a; J.C. Turner and Mahlberg, 1984). R.N. Smith and Vaughan (1977) demonstrated that results are also affected by the solvents used to extract the samples and the method of storage of the extracts (J.M. Parker et al., 1974; R.N. Smith and Vaughan, 1977). Chloroform (C.E. Turner and Henry, 1975) and methanol or ethanol (R.N. Smith and Vaughan, 1977) are efficient in the extraction of cannabinoids. Storage of the extracts in the dark and in the cold is essential to minimize changes in the samples (R.N. Smith and Vaughan, 1977).

The presence in *Cannabis* of the alkanes *n*-heptacosane and *n*-nonacosane as well as other straight-chain alkanes, ranging from C_{19} to C_{32}, was reported by de Zeeuw et al. (1973). These compounds can interfere with cannabinoid analysis when using GC alone. The authors noted a variation in the hydrocarbon concentrations with area of origin. C.E. Turner et al. (1973b) noted that the propyl homologs of CBN (cannabivarin), CBD (cannabidivarin), and THC (tetrahydrocannabivarin), in which the pentyl side chain is replaced with propyl, showed variations with geographical origin. Turner and Hadley (1973) reported the absence of CBD in an African variant. This was followed by an extensive study of cannabinoids in *Cannabis* from South Africa (Field and Arndt, 1980). de Zeeuw et al. (1972) also noted geographical variation of the propyl side chains. The ratios of concentrations of CBC, CBD, and THC were also correlated with geographical origin (Holley et al., 1975).

The bulk of earlier work on cannabinoid ratios utilized packed-column GC. The packed-column GC of *Cannabis* constituents has been reviewed (Fish, 1974; J.M. Parker and Stembal, 1974). Methods for qualitative and quantitative analysis of *Cannabis* products have also been reviewed (Vollner et al., 1986).

Since the ratios of the concentrations of the major cannabinoids are more a reflection of the origin of the seed than of the region where the crop is grown, these ratios are more useful for separating chemical races and as tactical intelligence than they are for strategic intelligence. Other constituents have been studied in order to determine their value in determining provenance. In a series of papers, Strömberg (1971, 1972a, 1972b, 1974a, 1974b, 1976) used packed-column GC to explore the separation and identification of what he termed minor components of *Cannabis* resin. He proposed the use of chromatograms showing components with both shorter and longer retention times than CBD in comparing hashish samples (Strömberg, 1972b). Volatile components sampled from the sealed headspace of solid *Cannabis* samples were explored by Hood et al. (1973) and Hood and Barry (1978). Three different packed-column GC analyses were used to identify three fractions consisting of oxygenated compounds (MW < 100), monoterpenes (MW > 100), and sesquiterpenes (MW < 100) (Hood et al., 1973). Eighteen compounds were identified by retention times. Chromatograms of headspace volatiles from 14 samples having different geographical origins were compared (Hood and Barry, 1978). The authors concluded that headspace-volatile analysis may be useful in comparing two seizures but that since they vary with handling and history, their utility in determining geographic origin is doubtful. Both Strömberg and Hood were hampered by an inability to resolve many constituents using packed columns.

3.2.2.2 Extraction

A wide variety of extraction solvents and methods have been used to separate the cannabinoids and other compounds of interest from the plant material or the resins. They include soaking in petroleum ether (Barni Comparini and Centini, 1983; Stephanou et al., 1984), chloroform (Kanter et al., 1979; J.C. Turner and Mahlberg, 1984), or methanol (Björkman, 1982; Wheals and Smith, 1975; Nakahara and Sekine, 1985). Soxhlet extraction with cyclohexane has been used (Novotny et al., 1976). R.N. Smith and Vaughan (1976) used methanol–chloroform (9:1), as did Brenneisen (1984). Baker et al. (1980) also used methanol–chloroform (4:1). Brenneisen and ElSohly (1988) compared various solvents and methods and concluded that methanol–chloroform (9:1) gave the overall best extraction efficiency for the wide range of analytes in *Cannabis*. Sonication at room temperature of powdered sample with this solvent has become the method of choice for comparison studies with *Cannabis*.

Veress (1994) used *Cannabis* as an example for a method of optimizing extraction efficiency in supercritical fluid extraction (SCF) for quantification. An evaluation of the effect of particle size on the SCF extraction of *Cannabis* showed that selection of a given sieve fraction leads to erroneous conclusions about the sample as a whole (Eory et al., 2001a). SCF has been applied to the measurement of THC and THCA concentrations in plant material (Eory et al., 2001b).

3.2.2.3 Derivatization

One approach to achieve increased resolution in packed-column GC and to allow simultaneous analysis of acid components is to derivatize the phenolic and carboxylic acid functions of the cannabinoids. Claussen et al. (1966) first used TMS derivatives to separate the cannabinoids from their acidic derivatives. TMS and trifluoroacetyl derivatives were described by Caddy and Fish (1967). Fetterman et al. (1971b) and K.H. Davis et al. (1970) described TMS derivatives in separations of THC, CBN, and CBD. The use of TMS derivatives to separate and identify cannabidiolic acid (CBDA) (Paris and Paris, 1973) and to separate CBD and CBC (C.E. Turner et al., 1974) was also reported. The use of silyl derivatives in routine analysis was advocated by C.E. Turner et al. (1974). Rasmussen (1975a, 1975b) explored the use of GC with solid injection and with on-column silation following solid injection with cold trapping.

Harvey and Paton (1975) combined packed-column GC with MS to explore silyl derivatives with longer alkyl groups to separate dihydroxy from monohydroxy cannabinoids. The tri-*n*-butyl silyl derivatives afforded complete separation. *t*-Butyldimethylsilyl, trimethylsilylacetate, and diethylphosphate derivatives were used in a study of the cannabinoids by GC, GC/MS, and HPLC (Knaus et al., 1976). The *t*-butyldimethylsilyl and trimethylsilylacetate derivatives were stable enough for use in HPLC. On-column methylation using dimethylformamide dimethylacetal in pyridine enabled Björkman (1982) to separate and identify at least 16 components of *Cannabis* extracts, by packed-column GCEIMS, compared with 6 without derivatization.

3.2.2.4 High-Performance Liquid Chromatography and Capillary Column Gas Chromatography

An alternative to derivatization of polar and acidic functions is to use a method that does not cause decomposition or rearrangement in thermally labile compounds. High-performance liquid chromatography (HPLC) fits this need. Although HPLC does not offer the resolving power of capillary-column GC, it is on a par with packed-column GC for the resolution of the main cannabinoids. The identification of the separated components requires either comparison to standards or isolation and analysis by mass spectrometry (Wheals and

Smith, 1975; R.N. Smith, 1975). Reversed-phase HPLC with UV detection has been utilized for provenance determination and specimen comparison (R.N. Smith and Vaughan, 1976; P.B. Baker et al., 1980; J.C. Turner and Mahlberg, 1982; Brenneisen, 1984, 1986). Nakahara and Sekine (1985) developed a method using electrochemical (EC) detection. Kanter et al. (1979) used HPLC in a method to quantitate THC and THCA based upon comparison of raw samples vs. decarboxylated samples, since the normal-phase separation being used did not enable direct measurement of the THCA. Veress et al. (1990) also used normal-phase HPLC and optimized the decarboxylation process to determine cannabinoid acids.

Novotny et al. (1976) used an 11-m by 0.26-mm glass capillary coated with SE-52 (methylsilicone) to separate cannabinoids. Soxhlet extraction with cyclohexane, followed by washing with nitromethane, was used to obtain samples for analysis. The cyclohexane was evaporated to dryness, and dichloromethane was used as the solvent for chromatography. The sample (4 μL) was injected into a precolumn that was flushed with helium to remove solvent. The precolumn was placed in the modified injection port of a GC, where it was thermally striped (250°C) onto the analytical column (room temperature). Temperature programming from 70°C to 240°C at 2°C was used for both FID and MS detection. The analysis lasted 110 minutes. The method separated 70 components, 38 of which were identified by EIMS. The authors demonstrated the discrimination of two samples that appeared identical by comparison of CBN, THC, and CBD using the same column under different conditions. Stephanou et al. (1984) used capillary-column GCEIMS to separate and identify the TMS derivatives of *Cannabis* extracts. Mass spectra of 18 components, including the TMS derivative of tetrahydrocannabinolic acid A (THCA-A), were reported. Barni Comparini and Centini (1983) compared packed-column GC, capillary-column GC, and HPLC for the analysis of *Cannabis* constituents and advocated the combination of capillary GC and HPLC.

Brenneisen and ElSohly (1988) used a comprehensive approach to developing chromatographic and spectral profiles of *Cannabis* of different origins. The samples (100 mg herb, 50 mg resin) were extracted by sonication in 1.0 mL of methanol–chloroform (9:1) containing 0.2 mg/mL of phenanthrene as internal standard. This solvent was chosen for its ability to rapidly extract, over a wide polarity range, the highest amount of cannabinoids and noncannabinoids compared with methanol, chloroform, dichlormethane, and cyclohexane. It was specifically recommended *not* to use a Soxhlet extraction, which can cause decomposition of thermolabile compounds. Gas chromatography was performed on 30-m × 0.25-mm fused silica columns coated with DB-1. Column temperature was programmed from 70°C to 250°C at 5°/min. The same column was used with an FID for generating profiles and with a GCEI (ion trap)

MS for identification. More than 100 different compounds were separated in a 70-minute analysis (Figures 3.5 and 3.6). This same GCMS procedure was used to identify TMS derivatives of acidic cannabinoids and polar noncannabinoids isolated by HPLC. HPLC profiles were generated using an isocratic mobile phase (CH$_3$OH:H$_2$O + 1% HOAc\77:23) in a 750- × 4.6-mm column packed with 3μm ODS-1. Detection was by UV at 230nm. Up to 45 different com-

Figure 3.5

GCMS profile (reconstructed ion chromatogram) of Cannabis "Mexico" Copyright ASTM. Reprinted with permission from Brenneisen and ElSohly (1988).

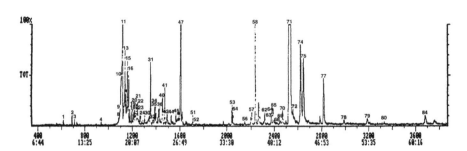

Figure 3.6

HPLC profile of Cannabis "Mexico" Copyright ASTM. Reprinted with permission from Brenneisen and ElSohly (1988).

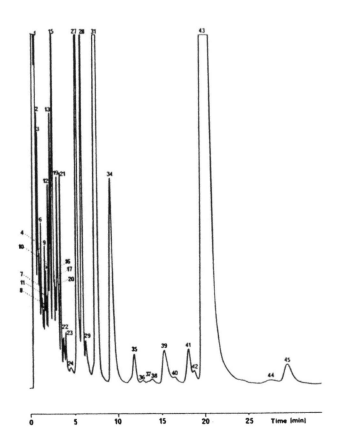

pounds were separated in a 35-minute analysis (Figure 3.6). Isolation followed by GCMS was used to identify 20 of these. The authors concluded that most of the diagnostically important peaks in the GC profiles are in the terpene region and that these profiles might be useful for determining geographic origin. They also concluded that HPLC is the preferred method of acquiring profiles of thermolabile and polar compounds such as THCA, CBDA, and CBCA and that these profiles are more useful for assessing the history of the samples. The combination of these two methods provided a very powerful tool for comparing samples (tactical intelligence) and showed great improvements over earlier methods.

Lehmann and Brenneisen (1995) developed an HPLC method with photodiode array detection (DAD) that allows qualitative and quantitative analysis of the neutral and acidic cannabinoids. Peaks were identified by comparison to standards and by DAD-UV spectra. A 200- × 2.0-mm column and a 20- × 2.0-mm precolumn packed with ODS-1(C_{18}), 3 µm, was used in combination with a complex-gradient elution to separate compounds with a wide variety of polarities (Figure 3.7). A limit of detection (LOD) of about 25 ng of cannabinoid per 1 mL of extract was reported. The method easily classifies the chemotypes and can be used to measure the psychotropic potency and to compare samples.

Much of the recent research in analytical methods for cannabinoids has focused on reducing the time of analysis and increasing the resolution and specificity. For developing profiles of *Cannabis*, including the terpenes and sesquiterpenes as well as the main cannabinoids, capillary-column GC and GCMS are excellent. However, in order to obtain a complete profile, a method that allows identification and quantification of the acid components without derivatization or decarboxylation is desirable. The method of Lehmann and Brenneisen (1995) is excellent for establishing chemotypes and provides a very good profile; however, it does not resolve all of the acidic components, and it requires a 60-minute run. Weinberger and Lurie (1991) explored the use of micellar electrokinetic capillary chromatography for the analysis of clandestinely manufactured drugs. They found the method provided great improvement over HPLC methods for heroin and cocaine seizures but lacked sufficient resolving power for *Cannabis* samples. Lurie et al. (1998) used capillary electrochromatography (CEC) to achieve excellent resolution of acidic, highly polar, and neutral cannabinoids in a 40-minute analysis (Figures 3.8 and 3.9).

Rustichelli et al. (1996) proposed HPLC-MS as a rapid method for separation and identification of hashish constituents. Reversed-phase C-18 columns were used with isocratic MeOH–H_2O (80:20) as the mobile phase. Excellent resolution of THC, CDB, and CBN was achieved, but the acid components were poorly resolved. Mass spectrometry (EI) utilized a Finnigan MAT SSQ 710A

Figure 3.7

HPLC profiles of chemotypes of Cannabis sativa L.: (a) Chemotype I (drug type); (b) chemotype II (intermediate type); (c) chemotype III (fiber/industrial type) Reprinted from Lehmann and Brenneisen (1995) by courtesy of Marcel Dekker, Inc.

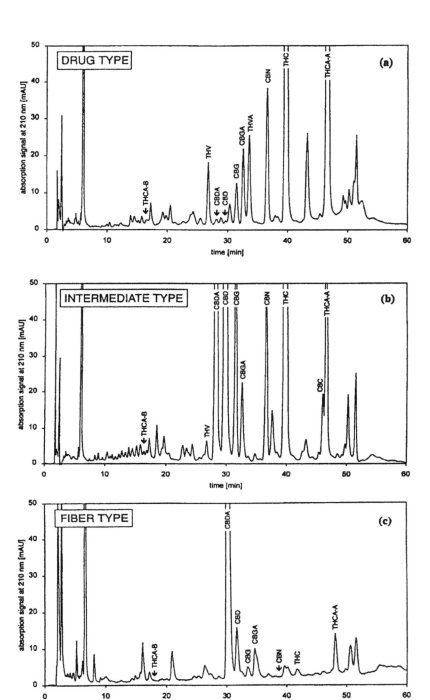

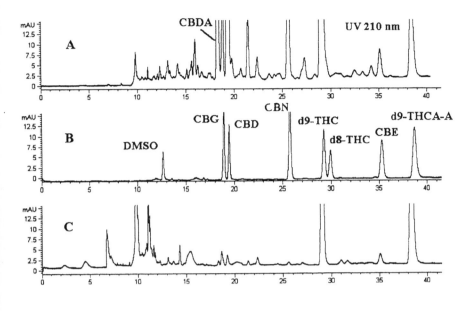

Figure 3.8

Capillary electrochromatography of (A) concentrated hashish extract, (B) standard mixture of cannabinoids, and (C) concentrated marijuana extract Reprinted with permission from Lurie et al. (1998). Copyright 1998 American Chemical Society.

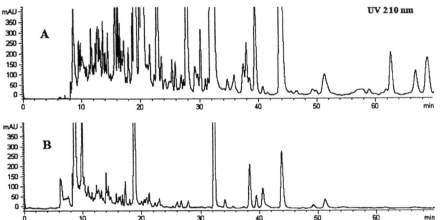

Figure 3.9

Capillary electrochromatography of (A) concentrated hashish extract and (B) concentrated marijuana extract Reprinted with permission from Lurie et al. (1998). Copyright 1998 American Chemical Society.

equipped with an interface particle beam (Finnigan) and a Jasco PU980 pump. Under the conditions used, the acid cannabinoids were decarboxylated. CBDA and CBNA coeluted. The same chromatographic system with UV detection was used (Rustichelli et al., 1998) in the analysis of cannabinoids in fiber hemp plant varieties. These analyses may be sufficient in differentiating chemotypes but would not suffice for forensic comparisons, due to the lack of resolution of acidic cannabinoids.

Ndjoko et al. (1998) used HPLC thermospray mass spectrometry (HPLC-TSMS) and HPLC-TSMSMS to separate and identify the major cannabinoids at the 100-pg level. A gradient elution (acetonitrile–H_2O, 50:50 to 100:0) was used to resolve the cannabinoids that gave intense molecular ions ([M + H]$^+$) in the TSMS with no fragment ions. Compounds recorded included THC (m/z 315), CBD (m/z 315), CBC (m/z 333), THCA (no attempt to define A or B; m/z 359), CBDA (m/z 359), CBN (m/z 311), and cannabichromevarinic acid (CBCVA, m/z 331). MSMS was used to obtain the characteristic fragments shown in Table 3.2.

Another approach to analysis of the thermolabile components of *Cannabis* without the need for derivatization was proposed by Bäckström et al. (1997). Supercritical fluid chromatography was used to separate CBD, CBN, Δ^8-THC, and Δ^9-THC in 8 minutes. THC-d_3 was used as an internal standard. Separation was achieved with a gradient elution consisting of 2% methanol in CO_2 going to 7% methanol in CO_2 over 15 minutes. A 250- × 4.6-mm cyanopropyl silica column was used. Analytes were detected by atmospheric pressure chemical ionization mass spectrometry (APCI-MS). At low cone voltages, intense molecular ions ([M + H]$^+$) ideal for quantitation were obtained. At higher voltages, characteristic fragmentation was observed. The authors noted in their introduction the limitation placed on GC analysis by decarboxylation of the cannabinoid acids but did not include any acids in their study. Application of this method to separation of mixtures such as those explored by Lurie et al. (1998) (Figure 3.8) and Lehmann and Brenneisen (1995) (Figure 3.7) should be of great interest.

The use of pyrolysis–gas chromatography to classify and compare hashish is another novel approach to determination of provenance (Hida et al., 1995). Dendrograms were developed from cluster analysis of the peaks in pyrograms of hashish from different sources and were effective in discriminating the samples. The method of pattern recognition of pyrograms has been widely used in forensic science to perform comparisons of polymeric materials such as paint, rubber, and plastic. In the case of hashish, however, it lacks the ability to focus on the individual components of the complex mixture.

Table 3.2

Thermospray MSMS of cannabinoids

	Parent Ion m/z	Daughter Ion m/z
THC	315	259, 247, 193
CBD	315	259, 247, 193
THCA	359	341, 295, 316
CBDA	359 (low intensity)	
CBN	311	296, 242, 232, 195, 181, 164
CBCVA	331	205
CBC	333	298, 287, 275, 263, 207, 166, 153

Source: Ndjoko et al. (1998).

The application of GC coupled with infrared spectrophotometric detection (GC-IR) has been investigated by Idilbi et al. (1985).

3.2.3 NONCHROMATOGRAPHIC APPROACHES

3.2.3.1 Carbon-13

J.H. Liu et al. (1979) explored variations in the ratio of ^{13}C to ^{12}C in *Cannabis* samples. Variations were found among the parts of the plant as well as among samples from different sources. In spite of the authors' suggestion that the addition of this approach to other (chromatographic) methods of comparing and sourcing *Cannabis* would "increase the chance of success," this approach has not attracted further research.

3.2.3.2 Inorganic Constituents in Determination of Provenance

The presence and relative concentrations of trace elements were used by Fagioli et al. (1986) to compare five hashish submissions. Atomic adsorption (AA) with sampling in a carbonaceous slurry was used to determine Na, K, Ca, Mg, Fe, Cu, Mn, and Zn. The submissions consisted of five different batches made up of multiple cakes of hashish. The within-cake variations and the within-batch variations were determined, and they demonstrated relative homogeneity within each. The elemental data clearly differentiated all of the batches. Lahl and Henke (1997) and Tenhagen et al. (1998) have used metals analysis to differentiate hashish samples. The authors quantified the elements in hashish samples by both inductively coupled plasma atomic absorption spectrometry (ICP-AES) and neutron activation analysis and found no significant difference in their power of discrimination when neural networks were used to interpret the data. Watling (1998) used laser ablation inductively coupled plasma mass spectrometry (LA-ICP-MS) to source the provenance of *Cannabis* crops in western Australia. LA-ICP-MS is not suitable for determining precise, accurate elemental concentrations, but it is excellent for developing "fingerprints" of elemental association patterns. The sample preparation is simple and does not require ashing or dissolution. The water-washed specimens are freeze-dried and ground to fine powder under liquid N_2. The powder is then compressed into a tablet in a cardboard mount. The cardboard mount is placed inside the laser cell, where a small portion is removed by multiple ablation (20 shots) and transferred to the plasma. The data can be presented as plots of raw data (Figure 3.10), as histograms (Figure 3.11), or as ternary ratio percentage plots that represent the direct comparison of the relationship between three analytes (Figure 3.12). This method should prove exceptionally valuable in determining provenance. Ferioli et al. (2000) used AA as one component of a multiple-method comparison of hashish samples.

Figure 3.10

Raw count data from laser ablation ICP-MS of four samples showing significant similarity and probable single source Reproduced by permission of the Royal Society of Chemistry from Watling (1998).

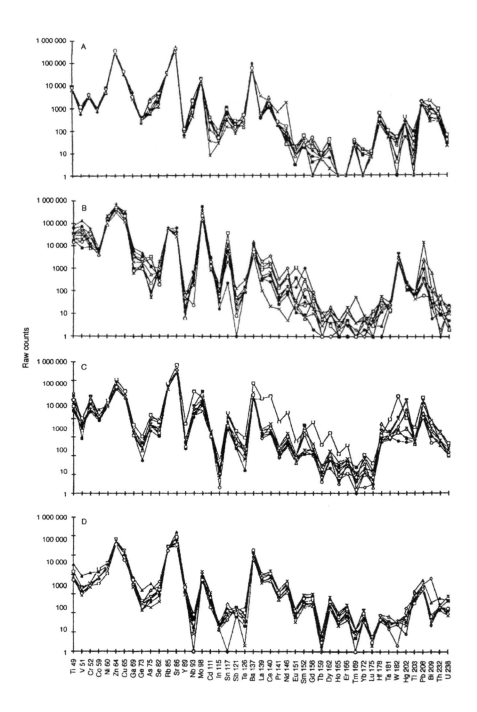

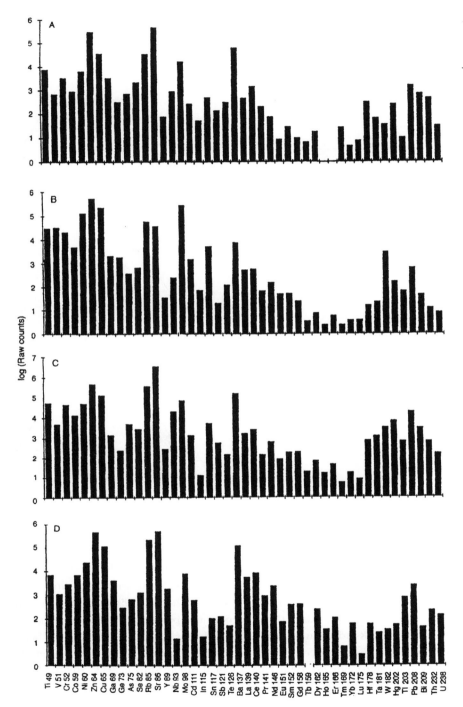

Figure 3.11
Simplified histogram plots
of median data from
four samples
Reproduced by permission
of the Royal Society of
Chemistry from Watling
(1998).

Figure 3.12

Ternary plots for four bulk samples recovered during a single raid showing difference in provenance (left) and four bulk samples showing similarity in provenance (right) Reproduced by permission of the Royal Society of Chemistry from Watling (1998).

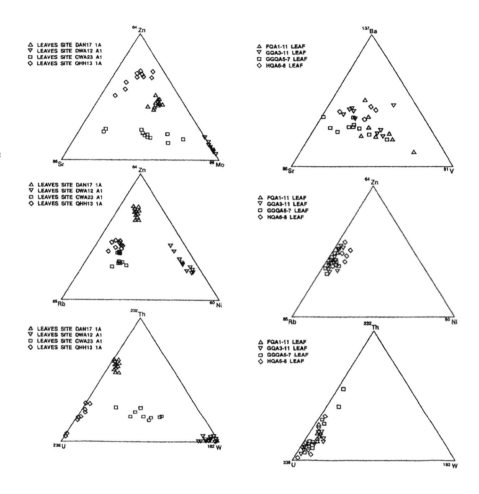

3.2.3.3 Molecular Biology Approaches

The application of molecular approaches to investigations of *Cannabis* has been reviewed (Siniscalco Gigliano, 2001). A variety of methods for identifying *Cannabis* using DNA technology have been developed (Siniscalco Gigliano, 1995, 1997, 1998, 1999; Siniscalco Gigliano and DiFinizio, 1997; Siniscalco Gigliano et al., 1997; Linacre and Thorpe, 1998). Wilkinson and Linacre (2000) have studied the detection and persistence of *Cannabis sativa* DNA on skin. Random amplification of polymorphic DNA (RAPD) has been explored as a means of comparing samples and assessing origin (Gillan et al., 1995; Siniscalco Gigliano, 1995; Jagadish et al., 1996; Shirota et al., 1988). Gillan et al. (1995) used five different primers to amplify DNA extracted from 17 different samples of herbal *Cannabis*. Only three of the primers led to sample

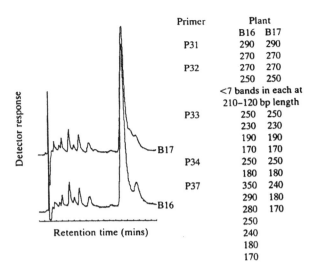

Primer	Plant	
	B16	B17
P31	290	290
	270	270
P32	270	270
	250	250
	<7 bands in each at	
	210–120 bp length	
P33	250	250
	230	230
	190	190
	170	170
P34	250	250
	180	180
P37	350	240
	290	180
	280	170
	250	
	240	
	180	
	170	

Figure 3.13

Example of differentiation by RAPD of two Cannabis samples that could not be differentiated by HPLC alone Reprinted from Gillan et al. (1995) by permission of the Forensic Science Society.

discrimination. Using these three primers (Genosys, 33: 5'-CTTGAGTGGA-3', 34: 5'-GGATCTGAAC-3', 37: 5'-CCACTTT-3'), all but 2 of the 17 samples could be distinguished. This included samples that were indistinguishable by HPLC (Figure 3.13) up to 10.

Kojoma et al. (2002) reported differentiation of *Cannabis* samples that were compared by HPLC using inter-simple sequence repeat (ISSR) amplification. The authors claim the method is easier than either RAPD or restriction fragment length polymorphism (RFLP) analyses.

Coyle et al. (2003) have reported a simplified method of DNA extraction using a commercially available plant DNA extraction kit manufactured by QIAGEN to replace a more difficult and time-consuming hexadecyltrimethylammonium bromide extraction (Doyle and Doyle, 1990). Amplified fragment length polymorphism was used to assess the quality of the extracts and the reproducibility of profiles from clonal *Cannabis*.

Single-strand conformation polymorphism (SSCP) using primers designed for the intergenic spacer region between *trnL* and *trnF* genes of *Cannabis sativa* chloroplast DNA was used to differentiate strains was reported by Kohjyouma et al. (2000).

3.2.4 SUMMATION

The determination of provenance is a complex undertaking for which there is no single ideal procedure that meets all the needs of the forensic science community. For the determination of chemotypes (differentiation of fiber- and drug-type material), HPLC procedures such as that published by Lehmann and Brenneisen (1995) are adequate (see Figure 3.7). For determining compliance with laws governing allowable concentrations of cannabinoids in crops, seeds, or seed-derived products, methods that concentrate on determination of THC alone or THC and THCA can be sufficient. HPLC procedures already described or recently published (Zoller et al., 2000) are ideal for determining the concentrations of THC and THCA without derivatization. GC or GC/MS methods in which THCA is converted to THC by decarboxylation (i.e., heating) work well when total THC is needed. Such a method (Ross et al., 2000) has been applied to the study of THC in seeds. When the task at hand is to determine whether samples could have a common origin or may be from a particular geographical location, high-resolution GC or GC/MS revealing not only the main cannabinoids but also the terpenes, sequiterpenes, and minor cannabinoids is needed. An additional profile by a method suitable for analysis of thermolabile compounds must also be used. These would include high-resolution HPLC, SCFC, or CEC. Elemental analysis may be called for, especially if a geographical location is the target of the investigation. An example of the combined approach is presented by Ferioli et al. (2000), who used HPLC, GC, GC/MS, and AA in an analytical characterization of hashish samples.

3.3 IMMUNOASSAYS FOR THE DETECTION OF CANNABINOIDS IN BIOLOGICAL MATRICES

3.3.1 OVERVIEW

Immunoassays for detecting *Cannabis* abuse are generally called cannabinoids assays or THC assays. Cannabinoids immunoassays are used to detect Δ^9-THC and its metabolites in biological and forensic matrices; therefore, the design and utility of immunoassays for different types of matrices have to take into consideration Δ^9-THC metabolism and pharmacokinetics. The administration, absorption, metabolism, and excretion profiles of cannabinoids have been extensively studied and reported (Hawks, 1982; Wall et al., 1983; Chiang and Barnett, 1984; Harvey, 1984; Law et al., 1984b; Alburges and Peat, 1986; Johansson et al., 1990; Moody et al., 1992b; Huestis et al., 1992a, 1992b, 1995, 1996; Cone and Huestis, 1993; Huestis and Cone, 1998a, 1998b; Smith-Kielland et al., 1999). It is generally concluded that THC is rapidly absorbed following marijuana smoking. The peak THC concentration in plasma is reached within 30 minutes and quickly declines due to redistribution into tissues, lipid stores, and metabolism. THC is extensively metabolized to a large number of compounds in humans; however, most of them are inactive. Notably, THC is trans-

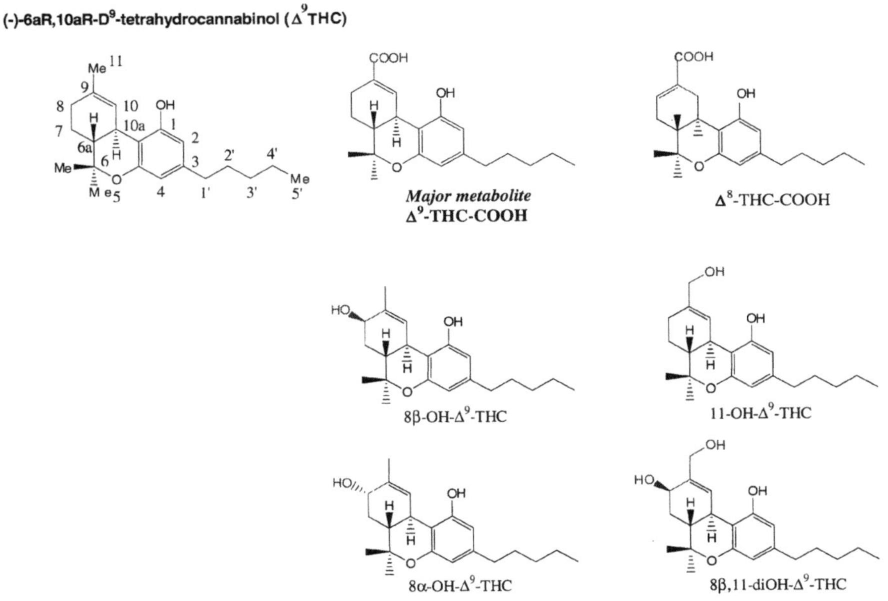

(-)-6aR,10aR-D^9-tetrahydrocannabinol (Δ^{9}THC)

Figure 3.14
Structures of THC and
selected THC metabolites

Major metabolite
Δ^9-THC-COOH

Δ^8-THC-COOH

8β-OH-Δ^9-THC

11-OH-Δ^9-THC

8α-OH-Δ^9-THC

8β,11-diOH-Δ^9-THC

formed to 11-hydroxy-Δ^9-THC (11-OH-THC), which is subsequently oxidized to 11-nor-Δ^9-tetrahydrocannabinol-9-carboxylic acid (THC-COOH). The major THC metabolite in urine is THC-COOH, which is present as both the free acid and its glucuronide conjugate (Williams and Moffat, 1980; Kanter et al., 1982b; Wall et al., 1983). Although the unconjugated THC-COOH is the "target analyte" for cannabinoids screening and confirmation, its glucuronide conjugate is present in considerably higher concentrations than the parent drug in urine and blood (Skopp and Potsch, 2002a, 2002b). Other metabolites found in urine (Figure 3.14) are 8-α-hydroxy-Δ^9-THC, 8-β-hydroxy-Δ^9-THC, 8-β,11-dihydroxy-Δ^9-THC, 11-hydroxy-Δ^9-THC, and a group of acid metabolites.

3.3.1.1 Cutoff Considerations

Commercial cannabinoids immunoassays can detect the presence of several THC metabolites via antibody cross-reactivities, although most assays for urine drug screening are calibrated only with THC-COOH. The overall sensitivity and specificity of an immunoassay is, to a certain extent, related to the characteristics of the antibody used in the assay (Teale et al., 1974a; Jones et al., 1984a; Peat, 1984; ElSohly et al., 1990; Salamone et al., 1998). The quantified value (assay result), as expressed in "apparent THC-COOH concentration" (i.e., calibrator-equivalent unit), is the "sum" of antibody immunoreactivities toward

THC-COOH and other structurally related THC metabolites in the testing specimen. Therefore, the "administrative cutoff" levels for THC initial tests are set at higher quantities than the associated confirmatory cutoff concentrations in order to accommodate the total contribution of antibody cross-reactivities. However, the correlation of total immunoreactivities to a single GC/MS value of the THC-COOH compound can vary to some extent. Such variations may influence the balance of clinical sensitivity and specificity for cannabinoids immunoassays, especially for testing specimens that contain near-cutoff concentrations of THC-COOH.

Regardless of the technology used, the analytical performance for a cannabinoids immunoassay is calibrated relative to the specified cutoff concentration and optimized for its comparative performance to the confirmation technologies. The screening cutoff of 100 ng/mL (or 100 μg/L) cannabinoids in urine was chosen at the inception of the SAMHSA drug-testing guidelines (53 FR 11970, 1988). This immunoassay cutoff was set partially due to the risk of passive exposure to marijuana smoke (Perez-Reyes et al., 1983; Law et al., 1984c; Morland et al., 1985; Cone and Johnson, 1986; Moffat, 1986b; Mulé et al., 1988). A comprehensive study of passive inhalation conducted by NIDA illustrated that it takes extensive exposure to extremely high concentrations under unrealistic conditions to cause a positive result (Cone et al., 1987). Additional factors, such as the cost and goals of the specific drug-testing programs, also influence the choice of cutoff levels (Sunshine, 1988). Several studies have since been conducted to demonstrate that lowering the initial testing cutoff in urine would increase the positive rates for marijuana detection (Wells and Barnhill, 1989; Rowland et al., 1994; Huestis et al., 1994; Wingert, 1997). Smith et al. (1989) showed that marijuana test sensitivity increased from 47% to 88% and specificity increased from 91% to 94% when the screening and confirming were lowered from 100 ng/mL and 15 ng/mL to 20 ng/mL and 5 ng/mL, respectively.

The current U.S. *Mandatory Guidelines* (59 FR 29916, 1994) specify a 50 ng/mL screening cutoff and a 15 ng/mL confirmation cutoff for cannabinoids testing. In case a retest is required for a specimen or for the testing of "Bottle B" of a split specimen, the retest quantification is not subject to a cutoff requirement; however, the retest "must provide data sufficient to confirm the presence of the drug or metabolite" (59 FR 29916, 1994). In general, many drug-testing programs in the nonregulated sectors also follow the cutoff defined by the *Federal Guidelines*. Depending on the drug-testing program goals and preference, four major cutoff concentrations have been used for urinary cannabinoids immunoassays: 20 ng/mL, 25 ng/mL, 50 ng/mL, and 100 ng/mL. Moreover, the screening immunoassay cutoff could be further decreased for detecting maternal and neonatal drug exposure (Hattab et al., 2000).

For any given cutoff, there can be substantial variability between subjects and between doses in the excretion profiles of THC-COOH. Huestis et al. (1996) demonstrated that mean detection times in urine following smoking varied considerably between individuals, even in highly controlled smoking studies. In addition, consecutive urine specimens may fluctuate below and above the cutoff during the terminal elimination phase, when THC-COOH concentrations approach the cutoff (Ellis et al., 1985; Huestis et al., 1996; Smith-Kielland et al., 1999). The "normalization" of drug excretion to urine creatinine concentration has been employed to predict new drug use and to reduce the variability of drug measurement attributable to urine dilution (Lafolie et al., 1991, 1994; Simpson et al., 1993; Huestis and Cone, 1998b; Fraser and Worth, 1999).

3.3.2 STABILITY OF CANNABINOIDS IN BIOLOGICAL FLUIDS

Results obtained from any given immunoassay for drugs of abuse can be determined either by qualitatively comparing the resulting signal output of the specimen to that of the "cutoff-level standard" solution or by semiquantitatively comparing to the calibration curve. Consequently, the stability of the analyte in calibrator solutions and in testing specimens is critical to the accuracy of the analytical system. The hydrophobic nature of the cannabinoids molecules can lead to the loss of the drugs in the specimen because of surface adsorption to the specimen-handling devices and storage containers. Thus the stability of cannabinoids in biological fluids has been evaluated in various container materials stored at different temperatures.

Dextraze et al. (1989) observed a 27% reduction in THC-COOH concentration due to adsorption to glass and reported that foaming of spiked urine caused by vigorous mixing resulted in a reversible 89% apparent reduction in THC-COOH concentration. Blanc et al. (1993) investigated cannabinoids loss from calibrators during the immunoassay testing process and found significant losses attributable to both the kind of pipette used and the surface contact in the analyzer cup. The loss of THC-COOH can be reduced by using appropriate pipette and maintaining a minimal surface-to-volume ratio in the analyzer cup. Roth et al. (1996) investigated the effects of solution composition and an assortment of container material types on the loss of THC-COOH using immunoassay and x-ray photoelectron spectroscopy. The authors also evaluated the effects of sample volume and sample handling and found that THC-COOH loss due to pipetting ranged from 1.1 ng to 7.9 ng per aliquot. Stout et al. (2000) observed rapid loss of THC-COOH at 4°C for polypropylene (maximal 14% loss) and polyethylene (maximal 17% loss), as well as a small loss (<5%) in polyethylene bottles at 25°C. All losses stabilized within 1 hour, and no further losses were seen over 1 week.

Paul et al. (1993) examined the effect of freezing on the concentration of abused drugs in urine and observed no significant loss of compounds except for THC-acid, which showed an average loss of 11% (ranging from 0 to 34%). Golding et al. (1998) observed appreciable losses (>22.4%) in some urine samples stored at room temperature for 10 days and approximately 8% loss when the samples were refrigerated for 4 weeks. The authors observed cannabinoids loss in frozen samples and postulated that the loss may be due to the decrease of the solubility of THC-COOH or the absorption process of cannabinoids molecules to the storage containers. Dugan et al. (1994) reanalyzed urine that had been stored at −20°C for 12 months and reported no extensive change in the average drug concentrations for THC-COOH. In contrast, Romberg and Past (1994) retested previously analyzed and frozen samples and found that 85 THC-COOH positive samples stored frozen for 1 to 10 months declined an average of 25% (ranging from −80% to +30%). The authors found that drugs partition into strata when frozen in urine because of the thermodynamics of the freezing process.

Skopp and Potsch (2002b) assessed the stability of THC-COOH glucuronides in urine and plasma by LC-tandem mass spectrometry. The glucuronide was stable in both matrices when stored frozen, whereas the glucuronide concentrations decreased at all other storage conditions. The authors reaffirmed that stability data derived from a particular biological matrix are important for reliable interpretation of the analytical results. The antibodies used in different cannabinoids immunoassays cross-react with THC-COOH and its glucuronide to different extents. Thus the specimen transportation and storage conditions following the collection procedure may affect the immunoassay results; however, the effect in general should not interfere with the screening result interpretation.

Johnson et al. (1984) reported that THC in blood was stable for up to 4 months at 4°C and −20°C. At room temperature, THC in blood decreased significantly at 2 months and dropped 90% after 6 months. By contrast, the concentration of THC-COOH was not significantly different from that of the control. McCurdy et al. (1989) assessed the stability of THC-COOH in whole blood while stored in four different kinds of blood collection tubes for up to 30 days at refrigeration and room temperature. Utilizing both radioimmunoassay and GC/MS, the authors reported that THC-COOH was stable in blood under all conditions studied. Skopp et al. (2000) demonstrated that cannabinoids usually measured in hair analysis are more affected by solar radiation than other drugs of abuse detected in hair. In addition to the deleterious effect of sunlight on the stability of cannabinoid constituents in hair, the weathering of hair, which damages the hair fiber at the ultrastructural level, may cause additional changes in drug concentrations in hair.

3.3.3 SPECIMEN VALIDITY AND INTEGRITY

Purposeful invalidation of the specimen by the donor can compromise specimen validity and integrity and, subsequently, negatively impact the accuracy of drug-testing results. Cook et al. (2000) reviewed the characterization of human urine for specimen validity determination. Cone et al. (1998) reported that the average detection times for marijuana metabolites appeared to be slightly shorter following ingestion of 1 gallon of fluids compared with ingestion of 12 oz of water. A popular means of sample adulteration is the addition of exogenous chemicals, such as glutaraldehyde, detergent, bleach, and various oxidizing agents (Baiker et al., 1994; Wu et al., 1995, 1999; George and Braithwaite, 1996; ElSohly et al., 1997; Urry et al., 1998; Tsai et al., 2000, 2001). THC-COOH is sensitive to oxidizing agents such as nitrite, peroxide, and chlorochromate. Because of the effect of oxidants on the cannabinoids molecules, by and large all immunoassay technologies can be affected. Specimens adulterated with oxidizing agents may give false-negative screening and escape further confirmation. For those that remain positive at the time of initial testing, the presence of oxidizing agents can interfere with subsequent GC/MS confirmation unless samples are treated with sodium bisulfite prior to the extraction procedure (ElSohly et al., 1997). The effectiveness of oxidizing agents can be affected by sample pH, original drug concentration, and the time between sample collection and sample testing. For example, Tsai et al. (2000) reported that significant decreases in the immunoassay results could be observed shortly after nitrite treatment in samples with acidic urinary pH values. In contrast, samples with neutral or higher pH values may remain immunoassay positive 3 days postnitrite spiking, even though some of these adulterated urine samples exhibited significant decrease in GC/MS recoveries following bisulfite treatment. Moreover, the decrease or loss of immunoassay-detectable cannabinoid crossreactives in acidic "THC positive samples" can be attenuated by chemically increasing the pH value of the samples to the basic pH range (Lewis et al., 1999; Tsai et al., 2000).

3.3.4 ALTERNATIVE MATRICES

The most commonly used biological matrices for cannabinoids analysis are urine, blood, serum, and plasma samples. Urine can readily be applied to various immunoassay analyses without sample pretreatment. Also, urine specimens can be obtained in relatively large quantities in comparison to other biological fluids. Therefore urine remains the most widely used specimen for initial screening tests, despite various issues such as variability of excretion profile, relationship to impairment, cutoff considerations, detection window, and collection and adulteration concerns. The use of alternative matrices may offer advantages in addressing some of the issues concerning urine drug testing (Schramm et al., 1992; Cone, 1993, 1997, 2001; Moeller, 1996; Kidwell et al., 1998; Skopp and Potsch, 1999; Jehanli et al., 2001; Caplan and Goldberg, 2001; Niedbala et al., 2001).

Analyses of THC and major metabolites in blood, including those involving immunoassay techniques, have been applied in a variety of pharmacokinetic and pharmacodynamic investigations, driving-impairment studies, and forensic cases (Hanson et al., 1983; Gjerde, 1991; Moody et al., 1992a, 1992b; Goodall and Basteyns, 1995). Interpretation of the significance of blood cannabinoids testing results and level of impairment or cannabis exposure has not been clearly established. However, various controlled studies have been conducted to correlate and predict these relationships (Huestis et al., 1992b; Cone, 1993).

Analysis of drugs in hair provides a longer detection window than urinalysis even though hair analysis for cannabinoids is one of the most difficult analyses (Nakahara, 1999). On the other hand, the detection of THC in saliva/oral fluids may indicate very recent marijuana use (Cone, 1993; Jehanli et al., 2001; Niedbala et al., 2001). It is generally postulated that cannabinoids in oral fluids were from residuals left in the oral cavity during the use of cannabis (Cone, 1993; Jehanli et al., 2001). Therefore, an ideal immunoassay for oral fluid THC should employ antibody produced against the parent THC compound instead of the traditional THC-COOH target analyte. Maseda et al. (1986) reported that saliva THC concentrations in subjects who drank beer after smoking marijuana were lower than those of nondrinking subjects. An earlier study in humans using radiolabeled THC administered by intravenous injection did not detect any radioactivity in saliva samples (Hawks, 1982). Although an advantage of oral fluid is the relative ease of collection, currently there is no standardized method for specimen collection. O'Neal et al. (2000b) demonstrated the impact of various collection devices on the measured drug concentrations in oral fluids. The chemical nature of the cannabinoids warrants caution in the specimen-collection mechanism. Alternative matrices are considered less vulnerable to adulteration due to the observed procedures of sample collection. However, there exist issues of environmental contamination, passive exposure, and bias concerns for some of the matrices (Nakahara, 1999; Kidwell et al., 2000; Skopp et al., 2000; Kidwell and Smith, 2001). A very small percentage of oral fluid sample substitution with canine or feline saliva was noticed when oral fluid sample integrity was checked for the presence of human IgG, indicating that the collection was not witnessed (Peat, 2000).

Compared to the urine matrix, oral fluid testing and sweat drug testing may have the limitations of the small amount of matrix collected and the lower levels of drugs in the specimen (Kintz et al., 2000). Oral fluid concentrations of THC vary over a wide range immediately after marijuana exposure and then rapidly decline over the first few hours. Thus the selection of a low cutoff for THC in oral fluid can increase the diagnostic sensitivity and allow a longer window of detection time. Niedbala et al. (2001) compared oral fluid THC testing to urine testing utilizing a screening cutoff of 1 ng/mL and a confirmation (GC/MS/MS) cutoff of 0.5 ng/mL. Although currently there is no standardized cutoff decision for alternative matrices, SAMHSA has been drafting a revision of the *Mandatory Guidelines* that will set cutoff levels and define requirements for alternative specimen drug screening and confirmation tests. The low drug concentration and hydrophobic feature of THC can present challenges for some of the screening technologies when applied to alternative matrices testing. Nevertheless, alternative matrix testing is an actively pursued area and more studies and reports are to be expected in the foreseeable future.

3.3.5 IMMUNOASSAY TECHNOLOGIES

Immunoassays utilize the high affinity and specificity of antibody–antigen binding interactions to detect minute amounts of molecules in complex biological materials. Immunoassays for drugs-of-abuse testing are generally used to eliminate negative samples, and to maximize the likelihood of finding the presence of a drug or a group of structurally related drugs in the specimen at, or above, a predetermined cutoff concentration. The following provides a brief overview of the commonly used cannabinoids immunoassay. The principles of these technologies were reviewed in greater detail in Chapter 2. Because most of the commercial immunoassays have been extensively evaluated in various comparative studies, the overall comparison of cannabinoids immunoassay technologies will be reviewed collectively in Section 3.3.6.

3.3.5.1 Radioimmunoassay (RIA)

An array of RIA tests has been developed or evaluated in the past three decades for the quantification of cannabinoids in urine, blood, serum, and plasma (Teale et al., 1974a, 1974b, 1975; Marks et al., 1975; Gross et al., 1974; Wall et al., 1976; Owens et al., 1981; Bergman et al., 1981; Zimmerman et al., 1983; Mason et al., 1983; Childs and McCurdy, 1984; Jones et al., 1984a, 1984b; D.E. Smith et al., 1989; Clatworthy et al., 1990; Altunkaya et al., 1991; Moody et al., 1992a). Hanson et al. (1983) compared ^{3}H-RIA and ^{125}I-RIA for cannabinoids with GC/MS and found that the three methods gave parallel but significantly different quantitative results. However, each technique was capable of measuring THC concentrations in blood and serum up to 3 hours after usage. Law et al. (1984a) described the confirmation of cannabis use through the analysis of blood and urine for THC-COOH and its O-ester glucuronide using combined

HPLC/RIA. An assortment of cannabinoids RIA kits was developed by Roche (Abuscreen RIA; now discontinued), Diagnostics Products Corporation (DPC, Los Angeles), the Immunalysis Corporation (Pomona, CA), and by Research Triangle Institute. The cross-reactivity profile, GC/MS comparison and regression analysis of RIA kits from different times and manufacturers have been analyzed in a number of studies (Bergman et al., 1981; Jones et al., 1984a; Peat, 1984; Weaver et al., 1991; R.H. Liu et al., 1994; R.H. Liu and Goldberger, 1995; Brendler and Liu, 1997).

In addition to blood and urine, RIA has been applied to the analysis of cannabis in oral fluids (Gross et al., 1985), fingernails (Lemos et al., 1999), hair (Mieczkowski, 1995), and meconium (Ostrea et al., 1989). Although RIA has the advantages of high analytical sensitivity for quantifying cannabinoids in a variety of biological and forensic matrices, there have been increasing concerns regarding the handling of radioactive materials and the disposal of radioactive waste. Currently the double-antibody cannabinoids RIA can be purchased from DPC. The THC Direct RIA available from Immunalysis Corporation has a 100 ng/mL cutoff for urine cannabinoids and claims a sensitivity of 2.5 ng/mL and a sharp and linear plot through 50 ng/mL from the low point through the high concentration point.

3.3.5.2 Enzyme-Linked Immunosorbent Assay (ELISA)

ELISA-based cannabinoids assays have the advantages of low detection limits and high versatility for various forensic and toxicological analyses. Diverse commercial ELISA kits can be used or tailored to test matrices such as urine, blood, serum, oral fluid, sweat, meconium, bile, vitreous humor, and tissue extracts (Perrigo and Joynt, 1995; K.A. Moore et al., 1999; Kerrigan and Phillips, 2001; Niedbala et al., 2001). ELISA has also been used to detect cannabinoids in plant tissue culture systems (Kanaka, et al., 1996).

Kerrigan and Phillips (2001) compared the performance of ELISA kits to detect drugs of abuse in blood with a selected cutoff for cannabinoids of 30 ng/mL. In comparative analysis of ELISAs from STC (now OraSure Technologies, Inc., Bethlehem, PA) and Immunalysis Corporation for six drugs-of-abuse classes in whole blood and urine, the authors concluded that Immunalysis assays offered superior binding characteristics and detection limits, whereas STC assays offered improved overall precision and lot-to-lot reproducibility. The STC serum cannabinoids assay is directed toward the carboxylic acid metabolite but is also reactive with parent THC. The percent cross-reactivity to Δ^9-THC for the ELISA kits used in the study (Kerrigan and Phillips, 2001) was 24.2% for STC and <5% for Immunalysis. By comparison, the respective percent cross-reactivity to Δ^9-THC and Δ^8-THC is reported as 10.4% and 125% for the Diagnostix cannabinoids assay and 35% and 200% for the Neogen cannabinoids

Compound	Approximate Percent (%) Cross-Reactivity Relative to the Specified THCA Equivalent Concentration of Each Assay			
	Immunalysis Direct ELISA (equivalent to 30 ng/mL THCA)[a]	Immunalysis Direct ELISA (equivalent to 10 ng/mL THCA)[b]	Immunalysis Ultrasensitive ELISA (equivalent to 25 pg/mL THCA)[b]	Immunalysis Sweat/Oral fluid ELISA (equivalent to 1 ng/mL THCA)[b]
	April 1998[c]	May 2001[c]	July 2001[c]	May 2001[c]
11-nor-9-Carboxy-Δ^9-THC	100	100	100	100
11-nor-9-Carboxy-Δ^8-THC	110	110	110	125
8 11-Dihydroxy-Δ^9-THC	<5	<5	<5	<1
11-Hydroxy-Δ^9-THC	<5	<5	16.6	<1
Δ^9-THC	<5	21	4.1	60
Δ^8-THC	NA[d]	45	NA[d]	66
Cannabinol	<5	<5	<1	<1
Cannabidiol	<5	<5	<1	<1

Table 3.3

Example of cross-reactivity profile of ELISA cannabinoids immunoassays

[a] Information was published by Kerrigan and Phillips (2001).
[b] Information was obtained from the specified package inserts, Immunalysis Corporation.
[c] Date of package insert or package insert revisions.
[d] NA—Not available.

assay (package inserts: 2001). In general, the cross-reactivity profile may vary in kits from the same company at different times and can be optimized for the specific requirements of different kit configurations. For example, the cross-reactivity profile of various ELISA kits from Immunalysis is shown in Table 3.3.

3.3.5.3 Enzyme-Multiplied Immunoassay Technique (EMIT)

The original formats of EMIT cannabinoids assay included the Emit-st assays, which utilized a single 100 ng/mL calibrator containing Δ^8-THC-COOH, and the Emit d.a.u. assays, which utilized a negative control, a low calibrator, and a medium calibrator (Irving et al., 1984; Bastiani, 1984; Ellis et al., 1985). O'Conner and Rejent (1981) confirmed EMIT cannabinoids assay with RIA and GC/MS and postulated that for routine screening applications, the heterogeneity of the EMIT cannabinoid antibody may be more sensitive than the other methods in detecting cannabinoid metabolites. Black et al. (1984) adapted EMIT for high-volume urine cannabinoids testing. Foltz and Sunshine

(1990) compared the analysis of urine specimens with TLC, EMIT, and GC/MS and reported that 63% of the urine specimens shown by GC/MS to contain greater than 20 ng/mL of THC-COOH were identified as positive by the Emit d.a.u. assay at the 100 ng/mL cannabinoids cutoff. Standefer and Backer (1991) investigated the precision, linearity, accuracy, and stability of quantitative results for five drugs of abuse by using Emit d.a.u. reagents and reported that the within-day and between-day coefficients of variation were between 10% and 20% for THC-COOH. The formulation of Emit II differs from earlier ones in the use of new drug–G6P-DH conjugates and new antibodies to improve performance at the cutoff level (Armbruster et al., 1993a). A comparative study indicated that both Emit 700 and Emit II assays detected approximately 90% of the urine samples screened positive by RIA and confirmed positive for marijuana (Armbruster et al., 1994). Smith-Kielland et al. (1999) compared results of the 1992 and 1993 testing of up to 20,000 urine specimens and concluded that there was no major difference in performance with the new formulation.

Currently the THC assays for both Emit d.a.u. (lyophilized) and Emit II Plus (liquid) are available in three cutoff levels: 20 ng/mL, 50 ng/mL, and 100 ng/mL.

In addition to Dade Behring Syva Emit products, cannabinoids assays that utilize similar enzyme immunoassay principles for urinary drug screening are also available from the companies Beckman Coulter, as Synchron THC-cannabinoids assay (Dietzen et al., 2001), and Microgenics, as DRI (formerly Diagnostic Reagents Inc.) cannabinoid (THC) assay (Broussard and Hanson, 1997). Besides urinary drug testing, EMIT assays have been applied to matrices such as blood and plasma (Peel and Perrigo, 1981; Mason and McBay, 1984; Asselin et al., 1988; Lewellen and McCurdy, 1988; Perrigo and Joynt, 1989; Blum et al., 1989; Bogusz et al., 1990; Gjerde et al., 1990), saliva (Peel et al., 1984), and meconium (Wingert et al., 1994; ElSohly et al., 1999). Gjerde (1991) reported the use of EMIT d.a.u. cannabinoid assay to test methanolic extracts of blood as a screening method in cases of suspected impairment by cannabis, provided that THC was analyzed in the subsequent assay. When a cutoff limit corresponding to 50 nM THC-COOH (17 ng/ml) was used, 86% of the EMIT positive blood samples contained THC concentrations above the cutoff limit of 1 nM (0.3 ng/mL).

3.3.5.4 Fluorescence Polarization Immunoassay (FPIA)

The Abbott (Abbott Park, IL) FPIA Cannabinoids assay is calibrated using either a master calibration (2-point) or a six-point calibration curve (0, 25, 40, 60, 80, and 135 ng/mL). Master calibrator concentrations were chosen that most accurately adjust the 0–135 ng/mL calibration curve with only two points. The FPIA cannabinoids assay is designed to perform at a variety of commonly used threshold levels. Analyzers for Abbott FPIA such as TDx, TDxFLx, and AXSYM have been "factory set" at a specified cutoff concentration. Instrument procedures are available for the users to configure the cutoff level if necessary. The reagent pack consists of bottles that contain antiserum, pretreatment solution, and cannabinoids fluorescein tracer, respectively. Previously the cross-reactivities of the Abbott TDx assay to various cannabinoid metabolites and a group of cannabinoids and noncannabinoid phenolic constituents of cannabis were also analyzed by ElSohly et al. (1990). In addition to urine samples, FPIA-based drug assays have been applied for the analysis of blood (Bogusz et al., 1990; Goodall and Basteyns, 1995; Cagle et al., 1997; Keller et al., 2000), meconium (ElSohly et al., 1999), synovial fluid of the knee joint and in vitreous humor (Felscher et al., 1998), and hair (Kintz et al., 1992).

3.3.5.5 Kinetic Interaction of Microparticles in Solution (KIMS)

The Roche (Indianapolis, IN) Abuscreen ONLINE and ONLINE DAT II products are KIMS-based immunoassays (Armbruster et al., 1993a, 1993b; Hailer et al., 1995; Crouch et al., 1998b; Boettcher et al., 2000). The cannabinoids qualitative applications utilize calibrators for cutoff at 20, 50, or 100 ng/mL, whereas the semiquantitative applications employ either four or five calibrators as appropriate for the respective cutoff levels. For example, calibrators 0, 20, 50, 100, and 300 ng/mL are used for the 50 ng/mL cutoff assay. For semiquantitative COBAS INTEGRA applications, the change in absorbance for each calibrator is plotted against its concentration and a lineal interpolation model is used to construct a calibration curve. For semiquantitative Roche/Hitachi applications, the analyzer computer constructs a calibration curve from absorbance measurements of the standards using a four-parameter logit-log fitting function, which fits a smooth line through the data points. The absorbance measurements of samples are then used to calculate drug or drug metabolite concentration by interpolation of the logit-log fitting function. The resulting curves are retained in analyzer memory and recalled for later use. In addition to urine drug testing, the ONLINE assays have also been applied to drugs-of-abuse analysis in serum (Moody and Medina, 1995) and other applications can be developed by the users for their specific drug-testing needs.

The design and selection of antibody have a significant impact on the specificity of an immunoassay. The immunogen structures can be designed to generate antibodies with different selectivity towards the cyclohexyl ring of the cannabinoid structure. Immunogens from benzpyran derivatives have been developed to elicit antibodies with broad cross-reactivity to cannabinoid metabolites (Salamone et al., 1998). The total cross-reactive cannabinoid values obtained with the benzpyran-elicited antibodies were 49% higher than the values obtained using the traditional immunogen structure. The broad-spectrum antibody has been used to develop the ONLINE DAT II cannabinoids assay. This antibody has also been utilized in an immunoaffinity extraction procedure for the simultaneous analysis of THC and its major metabolites in urine, plasma, and meconium by GC/MS (Feng et al., 2000).

3.3.5.6 Cloned Enzyme Donor Immunoassay (CEDIA)

The Microgenics (Fremont, CA) CEDIA DAU Multi-Level THC assays can be used for qualitative or semiquantitative determinations of cannabinoids at 25, 50, or 100 ng/mL cutoff levels. The data analysis using the Roche/Hitachi analyzers has been described in the previous section. The calibrators used for a 50 ng/mL cannabinoids assay are 0, 25, 75, and 100 ng/mL. The performance of CEDIA for urine drug testing was compared to that of RIA, TDx, ONLINE, and EMIT II (Armbruster et al., 1995).

Wu et al. (1995) compared CEDIA to EMIT II for its use in drug screening in urine and investigated the effect of various adulterants on the immunoassay performance. Cagle et al. (1997) evaluated CEDIA and FPIA for their combined effectiveness in the analysis of cannabinoids in acetone-pretreated whole blood. The authors reported that all blood samples that screened positive could be confirmed for the presence of THC-COOH by GC/MS at concentrations greater than the 10 ng/mL cutoff. However, the GC/MS results were found to correlate significantly better with those of the FPIA cannabinoids assay. Iwersen-Bergmann and Schmoldt (1999) demonstrated that the use of the CEDIA urine-screening technique without any adaptation can provide a sensitive serum/whole blood screening for several drugs of abuse, including cannabinoids.

3.3.5.7 Onsite (Point-of-Collection) Immunoassays

Various immunoassay technologies have been applied to develop onsite drug-testing products since the late 1980s. In a study that involved volunteers with a history of marijuana use, Jenkins et al. (1993) compared results of the enzyme immunoassay based EZ-SCREEN (Environmental Diagnostics, Burlington, NC) with GC/MS and reported that the test produced positive results at a standard THC-COOH concentration of 5 ng/mL. Overall agreement between the three analysts was approximately 80%. Delayed readings and photocopy readings tended to be less accurate than readings obtained at 3 minutes. Another example of multistep, point-of-collection drug screening is the Triage drugs-of-abuse testing panel (Biosite Diagnostics Inc., San Diego, CA) (Buechler et al., 1992; Wu et al., 1993; Rohrich et al., 1994; de la Torre et al., 1996).

The Roche Abuscreen OnTrak THC assay was based on the visual interpretation of qualitative results following a KIMS-like reaction (Schwartz et al., 1990; Cone et al., 1991; Armbruster et al., 1993a; Crouch et al., 1998a, 1998b). The manual, qualitative immunoassay system was shown to be sufficiently sensitive, and the results were found to agree well with those obtained from instrument-based screening and GC/MS confirmation (Armbruster and Krolak, 1992). (The product line was recently discontinued.) With the advantages of simple and rapid one-step testing as well as room temperature storage, a variety of lateral-flow assays have been gaining popularity in various drug-testing programs in the past few years. Most of these devices have been evaluated for onsite screening of abused drugs, including cannabinoids, in urine (Jenkins et al., 1995; Towt et al., 1995; Ros et al., 1998; Crouch et al., 1998b; Buchan et al., 1998; Wennig et al., 1998; Peace et al., 2000; Leino et al., 2001; Gronholm and Lillsunde, 2001). The lateral flow immunochromatographic assays were also adapted to drug screening for alternative matrices such as oral fluids (Kintz et al., 2000; Samyn and van Haeren, 2000). For example, the Cozart RapiScan (Abingdon, Oxfordshire, UK) is a hand-held reader that couples a lateral-flow test strip with digital photography for the detection of drugs of abuse in saliva. Jehanli et al. (2001) compared the use of Cozart RapiScan with that of enzyme immunoassays and GC/MS methods in blind clinical trials. The authors reported that the cutoff of the marijuana test at 10 ng/mL THC-COOH was too high to detect marijuana use for more than a few hours after smoking.

3.3.6 COMPARATIVE EVALUATIONS

With plenty of technological choices, a wide variety of studies have been carried out over the past decades to evaluate and compare the performance of various immunoassays. When comparing results from these studies, it is always important to recognize the variables that can influence the outcome and interpretation of the immunoassays and comparative studies (Baselt, 1984; Kricka, 2000). The contributing variations include, but are not limited to, physiological and biological factors (Huestis and Cone, 1998a, 1998b; Vandevenne et al., 2000) and potential interference with the assays by food or medication (Berkabile and Meyers, 1989; Rollins et al., 1990; Colbert, 1994; Wagener et al., 1994; Linder and Valdes, 1994; Joseph et al., 1995; ElSohly and Jones, 1995; Costantino et al., 1997; Lehmann et al., 1997; Struempler et al., 1997). Additional factors to be taken into consideration include market-segment goals on sensitivity and specificity, percentage of "near-cutoff" specimens evaluated, sample size, prevalence, the type of population selected for evaluation, and the study protocols.

As discussed in previous sections, the utility of combining a 50 ng/mL immunoassay cutoff and a 15 ng/mL GC/MS cutoff has been supported by several studies and chosen as the rule by the U.S. *Mandatory Guidelines*. However, the composition of total THC metabolites relative to the amount of THC-

Figure 3.15

Correlation of GC and immunoassay results for THC-COOH Reproduced with permission from Smith-Kielland et al. (1999).

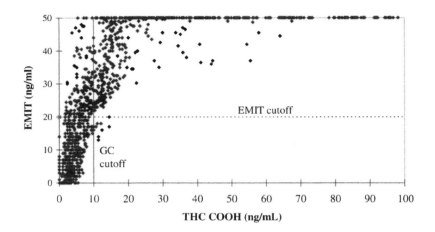

COOH can vary for any given specimen donor that provides a sample at any given time. Therefore, the balance of "analyte detection rate" and "confirmation rate" for samples that exhibit GC/MS values between the GC/MS cutoff and immunoassay cutoff can differ from study to study. Smith-Kielland et al. (1999) demonstrated the relationship between the GC analysis of urinary THC-COOH concentration (using a 10 ng/mL cutoff) and Syva Emit immunoassay values (using a 20 ng/mL cutoff). The results were obtained by screening 1432 samples, of which 1248 samples were further analyzed by GC. Although the cutoff levels chosen for EMIT and GC/MS were lower than those mandated by the current SAMHSA guidelines, the scatter plot (Figure 3.15) exemplifies a field scenario where there is correlation but not a directly linear relationship between the two types of results. Comprehensive studies that utilize regression analysis to explore the relationship of immunoassay screening and GC/MS confirmation have been presented in a series of scatter graph plots published by Weaver et al. (1991), R.H. Liu et al. (1994), R.H. Liu and Goldberger (1995), and Brendler and Liu (1997).

Baselt (1989) and Haver et al. (1991) raised questions regarding the utility of immunoassays as a quantitative tool. When used as a qualitative assay, the amount of drugs and metabolites detected in any given sample cannot be estimated from immunoassay results. Semiquantitative determinations of cannabinoids concentrations are possible by plotting the ΔA or mP values of the calibrators and comparing the ΔA or mP value of the positive sample to the standard curve. Armbruster et al. (1993a) reported that the slopes for the immunoassay calibration curves of KIMS and FPIA assays were significantly greater than those of the Emit II assays. Wu et al. (1995) reported that the rate separations by CEDIA assays between the negative and cutoff calibrators were greater than corresponding Emit II assays.

Frederick et al. (1985) compared GC/MS and five commercial cannabinoids immunoassays (Emit-st, Emit d.a.u., Abuscreen RIA, Immunalysis RIA, and Toxi-Lab TLC). The GC/MS method provided confirmation for all procedures except 2% or 3% of the positive EMIT-d.a.u. results. Abercrombie and Jewell (1986) evaluated EMIT and RIA "high volume test procedures" for THC metabolites in urine utilizing GC/MS confirmation and reported that EMIT and RIA results agreed for 91% of samples. The authors found that there is no relationship between quantitations determined by the two tests.

Budgett et al. (1992) compared the qualitative detection of cannabinoids in urine using Abbott FPIA and Roche RIA and concluded that the two technologies give comparable results. Karlsson and Strom (1988) applied the FPIA using TDx and the Emit assay using Cobas analyzer for detection of cannabinoids in urine from prison inmates. Their results indicated that the Emit assay detects a few more positive samples but also yields a higher rate of unconfirmed positive results compared to the TDx. Those additional "positives" by Emit had THC-COOH concentrations below 10 ng/mL.

Kintz et al. (1995c) compared GC/MS and immunological methods, including Syva Emit, Abbott FPIA, and Roche ONLINE immunoassay, for the determination of THC-COOH. The immunological methods compared favorably and are acceptable for detecting the presence of cannabis metabolites in urine. The authors stated that these results support the concept that all immunoassays for cannabinoids should be considered screening procedures. No concentration correlation between GC/MS and the immunoassays could be established because of the different cross-reactivities of the metabolites.

K.A. Moore et al. (1999) compared double antibody RIA kits (DPC and Immunalysis) and ELISA (STC Microplate EIA) for the screening of post-mortem blood and tissues for nine cases of drugs of abuse. The cutoff used for THC immunoassay and confirmation was 25 ng/mL and 10 ng/mL, respectively. The performances of EIA and RIA were comparable when 239 samples were tested for cannabinoids. Niedbala et al. (2001) compared ELISA-based cannabinoids assays for oral fluid testing (by using a 1 ng/mL cutoff) to ELISA-based cannabinoids assays for urine testing (by using a 50 ng/mL cutoff) in subjects who were administered single doses of marijuana by smoked and oral routes. The results supported the utility of oral fluid testing with the chosen cutoff concentration and hinted at the dependence of the detection time window for various matrices or assays on their cutoff level selection.

A few large-scale evaluations were carried out to examine and compare diverse drugs-of-abuse immunoassays that were conducted in the same study setting or comparable conditions. Ferrara et al. (1994) compared six immunochemical techniques and three chromatographic techniques and demonstrated the statistical approach and experimental comparison of these nine techniques. Among the seven immunoassays evaluated (the assays have different cutoffs), sensitivity for cannabinoids detection ranged from 56.8% to 97.6%, whereas specificity for corresponding tests ranged from 94.0% to 98.9%. The sensitivity results were inversely related to the cutoff concentrations for the assays evaluated.

Armbruster et al. (1993a) compared several immunoassays and showed that RIA, TDx, ONLINE, and EMIT II detected 99%, 95%, 99%, and 88% of the GC/MS-confirmed marijuana samples, respectively. In a separate study, Armbruster et al. (1995) showed that RIA, TDx, ONLINE, EMIT II, and CEDIA detected 100%, 87.2%, 88.8%, 85.5%, and 88.8% of the GC/MS-confirmed marijuana samples, respectively.

Huestis et al. (1995) evaluated the use of RIA, EMIT, FPIA, and KIMS immunoassays (at two cutoff concentrations) to monitor urine samples from six healthy subjects with a history of marijuana use when they had resided in the clinical ward of the Addiction Research Center for 4 to 6 weeks. Using 50 ng/mL and 15 ng/mL as the respective cutoff for immunoassays and GC/MS, the respective efficiency of these immunoassays ranged from 91.4% to 94.7%. In another study, Huestis et al. (1994) determined detection times of cannabinoids in urine using five cannabinoid immunoassays (EMIT, ONLINE, RIA, DRI, and ADx) with different cutoff concentrations and GC/MS and reported that urinary cannabinoid detection times varied substantially across assays, subjects, doses, and cutoff concentrations.

von Meyer et al. (1997) evaluated the performance of the following systems in accordance with the guidelines of the European Committee for Clinical Laboratory Standards (ECCLS): Abbott TDx and ADx (using Abbott AxSYM analyzer), Syva Emit d.a.u. (using Roche MIRA S Plus analyzer), Syva Emit d.a.u. (using Syva ETS Plus analyzer), Syva Emit II (using Hitachi 717 analyzer), and Roche Abuscreen (using MIRA S Plus analyzer). The test analytes, including cannabinoids, were each investigated in three laboratories on different systems. The authors reported that the imprecision of all systems in the series and from day to day was good, with CV values of less than 5% and 10%, respectively.

Studies have also been carried out to evaluate diverse onsite devices. A SAMHSA-sponsored study was conducted by the Center for Substance Abuse Prevention Division of Workplace Programs to evaluate 15 onsite devices and the instrument-based Emit assays (http://workplace.samhsa.gov/ResourceCenter/r362.htm). The evaluation was designed to challenge the devices on their accuracy around the cutoff. The report did emphasize that actual specimens from the field have much fewer specimens with drug concentrations near the cutoff. This means that a much higher percentage of confirmed positive results and fewer false-negative results should occur during actual testing in the field.

Another large study, a field test of onsite drug detection devices, was sponsored by the Department of Transportation National Highway Safety Administration (http://www.nhtsa.dot.gov/people/injury/research/pub/onsitedetection/Drug_index.htm). The study identified 30 onsite devices and rated 16 devices based on 14 criteria. From the rating results, 5 devices were selected to evaluate 800 samples in two high prevalence counties in New York and Texas, respectively. For THC assay, there were no false negatives for the samples that tested negative on all devices. However, false-negative results were obtained on samples that tested negative on some, but not all, of the devices for a given drug. These false-negative rates ranged from 0.12% to 0.37% for drug present in concentrations greater than the screening cutoff and ranged from 0.25% to 0.87% for drug present in concentrations greater than the confirmatory cutoff. The report indicated that when cutoff concentration and additional drugs are taken into consideration, the devices were accurate in identifying positive samples and rarely failed to identify a driver who had the target drugs in his/her urine. The report also stated that police officers who participated in the study generally favored the use of onsite devices in the enforcement of impaired driving laws, although the use of these devices should not supplant the officer's judgment regarding impairment.

Buchan et al. (1998) reported a field evaluation of onsite, multianalyte drug-testing devices to determine their accuracy, efficiency, and cost-effectiveness as a tool for identifying impaired drivers and determining prevalence of illicit drugs in reckless drivers in a county in Florida. For THC, results from testing 303 voluntary urine specimens indicated that the accuracy ranged from 97.4% to 98.0%. The authors observed that the four kits were in very close agreement on prevalence (15.5–15.8% for THC). Gronholm and Lillsunde (2001) evaluated the accuracy of 10 onsite testing devices for drug screening using urine or oral fluid specimens. The onsite test results were compared with GC/MS. A total of 800 people and eight onsite devices for urine and two for oral fluid testing were included in the study. The accuracy of the devices was in the range of 97% to 99% for cannabinoids, although there were differences in the ease of performance and interpretation of test results. For oral fluid onsite devices, the cannabinoids assay did not fulfill the needs of sensitivity. Leino et al. (2001) evaluated eight commercially available onsite drugs-of-abuse testing devices and reported sensitivities ranging from 88% to 98% and specificities ranging from 95% to 100% for THC-COOH. However, the devices differed markedly with respect to the interpretation of test results and to the ease of test performance, leading to the suggestion that different criteria should be used for selecting onsite devices for either emergency laboratories in hospitals or police stations and prisons. The authors also emphasized the importance of confirming any positive screening test result.

In 1989, Frings et al. reported results of a blind study designed to determine the accuracy of drugs-of-abuse testing in urine in 31 laboratories across the United States. The authors concluded that urine drug testing could be accurate when performed by qualified staff, using up-to-date screening and confirmation methods, appropriate quality assurance measures, and a chain of custody. The fundamental conclusions remain valid more than 10 years later. However, because the immunoassay reagent formulations may change over time and the evaluation protocols, goals, and sample populations may vary significantly, the relative performance of one immunoassay over the other may vary from study to study. Even though most studies showed that there is no absolute relationship between quantifications of various cannabinoids immunoassays, the majority of cannabinoids immunoassay evaluations demonstrated comparable performance. Most important, these immunoassays are cost-effective initial tests for the screening of abused drugs, provided that confirmatory tests of presumptive positives are performed to ensure reliability of forensic drug analysis results.

3.4 CONFIRMATION (CONFIRMATORY TEST) OF CANNABINOIDS IN URINE SPECIMENS

3.4.1 INTRODUCTION

Confirmations of drugs or metabolites detected by immunoassay require methods capable of quantifying a single chemical species and of excluding all other relevant species. By far the most commonly performed analysis in the toxicology of cannabinoids is the confirmation of THC-COOH in urine. This is the preponderant cannabinoid in urine, and it is the target of commercially available immunoassays used in screening.

In order for an analytical method to be of value in forensic cases, preemployment testing, postemployment testing, or probation testing it must be highly specific and it must be sensitive. In the United States the required cutoff for confirmation of THC-COOH in federally regulated drug testing is 15 ng/mL (Federal Register 59, 29908–29931, 1994). The method used must be capable of detecting THC-COOH at 6 ng/mL (40% of the cutoff) in reanalysis of challenged cases. In Europe, cutoff concentrations from 1 to 400 ng/mL are used, depending on the type of laboratory and the purpose of the analysis (Badia et al., 1998a, 1998b). A cutoff of 15 ng has been recommended in the European Union (de la Torre et al., 1997). Methods of analysis have been reviewed by ElSohly and Salem (2000).

3.4.1.2 Sample Preparation

3.4.1.2.1 Glassware/Plasticware/Pipettes

Adsorption of cannabinoids by the surface of containers and equipment has been reported (Garrett and Hunt, 1974; Fenimore et al., 1976a; Jones et al., 1984a; Christophersen, 1986; Joern, 1987; Dextraze et al., 1989; Blanc et al., 1993; Bond et al., 1990; Dugan et al., 1994). Such adsorption of THC-COOH can lead to a lack of linearity in analysis (Joern, 1987) and is one explanation for loss of THC-COOH in storage (Jones et al., 1984a). Joern (1992c) reported that loss occurs from standard solutions of THC-COOH in borosilicate glass tubes whether or not they are silanized and the adsorption is highly variable. The adsorption of THC-COOH is greatly reduced or nonexistent from basic solutions and organic solutions (Joern, 1987). Joern (1992c) proposed that standard THC-COOH solutions be prepared in drug-free urine made basic by addition of 10M sodium hydroxide to yield a final concentration of sodium hydroxide of 0.10 M. The solution must be centrifuged or filtered to remove precipitate. Additionally, it was suggested that the basic solutions used in hydrolysis be added to tubes before the addition of patient or control urines.

Roth et al. (1996) reported a comprehensive study on the effects of solution composition and container material type on the loss of THC-COOH. The authors measured losses in relation to surface area (ng/cm^2) for glass, acrylic, silanized glass, Kynar, Teflon-S, polystyrene, polypropylene, and high-density polyethylene and for three solvents: water, urine, and Abbott cannabinoids diluent. The authors' conclusions provide insight into methods to minimize loss of standard or analyte. The losses were greatest for high-density polyethylene and least for untreated glass. Water solutions were subject to greater loss than urine. The smaller the volume of solution (with a greater surface-to-volume ratio), the greater was the observed loss. Of particular interest is the observation that no loss was observed beyond the first hour.

Losses in pipetting were least for unsilanized glass and were determined by time of exposure and temperature, with less loss at lower temperatures. The authors concluded that exposure of THC-COOH solutions to new surfaces should be avoided during sample handling. The stability of THC in urine in high-density polyethylene is addressed by Giardino (1996).

3.4.1.2.2 Hydrolysis

Since THC-COOH is found in urine as both the free acid and the glucuronic acid conjugate (Kanter et al., 1982b; Law et al., 1984a, 1984b), the analysis generally starts with the hydrolysis of the sample. Either basic solutions or enzymes can be used to free the acid from its conjugate. A wide variety of conditions have been reported for the basic hydrolysis. Baker et al. (1984) compared recoveries of THC-COOH using a variety of hydrolysis conditions and concluded 1 mL of 1 N KOH for 5 mL of urine heated at 37°C for 15 minutes gave optimum recovery. They also concluded that β-glucuronidase (bovine liver) could completely hydrolyze the sample in 30 minutes at 37°C. It should be noted that many reported β-glucuronidase hyrolyses are carried out overnight (16 h) and that results are dependent on the source and the particular batch. Kemp et al. (1995b) reported that 2 N NaOH (0.5 mL) when added to a solution of unhydrolyzed urine (1 mL) and phosphate buffer (1 mL, for volume adjustment) followed by hexane : ethyl acetate extraction gave complete hydrolysis of THC-COOH without heat or incubation time. Kemp et al. (1995b) also demonstrated that base hydrolysis is ineffective in hydrolyzing ether glucuronides (as opposed to esters) and that hydrolysis with bacterial β-glucuronidase revealed significant concentrations of THC and 11-OH-THC in urine. The β-glucuronidase from bacteria (*Escherichia coli*) was shown to be much more effective than β-glucuronidase from mollusks (*Helix pomatia*) in hydrolyzing ether conjugates, such as found in THC-glucuronide. The choice of method will depend on the purpose of the analysis, with β-glucuronidase being essential if analytes other than THC-COOH are of interest. For routine analysis of THC-COOH, basic hydrolysis is the most widely used method.

3.4.1.2.3 Extraction

The extraction of cannabinoids from biological matrices can be achieved by liquid–liquid extraction or solid-phase extraction. The most commonly used solvent for extraction from urine is hexane–ethyl acetate (7 : 1, 9 : 1). For extraction from blood, plasma, serum, and other tissues, acetone and/or acetonitrile are often used. The supernatant after centrifugation is generally evaporated, and the extract is dissolved in base and the neutral and basic components extracted into an organic solvent, typically hexane–ethyl acetate (9 : 1). The aqueous layer is then acidified, and the acid components are extracted into organic solvent. Liquid–liquid extraction is still widely used in research studies. Solid-phase extraction is now the most frequently used method in urine drug testing (Gere and Platoff, 1995) and in many research studies. A widely used method for THC-COOH in urine (Paul et al., 1987) employs anion exchange resin. Solid-phase extraction (SPE) systems are commercially available from numerous manufacturers. Gere and Platoff (1995) have reviewed all facets of SPE, including the cartridges of specific manufacturers and automation of the process.

The trend in workplace and regulatory drug testing is toward systems that reduce the volume of organic solvents (O'Dell et al., 1997) and that can be automated. In this regard extraction discs in which the solvent is enmeshed in inert microfibrils have proved useful (Singh and Johnson, 1997). Wu et al.

(1993a) utilized such discs in a procedure where the THC-COOH that had been extracted onto the disc was eluted and derivatized by MSTFA in one step.

Solid-Phase Extraction (SPE)

A typical analysis for THC-COOH using SPE will include the following steps:

1. Measurement of aliquot of urine (1–3 mL)
2. Addition of base and internal standard (hydrolysis)
3. Adjustment of pH (acid)
4. Transfer of solution to appropriately prepared extraction cartridges
5. Passage of solution through the cartridge
6. One or more washes with appropriate solvents (dependent upon solid phase used)
7. Drying of solid phase
8. Elution with appropriate solvent
9. Evaporation
10. Derivatization (may be multiple steps)
11. Chromatography

Preparation of the SPE cartridges requires one or more washings with appropriate solutions, which are dependent on the specific packing. The cartridge preparation and steps 5 to 8 are often preformed by placing the cartridges in the top of a vacuum manifold that draws the liquids through the cartridges. These commercially available vacuum systems allow processing of 12 or more samples simultaneously.

An actual application of SPE is shown in the following example from Langen et al. (2000) using Bakerbond SPD NARC-1 3-mL extraction cartridges.

Step 1. 1 mL urine.

Step 2. 300 μL 10 M KOH, 2 mL H_2O, 25 μL IS (4 μg/mL THC-COOH-d_3) 15 min/60°C.

Step 3. 350 μL acetic acid (96%), adjust to pH 2.5 with 2 mL 50 mM phosphate buffer.

Step 4. Preparation of cartridges:
  a. 3 mL methanol
  b. 3 mL 50 mM phosphate buffer

Step 5. Draw sample through cartridge—do not dry.

Step 6–7. Wash—2 mL acetonitrile/0.1 M HCl (2:3 v/v)—dry (1 min)—0.5 mL hexane—dry 5 min.

Step 8. Elute—3 mL hexane/ethyl acetate (1:1 v/v).

Automation

Automation of the entire process or significant components of the process offers the possibility of improving throughput, reducing errors, reducing labor costs, and improving precision. One automation system, the Dupont Prep-1, has been widely used (Paul et al., 1987; Abercrombie and Jewell, 1986) in this regard but is no longer manufactured. Creative Technology has developed a successor (Xtrx Automated Processor) to the Prep-I. An early version of the Zymate, a complete robotic system manufactured by Zymark, was found by one author (CT) to take up too much space and to perform too slowly to justify its cost. A less ambitious instrument, Rapid Trace, by Zymark has, on the other hand, been successful in efficiently performing all the steps usually performed manually on the vacuum manifold (Polyniak, 2001). Stonebraker et al. (1998) reported the use of Rapid Trace to automate the SPE and GCMS analysis of THC in blood. Zymark also manufactures Confir Mate for robotic preparation of samples for GCMS.

Instruments designed to automate all or part of the sample preparations are manufactured by Tecan, Waters, Savant, Gilson, Hamilton, and Agilent. Whitter et al. (1999) have reported successful improvement of laboratory efficiency and reduction of costs using a Six-Head Probe Hamilton Microlab 2200 system to automate steps 1 through 8. Langen et al. (2000) have reported on the use of ASPECXL (Gilson) to automate the extraction procedure. The authors encountered difficulty in controlling absorption of the analyte in the tubing and glassware during the procedure. Throughput was slow, but the system could operate 24 h a day. The instrument can be used to perform the hydrolysis, evaporation, derivatization, and possibly the injection steps; however, no evaluation of these functions has been reported. Extraction procedures for analytes from matrices other than urine will be covered under specific matrices. Steinberg et al. (1997) evaluated Toxi-Prep to semiautomate SPE extractions of drugs in urine.

3.4.1.3 Standards

Certified urine-based standard reference material (SRM) for 11-nor-Δ^9-tetrahydrocannabinol-9-carboxylic acid (SRM 1507b) is available from the U.S. National Institute of Standards and Technology (NIST). The SRM 1507b consists of three concentration levels (approximately 12, 25, and 50 ng/mL). These certified reference standards can also be obtained from the College of American Pathologists (CAP). Standards of Δ^9-THC-COOH as well as Δ^8-THC-COOH, 11-hydroxy-Δ^9-tetrahydrocannabinol, cannabinol, and cannabidiol are available from Sigma (St. Louis, MO). Standards are also available in the United States from Research Triangle Institute (Research Triangle Park, NC), Alltech-Applied Science (State College, PA), and Cerilliant (Austin, TX).

3.4.1.4 Analytical Methods

Confirmation of THC-COOH by GC/MS is by far the most widely used method, especially for forensic examination and for regulated analyses (Bronner and Xu, 1992; Goldberger and Cone, 1994; Badia et al., 1998a). However, a wide variety of methods are used in unregulated testing or in countries where regulated testing does not mandate mass spectrometry (Badia et al., 1998a).

3.4.1.4.1 Thin-Layer Chromatography

The use of TLC to identify THC-COOH is widespread in clinical laboratories and has substantial use in forensic laboratories (Badia et al., 1998a). Kaistha and Tadrus (1982) advocated the use of silica gel plates with chloroform–methanol–concentrated ammonium hydroxide (85:15:2) as the mobile phase. Fast blue RR (0.5% w/v, in equal volumes of methanol and water) was used for detection. The limit of detection is approximately 50 ng/mL. Kanter et al. (1982b) developed a method for simultaneously detecting THC-COOH and THC-COOH glucuronide by extracting the free acid prior to hydrolysis of the glucuronide. The extracts were sequentially developed in two different solvent systems and detected with fast blue salt B. A method (Kanter et al., 1982a) for identifying total THC-COOH utilized silica gel G plates and sequentially developed them in acetone–chloroform–triethylamine (80:20:1) followed by petroleum ether–ether–glacial acetic acid (50:50:1.5). The procedure could detect a spot containing 0.5 µg of THC-COOH. High-efficiency thin-layer chromatography (HETLC) was utilized by Black et al. (1984) to aid in the confirmation of EMIT results. An internal standard (IS) (Δ^8-THC) was added to 10 mL of urine before basic hydrolysis. Solid-phase extraction (Bond-Elut-THC) was used to isolate the analyte and IS for HPLC and HETLC. Hexane–acetone–glacial acetic acid (70:30:1) was used to effect the separation on 10 × 10-cm HETLC-HL plates (Analtech). Visualization utilized alkaline fast blue B salt. The LOD was 20 ng/mL. Kogan et al. (1984) used SPE and 25 × 75-mm E. Merck silica gel 60 plates. A mobile phase of ethyl acetate–methanol–water–ammonium hydroxide (12:5:0.5:1) was used to chromatograph the extracts, and fast blue RR was used to visualize the cannabinoids. The LOD was 20 ng/mL in 10 mL of urine. Meatherall and Garriott (1988) used HPTLC plates from three different manufactures (Analtech, Whatman, and Merck Science) to detect THC-COOH with a LOD of 5 ng/mL in 2 mL of urine. Fast blue BB was used to visualize the analyte, and heptane–butanol–acetic acid (90:9:1) was used as the mobile phase. The hydrolyzed samples were made acidic and extracted with hexane. Foltz and Sunshine (1990) evaluated the Toxi-MS cannabinoid test (Toxi-Lab, Inc.). In this system the hydrolyzed samples are aspirated through a SPE layer and then through a silica gel phase to achieve separation. The first layer concentrates the sample at the beginning of the TLC plate, and a rapid development separates the THC-COOH from other components. Fast blue BB is used to visualize the analyte. The method was compared directly via EMIT and GC/MS. A LOD of 10 ng/mL was reported.

Brandt and Kovar (1997) developed a TLC method that is sensitive, quantitative, and specific enough for forensic identification of THC-COOH. SPE was performed with Isolute C_8-(EC), 500 mg, 10-mL columns. After passing the hydrolyzed urine through the column, the column was washed first with acetonitrile–water (4:6) and then with dichloromethane–n-hexane (2:8). Elution with diethyl ether–n-hexane (2:8) gave very clean extracts. Separation was achieved on 0.1-mm layers of silica gel 60 WRF_{254}[5] (Merck). Online detection and quantitation was carried out by UV (LOD 4 ng/mL) and IR (LOD 14 ng/mL). An IR spectrum of the THC-COOH is obtained.

3.4.1.4.2 High-Performance Liquid Chromatography

Between 10% and 11% of European Union laboratories reported the use of HPLC for identification of drugs in urine. Many laboratories (13%) reported HPLC as a method used for quantification (Badia et al., 1998a). Methods using UV detection (ElSohly et al., 1983; Posey and Kimble, 1984; Karlsson and Roos, 1984; Johansson and Halldin, 1989; Ferrara et al., 1992), electrochemical detection (Bourquin and Brenneisen, 1987; Craft et al., 1989; Fisher et al., 1996), and RIA (Law et al., 1984b) have been published. Breindahl and Andreasen (1999) developed an LC method using atmospheric pressure ionization electrospray mass spectrometry (API-ES-MS) for detection. This method overcomes the lack of specificity of the aforementioned methods and allows for isotope dilution for quantitative methods using THC-COOH-d_3 as the internal standard. A gradient elution varying the concentration of acetonitrile in a constant 4 mM formic acid solution through a 150×3.0-mm C_8 column was used. The instrument was used in the positive ion mode. A LOD of 15 ng/mL was obtained using the authors' acceptance criteria, which included the m/z 345 ion (THC-COOH-H$^+$) and the m/z 327 and 299 ions created by up-front collision-induced dissociation. These two ions must have ion ratios within ±20% of standards. Using the m/z 345 ion alone gave a LOD of 2 ng/mL. Tai and Welch (2000) used a C_{18} column and an isocratic mobile phase (0.05 M ammonium acetate in methanol–water, 75:25) in a LCESMS method to measure THC-COOH in SRM 1507b. The negative ion mode was used, and m/z 343 and 346 for THC-COOH and THC-COOH-d_3 were monitored. A LOD of 5 pg/mL is reported for this method on spiked urine. No hydrolysis was needed, and no qualifying ions were used since identification was not the goal of the analysis. A summary of HPLC methods is shown in Table 3.4.

Table 3.4

HPLC methods for THC-COOH identification and quantitation

Source	Column	Mobile Phase	Internal Standard	Detector	Run Time (min)	Limit of Detection (ng/mL)	Limit of Quantification (ng/mL)
ElSohly et al. (1983)	2.5 cm × 4.6-mm C-8	65% acetonitrile, 35% 50 mM H_3PO_4	CBN-COOH	UV 214 nm	6	25	
Posey and Kimble (1984)	30 cm × 3.9-mm C-18	45% ACN, 55% phosphate buffer pH 6.0	Δ^8-THC-COOH	UV 205 nm	8		20
Karlsson and Roos (1984)	125 × 4-mm C-8	50% acetonitrile, 50% 0.05 M $(NH_4)H_2PO_4$	Δ^8-THC-COOH	UV 220–225 nm, quant. by GC of eluate	15		20
Law et al. (1984a)	160 × 5-mm C-18	82.5% v/v MeOH in pH 1.95 buffer	None	UV 220 nm, monitor RIA	15	3.3 total cannabinoids	
Bourquin and Brenneisen (1987)	150 × 4.6-mm C-18	MeOH/5% HOAc (76:24)	Cannabinol	EC	16	5	
Johansson and Halldin (1989)	250 × 4.6-mm C-18	MeOH:50 mM H_3PO_4 3:1 (pH 3.2)	11-nor-Cannabinol-9-carboxylic acid	UV/EC	12	7	
Craft et al. (1989)	250 × 4.6-mm	Gradient	11-nor-11-Hydroxy-Δ^9-tetrahydro-cannabinol (not suitable in casework)	EC	25	Not reported	
Ferrara et al. (1992)	250 × 4-mm C-8	0.05 M H_3PO_4: acetonitrile 35:65 v/v		UV	13	50	
Breindahl and Andreasen (1999)	150 × 3-mm C-18	Gradient	THC-COOH-d_3	APIESMS positive ion	6	15	
Tai and Welch (2000)	C-18	0.05 M ammonium acetate in MeOH/H_2O (75:25)	THC-COOH-d_3	ESMS negative ion	7	0.005	

3.4.1.4.3 Gas Chromatography and Gas Chromatography–Mass Spectrometry

Many of the methods of TLC and HPLC already described lack the specificity required to meet the demands of modern forensic or regulated drug-testing laboratories (Federal Register 59, 299908-2993, 1994). In 1998 over 50% of the laboratories in the European Union (Badia et al., 1998b) and all of the federally regulated laboratories in the United States used GC/MS methods to confirm THC-COOH. In the European Union 14% of the laboratories use GC without MS to identify THC-COOH (Badia et al., 1998b). Several excellent reviews of analytical methodology related to cannabinoid analysis in biological samples have been published within the past 10 years. Cody and Foltz (1995) and Goldberger and Cone (1994) have published excellent reviews of GC/MS of drugs of abuse in body fluids. Bronner and Xu (1992) extensively covered the literature of GC/MS analysis of THC-COOH through the middle of 1991. Staub (1999) has reviewed chromatographic procedures for determination of cannabinoids in matrices other than urine.

Internal Standards

Most, if not all, GC methods for THC-COOH and other cannabinoids utilize an internal standard (IS). Ideally the IS is added to the specimen at the beginning of the analysis, i.e., before the extraction of the specimen. The standard should be chemically similar to the analyte. If the IS is chosen well, it will serve as a quantitative reference, as a monitor of the extraction and derivatization procedure, and as a means of compensating for analytical variables such as extraction efficiency, efficiency of derivative formation, and minor changes in gas chromatographic parameters. If GC is being used without MS, the IS must be chromatographically separable from the analyte. In the case of THC-COOH the IS should contain a carboxyl function and a phenolic function. Frederick et al. (1985) used Δ^8-THC-COOH as an internal standard, which has extraction characteristics identical to those of Δ^9-THC-COOH and which is separated by GC. Bronner and Xu (1992) cite numerous examples of internal standards that are inadequate. For analysis by GCMS, isotopically labeled THC and THC-COOH are available as internal standards for these analytes. Isotope dilution with single-ion monitoring is the preferred method for THC-COOH. When using multiple- or single-ion monitoring, these are the ideal internal standards. If full-scan spectra are being used, an IS that is chromatographically separable must be used. Common deuterated internal standards for THC-COOH analysis are shown in Table 3.5 along with the common ions observed in EIMS with various derivatives. The most commonly referenced IS is $5'$-($^2H_3$)-11-nor-Δ^9-tetrahydrocannabinol-9-carboxylic acid (THC-COOH-d_3) (Cerilliant, Sigma, Research Triangle Institute). This IS is still widely used as its methyl ester–methyl ether, in spite of a minor m/z 316 ion in the MS of the analyte.

Table 3.5
Internal standards commonly used in mass spectrometry of THC-COOH and the major ions of common derivatives

	Derivative	Ions D(H)	References
 5 (^{2}H$_3$)-11-nor-Δ^9- tetrahydrocannabinol-9- carboxylic acid THC-COOH-d$_3$	—CH$_3$, —CH$_3$	316, 360, 375 (313, 357, 372)	Paul et al. (1987)
	—C$_3$H$_7$, —C$_3$H$_7$	344, 388, 431 (341, 385, 428)	Mulé and Casella (1988)
	TMS, TMS	374, 476, 491 (371, 473, 488)	
	TBDMS, TBDMS	416, 518, 560, 575 (413, 515, 557, 572)	Clouette et al. (1993)
	—CH(CF$_3$)$_2$ / —O—CF$_2$CF$_3$	605 (432, 474, 602, 622)	Kintz et al. (1995a, 1995b)
 THC-COOH-d$_6$	—CH$_2$CF$_2$CF$_3$ / — C— CF$_2$CF$_3$	610, 625 (445, 459, 607, 622)	Joern (1987)
	—CH$_3$, —CH$_3$	319, 360, 378 (313, 357, 372)	ElSohly et al. (1992)
	TMS, TMS	377, 494 (371, 473, 488)	ElSohly and Feng (1998)
 THC-COOH-d$_9$	TBDMS, TBDMS	422, 524, 563, 581 (413, 515, 557, 572)	Clouette et al. (1993)
	—CH$_2$CF$_2$CF$_3$ / — C— CF$_2$CF$_3$	454, 468 (445, 459, 489, 622)	Stout et al. (2001)
 Δ^8-THC-COOH-d$_6$	—CH$_3$, CH$_3$	248, 322, 378 (313, 357, 372)	ElSohly et al. (1988)
	TMS, TMS	306, 438, 494 (371, 473, 488)	ElSohly et al. (1988)

The ratio of the m/z 313 ion in the analyte to the m/z 316 ion in the IS is used for quantitative analysis, and the presence of a minor m/z 316 ion in the analyte yields nonlinearity above 800 ng/mL.

ElSohly et al. (1988) developed ^{2}H$_6$-11-nor-Δ^8-tetrahydrocannabinol-9-carboxylic acid (Δ^8-THC-COOH-d$_6$) (ElSohly Labs, Meridian, MS) as an IS that has the same extraction properties as THC-COOH, can be separated chromatographically from THC-COOH, and does not suffer from the interference noted for THC-COOH-d_3 when used as the methyl ester–methyl ether derivative. Joern (1992a) successfully used this IS in the procedure of Paul et al. (1987).

ElSohly et al. (1992) reported $^2H_6$-11-nor-Δ^9-tetrahydrocannabinol-9-carboxylic acid as an IS and its use as the methyl ester–methyl ether derivative. With this IS the analysis was linear over a wide range. ElSohly and Feng (1998) reported the use of this IS as the TMS derivative.

Clouette et al. (1993) reported the use of 5′-$^2H_3$-11-nor-Δ^9-tetrahydro-6, 6-di(methyl-$^2H_3$)-cannabinol-9-carboxylic acid (THC-COOH-d_9) (Cerilliant, Austin, TX) and THC-COOH-d_3 in a study of the mechanism of fragmentation of the t-butyldimethylsilyl derivative of THC-COOH. Szirmai et al. (1996) reported the use of THC-COOH-d_{10}, with no apparent advantages over existing standards.

Stout et al. (2001) have developed a method, suitable for high-volume laboratories, using pentafluropropprionic acid and pentafluropropanol as derivitizing agents and THC-COOH-d_9 as the IS. An anion exchange SPE was used to give 95% recovery, 0.875 ng/ml LOD with 3-mL samples, and linearity to 900 ng/mL. With THC-COOH-d_9 there is negligible contribution from IS to very weak samples.

Derivatization

Analysis of THC-COOH by GC universally involves derivatizing the carboxyl and phenol functions of the molecule. A wide variety of approaches have been utilized (Bronner and Xu, 1992). The choice of derivatives will depend on several factors, including GC detectors, MS methods, number of samples, sensitivity, and stability required. A summary of published derivatives is shown in Table 3.6. These derivatives can be divided into four groups based on the chemistry utilized in preparing them.

Alkyl Ester–Alkyl Ether Derivatives   The most commonly reported method (since its first use and currently) is the esterification of the carboxyl function and alkylation of the phenolic group to give an alkyl ester–alkyl ether (Whiting and Manders, 1982). In this method the extract is treated with tetramethylammoniumhydroxide followed by iodomethane to yield the methyl ester–methyl ether. Ethyl, propyl, and butyl derivatives have been evaluated (McCurdy et al., 1986), and the propyl derivative has been widely used in the method of Mulé and Casella (1988). Baker et al. (1984) and Nakahara et al. (1995) have compared the methyl ester–methyl ether with TMS derivatives. Dimethyl sulfate has been used to methylate THC-COOH (Wall et al., 1979), and THC-COOH has been methylated on column using dimethylformamide dimethylacetal

Table 3.6

Commonly used derivatives of 11-nor-Δ⁹-tetrahydrocannabinol-9-carboxylic acid

R′	R″	m/z of Abundant Ions	References
—CH₃	—CH₃	313, 357, 372	Whiting and Mauders (1983)
—C₃H₇	—C₃H₇	341, 385, 413, 428	McCurdy et al. (1986)
CH₃ | —Si—CH₃ | CH₃	CH₃ | —Si—CH₃ | CH₃	371, 473, 488	Harzer and Kächele (1983) McCurdy et al. (1986)
CH₃ | —Si—tbutyl | CH₃	CH₃ | —Si—tbutyl | CH₃	413, 515, 572	Bourquin and Brenneisen (1987) Clouette et al. (1993)
—CH(CF₃)(CF₃)	O=C—CF₂CF₃	429, 477, 489, 640	O'Connor and Rejent (1981)
—CH(CF₃)(CF₃)	O=C—CF₂CF₂CF₃	344, 492 (daughter ions), 670 (parent ion) (NCI, MS-MS)	Baumgartner et al. (1995)
—CH₂CF₂CF₃	O=C—CF₂CF₃	445, 459, 607, 622	Joern (1987)
—CH₃	O=C—CF₃	454 (NCI)	Foltz et al. (1983)

(Björkman, 1982) or 4:1 methanol–10% tetramethylammonium hydroxide in methanol (Nakamura et al., 1985). The methyl ester–methyl ether is widely used in part due to its stability, ease of preparation, and lack of adverse effects on columns and MS sources (Paul et al., 1987; Mulé and Cassella, 1988). According to Cody and Foltz (1995), when using EIMS the alkyl derivatives provide maximum stability and sensitivity. Studies utilizing alkyl ester–alkyl ether derivatives are listed in Table 3.7.

Table 3.7

Publications demonstrating the use of common derivatizing agents in urine analysis

References	Reagent
Selected Studies Using Silyl Ester–Silyl Ether Derivatives	
Fredrick et al. (1985)	MSTFA
Craft et al. (1989)	BSA
Parry et al. (1990)	BSTFA
Clouette et al. (1993)	MTBSTFA
Kintz et al. (1995c)	BSTFA
Singh and Johnson (1997)	MSTFA
O'Dell et al. (1997)	BSTFA
Whitter et al. (1999)	MTBSTFA
Langen et al. (2000)	MTBSTFA
Selected Studies Using Alkyl Ester–Alkyl Ether Derivatives	
Whiting and Manders (1982, 1983)	TMAH/CH₃I
ElSohly et al. (1984)	PFBBr/BTMAH
McCurdy et al. (1986)	TMAH/C₃H₇I
Paul et al. (1987)	TMAH/CH₃I
Cone et al. (1987)	TMAH/CH₃I
Mulé and Casella (1988)	TMAH/C₃H₇I
Rosenfeld et al. (1989)	PFBBr (XAD-2)
Lisi et al. (1993)	THAH/CH₃I
Cone et al. (1993)	TMAH/CH₃I
Liu et al. (1994)	TMAH/CH₃I
Huestis et al. (1995)	TMAH/CH₃I
Jenkins et al. (1995)	TMAH/CH₃I
Huestis et al. (1996)	TMAH/CH₃I
Huestis and Cone (1998b)	TMAH/CH₃I
Fraser and Worth (1999)	TMAH/C₃H₇I
Selected Studies Using Alkyl Ester–Alkyl Ester Derivatives	
O'Conner and Rejent (1981)	PFPA/PFIP
Karlsson and Roos (1984)	PFPA/PFIP
Joern (1987)	PFPA/PFPOH
Stout et al. (2001)	PFPA/PFPOH

Silylester–Silyl Ether Derivatives   Silyl ester–silyl ether derivatives of THC-COOH have been widely used. The trimethylsilyl (TMS) derivative is the most common and is readily prepared using N-methyl-N-(trimethylsilyl)trifluoroacetamide (MSTFA), N,O-bis(trimethylsilyl)acetamide (BSA), or bis(trimethylsilyl)trifluoroacetamide (BSTFA), with or without 1% trimethylchlorosilane as a catalyst

(Bronner and Xu, 1992). Unlike the alkyl derivatives, the TMS derivatives are sensitive to moisture. The derivatives can be injected into GC or GC/MS without further cleanup. MSTFA has been used to elute sample from an extraction disc and simultaneously derivatize the THC-COOH (Wu et al., 1993). Clouette et al. (1993) published a study of the mechanism of MS fragmentation of THC-COOH derivatives using the *t*-butydimethylsilyl derivative first used by Bourquin and Brenneisen (1987). The derivative yields four characteristic ions and is exceptionally stable. It is insensitive to moisture to the extent that it has been used in HPLC (Knaus et al., 1976). Studies using silyl derivatives are listed in Table 3.7.

Alkyl Ester–Alky Ester Derivatives   The formation of alkyl ester–alkyl ester derivatives by esterification of the carboxyl group and acylation of the phenol group can be used to prepare fluoronated derivatives that aid in the formation of negative ions in NCIMS methods and give higher-mass fragments in EIMS. Reaction of THC-COOH, either sequentially or concurrently, with an acid anhydride and an alcohol yields an alkyl ester–alkyl ester derivative. Pentafluoropropionic anhydride and 2,2,3,3,3-pentafluoro-1-propanol were utilized by Karlsson et al. (1983) in a comparison of EI, PCI, and NCI mass spectrometric methods. Joern (1987) proposed this derivative for routine confirmations by EIMS in a substance-abuse treatment setting. A LOD of 1.8 ng/mL using 1 mL of sample was achieved. Although Karlsson et al. (1983) claimed that NCIMS was over 200 times as sensitive as EIMS, the LOD reported is only 0.7 ng/mL. McBurney et al. (1986) achieved subnanogram/mL detection limits for cannabinoid metabolites in urine and plasma using the pentafluoropropionyl–hexafluoroisopropyl derivatives and EIMS. W.A. Baumgartner et al. (1995) used derivatization with heptafluorobutyric anhydride and hexafluro-2-propanol to detect low picogram levels of metabolites in hair by NCIMSMS.

Alkyl ester–alkyl ester derivatives can also be prepared by methylating the carboxylic acid, followed by acylation of the phenol. A very sensitive method for analysis of THC-COOH in blood, plasma, serum, and urine was reported by Foltz et al. (1983). The carboxylic acid was methylated using methanolic-BF_3. The phenol was then acylated with trifluoroacetic anhydride. The derivative was used in an NCIGCMS method to detect 100 pg/mL concentrations of THC-COOH. Cano and Lykissa (1989) reported the use of the same derivative in a GCEIMS method.

Alkyl Ester–Trimethyl Silyl Ether Derivatives   The use of methyl ester–trimethylsilyl ether derivatives has been reported by Foltz and Hidy (1982), T.S. Baker et al. (1984), and Harvey et al. (1980). J.M. Rosenfeld et al. (1986, 1989) reported that THC-COOH extracted onto XAD-2 resin could be alkylated with pentafluorobenzyl bromide. The dialkyl derivative or each of the possible mono-alkyl derivatives could be obtained, depending on conditions. Treatment with BSTFA gave the two pentafluorobenzyl–TMS derivatives.

Chromatographic Parameters

Phenyl methyl silicone or cross-linked dimethyl silicone capillary columns (12–40 m) are nearly universally used in cannabinoid analysis in biological matrices. Column temperature is usually programmed, with starting temperatures at 65 to 150°C and ending temperatures of >300°C. Analysis times of less than 15 minutes are routine for THC-COOH in urine. For workplace testing and routine forensic testing of urine for THC-COOH, EIMS is by far the most popular detection method. PCIMS, NCIMS, and MSMS methods are used when enhanced sensitivity is needed for research or for detection of low concentrations found in alternate matrices, such as blood, hair, and saliva.

3.4.1.5 Potential Interferences Encountered in Urine Analysis of THC-COOH

3.4.1.5.1 Adulteration

The adulteration of urine specimens with nitrite ion can cause failure to confirm THC-COOH by GC/MS (ElSohly et al., 1997). The degradation of the THC-COOH has been shown to be pH dependent, with the metabolite being stable in neutral or basic urine and degraded in even weak (pH 6) acid (Tsai et al., 1998). Much of the degradation may come during the step where the metabolite is extracted from acidic solution. Degradation during processing can be avoided by adding 250 mg of sodium bisulfite to the specimen prior to hydrolysis (ElSohly et al., 1997). Frederick (1998) reports consistently good results by using sulfamic acid to adjust the pH from basic in the hydrolysis step to acidic prior to extraction.

3.4.1.5.2 Interference by Other Drugs

Brunk (1988) reported that high concentrations of ibuprofen can cause false-negative confirmations by consuming derivatizing agents. Interferences from ibuprofen or other acidic drugs can be removed by reanalyzing the samples with an excess of the derivatizing agent (ElSohly et al., 1997)

If a nontarget drug or metabolite coelutes with derivatized THC-COOH and has a fragmentation ion in common with either the THC-COOH-d$_3$ derivative or the derivatized THC-COOH, the ion ratios for these ions will not fall within acceptance tolerances, and thus the confirmation will fail. Two such interferences have been reported in THC-COOH confirmation analyses using the dimethyl derivative of THC-COOH. Podkowik et al. (1991a) reported that ritodrine, a beta-blocking drug used to prevent premature labor, has a metabolite that is not completely separated from THC-COOH in the system being used by the U.S. Army Laboratory in Wiesbaden, Germany, at that time. In the procedure used, the m/z 316, 360, 375 ions are monitored for the dimethyl derivative of THC-COOH-d$_3$. (m/z 313, 357, 372 are monitored for the THC-COOH derivative.) This coeluting metabolite interfered with the m/z 316 ion in the fragmentation of THC-COOH-d$_3$ (dimethyl derivative). Rerunning the samples with a lower-temperature program could eliminate the interference. An interference with the m/z 360 ion was also noted in some cases (Podkowik et al., 1991b). The interfering substance was identified as 8-hydroxy-3',4',5'-tris-nor-Δ^9-THC-2'-oic acid, a minor metabolite of THC. Joern (1992b) noted a significant number of cases that failed acceptance standards when using the dimethyl derivative. The failure was traced to an unidentified eluent that broadened the m/z 313 ion. Using the dipropyl derivative eliminated the interference.

3.4.1.6 Criteria for Positive Identification and Calculation of Concentrations

In order to positively identify an analyte using GCEI-MS, it is widely accepted that the full-scan spectrum should have a minimum of three characteristic ions whose ratios are within 20% of the same ion ratios run on standards on the same instrument. When using selected ion monitoring, a minimum of three ions in the analyte should be monitored and meet the same standards as for full-scan spectra. Most chemical ionization methods offer increased sensitivity but do not yield three characteristic peaks. These methods are more suitable to quantitative determinations of very low concentrations for research purposes. Soft ionization techniques coupled with tandem mass spectrometry offer a combination of extreme sensitivity and the opportunity to increase specificity by generating daughter ions. The majority of quantitative determinations of cannabinoids in urine or other biological matrices utilize coeluting deuterated internal standards, i.e., isotope dilution methods.

3.4.2 BLOOD, SERUM, AND PLASMA

The detection and quantitative analysis of cannabinoids in blood, serum, and plasma are of interest for both pharmacological studies (Foltz et al., 1983) and forensic studies (Agurell et al., 1973). The possibility of correlating concentrations of THC and THC metabolites with time of consumption (Huestis et al., 1992a, 1992b) is of particular interest in traffic law enforcement and forensic cases since urinanalysis is not useful in determining whether the subject was under the influence at a given time. In order to be useful, analytical methods must have appropriate sensitivity and selectivity. For forensic investigations, a LOD of 1.0 ng/mL of THC is generally sufficient. More sensitive techniques have been developed for pharmacological studies. The requisite selectivity for forensic purposes can be obtained only through mass spectrometric or infrared techniques. However, many less selective techniques are utilized for both forensic and clinical investigations in some jurisdictions (Badia et al., 1998a). In addition to immunoassay techniques, TLC, GC, and HPLC methods are used for screening of samples.

Methods of determination of drugs in blood, including *Cannabis*, have been reviewed for the years 1991 to 1997 (Moeller et al., 1998) and of cannabinoids from 1990 to 1999 (Staub, 1999). GC/MS methods for THC-COOH in biological matrices, including blood, have been comprehensively reviewed through 1991 (Bronner and Xu, 1992; Cody and Foltz, 1995). A review and specific methods can be found in ElSohly and Salem (2000). Older methods, including TLC methods, are reviewed by Foltz et al. (1980), Foltz (1984), Burstein (1979), and Harvey (1985).

3.4.2.1 Standards and Internal Standards
See Sections 3.4.1.3 and 3.4.1.4.3.

3.4.2.2 Glassware
All glassware and stoppers should be silanized.

3.4.2.3 Extraction
Effective extraction procedures must efficiently remove the analytes of interest from the matrix and separate them from endogenous materials that may interfere with the analytical method chosen. Blood and plasma contain lipids that are soluble in the lipohilic solvents that extract the neutral cannabinoids. They also contain proteins that can complicate the extractions. A wide variety of extraction procedures have been used. The procedure of choice will depend upon the analytes of interest and the analytical method chosen.

3.4.2.3.1 Liquid–Liquid Extraction
Early methods (Agurell et al., 1973; Ohlsson et al., 1976) utilized liquid–liquid extraction with petroleum ether or petroleum ether–isoamylalchol (1.5%) followed by separation by liquid chromatography on sephadex columns prior to actual analysis. Extraction from blood or plasma at pH 4 with hexane–isoamylalcohol (98:2), followed by shaking of the hexane layer with modified Claisen alkali (3.7 g of potassium hydroxide in 20 mL of water added to 100 mL of methanol), extracts cannabinoids and reduces the amount of lipids (Vinson et al., 1977; J.J. Rosenfeld et al., 1974). The alkali layer is acidified, and the solid that forms is dissolved in H_2O and extracted with hexane. See Figure 3.16.

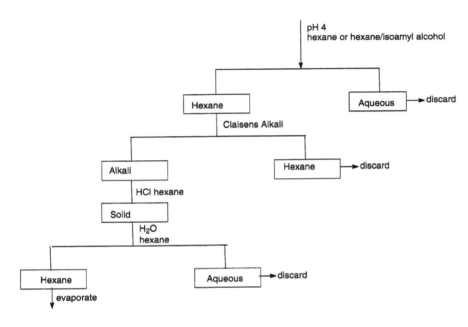

Figure 3.16

Extraction of cannabinoids from blood or plasma designed to optimize removal of lipids. Acids, as well as neutral compounds, are extracted

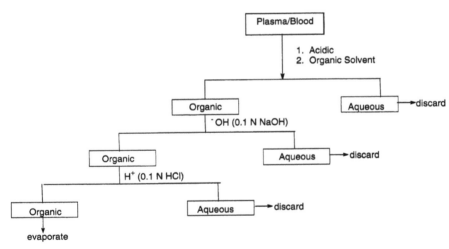

Figure 3.17

Extraction of cannabinoids: only neutral compounds remain in the extract

Liquid–liquid extractions from acidified blood or plasma using hexane, heptane, petroleum ether, diethyl ether, and chloroform have all been performed. If THC and 11-OH-THC are the target analytes, the organic extract is washed first with base and then with acid prior to derivatization or direct analysis (McCallum, 1973; Detrick and Foltz, 1976) (Figure 3.17).

If both acidic and basic analytes are wanted in the same extract, the basic wash is eliminated and a more polar extraction solvent (hexane–thyl acetate

Figure 3.18

Extraction of cannabinoids: acid and neutral compounds remain in the extract

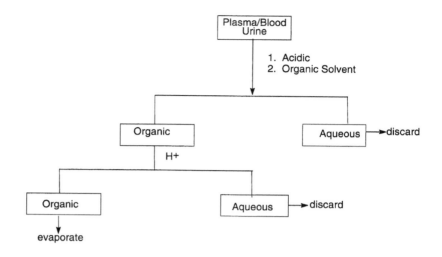

7:1) can be used (Foltz and Hidy, 1982) (see Figure 3.18). In a widely used method for analysis of THC and its metabolites, proteins in blood or plasma (1 mL) are precipitated by the addition of acetonitrile (2 mL) (Foltz et al., 1983). After centrifugation the supernatant is separated and reduced in volume (<1 mL). The solution is made basic by the addition of 0.2 N NaOH and extracted with 2 mL of hexane–ethyl acetate (9:1). The aqueous layer contains the acid constituents, and the organic layer contains the neutral constituents. The organic layer is washed with 2 mL of 0.1 N HCl and evaporated to dryness. The aqueous phase containing the acid components (THC-COOH) is acidified with 1 mL of 1 N HCl and extracted with 2 mL of hexane–ethyl acetate (9:1). The extract is then evaporated to dryness (see Figure 3.19). Kintz and Cirimele (1997) used hexane–ethyl acetate (9:1) extraction of acidified blood and no acid or base washes in a method for THC and THC-COOH, with a LOD of 1.0 ng/mL for THC and 0.05 ng/mL for THC-COOH.

3.4.2.3.2 Solid-Phase Extraction

SPE has also found wide application (Kelly and Jones, 1992; Moeller et al., 1992; Nelson et al., 1993; Felgate and Dinan, 2000; D'Asaro, 2000; Huang et al., 2001). Huang et al. (2001) achieved limits of quantitation for THC and THC-COOH of 0.5 ng/mL and 2.5 ng/mL, respectively, using SPE and NCI-GC-MS. This method offered major improvements over the liquid–liquid extraction procedure developed by the same laboratory and outlined earlier (Foltz et al., 1983). Both analytes were simultaneously derivatized with hexafluroisopropanol and trifluroacetic anhydride. Internal standard was THC-d_3 and THC-COOH-d_3.

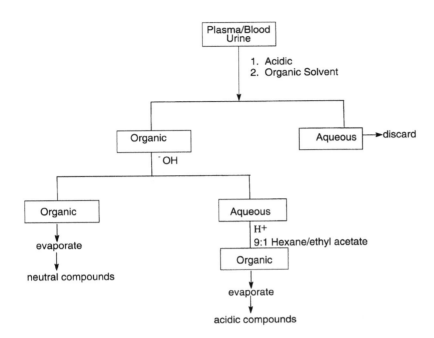

Figure 3.19

Extraction of cannabinoids: acid and neutral compounds are extracted separately

3.4.2.4 Thin-Layer Chromatography

A variety of TLC methods are available for screening blood or plasma. Vinson et al. (1977) used a fluorescent derivative to detect THC in concentrations of less than 0.4 ng/mL using 5 mL of blood. The residue from extraction was derivatized with 5 μL of a 1 mg/mL acetonitrile solution of 2-*p*-chlorosulfophenyl-3-phenylidone chloride (DIS-Cl). The derivative was chromatographed on Bakerflex 1B2 silica gel sheets using methanol–water (95:5) as the mobile phase. Visualization was achieved by spraying with a solution prepared by dissolving 8 g of sodium metal in 100 mL of methanol and 8 mL of dimethylsulfoxide. The plates were visualized while wet under long-wavelength UV light. A quantitative method for determining THC in plasma using dansylation with ^{14}C-labeled dansylchloride and [3]H$_2$-THC as IS was developed by Scherrmann et al. (1979). The plasma extract was derivatized and purified by TLC, and the spots were detected by UV and eluted for measurement of the ^{14}C activity. Chromatographic separations on silica gel in either one or two dimensions were good; however, dansyl breakdown products complicated the interpretation. Alemany et al. (1993) used high-performance thin-layer chromatography (HPTLC) on silica gel to separate the dansyl derivative of THC. A LOD of less than 0.5 ng/mL was achieved using fluorimetric scanning densitometry at 340 nm to quantitate the spots.

3.4.2.5 High-Performance Liquid Chromatography

Garrett and Hunt (1976) explored both normal-phase and reversed-phase HPLC using UV detection. Valentine et al. (1976) used normal-phase HPLC on 10-μm silica gel in 250 × 2-mm columns and heptane–dichloromethane gradient elution to separate cannabinoids. Detection was by UV at 273.7 nm. THC-d_3 was used as an IS that could be detected by the UV. The coeluted THC/THC-d_3 was then placed in a mass spectrometer by direct insertion probe to identify and quantify the analyte. A LOD of 1 ng/mL was obtained. Gerostamoulos and Drummer (1993) used a reversed-phase 250 × 50-mm (C_8) column and acetonitrile/methanol/0.01 M H_2SO_4 (45:20:35) as mobile phase to determine THC and 11-OH-THC in blood. Electrochemical detection (ED) was used to achieve a LOD of 1.0 ng/mL for each analyte. Abdul Rahman et al. (1995) used SPE and reversed-phase HPLC to determine THC and THC-COOH, with a LOD of 2.5 ng/mL for THC and 1 ng/mL for THC-COOH by ED and with 20 ng and 10 ng, respectively, by UV detection at 212 nm and 220 nm.

3.4.2.6 Gas Chromatography and Gas Chromatography/Mass Spectrometry

In early research on THC pharmakokinetics ^{14}C-labeled THC was administered and later measured in the plasma (Galanter et al., 1972). Agurell et al. (1973) published the first method to identify and accurately measure nonlabeled THC in the plasma of humans who smoked *Cannabis*. This work is described in detail in Ohlsson et al. (1976). Packed-column GCEIMS with selected ion monitoring was used to measure the m/z 299 and 314 ions from THC and the m/z 301 and 316 ions from a deuterated IS (THC-d_2) synthesized by the authors. A LOD of 1 ng/mL was reported. Fenimore et al. (1973, 1976a) used hexahydrocannabinol as IS and heptafluorobutyric anhydride as the derivatizing agent. A two-oven system with a packed precolumn followed by a cold trap and a capillary column enabled the authors to measure 0.1 ng/mL using an electron capture detector (ECD). McCallum (1973) used a packed column with a flame photometric detector to measure the diethyl phosphate ester of THC, with a LOD of 2 ng/mL (from 10 mL of blood or plasma). Garrett and Hunt (1973, 1976) used the pentafluorobenzoyl derivative and ECD to measure 0.1 ng/mL of THC in 5 mL of blood. The methods utilizing ECD have excellent detection limits but lack the specificity required for forensic analysis. Several methods using EIMS-SIM quickly followed the work of Agurell et al. (1973) (Harzer and Kächele, 1983; Bergman et al., 1981; Pirl et al., 1979; Rosenfeld et al., 1974). Methods using positive ion chemical ionization (PCI) MS were rapidly developed (Foltz et al., 1980; Rosenthal et al., 1978; Wall et al., 1976; Detrick and Foltz, 1976). These methods offer excellent sensitivity and selectivity for use in research but generally provide only one characteristic ion ($[M + H]^+$) and thus do not provide the minimum three characteristic ions generally associated with EI-SIM identification. The details of more recent methods are shown in Table 3.8. They include EI-SIM, PCI, NCI, and PCIMSMS. In each of these methods an appropriate deuterated IS is added prior to extraction. Most of the methods use 5% phenyl-methyl silicone or dimethyl silicone capillary columns of from 12 to 40 m. Separation is usually achieved by temperature programming between 150°C and 300°C. The method of Foltz et al. (1983) is widely used in research (Moody et al., 1992a, 1992b; Mason et al., 1983; Huestis et al., 1992a, 1992b; Johnson et al., 1984). In this method, liquid–liquid extraction is used to generate separate neutral and acidic fractions.

The neutral fraction is derivatized with trifluoroacetic anhydride (TFAA). The THC-COOH in the acidic fraction is derivatized by methylation with methanol and BF_3 followed by acylation with TFAA. Detection is by negative ion chemical ionization mass spectrometry. Limits of quantitation of 0.1 ng/mL of THC-COOH can be achieved in blood. Nelson et al. (1993) have used positive ion chemical ionization tandem mass spectrometry (PCIMSMS) to achieve 10 to 20 pg/mL sensitivity for THC and 11-OH-THC in plasma. By generating daughter ions this method offers positive identification and extreme sensitivity. Collins et al. (1997) used an ion trap to perform MSMS of cannabinoids in postmortem samples. A LOD for the method was not reported. Kintz and Cirimele (1997) have achieved excellent sensitivity using EIMS-SIM of the methyl derivative of THC and THC-COOH.

3.4.3 SALIVA

The analysis of drugs of abuse in saliva has been reviewed (Idowu and Caddy, 1982; Kidwell et al., 1998; Schramm et al., 1992; Samyn et al., 1999; Staub, 1999; Kintz and Samyn, 2000). The use of saliva for the detection of cannabinoids in impaired drivers is of particular interest because saliva is more easily obtained than blood and provides a better indication of recent use than urine. Whether the source of cannabinoids in saliva is from transport from blood or from direct absorption from smoke is an open question (Samyn et al., 1999). The detection of cannabinoids by way of TLC was reported in the early 1970s (Haeckel, 1972; Just et al., 1972, 1974). Candela and Marino (1979) reported detection of cannabinoids in hashish smokers for up to 4 hours using TLC and GC. Peel et al. (1984) modified the method of Foltz et al. (1983) to confirm THC in saliva by GCEIMS; the LOD of the method was 2 ng/mL. Hexahydrocannabinol was used as IS. For law enforcement purposes THC is of interest. The metabolites are present in very low concentrations if at all (Schramm et al., 1992). Hall et al. (1998) used SPME and GCEIMS (Quadrapole Ion Trap

Table 3.8

Recent methods of detection and confirmation of cannabinoids in blood, serum, and plasma by GC/MS

Reference	Matrix	Sample volume (mL)	Analyte(s)	IS	Extraction	Derivitization Reagent	GC Column	Detection	LOD (ng/mL)
Teske et al. (2002)	Blood plasma	0.025 (25 µL)	THC 11-OH-THC THC-COOH		SPE	CH$_3$I		EIMS	
Chu and Drummer (2002)	Blood	1	THC		Liq-Liq	PFPA PFPOH		EIMS	0.5
Huang et al. (2001)	Plasma	1	THC THC-COOH	THC-d$_3$ THC-COOH-d$_3$	SPE	HFPOH TFAA		NCIMS	0.5 2.5
Kintz and Cirimele (1997)	Blood	2	THC THC-COOH	THC-d$_3$ THC-COOH-d$_3$	Hexane: ethylacetate (9:1)	TBAH/CH$_3$I	30 m × 0.25-mm HP-5-MS	EISIM	0.4 0.2
Collins et al. (1997)	Blood	1	THC THC-COOH	THC-d$_3$ THC-COOH-d$_3$	1. ACN/acetone 2. Hexane/base 3. Hexane ethyl: acetate acid (9:1)	BSTFA	12 m × 0.18-mm D8-1	EISIM EISIM	1 2
							30 m × 0.25-mm DB-5	ITEIMSMS	?
Kemp et al. (1995a)	Plasma Urine	1	THC 8α-OH-THC 8β-OH-THC THC-COOH 8α, 11-di-OH-THC 8β, 11-di-OH-THC CBD CBN 11-OH-THC	THC-d$_3$ THC-COOH-d$_3$ 11-OH-THC-d$_3$	1. β-glucuronidase (E. coli) 2. ACN 3. LLE	BSTFA	30 m × 0.25-mm HP-5MS	EISIM	1.6 0.8 1.1 0.6 0.7 0.8 2.1 0.6 0.9
Goodall and Basteyns (1995)	Blood Plasma Urine	1	THC 11-OH-THC THC-COOH	THC-d$_3$ THC-COOH-d$_3$	1. ACN 2. LLE	BSTFA	12 m HP-1	EISIM	0.2 0.2 2.0

Reference	Matrix		Analytes	Internal standard	Extraction	Derivatization	Column	Detection	LOD
Nelson et al. (1993)	Plasma	2	THC, 11-OH-THC	THC-d$_3$, 11-OH-THC-d$_3$	1. ACN 2. SPE	BSTFA	12.5 × 0.2-mm 5% phenyl methyl silcone	PCI-MS-MS	10 × 10^{-3}, 20 × 10^{-3}
Kelly and Jones (1992)	Plasma Urine	1	THC-COOH, THC-COOH-glucuronide	THC-d$_3$, THC-COOH-d$_3$	1. Acetontrile 2. SPE	TFAA PFPA/HFIP	30 m × 0.25-mm DB-5	EISIM	1
McBurney et al. (1986)	Plasma	1	THC, 11-OH-THC, THC-COOH	None	1. β-glucuronidase 2. LLE pH 2.3, 1.5% isoamylalcohol in heptane	PFPA/HFIP	40 m × 0.5-mm SCOT, 3% OV17	EISIM	0.8, 0.8, 0.8
	Urine	1	THC-COOH, 8,11-diOH-THC	THC-COOH-d$_3$	1. β-glucuronidase 2. LLE, pH 2–3, hexane–ethyl acetate (7:1)	PFPA/HFIP	40 m × 0.5-mm SCOT, 3% OV17	EISIM	0.5, 0.8
J.M. Rosenfeld et al. (1986)	Plasma	1	THC, 11-OH-THC	CH$_3$(CH$_2$)$_{22}$CO$_2$PFB (external)	XAD-2	PFBBr	15 m DB-17N	EC	
			THC-COOH	THC-d$_3$, 11-OH-THC-d$_3$, THC-COOH-d$_3$			15-m DB-15W	NCIMS	0.3, 1.0, 0.3
Foltz and Hidy (1982)	Plasma	1	THC	THC-d$_3$	LLE (hexane) acid and base washes	BSTFA	1.8 m × 2-mm 3% OV17	PCIMS	0.2
			THC, 11-OH-THC, THC-COOH	THC-d$_3$, 11-OH-THC-d$_3$, THC-COOH-d$_3$	LLE Hexane:ethyl acetate (7:1) acid wash	1. CH$_2$N$_2$ 2. BSTFA	15 m × 0.25-mm SE-30	PCIMS	?
Foltz et al. (1983)	Blood Plasma Urine	1	THC, 11-OH-THC, THC-COOH	THC-d$_3$, 11-OH-THC-d$_3$, THC-COOH-d$_3$	LLE	TFAA 1. CH$_3$OH-BF$_3$ 2. TFAA	15 m × 0.32-mm DMS	NCIMS	0.2, 0.5, 0.1

Abbreviations: ACN = Acetonitrile.
ITEIMSMS = Ion Trap-EIMSMS.

Table 3.9

Chromatographic methods of detection of cannabinoids in saliva

Reference	Analytes	Internal Standard	Extraction	Derivatizing Reagent	Analytical Method	LOD (ng/mL)
Fucci et al. (2001)	THC	None	SPME	None	GC	NR
Kintz et al. (2000)	THC	THC-d$_3$	Hexane/ethyl acetate (9:1)	TBAH/CH$_3$I	GCEIMS	1.0
Hall et al. (1998)	CND Δ^8-THC Δ^9-THC CBN	THC-d$_3$	SPME	None	GCEIMS (ion trap)	1.0
Kircher and Parlar (1996)	THC CBN CND	None	On column Immunoaffinity	None	Tandem imunoaffinity HPLC-UV (220 nm)	1.0 0.8 2.0
Schramm et al. (1992)					HPLCTSMS	
Menkes et al. (1991)	THC	Δ^8-THC (heptyl analog)	Pentane	PFPA	GCEIMS	[a]
Thompson and Cone (1987)	THC				HPLC-ECD	1.0
Ohlsson et al. (1986)	CBN				GCEIMS	0.05
Maseda et al. (1986)	THC	DDT[b]	n-Hexane	PFPA	GC-ECD	0.5
Peel et al. (1984)	THC	Hexahydro-cannabinol	Hexane-ethyl acetate (9:1)	1. MeOH-BF$_3$ 2. TFAA	GCEIMS	Not reported

[a] Published method metabolites (McBurney et al., 1986).
[b] 1,1-Bis(4-chlorophenyl)-2,2,2-trichloroethane.

Instrument) to detect neutral cannabinoids at the 1 ng/mL level. The use of SPME completely avoids organic solvents and LLE or SPE extraction steps, and the 1.0 ng/mL LOD is reasonable for forensic purposes. This method should be considered, especially for large numbers of samples. Fucci et al. (2001) have reported the use of SPME-GC to detect THC in samples collected by the "EPITOPE" system (EPITOPE Inc.). No LOD was reported. Kintz et al. (2000) used GCEIMS and LLE to achieve a LOD of 1.0 ng/mL. The authors point out the need for standardized collection procedures if these analyses are to be used for traffic law enforcement. Recent methods of analysis are summarized in Table 3.9.

3.4.4 SWEAT

Very little research has been performed on the use of sweat as a sample for confirmation of recent use of *Cannabis*. Reviews (Kidwell et al., 1998; Staub, 1999; Kintz and Samyn, 2000) cover methods of collecting sweat as well as analysis. Devices marketed as PharmChek sweat patches have been used to collect sweat over an extended period of time. One study using these devices for cannabinoid analysis has appeared (Kintz, 1996). The patches were extracted with methanol in the presence of internal standards (THC-d_3 for cannabinoids). The extract was evaporated to dryness and the TMS derivatives were prepared for GCEIMS. Several drugs were analyzed simultaneously, and results for urine, sweat, and hair were compared. Kintz et al. (2000) reject the use of patches as an adjunct to traffic law enforcement/roadside testing since the sample represents collection over more than 1 day. In this study, commercially available cosmetic pads were used to wipe sweat from the forehead. Hexane–ethyl acetate (9:1) was used to extract the analyte and added IS (THC-d_3) from the pad. The analyte was chromatographed as the methyl derivative using EIMS as the detector. A LOD of 1 ng per pad was achieved.

3.4.5 HAIR

Interest in the detection of drugs in hair has grown since A.M. Baumgartner et al. (1979), Arnold and Pueschel (1980, 1981), and Valente et al. (1981) first reported the use of immunoassays for this purpose. Hair assays are of particular interest, compared with those of urine or blood, since they provide a longer window of detection and they provide information concerning the subject's overall exposure to drugs (Mieczkowski, 1995; Kintz, 1993). W.A. Baumgartner et al. (1995) thoroughly outline the advantages of hair analysis for detecting and monitoring drug abuse in workplace and forensic applications. Methods of drug detection and confirmation in hair have been reviewed (Moeller, 1992; Moeller et al., 1993; W.A. Baumgartner et al., 1995; Sachs and Kintz, 1998; Staub, 1999; Skender, 2000; ElSohly and Salem 2000; Kintz and Samyn, 2000).

Since the prevalent cannabinoid found in urine is THC-COOH, the commercially available immunoassays used in drug screens are quite specific for this major metabolite (Spiehler, 2000). In hair, however, the acid metabolites are found in very low concentrations (Nakahara et al., 1995; Wilkins et al., 1995; Mieczkowski, 1995). The neutral constituents THC and 11-OH-THC are found in higher concentrations (Wilkins et al., 1995), although they are much lower than the concentrations found with other drugs of abuse (W.A. Baumgartner et al., 1995). The choice of what constituents to look for will be determined by the goal of the investigation. Regardless of purpose, GC/MS has become the method of choice (Moeller, 1992).

A second analytical consideration is the potential contamination of hair from exposure to the drugs of interest by smoke or dust or other exogenous sources. These issues have been discussed extensively (Baumgartner and Hill, 1992, 1993; Kidwell and Blank, 1992; Blank and Kidwell, 1993, 1995). These concerns have led to the recognition of the need for stringent preanalysis procedures for preparing samples. Wilkins et al. (1995) studied washing regimes using methanol, methylene chloride, anhydrous isopropanol, and phosphate buffer. With each solvent the hair samples were sonicated for 15 s for each of three washes. Each solvent was evaluated by comparing analytical results of hair from the same subject, which was either unwashed or washed in one of the four wash solutions. In addition the solutions were evaluated with hair that had been fortified with cannabinoids. The phosphate buffer was ineffective in removing the fortified analytes from the hair. All three of the organic solvents completely removed the analytes by the third wash. As the authors point out, the results apply only to the specific conditions and concentrations utilized in their study.

Strano-Rossi and Chiarotti (1999) evaluated an aqueous surfactant followed by acetone, multiple dichloromethane washes, and multiple light petroleum ether washes. They concluded that three washes with light petroleum ether were most effective. However, they determined the effectiveness by analyzing the wash solution rather than the hair. Decontamination procedures based on wash kinetics and considerations of hair type and hair damage have been proposed by W.A. Baumgartner et al. (1995) and Kippenberger et al. (1995). Blank and Kidwell (1995) have questioned the sufficiency of this approach; however, *Cannabis* was not used in this study. W.A. Baumgartner et al. (1995) distinguish between routine clinical or workplace testing and forensic samples. Enzyme digestion and separation of the digests into fractions from various parts of the hair are utilized in forensic samples. However, Baumgartner (Cairns et al., 1995) used basic digestion for analysis of THC-COOH. A definitive study on a method that will remove all contamination (including analytes absorbed into the hair) without reducing the concentration of analytes acquired through ingestion or inhalation has not been published. This is not a problem if THC-COOH is the target analyte, since it is not present in smoke or dust from *Cannabis* and thus is unlikely to become an exogenous contaminant. The methods reported next all utilize basic hydrolysis, and they all utilize THC-COOH-d_3 as the IS when THC-COOH is an analyte. See Figure 3.10.

Methods of analysis for cannabinoids as part of a general drug analysis in hair have been reported (Moeller et al., 1993; Kauert, 1989; Sachs and Moeller,

1989; Jurado et al., 1995). Application of headspace solid-phase dynamic extraction, in which the analytes are absorbed on the polydimethyl siloxane-coated interior of a hollow fiber, by multiple aspiration of the sample headspace into the fiber has been coupled with on-fiber derivatization and MSMS to provide an automated and sensitive analysis of drugs, including cannabinoids (Lachenmeier et al., 2003). A method for the detection of THC in hair was reported by Balabanova et al. (1989) and critiqued by Käferstein and Sticht (1990). The signal-to-noise ratio in Balabanova's work is insufficient for identification. An extremely sensitive method for the quantitative analysis of THC, 11-OH-THC, and THC-COOH in hair was developed by Wilkins et al. (1995) to support research in the pharmacokinetics of drug disposition in hair. The method is a modification of the author's earlier reported method for serum, plasma, and urine (Foltz et al., 1983). Gas chromatography negative ion chemical ionization (GCNCIMS) is utilized to quantitatively detect the trifluroacetyl derivatives of THC and 11-OH-THC and the methyl trifluroacetyl derivative of THC-COOH. A limit of quantitation of 50 pg/mg of THC and THC-COOH is reported in 20-mg samples. Kintz et al. (1995a, 1995b) also used GCNCIMS in a sensitive method of identifying and quantitatively measuring THC-COOH. The pentafluropropyl, pentafluropropionyl derivative was used and the THC-COOH derivative was identified based on the m/z 602, 622, and 474 ions. The m/z 602 ion and the m/z 605 ion from THC-COOH-d_3 were used to quantify the analyte. A LOD of 5 pg/mg and a limit of quantitation of 10 pg/mg were reported in 100-mg samples. The rationale proffered for identifying THC-COOH rather than THC is that since it is a metabolite and not found in smoke or dust from *Cannabis* products it is positive proof of *Cannabis* use. The same authors (Cirimele et al., 1996; Kintz et al., 1995a) reported a method for simultaneous identification of THC, CBN, and CBD using GCEIMS and no derivatization and offered it as a rapid screen that would require the additional identification of THC-COOH for forensic purposes. The method utilizes THC-d_3 as the IS and CBN and CBD are measured from response factors to the IS. An exceptionally sensitive NCIMSMS method was reported by Baumgartner and coworkers (Cairns et al., 1995). This method was used in a study of confirmations versus RIA screens reported by Mieczkowski (1995). The method utilizes liquid–liquid extraction of the basic digest followed by derivatization by heptafluorobutyric anhydride and hexafluoroisopropanol. Negative ion chemical ionization MSMS gave a parent ion at m/z 670, which gave collision-induced dissociation (CID) (argon) to yield daughter ions of m/z 344 and 492. The IS (THC-COOH-d_3) gave corresponding ions at m/z 673, 347, and 495. The ratio of m/z 492/495 was used for quantitation. The authors report a limit of quantitation of 0.5 pg/10 mg and a LOD of 0.2 pg/10 mg. Uhl (1997) used PFPA/HFIP in a similar method. The parent ions selected for CID with argon were m/z 620 for the analyte and m/z 623 for IS. These gave daughter ions at m/z 383 and 386. Baumgartner et al. (1995) suggested that ion trap MSMS should make these MSMS methods more widespread; however, ion trap technology for NCIMSMS is only now becoming available.

A method using NCIGCMS and high-volume injection enabled C. Moore et al. (2001) to quantitate 0.5 pg/mg of THC-COOH in 20-mg samples. Solid-phase microextraction has been shown to provide a simple quantitative method for THC, CBD, and CBN in hair (Strano-Rossi and Chiarotti, 1999). In this procedure, 50 mg of hair spiked with THC-d_3 is digested in 1 M NaOH (200 μL). The digest is neutralized with 6 M HCL and 200 μL of phosphate buffer (pH 7.5). A 30-mm polydimethylsiloxane fiber is dipped into 200 μL of digest for 15 minutes. The fiber is then inserted directly into the GC injection port. Limits of detection in the range 0.1 to 0.2 ng/mg were reported. This method should prove to be exceptionally efficient as a screening technique. Headspace solid-phase microextraction was used by Musshoff et al. (2002) in a fully automated method for the neutral cannabinoids. EI-MS was used to obtain 0.05 ng/mg LOD on 10-mg samples (Table 3.10).

Capillary electrophoresis with electrochemical detection has been reported (Backofen et al., 2002).

3.4.6 FINGERNAILS

Cairns et al. (1995) reported the use of NCIMSMS to detect and identify THC-COOH in hair and fingernails (see previous section for details). They found that fingernails contained significantly higher concentrations of THC-COOH than did hair. What was referred to as a regulatory cutoff of 50 pg/g of sample was reported. A procedure for extraction and determination of cannabinoids in fingernails using GCEIMS has been published (Lemos et al., 1999). As with hair, removal of external contaminants is important. The authors report that a wash protocol consisting of sonication for 15 minutes once with 0.1% sodium-dodecyl sulfate solution, three times with distilled water, and three times with methanol resulted in the last wash's being completely negative by both RIA and GC/MS. Sample extraction for both RIA and GC/MS utilized hydrolysis in 1 mL of 1 M NaOH at 95°C. For RIA the hydrolysate was diluted with 3 mL of methanol and taken to dryness at 60°C. The residue was then reconstituted in phosphate buffer (pH 7.4) for analysis using the cannabinoids double-antibody procedure by Diagnostics Products Corp. (Gwynedd, UK).

For GC/MS the hydrolysis was carried out after addition of THC-d_3 and THC-COOH-d_3 as internal standards. Extraction with ethyl acetate proved effective for the recovery of THC. If instead of directly extracting the hydrolysate it was diluted with 3 M hydrochloric acid followed by extraction by ethyl acetate,

Table 3.10

Recent procedures for analysis of cannabinoids in hair

Reference	Sample Size (mg)	Analyte(s)	Internal Standard	Extraction[a,b]	Derivativization[c] Reagent	GC-MS Method	LOD (ng/mg)
Musshoff et al. (2002)	10	THC CBD CBN	THC-d$_3$	HSSPME	MSTFA	EI	0.05 0.08 0.14
Baptista et al. (2002)		THC THC-COOH CBN CBD	Ketroprofen Ketroprofen Ketamine Ketamine	LLE	PFPA/PFPOH	EI NCI EI EI	0.10 0.01 0.10 0.10
Moore et al. (2001)	20	THC-COOH	THC-COOH-d$_3$	SPE	TFAA HFIP	NCI	0.0005
Strano-Rossi and Chiarotti (1999)	50	CBN, CBD THC	THC-d$_3$	SPME	None	EI-SIM	0.1, 0.2 0.1
Uhl (1997)	15	THC-COOH	THC-COOH-d$_3$	SPE	PFPA/HFIP	NCI-MSMS	0.0002
Cirimele et al. (1996)	50	CBN, CBD THC	THC-d$_3$	LLE	None	EI-SIM	0.01, 0.02 0.1
Kauert and Röhrich (1996)	50–200	THC	Methaqualone	MeOH	PA	EI-SIM	0.1
Kintz et al. (1995a, 1995b)	100	THC-COOH	THC-COOH-d$_3$	LLE	PFPA/ PFP	NCI	0.005
Wilkins et al. (1995)	20	THC, 11-OH-THC THC-COOH	THC-d$_3$ 11-OH-THC-d$_3$ THC-COOH-d$_3$	LLE	TFAA MeOH-BF$_3$/ TFAA	NCI	0.05, 0.5 0.05
Cairns et al. (1995)	15–25	THC-COOH	THC-COOH-d$_3$	LLE	HFBA/ HFIP	NCIMSMS	2×10^{-5}
Cirimele et al. (1996)	100	THC THC-COOH	THC-d$_3$ THC-COOH-d$_3$	LLE	PFPA/ PFP	EI-SIM	0.1 0.1
Jurado et al. (1995)	?	THC THC-COOH	THC-d$_3$ THC-COOH-d$_3$	LLE	HFBA/ HFIP	EI-SIM	0.01 0.01

[a] All liquid–liquid extractions were performed with hexane–ethyl acetate (9:1).

[b] All samples for THC-COOH were hydrolyzed with strong base.

[c] Abbreviations of derivatizing agents: PFPA = pentafluoroproprionic acid anhydride, HFIP = hexafluoro2-propanol, PA = proprionic acid anhydride, PFP = pentafluoropropanol, TFAA = trifluoroacetic anhydride, HFBA = heptafluorobutyric acid anhydride, MeOH = methanol.

THC-COOH was effectively recovered. Both extracts were derivatized using BSTFA catalyzed with 1% TMCS. Limits of detection for both analytes were less than 0.1 ng/mg of sample, and results were obtained on samples ranging from 2.5 to 25 mg. Identification was based on m/z 371 and 386 for THC and m/z 371 and 488 for THC-COOH. Quantitation was based on the ratio of m/z 386 and 389 for THC and m/z 488 and 491 for THC-COOH. Using GC/MS the authors detected THC in 11 of 14 extracts, with a range from 0.13 to 6.97 ng/mg. They also detected THC-COOH in 2 of 3 acid extracts. Concentration ranged from 9.82 to 29.67 ng/mg.

3.4.7 MECONIUM

Prenatal exposure through maternal consumption of drugs has become a major concern to health professionals (Nair et al., 1994; Yawn et al., 1994). Although blood and urine may seem to be suitable specimens for determining these exposures, the meconium (first stool) has been shown to extend the window of detection to the last 20 weeks of gestation for some drugs (Callahan et al., 1992; Ryan et al., 1994). This window is only 2 or 3 days with blood (Ostrea et al., 1988) and urine (Ostrea et al., 1989). The relative merits of interviews, hair analysis, and meconium analysis have been reported by Ostrea et al. (2001). Meconium extracts that screened positive for cannabinoids by immunoassay techniques showed lower than expected confirmation rates for THC-COOH by GC/MS (Wingert et al., 1994; C. Moore et al., 1996; ElSohly et al., 1994). C. Moore et al. (1996) developed a method for confirmation of THC-COOH in meconium that had been screened by FPIA. The meconium was homogenized with methanol, IS (THC-COOH-d_3) was added, and the homogenate was made basic. After 15 minutes the homogenate was centrifuged and basic and neutral compounds were extracted with hexane–ethyl acetate and discarded. The solution was acidified and the THC-COOH was extracted with hexane–ethyl acetate. The extract was evaporated and derivatized with MTBSTFA. Since only 80% of FPIA-positive samples were confirmed, it was suggested that other metabolites of THC that cross-react in the immunoassays may be present in meconium. ElSohly and Feng (1998) established this to be the case. They reported that 11-hydroxy-Δ^9-tetrahydrocannabinol (11-OH-THC), 8β,11-dihydroxy-Δ^9-tetrahyhydrocannabinol (8β, 11-diOH-THC), 8α,11-dihydroxy-Δ^9-tetrahydrocannabinol, and Δ^9-THC all show significant cross-reactivity in the EMIT cannabinoid assay using low cutoff levels. They also reported the presence of THC-COOH, 8β,11-diOH-THC, 11-OH-THC, and 8-OH-THC in meconium. In addition they established that these compounds are present to some degree as their glucuronides.

The authors prepared Δ^9-THC-glucuronide and determined that hydrolysis by acid (pH 6.8–2.0) or 2 N KOH gave 0% recovery of Δ^9-THC. Hydrolysis with

5000 units of β-glucuronidase per gram of meconium, overnight at 37°C, gave 100% recovery. The analytical procedure adopted first homogenized 1 g of meconium and IS (Δ^9-THC-d_9 and THC-COOH-d_6) with 4 mL of methanol. The homogenate was centrifuged and the supernatant was taken to dryness. The residue was partitioned between 1 mL of saturated monobasic potassium phosphate and 10 mL of chloroform. The aqueous phase was discarded and the chloroform layer was evaporated to dryness. The residue was hydrolyzed at 37°C overnight with 5000 units of β-glucuronidase in 1 mL of 0.1 M phosphate buffer (pH 6.8). The solution was acidified and extracted into hexane–ethyl acetate (9:1). The organic layer was shaken with 1 N NaOH with acidic analytes (THC-COOH and 8β,11-diOH-THC) residing in the bottom aqueous layer and the neutral analytes (THC, 11-OH-THC, and 8-OH-THC) remaining in the organic layer. The neutral fraction was shaken with 0.2 N NaOH in methanol in order to separate the analytes from lipids. The bottom methanol layer was made acidic and diluted and the analytes were extracted into hexane–ethyl acetate (9:1). After solvent removal, the acetate derivatives were formed using 20 μL of pyridine and 60 μL of acetic anhydride. The aqueous solution containing the acid analytes was made acidic and extracted with hexane–ethyl acetate (9:1). After evaporating the solvent, the residue was derivatized using BSTFA. Both fractions were chromatographed on 25 m × 0.2-mm DB-5 MS columns. The separations and the ions monitored are shown in Table 3.11. The LODs for THC-COOH and 8β,11-diOH-Δ^9-THC were 2 and 5 ng/g, respectively. The LODs for 11-OH-THC and 8-OH-THC (α and β combined) were 10 and 15 ng/g, respectively. Interference with the m/z 313 ion made its use as a qualifying ion for THC difficult below 50 ng/g, although the quantitating ion (m/z 297) could be distinguished as low as 5 ng/g. Procedures for determination of cannabinoids in meconium have been reviewed (Staub, 1999; Moore et al., 1998; Kintz and Samyn, 2000).

Compound	Rt	Derivative	Ions Monitored
Δ^9-THC-d_9 (IS)	5.77	Acetate	306, 322
Δ^9-THC	5.83	Acetate	297, 313
8α- and 8β-OH-Δ^9-THC	8.35	Diacetate	312, 354
11-OH-Δ^9-THC	9.63	Diacetate	312, 354
8β11-diOH-Δ^9-THC	9.27	TMS	369, 459, 562
11-nor-Δ^9-THC-9-COOH	9.35	TMS	371, 473, 488
11-nor-Δ^9-THC-9-COOH-d_6 (IS)	9.28	TMS	377, 494

Table 3.11

Retention times and ions monitored for Δ^9-THC and its neutral metabolites analyzed as the acetate derivatives and for the acidic metabolites analyzed as the TMS derivatives

Reproduced by permission of Preston Publications, Division of Preston Industries, Inc., from ElSohly and Feng (1998).

3.4.8 OTHER MATRICES

Johansson et al. (1989) developed an extraction procedure for fat combining liquid–liquid extraction, Lipidex filtration, and preparative LC prior to HPLC and GC/MS of the *t*-butyldimethylsilyl derivatives of THC. A LOD of less than 0.4 ng/g was achieved by GCEIMS-SIM using ($1'$-^{2}H, $2'$-^{2}H, $3'$-^{2}H, $4'$-^{2}H, $5'$-^{2}H$_3$)-THC (THC-d$_7$) as IS.

Kudo et al. (1995) modified the extraction of Foltz et al. (1983) to accommodate solid samples. Adipose tissue, 0.1 g, or other tissue, 0.5 g, was homogenized in 3 mL of acetonitrile before extraction with 2 mL of hexane–ethyl acetate (9:1). The methyl derivative was used and THC-d$_3$ was used as the IS. A LOD of less than 1 ng/g was obtained in all tissues (i.e., blood, urine, brain, lung, kidney, muscle, liver, spleen, and adipose).

Manolis et al. (1983) developed a method for determination of THC in breath. Seven different trapping systems were evaluated, and absorption on Tenax-GC (2.6-diphenyl-*p*-phenylene oxide polymer) was determined to be the best. The perfluoropropyl derivative was used for GCEIMS using packed columns. The limit of detection was 250 pg per breath sample. Ten of 14 subjects had detectable levels of THC 10 minutes after smoking two marijuana cigarettes. All were below the detection limit at 20 minutes.

REFERENCES

INTERNET

American Board of Criminalists (ABC) (2001). Web page: www.criminalistics.com/abc/drugksa.htm.

Scientific Working Group for Seized Drug Analysis (SWGDRUG) (2001). Web page: www.swgdrug.org.

Fed. Regist. 59, 29908-29931. Mandatory guidelines for federal workplace drug-testing programs (1994). http://www.health.org/workplace/GDLNS-94.aspx.

Abdul Rahman, M.A., Anderson, R.A., MacDonald, M., and Williams, K. (1995). In *Advances in Forensic Science* (ed. G. Jacob and W. Bonte). Biomedical Publications, Foster City, CA, pp. 289–295.

Abercrombie, M.L., and Jewell, J.S. (1986). *J. Anal. Toxicol.* 10, 178–180.

Agurell, S. (1970). In *The Botany and Chemistry of Cannabis* (ed. C.R.B. Joyce and S.H. Curry). Churchill, London, pp. 57–59.

Agurell, S., Gustafsson, B., Holmstedt, B., Leander, K., Lindgren, J.-E., Nilsson, I., Sandberg, F., and Asberg, M. (1973). *J. Pharm. Pharmacol.* 25, 554–558.

Agurell, S., Halldin, M., Lindgren, J.E., Ohlsson, A., Widman, M., Gillespie, H., and Hollister, L. (1986). *Pharmacology* 38, 21–43.

Alburges, M.E., and Peat, M.A. (1986). *J. Forensic Sci.* 31(2), 695–706.

Alemany, G., Gamundi, A., Nicolau, M.C., and Sano, D. (1993). *Biomed. Chromatogr.* 7, 273–274.

Altunkaya, D., Clatworthy, A.J., Smith, R.N., and Start, I.J. (1991). *Forensic Sci. Int.* 50, 15–22.

Armbruster, D.A., and Krolak, J.M. (1992). *J. Anal. Toxicol.* 16, 172–175.

Armbruster, D.A., Schwarzhoff, R.H., Hubster, E.C., and Liserio, M.K. (1993a). *Clin. Chem.* 39, 2137–2146.

Armbruster, D.A., Schwarzhoff, R.H., Pierce, B.L., and Hubster, E.C. (1993b). *J. Forensic Sci.* 38, 1326–1341.

Armbruster, D.A., Schwarzhoff, R.H., Pierce, B.L., and Hubster, E.C. (1994). *J. Anal. Toxicol.* 18, 110–117.

Armbruster, D.A., Hubster, E.C., Kaufman, M.S., and Ramon, M.K. (1995). *Clin. Chem.* 41, 92–98.

Arnold, W., and Pueschel, K.Z. (1980). *Rechtsmedizin* 20, 13–14.

Arnold, W., and Pueschel, K. (1981). *J. Forensic Sci. Soc.* 21, 83.

ASCLD News, Summer (2001). "A New Resource: The National Forensic Laboratory Information System (NFLIS)."

Asselin, W.M., Leslie, J.M., and McKinley, B. (1988). *J. Anal. Toxicol.* 12, 207–215.

Backofen, U., Matysik, F.-M., and Lunte, C.E. (2002). *J. Chromatogr. A* 942(1–2), 259–269.

Bäckstrom, B., Cole, M.D., Carrott, M.J., Jones, D.C., Davidson, G., and Coleman, K. (1997). *Sci. Justice* 37(2), 91–97.

Badia, R., de la Torre, R., Corcione, S., and Segura, J. (1998a). *Clin. Chem.* 44, 790–799.

Badia, R., Segura, J., Artla, A., and de la Torre, R. (1998b). *J. Anal. Toxicol.* 22, 117–126.

Baiker, C., Serrano, L., and Lindner, B. (1994). *J. Anal. Toxicol.* 18, 101–103.

Bailey, K. (1979). *J. Forensic Sci.* 24, 817–841.

Baker, P.B., Fowler, R., Bagon, K.R., and Gough, T.A. (1980). *J. Anal. Toxicol.* 4, 145–152.

Baker, T.S., Harry, J.V., Russell, J.W., and Myers, R.L. (1984). *J. Anal. Toxicol.* 8, 255–259.

Balabanova, S., Arnold, P.J., Luckow, V., Brunner, H., and Wolf, H.U. (1989). *Zeitschrift Rechtsmedizin* 102, 503–508.

Baptista, M.J., Monsanto, P.V., Pinho Marques, E.G., Bermejo, A., Avila S., Castanheira, A.A., Margalho, C., Barroso, M., and Vieira, D.N. (2002). *Forensic Sci. Int.* 128(1–2), 66–78.

Barbato, J.J. (1978). *DEA Laboratory Notes* 10, 1–2.

Barni Comparini, I., and Centini, F. (1983). *Forensic Sci. Int.* 21, 129–137.

Baselt, R.C. (1984). In *Advances in Analytical Toxicology, Vol. 1* (ed. R.C. Baselt). Biomedical Publications, Foster City, CA, pp. 81–123.

Baselt, R.C. (1989). *J. Anal. Toxicol.* 13, 1.

Bastiani, R.J. (1984). In *The Cannabinoids: Chemical, Pharmacologic, and Therapeutic Aspects* (ed. S. Agurell, W.L. Dewey, and R.E. Willette). Academic Press, New York, pp. 263–280.

Baumgartner, A.M., Jones, P.F., Baumgartner, W.A., and Black, C.T. (1979). *J. Nucl. Med.* 20, 748–752.

Baumgartner, W.A., and Hill, V.A. (1992). In *Recent Developments in Therapeutic Drug Monitoring and Clinical Toxicology* (ed I. Sunshine). Marcel Dekker, New York, pp. 577–597.

Baumgartner, W.A., and Hill, V.A. (1993). *Forensic Sci. Int.* 63, 121–135.

Baumgartner, W.A., Cheng, C.-C., Donahue, T.D., Hayes, G.F., Hill, V.A., and Scholtz, H. (1995). In *Forensic Application of Mass Spectrometry* (ed. J. Yinon). CRC Press, Boca Raton, FL, pp. 61–94.

Bergman, R.A., Lukaszewski, T., and Wang, S.Y.S. (1981). *J. Anal. Toxicol.* 5, 85–89.

Berkabile, D.R., and Meyers, A. (1989). *J. Anal. Toxicol.* 13, 63.

Björkman, S. (1982). *J. Chromatogr.* 237, 389–397.

Black, D.L., Goldberger, B.A., Isenschmid, D.S., White, S.M., and Caplan, Y.H. (1984). *J. Anal. Toxicol.* 8, 224–227.

Blanc, J.A., Manneh, V.A., Ernst, R., Berger, D.E., de Keczer, S.A., Chase, C., Centofanti, J.M., and DeLizza, A.J. (1993). *Clin. Chem.* 39, 1705–1712.

Blank, D.L., and Kidwell, D.A. (1993). *Forensic Sci. Int.* 63, 145–156.

Blank, D.L., and Kidwell, D.A. (1995). *Forensic Sci. Int.* 70, 13–38.

Blum, L.M., Klinger, R.A., and Rieders, F. (1989). *J. Anal. Toxicol.* 13, 285–288.

Boettcher, M., Haenseler, E., Hoke, C., Nichols, J., Raab, D., and Domke, I. (2000). *Clin. Lab.* 46, 49–52.

Bogusz, M., Aderjan, R., Schmitt, G., Nadler, E., and Neureither, B. (1990). *Forensic Sci. Int.* 48, 27–37.

Bond, G.D., Chand, P., Walia, A.S., and Liu, R.H. (1990). *J. Anal. Toxicol.* 14, 389–390.

Bourquin, D., and Brenneisen, R. (1987). *J. Chromatogr.* 414(1), 187–191.

Brandt, C., and Kovar, K.-A. (1997). *J. Planar Chromatogr.* 10, 348–352.

Breindahl, T., and Andreasen, K. (1999). *J. Chromatogr. B Biomed. Sci. Appl.* 732(1), 155–164.

Brendler, J., and Liu, R.H. (1997). *Clin. Chem.* 43, 688–690.

Brenneisen, R. (1984). *Pharm. Acta Helv.* 59, 247–259.

Brenneisen, R. (1986). *Arch. Kriminol.* 177, 95–104.

Brenneisen, R., and ElSohly, M.A. (1988). *J. Forensic Sci.* 33(6), 1385–1404.

Bronner, W.E., and Xu, A.S. (1992). *J. Chromatogr.* 580, 63–75.

Bronner, W.E., Nyman, P., and von Minden, D. (1990). *J. Anal. Toxicol.* 14, 368–371.

Broussard, L.A., and Hanson, L. (1997). *Clin. Lab. Sci.* 10, 83–86.

Brunk, S.D. (1988). *J. Anal. Toxicol.* 12, 290–291.

Buchan, B.J., Walsh, J.M., and Leaverton, P.E. (1998). *J. Forensic Sci.* 43, 395–399.

Budgett, W.T., Levine, B., Xu, A., and Smith, M.L. (1992). *J. Forensic Sci.* 37, 632–635.

Buechler, K.F., Moi, S., Noar, B., McGrath, D., Villela, J., Clancy, M., Shenhav, A., Colleymore, A., Valkirs, G., and Lee, T. (1992). *Clin. Chem.* 38, 1678–1684.

Burstein, S. (1979). In *Cannabinoid Analysis in Physiological Fluids.* ACS Symposium Series 98 (ed. J.A. Vinson). American Chemical Society, Washington, DC, pp. 1–12.

Caddy, B., and Fish, F. (1967). *J. Chromatogr.* 31, 584–587.

Cagle, J.C., McCurdy, H.H., Pan, Y.M., Ayton, K.J., Wall, W.H., and Solomons, E.T. (1997). *J. Anal. Toxicol.* 21, 213–217.

Cairns, T., Kippenberger, D.J., Scholtz, H., and Baumgartner, W.A. (Nov. 1995). In *Proceedings of the 1995 International Conference and Workshop for Hair Analysis in Forensic Toxicology* (ed. R.A. de Zeeuw, I. Al Hosani, S. Al Munthiri, and A. Maqbool). Abu Dhabi, pp. 185–193.

Callahan, C.M., Grant, T.M., and Phipps, P. (1992). *J. Pediatr.* 120, 763–768.

Candela, R.G., and Marino, C. (1979). *Boll. Ital. Biol. Sper.* 65, 32–37.

Cano, C., and Lykissa, E.D. (1989). Abstract 492. *Clin. Chem.* 35, 1170.

Caplan, Y.H., and Goldberger, B.A. (2001). *J. Anal. Toxicol.* 25, 396–399.

Chiang, C.W., and Barnett, G. (1984). *Clin. Pharmacol. Ther.* 36, 234–238.

Chiesa, E.P., Rondina, R.V.D., and Coussio, J.D. (1973). *J. Chromatogr.* 87, 298–299.

Childs, P.S., and McCurdy, H.H. (1984). *J. Anal. Toxicol.* 8, 220–223.

Christophersen, A.S. (1986). *J. Anal. Toxicol.* 10, 129–131.

Chu, M.H.C., and Drummer, O.H. (2002). *J. Anal. Toxicol.* 26(8), 575–581.

Cirimele, V., Sachs, H., Kintz, P., and Mangin, P. (1996). *J. Anal. Toxicol.* 20, 13–16.

Clatworthy, A.J., Oon, M.C., Smith, R.N., and Whitehouse, M.J. (1990). *Forensic Sci. Int.* 46, 219–230.

Claussen, V., Berger, W., and Korte, F. (1966). *Ann. Chem.* 693, 158–162.

Clouette, R., Jacob, M., Koteel, P., and Spain, M. (1993). *J. Anal. Toxicol.* 17, 1–4.

Cody, J.T., and Foltz, R.L. (1995). In *Forensic Application of Mass Spectrometry* (ed. J. Yinon). CRC Press, Boca Raton, FL, pp. 1–59.

Coffman, C., and Gentner, W. (1975). *Agronomy J.* 67, 491–495.

Colbert, D.L. (1994). *Br. J. Biomed. Sci.* 51, 136–146.

Collins, M., Easson, J., Hansen, G., Hodda, A., and Lewis, K. (1997). *J. Anal. Toxicol.* 21, 538–542.

Cone, E.J. (1993). *Ann. N.Y. Acad. Sci.* 694, 91–127.

Cone, E.J. (1997). *NIDA Research Monograph*, Vol. 167. National Institute on Drug Abuse, Rockville, MD, pp. 108–129.

Cone, E.J. (2001). *Forensic Sci. Int.* 121, 7–15.

Cone, E.J., and Huestis, M.A. (1993). *Ther. Drug. Monit.* 15, 527–532.

Cone, E.J., and Johnson, R.E. (1986). *Clin. Pharmacol. Ther.* 40, 247–255.

Cone, E.J., Johnson, R.E., Darwin, W.D., Yousefnejad, D., Mell, L.D., Paul, B.D., and Mitchell, J. (1987). *J. Anal. Toxicol.* 11, 89–96.

Cone, E.J., Darwin, W.D., and Dickerson, S.L. (1991). *Clin. Chem. Newslett.* 17, 40.

Cone, E.J., Huestis, M.A., and Mitchell, J.M. (1993). *J. Anal. Toxicol.* 17, 186–187.

Cone, E.J., Lange, R., and Darwin, W.D. (1998). *J. Anal. Toxicol.* 22, 460–473.

Cook, J.D., Caplan, Y.H., LoDico, C.P., and Bush, D.M. (2000). *J. Anal. Toxicol.* 24, 579–588.

Costantino, A., Schwartz, R.H., and Kaplan, P. (1997). *J. Anal. Toxicol.* 21, 482–485.

Coyle, H.M., Shutler, G., Abrams, S., Hanniman, J., Neylon, S., Ladd, C., Palmbach, T., and Lee, H.C. (2003). *J. Forensic Sci.* 48(2), 343–347.

Craft, N.E., Byrd, G.D., and Hilpert, L.R. (1989). *Anal. Chem.* 61, 540–544.

Crouch, D.J., Cheever, M.L., Andrenyak, D.M., Kuntz, D.J., and Loughmiller, D.L. (1998a). *J. Forensic Sci.* 43, 35–40.

Crouch, D.J., Frank, J.F., Farrell, L.J., Karsch, H.M., and Klaunig, J.E. (1998b). *J. Anal. Toxicol.* 22, 493–502.

Cunniff, P. (ed.) (1997). *Official Methods of Analysis of AOAC International*, Vol. 1. AOAC International, Gaithersburg, MD, Chap. 22, p. 4.

D'Asaro, J.A. (2000). *J. Anal. Toxicol.* 24, 289–295.

Davis, K.H., Jr., Martín, N.H., Pitt, C.G., Wildes, J.W., and Wall, M.E. (1970). *Lloydia* 33(4), 453–460.

Davis, T.W.M., Farmilo, C.G., and Osadchuk, M. (1963). *Anal. Chem.* 35, 751–755.

DeFaubert Maunder, M.J. (1969). *Bull. Narc.* 21(4), 37–41.

DeFaubert Maunder, M.J. (1974). *Bull. Narc.* 26(4), 19–26.

DeForest, P.R., and Morton, C.V. (1972). *J. Forensic Sci.* 19, 29–33.

de la Torre, R., Domingo-Salvany, A., Badia, R., Gonzalez, G., McFarlane, D., San, L., and Torrens, M. (1996). *Clin. Chem.* 42, 1433–1438.

de la Torre, R., Segura, J., de Zeeuw, R., and Williams, J. (1997). *Ann. Clin. Biochem.* 34, 339–344.

de Zeeuw, R.A., Wijsbeek, J., Breimer, D.D., Vree, T.B., van Ginneken, C.A.M., and van Rossum, J.M. (1972). *Science* 175(4023), 778–779.

de Zeeuw, R.A., Wijsbeek, J., and Malingre, T.M. (1973). *J. Pharm. Pharmacol.* 25, 21–26.

Detrick, R., and Foltz, R.L. (1976). In *Cannabinoid Assays in Humans NIDA Research Monograph, Vol. 7* (ed. R.E. Willette). National Institute on Drug Abuse, Rockville, MD, pp. 88–95.

Dextraze, P., Griffiths, W.C., Camara, P., Audette, L., and Rosner, M. (1989). *Ann. Clin. Lab. Sci.* 19, 133–138.

Dietzen, D.J., Ecos, K., Friedman, D., and Beason, S. (2001). *J. Anal. Toxicol.* 25, 174–178.

Doorenbos, N., Fetterman, P., Quimby, M., and Turner, C. (1971). *Ann. N.Y. Acad. Sci.* 191, 3–14.

Doyle, J.J., and Doyle, J.L. (1990). *Focus* 12, 13–15.

Drandliker, W.B., and De Saussure, V.A. (1970). *Immunochemistry* 7, 799–828.

Drandliker, W.B., and Feigen, G.A. (1961). *Biochim. Biophys. Res. Commun.* 5, 299–304.

Drover, D.P., and Lacienta, E. (1980). *Sci. New Guinea* 7(1), 33–36.

Dugan, S., Bogema, S., Schwartz, R.W., and Lappas, N.T. (1994). *J. Anal. Toxicol.* 18, 391–396.

Duke, E.L., and Reimann, B.E.F. (1973). *Toxicology* 1(4), 289–300.

El-Darawy, A.I., Ali, M.I., and Mobarak, A.M. (1972). *Qual. Plant. Mater. Veg.* 22(1), 7–13.

Ellis, G.M., Jr., Mann, M.A., Judson, B.A., Schramm, N.T., and Tashchian, A. (1985). *Clin. Pharmacol. Ther.* 38, 572–578.

ElSohly, M.A., and Feng, S. (1998). *J. Anal. Toxicol.* 22, 329–335.

ElSohly, M.A., and Jones, A.B. (1995). *J. Anal. Toxicol.* 19, 450–458.

ElSohly, M.A., and Salem, M. (2000). In *Handbook of Analytical Separations, Vol. 2 Forensic Science* (ed. M.J. Bogusz). Elsevier, Amsterdam, pp. 163–193.

ElSohly, M.A., ElSohly, H.N., and Jones, A.B. (1983). *J. Anal. Toxicol.* 7, 262–264.

ElSohly, M.A., Stanford, D.F., and Little, T.L., Jr. (1988). *J. Anal. Toxicol.* 12, 54.

ElSohly, M.A., Jones, A.B., and ElSohly, H.N. (1990). *J. Anal. Toxicol.* 14, 277–279.

ElSohly, M.A., Little, T.L., Jr., and Stanford, D.F. (1992). *J. Anal. Toxicol.* 16, 188–191.

ElSohly, M.A., Walls, C., Lester, M.B., Bauer, C.Z., Shankaran, S., Bada, H., Wright, L., Smeriglio, V., and Kraus-Steinrauf, H. (1994). *Pediatr. Res.* 35, 83A.

ElSohly, M.A., Feng, S., Kopycki, W.J., Murphy T.P., Jones, A.B., Davis, A., and Carr, D. (1997). *J. Anal. Toxicol.* 21, 240–242.

ElSohly, M.A., Stanford, D.F., Murphy, T.P., Lester, B.M., Wright, L.L., Smeriglio, V.L., Verter, J., Bauer, C.R., Shankaran, S., Bada, H.S., and Walls, H.C. (1999). *J. Anal. Toxicol.* 23, 436–445.

ElSohly, M.A., Ross, S.A., Mehmedic, A., Arafat, R., Yi, B., and Banahan, B.F., III (2000). *J. Forensic Sci.* 45(1), 24–30.

ElSohly, M.A., Walls, C., Lester, M.B., Bauer, C.Z., Shankaran, S., Bada, H., Wright, L., Smeriglio, V., and Kraus-Steinrauf, H. (1994). *Pediatr. Res.* 35, 83A.

Engel, W.D., and Khanna, P.L. (1992). *J. Immunol. Methods* 150, 99–102.

Eory, L., Danos, B., and Veress, T. (2001a). *Z. Zagadnien Nauk Sadowych* 47, 322–327.

Eory, L., Szalay, V., and Veress, T. (2001b). *Z. Zagadnien Nauk Sadosych* 47, 328–332.

Fagioli, F., Locatelli, C., Scanavini, L., Landi, S., and Berti Donini, G. (1986). *Anal. Sci.* 2(3), 239–242.

Fairbairn, J.W. (1972). *Bull. Narc.* 24(4), 29–33.

Fairbairn, J.W., and Liebmann, J.A. (1974). *J. Pharm. Pharmacol.* 26(6), 413–419.

Felgate, P.D., and Dinan, A.C. (2000). *J. Anal. Toxicol.* 24, 127–132.

Felscher, D., Gastmeier, G., and Dressler, J. (1998). *J. Forensic Sci.* 43, 619–621.

Feng, S., ElSohly, M.A., Salamone, S., and Salem, M.Y. (2000). *J. Anal. Toxicol.* 24, 395–402.

Fenimore, D.C., Freeman, R.R., and Loy, P.R. (1973). *Anal. Chem.* 45(14), 2331–2335.

Fenimore, D.C., Davis, C.M., and Horn, A.H. (1976a). In *Cannabinoid Assays in Humans NIDA Research Monograph, Vol. 7* (ed. R.E. Willette). National Institute on Drug Abuse, Rockville, MD, pp. 42–47.

Fenimore, D.C., Davis, C.M., Whitford, J.H., and Harrington, C.A. (1976b). *Anal. Chem.* 48, 2289–2290.

Ferioli, V., Rustichelli, C., Pavesi, G., and Gamberini, G. (2000). *Chromatographia* 52(1/2), 39–44.

Ferrara, S.D., Tedeschi, L., Frison G., and Castagna R. (1992). *J. Anal. Toxicol.* 16, 217–222.

Ferrara, S.D., Tedeschi, L., Frison, G., Brusini, G., Castagna, F., Bernardelli, B., and Soregaroli, D. (1994). *J. Anal. Toxicol.* 18, 278–291.

Ferrara, S.D., Brusini, G., Maietti, S., Frison, G., Castagna, F., Allevi, S., Menegus, A.M., and Tedeschi, L. (1999). *Int. J. Legal Med.* 113, 50–54.

Fetterman, P., Keith, E., Waller, C., Gerrero, O., Doorenbox, N., and Quimby, M. (1971a). *J. Pharm. Sci.* 60, 1246–1249.

Fetterman, P.S., Doorenbos, N.J., Keith, E.S., and Quimby, M.W. (1971b). *Experientia* 27, 988–990.

Field, B.I., and Arndt, R.R. (1980). *J. Pharm. Pharmacol.* 32(1), 21–24.

Fish, F. (1974). *Chromatographia* 7, 302.

Fisher, D.H., Broudy, M.I., and Fisher, L.M. (1996). *Biomed. Chromatogr.* 10, 161–166.

Fochtman, F.W., and Winek, C.L. (1971). *Clin. Toxicol.* 4(2), 287–289.

Foltz, R.L. (1984). In *Advances in Analytical Toxicology, Vol. 1* (ed. R.C. Baselt). Biomedical Publications, Davis, CA, pp. 125–130.

Foltz, R.L., and Hidy, B.J. (1982). In *The Analysis of Cannabinoids in Biological Fluids NIDA Research Monograph, Vol. 42* (ed. R.L. Hawks). National Institute on Drug Abuse, Rockville, MD, pp. 99–118.

Foltz, R.L., and Sunshine, I. (1990). *J. Anal. Toxicol.* 14, 375–378.

Foltz, R.L., Fentiman, A.F., Jr., and Foltz, R.B. (1980). In *GC/MS Assays for Abused Drugs in Body Fluids, NIDA Research Monograph 32.* National Institute on Drug Abuse, Rockville, MD, pp. 62–89.

Foltz, R.L., McGinnis, K.M., and Chinn, D.M. (1983). *Biomed. Mass Spectrom.* 10(5), 316–323.

Fonseka, K., Widman, M., and Agurell, S. (1976). *J. Chromatogr.* 120, 343–348.

Forrester, D.E. (1998). *Diss. Abstr. Int. B* 58(7), 3603.

Fowler, R., Gilhooley, R.A., and Baker, P.B. (1979). *J. Chromatogr.* 171, 509–511.

Fraser, A.D., and Worth, D. (1999). *J. Anal. Toxicol.* 23(6), 531–534.

Frederick, D.L. (1998). *J. Anal. Toxicol.* 22, 255–256.

Frederick, D.L., Green, J., and Fowler, M.W. (1985). *J. Anal. Toxicol.* 9, 116–120.

Frings, C.S., Battaglia, D.J., and White, R.M. (1989). *Clin. Chem.* 35, 891–894.

Fucci, N., De Giovanni, N., Chiarotti, M., and Scarlata, S. (2001). *Forensic Sci. Int.* 119(3), 318–321.

Fulton, C.C. (1970). *Bull. Narc.* 22(2), 33.

Galanter, M., Wyatt, R.J., Lemberger, L., Weingartner, H., Waughan, T.B., and Roth, W.T. (1972). *Science* 176, 934–936.

Gaoni, Y., and Mechoulam, R. (1966). *Chem. Commun.* 1, 20.

Gaoni, Y., and Mechoulam, R. (1971). *J. Am. Chem.* Soc. 93, 217.

Garrett, E.R., and Hunt, C.A. (1973). *J. Pharm. Sci.* 62, 1211–1214.

Garrett, E.R., and Hunt, C.A. (1974). *J. Pharm. Sci.* 63, 1056–1064.

Garrett, E.R., and Hunt, C.A. (1976). In *Cannabinoid Assays in Humans NIDA Research Monograph, Vol. 7* (ed. R.E. Willette). National Institute on Drug Abuse, Rockville, MD, pp. 33–41.

George, S., and Braithwaite, R.A. (1996). *J. Anal. Toxicol.* 20, 195–196.

Gere, J.A., and Platoff, G.E. (1995). In *Handbook of Workplace Drug Testing* (ed. R.H. Liu and B.A. Goldberger). AACC Press, Washington, DC, pp. 23–34.

Gerostamoulos, J., and Drummer, O.H. (1993). *J. Forensic Sci.* 38(3), 649–656.

Giardino, N.J. (1996). *J. Anal. Toxicol.* 20, 275–276.

Gillan, R., Cole, M.D., Linacre, A., Thorpe, J.W., and Watson, N.D. (1995). *Sci. Justice* 35, 169–177.

Gjerde, H. (1991). *Forensic Sci. Int.* 50, 121–124.

Gjerde, H., Christophersen, A.S., Skuterud, B., Klemetsen, K., and Morland, J. (1990). *Forensic Sci. Int.* 44, 179–185.

Goldberger, B.A., and Cone, E.J. (1994). *J. Chromatogr. A* 674, 73–86.

Golding, F.S., Diaz-Flores, E.J., and Diaz, R.C. (1998). *Ann. Clin. Lab. Sci.* 28, 160–162.

Gooch, J.C., Caldwell, R., Turner, G.J., and Colbert, D.L. (1992). *J. Immunoassay.* 13, 85–96.

Goodall, C.R., and Basteyns, B.J. (1995). *J. Anal. Toxicol.* 19, 419–426.

Gronholm, M., and Lillsunde, P. (2001). *Forensic Sci. Int.* 121, 37–46.

Gross, S.J., Soares, J.R., Wong, S.L., and Schuster, R.E. (1974). *Nature* 252, 581–582.

Gross, S.J., Worthy, T.E., Nerder, L., Zimmerman, E.G., Soares, J.R., and Lomax, P. (1985). *J. Anal. Toxicol.* 9, 1–5.

Gupta, R.N. (ed.) (1981). *CRC Handbook of Chromatography Drugs*, Vol. 1. CRC Press, Boca Raton, FL, pp. 120–122.

Haeckel, R. (1972). *Arch. Toxikol.* 29, 341–344.

Hailer, M., Glienke, Y., Schwab, I.M., and von Meyer, L. (1995). *J. Anal. Toxicol.* 19, 99–103.

Hall, B.J., Satterfield-Doerr, M., Parikh, A.R., and Brodbelt, J.S. (1998). *Anal. Chem.* 70(9), 1788–1796.

Haney, A., and Kutscheid, B. (1973). *Econ. Botany* 27, 193–203.

Hanson, V.W., Buonarati, M.H., Baselt, R.C., Wade, N.A., Yep, C., Biasotti, A.A., Reeve, V.C., Wong, A.S., and Orbanowsky, M.W. (1983). *J. Anal. Toxicol.* 7, 96–102.

Harvey D.J. (1984). In *Marihuana in Science and Medicine* (ed. G.G. Nahas). Raven Press, New York, pp. 37–107.

Harvey, D.J. (1985). In *Analytical Methods in Human Toxicology* (ed. A.S. Curry). Verlag Chemie, Weinheim, pp. 257–310.

Harvey, D.J., and Paton, W.D.M. (1975). *J. Chromatogr.* 73, 109.

Harvey, D.J., Martín, B.R., and Paton, W.D.M. (1980). *J. Pharm. Pharmacol.* 32, 267–271.

Harzer, K., and Kächele, M. (1983). *J. Chromatogr.* 278(1), 63–70.

Hattab, E.M., Goldberger, B.A., Johannsen, L.M., Kindland, P.W., Ticino, F., Chronister, C.W., and Bertholf, R.L. (2000). *Ann. Clin. Lab. Sci.* 30, 85–91.

Hauber, D.J. (1992). *J. Forensic Sci.* 37, 1656–1661.

Haver, V.M., Romson, J.L., and Sadrzadeh, S.M. (1991). *J. Anal. Toxicol.* 15, 98–100.

Hawks R.L. (1982). *NIDA Res. Monogr.* 42, 125–137.

Hemphill, J., Turner, J., and Mahlberg, P. (1980). *J. Nat. Prod.* 43, 112–122.

Henderson, D.R., Friedman, S.B., Harris, J.D., Manning, W.B., and Zoccoli, M.A. (1986). *Clin. Chem.* 32, 1637–1641.

Hida, M., Mitui, T., Minami, Y., and Fujimura, Y. (1995). *J. Anal. Appl. Pyrolysis* 32, 197–204.

Holley, J.H., Hadley, K.W., and Turner, C.E. (1975). *J. Pharm. Sci.* 64(5), 892–894.

Hood, L.V.S., and Barry, G.T. (1978). *J. Chromatogr.* 166, 499–506.

Hood, L.V.S., Dames, M.E., and Barry, G.T. (1973). *Nature* 242, 402–403.

Huang, W., Moody, D.E., Andrenyak, D.M., Smith, E.K., Foltz, R.L., Huestis, M.A., and Newton, J.R. (2001). *J. Anal. Toxicol.* 25, 531–537.

Huestis, M.A., and Cone, E.J. (1998a). *Ther. Drug Monit.* 20, 570–576.

Huestis, M.A., and Cone, E.J. (1998b). *J. Anal. Toxicol.* 22, 445–454.

Huestis, M.A., Henningfield, J.E., and Cone, E.J. (1992a). *J. Anal. Toxicol.* 16, 276–282.

Huestis, M.A., Henningfield, J.E., and Cone, E.J. (1992b). *J. Anal. Toxicol.* 16, 283–290.

Huestis, M.A., Mitchell, J.M., and Cone, E.J. (1994). *Clin. Chem.* 40, 729–733.

Huestis, M.A., Mitchell, J.M., and Cone, E.J. (1995). *J. Anal. Toxicol.* 19(6), 443–449.

Huestis, M.A., Mitchell, J.M., and Cone, E.J. (1996). *J. Anal. Toxicol.* 20, 441–452.

Hughes, R.B., and Warner, V.J. (1976). *Microgram,* IX (July).

Idilbi, M.M., Huvenne, J.P., Eleury, G., Tran V., Ky, P., Muller, P.H., and Moschetto, Y. (1985). *Bull. Soc. Pharm. Lille* 41(4), 33–35.

Idowu, O.T., and Caddy, G. (1982). *J. Forensic Sci. Soc.* 22, 123–135.

Irving, J., Leeb, B., Foltz, R.L., Cook, C.E., Bursey, J.T., and Willette, R.E. (1984). *J. Anal. Toxicol.* 8, 192–196.

Iwersen-Bergmann, S., and Schmoldt, A. (1999). *J. Anal. Toxicol.* 23, 247–256.

Jagadish, V., Robertson, J., and Gibbs, A. (1996). *Forensic Sci. Int.* 79, 113–121.

Jarzen, R.A. (1977). *Microgram,* X (December).

Jehanli, A., Brannan, S., Moore, L., and Spiehler, V.R. (2001). *J. Forensic Sci.* 46, 1214–1220.

Jenkins, A.J., Mills, L.C., Darwin, W.D., Huestis, M.A., Cone, E.J., and Mitchell, J.M. (1993). *J. Anal. Toxicol.* 17, 292–298.

Jenkins, A.J., Darwin, W.D., Huestis, M.A., Cone, E.J., and Mitchell, J.M. (1995). *J. Anal. Toxicol.* 19(1), 5–12.

Joern, W.A. (1987). *J. Anal. Toxicol.* 11, 49–52.

Joern, W.A. (1992a). *Clin. Chem.* 38(5), 717–719.

Joern, W.A. (1992b). *J. Anal. Toxicol.* 16, 207.

Joern, W.A. (1992c). *J. Anal. Toxicol.* 16, 401.

Johansson, E., and Halldin, M.M. (1989). *J. Anal. Toxicol.* 13, 218–223.

Johansson, E., Noren, K., Sjoevall, J., and Halldin, M.M. (1989). *Biomed. Chromatogr.* 3(1), 35–38.

Johansson, E., Gillespie, H.K., and Halldin, M.M. (1990). *J. Anal. Toxicol.* 14, 176–180.

Johnson, J.R., Jennison, T.A., Peat, M.A., and Foltz, R.L. (1984). *J. Anal. Toxicol.* 8, 202–204.

Jones, A.B., ElSohly, H.N., Arafat, E.S., and ElSohly, M.A. (1984a). *J. Anal. Toxicol.* 8, 249–251.

Jones, A.B., ElSohly, H.N., and ElSohly, M.A. (1984b). *J. Anal. Toxicol.* 8, 252–254.

Joseph, R., Dickerson, S., Willis, R., Frankenfield, D., Cone, E.J., and Smith, D.R. (1995). *J. Anal. Toxicol.* 19, 13–17.

Jurado, C., Gimenez, M.P., Menendez, M., and Repetto, M. (1995). *Forensic Sci. Int.* 70, 165–174.

Just, W.W., Werner, G., and Weichmann, M. (1972). *Naturwiss* 59, 222–226.

Just, W.W., Filipovic, N., and Werner, G. (1974). *J. Chromatogr.* 96, 189–193.

Käferstein, H., and Sticht, G. (1990). *Zeitschrift Rechtsmedizin* 103, 393–396.

Kaistha, K.K., and Tadrus, R. (1982). *J. Chromatogr.* 237, 528–533.

Kaistha, K.K., Tadrus, R., and Janda, R. (1975). *J. Chromatogr.* 107, 359–379.

Kanter, S.L., Musumeci, M.R., and Hollister, L.E. (1979). *J. Chromatogr.* 171, 504–508.

Kanter, S.L., Hollister, L.E., and Musumeci, M. (1982a). *J. Chromatogr.* 234, 201–208.

Kanter, S.L., Hollister, L.E., and Zamora, J.U. (1982b). *J. Chromatogr.* 235, 507–512.

Karlsson, L., and Roos, C. (1984). *J. Chromatogr.* 306, 183–189.

Karlsson, L., and Strom, M. (1988). *J. Anal. Toxicol.* 12, 319–321.

Karlsson, L., Jonsson, J., Aberg, K., and Ross, C. (1983). *J. Anal. Toxicol.* 7, 198–202.

Kauert, G.F. (1989). *Zentralblatt Rechtsmedizin*, 40, 237.

Kauert, G.F., and Röhrich, J. (1996). *Int. J. Legal Med.* 108, 294–299.

Keller, T., Schneider, A., Dirnhofer, R., Jungo, R., and Meyer, W. (2000). *Med. Sci. Law* 40, 258–262.

Kelly, P., and Jones, R.T. (1992). *J. Anal. Toxicol.* 16, 228–235.

Kemp, P.M., Abukhalaf, I.K., Manno, J.E., Manno, B.R., Alford, D., and Abusada, G.A. (1995a). *J. Anal. Toxicol.* 19, 285–291.

Kemp, P.M., Abukhalaf, I.K., Manno, J.E., Manno, B.R., Alford, D.D., McWilliams, M.E., Nixon, F.E., Fitzgerald, M.J., Reeves, R.R., and Wood, M.J. (1995b). *J. Anal. Toxicol.* 19, 292–298.

Kempe, C.R., Tannert, W.K., and Sterngast, A. (1972). *J. Crim. Law Criminol. Police Sci.* 63, 593–594.

Kerrigan, S., and Phillips, W.H., Jr. (2001). *Clin. Chem.* 47, 540–547.

Khanna, P.L., Dworschack, R.T., Manning, W.B., and Harris, J.D. (1989). *Clin. Chim. Acta.* 185, 231–239.

Kidwell, D.A., and Blank, D.L. (1992). In *Recent Developments in Therapeutic Drug Monitoring and Clinical Toxicology* (ed. I. Sunshine). Marcel Dekker, New York, pp. 555–563.

Kidwell, D.A., and Smith, F.P. (2001). *Forensic Sci. Int.* 116, 89–106.

Kidwell, D.A., Holland, J.C., and Athanaselis, S. (1998). *J. Chromatogr. B* 713, 111–135.

Kidwell, D.A., Lee, E.H., and DeLauder, S.F. (2000). *Forensic Sci. Int.* 107, 39–61.

Kimura, M., and Okamoto, K. (1970). *Experientia* 26, 819–820.

Kintz, P. (1993). In *Forensic Sciences* (ed. C. Wecht). Matthew Bender, New York, Chap. 37D, pp. 1–32.

Kintz, P. (1996). *Ther. Drug Monit.* 18, 450–455.

Kintz, P., and Cirimele, V. (1997). *Biomed. Chromatogr.* 11, 371–373.

Kintz, P., and Samyn, N. (2000). In *Handbook of Analytical Separations, Vol. 2, Forensic Science* (ed. M.J. Bogusz). Elsevier, Amsterdam, pp. 459–488.

Kintz, P., Ludes, B., and Mangin, P. (1992). *J. Forensic Sci.* 37, 328–331.

Kintz, P., Cirimele, V., and Mangin, P. (1995a). *J. Forensic Sci.* 40(4), 619–622.

Kintz, P., Cirimele, V., and Mangin, P. (1995b). In *Proceedings of the 1995 International Conference and Workshop for Hair Analysis in Forensic Toxicology* (ed. R.A. de Zeeuw, I. Al Hosani, S. Al Munthiri, and A. Maqbool). Abu Dhabi, pp. 194–202.

Kintz, P., Machart, D., Jamey, C., and Mangin, P. (1995c). *J. Anal. Toxicol.* 19, 304–306.

Kintz, P., Cirimele, V., and Ludes, B. (2000). *J. Anal. Toxicol.* 24(7), 557–561.

Kippenberger, D.J., Cairns, T., and Baumgartner, W. (Nov. 1995). In *Proceedings of the 1995 International Conference and Workshop for Hair Analysis in Forensic Toxicology* (ed. R.A. de Zeeuw, I. Al Hosani, S. Al Munthiri, and A. Maqbool). Abu Dhabi, pp. 299–325.

Knaus, E.E., Coutts, R.T., and Kazakoff, C.W. (1976). *J. Chromatogr. Sci.* 14, 525–530.

Kircher, V., and Parlar, H. (1996). *J. Chromatogr. B.* 677, 245–255.

Kogan, M.J., Newman, E., and Wilson, N.J. (1984). *J. Chromatogr.* 306, 441–443.

Kohjyouma, M., Lee, I-J., Iida, O., Sekita, S., Satake, M., and Makino, Y. (2000). *DNA Takei* 8, 87–90.

Kojoma, M., Ikda, O., Makino, Y., Sekita, S., and Satake, M. (2002). *Plant Med.* 68, 60–63.

Korte, F., and Sieper, H. (1964). *J. Chromatogr.* 13, 90.

Kranzler, H.R., Stone, J., and McLaughlin, L. (1995). *Drug Alcohol Depend.* 40, 55–62.

Krejčí, Z. (1970). In *The Botany and Chemistry of Cannabis* (ed. C.R.B. Joyce and S.H Curry). J. & A. Churchill, London, pp. 49–55.

Kricka, L.J. (2000). *Clin. Chem.* 46, 1037–1038.

Kudo, K., Nagata, T., Kimura, K., Imamura, T., and Jitsufuchi, N. (1995). *J. Anal. Toxicol.* 19, 87–90.

Lachenmeier, D.W., Kroener, L., Musshoff, F., and Madea, B. (2003). *Rapid Commun. Mass Spectrom.* 17(5), 472–478.

Lafolie, P., Beck, O., Blennow, G., Boreus, L., Borg, S., Elwin, C.E., Karlsson, L., Odelius, G., and Hjemdahl, P. (1991). *Clin. Chem.* 37, 1927–1931.

Lafolie, P., Beck, O., Hjemdahl, P., and Borg, S. (1994). *Clin. Chem.* 40, 170–171.

Lahl, H., and Henke, G. (1997). *Pharmazie* 52, 848–851.

Langen, M.C.J., De Biji, G.A., and Egberts, A.C.G. (2000). *J. Anal. Toxicol.* 24(6), 433–437.

Latta, R., and Eaton, B. (1975). *Econ. Botany* 29, 153–162.

Lau-Cam, C.A. (1978). *Clin. Toxicol.* 12(5), 535–541.

Lau-Cam, C.A., and McDonnell, J. (1978). *Bull. Narc.* 30(2), 63–68.

Law, B., Mason, P.A., Moffat, A.C., and King, L.J. (1984a). *J. Anal. Toxicol.* 8, 14–18.

Law, B., Mason, P.A., Moffat, A.C., and King, L.J. (1984b). *J. Anal. Toxicol.* 8, 19–22.

Law, B., Mason, P.A., Moffat, A.C., Gleadle, R.I., and King, L.J. (1984c). *J. Pharm. Pharmacol.* 36, 289–294.

Law, B., Mason, P.A., Moffat, A.C., King, L.J., and Marks, V. (1984d). *J. Pharm. Pharmacol.* 36, 578–581.

Lehmann, T., and Brenneisen, R. (1995). *J. Liquid. Chromatogr.* 18(4), 689–700.

Lehmann, T., Sager, F., and Brenneisen, R. (1997). *J. Anal. Toxicol.* 21, 373–375.

Leino, A., Saarimies, J., Gronholm, M., and Lillsunde, P. (2001). *Scand. J. Clin. Lab. Invest.* 61, 325–331.

Lemos, N.P., Anderson, R.A., and Robertson, J.R. (1999). *J. Anal. Toxicol.* 23, 147–152.

Lewellen, L.J., and McCurdy, H.H. (1988). *J. Anal. Toxicol.* 12, 260–264.

Lewis, S.A., Lewis, L.A., and Tuinman, A. (1999). *J. Forensic Sci.* 44, 951–955.

Linacre, A., and Thorpe, J. (1998). *Forensic Sci. Int.* 91, 71–76.

Linder, M.W., and Valdes, R., Jr. (1994). *Clin. Chem.* 40, 1512–1516.

Lisi, A.M., Kazlauskas, R., and Trout, G.J. (1993). *J. Chromatogr.* 617, 265–270.

Liu, J.H., Lin, W.F., Fitzgerald, M.P., Saxena, S.C., and Shieh, Y.N. (1979). *J. Forensic Sci.* 24(4), 814–816.

Liu, R.H., and Goldberger, B.A. (eds.) (1995). *Handbook of Workplace Drug Testing*. AACC Press, Washington, DC.

Liu, R.H., Edwards, C., Baugh, L.D., Weng, J.-L., Fyte, M.J., and Walla, A.S. (1994). *J. Anal. Toxicol.* 18, 65–70.

Lurie, I.S., Meyers, R.P., and Conver, T.S. (1998). *Anal. Chem.* 70, 3255–3260.

Machata, G. (1969). *Arch. Toxikol.* 25, 19.

Mahlberg, P.G., and Hemphill, J.K. (1983). *Botany Gazette* 144, 43–48.

Manno, S., Manno, B., Walsworth, D., and Herd, R. (1974). *J. Forensic Sci.* 19, 884–890.

Manolis, A., McBurney, L.J., and Bobbie, B.A. (1983). *Clin. Biochem. (Ottawa)* 16(4), 229–233.

Marks, V., Teale, D., and Fry, D. (1975). *Br. Med. J.* 3, 348–349.

Maseda, C., Hama, K., Fukui, Y., Matsubara, K., Takahashi, S., and Akane, A. (1986). *Forensic Sci. Int.* 32(4), 259–266.

Mason, A.P., and McBay, A.J. (1984). *J. Forensic Sci.* 29, 987–1026.

Mason, A.P., Perez-Reyes, M., McBay, A.J., and Foltz, R.L. (1983). *J. Anal. Toxicol.* 17(4), 172–174.

Mausolf, N. (2001). *Microgram* XXXIV, 235.

McBay, A.J., Dubowski, K.M., and Finkle, B.S. (1983). *JAMA* 249, 881.

McBurney, L.J., Bobbie, B.A., and Sepp, L.A. (1986). *J. Anal. Toxicol.* 10, 56–64.

McCallum, N.K. (1973). *J. Chromatogr. Sci.* 11, 509–511.

McCurdy, H.H., Lewellen, L.J., Callahan, L.S., and Childs, P.S. (1986). *J. Anal. Toxicol.* 10, 175–177.

McCurdy, H.H., Callahan, L.S., and Williams, R.D. (1989). *J. Forensic Sci.* 34, 858–870.

Meatherall, R.C., and Garriott, J.C. (1988). *J. Anal. Toxicol.* 12, 136–140.

Mechoulam, R. (ed.) (1973). *Marijuana Chemistry Pharmacology Metabolism and Clinical Effects*. Academic Press, New York.

Menkes, D.B., Howard, R.C., Spears, G.F., and Cairris, E.R. (1991). *Psychopharmacol.* 103, 277–279.

Mieczkowski, T. (1995). *Forensic Sci. Int.* 70(1–3), 83–91.

Mills, T., and Roberson, C.J. (1993). *Instrumental Data for Drug Analysis*, Vols. 1 & 3., CRC Press, Boca Raton FL.

Mitosinka, G.T., Thornton, J.I., and Hayes, T.L. (1972). *J. Forensic Sci. Soc.* 12, 521–529.

Moeller, M.R. (1992). *J. Chromatogr.* 580, 125–134.

Moeller, M.R. (1996) *Ther. Drug Monit.* 18, 444–449.

Moeller, M.R., Doerr, G., and Warth, S. (1992). *J. Forensic Sci.* 37, 969–983.

Moeller, M.R., Fey, P., and Sachs, H. (1993). *Forensic Sci. Int.* 63, 43–53.

Moeller, M.R., Steinmeyer, S., and Kraemer, T. (1998). *J. Chromatogr. B* 713, 91–109.

Moffat, A.C. (1986a). *Arch. Toxicol. Suppl.* 9,103–110.

Moffat, A.C. (ed.) (1986b). *Clarke's Isolation and Identification of Drugs*, 2nd ed. Pharmaceutical Press, London, p. 172.

Moody, D.E., and Medina, A.M. (1995). *Clin. Chem.* 41, 1664–1665.

Moody, D.E., Rittenhouse, L.F., and Monti, K.M. (1992a). *J. Anal. Toxicol.* 16, 297–301.

Moody, D.E., Monti, K.M., and Crouch, D.J. (1992b). *J. Anal. Toxicol.* 16, 302–306.

Moore, C., Lewis, D., Becker, J., and Leikin, J. (1996). *J. Anal. Toxicol.* 20(1), 50–51.

Moore, C., Negrusz, A., and Lewis, D. (1998). *J. Chromatogr. B* 713, 137–146.

Moore, C., Guzaldo, F., and Donahue, T. (2001). *J. Anal. Toxicol.* 25, 555–558.

Moore, K.A., Werner, C., Zannelli, R.M., Levine, B., and Smith, M.L. (1999). *Forensic Sci. Int.* 106, 93–102.

Morland, J., Bugge, A., Skuterud, B., Steen, A., Wethe, G.H., and Kjeldsen, T. (1985). *J. Forensic Sci.* 30, 997–1002.

Mulé, S.J., and Casella, G.A. (1988). *J. Anal. Toxicol.* 12, 102–107.

Mulé, S.J., Lomax, P., and Gross, S.J. (1988). *J. Anal. Toxicol.* 12, 113–116.

Musshoff, F., Junker, H.P., Lachenmeier, D.W., Kroener, L., and Madea, B. (2002). *J. Anal. Toxicol.* 26(8), 554–560.

Nair, P., Rothblum, B.A., and Hebel, R. (1994). *Clin. Pediatr.* 33(5), 280–285.

Nakahara, Y. (1999). *J. Chromatogr. B Biomed. Sci. Appl.* 733, 161–180.

Nakahara, Y., and Sekine, H. (1985). *J. Anal. Toxicol.* 9(3), 121–124.

Nakahara, Y., Takahashi, K., and Kikura, R. (1995). *Biol. Pharm. Bull.* 18, 1223–1227.

Nakamura, G.R. (1969). *J. Assoc. Off. Anal. Chem.* 52, 5–16.

Nakamura, G.R., and Thornton, J.I. (1973). *J. Police Sci. Admin.* 1, 102–112.

Nakamura, G.R., Stall, W.J., Masters, R.G., and Folen, V.A. (1985). *Anal. Chem.* 57(7), 1492–1494.

Ndjoko, K., Wolfender, J.L., and Hostettmann, K. (1998). *Chromatographia* 47(1/2), 72–76.

Nelson, C., Fraser, M., Wifahrt, J., and Foltz, R. (1993). *Ther. Drug Monit.* 15, 557–562.

Niedbala, R.S., Kardos, K.W., Fritch, D.F., Kardos, S., Fries, T., Waga, J., Robb, J., and Cone, E.J. (2001). *J. Anal. Toxicol.* 25, 289–303.

Novotny, M., Lee, M.L., Low, C.E., and Raymond, A. (1976). *Anal. Chem.* 48(1), 24–29.

O'Connor, J.E., and Rejent, T.A. (1981). *J. Anal. Toxicol.* 5, 168–173.

O'Dell, L., Rymut, K., Chaney, G., Darpino, T., and Telepchak, M. (1997). *J. Anal. Toxicol.* 21, 433–437.

O'Neal, C.L., Crouch, D.J., and Fatah, A.A. (2000a). *Forensic Sci. Int.* 109(3), 189–201.

O'Neal, C.L., Crouch, D.J., Rollins, D.E., and Fatah, A.A. (2000b). *J. Anal. Toxicol.* 24, 536–542.

Ohlsson, A., Abou-Chaar, C.I., Agurell, S., Nilsson, I.M., Olofsson, K., and Sandberg, R. (1971). *Bull. Narc.* 23(1), 29–32.

Ohlsson, A., Lindren, J.-E., Leander, K., and Agurell, S. (1976). In *Cannabinoid Assays in Humans NIDA Research Monograph, Vol. 7* (ed. R.E. Willette). National Institute on Drug Abuse, Rockville, MD, pp. 48–63.

Ohlsson, A., Lindgren, J.-E., Andersson, S., Aguerri, S., Gillespie, H., and Holister, L.E. (1986). *Biomed. Environ. Mass Spectrom.* 13, 77–83.

Oroszlan, P., Verzar-Petri, G., Mincsovics, E., and Szekely, T. (1987). *J. Chromatogr.* 388(1), 217–224.

Ostrea, E.M., Jr., Subramanian, M.G., and Abel, E.L. (1988). In *Marijuana: An International Research Report, Monograph Series No. 7* (ed. G. Chesher, P. Consroe, and R. Musty). Australian Gov. Publ. Service, Canberra, Australia, pp. 103–106.

Ostrea, E.M., Jr., Brady, M.J., Parks, P.M., Assensio, D.C., and Naluz, A. (1989). *J. Pediatr.* 115(3), 474–477.

Ostrea, E.M., Jr., Knapp, D.K., Tannenbaum, L., Ostrea, A.R., Romero, A., Salari, V., and Ager, J. (2001). *J. Pediatr.* 138, 344–348.

Owens, S.M., McBay, A.J., Reisner, H.M., and Perez-Reyes, M. (1981). *Clin. Chem.* 27, 619–624.

Paris, M.R., and Paris, R.R. (1973). *Bull. Fr. Chem. Soc.* 1, 118–122.

Parker, J.M., and Fiske, H.L. (1972). *J. Assoc. Off. Anal. Chem.* 55, 876–879.

Parker, J.M., and Stembal, B.L. (1974). *J. Assoc. Off. Anal. Chem.* 57(4), 888–892.

Parker, J.M., Borke, M.L., Block, L.H., and Cochran, T.G. (1974). *J. Pharm. Sci.* 63, 970–971.

Parker, K.D., Wright, J.A., Halpern, A.F., and Hine, C.H. (1968). *Bull. Narc.* 20(4), 9–14.

Parry, R.C., Nolan, L., Shirey, R.E., Wachob, G.D., and Gisch, D.J. (1990). *J. Anal. Toxicol.* 14, 39–44.

Paul, B.D., McKinley, R.M., Walsh, J.K., Jr., Jamir, T.S., and Past, M.R. (1993). *J. Anal. Toxicol.* 17, 378–380.

Paul, B.D., Mell, L.D.Jr., Mitchell J.M., McKinley R.M., and Irving, J. (1987). *J. Anal. Toxicol.* 11, 1–5.

Peace, M.R., Tarnai, L.D., and Poklis, A. (2000). *J. Anal. Toxicol.* 24, 589–594.

Peat, M.A. (1984). In *Advances in Analytical Toxicology, Vol. 1* (ed. R.C. Baselt). Biomedical Publications, Foster City, CA, pp. 59–80.

Peat, M.A. (2000). "A brief introduction to oral fluid drug testing." http://www.4intercept.com/clinicals/brief_intro.html.

Peel, H.W., and Perrigo, B.J. (1981). *J. Anal. Toxicol.* 5, 165–167.

Peel, H.W., Perrigo, B.J., and Mikhael, N.Z. (1984). *J. Forensic Sci.* 29(1), 185–189.

Perez-Reyes, M., DiGuiseppi, S., Mason, A.P., and Davis, K.H. (1983). *Clin. Pharmacol. Ther.* 34, 36–41.

Perillo, B.A., Klein, R.F.X., and Franzosa, E.S. (1994). *Forensic Sci. Int.* 69, 1–6.

Perrigo, B.J., and Joynt, B.P. (1989). *J. Anal. Toxicol.* 13, 235–237.

Perrigo, B.J., and Joynt, B.P. (1995). *Can. Soc. Forensic Sci. J.* 28, 261–269.

Phillips, R., Turk, R., Manno, J., Jain, N., Crim, D., and Forney, R. (1970). *J. Forensic Sci.* 15, 191–200.

Pirl, J.N., Papa, V.M., and Spikes, J.J. (1979). *J. Anal. Toxicol.* 3, 129–132.

Pitt, C.G., Hendron, R.W., and Hsia, R.S. (1972). *J. Forensic Sci.* 17(4), 693–700.

Podkowik, B.-I., Repka, M.L., and Smith, M.L. (1991a). *Clin. Chem.* 37, 1305–1306.

Podkowik, B.-I., Kippenberger, D.J., and Smith, M.L. (1991b). *Clin. Chem.* 37, 1307–1308.

Poklis, A., and O'Neal, C.L. (1996). *J. Anal. Toxicol.* 20, 209–210.

Polyniak, J. (2001). New Jersey State Police, North Regional Laboratory, personal communication.

Posey, B.L., and Kimble, S.N. (1984). *J. Anal. Toxicol.* 8, 234–238.

Rasmussen, K.E. (1975a). *J. Chromatogr.* 109, 175.

Rasmussen, K.E. (1975b). *J. Chromatogr.* 114, 250.

Rodgers, R., Crowl, C.P., Eimstad, W.M., Hu, M.W., Kam, J.K., Ronald, R.C., Rowley, G.L., and Ullman E.F. (1978). *Clin. Chem.* 24, 95–100.

Rohrich, J., Schmidt, K., and Bratzke, H. (1994). *J. Anal. Toxicol.* 18, 407–414.

Rollins, D.E., Jennison, T.A., and Jones, G. (1990). *Clin. Chem.* 36, 602–606.

Romberg, R.W., and Past, M.R. (1994). *J. Forensic Sci.* 39, 479–485.

Ros, J.J., Pelders, M.G., and Egberts, A.C. (1998). *J. Anal. Toxicol.* 22, 40–44.

Rosenfeld, J.J., Bowins, B., Roberts, J., Perkins, J., and Macpherson, A.S. (1974). *Anal. Chem.* 46(14), 2232–2234.

Rosenfeld, J.M., McLeod, R.A., and Foltz, R.L. (1986). *Anal. Chem.* 58, 716–721.

Rosenfeld, J.M., Moharir, Y., and Sandler, S.D. (1989). *Anal. Chem.* 61, 925–928.

Rosenthal, D., Harvey, T.M., Bursey, J.T., Brine, D.R., and Wall, M.E. (1978). *Biomed. Mass Spectrom.* 5, 312–316.

Ross, S.A., Mehmedic, Z., Murphy, T.P., and ElSohly, M.A. (2000). *J. Anal. Toxicol.* 24(8), 715–717.

Roth, K.D.W., Siegel, N.A., Johnson, R.W., Jr., Litauszki, L., Salvati, L., Jr., Harrington, C.A., and Wray, L.K. (1996). *J. Anal. Toxicol.* 20, 291–300.

Rowan, M.G., and Fairbairn, J.W. (1977). *J. Pharm. Pharmacol.* 29, 491–494.

Rowland, B.J., Irving, J., and Keith, E.S. (1994). *Clin. Chem.* 40, 2114–2115.

Rubenstein, K.E., Schneider, R.S., and Ullman, E.F. (1972). *Biochem. Biophys. Res. Commun.* 47, 846–851.

Rustichelli, C., Fefioli, V., Vezzalini, F., Rossi, M.C., and Gamberini, G. (1996). *Chromatographia* 43(3/4), 129–134.

Rustichelli, C., Ferioli, V., Baraldi, M., Zanoli, P., and Gamberini, G. (1998). *Chromatographia* 47(3/4), 215–222.

Ryan, R.M., Wagner, C.L., Schultz, J.M., Varley, J., DiPreta, J., Sherer, D.M., Phelps, D.L., and Karong, T. (1994). *J. Pediatr.* 125, 435–440.

Sachs, H., and Kintz, P. (1998). *J. Chromatogr. B* 713, 147–161.

Sachs, H.W., and Moeller, M.R. (1989). *Fresenius Z. Anal. Chem.* 334, 713.

Saferstein, R. (2001). *Criminalistics: An Introduction to Forensic Science,* 7th ed. Prentice Hall, Upper Saddle River, NJ.

Salamone, S.J., Bender, E., Hui, R.A., and Rosen, S. (1998). *J. Forensic Sci.* 43, 821–826.

Samyn, N., and van Haeren, C. (2000). *Int. J. Legal. Med.* 113, 150–154.

Samyn, N., Verstraete, A., van Haemen, C., and Kintz, P. (1999). *Forensic Sci. Rev.* 11, 1–19.

Scherrmann, J.M., Hoellinger, H., Nguyen-Hoang-Nam, Bourdon, R., and Fournier, E. (1979). In *Cannabinoid Analysis in Physiological Fluids, ACS Syjmposium Series 98* (ed. J.A. Vinson). American Chemical Society, Washington, DC, pp. 207–224.

Schramm, W., Smith, R.H., Craig, P.A., and Kidwell, D.A. (1992). *J. Anal. Toxicol.* 16, 1–9.

Schwartz, R.H., Bogema, S., and Thorne, M.M. (1990). *J. Pediatr.* 117, 670–672.

Shirota, O., Watanabe, A., Yamazaki, M., Saito, K., Shibaano, K., Sekita, S., and Satake, M. (1988). *Nat. Med.* 52, 160–166.

Siegel, J.A. (1993). In *Forensic Science Handbook, Vol. II* (ed. R. Saferstein). Prentice Hall, Englewood Cliffs, NJ, pp. 68–160.

Simpson, D., Jarvie, D.R., and Moore, F.M. (1993). *Clin. Chem.* 39, 698–699.

Singh, J., and Johnson, L. (1997). *J. Anal. Toxicol.* 21, 384–387.

Siniscalco Gigliano, G. (1984). *Boll. Chim. Farm.* 123, 352–356.

Siniscalco Gigliano, G. (1995). *Delpinoa ns* 37, 85–57.

Siniscalco Gigliano, G. (1997). *Delpinoa ns,* 39, 3–7.

Siniscalco Gigliano, G. (1998). *Sci. Justice* 38(4), 225–230.

Siniscalco Gigliano, G. (1999). *J. Forensic Sci.* 44(3), 475–477.

Siniscalco Gigliano, G. (2001). *Forensic Sci. Rev.* 13(1), 2–17.

Siniscalco Gigliano, G., and DiFinizio, A. (1997). *Bull. Narc.* 49(1/2), 129–137.

Siniscalco Gigliano, G., Caputo, P., and Cozzolino, S. (1997). *Sci. Justice* 37, 171–174.

Skender, L. (2000). *Arh. Hig. Rada Toksikol.* 51(4), 409–420.

Skopp, G., and Potsch, L. (1999). *Int. J. Legal Med.* 112, 213–221.

Skopp, G., and Potsch, L. (2002a). *Clin. Chem.* 48, 301–306.

Skopp, G., and Potsch, L. (2002b). *Forensic Sci. Int.* 126, 17–23.

Skopp, G., Pötsch, L., and Mauden, M. (2000). *Clin. Chem.* 46, 1846–1848.

Small, E., and Beckstead, H.D. (1973a). *Lloydia* 36, 144.

Small, E., and Beckstead, H.D. (1973b). *Nature* 245, 147–148.

Small, E., Beckstead, H.D., and Chan, A. (1975). *Econ. Bot.* 29, 219–232.

Smith, D.E., Gutgesell, M.E., Schwartz, R.H., Thorne, M.M., and Bogema, S. (1989). *Arch. Pathol. Lab. Med.* 113, 1299–1300.

Smith, R.N. (1975). *J. Chromatogr.* 115(1), 101–106.

Smith, R.N. (1988). In *Radioimmunoassay of Drugs in Body Fluids in a Forensic Context* (ed. A. Maehly and R.L. Williams). Springer-Verlag, Berlin, pp. 1–89.

Smith, R.N., and Vaughan, C.G. (1976). *J. Chromatogr.* 129, 347–354.

Smith, R.N., and Vaughan, C.G. (1977). *J. Pharm. Pharmacol.* 29(5), 286–290.

Smith-Kielland, A., Skuterud, B., and Morland, J. (1999). *J. Anal. Toxicol.* 23, 323–332.

Spiehler, V. (2000). *Forensic Sci. Int.* 107(1–3), 249–259.

Spiehler, V.R., Collison, I.B., Sedgwick, P.R., Perez, S.L., Le, S.D., and Farnin, D.A. (1998). *J. Anal. Toxicol.* 22, 573–579.

Standefer, J.C., and Backer, R.C. (1991). *Clin. Chem.* 37, 733–738.

Staub, C. (1999). *J. Chromatogr. B* 733, 119–126.

Steinberg, D.M., Sokoll, L.J., Bowles, K.C., Nichols, J.H., Roberts, R., Schultheis, S.K., and O'Donnell, C.M. (1997). *Clin. Chem.* 43(11), 2099–2105.

Stephanou, E., Lawi-Berger, C., and Kapetanidis, I. (1984). *Pharm. Acta Helv.* 59(8), 216–224.

Stonebraker, W.E., Lamoreaux, T.C., Bebault, M., Rasmussen, S.A., Jepson, B.R., and Beck, B.K. (1998). *Am. Clin. Lab.* 17(6), 18–19.

Stout, P.R., Horn, C.K., and Lesser, D.R. (2000). *J. Anal. Toxicol.* 24, 567–571.

Stout, P.R., Horn, C.K., and Klette, K.L. (2001). *J. Anal. Toxicol.* 25, 550–554.

Strano-Rossi, S., and Chiarotti, M. (1999). *J. Anal. Toxicol.* 23, 7–10.

Strömberg, L. (1971). *J. Chromatogr.* 63, 391–396.

Strömberg, L. (1972a). *J. Chromatogr.* 68, 248–252.

Strömberg, L. (1972b). *J. Chromatogr.* 68, 253–258.

Strömberg, L. (1974a). *J. Chromatogr.* 96(1), 99–114.

Strömberg, L. (1974b). *J. Chromatogr.* 96(2), 179–187.

Strömberg, L. (1976). *J. Chromatogr.* 121(2), 313–322.

Struempler, R.E., Nelson, G., and Urry, F.M. (1997). *J. Anal. Toxicol.* 21, 283–285.

Sunshine, I. (1988). *Clin. Chem.* 34, 331–334.

Szirmai, M., Beck, O., Stephannsson, N., and Halldin, M.M. (1996). *J Anal. Toxicol.* 20, 573–578.

Tai, S.S.-C., and Welch, M.J. (2000). *J. Anal. Toxicol.* 24(6), 385–389.

Teale, J.D., Forman, E.J., King, L.J., and Marks, V. (1974a). *Nature* 249, 154–155.

Teale, J.D., Forman, E.J., King, L.J., and Marks, V. (1974b). *Lancet* 2, 553–555.

Teale, J.D., Forman, E.J., King, L.J., Piall, E.M., and Marks, V. (1975). *J. Pharm. Pharmacol.* 27, 465–472.

Tenhagen, A., Feuring, Th., and Lippe, W.M. (1998). *Pharmazie* 53, 39–42.

Teske, J., Putzbach, K., Engewald, W., and Muller, R.K. (2002). *J. Chromatogr. B* 772(2), 299–306.

Tewari, S.N., and Sharma, J.D. (1983). *Bull. Narc.* 35(1), 63–67.

Tewari, S.N., Harpalani, S.P., and Sharma, S.C. (1974). *Mikrochim Acta* 6, 991–995.

Thompson, L.K., and Cone, E.J. (1987). *J. Chromatogr.* 421, 91–97.

Thornton, J.I., and Nakamura, G.R. (1972). *J. Forensic Sci. Soc.* 12(3), 461–519.

Toffoli, G., Avico, U., and Signoretti Ciranni, E. (1966). *Bull. Narc.* 20(1), 55–59.

Towt, J., Tsai, S.-C.J., Hernandez, M.R., Klimov, A.D., Kravec, C.V., Rouse, S.L., Subuhi, H.S., Twarowska, B., and Salamone, S.J. (1995). *J. Anal. Toxicol.* 19, 504–510.

Tsai, J.S.-C., ElSohly, M.A., Dubrovsky, T., Twarowska, B., Towt, J., and Salamone, S.J. (1998). *J. Anal. Toxicol.* 22, 474–480.

Tsai, J.S.-C., ElSohly, M.A., Tsai, S.F., Murphy, T.P., Twarowska, B., and Salamone, S.J. (2000). *J. Anal. Toxicol.* 24, 708–714.

Tsai, J.S.-C., ElSohly, M.A., Tsai, S.F., Murphy, T.P., and Salamone, S.J. (2001). *Proc. Am. Acad. Forensic Sci.* 7, 329.

Turner, C.E., and Hadley, K.W. (1973). *J. Pharm. Sci.* 62, 251–255.

Turner, C.E., and Henry, J.T. (1975). *J. Pharm. Sci.* 64(2), 357–359.

Turner, C.E., Hadley, K.W., Fetterman, P.S., Doorenbos, N.J., Quimby, M.W., and Waller, C. (1973a). *J. Pharm. Sci.* 62(10), 1601–1605.

Turner, C.E., Hadley, K., and Fetterman, P.S. (1973b). *J. Pharm. Sci.* 62, 1739–1741.

Turner, C.E., Hadley, K.W., Jenry, J., and Mole, M.L. (1974). *J. Pharm. Sci.* 63(12), 1872–1876.

Turner, C.E., Hadley, K.W., Holley, J.H., Billets, S., and Mole, M.L., Jr. (1975). *J. Pharm. Sci.* 64(5), 810–814.

Turner, C.E., Hsu, M.H., Knapp, J.E. Schiff, P.L., Jr., and Slatkin, D.J. (1976). *J. Pharm. Sci.* 65(7), 1084–1085.

Turner, J.C., and Mahlberg, P.G. (1982). *J. Chromatogr.* 253(2), 295–303.

Turner, J.C., and Mahlberg, P.G. (1984). *J. Chromatogr.* 283, 165–171.

Turner, J.C., Hemphill, J., and Mahlberg. (1977). *Am. J. Bot.* 64, 687–693.

Uhl, M. (1997). *Forensic Sci. Int.* 84, 281–294.

United Nations (1991). *Recommended Methods for Testing Cannabis.* Division of Narcotic Drugs, Vienna, Austria, pp. 1–38.

Urry, F.M., Komaromy-Hiller, G., Staley, B., Crockett, D.K., Kushnir, M., Nelson, G., and Struempler, R.E. (1998). *J. Anal. Toxicol.* 22, 89–95.

U.S. Treasury Department, Bureau of Narcotics (1948). *Marihuana: Its Identification.* U.S. Government Printing Office, Washington, DC.

Valente, D., Cassani, M., Pigliapochi, M., and Vansetti, G. (1981). *Clin. Chem.* 27, 1952–1953.

Valentine, J.L., Bryant, P.J., Gutshall, P.L., Gan, O.H.M., Thompson, E.D., and Niu, H.C. (1976). In *Cannabinoid Assays in Humans NIDA Research Monograph, Vol. 7* (ed. R.E. Willette). National Institute on Drug Abuse, Rockville, MD, pp. 96–106.

Valle, J., Vieira, J. Aucelio, J., and Valio, I. (1978). *Bull. Narc.* 30(1), 67–68.

Vandevenne, M., Vandenbussche, H., and Verstraete, A. (2000). *Acta Clin. Belg.* 55, 323–333.

Veress, T. (1994). *J. Chromatogr. A* 668(2), 285–291.

Veress, T., Szanto, J.I., and Leisztner, L. (1990). *J. Chromatogr.* 520, 339–347.

Vinson, J.A., Patel, D.D., and Patel, A.H. (1977). *Anal. Chem.* 49(1), 163–165.

Vollner L., Bieniek, D., and Korte, F. (1986). *Regul. Toxicol. Pharmacol.* 6, 348–358.

von Meyer, L., Hanseler, E., Lardet, G., Scholer, A., and Sieghart, W. (1997). *Eur. J. Clin. Chem. Clin. Biochem.* 35, 133–140.

Vree, T.B., Breimer, D.D., vanGinneken, C.A.M., and van rossum, J.M. (1972). *J. Chromatogr.* 74, 209–224.

Wagener, R.E., Linder, M.W., and Valdes, R., Jr. (1994). *Clin. Chem.* 40, 608–612.

Wall, M.E., Harvey, T.M., Bursey, J.T., Brine, D.R., and Rosenthal, D. (1976). In *Cannabinoid Assays in Humans NIDA Research Monograph, Vol. 7* (ed. R.E. Willette). National Institute on Drug Abuse, Rockville, MD, pp. 107–117.

Wall, M.E., Brine, D.R. Bursey, J.T., and Rosenthal, D. (1979). In *Cannabinoid Analysis in Physiological Fluids* (ed. J.A. Vinson). American Chemical Society, Washington, DC, pp. 39–57.

Wall, M.E., Sadler, B.M., Brine, D., Taylor, H., and Perez-Reyes, M. (1983). *Clin. Pharmacol. Ther.* 34, 352–363.

Watling, R.J. (1998). *J. Anal. At. Spectrom.* 13(9), 917–926.

Weaver, M.L., Gan, B.K., Allen, E., Baugh, L.D., Liao, F.Y., Liu, R.H., Langner, J.G., Walia, A.S., and Cook, L.F. (1991). *Forensic Sci. Int.* 49, 43–56.

Weinberger, R., and Lurie, I.S. (1991). *Anal. Chem.* 63, 823–827.

Wells, D.J., and Barnhill, M.T., Jr. (1989). *Clin. Chem.* 35, 2241–2243.

Wennig, R., Moeller, M.R., Haguenoer, J.M., Marocchi, A., Zoppi, F., Smith, B.L., de la Torre, R., Carstensen, C.A., Goerlach-Graw, A., Schaeffler, J., and Leinberger, R. (1998). *J. Anal. Toxicol.* 22, 148–155.

Wheals, B.B., and Smith, R.N. (1975). *J. Chromatogr.* 105, 396–400.

Whiting, J.D., and Manders, W.W. (1982). *J. Anal. Toxicol.* 6, 49–52.

Whiting, J.D., and Manders, W.W. (1983). *Aviation Space Environ. Med.* Nov., 1031–1033.

Whitter, P.D., Cary, P.L., Leaton, J.I., and Johnson, J.E. (1999). *J. Anal. Toxicol.* 23, 286–289.

Wilkins, D., Haughey, H., Cone, E., Huestis, M., Foltz, R., and Rollins, D. (1995). *J. Anal. Toxicol.* 19(6), 483–491.

Wilkinson, M., and Linacre, A.M.T. (2000). *Sci. Justice* 40(1), 11–14.

Williams, P.L., and Moffat, A.C. (1980). *J. Pharm. Pharmacol.* 32, 445–448.

Wingert, W.E. (1997). *Clin. Chem.* 43, 100–103.

Wingert, W.E., Feldman, M.S., Kim, M.H., Noble, L., Hand, I., and Yoon, J.J. (1994). *J. Forensic Sci.* 39(1), 150–158.

Wu, A.H., Wong, S.S., Johnson, K.G., Callies, J., Shu, D.X., Dunn, W.E., and Wong, S H. (1993). *J. Anal. Toxicol.* 17, 241–245.

Wu, A.H., Forte, E., Casella, G., Sun, K., Hemphill, G., Foery, R., and Schanzenbach, H. (1995). *J. Forensic Sci.* 40, 614–618.

Wu, A.H.B., Bristol, B., Sexton, K., Cassella-McLane, G., Holtman, V., and Hill, D.W. (1999). *Clin. Chem.* 45, 1051–1057.

Yawn, B.P., Thompson, L.R., Lupo, V.R., Googins, M.K., and Yawn, R.A. (1994). *Arch. Fam. Med.* 3, 520–527.

Zimmerman, E.G., Yeager, E.P., Soares, J.R., Hollister, L.E., and Reeve, V.C. (1983). *J. Forensic Sci.* 28, 957–962.

Zoller, O., Rhyn, P., and Zimmerli, B. (2000). *J. Chromatogr. A* 872, 101–110.

CHAPTER 4

ANALYSIS OF THE HALLUCINOGENS

John Hugel, John A. Meyers & David C. Lankin
Drug Analysis Service, Health Canada;
U.S. Drug Enforcement Agency;
Pharmacia Corporation

This chapter was previously published as Chapter 5 in *Hallucinogens: A Forensic Drug Handbook*, Richard Laing (Ed.), Academic Press, Copyright 2003. Used with permission.

Contents

Handbook of Forensic Drug Analysis
Frederick P. Smith, Editor

PART I: INFRARED (IR) SPECTROSCOPY

Since the 1960s, infrared spectroscopy has been used as a powerful confirmatory test for the identification of organic compounds, including the hallucinogens and other drugs of abuse. As with the application of any technique to illicit drug analysis, the forensic chemist must understand how the technique works and how it can be applied, and its strengths and weaknesses.

4.0 THEORETICAL BASIS

An organic molecule is characterized by the composition of its atoms and the bonds they form. These bonds can absorb wavelengths of infrared light causing their vibration, stretching, bending and wagging. The infrared (IR) spectrometer is an analytical instrument in which organic compounds are irradiated with infrared light typically with wavelengths of 4000–400 cm^{-1}. When the molecule absorbs at a certain wavelength, depending upon the type of bond, it creates a peak at that wavelength in its infrared spectrum. Slight variations in a molecule such as the positions of bonds (as with isomers), different composition of atoms, and even salt or crystalline forms will change the manner in which the molecule absorbs the IR radiation. With this, the IR spectrum can be used to distinguish small differences between two similar molecules. It also follows that the same compound will yield the same infrared spectrum ostensibly unchanged by time and instrument constraints. This further means that if one obtains an infrared spectrum of an analyte which matches that of a known molecule, then the analyte is that known molecule. As can be expected, there are pitfalls to be avoided in making such sweeping statements, but with the application of knowledge and care, the statement will hold when applied to the identification of hallucinogens.

Isomers yield different IR spectra. One exception to this rule is optical isomers which cannot be differentiated. Diastereomers (optical isomers with more than one chiral center) do, however, exhibit different spectra. For example, the spectra of D-lysergic acid diethylamide (LSD) is identical to L-LSD, but the differences between the infrared spectra of LSD and iso-LSD are remarkable. The same applies to lysergic acid sec-butylamide (LSB) which is a structural isomer of LSD and iso-sec-LSB. The structures and infrared spectra of LSD/iso-LSD and LSB/iso-sec-LSB are shown in Figure 4.1.

Occasionally the spectrum of the optically pure isomer in the solid phase will not be the same as that of a racemic mixture. This is caused by intermolecular interactions between the two racemates changing the way they vibrate, stretch, bend or wag. This has been examined as a way of determining the optical purity of phenethylamines (CND Analytical, 1994). It, however, was concluded that it is not a reliable technique.

Figure 4.1 (opposite)

Infrared spectra of LSD-related diastereomers:
(a) LSD amorphous;
(b) iso-LSD amorphous;
(c) sec-LSB amorphous;
(d) iso-sec-LSB amorphous

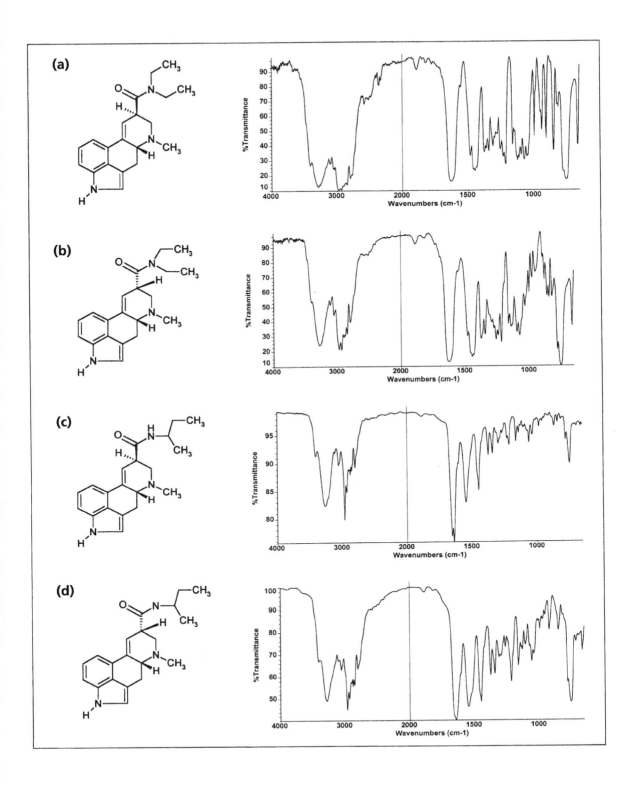

A problem with infrared spectroscopy, which appears occasionally in the identification of hallucinogens, is polymorphism. That is, some analytes in the solid phase can crystallize in different ways. Since the different crystal forms will change the intermolecular interactions, there can be significant changes in the infrared spectrum. It is important to remember that even if an analyte is polymorphic, as long as the spectrum of the analyte matches the spectrum of the known compound, its identity is established. If the spectrum does not match, it does not necessarily rule out that the analyte is, in fact, the known compound.

A powerful feature of infrared spectroscopy is that it can be used in elucidating the structure of a molecule since functional groups absorb at characteristic wavelengths. For example, carbonyls (–C=O) exhibit a strong absorption in the 1780–$1630 \, cm^{-1}$ region of the infrared spectrum. This feature means that analytes with the same functional groups will present an absorption at similar wavelengths. In addition, information about which functional groups are present or absent can be gained from the infrared spectrum. This is particularly helpful when dealing with an analyte whose identity is unknown. For a list of texts which include tables of absorption frequency versus functional group, see the further reading heading at the end of the IR spectroscopy section.

One general principle that holds true is that solid phase spectra of the same analyte will have more features than the analyte's liquid phase spectrum, which in turn will have more features than the analyte's vapor phase spectrum. Figure 4.2 illustrates the infrared spectrum of 3,4-methylenedioxymethamphetamine hydrochloride (MDMA.HCl)–solid phase, MDMA base–liquid phase, and MDMA vapor phase at 225°C.

4.1 INFRARED SPECTROMETER INSTRUMENTATION

Infrared spectrometers are divided into two groups—dispersive and Fourier transform instruments. The former scans each wavelength sequentially and plots the absorption on a chart. The latter obtains an interferogram of all infrared wavelengths simultaneously and then performs a mathematical function called a Fourier transform to obtain the plot of absorption versus wavelength. Performing the Fourier transform requires some computing power which, nowadays, is easily obtained. Since Fourier transform instruments are faster and more sensitive, they now dominate the market. Fourier transform instruments also have the advantage of having only one moving part. The optical benches of Fourier transform infrared (FTIR) spectrometers usually last much longer than any controlling computer system.

Dispersive instruments are often double beam, which means that the infrared spectrum of the analyte is automatically ratioed against a background infrared

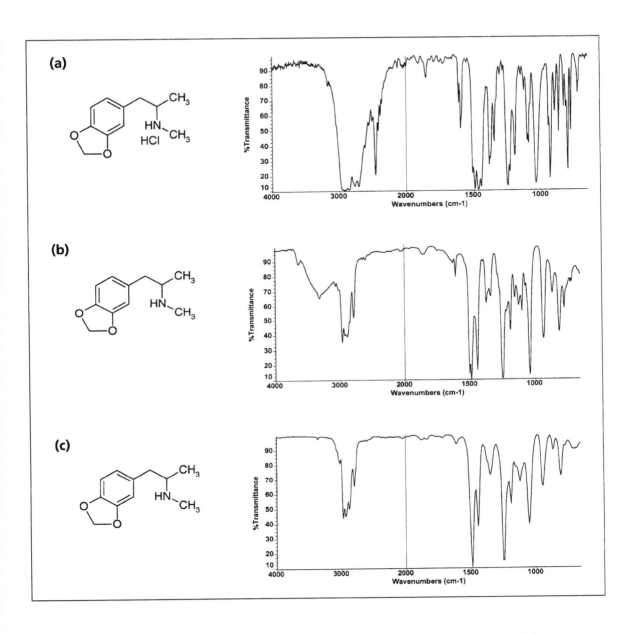

spectrum. This automatically eliminates the effects of ambient infrared absorbing water vapor and carbon dioxide. Fourier transform instruments, on the other hand, are single beam instruments which measure the spectrum of the analyte and the ambient interferences together. To eliminate the water vapor and carbon dioxide spectrum, a background spectrum is obtained and ratioed mathematically against the analyte spectrum. A further measure, which can be

Figure 4.2
IR spectra of MDMA:
(a) solid—MDMA.HCl;
(b) liquid—MDMA base;
(c) vapor MDMA at
225°C

taken to reduce this effect, is to purge the spectrometer with dry, carbon dioxide-free air. This will also lengthen the life of any moisture-sensitive parts in the infrared spectrometer, namely the beam splitter. In the case of a purged sample compartment, whenever adding an analyte to the sample compartment, one must wait for the purge to be re-established. This is usually a matter of a minute or so.

Infrared spectrometers, dispersive or Fourier transform, measure the analyte that is placed in the infrared beam. Contaminants in an analyte will affect the obtained infrared spectrum. The extent of the effect depends on the infrared spectra of the analyte and the contaminant. In the worst case, where the contaminant has a strong infrared spectrum and the analyte a weak spectrum, a few percent of the contaminant will badly affect the analyte spectrum. In the best case, where the reverse is true, seemingly unaffected spectra are observed even though the analyte might be only 80% pure. An effective way of getting around this problem is the use of the gas chromatograph/Fourier transform infrared (GC-FTIR) spectrometer.

The biggest problem with applying infrared spectroscopy to the analysis of hallucinogens is ensuring that the analyte being placed in the infrared beam is sufficiently pure that the analyte spectrum is free of interferences from contaminants. It is for this reason that the following discussion on the applications of infrared spectroscopy to the analysis of hallucinogens includes outlines of extraction procedures to purify samples.

4.1.1 Obtaining Condensed Phase Infrared Spectra

For the purposes of IR spectroscopy, analytes that are solids or liquids are considered to be in the condensed phase.

The classical spectrum of a solid phase analyte is obtained by making a paste of the analyte and a mulling agent and spreading the paste between two salt (usually NaCl or KBr) plates. The most common mulling agent is nujol (mineral oil). Alternatively, the analyte is mixed with a salt (usually KBr), ground and pressed into a pellet which is placed into the infrared beam. Both techniques have their pros and cons, but for hallucinogen identification, either will function well. Terry Gough (1991) includes a discussion on the two techniques. Other techniques which do not require the dilution of the sample in a mulling agent include attenuated total reflectance (ATR) and diffuse reflectance. ATR uses an IR inert crystal whose internal reflectance does not allow the IR radiation to exit the crystal but rather to bounce within the crystal and sample the analyte which is in contact with the surface. This technique is perfectly suited for films, liquids and polymers. It is also used in IR microscopy and with "diamond" cells which enable crystalline materials or powders to be sampled under pressure as a film. Diffuse reflectance, on the other hand, can be used to collect the spectra of powders directly through the focusing of the IR radiation using ellipsoid mirrors onto the sample and processing the resulting reflected radiation (Griffiths and de Haseth, 1986).

A spectrum of a (non-aqueous) liquid phase analyte can be obtained by placing the analyte between two salt (usually NaCl or KBr) plates and placing the analyte in the infrared beam. The two cells can be, but do not necessarily have to be, separated by a spacer of known width. Specialized cells with a cell cavity of known volume can also be used. By knowing the width of the spacer and the volume of the cell, quantitative experiments can be performed. Using two cells with no spacer that are pressed together is effective for identification work.

Both solids and liquids can be dissolved in appropriate solvents and the spectra obtained. The spectrum of the solvent will be superimposed on that of the analyte but can sometimes be removed using a reference spectrum and through the data manipulation of a subtraction algorithm. For routine hallucinogen identification work, this is normally unnecessary.

4.1.2 Vapor Phase Infrared Spectroscopy

Vapor phase IR spectroscopy can be applied to the identification of analytes which have a sufficient vapor pressure at room temperature such that the headspace of the analyte in a container can be introduced into an evacuated gas cell and a useful spectrum obtained. Almost all solvents can be identified by this method without difficulty. This technique can be easily and successfully applied to those solvents which have a boiling point of less than 100°C. With the use of multi-pass gas cells, the technique can be applied to less volatile analytes. Since solvents are always used in the production of hallucinogens, this technique can be useful in clandestine laboratory investigations.

Another method of obtaining vapor phase spectra of hallucinogens is the use of gas chromatography–Fourier transform infrared (GC-FTIR) spectroscopy. (Dispersive IR spectrometers cannot scan quickly enough to obtain infrared spectra of peaks eluting from capillary columns.) The technique combines the separating power of the gas chromatograph with the identifying power of the FTIR spectrometer. The analyte along with contaminants is injected into a gas chromatograph which separates the components based upon physical characteristics. As the components elute from the GC, they enter a light pipe through which the infrared beam has been focused. The light pipe consists of a gold-lined heated tube with IR inert crystals on either end permitting the IR radiation to traverse through the vaporized sample. This technique requires the use of a liquid nitrogen cooled mercury-cadmium-telluride (MCT) detector for the required sensitivity and speed also to obtain the spectra of the fast eluting components from a capillary column.

Vapor phase FTIR spectra have the characteristics of condensed phase spectra such as same functional group absorptions, except that they generally show fewer features.

Subtle differences in vapor phase spectra become very significant when comparing homologous series of IR spectra of hallucinogens. Figure 4.3 illustrates the structures and vapor phase infrared spectra of 3,4-methylenedioxymethamphetamine (MDMA) versus that of N-methyl-1-(3,4-methylenedioxyphenyl)-2-butanamine (MBDB).

Minor, but reproducible, differences can be seen in the spectra in the 2950, 1350, and $1100\,cm^{-1}$ areas of the spectrum. On the other hand, structural isomers exhibit remarkably different spectra. Figure 4.4 illustrates the vapor phase IR spectra of 2,3-methylenedioxyamphetamine versus 3,4-methylenedioxyamphetamine (MDA).

Figure 4.5 demonstrates the differences between the homologous series related to MDA (Figure 4.4):

- 3,4-methylenedioxyphenethylamine;
- 1-(3,4-methylenedioxyphenyl)-2-butanamine; and
- 1-(3,4-methylenedioxyphenyl)-2-pentanamine.

As the homologue side chain grows in length, the differences become more subtle.

A skilled and knowledgeable forensic chemist can make use of the vapor phase FTIR spectra to distinguish among isomers and homologous series of hallucinogens.

Figure 4.3 (p. 159, top)

Vapor phase infrared spectra of homologues: (a) MDMA at 225°C; (b) MBDB at 225°C

Figure 4.4 (p. 159, bottom)

Vapor phase IR spectra of structural isomers: (a) 2,3-methylenedioxyamphetamine at 225°C; (b) 3,4-methylenedioxyamphetamine (MDA) at 225°C

Another problem which arises when using GC-FTIR is the effect that temperature can have on vapor phase spectra. Since the differentiation and identification of vapor phase infrared spectra is often performed on the basis of subtle differences in the spectra, and since temperature can subtly affect the infrared spectrum, the temperature at which the vapor phase spectrum is obtained is a crucial parameter when identifying hallucinogens. Figure 4.6 illustrates the spectra of MDMA at 150°C.

The spectrum of MDMA at 225°C is found in Figure 4.3. The key to working around this problem is to have a spectrum of the standard and the sample obtained at the same temperature.

The sensitivity of GC-FTIR is typically in the 10 ng range dependent on the instrument's characteristics and the intensity of the analyte's IR spectrum. The gas chromatograph should be equipped with a capillary column. The use of wide bore (about 0.3 mm ID diameter) or mega-bore (about 0.5 mm ID diameter)

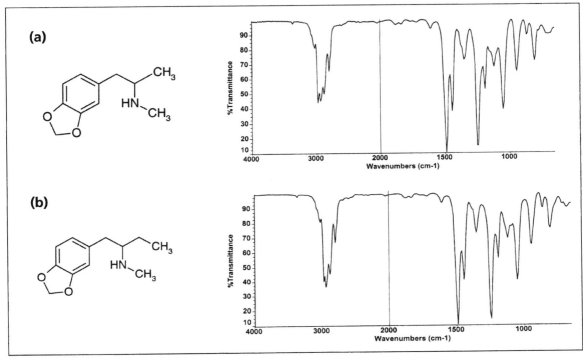

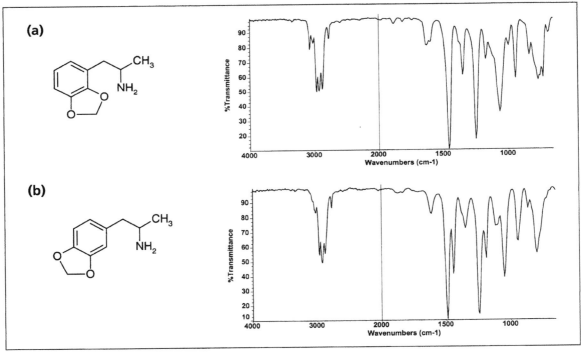

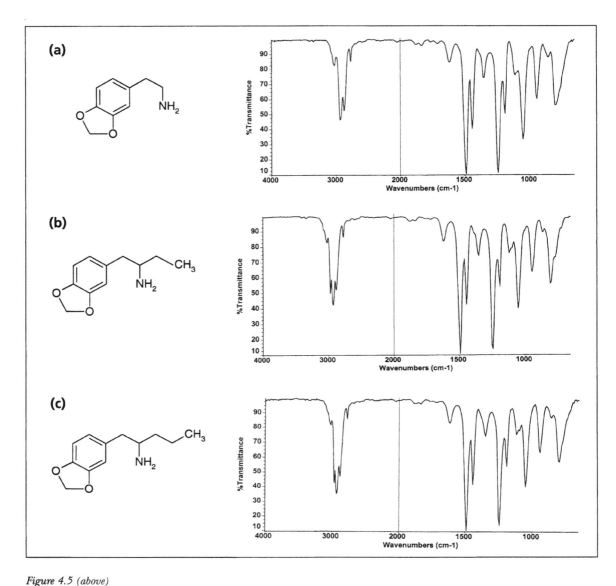

Figure 4.5 (above)

Vapor phase IR spectra of the homologous series related to MDA: (a) 3,4-methylenedioxyphenethyl-amine at 225°C, (b) 1-(3,4-methylenedioxyphenyl)-2-butanamine at 225°C; (c) 1-(3,4-methylenedioxyphenyl)-2-pentanamine at 225°C

columns is recommended for GC-FTIR work. The common capillary dimethylpolysiloxane and (5% phenyl)methylpolysiloxane columns will work well.

Unlike gas chromatography–mass spectrometry, there is no need to turn off the FTIR spectrometer at any time during the GC run. This means that low boiling contaminants and solvent mixtures can be identified in or near the solvent front. Another characteristic of vapor phase FTIR spectrometry is that all wavelengths are being measured concurrently. The implication of this is that as the concentration of the analyte increases as on the up slope of an eluting

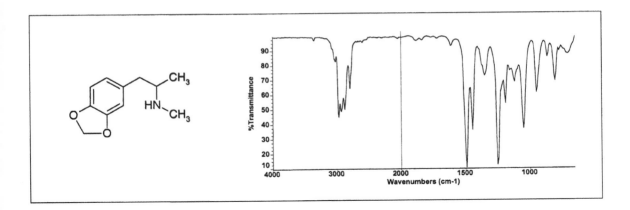

Figure 4.6

Vapor phase IR spectrum of MDMA at 150°C

chromatographic peak or decreasing as on the down slope of an eluting chromatographic peak, the obtained spectrum is unaffected. This is an important feature which leads to vapor phase IR spectra which are remarkably reproducible.

Since the FTIR spectrometer collects the GC-FTIR data as spectra, an algorithm called a Gram–Schmidt orthogonalization is used to generate an analyzable chromatogram where the peak height and area are representative of the analyte's concentration.

Since GC-FTIR spectroscopy is less sensitive than gas chromatography–mass spectrometry (GC-MS), GC-MS is much more popular. The mass spectra of structural isomers are often very similar (see section in this chapter on GC-MS). On the other hand, the mass spectra of a homologous series of compounds are usually different. The two techniques, GC-FTIR and GC-MS, are therefore complimentary.

4.1.3 Spectral Compilations

In order to identify the infrared spectrum of various hallucinogens, the easiest way is to search a library of infrared spectra. This has led to compilations of infrared spectra which are available in electronic or hard copy (book) form. Electronic libraries have the advantage that they can be searched by FTIR instrument manufacturer's software. A good match when working with condensed phase spectrum is one which has a significantly better match value than the next. The absolute value of the obtained numbers is not necessarily a good indication of the identity of the unknown. It is always important to remember that, regardless of how "good" a match is, visual comparison of the analyte spectrum against that of the appropriate standard is an absolute requirement.

As discussed earlier, analytes which include the same functional groups will give similar infrared spectra. Infrared search results will reflect this similarity.

This means that, if the analyte's spectrum is not in the IR spectral library, the best search results will be of compounds containing similar functional groups.

4.2 INFRARED SPECTROSCOPY OF LYSERGIC ACID DIETHYLAMIDE (LSD)

Lysergic acid diethylamine (LSD) is well known as a powerful hallucinogen. The dose of LSD necessary to have a hallucinogenic effect is about 100 µg. Tablets and pieces of blotter will normally contain between 20 and 100 µg of LSD tartrate. The common sample preparation techniques for condensed phase infrared spectroscopy, that is pellet formation and mulling, normally require a few milligrams. This means that extraordinary means are needed to obtain usable infrared spectra of LSD. Techniques such as preparing a micropellet—1 to 3 mm in diameter—for insertion into a beam condenser are often needed. The placing of a small spot of LSD amorphous solid on a small silver chloride disk and inserting it into the focus of a beam condenser also works well. With these techniques quantities as low as a single dose of LSD should be identifiable.

In addition, LSD when isolated as the base, does not crystallize well. It forms what it is termed an amorphous solid. The one saving grace of this formation is that the spectrum amorphous solid is reproducible. Mesley and Evans (1969) characterized the infrared spectrum of the amorphous solid LSD.

The isomers of LSD are all quite distinguishable by infrared spectroscopy. Iso-LSD as well as lysergic acid methyl propyl amide (LAMPA) are all readily distinguishable by the infrared spectra of their amorphous solids. Figure 4.1 illustrates the differences between LSD and iso-LSD. Bailey et al. (1973) published the infrared spectra of iso-LSD and LAMPA. Neville et al. (1992) included the infrared spectra of LSD and LAMPA.

Infrared spectroscopy is an excellent method for the identification of LSD. The problem to be overcome is isolating the LSD in a sufficiently pure form that a suitable infrared spectrum is obtained. LSD acts as a base and is extracted from aqueous basic solutions by organic solvents. The use of very strong bases such as sodium or potassium hydroxide is not, however, recommended as LSD will decompose in their presence. For LSD soaked or spotted onto papers the following method will often work to isolate the LSD:

- cut the paper up into small pieces;
- soak the paper in dilute sulfuric acid solution;
- extract the sulfuric acid solution with an organic solvent such as chloroform to remove any acidic or neutral dyes;
- make the aqueous solution basic with ammonia;
- extract with chloroform;
- evaporate the solvent.

For LSD in tablets, crushing the tablet and following the same procedure will often work. In some cases, however, an emulsion will result. The alternative is a basic celite column which is described as follows:

- crush tablets and triturate with dilute sulfuric acid;
- add sodium bicarbonate and mix;
- add acid washed celite and mix;
- pack dry mixture is packed in column stoppered with chloroform washed cotton or glass wool;
- elute column with water washed chloroform;
- extract chloroform twice with dilute sulfuric acid (chloroform is discarded);
- make dilute sulfuric basic with ammonia;
- extract basic solution twice with chloroform;
- evaporate chloroform to yield LSD.

Because LSD is present in such small doses, either technique is very sensitive to sources of contamination. All glassware should be carefully inspected and rinsed and care used in handling solvents in that a small contamination of plasticizer or grease will mask the LSD spectrum.

If the above technique does not yield LSD of sufficient purity that the spectrum is contaminated, preparatory thin layer chromatography using a silica gel plate in a solvent system of chloroform:methanol 90:10 will often work.

There are other approaches on the use of infrared spectroscopy to identify LSD. Harris and Kane (1991) outlined the use of a microscope sampling device attached to an FTIR instrument in conjunction with thin layer chromatography to distinguish among LSD, iso-LSD and LAMPA. Kovar et al. (1995) and Pfiefer and Kovar (1995) discussed the application of high performance thin layer chromatography-ultraviolet (HPTLC-UV)/ FTIR on line coupling to LSD identification. Kempfert (1988) included the identification of LSD and its isomers in his discussion of the applications of GC-FTIR.

4.3 INFRARED SPECTROSCOPY OF PHENYLALKYLAMINES

The phenylalkylamines are good examples of several of the general principles discussed earlier in the chapter. For instance, the rule that the number of spectral features decreases from the condensed phase to the vapor phase is demonstrated in Figure 4.2 on the phenylalkylamine 3,4-methylenedioxymethamphetamine (MDMA). The power of FTIR spectroscopy to distinguish among structural isomers is illustrated in Figure 4.4 using the example of 2,3-methylenedioxyamphetamine versus 3,4-methylenedioxyamphetamine (MDA). Distinguishing among homologues is demonstrated with the example of the vapor phase spectra of MDMA versus *N*-methyl-1-(3,4-methylene-dioxyphenyl)-2-butanamine (MBDB) in Figure 4.3 and MDA and its homologues in Figure 4.5. It is important to note that while the vapor phase spectra of MDMA and MBDB show few differences, the liquid phase spectra, also termed a film of the base extract, of MDMA and MBDB show more (Figure 4.7).

The hydrochloride spectra of the two isomers are even more distinctly different, as Figure 4.8 illustrates.

It follows from the previous discussion that the easiest way of identifying phenylalkylamines is to obtain an uncontaminated spectrum of their hydrochloride salts. Liquid and vapor phase spectra can be used quite effectively in identifying phenylalkylamines as long as the techniques are applied with care and knowledge. The problem then becomes how to isolate the phenylalkylamine from the sample matrix. One of the best ways is by extraction.

A dry extraction technique which will isolate the salt of the phenylalkylamine directly is as follows:

- grind the tablet or other matrix into a fine powder;
- extract the dry powder with diethyl ether to extract any tablet lubricant such as methyl stearate. The ether can usually be discarded;
- extract the powder with chloroform and filter the chloroform;
- evaporate the chloroform;
- in some cases, methanol is a better choice than chloroform.

The above technique will work using chloroform with most phenylalkylamines including MDA.HCl and MDMA.HCl. Methanol can be used in place of chloroform, but some of the tablet excipients may contaminate the spectrum.

A second extraction technique which is a liquid–liquid extraction is as follows:

- grind the tablet or other matrix into a fine powder;
- add the powder to a separatory funnel;
- add dilute sulfuric acid;
- extract at least twice with an organic solvent (chloroform works well);
- render solution basic with sodium hydroxide solution or ammonia;
- extract twice with an organic solvent;
- evaporate the solvent;
- add a few drops of concentrated hydrochloric acid before all the solvent has evaporated.

Figure 4.7 (opposite, top)

Liquid phase infrared spectra of: (a) MDMA base; (b) MBDB base

Figure 4.8 (opposite, bottom)

Solid phase IR spectra of: (a) MDMA.HCl; (b) MBDB.HCl

The second technique can be used to obtain the base in the liquid phase by not adding hydrochloric acid. The base can also be diluted with an organic

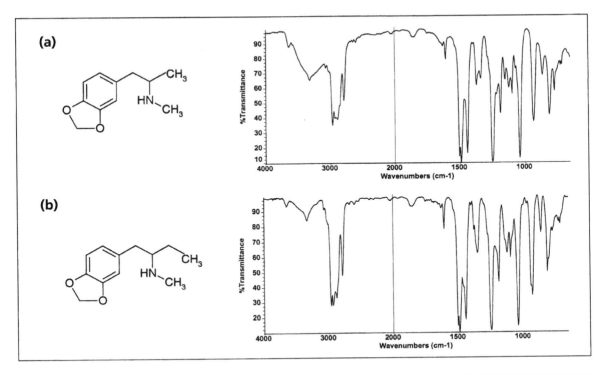

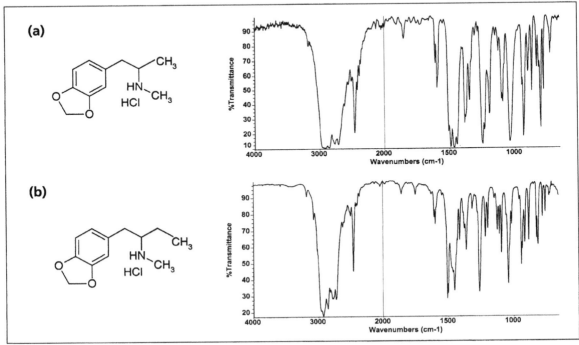

solvent and injected into a GC-FTIR spectrometer. It is important to evaporate the solvent carefully; some of the phenylalkylamines are sufficiently volatile that they can be lost if heated unduly after all solvent has been evaporated.

It is also important to not use methanol or ethanol as the solvent when injecting onto a gas chromatograph. Clark et al. (1992) detailed the formation of condensation products of phenylalkylamines with methanol or ethanol.

There are several articles on the infrared spectra of the base and hydrochloride forms of the phenylalkylamines. Dal Cason (1989) published several spectra of MDA and MDMA and their analogues. Bailey et al. (1975) published the spectra of the *N*-methylated analogues of the methoxyamphetamines and MDA. Noggle et al. (1986) published the spectra of MDA, MDMA, and 3,4-methylenedioxy-*N*-ethylamphetamine (MDEA) and their hydrochloride salts. Hugel and Weaver (1988) published the infrared spectra of 2-methoxy-3,4-methylenedioxyamphetamine, *N,N*-dimethyl-MDA and MDEA. Veress et al. (1994) published the solid phase and vapor phase spectra of MDEA. CND Analytical (1988, 1991) published many of the infrared spectra of the phenylalkylamines related to MDA.

4.4 INFRARED SPECTROSCOPY OF PHENCYCLIDINE AND ANALOGS

The approach and comments outlined in the phenylalkylamines hold true for phencyclidine and its analogues with a few notable differences. The generalization that the number of spectral features decreases from the condensed phase to the vapor phase is demonstrated by Figure 4.9 where the spectra of phencyclidine HCl—solid phase, phencyclidine base—liquid phase, and phencyclidine base at 225°C vapor phase are presented.

Some methods for the synthesis of phencyclidine involve the use of hydrobromic acid near the end of the reaction. This will sometimes result in the occurrence of phencyclidine hydrobromide (PCP.HBr) in street samples in place of the more common phencyclidine hydrochloride (PCP.HCl). Figure 4.10 illustrates the spectra of PCP.HBr in comparison to the spectrum of PCP.HCl in Figure 4.9.

Note the differences in the spectra in the 2600 to 2900 cm^{-1} region of the spectrum.

The spectra of the base films of the following homologous series are presented in Figure 4.11:

- *N*-(1-phenylcyclohexyl)methylamine;
- *N*-(1-phenylcyclohexyl)ethylamine;
- *N*-(1-phenylcyclohexyl)propylamine;
- *N*-(1-phenylcyclohexyl)isopropylamine.

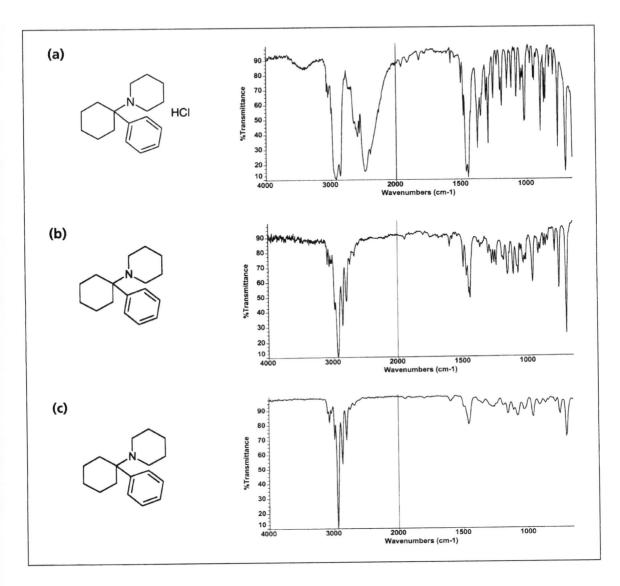

The series of spectra demonstrate why IR spectroscopy is an excellent technique in distinguishing phencyclidine and its analogues.

Phencyclidine and analogues can be extracted as outlined in the phenylalkylamines section with a few exceptions. Phencyclidine HCl is so soluble in chloroform that it will extract from the aqueous acid solution in the liquid–liquid extraction method. 1-Phenylcyclohexene is a common gas chromatographic artifact when phencyclidine is injected into the gas chromatograph.

Figure 4.9

Infrared spectra of phencyclidine (PCP): (a) solid—phencyclidine HCl; (b) liquid—phencyclidine base; (c) vapor— phencyclidine at 225°C

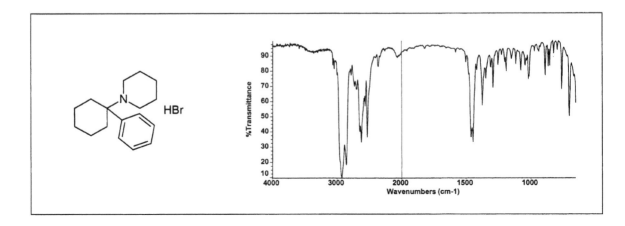

Figure 4.10

IR spectra of phencyclidine HBr

There are several articles on the identification of phencyclidine and its analogues by infrared spectroscopy. Bailey et al. (1976) published the base and base hydrochloride spectra of six phencyclidine analogues observing that the base or hydrochloride spectra were all distinguishable. Bailey et al. (1979) argued that while the base spectra of some of the analogues of *N*-(1-phenylcyclohexyl)ethylamine (cyclohexylamine) were similar they could be distinguished. Allen et al. (1980) presented infrared spectra of 1-(1-phenylcyclohexyl)-4-methylpiperidine. Lodge et al. (1992) presented the hydrochloride spectra of analogues of phencyclidine where the phenyl group had been replaced by a benzyl, 2-methylphenyl, 3-methylphenyl, and 4-methylphenyl. The spectra were readily distinguishable.

4.5 INFRARED SPECTROSCOPY OF TRYPTAMINES

The techniques outlined in the phenylalkylamine section also hold for the identification of the tryptamines. Spectra of *N*,*N*-dimethyltryptamine, *N*,*N*-diethyltryptamine and *N*,*N*-dipropyltryptamine are illustrated in Figure 4.12 and are easily distinguishable.

Figure 4.11 (opposite)

IR spectra of phencyclidine homologues in liquid form are: (a) N-(1-phenylcyclohexyl) methylamine; (b) N-(1-phenylcyclohexyl) ethylamine; (c) N-(1-phenylcyclohexyl) propylamine; (d) N-(1-phenylcyclohexyl) isopropylamine

The newest member of the tryptamine family, 5-methoxy-*N*,*N*-diisopropyltryptamine, is easily identified using the infrared spectrometer (Figure 4.13).

Most tryptamines will extract as described in the phenylalkylamine section. A notable exception is psilocybin which has a labile phosphate group. The phosphate group is easily removed from the psilocybin molecule to make psilocin. The phosphate group will hydrolyze under acidic, basic, and high temperature treatment. Psilocybin is isolated from its matrix (usually mushrooms or mycelia) by preparatory HPLC (Hugel, 1984). The spectrum of the purified analyte can be obtained as an amorphous solid on a silver chloride disk

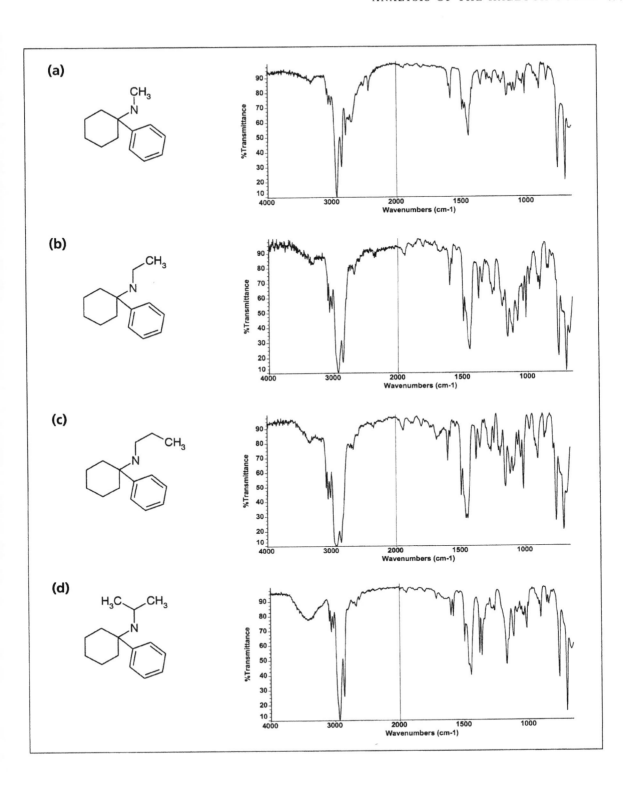

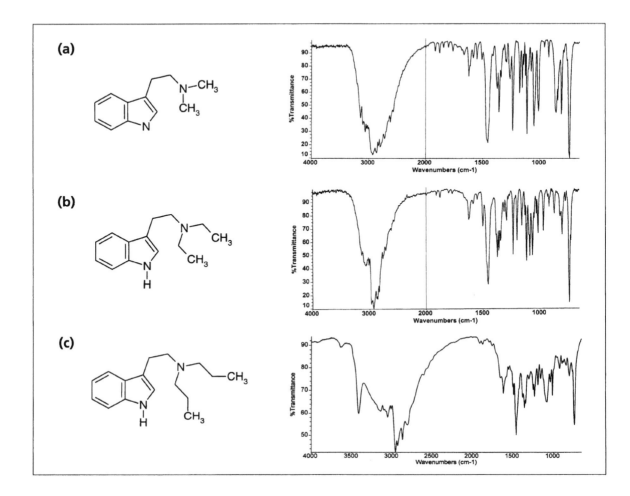

Figure 4.12

IR spectra of tryptamine homologues: (a) solid— N,N-dimethyltryptamine; (b) solid—N,N-diethyltryptamine; (c) liquid—N,N-dipropyltryptamine

or as a KBr micropellet. Spectra of psilocin, psilocybin standards as KBr pellets as well as a spectrum of psilocybin as an amorphous solid are presented in Figure 4.14.

4.6 FURTHER READING

Detailed discussions on the theoretical basis of infrared spectroscopy can be found in many university level textbooks. In particular, Fifield and Kealey (1995) and Ege (1999) discussed the theoretical basis of infrared spectroscopy and its application to the identification of organic molecules. The assignment of absorption frequencies to particular functional groups was also outlined. The text edited by Gough (1991) similarly contained a chapter which includes the theoretical basis of infrared spectroscopy in the context of illicit drug analysis.

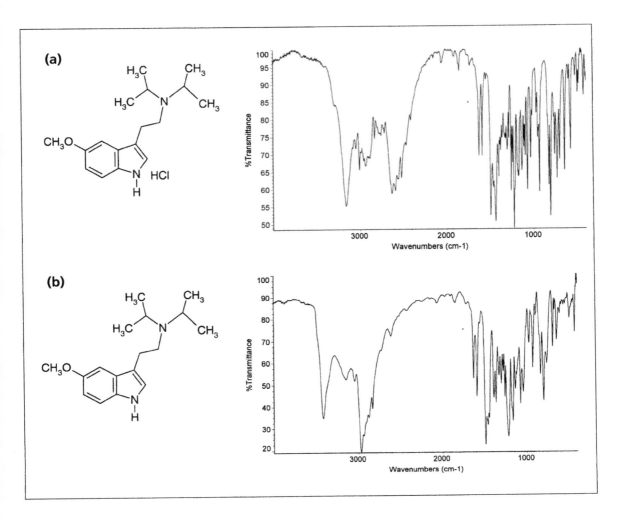

CND Analytical (1994) provided a similar discussion in the context of the analysis of phenylalkylamines.

Texts which outline the absorption frequencies of functional groups include:

- *The Analysis of Drugs of Abuse* (1991) by T. Gough (editor).
- *Handbook of Spectrophotometric Analysis of Drugs* (1981b) by I. Sunshine (editor).
- *Spectroscopic Methods in Organic Chemistry* (1966) by D.H. Williams and I. Fleming.
- *Applications of the Absorption Spectroscopy of Organic Compounds* (1965) by J.R. Dyer.

Figure 4.13
IR spectra of 5-methoxy-N,N-diisopropyl tryptamine: (a) solid—as HCl salt; (b) liquid—freebase

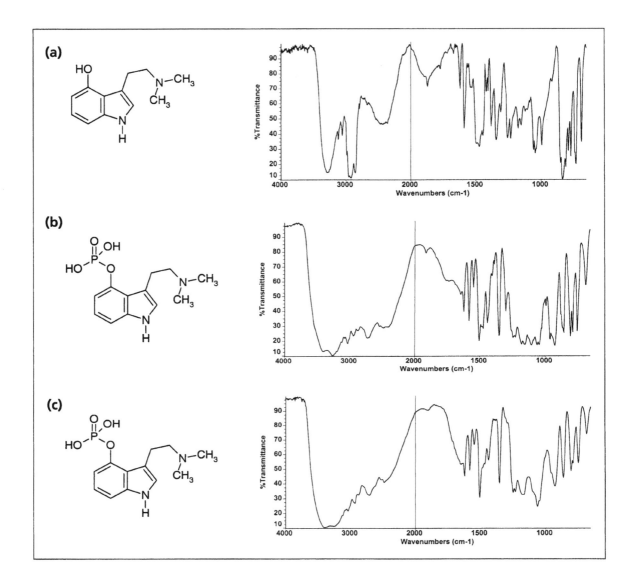

Figure 4.14

Infrared spectra of psilocin and psilocybin: (a) solid—psilocin; (b) solid—psilocybin; (c) solid—amorphous psilocybin

Less common ways of obtaining condensed phase spectra are specular reflectance and photoacoustic spectroscopy. All are discussed in the text by Gough (1991). These techniques can be effective for the analysis of unusual analytes but are not in general use for hallucinogen analysis.

Electronic compilations of condensed phase infrared spectra which include hallucinogens and/or their precursors include:

- Georgia State Crime Laboratory Drug Library containing 1900 spectra which includes abused drugs, isomers, and precursors;
- Toronto Forensic FTIR Library containing 3400 spectra which focuses on abused drugs, pharmaceuticals, precursors, and reagents;
- Nicolet/Aldrich Spectral Library containing 18,500 spectra which includes precursors, essential chemicals, and solvents used in the clandestine production of hallucinogens;
- Nicolet/Sigma Library containing 10,400 spectra which includes many biochemicals as well as spectra of many abused drugs;
- Sadtler/Bio-Rad Condensed Phase IR Standards containing 75,500 spectra which includes precursors, essential chemicals, and solvents used in the clandestine production of hallucinogens.

Electronic compilations of vapor phase infrared spectra which include hallucinogens and/or their precursors include:

- Sadtler/Bio-Rad Vapor Phase IR Standards containing 9100 spectra which includes precursors, essential chemicals, and solvents used in the clandestine production of hallucinogens;
- Nicolet Vapor Phase Library containing 8600 spectra which includes precursors, essential chemicals, and solvents used in the clandestine production of hallucinogens;
- Aldrich FTIR Vapor Phase Library containing 5000 spectra which includes precursors, essential chemicals, and solvents used in the clandestine production of hallucinogens;
- EPA Vapor Phase Library containing 3300 spectra which includes essential chemicals and solvents used in the clandestine production of hallucinogens.

Hard copy (text form) compilations of condensed phase infrared spectra which include hallucinogens and their precursors include:

- *Instrumental Data for Drug Analysis Volumes 1 to 4* (1987) by Mills and Roberson;
- *Instrumental Data for Drug Analysis Volume 5* (1992) by Mills et al.;
- *Instrumental Data for Drug Analysis Volumes 6 and 7* (1996) by Mills et al.;
- *Clarke's Isolation and Identification of Drugs* (1986) by Moffat et al. (editors);
- *Sigma Library of FT-IR Spectra* (1987) by Keller;
- *The Aldrich Library of FT-IR Spectra* (1985) by Pouchert;
- *Analytical Profiles of Amphetamines and Related Phenethylamines* (1989) by CND Analytical;

- *Analytical Profiles of Designer Drugs Related to the 3,4-Methylenedioxyamphetamines (MDA's)* (1991) by CND Analytical;
- *Analytical Profiles of Substituted 3,4-Methylenedioxyamphetamines: Designer Drugs Related to MDA* (1988) by CND Analytical;
- *Analytical Profiles of Precursors and Essential Chemicals* (1990) by CND Analytical;
- *Analytical Profiles of the Hallucinogens* (1991) by CND Analytical;
- *Forensic and Analytical Chemistry of Clandestine Phenethylamines* (1994) by CND Analytical.

Hard copy (text form) compilations of vapor phase infrared spectra which include hallucinogens and their precursors include:

- *The Aldrich Library of FT-IR Spectra Volume 3* (1989) by Pouchert;
- *Instrumental Data for Drug Analysis Volumes 6 and 7* (1996) by Mills et al.

PART II: MASS SPECTROMETRY

The application of gas chromatography–mass spectrometry (GC-MS) has become a common tool in most forensic labs charged with the identification of illicit drugs seized by law enforcement agencies. Being a sensitive technique, only small quantities of analyte are required in order to obtain a usable spectrum. It is also a quick technique and, with advances in computer technology, easy to operate. As with the application of any technique in illicit drug analysis, the forensic chemist must understand how GC-MS works, how it can be applied, and the strengths and weaknesses of the technique.

4.7 THEORETICAL BASIS

Classical electron impact mass spectroscopy works by introducing the analyte to the mass spectrometer at a very low pressure. At this low pressure, inside the mass spectrometer's source, the analyte is bombarded by an electron beam. The high energy electrons when passing in close proximity to the molecule can cause it to lose an electron. The molecule, carrying a positive charge, then becomes unstable (termed metastable) and fragments. The positively charged fragments are repelled from the source into the mass analyzer. The mass analyzer, based upon the generation of electromagnetic or similar fields, allows only one fragment at a time to enter the detector, an electron multiplier. The mass analyzer rapidly scans through the atomic mass range of interest. In this process, the ions that are being selected reach the electron multiplier and their mass to charge ratio can be calculated by knowing what electromagnetic field strength allowed them to reach the detector. The resulting data is plotted as ion intensity, or abundance, versus the mass to charge ratio of the fragment. For simple organic molecules normally only one positive charge can be accommodated and therefore the mass to charge ratio can be referenced as mass only.

The formation of fragment ions is dependent upon several factors including the stability and amount of energy imparted upon the molecular ion (M^+). The molecular ion degrades through various pathways dependent upon the formation of energetically favored intermediates. Structural differences from one analyte to another mean that different pathways and fragment ions form. This in turn means that the mass spectrum will be different. In the application of GC-MS to hallucinogen analysis, this description holds true for most but not all applications. In particular, distinguishing isomers by mass spectra is often problematic. Optical isomers are not distinguishable. Diastereomers are sometimes distinguished by their mass spectra. In some cases, structural isomers are not distinguished. For instance, the mass spectra of lysergic acid diethylamine (LSD) and iso-LSD, lysergic acid methyl-propylamide (LAMPA), and lysergic acid sec-butylamide (LSB) are virtually identical as illustrated in Figure 4.15.

On the other hand, the addition of a methylene group to an analyte will invariably change its mass spectrum relative to its nonmethylated homologue. For example, as shown in Figure 4.16 the easily distinguished mass spectra of the following homologous series is presented:

- 3,4-methylenedioxyphenethylamine;
- 3,4-methylenedioxyamphetamine (MDA);
- 1-(3,4-methylenedioxyphenyl)-2-butanamine;
- 1-(3,4-methylenedioxyphenyl)-2-pentanamine.

One common way of dealing with the problems of isomers having the same mass spectra is the use of GC retention times. Examples abound where the mass spectra are identical, but the GC retention time is different enough that the two isomers can be distinguished. For example, the mass spectra of LSD, iso-LSD and lysergic acid methyl propyl amide (LAMPA) are all identical. It is, however, a relatively simple matter to develop a method using either a dimethylpolysiloxane or (5% phenyl)methylpolysiloxane capillary column to separate the three isomers.

The sensitivity of mass spectrometers is nothing short of remarkable. Some instruments are more sensitive than others and some analytes intrinsically provide more intense and more featured mass spectra than others. To obtain full scans of hallucinogens where the features of the mass spectrum are clear enough to allow conclusive identification generally requires sensitivity in the nanogram range. The downside to this sensitivity is that the analyst must be

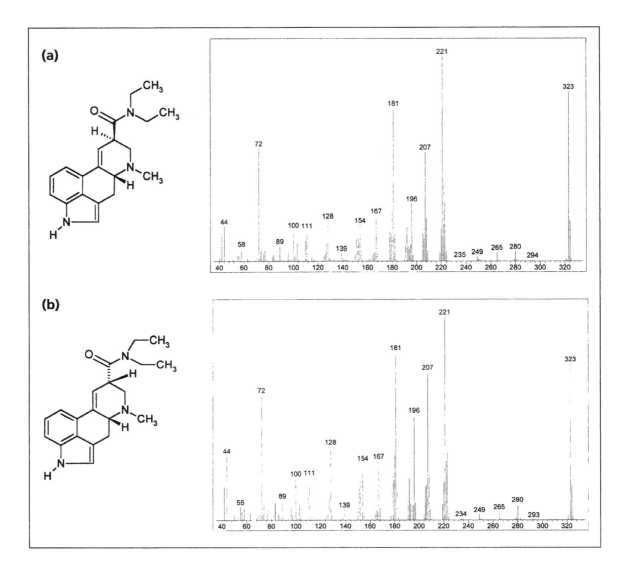

Figure 4.15

Mass spectra of LSD-related compounds: (a) LSD; (b) iso-LSD; (c) Lysergic acid N,N-methyl propylamide (LAMPA); (d) Lysergic acid sec-butylamide (sec-LSB)

sure that the small amount of drug that is being detected was not caused by inadvertent contamination.

The resolution of a mass spectrometer is a measure of the accuracy of the mass that is measured by the mass analyzer. Unit resolution means that the mass analyzer can distinguish between a mass of 323 and 322 or 324. It cannot distinguish between a mass of 323.2 and 323.5. If the mass of a peak is 43.0184 daltons, then the peak is that of $C_2H_3O^+$ and not $C_3H_7^+$ (43.0547 daltons) or $C_2H_5N^+$ (43.0421 daltons) (McLafferty, 1980). A unit resolution mass spectrometer cannot make this distinction. However, this differentiation is beyond

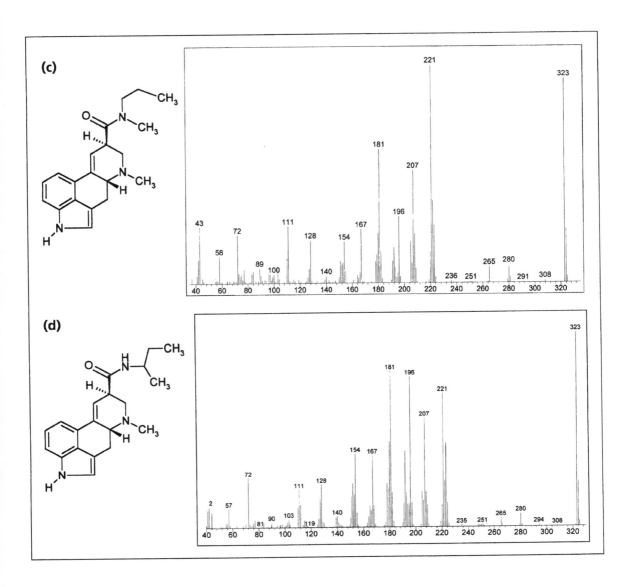

Figure 4.15 (continued)

the capabilities of many common GC-MS instruments. There are mass analyzers which can obtain resolution in the tens of thousands range. Popular mass analyzers that are used in forensic laboratories are normally unit resolution.

4.7.1 Mass Analyzers

A magnetic sector instrument deflects the ion fragments based on their mass to charge (m/z) ratio by means of a magnetic field. By varying the magnetic field, only one m/z will reach the detector at a time. Magnetic field instruments

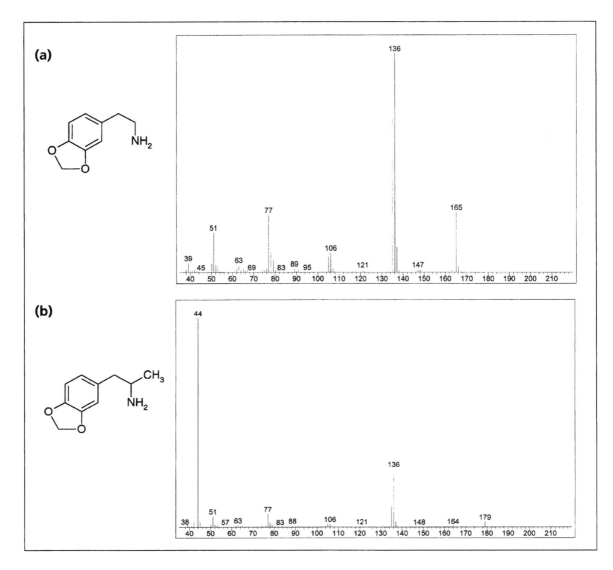

Figure 4.16

Mass spectra of the homologous series based on MDA: (a) 3,4-methylenedioxyphenethyl-amine; (b) MDA; (c) 1-(3,4-methylenedioxyphenyl)-2-butanamine; (d) 1-(3,4-methylenedioxyphenyl)-2-pentanamine

when coupled with an electrostatic field analyzer are capable of much better than unit resolution. These double focusing instruments are not typically used in the identification of routine drug exhibits.

The mass analyzer in quadrupole instruments consist of four precisely aligned parallel rods to which radio frequency and direct current voltages are applied. By varying the frequency and voltage only one mass unit can travel among the quadrupoles and hit the electron multiplier detector. These instruments have enjoyed increasing popularity over the past few years.

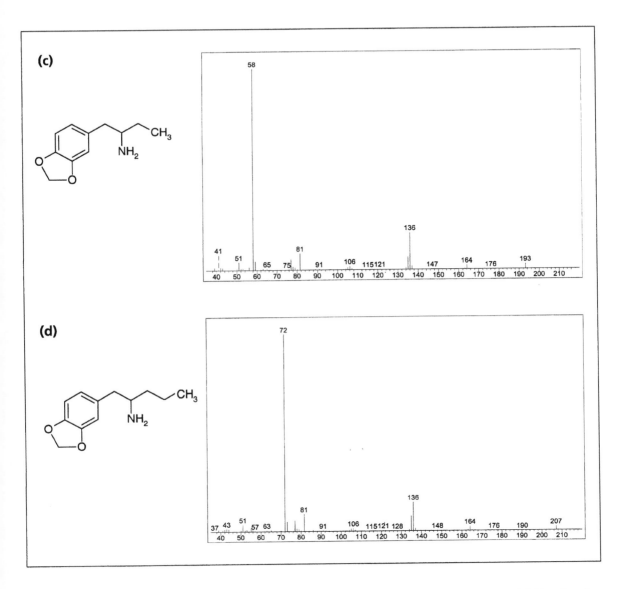

Figure 4.16 (continued)

Ion trap mass analyzers have the sample ionization and mass analysis occur in the same region. A radio frequency is applied to a ring electrode which traps the ions. The ions are selectively expelled by varying the radio frequency. This, as with the quadrupole, is a unit resolution instrument and is commonly used for drug analysis.

In time of flight mass analyzers ion fragments are accelerated into the mass analyzer. The ions drift through a field free region and arrive at the detector at different times based on their velocity and hence their mass can be calculated. These types of instruments are typically of low resolution and, to date have not been popular.

4.7.2 Ionization Techniques

In electron impact (EI) ionization, electrons are accelerated to 70 eV and focused on the analyte in the vapor phase in the mass spectrometer's source. The electrons hit the analyte and remove an electron from the analyte causing fragmentation. Most of the published work to date on the mass spectra of illicit drugs, including hallucinogens, has been electron impact data with ionization energy of 70 eV. Libraries of mass spectra consisting of several hundred thousand spectra have been accumulated from such data. This continues to be the ionization method of choice for most hallucinogen analyses. In some cases, the positively charged molecular ion fragments so readily that molecular ions are not seen. This can be a problem when attempting to identify an unknown compound using its mass spectrum.

In chemical ionization (CI), a positively charged reagent gas such as methane, isobutane, or ammonia collides with the analyte transferring a proton (H^+) from the reagent gas to the analyte (A). The $(A+H)^+$ ion is quite stable and is often the base peak in the CI spectrum. This can be an important characteristic for determining the molecular ion for those hallucinogens, such as the phenethylamines, which do not have strong molecular ions in their EI spectra.

4.7.3 Analyte Introduction

There are several techniques for introducing the analyte to the mass spectrometer.

4.7.3.1 Direct Insertion Probe

The analyte is coated onto a glass holder which is introduced directly into the mass spectrometer source through a vacuum lock. The end of the probe can be temperature programmed to selectively desorb any components that have been deposited on the glass holder. Most often, however, the technique is used with pure analytes. This technique is quite often employed when the analyte is not chromatographable and as such will decompose in the GC inlet. It does not lend itself to routine analysis or automation.

4.7.3.2 Gas Chromatography (GC)

The components, including the analyte of interest, are injected onto a capillary column gas chromatograph. The gas chromatograph separates the components which are sequentially introduced to the mass spectrometer. Before the commercial availability of capillary GC columns there was a need for separators to eliminate the carrier gas before the components reached the mass analyzer (Gough, 1991). In almost all cases now, the end of the GC capillary column is inserted directly into the mass spectrometer source with the pumping system able to handle the carrier gas flow rates. Helium or hydrogen are typical GC carrier gases providing the best chromatographic separation characteristics.

The technique of gas chromatography–mass spectrometry (GC-MS) is the most common mass spectral technique used in the identification of hallucinogens. The most common columns are dimethylpolysiloxane and (5%phenyl)methylpolysiloxane. With few exceptions, either of these columns will separate the mixtures of hallucinogens and contaminants such that the analyte of interest can be identified. One consideration in determining the internal diameter of the gas chromatograph capillary column to be used is the ability of the mass spectrometer vacuum pumps to remove the carrier gas from the source. Generally, for an instrument that is capable of handling a few mL/min carrier gas and can obtain a full scan in less than a second, the internal diameter of the capillary columns should be in the 0.15- to 0.25-mm range. The length of the column should be determined by the resolving power required to separate analytes of similar composition. Columns of length between 10 and 30 m are quite satisfactory for normal hallucinogen identification.

The problems associated with GC-MS are that the analyte must be gas chromatographicable. Compounds which are not volatile and which are thermally labile fall into the category of analytes which are not suitable for GC-MS.

4.7.3.3 Liquid Chromatography (LC)

The use of liquid chromatography permits the analysis of thermally labile and involatile analytes.

The major difficulty with LC-MS has been sample introduction where the liquid mobile phase cannot be directly introduced into the mass spectrometer. One of the first techniques for LC-MS was the moving belt system. The eluant from the LC is sprayed onto a moving belt which is heated to remove the mobile phase and which then passes through a vacuum lock to the mass analyzer source. This technique suffered from low sensitivity and the possibility of contamination of the belt.

Another early direct liquid introduction technique involved forcing the LC column elute through a diaphragm orifice which then enters a chamber where most of the liquid is turned into vapor. The solvent vapor acts as the CI gas and ionization takes place.

A technique that has had commercial success is the thermospray technique. The eluate is introduced into the mass spectrometer through a heated capillary tube. The aqueous mobile phase contains electrolytes which are charged and in turn cause ionization of the sample molecules. This is a mild form of ionization which means that there is little fragmentation. In addition, however, if the molecule is thermally labile it could decompose in the heated inlet.

Another recent technique which does not require heating the sample is atmospheric pressure ionization (API). The sample and the mobile phase are vaporized through a nebulizer which then passes through a veil of nitrogen gas before entering the source where the bulk of the solvent is removed and soft ionization of the analyte takes place.

A more recent sample introduction technique involves the use of a particle beam interface. From a conventional reverse phase LC, the low volatility analyte is enriched in concentration as it passes through the interface. Classical EI spectra can then be obtained as the analyte is introduced into the mass analyzer. The advantage of this technique is that the obtained EI spectra can be compared with the vast amount of published EI spectra.

4.7.4 Tandem Mass Spectrometry

Tandem mass spectrometers involve the use of two mass spectrometers in series. The first mass spectrometer purifies the introduced mixture by focusing only the molecular ion of the analyte of interest. That molecular ion then collides with neutral gas molecules which cause fragmentation of the molecular ion, which fragments and is measured by the second mass spectrometer. The advantage of this technique is that there is no need to have a chromatograph at the front end of the mass analyzer. Mixtures can be introduced directly to the first mass analyzer. Tandem mass spectrometers are perfectly suited for studying the origin of an ion and their fragmentation pathways through MS-MS or "linked-scan" studies.

4.7.5 Data Acquisition and Manipulation

In order to obtain usable information from the mass spectrometer, the data must be in an easy-to-use format. With the advances in computer technology within the last few years, this has been effectively obtained. One of the techniques that is important to working with GC-MS or LC-MS data is obtaining a chromatogram from the data. The ions that are obtained by the mass spectrometer are summed by the computer, referred to as the total ion current (TIC), to derive an analyzable chromatogram which is analogous to a gas chromatographic (or liquid chromatographic) run. For low level analyses where interferences from numerous extraneous sources are possible the mass spectrometer can be programmed to analyze for a small set of ions characteristic to the analyte(s) in question (selected ion monitoring: SIM).

In most cases, however, for the identification of hallucinogens, it is best to obtain full scan spectra. This is accomplished by most modern systems at a rate of about one complete scan a second. This speed is quite satisfactory to identify the peaks eluting from a capillary column. Even if only a few scans are obtained per peak, there is no difficulty in obtaining good spectra providing there is enough sample.

One of the implications of the use of a capillary column gas chromatograph as a separation tool for the mass spectrometer is that the concentration of the analyte as it elutes from a column is constantly changing. As the analyte begins to appear at the mass spectrometer, its concentration is increasing. After reaching the peak maximum the concentration of the analyte begins to decrease. Since the mass spectrometer is measuring individual masses sequentially and those masses are changing with time, it follows that the mass spectrum can be skewed depending on the changing analyte concentration. For example, on the upside of a peak when the mass spectrometer scans from high to low masses, the lower masses will be stronger in relative intensity. Conversely, on the downside of the peak, the higher masses will be weaker in relative intensity. The problem is exacerbated by the narrow peak shapes that are characteristic of modern capillary columns. The problem of skewed spectra can be overcome by averaging scans on the upside, at the apex of the peak, and on the downside of the peak. Modern software will accomplish this with minimal effort on the user's part and can be automated.

4.7.6 Spectral Compilations

In order to identify the mass spectra of the hallucinogens, the easiest way is to search a library of mass spectra. This has led to compilations of 70 eV electron impact mass spectra which are available in electronic or hard copy (book) form. Electronic libraries have the advantage that they can be searched by instrument manufacturer's software. A good match is one which has a significantly better hit value than the next. As with the case of the IR library searches, proper care must be taken to interpret the search results. It is always important to visually compare the sample spectrum with the appropriate standard spectrum to identify an analyte. The heading on further reading details electronic and hard copy compilations of mass spectra.

4.8 MASS SPECTROSCOPY OF LYSERGIC ACID DIETHYLAMIDE (LSD)

As noted earlier in the chapter in the section on infrared spectroscopy, lysergic acid diethylamine (LSD) dosage units are typically in the 30 to 100 µg range. An alternative to obtaining a condensed phase infrared spectrum is to obtain a mass spectrum using a GC-MS. In order to properly interpret the obtained mass spectrum, there are pitfalls to avoid.

LSD is particularly sensitive to contamination in the injection port. If the injection port is dirty, the mass spectrum of LSD will not be obtained. Changing the injection port insert is an excellent idea before attempting to obtain a mass spectrum of LSD using a GC-MS.

Isomers of LSD can be problematic when obtaining mass spectra. In particular, iso-LSD, lysergic acid methyl propyl amide (LAMPA), and lysergic acid sec-butylamide (sec-LSB) give essentially identical spectra. See Figure 4.15 at the beginning of the GC-MS section. The way to conclusively identify which isomer is present is to determine the retention times of the standards. As long as the isomers are well separated, the retention time and the mass spectrum form a conclusive identification. It is also important to either run a standard LSD in the same sequence as the sample or run the sample with an internal standard to ensure that the analyte retention time does indeed match that of LSD. As far as which columns are the best to use, the standard dimethylpolysiloxane and (5% phenyl)methylpolysiloxane columns both work.

The similarity of the spectra of LSD and its isomers has been discussed in several articles. Bailey et al. (1973) observed that the distinction between LSD, iso-LSD, and the methyl propyl amides of lysergic acid by mass spectrum alone is not satisfactory. Ardrey and Moffat (1979) published spectra of several ergot alkaloids as well as iso-LSD and LSD. Nichols et al. (1983) noted that while the mass spectra of LSD and LAMPA are similar, they could be separated by capillary column gas chromatography. Japp et al. (1987), Kessler (1988), and Boshears (1990) made similar observations. Clark (1989) published many mass spectra related to LSD and outlined reproducible minor differences in the iso-LSD and LAMPA mass spectra but went on to recommend the use of other techniques in addition to MS for positive identification. Neville et al. (1992) published the spectra of LSD and LAMPA. Blackwell (1998) demonstrated the retention time difference between LSD and LAMPA.

Since LSD is present in such small quantities in dosage units, it follows that the amount of LSD to be detected in biological samples is likewise very small. This has led to the application of several innovative approaches to LSD analysis. Francom et al. (1988) discussed the derivatization of LSD and then the application of GC-MS to identify LSD in urine. Paul (1990) discussed a similar procedure for the quantitation of LSD in urine. Sun (1989) and Bukowski and

Eaton (1993) outlined a procedure for the quantitation of LSD using trimethylsilyl derivatives. Papac and Foltz (1990) described a method for the measurement of LSD in plasma using capillary column negative ion mass spectrometry. Nelson and Foltz (1992) discussed the use of gas chromatography/tandem mass spectrometry (MS/MS) for the identification of LSD, iso-LSD and N-demethyl-LSD. Several ionization techniques are discussed along with various derivatization techniques. Ohno and Kawabata (1988) outlined the use of direct inlet chemical ionization mass spectrometry for LSD analysis. Duffin et al. (1992) discussed several applications of liquid chromatography/mass spectrometry including to the identification of LSD. Rule and Henion (1992) and Cai and Henion (1996) use an immunoaffinity chromatograph before the LC/MS in their approach. Hopfgartner et al. (1993) used a high flow ion spray LC/MS to identify LSD. Pseudo-chemical ionization mass spectra were obtained using this method. Bogusz et al. (1998) discussed the LC-MS of LSD in biological samples using atmospheric pressure chemical ionization mass spectrometry.

4.9 MASS SPECTROSCOPY OF PHENYLALKYLAMINES

The spectrum of phenylalkylamines is dominated by the amine-containing fragment formed by cleavage of the bond beta to the amine group. Figure 4.17 shows this α-cleavage for a number of the phenylalkylamines.

In Figure 4.17 the R substitution can be any functional group on the phenyl ring. One of the problems that is immediately evident from Figure 4.17 is that some of the structural isomers can generate the same base peak. This problem is further exacerbated by the possibility that other amines which are attached to the carbon alpha to the phenyl group give base peaks in an analogous manner. Figure 4.18 illustrates three other amines that would give base peaks at 58 daltons.

Another characteristic of the mass spectra of phenylalkylamines is that the molecular ion is weak but usually present. Figure 4.19 illustrates the spectra of 3,4-methylenedioxyamphetamine (MDA), 3,4-methylenedioxymethamphetamine (MDMA), and 3,4-methylenedioxy-N-ethylamphetamine (MDEA).

The forensic drug chemist must determine the identification of the analyte among the possible structural isomers. In some cases, scale expansion of the mass spectrum will assist. (This would be done by making the base peak well off scale.) This is demonstrated in Figure 4.19 by comparing the spectra with the scale expanded spectra of the same three analytes in Figure 4.20.

Using this technique along with a comparison of the spectra of the possible structural isomers can sometimes be sufficient to obtain a positive identification. Literature spectra can be used with this technique, but spectra in libraries are often obtained using several different instruments, including different mass

Figure 4.17

α-Cleavage of the aliphatic amine side chain of several phenylalkylamines

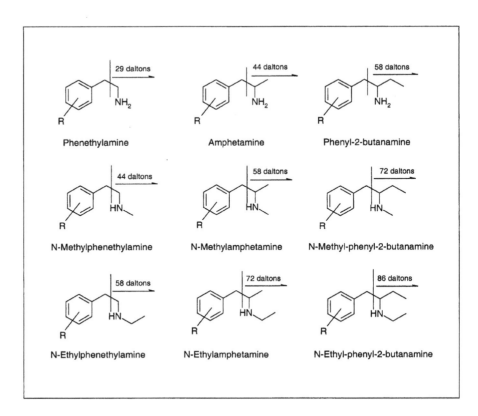

analyzers. It is best, but often impractical, to obtain or synthesize possible isomers and obtain their spectra on the forensic laboratory's instruments.

Another technique to differentiate among the mass spectra of structural isomers is to obtain the gas chromatograph retention time of the analyte and of the suspected hallucinogen. With modern capillary column gas chromatography, the separation among even closely related structural isomers is usually significant. Again the use of standards run at one time to establish the separation among isomers is necessary. As well, the retention time of the standard must be established in the current sequence either by obtaining its retention time by its injection or by establishing the analyte's relative retention time by use of internal standard.

It is best practice to inject the bases of phenylalkylamines into gas chromatographs (including GC-MSs) in order to obtain best chromatography. Phenylalkylamine hydrochlorides lose the hydrochloride when injected, the chromatography suffers, but the spectra so obtained are quite usable. The caveat mentioned in the infrared section of the chapter that alcohols are poor choices of solvent for the injection of phenylalkylamines into a GC-MS should always be kept in mind. See the article by Clark et al. (1992) for details.

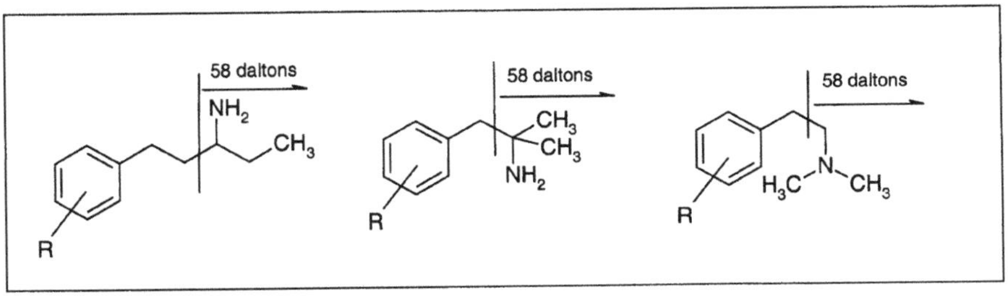

Figure 4.18

Other amines which give rise to 58 m/z base peaks

There were several articles on the mass spectra of phenylalkylamines. Dal Cason (1989) published classical EI spectra and methane chemical ionization spectra of MDA and MDMA and its analogues. He observed that most of these analogues have weak molecular ions. CND Analytical (1994) discussed the analysis of phenylalkylamines by GC-MS. They pointed out the formation of the 44, 58, and 72 dalton ions that dominate the spectra of phenylalkylamines and the difficulty in distinguishing among regioisomeric phenethylamines. An example given in their text was the isomers of methamphetamine. Renton et al. (1993) presented the mass spectrum of the trifluoroacetic anhydride (TFA) derivative of MDA and N,N-dimethyl-MDA. Bailey et al. (1975) presented the N-methylated analogues of methoxyamphetamine and MDA and noted the similarity of mass spectra of some of the isomers. Hugel and Weaver (1988) published the infrared spectra of 2-methoxy-3,4-methylenedioxyamphetamine, N,N-dimethyl-MDA and MDEA. Veress et al. (1994) published the EI and CI spectrum of MDEA.

4.10 MASS SPECTROSCOPY OF PHENCYCLIDINE AND ANALOGS

Phencyclidine and its analogues are well distinguished by their mass spectra. Figure 4.21 illustrates the structure of phencyclidine, which is 1-(1-phenylcyclohexyl)piperidine, and its analogues where the phenyl group has been substituted.

Figure 4.22 illustrate the structure of the analogues of phencyclidine where the piperidine group has been substituted.

The mass spectra of phencyclidine, along with 1-(1-(2-thienyl)cyclohexyl) piperidine, are presented in Figure 4.23.

To further demonstrate the ability of mass spectroscopy to identify phencyclidine and its analogues, Figure 4.24 includes the following mass spectra:

- N-(1-phenylcyclohexyl)methylamine;
- N-(1-phenylcyclohexyl)ethylamine;

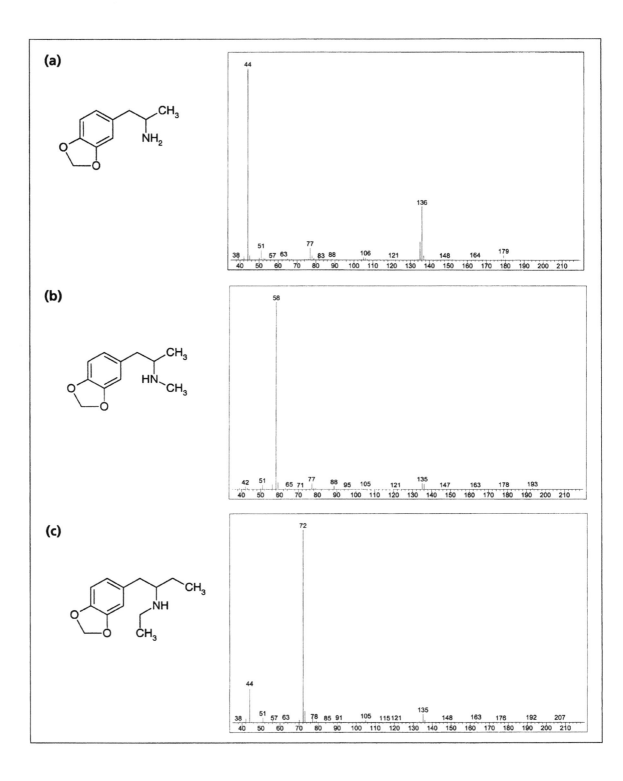

- *N*-(1-phenylcyclohexyl)propylamine;
- *N*-(1-phenylcyclohexyl)isopropylamine.

There were several literature references on the mass spectra of phencyclidine and its analogues. Bailey et al. (1976) detailed that changing the piperidine to pyrrolidine or to morpholine in the phencyclidine molecule creates easily distinguishable spectra. The article went on to discuss replacing the phenyl group with thienyl in the phencyclidine molecule. The mass spectra so obtained were again easily distinguished. The mass spectra of these analogues exhibit moderate to strong molecular ions. Lodge et al. (1992), on the other hand, found that replacing the phenyl group with a benzyl moiety yielded a mass spectrum with no molecular ion. Close examination of that mass spectrum along with the mass spectra of the structural isomers where the phenyl group has been replaced by 2-, 3-, and 4-methylphenyl revealed significant differences. Bailey et al. (1979) investigated the mass spectra of the analogues of *N*-(1-phenylcyclohexyl)ethylamine and again concluded that the mass spectra were easily distinguishable and that GC-MS was a good technique to distinguish among the analogues. Allen et al. (1980) discussed the mass spectrum of 1-(1-phenylcyclohexyl)-4-methylpiperidine and also came to the same conclusion.

The extraction of phencyclidine and its analogues is discussed in the infrared spectroscopy section of this chapter. In general terms, the extraction is straightforward except that phencyclidine hydrochloride will extract from acid solutions. The formation of the GC artifact 1-phenylcyclohexene from the injection of phencyclidine should also be kept in mind.

4.11 MASS SPECTROSCOPY OF TRYPTAMINES

The mass spectra of dimethyltryptamine and diethyltryptamine are dominated by the fragment formed by cleavage beta to the amino group. Figure 4.25 illustrates this.

The molecular ions are either very weak or missing. The mass spectra of dimethyltryptamine (DMT), diethyltryptamine (DET) and dipropyltryptamine (DPT) in expanded scale are presented in Figure 4.26.

In Figure 4.27, 5-methoxy-diisopropyltryptamine is presented in both normal and expanded scales.

As mentioned in the section on the infrared spectroscopy of tryptamines, psilocybin easily loses its phosphate group to form psilocin. Derivatization of psilocybin with *N,O*-bis-(trimethylsilyl)trifluoroacetamide (BSTFA) will yield a derivatized spectrum which is easily distinguished from psilocin. Figure 4.28 presents the mass spectrum of underivatized psilocin as well as derivatized psilocybin and psilocin.

Figure 4.19 (opposite)

Mass spectra of:
(a) MDA; (b) MDMA;
(c) MDEA

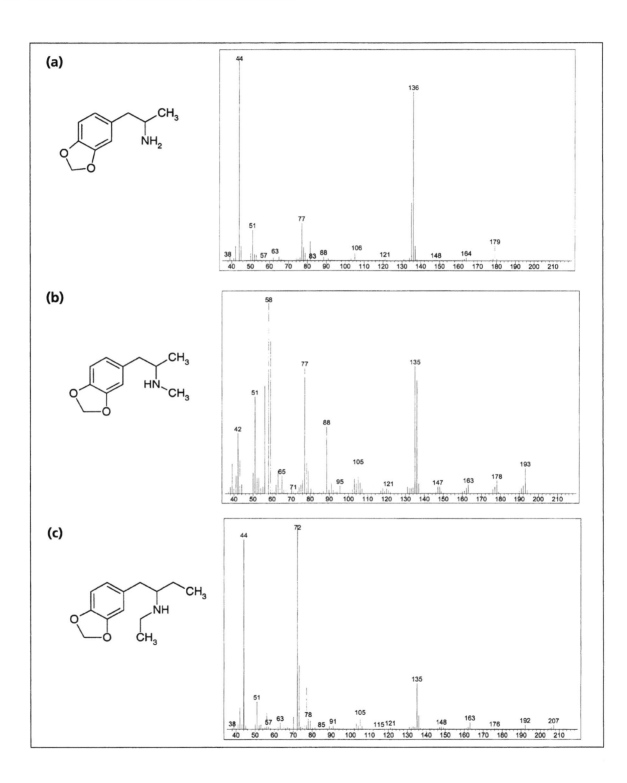

There are a few references on the identification of psilocybin. Repke et al. (1977) outlined the need to derivatize psilocybin to identify it by mass spectrometry. Hugel (1984) described the separation and identification of psilocybin from chocolate cookies containing psilocybin mycelia. Redhead (1984) described how the mycelia in the chocolate cookies was biologically identified. Timmons (1984) published a method using the described derivatizing technique to identify psilocybin and psilocin in mushrooms.

Figure 4.20 (opposite)

Mass spectra of Figure 4.19 with expanded y-scale: (a) MDA; (b) MDMA; (c) MDEA

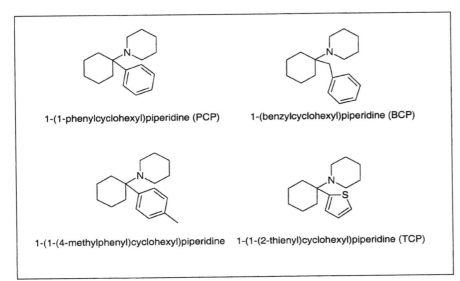

1-(1-phenylcyclohexyl)piperidine (PCP)

1-(benzylcyclohexyl)piperidine (BCP)

1-(1-(4-methylphenyl)cyclohexyl)piperidine

1-(1-(2-thienyl)cyclohexyl)piperidine (TCP)

Figure 4.21

Phencyclidine and street analogues where the phenyl group is substituted

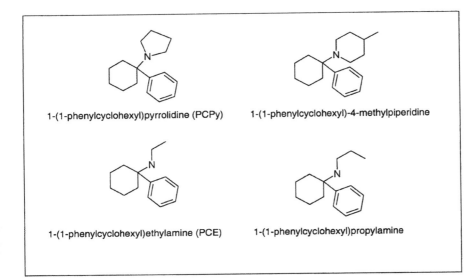

1-(1-phenylcyclohexyl)pyrrolidine (PCPy)

1-(1-phenylcyclohexyl)-4-methylpiperidine

1-(1-phenylcyclohexyl)ethylamine (PCE)

1-(1-phenylcyclohexyl)propylamine

Figure 4.22

Street analogues of phencyclidine where the piperidine group is substituted

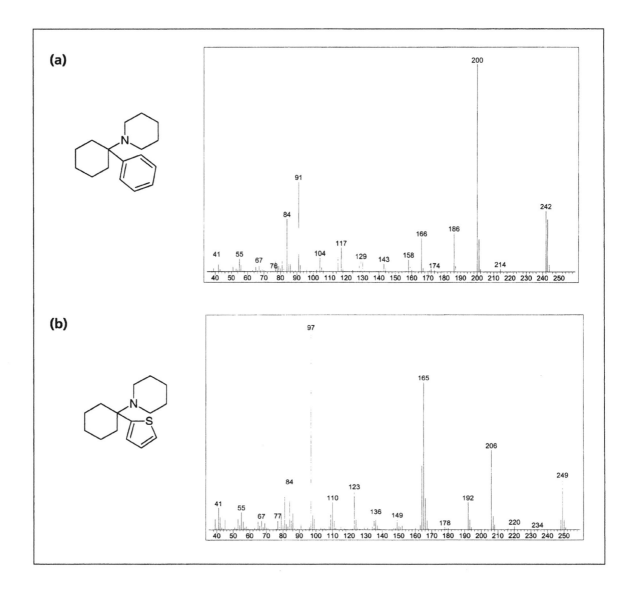

Figure 4.23

Mass spectra of:
(a) phencyclidine;
(b) 1-(2-thienylcyclohexyl)
piperidine (TCP)

Most of the common hallucinogens chromatograph readily on a gas chromatograph. In Figure 4.29 a text mix of several amphetamine, phenthylamine and tryptamine based compounds were effectively separated on a 15-m DB-1 (J & W) using routine conditions.

The tryptamines and LSD analogues are easily chromatographed on thin layer chromatographic systems (TLC) and will fluoresce under ultraviolet light.

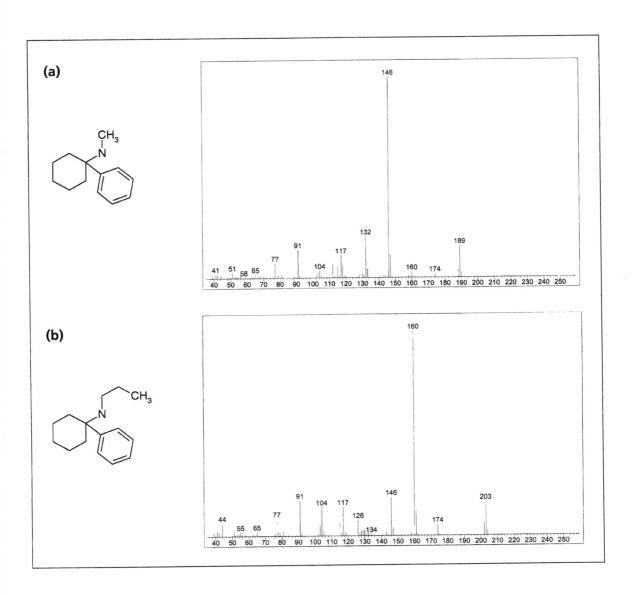

These compounds will also react with highly selective color reagents such as DMBA and Erelich's reagent.

4.12 FURTHER READING

More detailed discussion on mass spectrometry and the interpretation of mass spectra can be found in the text by McLafferty (1980). The university textbook by Ege (1999) includes a description of the technique as it relates to the iden-

Figure 4.24

Mass spectra of a homologous series of phencyclidine-related compounds: (a) N-(1-phenylcyclohexyl) methylamine; (b) N-(1-phenylcyclohexyl)ethyl-amine; (c) N-(1-phenyl-cyclohexyl)propylamine; (d) N-(1-phenylcyclohexyl) isopropylamine

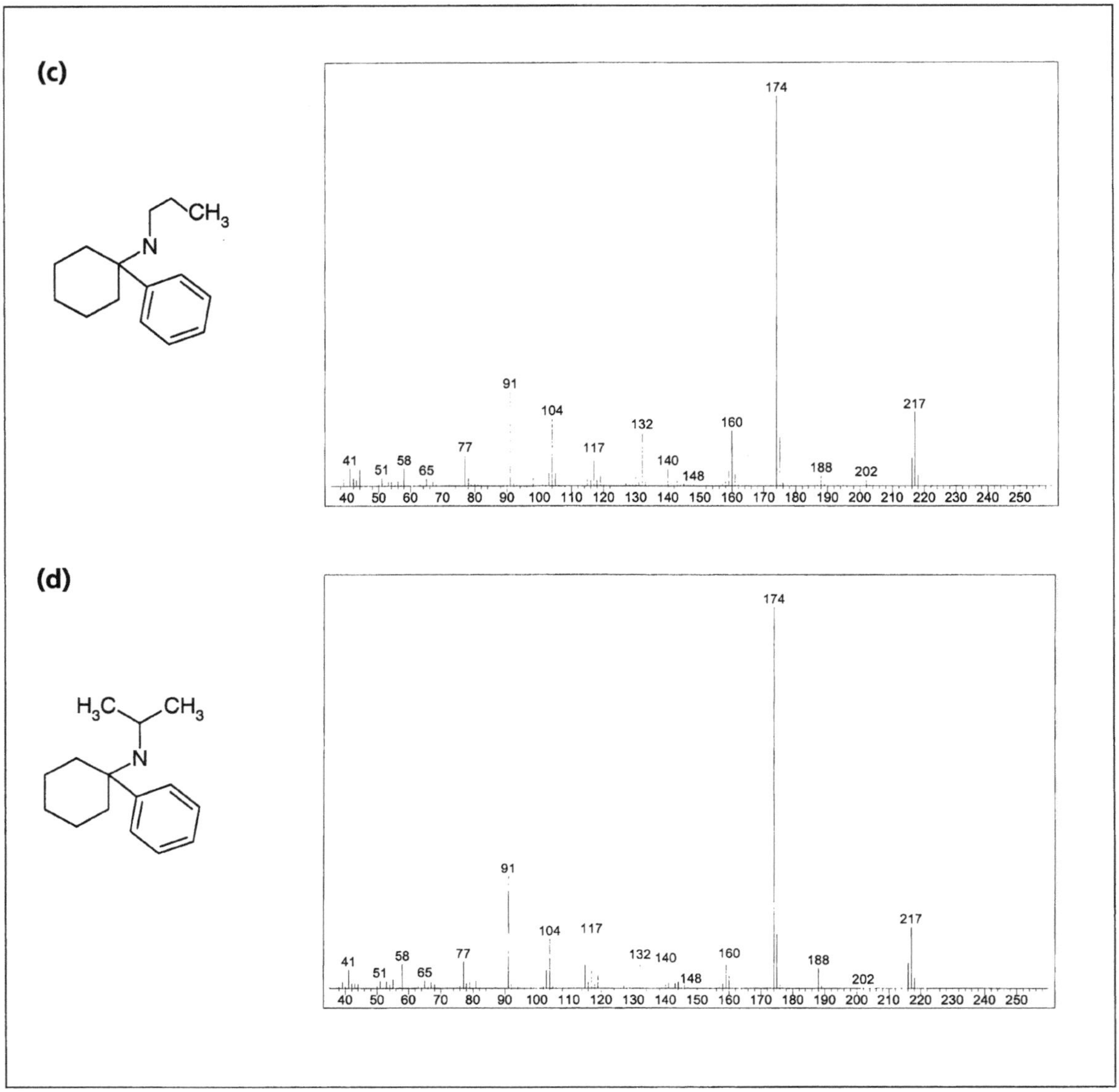

(c)

(d)

Figure 4.24 (continued)   tification of organic compounds. The chapter in the book by Gough (1991) detailed the mass analyzers as well as other ionization techniques such as field ionization/field desorption techniques, fast atom bombardment, and atmospheric pressure ionization techniques as well as LC-MS. Willoughby et al. (1998) present a modern view of the technique of LC-MS and include a discussion on the particle beam interface.

(a)

(b)

(c)

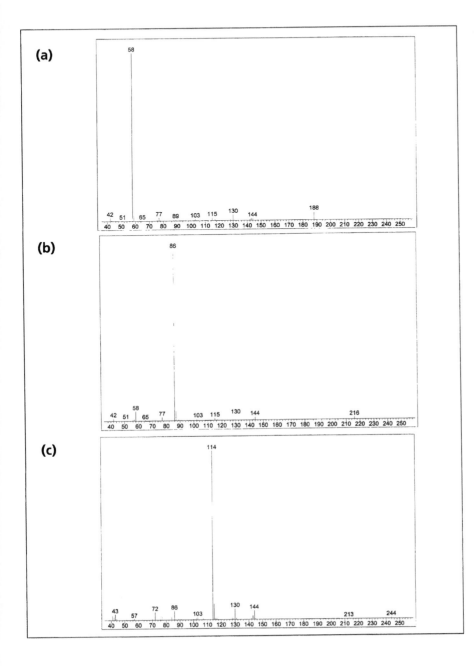

Figure 4.25

Mass spectra of: (a) dimethyltryptamine; (b) diethyltryptamine; (c) dipropyltryptamine; (d) origin of base peak in the mass spectrum of DMT, DET and DPT

Figure 4.25 (continued)

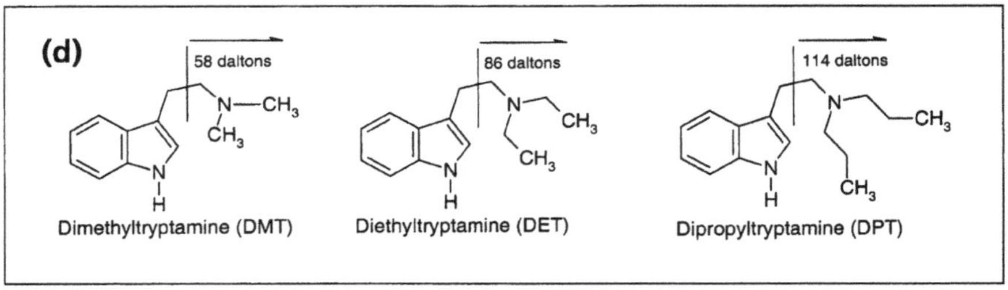

(d)

58 daltons
Dimethyltryptamine (DMT)

86 daltons
Diethyltryptamine (DET)

114 daltons
Dipropyltryptamine (DPT)

Electronic compilations of mass spectra which include hallucinogens and their precursors are:

- Pfleger/Maurer/Weber Library consisting of 6300 spectra of drugs and metabolites;
- Wiley Mass Spectral Data 7th Edition consisting of 390,000 spectra library which include hallucinogens, precursors, essential chemicals, and reagents;
- NIST/EPA/NIH Mass Spectral Library consisting of 107,800 spectra which include hallucinogens, precursors, essential chemicals, and reagents.

Hard copy (text form) compilations of infrared spectra which include hallucinogens and their precursors are:

- *Instrumental Data for Drug Analysis Volumes 1 to 4* (1987) by Mills and Roberson.
- *Instrumental Data for Drug Analysis Volume 5* (1992) by Mills et al.
- *Instrumental Data for Drug Analysis Volumes 6 and 7* (1996) by Mills et al.
- *Clarke's Isolation and Identification of Drugs* (1986) by Moffat et al. (editors).
- *Handbook of Mass Spectra of Drugs* (1981a) by I. Sunshine.
- *Analytical Profiles of Amphetamines and Related Phenethylamines* (1989) by CND Analytical.
- *Analytical Profiles of Designer Drugs Related to the 3,4-Methylenedioxyamphetamines (MDA's)* (1991) by CND Analytical.
- *Analytical Profiles of Substituted 3,4-Methylenedioxyamphetamines: Designer Drugs Related to MDA* (1988) by CND Analytical.
- *Analytical Profiles of Precursors and Essential Chemicals* (1990) by CND Analytical.
- *Analytical Profiles of the Hallucinogens* (1991) by CND Analytical.
- *Forensic and Analytical Chemistry of Clandestine Phenethylamines* (1994) by CND Analytical.

Figure 4.26 (opposite)

Mass spectra of Figure 4.25 with expanded y-scale: (a) dimethyl-tryptamine; (b) diethyltryptamine; (c) dipropyltryptamine scale expanded

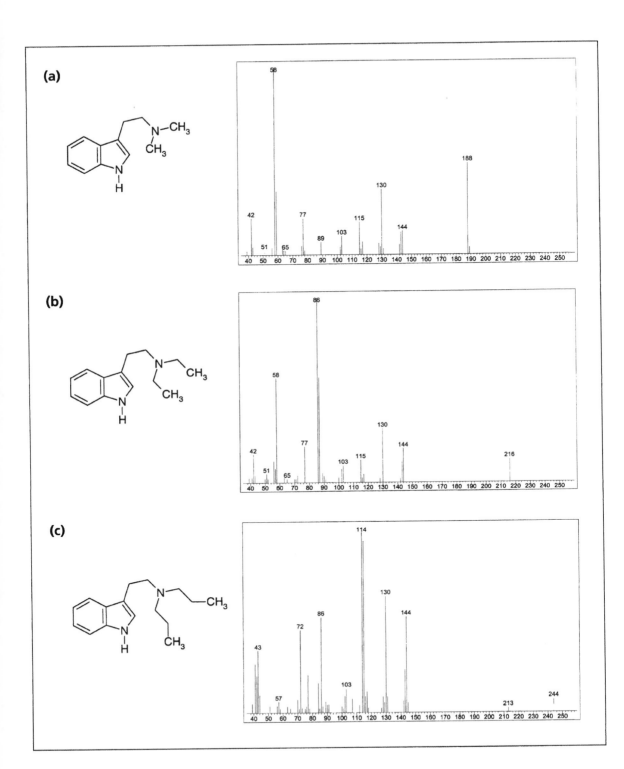

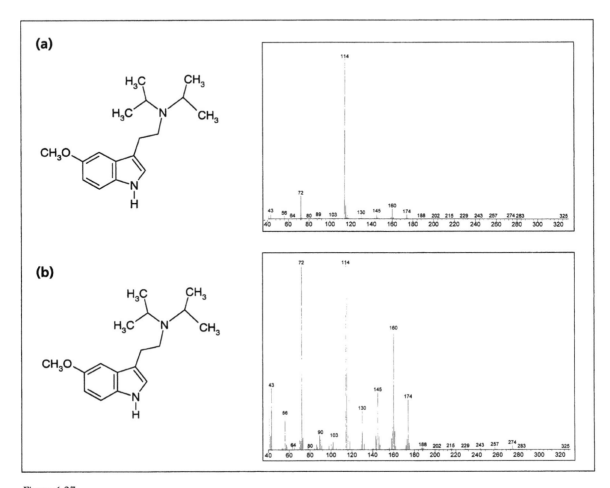

Figure 4.27

Mass spectra of: (a) 5-methoxy-N,N- diisopropyl-tryptamine; (b) 5-methoxy-N,N- diisopropyl-tryptamine scale expanded

Figure 4.28 (opposite)

Mass spectra of derivatized psilocin and psilocybin: (a) BSTFA derivatized psilocin; (b) BSTFA derivatized psilocybin; (c) BSTFA derivatized psilocybin expanded scale

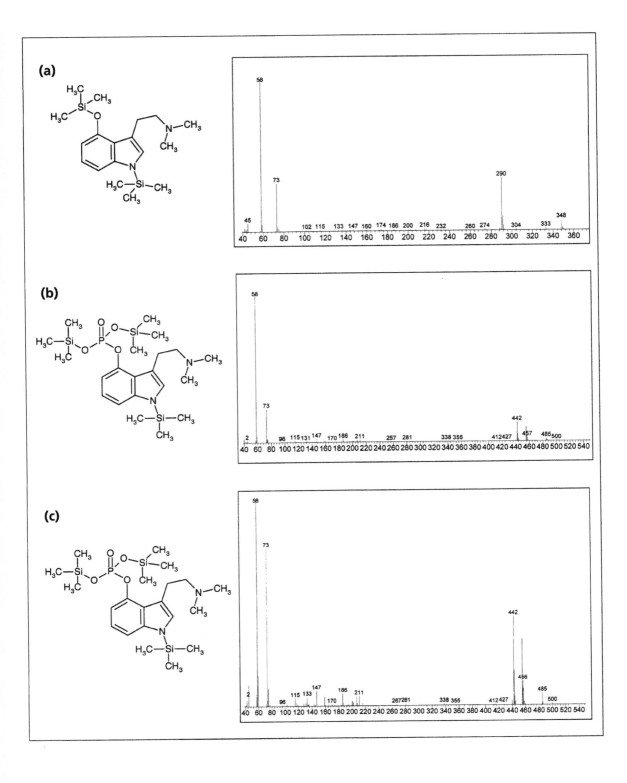

Figure 4.29

A gas chromatogram of a mixture of several hallucinogenic compounds

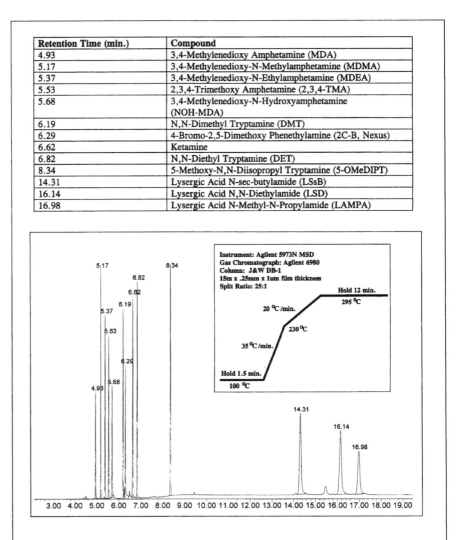

Retention Time (min.)	Compound
4.93	3,4-Methylenedioxy Amphetamine (MDA)
5.17	3,4-Methylenedioxy-N-Methylamphetamine (MDMA)
5.37	3,4-Methylenedioxy-N-Ethylamphetamine (MDEA)
5.53	2,3,4-Trimethoxy Amphetamine (2,3,4-TMA)
5.68	3,4-Methylenedioxy-N-Hydroxyamphetamine (NOH-MDA)
6.19	N,N-Dimethyl Tryptamine (DMT)
6.29	4-Bromo-2,5-Dimethoxy Phenethylamine (2C-B, Nexus)
6.62	Ketamine
6.82	N,N-Diethyl Tryptamine (DET)
8.34	5-Methoxy-N,N-Diisopropyl Tryptamine (5-OMeDIPT)
14.31	Lysergic Acid N-sec-butylamide (LSsB)
16.14	Lysergic Acid N,N-Diethylamide (LSD)
16.98	Lysergic Acid N-Methyl-N-Propylamide (LAMPA)

ACKNOWLEDGMENT

We gratefully acknowledge permission given by Health Canada to include data generated by their Drug Analysis Service.

REFERENCES

Allen, A., Carr, S., Cooper, D., Fransoza, E., Koles, J., Kram, T., and Solon, E. (1980). *Microgram*, 13, pp. 44–46.

Ardrey, R.E., and Moffat, A.C. (1979). *Jour. For. Sci. Soc.*, 19, pp. 253–282.

Bailey, K., By, A.W., Legault, D., and Verner, D. (1975). *Jour. Assoc. Off. Anal. Chem.*, 58, pp. 62–69.

Bailey, K., Gagne, D.R., and Pike, R.W. (1976). *Jour. Off. Anal. Chem.*, 59, pp. 81–89.

Bailey, K., and Legault, D. (1979). *Jour. Assoc. Off. Anal. Chem.*, 62, pp. 1124–1137.

Bailey, K., Verner, D., and Legault, D. (1973). *Jour. Assoc. Off. Anal. Chem.*, 56, pp. 88–99.

Blackwell, T.M. (1998). *Microgram*, 31, pp. 51–61.

Bogusz, M.J., Maier, R-D., Kruger, K-D., and Kohls, U. *Jour. Anal. Toxicol.*, 22, pp. 549ff.

Boshears, F.E. (1990). *Microgram*, 23, pp. 99–100.

Bukowski, N., and Eaton, A.N. (1993). *Rapid Commun. Mass Spectrom.*, 7, pp. 106–108.

Cai, J., and Henion, J. (1996). *Anal. Chem.*, 68, pp. 72–78.

Clark, C.C. (1989). *Jour. For. Sci.*, 34, pp. 532–546.

Clark, C.R., Noggle, F.T., and DeRuiter, J. (1992). *Microgram*, 25, pp. 330–340.

CND Analytical (1988). *Analytical Profiles of Substituted 3,4-Methylenedioxyamphetamines: Designer Drugs Related to MDA*, Auburn, AL: CND Analytical.

CND Analytical (1989). *Analytical Profiles of Amphetamines and Related Phenethylamines*, Auburn, AL: CND Analytical.

CND Analytical (1990). *Analytical Profiles of Precursors and Essential Chemicals*, Auburn, AL: CND Analytical.

CND Analytical (1991). *Analytical Profiles of Designer Drugs Related to the 3,4-Methylenedioxyamphetamines (MDA's)*, Auburn, AL: CND Analytical.

CND Analytical (1991). *Analytical Profiles of the Hallucinogens*, Auburn, AL: CND Analytical.

CND Analytical (1994). *Forensic and Analytical Chemistry of Clandestine Phenethylamines*, Auburn, AL: CND Analytical.

Dal Cason, T. (1989). *Jour. For. Sci.*, 34, pp. 928–961.

Duffin, K.L., Wachs, T., and Henion, J.D. (1992). *Anal. Chem.*, 64, pp. 61–68.

Dyer, J.R. (1965). in *Applications of the Absorption Spectroscopy of Organic Compounds*, Englewood Cliffs, NJ: Prentice-Hall Inc.

Ege, S. (1999). in *Organic Chemistry Structure and Reactivity*, 4th edn, New York: Houghton Mifflin Company.

Fifield, F.W., and Kealey, D. (1995). in *Principles and Practices of Analytical Chemistry*, 4th edn, Glasgow: Blackie Academic and Professional.

Francom, P., Andrenyak, D., Lim, H-K., Bridges, R.R., Foltz, R.L., and Jones, R.T. (1988). *Jour. Anal. Toxicol.*, 12, pp. 1–8.

Gough, Terry (ed.) (1991). in *The Analysis of Drugs of Abuse*, West Sussex, England: John Wiley & Sons Ltd.

Griffiths, P.R., and de Haseth, J.A. (1986). in *Fourier Transform Infrared Spectrometry*, New York: John Wiley & Sons, p. 191.

Japp, M., Gill, R., and Osselton, M.D. (1987). *Jour. For. Sci.*, 32, pp. 933–940.

Harris, H.A., and Kane, T. (1991). *Jour. For. Sci.*, 36, pp. 1186–1191.

Hopfgartner, G., Wachs, T., Bean, K., and Henion, J. (1993). *Anal. Chem.*, 65, pp. 439–446.

Hugel, J. (1984). *Microgram*, 17, pp. 111–119.

Hugel, J., and Weaver, K. (1988). *Microgram*, 21, pp. 681–686.

Keller, R.J. (1986). in *The Sigma Library of FT-IR Spectra*, St Louis, MO: Sigma Chemical Company.

Kempfert, K. (1988). *App. Spectrosc.*, 42, pp. 845–849.

Kessler, R.R. (1988). *Microgram*, 21, pp. 217–221.

Kovar, K.A., Dinkelacker, J., Pfiefer, A.M., Pisternick, W., and Woessener, A. (1995). *GIT Spez. Chromatog.*, 15, pp. 19–24.

Kovar, K.A., Dinkelacker, J., Pfiefer, A.M., Pisternick, W., and Woessener, A. (1995). *Chem. Abstr.*, 123, p. 248677y.

Lodge, B.A., Duhaime, R., Zamecnik, J., MacMurray, P., and Brousseau, R. (1992). *For. Sci. Int'l*, 55, pp. 13–26.

McLafferty, F.W. (1980). *Interpretation of Mass Spectra*, Mill Valley, CA: University Science Books.

Mesley, R.J., and Evans, W.H. (1969). *Jour. Pharm. Pharmac.*, 21, pp. 713–720.

Mills, T., and Roberson, J.C. (1987). *Instrumental Data for Drug Analysis*, Volumes 1 to 4, 2nd edn, New York: Elsevier Science Publishing.

Mills, T., Roberson, J.C., McCurdy, H.H., and Hall, W.H. (1992). in *Instrumental Data for Drug Analysis*, Volume 5, 2nd edn, New York: Elsevier Science Publishing.

Mills, T., Roberson, J.C., Wall, W.H., Lothridge, K.L., McDougall, W.D., and Gilbert, M.W. (1996). *Instrumental Data for Drug Analysis*, Volumes 6 and 7, New York: CRC Press.

Moffat, A.C., Jackson, J.V., Moss, M.S., and Widdop, B. (1986). in *Clarke's Isolation and Identification of Drugs*, London: The Pharmaceutical Press.

Nelson, C.C., and Foltz, R.L. (1992). *Anal. Chem.*, 64, pp. 1578–1585.

Neville, G.A., Beckstead, H.D., Black, D.B., Dawson, B.A., and Ethier, J.-C. (1992). *Can. Jour. App. Spectrosc.*, 37, pp. 149–157.

Nichols, H.S., Anderson, W.H., and Stafford, D.T. (1983). *Jour. High Res. Chromatog. & Chromatog. Comm.*, 6, pp. 101–103.

Noggle, F.T., DeRuiter, J., and Long, M.J. (1986). *Jour. Assoc. Off. Anal. Chem.*, 69, pp. 681–686.

Ohno, Y., and Kawabata, S. (1988). *Chem. Abstr.*, 108, p. 89060p.

Papac, D.I., and Foltz, R.L. (1990). *Jour. Anal. Toxicol.*, 14, pp. 189–191.

Paul, B.D., Mitchel, J.M., Burbage, R., Moy, M., and Sroka, R. (1990). *Jour. Chromatog.*, 529, pp. 103–112.

Pfiefer, A.M., and Kovar, K.A. (1995). *Jour. Planar Chromatogr.—Mod. TLC*, 8, pp. 388–392.

Pouchert, C.J. (1985). in *The Aldrich Library of FT-IR Spectra*, Volumes 1 and 2, Milwaukee, WI: Aldrich Chemical Company.

Pouchert, C.J. (1989). in *The Aldrich Library of FT-IR Spectra Volume 3 Vapor Phase*, Milwaukee, WI: Aldrich Chemical Company.

Redhead, S.A. (1984). *Microgram*, 17, pp. 120–122.

Renton, R.J., Cowie, J.S., and Oon, M.C.H. (1993). *For. Sci. Int'l*, 60, pp. 189–202.

Repke, D.B., Leslie, D.T., Mandell, D.M., and Kish, N.G. (1977). *Jour. Pharm. Sci.*, 66, pp. 743–744.

Rule, G.S., and Henion, J.D. (1992). *Jour. Chromatog.*, 582, pp. 103–112.

Sun, J. (1989). *Chem. Abstr.*, 111, p. 72627t.

Sunshine, I. (1981a). in *Handbook of Mass Spectra of Drugs*, Boca Raton, FL: CRC Press Inc.

Sunshine, I. (1981b). in *Handbook of Spectrophotometric Data of Drugs*, Boca Raton, FL: CRC Press Inc.

Timmons, J.E. (1984). *Microgram*, 17, pp. 28–32.

Veress, T., Gal, T., Nagy, G., Nagy, J., and Korosi, A. (1994). *Microgram*, 27, pp. 48–57.

Williams, D.H., and Fleming, I. (1966). in *Spectroscopic Methods in Organic Chemistry*, London: McGraw-Hill Publishing Co.

Willoughby, R., Sheehan, E., and Mitrovich, S. (1998). in *A Global View of LC/MS*, Pittsburgh, PA: Global View Publishing.

PART III: NUCLEAR MAGNETIC RESONANCE SPECTROSCOPY

4.13 THEORETICAL BASIS

Infrared spectroscopy (IR) and gas chromatography/mass spectrometry (GC/MS) are considered the preferred instrumentation used in forensic laboratories for the identification of drugs of abuse. Certain laboratories, however, have greatly enhanced their identification capabilities with the use of nuclear magnetic resonance (NMR) spectroscopy. IR spectroscopy can only provide a single element of structural information—that of functional group frequencies. However, the IR spectra taken together with GC/MS data can provide additional components of structural information—that of the mass spectrum which provides MW information, structural fragments and the GC retention time along with the IR functional group frequencies. NMR can provide multiple structural elements of information, including carbon/proton count, types of protons and carbons in the molecule, carbon framework, information deduced from carbon-13 chemical shift measurements and correlated with IR data, leading to the formal assembling of molecular structure. IR and NMR represent nondestructive analytical techniques, whereas with GC/MS the samples consumed during the analysis, albeit in a low level, amount.

Early NMR instrumentation suffered from low sensitivity that precluded rapid identification. Generally speaking, ^{1}H NMR results obtained in the 1960s and 1970s were reported at 60, 90, and 100 MHz. During the 1980s, with the development of commercial superconducting magnets, NMR results were being reported at ^{1}H frequencies of 200, 300, 400, and 500 MHz. In the 1990s to the present day, the majority of NMR results have reported at ^{1}H frequencies of 400–600 MHz and more recently at ultrahigh magnetic fields for biological NMR where proton frequencies are 700, 750, 800, and 900 MHz. Carbon data was introduced as a routine technique in the late 1970s and ^{13}C frequencies of 20 MHz (80 MHz for proton) to 125 MHz (500 MHz for proton) were the most common frequencies to be reported well into the 1990s. The technology has evolved dramatically over the past 30 years as much higher magnetic fields, more stable RF components and more sensitive probes have become readily available. More recently the use of cryogenic probe technology has evolved and this has permitted NMR results to be obtained on lower levels of more complex samples. Additionally, the advent of two-dimensional NMR (2-D NMR) in the late 1970s and early 1980s has become an invaluable tool for the identification and structure elucidation of complete unknowns. The introduction of pulsed field gradients (PFG) has introduced new experiments probing different kinds of information and has significantly reduced the time for 2-D data collection. As a result, the use of 2-D NMR for structural problems has become almost as common as 1-D methods.

NMR spectroscopy continues to be the premiere tool for structure elucidation. It has the greatest usable information content of all of the forms of spectroscopy (Claridge, 1999). In recent years, NMR experiments have been developed which permit gross structure elucidation and stereochemical determination, and exact assignments of NMR resonance signals (^{1}H, ^{13}C, ^{19}F, ^{31}P). The principal caveat to NMR as a technique is that of sensitivity and its limitations, which are imposed by potential low sample availability. This general problem, as noted earlier, is being addressed with the use of cryogenic NMR probes as well as with the use of proton-detected experiments for 2-dimensional NMR. For the forensic area, lack of sample availability is generally not a problem. Therefore, NMR can provide rapid and *definitive* structural answers to problems which arise. Most of the NMR analyses in the forensic area will fall into one of two categories:

1. 1-dimensional proton and carbon-13 NMR spectra which are obtained on a sample of suspected unknown or actual known structure where comparison of the resultant spectra is made to a spectral library or to spectra produced from authentic samples for the purposes of identification, both qualitatively and quantitatively; and
2. appropriate 1- and 2-dimensional NMR spectra are obtained on a complete unknown and the structure is deduced from the NMR data (as well as from the results of other complementary structural techniques, e.g., IR and MS and possibly chemical synthesis).

The purpose of this section is to:

1. provide a very brief overview of the NMR technique as it is currently practiced and
2. summarize some of the specific applications of NMR spectroscopy to forensic analysis of hallucinogenic drugs and provide key useful resources for practitioners of forensic drug analysis.

For pure structure elucidation, we will restrict the NMR discussion to the uses of proton (^{1}H) and carbon-13 (^{13}C) NMR. These nuclei represent the principle NMR active nuclei, which are traditionally employed for organic structure elucidation. Other NMR active nuclei (e.g., ^{15}N, ^{19}F, ^{31}P) can provide additional and complementary structural information to that obtained from proton and carbon-13, but they will not be discussed here.

4.14 THE NMR EXPERIMENT

The measurement of NMR spectra is generally performed in solution, although extensive applications using solid-state NMR (principally ^{13}C) are well known (Fyfe, 1983; Mehring, 1983). The sample is usually dissolved in a solvent, which is generally deuterated to provide a deuterium (^{2}H) source for internal field frequency lock of the spectrometer and is placed in a strong magnetic field. The sample is then pulsed with a burst of radio frequency (rf). The wavelength of the frequency (MHz) corresponds to the radio frequency of the nucleus at a given magnet field. The result is a "free-induction decay" or FID, which is a time domain response to the rf excitation. A FID records the free precession of nuclei after the pulse and represents the change in voltages induced in the receiver coil in the probe versus time. The FID information is digitized and stored in a computer. The digitized FID is then converted to a frequency domain spectrum by applying a Fourier transformation to the time domain FID information. The result is the typical NMR spectrum we are used to viewing for interpretative purposes. The result of a typical proton (^{1}H) NMR experiment is shown in Figure 4.30.

The information contained in a survey spectrum, in this instance a 1-dimensional proton NMR spectrum, provides three pieces of basic information:

1. the position of the various resonance patterns corresponds to the different chemical environment that the protons find themselves;
2. spin-spin splitting (coupling), the multiplicity of lines in the spectrum, relates to how the protons are bonded within the molecule; and
3. electronic integration of the spectrum, in particular the resonance patterns, provides a quantitative relationship of the relative numbers and types of protons in the molecule.

Thus the proton NMR spectrum and the pattern(s) which are observed are characteristic of the structure of a pure chemical compound or perhaps a mixture of chemical compounds found in the sample.

Figure 4.30

Proton NMR spectrum (300 MHz, CDCl₃) of N-(n-propyl) MDA hydrochloride

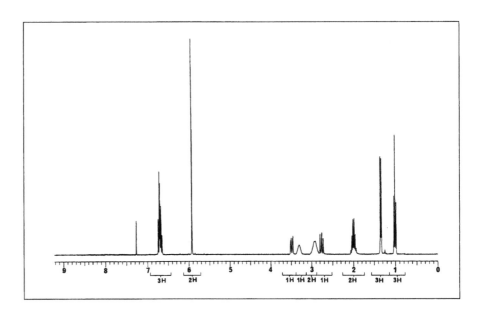

The patterns observed in proton NMR are sensitive to solvent effects and temperature. The same compound dissolved in different deuterated solvents or obtained at different temperatures may give slightly different proton NMR spectra due to shifting of the resonance positions and/or broadening of the lines. Thus, when making comparative analysis by proton NMR it is important to be sure that the same solvent is used in all cases and the same data acquisition parameters (instrument parameters) are used and that the temperature be regulated. Obtaining a survey proton NMR spectrum is usually the first logical step in using NMR for structural identification. All proton NMR spectra run in organic deuterated solvents, e.g., deuterochloroform, deuteromethanol, and deuteroacetone are internally referenced to tetramethylsilane (TMS). This internal reference is assigned 0.00 ppm (the ppm scale is used for NMR spectra and the resonance positions, or chemical shifts as they are referred to, is expressed relative to internal TMS). For deuterium oxide trimethylsilylpropionate sodium salt (TSP) is used as the internal reference.

The next logical step would be to obtain a survey carbon-13 (^{13}C) NMR (Wehrli, 1988) spectrum of the sample in question. Carbon-13 NMR spectra are more difficult to obtain than proton NMR spectrum. The natural abundance of natural NMR active nucleus of carbon (i.e., ^{13}C) in a molecule is 1.1% (as compared to 99.6% for proton). NMR also more easily detects the hydrogen nucleus than the carbon-13. These two factors make carbon-13 less sensitive than proton to NMR detection by a factor of 5600. Carbon-13 spectra are obtained under conditions where the spin-coupling effects from the protons directly attached to the carbons as well as long-range couplings effects (2 and 3 bonds away) are removed. This is done by irradiating the protons at their appropriate precessional frequency with radio frequency (rf). This effectively removes the proton coupling effects on the carbon-13 signals and the resulting carbon signals appear as single sharp lines. There is no mutual coupling from other carbon-13 nuclei since each line which is observed arises from an ensemble of molecules in solution which is rich in carbon-13 *at only one carbon site*, i.e., each resonance line in the spectrum arises from molecules in solution which have a single carbon-13 in the molecule all located at a specific carbon site (isolated carbon-13 nuclei). Protonated carbon-13 nuclei generally give more intense signals due to a phenomenon known as the nuclear Overhauser effect (Claridge, 1999). This phenomenon aids in the detection of carbon-13 spectra and serves to improve the detectability of carbon-13 NMR data.

The next logical step after obtaining the 1-dimensional carbon spectrum would be to assign the multiplicity of the carbon-13 resonances. This is done by using one of two experiments: attached proton test (APT) (Patt, 1982) or distortionless enhancement by polarization transfer (DEPT) (Doddrell, 1982; Richarz, 1982). Both experiments provide information about the types of carbons typically found in a molecule (quaternary, methine, methylene, and methyl). Both experiments have advantages and disadvantages.

The APT is a variation of a class of experiments known as spin echo J-modulation experiments. In the APT experiment, the spectrum which is obtained consists of signals which are either phased up (quaternary and methylene) or phased down (methine and methyl) and relate to the odd or even number of protons attached to carbon. Quaternary and methylene carbons have an even number (0 and 2) of protons attached to them whereas methine and methyl carbons have an odd number (1 and 3) of protons attached to them. The multiplicity of the carbon atom is thus implied from the position of the carbon resonance (chemical shift) and the phasing of the resonance line. Figure 4.31 shows the results of an APT experiment together with a plot of a carbon spectrum (bottom) and the corresponding APT spectrum (top).

A caveat to the APT experiment involves its sensitivity (slightly less than a normal proton decoupled carbon-13 spectrum) and the fact that since this is a spin echo experiment, the spin echo scheme discriminates with respect to broad lines. If you have a sample whose carbon resonances are broadened due to some exchange process (known as exchange broadening) the carbon resonances can be eliminated completely. By changing solvents, adding a proton

Figure 4.31

Carbon-13 NMR spectrum (75 MHz, CDCl₃) of N-(n-propyl)MDA hydrochloride; (top) proton decoupled attached proton test (APT) spectrum, (bottom) proton decoupled carbon-13 spectrum

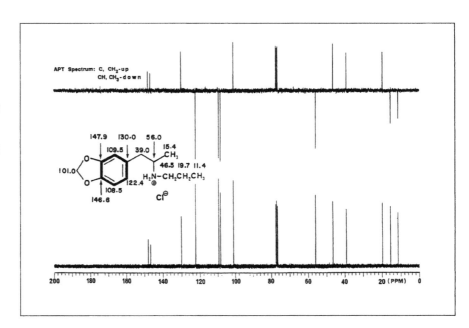

source (H⁺), or changing the temperature of the probe (sample), you can alter the dynamics of the experiment. The practitioner should be aware of this as it represents a potentially serious problem.

The other standard experiment for determining carbon multiplicity, the DEPT experiment (Doddrell, 1982), involves a polarization transfer scheme in which proton polarization (abundant nucleus) is transferred to the carbon-13 nucleus (rare spin nucleus) and modulated by the one bond coupling constant (^{1}JCH).

In this experiment, only protonated carbons will appear (quaternary carbons including residual solvent resonances are suppressed). The "raw" DEPT data results in three types of subspectra:

1. an all protonated carbon spectrum;
2. a methine carbon only spectrum; and
3. a spectrum in which the methine and methyl carbon resonances are phased up and the methylene carbon resonances are phased down.

These spectra may be subsequently combined to generate a set of what are referred to as "edited" DEPT spectra. For the purposes of identification, a normal proton decoupled carbon-13 spectrum needs to be collected and plotted along with, in this case, the edited DEPT data. Figure 4.32 illustrates

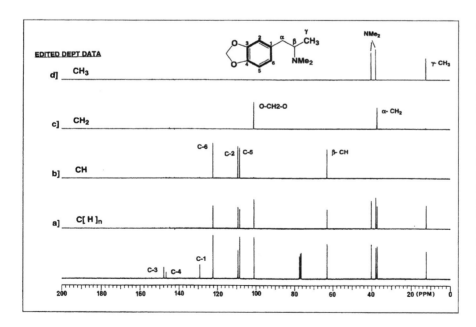

Figure 4.32
Carbon-13 NMR spectra (75 MHz, CDCl₃) of N,N-dimethyl MDA. Bottom spectrum. proton decoupled carbon-13 spectrum showing all carbon resonances. Upper spectra (a)–(d). Proton decoupled edited DEPT data (a) all protonated carbon resonances (Note: the absence of the quaternary carbons C-1, C-3, and C-4 as well as the solvent 3-line pattern centered at 77 ppm), (b) CH—subspectrum, (c) CH₂—subspectrum, (d) CH₃—subspectrum

a typical result including proton decoupled carbon-13 spectrum together with the corresponding edited DEPT data.

The advantage of the DEPT experiment is that data can be obtained very quickly with good sensitivity relative to the simple proton decoupled carbon-13 spectra and the solvent peak in this instance is suppressed. The solvent behaves like a quaternary carbon resonance. There is no proton attached to the solvent and therefore no polarization transfer takes place. This is an advantage since the solvent signal may very well obscure carbon resonances that are of interest which are present in the carbon spectrum of the sample. A disadvantage of the DEPT experiment generally occurs when the proton resonances of the sample are dynamically broadened due to some exchange process (exchange broadening). The spin-spin relaxation (T_2), which is related to the line width-at-half-height ($v_{1/2}$), is short and the dynamics of the polarization transfer in the DEPT experiment competes with T_2 relaxation. The result is that the carbon signals from these protonated carbons can disappear (no polarization transfer takes place). This is a potentially serious caveat to the DEPT experiment since, as we saw with the APT experiment, chemical information about the sample is being deleted. The practitioner needs to be aware of this.

Survey proton and carbon-13 data together with the carbon-13 multiplicity information (APT and/or DEPT) represent the essential minimum data necessary for the identification and structural characterization of a complete unknown. For a sample containing a substance of potentially known structure, a comparative analysis of the simple proton and/or carbon-13 spectrum with spectra obtained from an authentic sample may be all that is necessary.

The development of 2-dimensional (2-D) NMR (Claridge, 1999; Richarz, 1982; Ernst, 1992; van der Ven, 1995) in the late 1970s and to the present day has revolutionized the process of structure elucidation by NMR. The 2-D experiment allows the correlation information to be obtained via a variety of mechanisms and spread into two frequency dimensions which involves manipulation (Freeman, 1997) of the three basic characteristics of any NMR spectrum: chemical shift, spin-spin coupling, and spin lattice relaxation (T_1). Table 4.1 provides a brief summary of a few of the useful 2-D experiments which are currently in use together with the chemical information that is associated with the NMR experiment.

Experiments with a "g" in front are a pulsed field gradient variant. They provide the same chemical information as their carbon detected counterpart but data collection is generally faster and lower level (small) samples can be done. Experiments that are in italics are proton (as opposed to carbon) detected experiments.

2-D Experiment	Correlation Observed	Information Content
COSY, gCOSY	H,H correlation	H,H spin coupling
DQCOSY, gDQCOSY		
TOSCY, gTOCSY		
ECOSY, PECOSY		
HOM2DJ	H, J correlation	H,H couplings
HET2DJ	C, J correlation	$^1J_{C-H}$ couplings
HETCOR, *HMQC*	H,C correlation	direct $^1J_{C-H}$ bonding
gHMQC		
FLOCK, COLOC	H,C correlation	long-range $^nJ_{C-H}$
HMBC, gHMBC	H,C correlation	long-range $^nJ_{C-H}$
NOESY, ROESY	H,H correlation	stereochemistry,
		H-H distance
INADEQUATE	$^{13}C,^{13}C$ correlation	carbon framework

Table 4.1

Summary of useful 2-D experiments

All 2-D experiments share common elements. There is a preparation period, an incremented evolution period (t_1), a mixing period, and a detection period (t_2). The preparation period can be as simple as a fixed delay and a pulse applied repetitively and in a reproducible manner for each increment of t_1 or it can be as complex as the double quantum filter elements found in the 2-D INADEQUATE (Buddrus, 1987) experiment. The evolution time (t_1, usually an incremented evolution time, but there are constant time evolution periods used in certain heteronuclear 2-D experiments, e.g., COLOC) is a time period during which evolution of an NMR measurable parameter occurs based on what information is being sought. The mixing time can be a simple fixed delay (e.g., as in NOESY) or a pulse (e.g., COSY). A pulse usually (but not always) precedes the detection period (t_2) and the final FID is collected. The resulting information is Fourier transformed to create a 3-dimensional plot that resembles a topographical map.

The 2-D experiments permit elucidation of structural details, sometimes subtle details that show themselves. For simple assignments of ^1H and ^{13}C res-

Figure 4.33

The 2-dimensional ^1H, ^1H—COSY spectrum (300 MHz, CDCl₃) of the phencyclidine analogue (PCM)

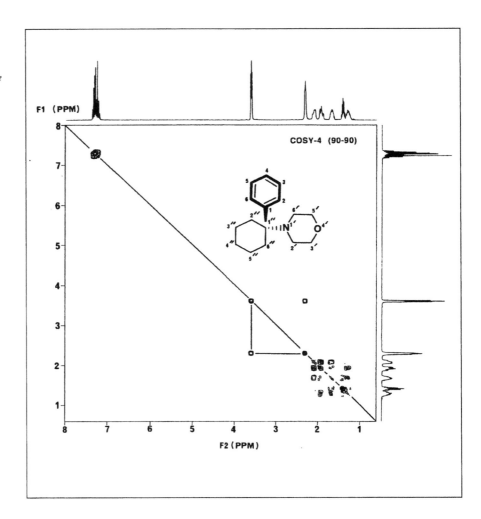

onances, one of the appropriate homonuclear proton correlations would be run in order to deduce proton coupling patterns and tell which protons are spin coupled to one another. It is this kind of information that would be characteristic of a particular structure. Figures 4.33 and 4.34 illustrate a simple COSY (Claridge, 1999) spectrum together with an expansion of the high field region of a PCP analogue (PCM). The proton resonances for the morpholine ring are clearly evident. There is no "cross coupling" between the cyclohexane ring protons and the protons on the morpholine ring. The complexity of the cyclohexane ring protons is also clearly evident from Figure 4.34.

The coupling complexity of the cyclohexane ring protons can be partially resolved and in the process a self-consistent assignment of both the ^1H spectrum and the ^{13}C spectrum can be confirmed.

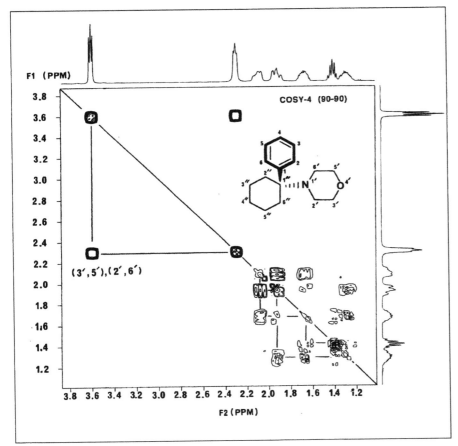

F1 (PPM)

COSY-4 (90-90)

$(3', 5'), (2', 6')$

F2 (PPM)

Figure 4.34

Expansion of the 2-dimensional COSY spectrum from Figure 4.33 showing the detailed correlation information from the respective non-aromatic six-membered rings

Figure 4.35 shows the results of the carbon-detected proton–carbon hetero-correlation experiment HETCOR (Bax, 1981, 1983; Rutar, 1984; Martin, 1988) ($J = 140$ Hz) for the PCP analogue (PCM). The connectivity (one-bond) correlation of the protons and the carbons of the morpholine ring are quite obvious. Expansion of the high-field region of the HETCOR data (Figure 4.36) actually allows both the carbon-13 resonances to be assigned and in the process the proton assignments become apparent. The geminal pairs of protons attached to C-2 and C-6 can be identified from the two correlation cross peaks corresponding to two protons having different chemical shifts but which correlate to the *same* carbon resonance. Similarly, the shift position of the geminal pairs of protons attached to C-3 and C-5 are also evident and are characterized by two correlation cross peaks, both of which correlate with the same carbon resonance. The C-4 carbon resonance may be assigned because of its intensity relative to the intensities of C-3/C-5 and C-2/C-6.

Figure 4.35

The carbon-detected ^1H, ^{13}C correlation spectrum (HETCOR) (75 MHz, CDCl$_3$, J = 140 Hz) for the phencyclidine analogue (PCM)

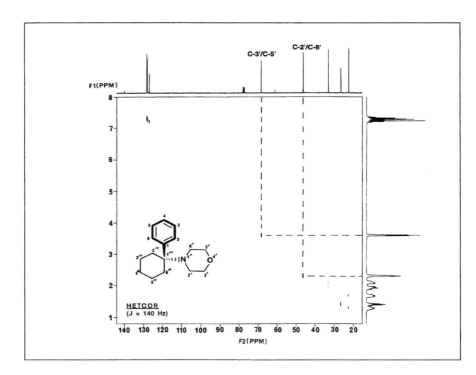

Figure 4.36

Expansion of the HETCOR spectrum from Figure 4.35 showing the detailed correlation information for the two non-aromatic six-membered rings

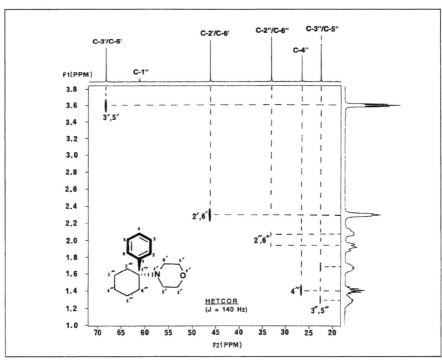

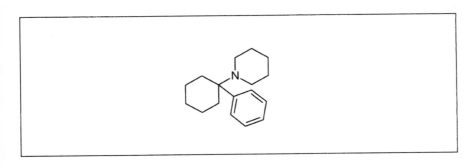

Figure 4.37
Chemical structure of
PCP

Clearly, the ability of 2-dimensional NMR experiments to establish structure and stereochemistry and to confirm, in this instance, proton and carbon-13 spectral assignments and, in a self-consistent manner, serve as a reliable structural tool for the structural elucidation of complete unknowns is of considerable importance to the forensic community. In the next few sections, you will see some of the specific applications that have been addressed in the area of forensic analysis of hallucinogenic drugs and the impact that 2-dimensional NMR is making in this important area.

Pharmaceutical laboratories and other researchers conducted much of the early NMR structural work reported on various drug molecules. Some of the compounds that exhibited pharmacological activity were ultimately investigated and results reported. A number of studies on these molecules have been summarized in comprehensive review articles that include literature citations to the work on the NMR of drugs of abuse (Groombridge, 1996).

Hallucinogens represent one of the challenges to forensic identification as most of the analogues seen have occurred in this area. This is a challenge because the primary identification tools, IR and GC/MS, used in forensic laboratories today have difficulty in providing definitive confirmation of identity of a substance when the compounds are structurally closely related. More than 200 psychotropic drugs have been reported (Shulgin, 1997, 2000) and their synthesis listed. Many of these are very similar in chemical structure. Many of the compounds do not have published spectral information. Without the use of NMR, these compounds could not be reliably and rapidly identified. The rapid growth of the Internet has made this information more readily available to a large portion of the population.

4.15 PHENCYCLIDINE AND RELATED SUBSTANCES

Parke Davis marketed phencyclidine (1-[1-phenylcyclohexyl]piperidine, PCP), Figure 4.37, as an anesthetic from 1958 to 1967. Because of its unpredictable

Figure 4.38

Chemical structure of PCC

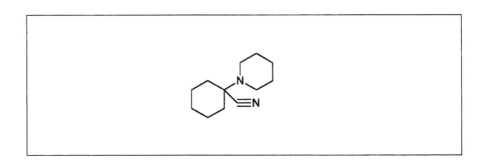

adverse effects, PCP was subsequently withdrawn from the commercial market. Since 1967, PCP, because of the hallucinogenic and stimulant qualities, has been manufactured primarily in clandestine laboratories. There are, however, neurotoxic side effects of PCP which can lead to "a psychosis clinically indistinguishable from schizophrenia" (Reynolds, 1989).

Most of the early NMR work on phencyclidines was directed toward establishing the conformational equilibrium dynamics of structurally modified phencyclidines. These investigations attempted to control receptor binding through appropriate substitution on the ring components. This provided valuable information about the biological effects of various substituted phencyclidine analogues that has been of considerable forensic value. As new analogues of PCP appeared on the street, they were subsequently identified and the spectra (IR, MS, NMR) reported. Other analogues were studied because of their ease of manufacture and for the potential to be seen in forensic samples.

The ^{1}H spectrum of PCP as well as some of its analogues exhibits complex overlapping resonances because of the presence of the two saturated rings (Eaton, 1983). Only with the advent of 2-D NMR techniques has the complexity of the patterns been sorted out. The free base of PCP shows line broadening due to certain molecular motions (ring flipping dynamics) at room temperature. The spectra of PCP and its analogues can easily be differentiated and can be compared against spectra of standards for identification. The ^{13}C spectrum is conceptually easier to comprehend (Eaton, 1983), although the chemical shifts of phenyl ring carbons were demonstrated to exhibit solvent and temperature dependence, presumably due to their influence on the conformational populations within the PCP molecule (Manoharan, 1983; Kamenka, 1987).

Often, samples submitted to forensic laboratories are for analysis and are not highly purified. Thus, the starting ingredients, intermediates and by-products of the synthesis are frequently present. The immediate precursor, 1-piperidino-cyclohexylcarbonitrile (PCC), Figure 4.38, has been characterized by proton (Bailey, 1976; Gagné, 1977) and carbon-13 NMR (Bailey, 1981). NMR has also

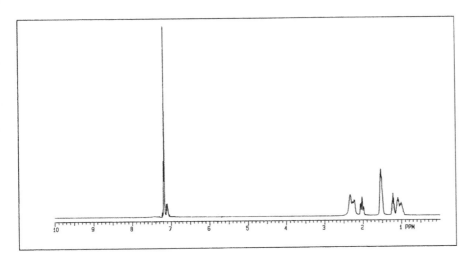

Figure 4.39
^{1}H spectra of phencyclidine hydrochloride

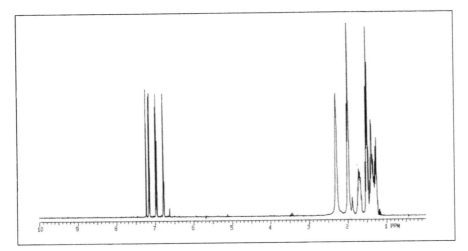

Figure 4.40
^{1}H spectra of thiophene analogue of phencyclidine hydrochloride

been used to characterize the starting ingredients and by-products. Often the presence of one by-product can help in the identification of the synthetic route used to prepare the PCP or its analogue.

More recently, the NMR spectra of PCP, PCC and analogues obtained at higher magnetic fields have been reported in the literature thus allowing better discrimination among the various compounds. Some of the analogues have appeared on the illicit drug market and some have been synthesized in an effort to facilitate the identification of additional new analogues. Figures 4.39, 4.40, and 4.41 show the ^{1}H spectra of PCP, 1-thienylcyclohexylpiperidine (TCP) and

Figure 4.41

¹H spectra of morpholine analogue of phencyclidine hydrochloride

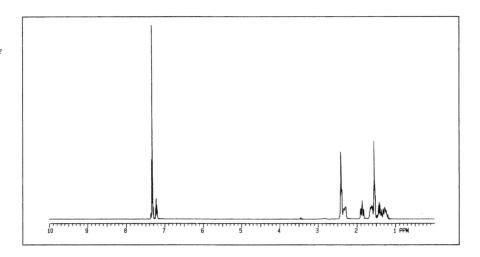

Figure 4.42

¹³C spectra of phencyclidine hydrochloride

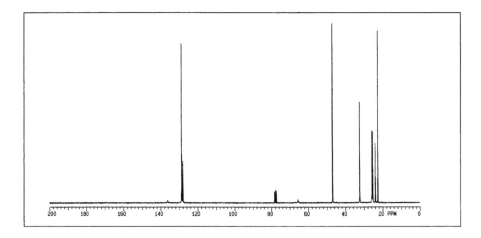

1-phenylcyclohexylpyrrolidine (PCPy), respectively. Figures 4.42, 4.43 and 4.44 show the ¹³C spectra of PCP, TCP and PCPy, respectively.

4.16 MDA AND ANALOGS

In the early 1970s Bailey et al. conducted a systematic investigation of methoxy- and methyl-substituted amphetamines. Initially, only the ¹H NMR (60 MHz) (Bailey, 1971, 1974, 1975, 1976, 1977) data was reported followed by reports of ¹³C NMR (Bailey, 1981, 1983) data in the 1980s. In many of these papers, NMR was used to confirm the structures suggested by IR and MS data. This is especially true in the identification of aromatic ring substitution

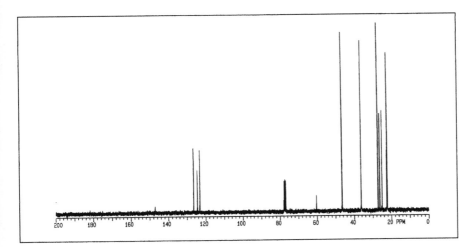

Figure 4.43
^{13}C spectra thiophene
analogue of phencyclidine
hydrochloride

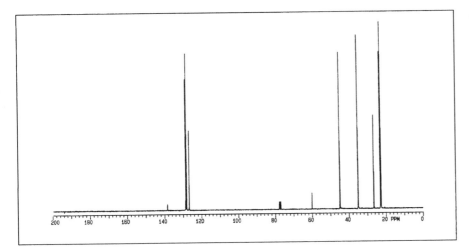

Figure 4.44
^{13}C spectra morpholine
analogue of phencyclidine
hydrochloride

patterns (Dawson, 1987, 1989; Delliou, 1983). This body of information is of particular importance when new analogues such as 4-bromo-2,5-dimethoxyamphetamine (DOB) (Figure 4.45), or phenethylamines such as 4-bromo-2,5-dimethoxyphenethylamine (2C-B) (Figure 4.46), were introduced into the illicit drug market (Ragan, 1985). The use of NMR, especially employing 2-D techniques, can reduce the time for identification of new compounds without the need for the synthesis of all possible combinations. NMR can be used to direct what compounds need to be synthesized for authentic comparison (Dal Cason, 1997).

Figure 4.45

Chemical structure of 4-bromo-2,5-dimethoxyamphetamine (DOB)

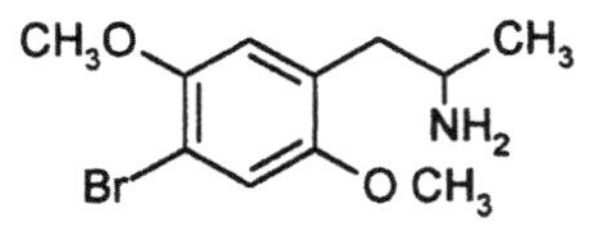

Figure 4.46

Chemical structure of 4-bromo-2,5-dimethoxyphenylethy-lamine (2C-B)

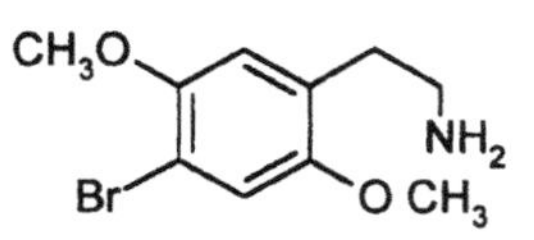

Figure 4.47

Chemical structure of MDA

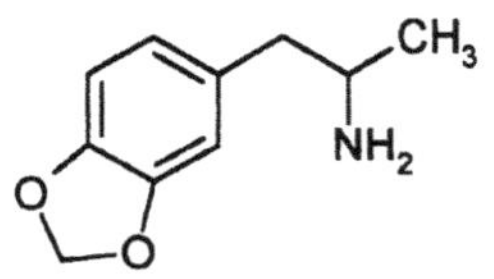

Dimethoxyamphetamines were reported as early as 1967. The earliest use of NMR to identify a new drug was to aid in the identification of 4-methyl-2,5-dimethoxyamphetamine (DOM or STP) (Martin, 1968). The various isomeric forms 2,3-, 2,4-, 2,5-, 3,4-, 3,5- were investigated to determine whether or not they could be distinguished (Bailey, 1971). 2-, 3-, 4-methoxy amphetamines were reported in 1971. All of the ^{1}H work was performed at 60 MHz (Bailey, 1974). Later, other substituted dimethoxyamphetamines—namely 4-methyl-2,5-dimethoxy amphetamine (Ono, 1970), 2,5-dimethoxy-4-bromoamphetamine, 2,5-dimethoxy-4-ethyloxyamphetamine, 2,5-dimethoxy-4-propylamphetamine, 2,5-dimethoxy-4-methylthioamphetamine—were reported (Bailey, 1971, 1974, 1975,1976, 1977, 1981, 1983).

3,4-Methylenedioxyamphetamine (MDA) (Figure 4.47) first appeared on the illicit drug market in the 1960s with its NMR data being reported as early as

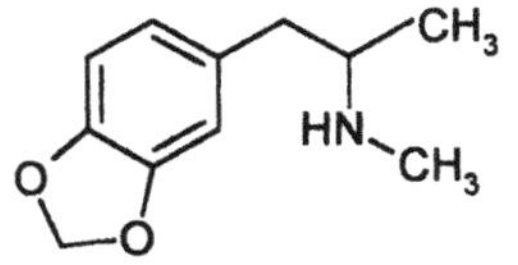

Figure 4.48
Chemical structure of
MDMA

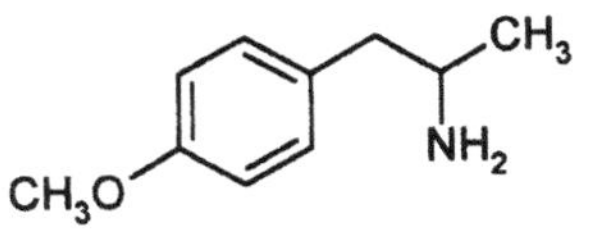

Figure 4.49
Chemical structure of
PMA

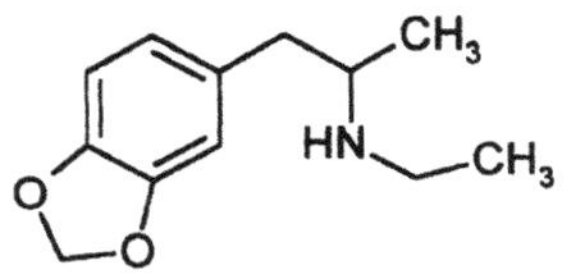

Figure 4.50
Chemical structure of
MDEA

1970 (Bellman, 1970; Lukaszewski, 1978). 3,4-Methylenedioxy-methamphet-amine (MDMA) (Bailey, 1975) (Figure 4.48) and 4-methoxyamphetamine (PMA) (Bailey, 1974) (Figure 4.49), among other MDA analogues, have been seen more recently with a huge increase in the number of tablets seized in the late 1990s. Other analogues such as 3,4-methylenedioxyethylamphetamine (MDEA) (Figure 4.50), *N*-propyl-MDA, *N*-isopropyl-MDA, *N*-butyl-MDA, *N*-isobutyl-MDA, and *N*-neobutyl-MDA, have been reported (Noggle, 1986). It was shown that the early NMRs (^{1}H 90 MHz) did not have the resolution sufficient to differentiate between MDA and 2,3-methylene dioxyamphetamine. As higher magnetic field NMR instrumentation became available this problem was resolved. Table 4.2 and Figure 4.51 provide a summary of the assigned ^{1}H chemical shifts for some MDA analogues and ^{13}C chemical shifts for the free bases and the hydrochloride salts, respectively. Table 4.3 provides a summary of the assigned ^{13}C chemical shifts for some MDA analogues.

Figure 4.51

Provides a summary of the assigned ^{13}C chemical shifts for some MDA analogues

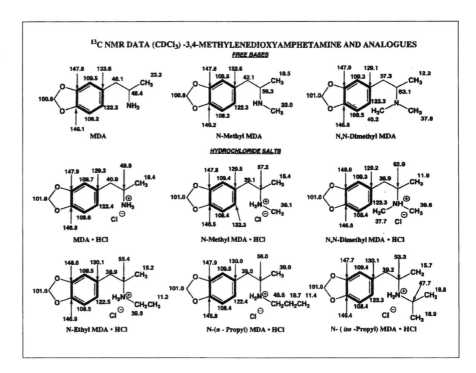

Table 4.2

^1H table of chemical shifts for several MDA analogues as the free bases

3,4-Methylenedioxyamphetamines — ^{1}H-NMR data (CDCl$_3$, 25°C) free bases

Proton	Proton chemical shifts, ppm (coupling constants, Hz)		
	(N=2)	(N=1)	(N=0)
H-2	6.61 d	6.65 d	6.66 d
	(1.2)	(1.2)	(1.6)
H-5	6.67 d	6.67 d	6.66 d
	(7.8)	(7.8)	(7.9)
H-6	6.56 dd	6.56 dd	6.60 dd
	(7.8, 1.2)	(7.8, 1.2)	(7.9, 1.6)
H-α	2.54 dd		3.41 dd
	(5.2, −13.4)		(3.1, −12.8)
H-α	2.36 dd	2.4–2.7 m	2.46 dd
	(8.2, −13.4)		(11.0, −12.8)
H-β	3.03 br.m.		3.39 br.m.
	(6.2, 5.2, 8.2)		
H-γ	1.03 d	1.00 d	1.19 d
	(6.2)	(6.2)	(7.0)
–O–CH$_2$–O–	5.85 s	5.88 s	5.86 s
N–CH$_3$	—	2.34 s	2.74 s
			2.72 s
			2.71 s
			2.69 s
N–H	1.4 br.s.	1.7 br.s.	—

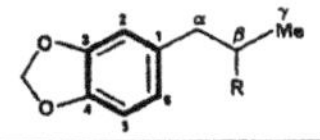

3,4-Methylenedioxyamphetamines — ¹H-NMR data (CDCl₃, 25°C) hydrochloride salts

R	Chemical shifts, ppm (coupling constants, Hz)										
	H-2	H-5	H-6	H-α	H-α	H-β	H-γ	-OCH₂O-	-NH	-N-CH₃	Other
$-N^+H_3$, Cl⁻*	6.66 d (1.4)	6.72 d (7.8)	6.62 dd (7.8, 1.4)	2.89 dd (7.5)	2.81 dd (7.0)	3.58 br.m.	1.37 d (6.6)	5.90 (s)	7.1 br.s.	—	—
$-N^+H_2-CH_3$, Cl⁻	6.65 d (1.6)	6.69 d (7.8)	6.61 dd (7.8, 1.6)	3.30 dd (−13.0) (4.0)	2.70 dd (−13.0) (4.0)	3.22 br.m.	1.28 d (6.5)	5.88 (s)	9.6 br.s.	2.65 (s)	—
$-N^+H(CH_3)_2$, Cl⁻	6.66 d (1.5)	6.66 d (7.8)	6.60 dd (7.8, 21.5)	3.40 dd (−12.4) (2.9)	2.45 dd (−12.4) (10.9)	3.35 br.m.	1.18 d (6.8)	5.86 (s)	12.3 br.s.	2.72 s 2.73 s 2.71 s 2.70 s	—
$-N^+H_2-CH_2CH_3$, Cl⁻	6.66 d (1.5)	6.68 d (7.9)	6.62 dd (7.9) (1.5)	3.42 dd (−13.0) (3.6)	2.72 dd (−13.0) (11.0)	3.22 br.m.	1.29 d (6.5)	5.89 (s)	9.65 br.s	—	CH₃, 1.48 d (7.3) CH₂, 3.35 br.m
$-N^+H_2-CH_2CH_2CH_3$, Cl⁻	6.70 dd (1.8, 0.5)	6.15 dd (7.8, 0.5)	6.66 dd (7.8, 1.8)	3.48 dd (−12.8) (3.5)	2.76 dd (−12.8) (11.0)	3.30 br.m.	1.34 d (6.5)	5.90 (s)	9.64 br.s.	—	CH₃, 0.99 d (7.4) CH₂, 1.99 dq (7.4, 7.8) CH₂, 2.98 br.m.
$-N^+H_2-CH(CH_3)_2$, Cl⁻	6.36 dd (1.8, 0.8)	6.68 dd (7.8, 0.8)	6.62 dd (7.8, 1.8)	3.43 dd (−13.0) (3.5)	2.80 dd (−13.0) (11.0)	3.30 br.m.	1.29 d (6.4)	5.87 (s)	9.39 br.s.	—	CH, 3.35 br.m. CH₃, 1.51 d (6.5) CH₃, 1.43 d (6.5)

*CF₃CO₂H added to enhance solubility in CDCl₃ solution.

Table 4.3
¹³C table of chemical shifts for several MDA analogues as the bases

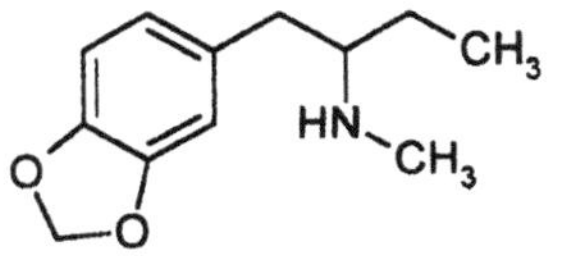

Figure 4.52
Chemical structure of MBDB

As can be expected, the proton spectra of MDA and N-hydroxy-MDA are similar (Dal Cason, 1989; Shimamine, 1990, 1993) but can be clearly differentiated by NMR spectroscopy. The hydroxy proton resonance was too broad to observe which contrasted the resonance measurements observed earlier for N-hydroxy-amphetamines, dimethoxyamphetamines, and others (Beckett, 1975; Mourad, 1985).

One of the areas where NMR is more readily suited is the identification of isomers. This has been demonstrated by the occurrence in Europe of N-methyl-1-(1,3-benzodioxol-5-yl)-2-butanamine (MBDB) (Figure 4.52). When compared to the isomeric forms 3,4-methylenedioxy-N-ethylamphetamine (MDEA) or N,N-dimethyl-MDA (Figure 4.53), the three compounds can be differentiated by careful comparison of MS but the ¹H NMR spectra are very different (Nichols, 1986; Azafonov, 1990).

Figure 4.53

Chemical structure of N,N-dimethyl MDA

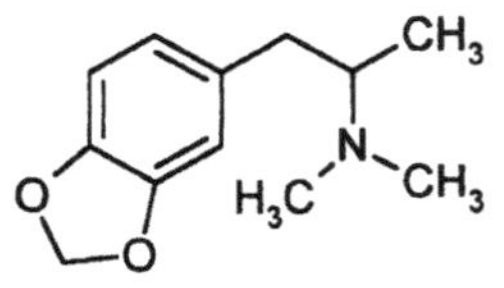

Figure 4.54

Chemical structure of mescaline

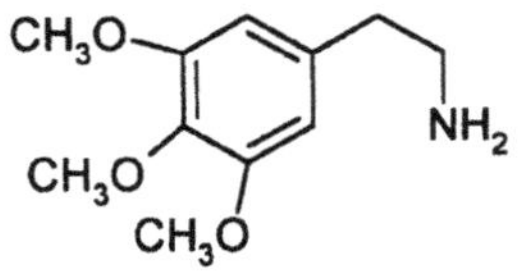

Figure 4.55

Chemical structure of 2,4,5-TMA

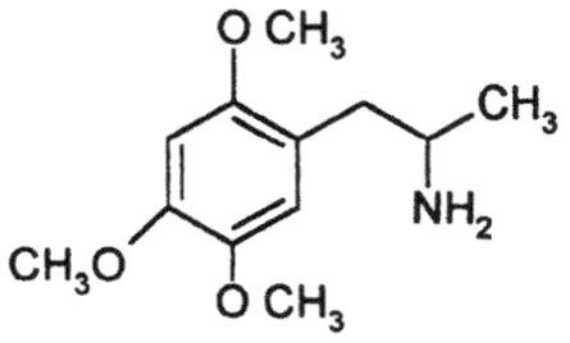

Other related compounds—mescaline (3,4,5-trimethoxyphenethylamine) (Ono, 1970) (Figure 4.54), 2,4,5-trimethoxyamphetamine (Foster, 1992) (Figure 4.55), 4-bromo-2,5-dimethoxyphenethylamine (2C-B) (Ragan, 1985) (Figure 4.46)—as well as other ring substituted compounds have been studied and data reported. NMR provides a definitive solution to the identification of these compounds provided the nonproton compound or group is identified by other means (e.g., halogens). 2,4,5-Trisubstituted permutations (16 possible combinations) have been resolved using lanthanide shift behavior (Dawson, 1987, 1989) or nuclear Overhauser effect (NOE) difference methods (Dawson, 1989). NMR is the only technique that can provide a variety of different means to attack and resolve an identification problem. Figure 4.56 and Figure 4.57 show the ^{1}H and ^{13}C spectra of mescaline, respectively.

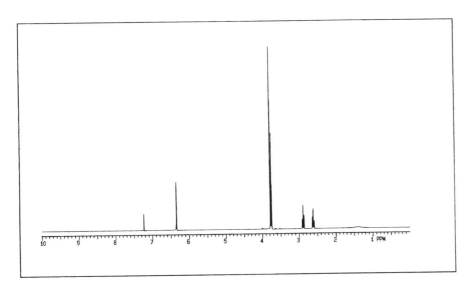

Figure 4.56
^1H spectra of mescaline

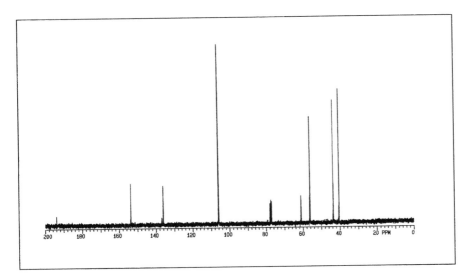

Figure 4.57
^{13}C spectra of mescaline

4.17 ERGOT AND OTHER INDOLE ALKALOIDS

Ergot is the dried material of the parasitic fungus *Claviceps purpurea*, which grows on rye and other grain. It yields four main alkaloid classes: clavines, lysergic acids, lysergic amides, and ergot peptides. Ergot alkaloids have also been found in many plant species, with the *Convolvulacea* (morning glories) also having mixed lysergic acid substances. Lysergic acid diethylamide (LSD)

(Figure 4.58) is derived from ergot. Its discovery by Hofmann in 1943 was the result of investigation of lysergic acid derivatives for the treatment of migraine headaches.

The abuse of LSD for its hallucinogenic quality was extensive in the 1960s, encompassing worldwide use. There was a subsequent decline in the 1970s when it was controlled in virtually every country around the world. However, it reemerged in the 1980s more often on impregnated paper ("blotter acid") or gelatin squares. The analysis of LSD poses a unique set of problems owing to, first, the relative small amounts required for a typical dosage (10–100 μg) as well as its sensitivity to light and/or high temperatures and to the presence of moisture. Detection of amounts of LSD below 10 μg is feasible with ^{1}H NMR at 400 MHz using 1–2 hour accumulation on a 5 mm probe. Application of micro-probe technology in conjunction with cryoprobe technology can significantly reduce the analysis time at this level and permit a whole host of proton-detected 2-D homonuclear and heteronuclear experiments to be run on LSD to further confirm structure. Applications of this technology would also push the limits of detection of LSD even lower (e.g., Varian and Nalorac Web site).

The ^{1}H spectrum of LSD has been discussed in only a few publications, with the ^{1}H NMR assignments suggested by Hoffman and Nichols (1985) based on the earlier detailed work of Bailey and Grey (1972). Rings C and D both adopt half-chair conformations, with the D ring in a "flap-up" mode. Coupling constants between H-8 and the two protons H-7 provide evidence for the conformational disposition. The spectra are made more complex due to the ergoline framework which exhibits significant long-range coupling pathways.

Proton spectra of LSD in aqueous solution are more poorly resolved than for the free base, and it is apparent that there is some variation from sample to sample. This variation reflects small changes in pH evident in the $N6$ protonation at near neutral pH.

Figure 4.58
Chemical structure of LSD

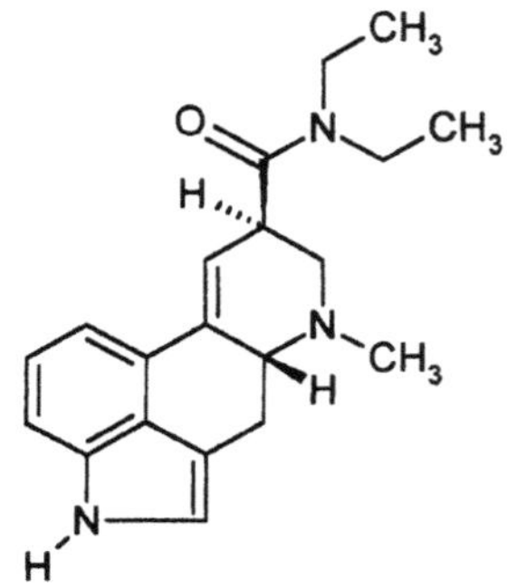

Proton NMR data has been used to reveal a problem with supposed pure reference material of LSD tartrate. Neville et al. (1992) showed that a reference standard supplied from a commercial firm contained a stoichiometric excess of tartrate (65%). It is customary for forensic laboratories to use certified commercial samples for qualitative and quantitative analyses. Problems such as this can lead to the overestimation of LSD quantity. NMR can be used to verify the validity of the standard and provide an alternate method to check the accuracy of the quantitative determination.

The ^{13}C spectra of LSD (free base and tartrate) have been reported by Neville et al. (1992) and there were earlier partial data and assignments given by Kidric and Kocjan (1982). Shift differences between LSD and iso-LSD were up to 5.5 ppm.

Because forensic evidence can be challenged in court by an isomer defense, work was done to establish the analysis for the differentiation of LSD and lysergic acid methylpropylamide (LAMPA). The chromatographic analytical techniques had problems distinguishing between the two; MS fragmentation patterns had only significant small differences (Clark, 1989); the ^{1}H NMR showed a simple distinction between LSD and LAMPA (Figure 4.59), even at lower magnetic fields (Bailey, 1972, 1973; Neville, 1992). The same is true for the epimers LSD and iso-LSD. Although no data has been presented for the methyl-isopropylamide analogue of LSD, new prediction software has demonstrated the possibility for ease of identification.

4.18 TRYPTAMINES

Psilocin (Figure 4.60), psilocybin (Figure 4.61) (from *Psilocybe* mushroom) and bufotenine (Figure 4.62) are the best-known naturally occurring indoles.

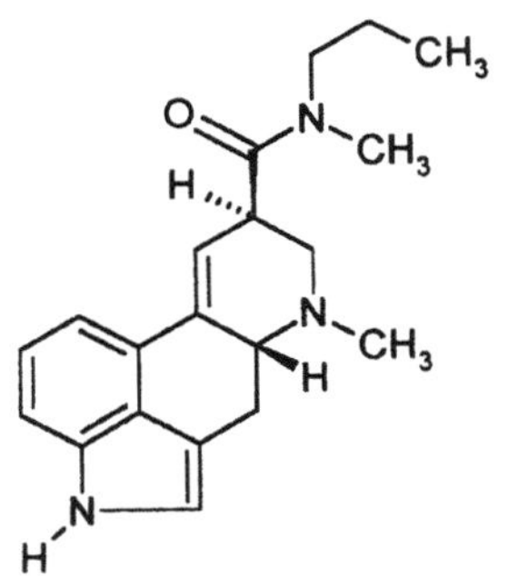

Figure 4.59

Chemical structure of LAMPA

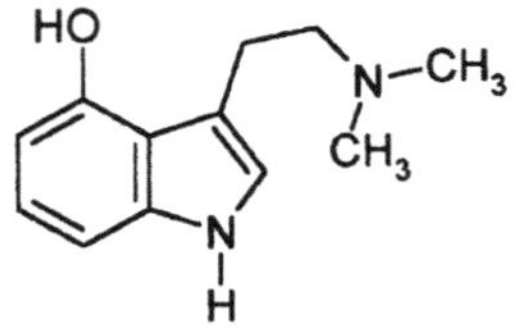

Figure 4.60

Chemical structure of psilocin

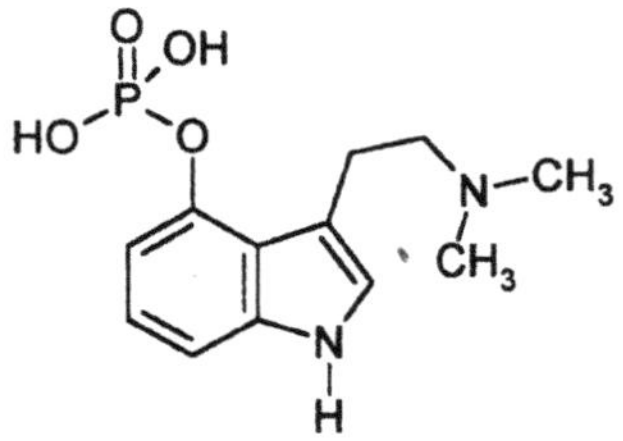

Figure 4.61

Chemical structure of psilocybin

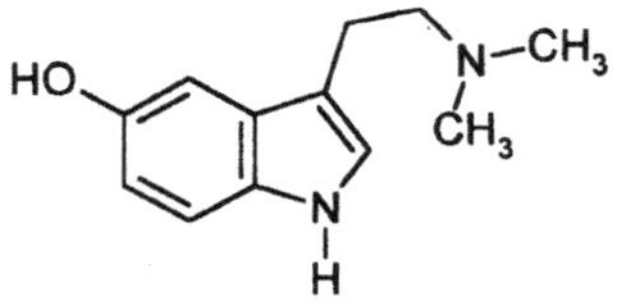

Figure 4.62

Chemical structure of bufotenine

Psilocin and bufotenine are isomers which give similar MS fragmentation patterns and have small differences in GC retention times. They should give readily discernable ^{1}H spectra, but the only reported spectrum of bufotenine (Bailey, 1975) is unclear.

Other research into natural product isolation has reported ^{1}H and ^{13}C spectra of other indoles. Among others, the ^{13}C shift data for *N*-methyl- and *N,N*-dimethyltryptamine (Mills, 1993) and the ^{1}H spectra of *N,N*-dimethyltryptamine (Poupat, 1976). Morales-Rios (1987) has published an extensive review of indole ^{13}C NMR data. Ranc and Jurs (1993) developed models for the prediction of ^{13}C shifts for this class of compounds.

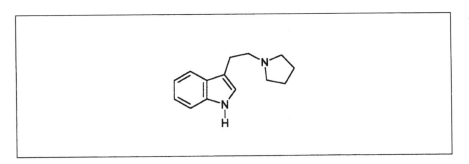

Figure 4.63
Chemical structure of
tetramethylene tryptamine

Tetramethylene tryptamine (Figure 4.63), a highly unusual tryptamine substance, was identified by Cowie et al. (1982) using MS and ^{1}H NMR. An intermediate from incomplete reduction was also identified, *N*-[1-hydroxy-2(3-indolyl)ethyl]pyrrolidine.

REFERENCES

Azafonov, N.E., Sedishev, I.P., and Zhulin, V.M. (1990) *Bull. Acad. Sci. USSR Div. Chem. Sci.*, 738. English translation of *Izv. Akad. Nauk SSSR, Ser. Khim.*, p. 829.

Bailey, K. (1971) *J. Pharm. Sci.*, 60, p. 1232.

Bailey, K., and Grey, A.A. (1972) *Can. J. Chem.*, 50, p. 3876.

Bailey, K., and Legault, D. (1981) *Anal. Chim. Acta*, 123, p. 75.

Bailey, K., and Legault, D. (1981) *J. Forens. Sci.*, 26, p. 27.

Bailey, K., and Legault, D. (1981) *J. Forens. Sci.*, 26, p. 368.

Bailey, K., and Legault, D. (1981) *Org. Magn. Reson.*, 15, p. 68.

Bailey, K., and Legault, D. (1983) *Org. Magn. Reson.*, 21, p. 391.

Bailey, K., Beckstead, H.D., Legault, D., and Verner, D. (1974) *J. Assoc. Off. Anal. Chem.*, 57, p. 1134.

Bailey, K., By, A.W., Graham, K.C., and Verner, D. (1971) *J. Assoc. Off. Anal. Chem.*, 49, p. 3143.

Bailey, K., By, A.W., Legault, D., and Verner, D. (1975) *J. Assoc. Off. Anal. Chem.*, 58, p. 62.

Bailey, K., Chow, A.Y.K., Downie, R.H., and Pike, R.K. (1976) *J. Pharm. Pharmacol.*, 28, p. 713.

Bailey, K., Gagné, D.R., and Pike, R.K. (1976) *J. Assoc. Off. Anal. Chem.*, 59, p. 1162.

Bailey, K., Gagné, D.R., Legault, D., and Pike, R.K. (1977) *J. Assoc. Off. Anal. Chem.*, 60, p. 642.

Bailey, K., Legault, D., and Verner, D. (1974) *J. Assoc. Off. Anal. Chem.*, 57, p. 70.

Bailey, K., Verner, D., and Legault, D. (1973) *J. Assoc. Off. Anal. Chem.*, 53, p. 88.

Bax, A., and Morris, G.A. (1981) *J. Magn. Res.*, 42, p. 501.

Bax, A. (1983) *J. Magn. Res.*, 53, p. 517.

Beckett, A.H., Haya, K., Jones, G.R., and Morgan, P.H. (1975) *Tetrahedron*, 31, p. 1531.

Bellman, S.W., Turczan, J.W., and Kram, T.C. (1970) *J. Forens. Sci.*, 15, p. 261.

Buddrus, J., and Bauer, H. (1987) *Angew. Chem. Int. Ed. Engl.*, 26, p. 625.

Claridge, T.D.W. (1999) *High Resolution NMR Techniques in Organic Chemistry*, Oxford: Pergamon (Elsevier).

Claridge, T.D.W. (1999) in *High Resolution NMR Techniques in Organic Chemistry*, Chapter 8, pp. 277–339. Pergamon (Elsevier), Oxford.

Claridge, T.D.W. (1999) in *High Resolution NMR Techniques in Organic Chemistry*, Chapter 5, pp. 148–220. Pergamon (Elsevier), Oxford.

Clark, C.C. (1989) *J. Forens. Sci.*, 34, p. 532.

Cowie, J.S., Holtman, A.L., and Jones, L.V. (1982) *J. Forens. Sci.*, 27, p. 527.

Dal Cason, T.A. (1989) *J. Forens. Sci.*, 34, p. 928.

Dal Cason, T.A., Meyers, J.A., and Lankin, D.C. (1997) *Forens. Sci. Int.*, 86, pp. 15–24.

Dawson, B.A., and Avdovich, H.W. (1987) *Can. Soc. Forens. Sci. J.*, 20, p. 29.

Dawson, B.A., and Neville, G.A. (1989) *Can. Soc. Forens. Sci. J.*, 22, p. 195.

Delliou, D. (1983) *Forens. Sci. Int.*, 21, p. 259.

Doddrell, D.M, Pegg, D.T., and Bendall, M.R. (1982) *J.Magn.Res.*, 48, p. 323.

Eaton, T.A., Houk, K.N., Watkins, S.F., and Fronczek, F.R. (1983) *J. Med. Chem.*, 26, p. 479.

Ernst, R.R, Bodenhausen, G., and Wokaun, A. (1992) *Principles of Nuclear Magnetic Resonance in One and Two Dimensions*, Oxford: Clarendon Press.

Foster, B.C., McLeish, J., Wilson, D.L., Whitehouse, L.W., Zamecnik, J., and Lodge, B.A. (1992. *Xenobiotica*, 22, p. 1383.

Freeman, R. (1997) *Spin Choreography. Basic Steps in High Resolution NMR*, Oxford: Spektrum Academic Publishers and University Press.

Fyfe, C. (1983) *Solid State NMR for Chemists*, Guelph, Ontario, Canada: C.F.C. Press.

Gagné, D.R., and Pike, R.K. (1977) *J. Assoc. Off. Anal. Chem.*, 60, p. 32.

Groombridge, C.J. (1996) *NMR Spectroscopy in Forensic Sciences*, Annual Reports on NMR Spectroscopy, Volume 12.

Hoffman, A.J., and Nichols, D.E. (1985) *J. Med. Chem.*, 28, p. 1252.

Kamenka, J.M., and Chicheportiche, R. (1987) *Eur. J. Med. Chem.*, 22, p. 193.

Kidrič, J., and Kocjan, D. (1982) *Stud. Phys. Theor. Chem.*, 18, p. 35.

Lukaszewski, T. (1978) *J. Assoc. Off. Anal. Chem.*, 61, p. 1978.

Manoharan, M., Eliel, E.L., and Carroll, F.I. (1983) *Tetrahedron Lett.*, 24, p. 1855.

Martin, G.E., and Zektzer, A.S. (1988) *Two Dimensional NMR Methods for Establishing Molecular Connectivity. A Chemist's Guide to Experiment Selection, Performance, and Interpretation*, New York: VCH Publishers.

Martin, G.E., and Zektzer, A.S. (1988) *Magn. Res. Chem.*, 26, p. 631

Martin, R.J., and Alexander, T.G. (1968) *J. Assoc. Off. Anal. Chem.*, 51, p. 159.

Mehring, Michael (1983) *High Resolution NMR in Solids*, Berlin/Heidelberg/New York: Springer-Verlag.

Mills III, T., and Roberson, J.C. (1993) *Instrumental Data for Drug Analysis*, Vols 1–5, 2nd edn, New York: Elsevier.

Morales, M.S., Espinera, J., and Joseph-Nathan, P. (1987) *Magn. Reson. Chem.*, 25, p. 377.

Mourad, M.S., Varma, R.S., and Kabalka, G.W. (1985) *J. Org. Chem.*, 50, p. 133.

Neville, G.A., Beckstead, H.D., Black, D.B., Dawson, B.A., and Ethier, J.-C. (1992) *Can. J. Appl. Spectrosc.*, 37, p. 149.

Nichols, D.E., Hoffman, A.J., Oberlender, R.A., Jacob, P., and Shulgin, A.T. (1986) *J. Med. Chem.*, 29, p. 2009.

Noggle, F.T., DeRuiter, J., and Long, M.J. (1986) *J. Assoc. Off. Anal. Chem.*, 69, p. 681.

Ono, M. (1970) *Nippon Hoigaku Zasshi*, 33, p. 339.

Patt, S.L., and Shoolery, J.N. (1982) *J. Magn. Res.*, 46, p. 535.

Poupat, C., Ahond, A., and Sévenet T., (1976) *Phytochem.*, 15, p. 2019.

Ragan, F.A., Hite, S.A., Samuels, M.S., and Garey, R.E. (1985) *J. Anal. Toxicol.*, 9, p. 91.

Ranc, M.L., and Jurs, P.C. (1993) *Anal. Chim. Acta*, 280, p. 145.

Reynolds, J.E.F. (ed.) (1989) *Martindale. The Extra Pharmacopoeia*, London: The Pharmaceutical Press.

Richarz, R., Ammann, W., and Wirthlin, T. (1982) No. Z-15 in *Varian Instruments at Work*, pp. 1–19 and references cited therein.

Rutar, V. (1984) *J. Magn. Res.*, 58, p. 306.

Shimamine, M., Takahashi, K., and Nakahara, Y. (1990) *Eisei Shikensho Hokoku*, 108, p. 118.

Shimamine, M., Takahashi, K., and Nakahara, Y. (1993) *Eisei Shikensho Hokoku*, 111, p. 66.

Shulgin, A.T., and Shulgin, A. (1991) *PIHKAL, A Chemical Love Story*, Berkeley, CA: Transform Press.

Shulgin, A.T., and Shulgin, A. (1997) *TIHKAL, The Continuation*, Berkeley, CA: Transform Press.

van de Ven, F.J.M. (1995) in *Multidimensional NMR in Liquids. Basic Principles and Experimental Methods*, New York: Wiley-VCH.

Wehrli, F.W., and Marchand, A.P. (1988) in *Interpretation of Carbon-13 NMR Spectra*, 2nd edn, New York: John Wiley & Sons.

CHAPTER 5

COCAINE: METHODS OF FORENSIC ANALYSIS

David A. Kidwell & Sotiris A. Athanaselis

U.S. Naval Research Laboratory, Washington, DC

University of Athens, Athens, Greece

Contents

5.1 INTRODUCTION

Cocaine is an odorless white crystalline powder usually found in the form of a salt, such as cocaine hydrochloride. It is considered the purification product of coca paste, an extract of the leaves of the coca bush (*Erythroxylum coca* or *Erythroxylum novogranatense*), where it is found as a natural alkaloid. Cocaine is purified from coca paste by dissolving the paste in dilute sulfuric acid, oxidizing impurities with potassium permanganate, filtering, and adding aqueous ammonia to precipitate the cocaine free base (Casale and Klein, 1993). The free base is dissolved in either acetone or ether, and the cocaine hydrochloride is precipitated by addition of concentrated hydrochloric acid. Cocaine can also be prepared by synthesis from ecgonine or by total synthesis via the Mannich reaction (Mannich, 1934; Casale, 1987). Cocaine is an optical active molecule (contains two optical centers, so there are four possible isomers) when isolated from natural sources but may be racemic when synthesized via the Mannich reaction (Allen et al., 1981). The optical isomers are much less physiologically active than is the natural material (Carroll et al., 1991).

Coca paste is an off-white, beige, or cream-colored powder. It is generally damp and coarse and contains aggregates. It is the initial extraction product of the coca leaf. Coca paste is prepared from the coca leaf by placing the leaves in lime water and macerating, usually by foot, with kerosene or other hydrocarbon solvent. The kerosene is removed and extracted with dilute sulfuric acid.

Handbook of Forensic Drug Analysis

Frederick P. Smith, Editor

The acid extract is made basic with either limestone or lime, thereby precipitating the coca paste.

Crack is cocaine base (also called *freebase*) obtained from the cocaine salt in order to be suitable for smoking. The name *crack* refers to the noise made by the crystals as they pop when heated. Crack is obtained by dissolving the cocaine salt in water, adding baking soda or ammonia, and collecting the precipitated powder. It is important to mention that this method does not require the involvement of any solvent, so the danger of explosion or fire is minimal. A hard, flaky material is produced, in contrast to the "freebase process," where ether or other flammable solvent is used and the material produced is powdery. Because of the volatile solvents, the possibilities for explosion or fire is considerable. The most common method to prepare crack in the U.S. is to heat cocaine hydrochloride in a microwave with baking soda and a limited amount of water. This method is very rapid and avoids collecting precipitates or evaporating solvents but produces less pure material. Crack is usually found in the form of white chips, chunks, or rocks and is often sold in vials. It is either smoked in specially designed water pipes or sprinkled on tobacco or marijuana to be smoked as a cigarette. Crack is sometimes used with heroin to lengthen the physiological high.

The most common street names for cocaine products are coco, coke, koks, bazooka, bazucos, speedball, C-dust, flake, crack, rock, stardust, lady, snow, big C, gin, candy, and blanche (U.S. Department of Justice, 1994).

5.2 ORIGIN OF COCAINE SAMPLES

The origin of cocaine samples can be determined through the analytical determination of the presence or absence of other coca alkaloids, manufacturing by-products from its synthesis, adulterants, or diluents (Cooper and Allen, 1984; Casale and Waggoner, 1991). The presence of other coca alkaloids, such as *cis*- and *trans*-cinnamoylcocaine, -tropococaine, and -truxillines, indicates the natural origin of the sample. Truxillic and truxinic acids may also be produced as a result of the hydrolysis of truxilline. Cuscohygrine and hygrine are two other alkaloids found only in coca leaf and not in cocaine. Benzoylecgonine, methylecgonine, and ecgonine can be found as a result of the hydrolysis of cocaine. Methyl ecgonidine is also a hydrolysis product of cocaine, but it can also result from the thermal degradation of cocaine or the truxillines in the injection port of the GC (Schlesinger, 1985). Benzoic acid is also detected when this decomposition occurs. If potassium permanganate has been used for the purification of cocaine, *N*-formyl cocaine may be detected due to oxidation of the *N*-methyl group of cocaine. Additionally, norcocaine resulting from a Schiff's base intermediate during the permanganate oxidation or from the

N-demethylation of cocaine, may be produced. More recently, through the analysis of carbon and nitrogen isotopes, the region where the cocaine leaf was grown may be identified (Ehleringer et al., 2000).

5.3 NONINSTRUMENTAL METHODS FOR DETECTION OF COCAINE

5.3.1 CHECK FOR ADULTERATION

Most cocaine samples are totally soluble in ethanol. If the samples are adulterated ("cut") by a carbohydrate such as lactose, glucose, mannitol, or sorbitol, insoluble colorless crystals appear in the solution. This insoluble material can be isolated and further analyzed by IR spectroscopy. All carbohydrates are soluble in ethanol to various extents, so the amount of the insoluble material gives only a rough idea about the extent to which the cocaine samples have been adulterated.

5.3.2 CRYSTALLINE PRECIPITATES (Allen et al., 1981; Clarke, 1969; Julian and Plein, 1983; U.S. Dept. of Justice, 1986; U.N., 1986)

Although still widely used as a preliminary positive test, better and less subjective analyses are available for screening. The crystals for observation are prepared on microscope slides. A very small amount of the suspicious sample is placed on a microscope slide, and one drop of the relative reagent is added. Crystals appear in seconds to minutes on the slide and then are covered with a coverslip. A polarizing microscope should be used for the observation of the crystals; however, a standard, bright-field microscope can also be used for the evaluation of crystal morphology.

In making an identification, the crystals given by an "unknown" and a known sample are compared under the same magnification, normally from 80 to 125×. A casual glance at each is not sufficient. One must know how to observe microcrystals, with attention to details. Taking photos for future evaluation can be extremely useful.

It must be kept in mind that the results of the crystal tests performed on a street sample must be compared with those of standard cocaine and must always be confirmed with a more appropriate analytical method. Crystal tests are subjective and thus open to question in court. If used routinely, the analyst should be able to articulate his/her reasons for the similarity of the questioned precipitate to that prepared from a standard.

Platinic chloride test (microcrystal test): Two milligrams of the sample are placed on a microscope slide and dissolved in one drop of 1 N hydrochloric acid. One

Figure 5.1

Crystals obtained from reaction of cocaine hydrochloride with platinum chloride: If formed rapidly, the platinum chloride cocaine crystals form numerous small, multibladed swords, as shown in the upper left of this collage; if formed slowly, the crystals produce long, slender swords, as shown in the middle.

drop of a 5% (aqueous, in 3 N HCL, or in 10% glycerol in water) solution of platinic chloride is added. The instantly resulting pointed, pale yellow crystals are viewed under a microscope and are compared to crystals formed by standard cocaine (see Figure 5.1). For optimum results, different dilutions of the test material or the hydrochloric acid should be tried. This is a sensitive test, and crystals are formed in dilutions up to 1:4000.

Gold chloride test: A highly sensitive and more characteristic crystal test for cocaine than the platinic chloride test is with *gold chloride* (5% aqueous gold chloride or 3–5% acid gold chloride in 25% acetic acid). A few small crystals are formed, even in a dilution of 1:20,000. When formed slowly, they are long rods with many short plates running out at right angles from the main axis (see Figure 5.2). However, their shapes vary according to the concentration.

Gold bromide test: Similar to the gold chloride crystals, variously skeletonized crystals (often crosses or Xs with ragged blade arms) are formed when gold bromide solution reacts with cocaine (see Figure 5.3). Gold bromide solution is prepared by dissolving 5 g of gold chloride and 5 g of sodium bromide in 100 mL of water.

Lead iodide test: Cocaine with lead iodide solution gives spiked balls (see Figure 5.4). The sensitivity of the test is 1:3000. For the preparation of lead iodide solution, a 30% w/v solution of potassium acetate in water is adjusted to pH 6 with 2 N acetic acid and is saturated with lead iodide. The lead iodide takes some time to dissolve and rapid shaking helps.

Figure 5.2

Crystals obtained from reaction of cocaine hydrochloride with gold chloride: This image is the sum of several images; if formed rapidly, the crystals have a shorter center axis.

Figure 5.3

Crystals obtained from reaction of cocaine hydrochloride with gold bromide: The crystals are yellow in color and show strong polarization. This figure is a collage of three separate figures taken with crossed polarizers and the image colors inverted.

Figure 5.4

Crystals obtained from reaction of lead iodide with cocaine hydrochloride in potassium acetate.

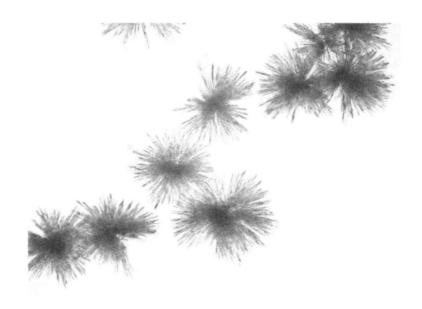

The foregoing tests are the more recently suggested crystal tests. Earlier, Fulton (1969) had proposed the use of $HAuBr_4$, $HAuCl_4$, H_2PtCl_6, and H_2PtBr_6 solutions in water or in mixtures of acids such as acetic, sulfuric, hydrochloric, or phosphoric, with similar results.

5.3.3 COLOR/SPOT TESTS

Positive color tests are presumptive indications of the possible presence of cocaine. A number of harmless materials or other controlled drugs (e.g., methaqualone) or the synthetic anesthetics that are often substituted for cocaine in the illicit market may give similar colors. Such results should always be confirmed by the use of alternative analytical techniques.

The most common method for the performance of a color test on a suspected drug material employs a white spot plate (for the enhancement of perception of the test's color), where the sample is placed in a depression and treated with the necessary reagents. The spot plate must be washed thoroughly with water and an organic solvent (preferably methanol or acetone) after each use to prevent contamination. Filter paper, test strips, or premeasured and prepackaged reagents in ampoules can also be used with comparable success. Some color tests can also be performed in open (and clean) test tubes. The presence of impurities or adulterants in cocaine samples can change slightly the color of the test.

A few grains or particles should be used for the test. If it is necessary to repeat the test, the amount of the sample should be increased up to the size of a match head. Only the color(s) indicated for each test should be interpreted as a positive result, which, in any case, means only the *possible* presence of cocaine in the sample. When a test yields negative or doubtful results, a second test suggested for cocaine should be performed. If the second test is also negative it can be concluded that the sample is unlikely to contain cocaine. If the amount of the suspected material is too small to be subjected to both a color test and a laboratory examination, the entire sample should be submitted to the laboratory. It must be kept in mind that although color tests are used worldwide for screening purposes in the field, they are not substitutes for more specific identification techniques, such as chromatography and spectroscopy.

Cobalt thiocyanate test (Young, 1931; U.N., 1994): A small amount of the suspected material is placed in a test tube. One drop of a 16% aqueous hydrochloric acid solution is added, and the tube is shaken for 10 seconds. Then one drop of a 2.5% aqueous solution of cobalt(II) thiocyanate is added, and the tube is shaken again for 10 seconds. A *blue* color indicates the possible presence of cocaine, including cocaine base preparations as crack. A similar color may appear in the presence of other controlled drugs, such as methaqualone, phencyclidine, and highly pure heroin.

Modifications of this test that have been suggested in the literature (Alliston et al., 1972) include:

- Acidified $Co(SCN)_2$: 2 g of cobalt thiocyanate are dissolved in 100 mL of 1% HCl.
- 1.6% $Co(SCN)_2$ in 10% methanolic solution of HCl.
- 2% $Co(SCN)_2$ in 2 N HCl.
- 0.8% $Co(SCN)_2$ in 1% orthophosphoric acid.
- 0.8% $Co(SCN)_2$ in 2:3 (v/v) mixture of methanol with 1% orthophosphoric acid.

In all cases the development of blue color indicates the presence of cocaine.

Scott test (modified cobalt thiocyanate test) (Scott, 1973): A small amount of the suspected material is placed in a test tube. Five drops of Scott reagent (1 g of cobalt(II) thiocyanate dissolved in 50 mL of 10% (v/v) acetic acid, and then 50 mL of glycerin added) are added, and the tube is shaken for 10 seconds. If cocaine is present, a blue color develops immediately. If no blue color appears, an equal amount of the suspected material to the amount first used is added. If a blue color still does not develop, the result of the test is considered negative.

If a blue color appears after addition of the Scott reagent, one drop of concentrated hydrochloric acid is added and the mixture shaken for a few seconds. If cocaine is present, the blue color will turn pink. If the color change is incomplete, an additional drop of HCl might be needed. If the color turns completely to pink, after addition of the HCl, then five drops of chloroform are added and the mixture shaken again. If cocaine is present, the blue color should reappear in the chloroform layer. Butacaine, dibucaine, phencyclidine, and methapyrilene (although they give the same color as cocaine with the Scott reagent) are all distinguished from it by the HCl and chloroform extraction, where only cocaine gives a blue color in the chloroform layer.

Logan test (Logan et al., 1989)—to identify the salt form of cocaine:

1. Place 5–10 mg of the sample in a test tube with 1 mL of hexane. Leave the sample to precipitate. Transfer 6–10 drops of the supernatant to another test tube, and add 4–6 drops of a 2% solution of $Co(SCN)_2$ in aqueous solution (1:1) of glycerin. A blue precipitate indicates the presence of cocaine free base.

2. Add 1 mL of water to the rest of the hexane solution and stir the mixture. Transfer 6–10 drops of the aqueous layer to another test tube that contains 0.5 mL of chloroform. Add 4–6 drops of the $Co(SCN)_2$ solution. A blue color indicates the presence of cocaine salt.

3. If steps 1 and 2 are negative, mix 6–10 drops of the rest of the hexane with 4–6 drops of the $Co(SCN)_2$ solution. A blue color indicates that the initial sample was a mixture of cocaine HCl and Na_2CO_3.

p-Dimethylaminobenzaldehyde test (Stevens, 1986): Freshly prepare 1% *p*-dimethylaminobenzaldehyde in a mixture of ethanol and sulfuric acid (60:40). Add a few drops of the reagent to the sample in a test tube and warm the mixture to 100°C for 3 minutes. A red color, that does not change to violet on dilution with water, indicates the presence of cocaine. Phencyclidine gives also a positive result with this test.

Travnikoff test (semiquantitative screening test) (Travnikoff, 1983a and 1983b): Place 10 mg of the sample in a test tube with 1 mL of 2% cupric sulfate pentahydrate ($CuSO_4·5H_2O$) in 0.1 N HCl and 1 mL of 2% potassium thiocyanate (KSCN). Add 2 mL of chloroform and shake the tube. The chloroform layer displays a brown color the intensity of which is relative to the amount of cocaine present. The procedure was checked with heroin, methaqualone, PCP, quinine, methamphetamine, barbiturates, procaine, benzocaine, tetracaine, lignocaine, butacaine, and methapyrilene. None of these substances gave a positive test.

Odor test (methyl benzoate test) (Grant et al., 1975; Kovar and Laundszun, 1989): A small amount of the suspected material is placed in a test tube. Ten drops of a 5% methanolic solution of potassium hydroxide are added and the tube is shaken for 10 seconds. The smell of the sample is then compared with that of a reference methyl benzoate sample. A brief sniff from a safe distance of 15–20 cm is recommended. If the smell is the same, this is a strong indication of the possible presence of cocaine. Only piperocaine (a benzoate ester) was found to give a positive result with this test. No controlled drugs give a similar odor with this test.

5.3.3.1 Differentiation of Cocaine Salts (U.N., 1986)

When mixed with a silver nitrate solution, a solution of cocaine hydrochloride yields a white, curdy precipitate that is insoluble in nitric acid but soluble in a diluted ammonia solution from which it is reprecipitated when nitric acid is added (essentially a chloride test). A solution of cocaine sulfate when mixed with a barium chloride solution yields a white precipitate that is insoluble in hydrochloric acid (essentially a sulfate test). Both tests will produce incorrect information if the cocaine is in the presence of other ionic materials, such as cocaine sulfate mixed with sodium chloride.

5.3.3.2 Differentiation of Cocaine HCl from Cocaine Freebase

Wagner test (U.N., 1994): A small amount of the suspected material is placed in a test tube. Five drops of water are added and the tube is shaken for a few seconds. Then two drops of Wagner reagent (1.27 g of iodine and 2 g of potassium iodide in 100 mL of water) are added. A brown precipitate indicates the possible presence of cocaine hydrochloride. Crack does not give a precipitate with this reagent. This test is not specific for cocaine because many other controlled and uncontrolled drugs give a positive result, but it is extremely useful as a differentiating test for cocaine hydrochloride from cocaine base.

Sodium hypochlorite test (Kaufman, 1990): Fill a transparent, colorless glass with 10–15% sodium hypochlorite solution. Put 10–30 mg of the sample on the surface. Cocaine HCl precipitates slowly and forms well-distinguished zones, while cocaine freebase floats and becomes oily.

The color tests just described are intended to be used as field tests or as screening tests in the lab. Only the colors indicated for each test should be interpreted as a positive result. Results from these tests are only a presumptive identification of the suspected material and not a definitive proof. In all cases where positive or doubtful results are obtained, the suspected material must be submitted to a more detailed analysis. Raman and I.R. spectroscopy may be useful for instrumental differentiation of cocaine free base from the salt.

5.3.3.3 Differentiation of Cocaine Enantiomers (Ruybal, 1982; U.N., 1986)

l-Cocaine is the only enantiomer of cocaine that occurs naturally. The procedure for synthesis of cocaine usually results in a racemic mixture. Therefore, the detection of the *d*-isomer of cocaine is a proof of synthetic production of cocaine. Courts in some countries have ruled that only the *l*-isomer of cocaine is an illegal drug; if the analyst fails to prove that the cocaine determined was *l*-cocaine, the prosecution may fail.

A microcrystal test has been suggested to differentiate cocaine enantiomers: Dissolve 10 mg of di-*p*-toluoyl-*d*-tartaric acid (TDTA) and 10 mg of di-*p*-toluoyl-*l*-tartaric acid (TLTA) in 1 mL of ethyl alcohol in separate 10-mL volumetric flasks, and then make to volume by adding 8 mL of water and 1 mL of glycerin. The test is performed on a microscope slide and viewed through a polarizing microscope at 100–125 times magnification, both with and without the analyzer inserted. A drop of reagent is placed on the slide; then a small quantity of sample is added to the reagent and stirred. Note that cocaine must be in its hydrochloric salt form. (If it isn't, it has to be converted.)

After 1 minute, *l*-cocaine HCl gives with TDTA almost perfectly symmetrical rosettes. The crystals have a grayish white to white color under polarized light when first formed. After a few minutes some rosettes show different colors (blue, red, green, yellow) on the arms of the rosettes, depending on orientation.

With TLTA, *l*-cocaine HCl forms grayish white crystals immediately. The formation of these crystals varies from a multitude of single needles to tufts, to fan shaped, to sheaves. *d*-Cocaine HCl gives the complete opposite crystal formation as *l*-cocaine HCl. About 1 minute after, it gives almost perfectly symmetrical rosettes with TLTA and crystals of various shapes with TDTA.

Again note the great importance of the extraction of cocaine from the sample matrix and its conversion to its hydrochloric salt. Other synthetic local anesthetics do not appear to interfere with this test.

Sorgen (1983) extracts cocaine through an alumina column with dichloromethane and reacts with TDTA in acetone and analyzes the precipitate by IR spectroscopy.

Eskes (1978) suggests a TLC method for the differentiation of the optical isomers of cocaine. The concept again is that *l*-cocaine is the natural alkaloid, while *dl*- and *d*-forms suggest a synthetic preparation of the cocaine sample. Cocaine is hydrolyzed to ecgonine and then is esterified with the enantiomeric 2-octanols to give the necessary diastereoisomeric derivatives, which may be distinguished by TLC (mobile phase: methanol).

Allen et al. (1981) suggests the differentiation of the four diastereoisomers of 2-carbomethoxy-3-benzoyloxytropane (cocaine, pseudococaine, allococaine, and pseudoallococaine) either by TLC (mobile phase: acetonitrile) or by microcrystalline tests using gold chloride, as described earlier in this chapter. Cocaine is the only one of the four diastereoisomers that gives a crystalline precipitate with the gold reagent. (Note: Gold chloride should *not* be able to distinguish between all the isomers of cocaine because it is not optically active. Therefore, this test should be suspect.)

The differentiation of cocaine enantiomers can be also made by use of conventional TLC, HPLC, GC, GC/MS (EI and CI), IR, and NMR methods.

5.3.4 THIN-LAYER CHROMATOGRAPHY (Davidow et al., 1968; Wallace et al., 1975; Baker and Gough, 1979; Jukofsky et al., 1980; Tandon, 1978; Clarke, 1986; U.N., 1986; Hussain, 1988; Ensing and de Zeeuw, 1991; Lillsunde and Korte, 1991)

For the thin-layer chromatography of cocaine, activated silica gel G on glass-backed plates should be used. The coating should contain a fluorescing additive (at 254-nm excitation). The plates (stored in a dry place) should be activated before use at 110°C for a minimum of 30 minutes. The size of the plates that should be used (20 × 20 cm, 20 × 10 cm, 10 × 5 cm) depends on the number of the samples that will be developed simultaneously.

The *spotting line* (the starting point of the run) should be 1 cm from the bottom of the plate, while the depth of developing solvent in TLC tank should be no more than 0.5 cm and not less than 0.3 cm. The spots should be placed at least 1.5 cm from the side of the plate in order to avoid the "side effect." The distance between them should be about 1 cm but never less than 0.8 cm.

Ideally the spots will be no more than 2 mm in diameter. This can be achieved by applying the sample solutions in aliquots rather than by a single discharge. The aliquots should be dried between discharges by air, preferably cold, in order to avoid the decomposition of thermally labile components of the sample. Glass pipettes, drawn out over a flame, make convenient, disposable applicators.

The TLC tank and the lid should be made of glass, and the tank should be lined with adsorbent paper to assist saturation of the solvent. The glass top should be ground and/or a smear of petroleum jelly should be applied to the rim for minimization of solvent evaporation.

If the developing solvent is a mixture, it should be made as accurately as possible by the use of graduated cylinders. Automatic dispensers can also be used, and the mixing can be done in the TLC tank. For most of the developing systems, the solvent must be renewed after each development or at least after two to three runs. The developing solvent should stay in the tank for about 15 minutes before the development in order for vapor saturation to be achieved.

Normally a 10-cm run is allowed (for better calculation of R_f values) by drawing a "development line" 11 cm from the bottom of the plate, although a run up to the top of the plate gives better separation results. In any case, plates should be removed from the TLC tank as soon as the solvent reaches the development line or the top of the TLC plate; otherwise, diffuse spots will result.

The most common developing systems suggested in the literature for TLC analysis of cocaine are given in Table 5.1.

Table 5.1

Reported system for TLC analysis

System	Solvents	Solvent Proportions	Rf (×100)
A	Methanol : ammonia	100 : 1.5	65
B	Cyclohexane : toluene : diethylamine	75 : 15 : 10	56
C	Chloroform : methanol	90 : 10	47
D	Chloroform : methanol : ammonia	100 : 20 : 1	87
E	Chloroform : dioxane : ethyl acetate : ammonia	25 : 60 : 10 : 5	81
F	Acetone		54
G	Ethyl acetate : methanol : water : ammonia	86 : 10 : 3 : 1	86
H	Ethyl acetate : methanol : ammonia	85 : 10 : 5	96
I	Hexane : benzene : diethylamine	75 : 25 : 10	44
J	Methylene chloride : methanol	50 : 50	35
K	Methylene chloride : methanol : acetone	40 : 40 : 20	41
L	Methylene chloride : methanol : acetone	50 : 25 : 25	12
M	Methanol : ammonia 2 N : ammonium nitrate	88 : 8 : 4	83

For the visualization of cocaine spots in most of the preceding cases, Dragendorff's reagent is used in combination with acidified potassium iodoplatinate reagent. However, if fluorescent plates are used, the spots should be observed under UV light (as dark spots against a green background) and marked with a pencil before spraying with visualization reagents.

Dragendorff's reagent. Solution A: Dissolve 2 g bismuth subnitrate in 25 mL of glacial acetic acid and add 100 mL of water. *Solution B:* Dissolve 40 g of potassium iodide in 100 mL of water. To produce Dragendorff's reagent, mix 10 mL of Solution A, 10 mL of Solution B, 20 mL of glacial acetic acid, and 100 mL of water.

Acidified potassium iodoplatinate reagent. Dissolve 0.25 g platinic chloride and 5 g of potassium iodide in water to 100 mL, and add 2 mL of concentrated hydrochloric acid. It is important for proper color development that all traces of ammonia or other bases used in the developing solvent be removed from the plate by thorough drying.

When the TLC plate is sprayed with Dragendorff's reagent, cocaine appears as an orange spot. When the plate is sprayed afterwards with acidified potassium iodoplatinate reagent, cocaine appears as an orange-brown to dark brown spot, with the color depending on the amount of cocaine present.

Jukofsky et al. (1980) suggest to develop the TLC plates by spraying with 5% H_2SO_4 followed by iodoplatinate. The immediate color of the cocaine spot is a purple blue; on standing, the spot becomes brown, with the presence of a very light purple ring that fades over time. Spraying only with iodoplatinate gives a blue spot for cocaine (Tandon, 1978).

The visualization of cocaine can also be made by examination of the TLC plate under UV light (366 nm and 254 nm) after spraying with H_2SO_4–$FeCl_3$ reagent (2 mL 5% $FeCl_3$ + 40 mL H_2O + 60 mL H_2SO_4). Cocaine shows a blue fluorescence.

It must be kept in mind that the unknown samples should always be run against cocaine standards; and the R_f and the colors developed should be compared. For positive identification, two or more solvent systems should be used. Also for legal purposes, the R_f precision should be articulated. It is often helpful to run the unknowns separately between two standards as well as mixed with standards. In this way, slight variations in solvent migration can be compensated. The form of standard used, salt or base, is not important. On the TLC plate the compounds always move as the freebase *if* the solvent contains a base.

The melting point of cocaine hydrochloride is 187–197°C and that of cocaine base is 98°C.

5.4 TRACE AND INSTRUMENTAL ANALYSIS

The instrumental techniques are discussed in order of increasing cost.

5.4.1 IMMUNOASSAYS

The alternative method for cocaine screening is an immunoassay. All immunoassays employ antibodies. *Antibodies* are proteins made in mammals that recognize, bind to, and elicit defenses against foreign substances. The compound that an antibody binds is termed the *antigen*. Two general types of antibodies are employed in immunoassays, polyclonal and monoclonal. Polyclonal antibodies are isolated from animal serum (usually rabbit or goat) and are often mixtures of antibodies with different specificities. In contrast, monoclonal antibodies (usually mouse) are frequently single protein molecules grown in cell culture and have a single specificity. In a mixture of polyclonal antibodies there are generally antibodies that will recognize and bind different parts of an antigen. In contrast, monoclonal antibodies, being a single compound, will recognize and bind only one type or part of an antigen. Therefore, monoclonal antibodies may not recognize related compounds, such as metabolites. The cross-reactivity of the antibody is often stated on the commercial package insert.

As employed in immunoassays, antibodies may be considered to function as a lock and key. The antibodies are the lock and the drug is the key. The specificity of the lock will determine the number of keys that will fit. The more specific the antibody, the less interference from other materials of similar structure will occur. However, with a very specific assay there is little chance of observing related compounds, such as metabolites or designer drugs. Therefore, the researcher should select the immunoassay to match their goals. If detection of only a single compound, such as cocaine, is desired, a monoclonal-based immunoassay should be used. If detection of cocaine and its metabolites, such as ecgonine, benzoylecgonine, and methylecgonine, is desired, then a polyclonal immunoassay should be used.

The binding of an antibody, be it monoclonal or polyclonal, is the fundamental part of any immunoassay. The distinction between all immunoassays is the manner in which this binding is measured. The four different immunoassays described in the following sections employ different techniques to measure binding of the antibody to its antigen.

A number of different immunoassays are commercially available to detect cocaine and benzoylecgonine. Because most immunoassays are used to screen for drugs in urine, they are highly selective to benzoylecgonine, the principal metabolite of cocaine. Therefore, their cross-reactivity and sensitivity for cocaine must be evaluated. Frequently this information is available from the manufacturer.

5.4.1.1 Radioimmunoassay (RIA)

Radioimmunoassay was first described in 1959 by Rosalyn Yalow as a method to detect insulin (Yalow and Berson, 1960). For her work in this area, she received the 1977 Nobel Prize in medicine. To perform the test, a known amount of radioactively labeled drug (antigen) is mixed with a small quantity (10–100 µL) of biological matrix (urine, sweat, saliva, tears, or buffer with solid sample added). Then an antibody to the drug is added. The antibody is not able to distinguish between that radioactively labeled drug and that drug that may be present in the urine. The antibody and drug–antibody complex are separated from the urine and the radioactivity is measured. The more radioactivity bound to the antibody, the less drug present in the test sample. The steps employed in RIA can be seen schematically in Figure 5.5.

The separation of bound drug from unbound drug, the labor-intensive part of RIA, may be performed in many ways (Skelley et al., 1973). One method relies upon the addition of a second antibody, which is directed against the first antibody. Because the second antibody cross-links the first antibody, an insoluble molecule is formed. This precipitate is pelleted by centrifugation, and the supernatant containing the unbound antigen is discarded. Then the radioactivity in the pellet is counted directly in the tube.

Another method for separating the bound from the unbound antigen relies upon binding the antibody to the walls of the reaction vessel. After the initial drug–antibody reaction, the unbound materials are poured out. The radioactivity bound to the antibodies that are coated on the walls of the tube is then determined.

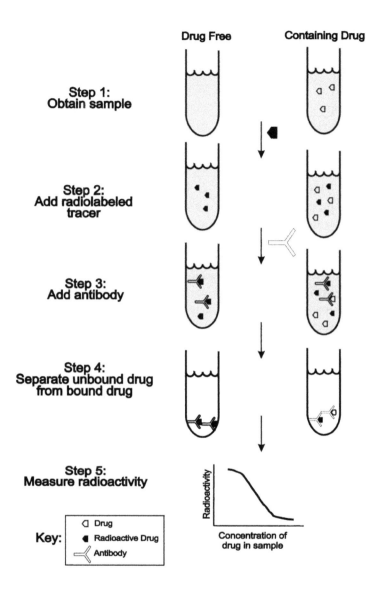

Figure 5.5

Steps used in typical radioimmunoassays.

The last method relies upon adsorption of the unbound antigen onto activated charcoal. The charcoal is coated with a dextran polymer, which allows only the smaller antigens to pass through and to be absorbed onto the charcoal. The charcoal is then removed, and the radioactivity in the urine or the charcoal is determined.

A typical plot of radioactivity observed versus concentration of antigen is shown in Figure 5.6a. This curve is very similar in shape and principle to an acid–base titration curve. The linear working range is on the S-shaped portion

Figure 5.6

Typical data generated by RIA: (a) a raw calibration curve; (b) a calibration curve after mathematical processing.

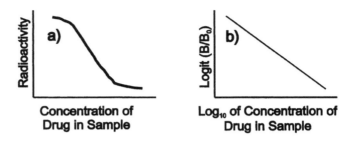

of the plot. This curve also may be made linear, as shown in Figure 5.6b (Henson et al., 1985). Note that the linear curve generated mathematically in Figure 5.6b from the normal binding curve is somewhat misleading. The precision near either end of this curve can be poor. Therefore, severe errors may occur in measuring either small drug concentrations or very high ones. High concentrations must be measured by diluting them into the working range of the RIA. In contrast, low concentrations are problematic, since the binding of the antibody may be affected, depending on the matrix being analyzed. An extraction-and-concentration step can be used to reduce the matrix effect and to increase the concentration of the analyte to a more precise part of the working curve. However, this is considerably extra work for a screening test. For most samples encountered in the forensic laboratory, concentration is not a problem—using too much is. Immunoassays are so sensitive that great dilution should be used. Typically, 1 mg of a sample can be diluted to 1000 mL with a buffer (1 μg/mL). Dilution also helps reduce interferences.

The advantage of RIA lies in its sensitivity; 10^{-12}–10^{-15} moles of antigen can be routinely determined. This sensitivity is the result of the low radioactive background of most materials and the high sensitivity of radioactive measurements. Also, RIA is very rugged; as long as the antibody–antigen reaction is specific, few false negatives will occur. The major disadvantage of RIA is the risk of exposure to radiation and the restrictive laws regulating the distribution, use, and disposal of the low-level radioactive waste generated.

Adulteration of samples to generate a false negative is a potential concern in any drug-screening program. Considering the principle of RIA, as shown in Figure 5.5, there are few, if any, adulterants that would allow the antibody to preferentially bind to the radiolabeled drug and not to a drug in the sample. Adulterating the sample by adding antidrug antibodies or radioactively labeled drugs would cause false negatives, but these materials would not be readily available to the average drug user. The addition of common adulterants such as salt, organic solvents, acids or bases to prevent antibody binding would prevent the antibody from binding to both radiolabeled drug and the drug present in the sample matrix and cause a *false* positive. For example, making the sample quite acidic (pH < 2) would cause a false positive. Dilution of the sample in a buffer helps prevent these rare occurrences.

5.4.1.2 Enzyme Multiplied Immunoassay Technique (EMIT)

In 1972, Rubenstein developed the homogeneous assay upon which EMIT is based (Rubenstein et al., 1972). EMIT employs enzymes rather than radioactivity as the determinant of antibody binding. A common enzyme system used for EMIT is glucose-6-phosphate dehydrogenase (G6PD). G6PD uses nicotine adenine dinucleotide phosphate (NADP) as a cofactor to oxidize glucose and to reduce the NADP. The reduced NADP absorbs UV light at a longer wavelength (340 nm) than the oxidized form. The activity of the enzyme can be measured as a rate of increase in absorbance due to the production of reduced NADP. The binding of the antibody to an enzyme-labeled drug decreases the activity of that enzyme. Only a few enzymes with the active site close to the surface show this effect (Rubenstein, 1978).

The principle behind EMIT is depicted in Figure 5.7. To perform the assay, the rate of turnover of the enzyme must be measured spectrophotometrically. The decrease in activity is measured as a decrease in absorbance after a set period of time compared to a standard. If no drugs are present in the test sample, then all the enzyme-labeled drug is bound to the antibodies and the activity of the enzyme is reduced. The bound enzyme-labeled drug produces little reduced NADP, and the absorbance at 340 nm is correspondingly low. If a detectable quantity of drug is present in the test sample, then the enzyme-labeled drug competes with the drug–enzyme conjugate for the antibody-binding sites (recall the earlier discussion of RIA). This prevents binding of some of the enzyme-labeled drug, restores its activity, and produces more reduced NADP. Therefore the absorbance at 340 nm increases. The drug concentration is computed by comparing the sample's rate of absorbance change to absorbance change values of a set of standards. The rate of enzyme activity is directly proportional to the concentration of drug in the sample. High concentrations of drug in the sample cause many antibody-binding sites to be occupied, leaving more enzyme-labeled drug unbound and active. Conversely, less drug in the sample allows more enzyme-labeled drug to bind with the antibody, resulting in less enzyme activity.

EMIT may be run in two ways. The method most analogous to RIA is depicted in Figure 5.7. In step 1, the enzyme-labeled drug is added to the sample. In step 2, antibodies specific to the drug of interest are added to the sample. Alternatively, for more sensitivity, steps 1 and 2 may be reversed. The antibody sites not occupied by drug from the sample may become occupied by enzyme-labeled drug. Because the off-rate of the antibody–drug complex is slow (10^4–10^5 seconds), equilibrium is not reached. In this rendition, by adding the

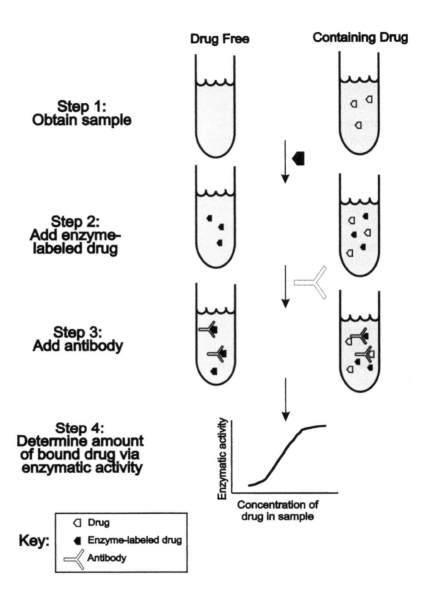

Figure 5.7

Steps used in an EMIT immunoassay.

antibody first, the EMIT assay is no longer a true competitive assay. This has the effect of shifting the sigmoidal curve, shown in step 4 of Figure 5.7, to the left (to more sensitivity).

The advantage of EMIT over RIA is that no radioactivity is involved. This makes disposal of waste products relatively easy. Also, the shelf life of the reagents is increased, since no radioactive decay is present for loss of the label. Therefore the signal generation (enzymatic activity) can be started when

Table 5.2

Common adulterants used to generate false negatives in EMIT

Salt
Acids (such as vinegar)
Bases (such as lye)
Oxidants (such as bleach)
Enzyme inhibitors (such as heavy metals)

desired, often by reconstituting the freeze-dried reagents. In addition, labor can be saved, since there is no need for separation of bound from unbound drugs as with RIA. A disadvantage of EMIT is that it cannot be used if the test sample is cloudy or has interfering substances that absorb at 340 nm. However, again dilution of the original sample avoids most problems. Since binding of antibodies is necessary, all the discussion about the cautions in measuring very high or low concentrations of analyte that apply to RIA also apply to EMIT.

EMIT is the one test that has had the most publicity about its susceptibility to adulteration. Like RIA, an adulterant that prevents binding of the antibody to the drug-labeled enzyme would generate a false positive. Unlike RIA, EMIT is vulnerable to generating a false *negative* by reducing the activity of the enzyme or changing the NADP cofactor. Some of the common adulterants that may be used to generate a false negative are listed in Table 5.2 (Kim and Cerceo, 1976).

Adulterants should not be a problem with trace analysis because the sample must be dissolved in a buffer before applying the EMIT test. Unless the trace analysis was in the presence of a large amount of interferent, the buffer should dilute any interferent. The applicability of EMIT depends on the interferent. Oxidants and strong acids/bases are particularly troublesome. For example, cocaine mixed with salt >1% should be testable. In contrast, 1% cocaine mixed with an oxidant, such as laundry detergent, will likely generate a false negative. This must be kept in mind if one is using an EMIT test to sample wipes of an area where cleaning agents may have been applied. One method that could be used to evaluate false negatives in tests that employ EMIT technology is to monitor the initial rate of the enzyme reaction before the antibody is added. If this rate was too low, then that sample would be flagged as untestable. Few laboratories use this method because it increases slightly the complexity of the analysis. Alternatively, a known amount of material may be added (similar to the standard addition method) and the sample assayed again. If the result is correct, then the sample is not adulterated and is testable.

5.4.1.3 Fluorescent Polarization Immunoassay (FPI)

The principles of fluorescent polarization were first developed by Perrin in the 1920s (Perrin, 1926), and its application to the detection of antigens bound to antibodies was first described in 1961 (Dandliker and Feigen). The principles

Figure 5.8
Principle of fluorescence polarization immunoassay.

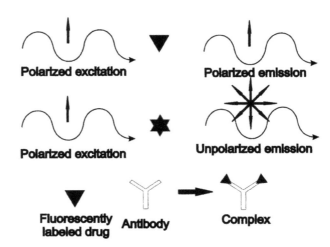

and practice of fluorescent polarization and its application to biological systems have been the subject of several review articles (Soini and Hemmila, 1979; Dandliker and de Saussure, 1970; O'Donnell and Suffin, 1979).

The basis of FPI can be seen in Figure 5.8. Fluorescent polarization is related to light scattering. If a polarized light beam excites a stationary, fluorescent molecule, the molecule will emit light that is polarized. If the molecule rotates before the light is emitted, then the polarization of the emitted light is lost. Small molecules, such as drugs, rotate faster than larger molecules, such as antibodies. An antibody binding to the smaller, fluorescent molecule would make a large complex with a slower rotational period. This large complex would not rotate significantly before fluorescence of the molecule had occurred; therefore, the polarization of the initial exciting light would be retained. If the antibody is prevented from binding the fluorescently labeled drug (because other molecules fill the site), then the polarization is lost. The steps used in FPI (Figure 5.8) are very similar to those used in EMIT, with the only difference being how the signal is interpreted.

The shelf life of the reagents in FPI is increased over that in both EMIT and RIA because no radioactivity or enzymes are involved with this analysis. Like EMIT, labor can be saved, since the assay is performed without a separation step. However, the sensitivity of FPI is somewhat less than can be achieved by RIA and EMIT, although it is sufficient for most drug assays. The sensitivity is limited by the theoretical maximum of polarization (0.4, due to the random distribution of molecules) and by the inherent fluorescence of the sample. This is especially severe if proteins (as in blood plasma) or certain vitamins are present.

Fluorescent polarization also is sensitive to a number of adulterants. Considering the principle behind fluorescent polarization, any high-molecular-weight material that nonspecifically binds the fluorescent label would generate a false negative. This nonspecific binding would reduce the rotation of the molecule and increase the polarization, just as if the antibody had bound to the drug-labeled fluorophore. Proteins are known to interfere with fluorescent polarization in this manner.

If the fluorescent lifetime were significantly reduced, even unbound molecules would appear stationary. Heavy metals are efficient fluorescent quenchers that can reduce lifetimes in high-enough local concentrations. These should generate false negatives with this assay.

The TD_x system used by Abbott Laboratories reduces or eliminates all these known interferences by a large, 250-fold dilution of the sample in buffer before an assay is performed and a careful background subtraction routine. We have tested samples with large amounts of protein, salt, and various quenchers without generating a false negative. However, fluorescent materials, such as endogenous riboflavin metabolites or surreptitiously added fluorescence dyes, still present a problem. Abnormally high levels of such species are indicated by the TD_x instrument, and that specimen cannot be tested. A policy decision must be made in these cases as to whether such a sample should be tested by alternative technology to avoid discarding a potential positive sample.

5.4.1.4 Immunochromatography (Mura et al., 1999; Samyn and van Haeren, 2000)

Lateral flow immunoassays, examplified by the Roche Teststik™ and the Securetech DRUGWIPE®, are the newest, fieldable techniques. All lateral flow techniques rely upon technology patented in 1982 (Leuvering, 1982) and more recently by a large number of inventors, as exemplified by Campbell et al. (1987), Rosenstein (1987), and May (2000).

They are in principle the same technology as used in most home pregnancy tests. The sample, dissolved in water or buffer, is applied to an absorbent pad (see Figure 5.9), where the solution mobilizes colored particles that are coated with antibodies. The particles move in the chromatography paper (often nitrocellulose) and are captured on an immobilized antigen line. Thus for detecting cocaine, the coated particles are coated with anticocaine antibodies and the immobilized antigen is cocaine-derivatized protein. If there are no cocaine molecules in the sample solution, then some of the particles bind to the immobilized cocaine and a visual line appears. Any cocaine molecules in the sample solution inhibit this binding and either reduce the line intensity or inhibit it entirely. Because a lateral flow immunoassay is an antibody–antigen assay, anything that inhibits antibody binding, such as strongly acidic or basic materials, would cause a false positive (lack of sample line). For a control, antibodies against a second protein on the colored particle are employed. The control

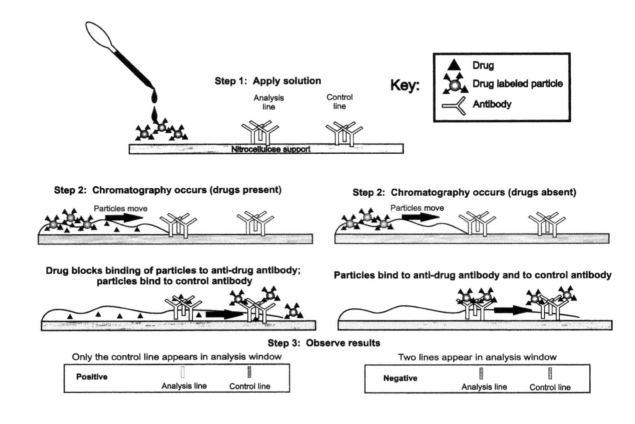

Figure 5.9

Principle of lateral flow immunoassays: The particles used for visualization may be blue (colored latex) or red (colloidal gold or selenium). For most lateral flow immunoassays, note the inverse nature of the signal—absence of a line is a positive. Because antibodies are employed, only aqueous solutions at neutral pH may be analyzed.

line, often present, serves as an indicator that the sample solution mobilized the particles and that additives were not present that inhibited antibody binding.

Generally, cocaine, methamphetamine, and opiates are difficult to detect by quick observations; therefore individuals may be driving under the influence of drugs and not be easily observed. On the other hand, alcohol and marijuana are readily detectable by smell. Consider a traffic stop made for erratic driving. The individual may have alcohol present but below legal limits. Would an officer detain that individual (spending several hours) and take a biological sample, such as blood or urine, without good evidence that the behavior was due to drug use?

Lateral flow assays are being proposed for sampling individuals at traffic stops to generate probable cause that they had used drugs (Mura et al., 1999). However, most of the lateral flow assays are sensitive to nanogram quantities of materials. This sensitivity is such that contamination by previous exposure to drugs (being around drug use or in an environment where prior drug use had occurred) is sufficient to generate a positive. Thus, lateral flow systems should be considered as presumptive positives rather than true indicators of drug use.

Lateral flow assays can also be used as a test of suspicious powders, being more selective than colorimetric tests. However, their cost of several to tens of dollars per test may make them too expensive for routine use when cheaper tests are available. The cost is related mainly to the ease of use. For larger-scale, laboratory testing, an instrumental technique would be preferable if the analyst wanted to employ immunoassays as a preliminary screen. Also, each test is specific for a given drug or maybe drug class. Therefore, the test user would need to have some idea of the substance being sought or else run a number of tests at increased cost.

A useful example of the sensitivity of lateral flow immunoassays is to test drug residues on currency. Most used $1 bills in the U.S. are contaminated with 1–10 μg of cocaine. A simple test is to extract a single bill with 10 μL of water and preform the assay on a small aliquot. The visual result of a positive with most of the lateral flow devices can be useful in legal settings.

5.4.2 ION SELECTIVE ELECTRODES (ISEs)

ISEs have been developed that provide some selectivity to cocaine over other drugs of abuse (Elnemma et al., 1992; Campanella et al., 1995, 1998; Watanabe et al., 1997). ISEs offer the advantage of very rapid identification (<30s), very good quantitation, and low cost. Unfortunately, commercial versions of ISEs for drug analysis are not available, and any systems must be fabricated in the laboratory. Nevertheless, the materials to prepare an ISE for cocaine can be purchased for under $300, and a laboratory pH meter can be employed for the measurement system. Thus an instrument can be constructed for the rapid identification and quantitation of a large number of seized samples. The principle behind an ion selective electrode is shown in Figure 5.10. Analysis is as simple as using a pH meter. An aliquot of an unknown is weighed and dissolved to about 1–10 μg/mL in a known volume of buffer. First dissolving the cocaine in water can tell if it is crack cocaine, which is almost insoluble without acid present. Then the ion selective electrode is inserted and the voltage produced measured. The quantitation may be calculated from a calibration curve (see Figure 5.11). Other drugs are unlikely to interfere, but common surfactants (especially long-chain quaternary ammonium salts), such as found in some shampoos, do interfere. A low-cost approach to cocaine identification and purity measurement may be the use of TLC in a two-solvent system followed by ISE analysis to confirm the identity and measure the purity. Analysis can be very rapid (see Figure 5.12).

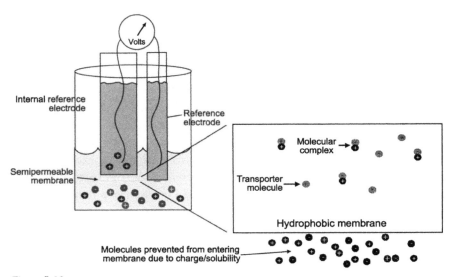

Figure 5.10

Principle of an ion selective electrode: An ion selective electrode is equivalent to a pH meter. A semipermeable membrane separates parts of a battery. Ions are carried across the semipermeable membrane with a selective transporter molecule—the driving force being a concentration gradient on either side of the membrane. Because the transport molecule carries only one part of the ion part (i.e., the cocaine cation), a charge build-up occurs inside the ion selective electrode solution. This charge buildup generates a voltage that can be measured and resists the further diffusion of cocaine cations. The larger the concentration of cocaine, the higher the voltage.

5.4.3 GAS CHROMATOGRAPHY–NITROGEN/PHOSPHOROUS DETECTION (GC-NPD) (Alm et al., 1983; Armstrong et al., 1987)

Of all analytical instruments, GC is the least expensive and lowest maintenance, and yet it provides a wealth of information. Gas chromatography with selective (flame ionization) or specific (nitrogen–phosphorous) detectors has been used to identify and quantitate cocaine. Early work centered on packed columns, which were soon supplemented and then replaced by capillary columns. Capillary columns, with their high resolution (3000 plates/meter) offer much more informational content (Kidwell, 2004) than does TLC for the identification of suspected materials. Cocaine does not need to be derivatized for analysis by GC, although it must be in the freebase form. GC also offers the advantage of fingerprinting the impurities in illicit cocaine samples, which are at trace levels and can be used to compare sources of cocaine (Comparini et al., 1983, 1984; Casale, 1992). Some authors have advocated the use of two columns with different polarities to confirm the identification of cocaine (Alm et al., 1983).

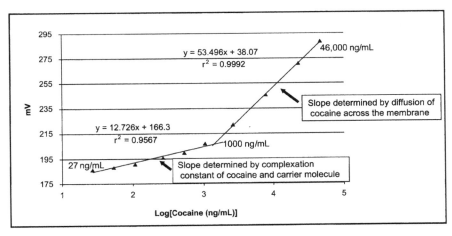

Figure 5.11

Typical data from a wire-coated ion selective cocaine electrode: The limit of detection is normally considered to be when the response is dominated purely by diffusion of cocaine across the membrane, and it is calculated from where the two lines cross. However, the ion selective electrode still responds to lower concentrations, where the response is dominated by the complexation constant of the transporter molecule. This region, although drawn as a straight line, is in reality a curve. A curve may be used for quantitation if higher-order curve-fitting routines are employed. With current electrode designs, drift in the absolute mV readings occurs, so the electrode should be calibrated immediately before use. A single point calibration is sufficient.

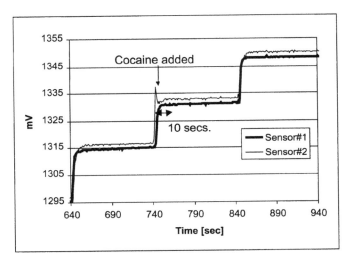

Figure 5.12

Rapid response of an ion selective electrode to cocaine: Aliquots of cocaine were added to a stirred, buffer solution. Typical response is under 30 s after addition of the cocaine, with some delay due to mixing of the solution.

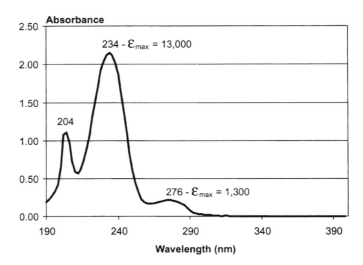

Figure 5.13

*UV spectrum of 1.65 e-4 M cocaine in 0.1 M HCl was Spectra: taken on a Hewett Packard 8451A Diode array spectrometer. From the calculated extinction coefficents and using Beers' law (A = εbc) one can calculate the minimium detectable quantity of cocaine. Assume that the HPLC detector can see an absorbance of 0.01 and has a 1 cm pathlength. Further assume that the flow is 1 mL/min and that the peak has a peak width of 30 seconds, then injection of 70 ng of cocaine should be observable at λ = 234 nm [0.01 (min. detectable absorbance)/13,000 (extinction coefficient) * 303 (molecular weight) * 0.0005 (elution volume) * 0.6 (peak factor)]. Of course, much more should be analyzed to ensure detection.*

5.4.4 HIGH-PRESSURE LIQUID CHROMATOGRAPHY (HPLC) (Chan et al., 1974; Wheals and Jane, 1977; Chiarotti and Fucci, 1990; de Zeeuw et al., 1994; Hill et al., 1987)

HPLC provides more information than does TLC due to the higher resolution attainable and the information content of the detection system (especially if multiple wavelengths or diode array detection is available). However, maintenance of HPLC can be much more expensive than a GC, and unless nonvolatile cutting agents (such as sugar) must be identified, GC would be the preferred analysis technique in the low-cost arena. The UV spectra of cocaine is shown in Figure 5.13 to aid in selection of wavelengths for detection if a fixed-array system is used. The ratio of absorbances at two or more wavelengths also helps in the identification of cocaine by comparison to a standard (for example: $A_{234\,nm}/A_{276\,nm} = 9.75$). Of course, for the detection of cutting agents, such as sugar, that have little or no useful UV aborbances, a refractive index detector must be used. Detectors can also be placed in series for added information.

5.4.5 CAPILLARY ZONE ELECTROPHORESIS (CZE)

Capillary zone electrophoresis, or just capillary electrophoresis, has been employed in the analysis of a wide range of drugs (Tagliaro et al., 1996; Lurie, 1998). The complexity and maintenance requirements are similar to those for HPLC, but CZE offers much higher chromatographic resolution, which can translate into more certain identification. Also, because the peak elutes in a smaller volume, the sensitivity can be higher than for HPLC. For example, assuming detection sensitivity of (0.01 absorbance units) for the CZE detector with a volume of 20 μL (diameter 1 cm × 50 μm) and that the peak is entirely contained in this volume, injection of 4.7 ng would then be detectable [0.01 (min. detectable absorbance)/13,000 (extinction coefficient)*303 (molecular weight)*20 e-6 (elution volume)]. This is 15 times more sensitive than HPLC with similar assumptions. CZE also has the advantages over HPLC of having many different modes of separation, which allows some flexibility for difficult analyses and drastically less solvent usage.

5.4.6 ION MOBILITY MASS SPECTROMETRY (IMS)

Ion mobility mass spectrometry is related to higher vacuum mass spectrometry but provides less information. It consists of introducing the sample (usually by thermal desorption) into the ion source of an atmospheric mass spectrometer. In the ion source, the molecules are normally ionized by charge exchange, similar to chemical ionization, with the reagent ions being formed by either a glow discharge or beta particles from a radioactive source (usually ^{63}Ni). The reagent ions can be adjusted in their proton affinity to provide some selectivity of nitrogen-containing compounds, such as cocaine, over hydrocarbons. Once ionized, the ions are pulsed into a drift region of the mass spectrometer, where the time necessary to reach a Faraday-type detector is measured. The drift time is related to the mass of the ions and their mobility (relating to size and shape) in the drift region. As such, an IMS does not give true mass-to-charge ratios. Nevertheless, an IMS can be selective because of the selectivity of the ionization and the drift time. The big advantage of IMS is that no vacuum is required. This allows handheld instruments to be constructed. Also, the sensitivity of most commercial instruments is less than 1 ng introduced, rivaling conventional mass spectrometry in a small, inexpensive package. At least three commercial variations are available.

5.4.7 GAS CHROMATOGRAPHY/MASS SPECTROMETRY (GC/MS)

GC/MS is the gold standard for cocaine analysis. By coupling a capillary gas chromatograph with a mass spectrometer an instrument is produced by which

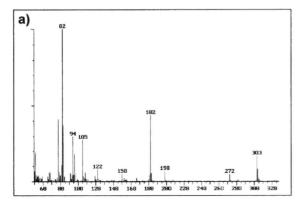

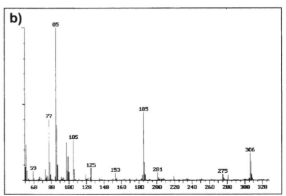

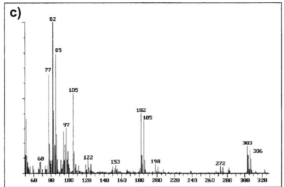

Figure 5.14

Electron impact spectrum of (a) d₀-cocaine, (b) N-methyl-d₃-cocaine, and (c) an approximately equal mixture of d₀-cocaine and N-methyl-d₃-cocaine. Spectra were obtained on a Varian 4 ion trap. The absolute intensities of the peaks may vary, depending on the instrument and its tuning. Diagnostic peaks for cocaine are at m/z 303, 182, and 82.

substantial information can be obtained (Kidwell, 2004). To consider a substance to be cocaine, both the retention time and mass spectrum must match those of a reference compound. Either chemical ionization or electron impact ionization may be used to ionize the cocaine molecule. Because electron impact provides fragmentation information, it is preferred. Normally at least three ions and the ratios between them must match a standard for a substance to be called positive. With newer mass spectrometers, based on ion traps, full-scan spectra can be obtained without substantial loss of sensitivity. Comparison of a full-scan spectrum of an unknown to that of a standard offers further proof of identity (Figure 5.14 for reference spectra). Although additional ions present in the unknown, due to coeluting impurities, that are not in the known may be acceptable, the reverse is not. Thus, the analyst must have written criteria for such comparisons because differences in intensity or additional peaks often occur. Because of the analysis capabilities of the mass spectrometer, deuterated internal standards are preferred. Deuterated cocaine, for the most part, is chemically identical to the undeuterated material, and thus losses in extraction and analysis are compensated. Likewise, the retention time of the deuterated standard on

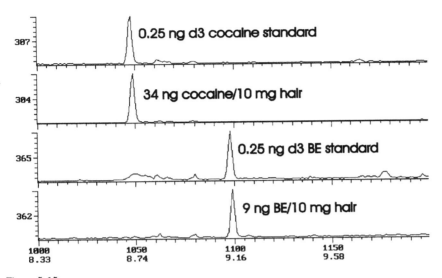

Figure 5.15

Methylamine CI/GC/MS of a hair extract from a 6-year-old African-American male: Methylamine was used as the CI reagent gas. Although methylamine produces cleaner spectra because its proton affinity is similar to cocaine, it is very corrosive. Isobutane or acetonitrile is the preferred reagent gas. Note that the deuterated standards elute slightly before the undeuterated analytes. Also, Gaussian peaks without shoulders can be obtained. The benzoylecgonine was derivatized as a trimethylsilyl derivative. TMS derivatives are easy to make and produce good sensitivity by CI because of their low proton affinity. However, TMS derivatives are moisture sensitive (thus they do not always remain intact on the autosampler for reruns), and some derivatization reagents degrade column performance (normally those containing TMS-CI). Fluorinated esters (such as pentafluoropropionyl) are now preferred for derivatization of benzoylecgonine. Cocaine is not derivatized. The information content of a CI-GC/MS analysis is lower than that of EI-GC/MS or CI-GC/MS/MS and is similar to that of packed-column GC/MS. Chemical ionization with only a single ion detection should not be used as proof of a substance identity for legal proceedings (Kidwell and Smith, 2000), especially in trace analysis.

the GC column serves as a standard to compare the unknown (Figure 5.15). Normally on a high-resolution GC column, deuterated materials elute slightly ahead of their corresponding undeuterated materials, and this further confirms the identity. Because GC is used to introduce the sample, all the requirements of GC must be followed. The sensitivity of most modern instruments can easily reach 1 ng injected, so most samples must be diluted. Generally, if you can see it, it is too much for analysis by mass spectrometry.

5.4.8 TANDEM MASS SPECTROMETRY, OR MS/MS (Kidwell, 1993)

MS/MS increases the information content in a spectrum, thereby increasing the certainty of identification (Fetterolf and Yost, 1984). MS/MS works by selecting

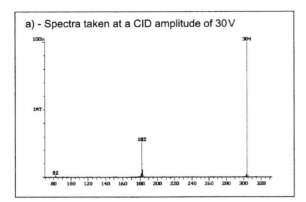

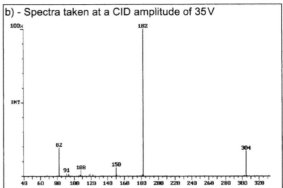

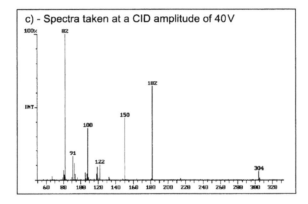

Figure 5.16

MS/MS spectra of cocaine: The spectra were obtained on a Varian 4 ion trap operating in positive CI mode using isobutane as the reagent gas. The excitation energy was nonresonant and was varied. Note the increase in fragmentation with increasing energy. Generally the window for fragmentation is small; too little energy produces little fragmentation, and too much scatters the ions, greatly reducing the sensitivity. Because the ion intensities vary with slight changes in instrumental conditions, MS/MS spectra are not as reproducible as electron impact spectra. However, running standards before/after the material in question usually produces a good spectral match. Alternatively, a comparison with the d_3 standards, run simultaneously, also is useful. In this case, ratios of the peaks to the corresponding peaks in the deuterated standard and then ratioing the ratios should produce reliable precision on day-to-day data. Spectra (b) is the most diagnostically useful.

an ion (usually the protonated molecular ion generated by chemical ioniza-tion—called the *parent* ion), fragmenting that ion, and examining the daughter ions produced (Figures 5.16 and 5.17). MS/MS is *not* a more sensitive technique than a single MS analysis. In fact, the signal levels obtained are actually *lower* than a single mass spectrum (due to ion scattering). However, by reducing the contribution from other ions in the spectra due to coeluting materials, MS/MS

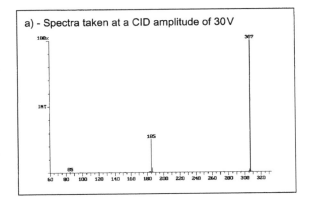

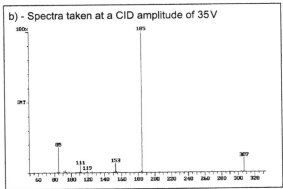

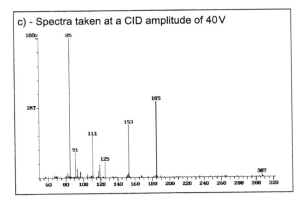

Figure 5.17

MS/MS spectra of N-methyl-d₃-cocaine: The spectra were obtained using the same conditions as for Figure 5.16. An example of the power of MS/MS is that any peaks may be used for quanitation even if they are isobaric (same m/z) to those of d₀ cocaine. This is because in the MS/MS process the molecular ion is isolated and fragmented in a sequential fashion. For example: m/z 304 is isolated and fragmented and the daughter ions measured. Then, m/z 307 is isolated and fragmented and the daughter ions measured. Even though m/z 91 is common to both d₃ and d₀ cocaine (spectra c in Figures 5.16 and 5.17), its origin can be determined by which parent ion is isolated to be fragmented. Although this example illustrates the power of MS/MS, for cocaine the major fragments all retain the deuterated label, so isobaric ions are not a consideration.

increases the signal-to-noise (S/N) ratio of an analysis. This increase in S/N allows the analyst to increase the instrumental sensitivity by increasing the gain on the electron multiplier. In a normal, single mass spectrum, increasing the gain of the electron multiplier increases the background in tandem with the signals of interest, so little increase in information is obtained. What is often relied upon in performing MS/MS is that coeluting materials will not have the same ions as the molecule of interest (or their ionization efficiency will be reduced by judicious selection of the CI reagent gas), and therefore the coeluting ions can be discriminated against by the MS/MS technique. If the coeluting peaks had the same ions (for example, m/z 304 for protonated cocaine) as the molecule of interest, MS/MS could still produce a valid spectrum because the coeluting molecules are unlikely ·to have similar fragments. However, if neither condition is met (different parent or fragment ions), then MS/MS will not work. For ion trap instruments, MS/MS is quite easy to accomplish, being done in software with minimal hardware modifications. However, the analyst must recognize that MS/MS spectra vary more with instrumental conditions than do the equivalent electron impact spectra (Figure 5.14).

5.4.9 INFRARED AND FOURIER TRANSFORM INFRARED (IR/FTIR)

IR is one of the more informative light-absorption techniques and provides a wealth of information on pure materials, especially in the fingerprint region of 1400–400 wave numbers. The spectra produced by an FTIR are identical to those of standard grading instruments, but frequently at higher resolution, with more accurate absorbances and more rapid spectral acquisition. Because no separation technique is usually used (although GC-FTIRs are commercially available), impurities may cloud the interpretation of the spectra. As in GC/MS, the analyst should have clear criteria for identification. The presence of extra absorbances may be acceptable, but missing absorbances should never be acceptable. Purification by acid/base extraction may be necessary before the IR spectrum is taken, to remove diluents. The salt form (freebase or hydrochloride) will affect the IR spectrum, thus this may be diagnostic of the form of the cocaine (Figure 5.18).

5.4.10 RAMAN IR

Raman provides much the same type of information as IR, except it relies on scattering of infrared radiation rather than absorption. One advantage is that it is capable of examining nontransparent surfaces and materials through packaging. This allows cocaine to be confirmed while in the bulk state without opening the package.

A disadvantage of Raman spectroscopy is that Raman signals are very weak as compared to IR absorptions. Because of this weakness, Raman spectroscopy is normally just used for bulk drugs. Particles may be examined with a micro-Raman instrument (Figure 5.19), although the intense laser light may change or burn the particles, especially if they are colored. Fluorescence is the biggest

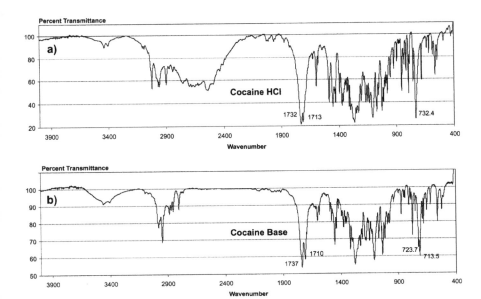

Figure 5.18

FTIR spectrum of cocaine hydrochloride (a) and cocaine base (b) in a KBr pellet: The baseline was corrected and the water and carbon dioxide bands were subtracted. Absorbances at 732, 1713, and 1732 wave numbers are characteristic of cocaine hydrochloride. Absorbances at 713, 723, 1710, and 1737 wave numbers are characteristic of cocaine freebase. These absorbances are slightly different than those in the literature (Morales, 2000). The broad absorbance between 2300–2900 wave numbers is also indicative of cocaine hydrochloride. However, the other peaks indicated are less obscured by adulterants. Some analysts use the small peaks at 3400 and the broad absorbance between 2400 and 2800 as indicative of cocaine hydrochloride. However, it is more difficult to articulate in court how something looks different than just to state that two numbers are different. The spectra were taken on a Nicolet 760 Manga-IR spectrometer.

interference in Raman spectroscopy. Besides fluorescent dyes, many natural substances in the environment fluoresce, chlorophyll being a good example. Also, many papers and cloths contain a fluorescent bluing agent to counteract their inherent yellow absorption. Examining cloth under UV light gives a dramatic visual impression of fluorescent brightening agents in most detergents. Thus, some samples may be masked by fluorescence. Using longer-wavelength lasers as excitation sources reduces fluorescence because most materials in the environment must be excited in the visible or UV. However, the intensity of Raman scattering decreases as λ^4, so a penalty in sensitivity is paid when using near-IR lasers. For example, using a 670-nm laser diode rather than a 540-nm argon laser would reduce the Raman scattering by a factor of 2.4. Laser wavelength should be considered in the choice of an instrument.

Figure 5.19

Raman spectrum of cocaine hydrochloride (a) and cocaine freebase (b): The spectrum was taken and baseline zeroed, and the fluorescence was removed. The spectra were taken on a Renishaw Ramascope. Carter et al. (2000) have used the differences in the 800–900 cm^{-1} region rather than the indicated absorbances to different cocaine HCl and cocaine base.

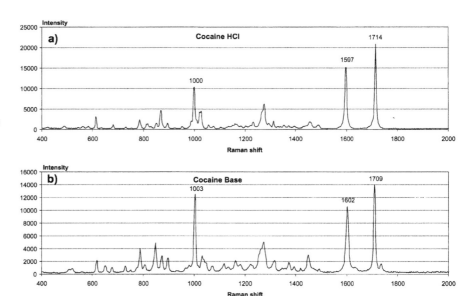

Like the IR spectra, the Raman emissions shift slightly depending on the salt form of cocaine (Figure 5.19). Also, like IR, impurities may cloud the interpretation of the Raman spectra. Certain colloidal metals enhance the Raman spectra (surface enhanced Raman spectroscopy—SERS), often by several orders of magnitude. SERS has been proposed to examine trace drug levels. It has the advantage over lateral flow assays of providing a fingerprint to match against a standard and thereby identifying an unknown from a single spectrum. Unfortunately, not all materials show the SERS effect, and research is still ongoing to extend SERS to trace-drug analysis. In addition, benzoylecgonine, a frequent impurity in cocaine base, shows a similar Raman spectrum to cocaine HCl (compare Figure 5.20 with Figure 5.19a). Mixtures of the two substances may broaden the Raman absorbances and cloud the interpretation of the results.

5.4.11 NUCLEAR MAGNETIC RESONANCE (NMR)

NMR is one of the more expensive techniques. However, it can be used for any sample that is reasonably pure and, like GC/MS, is definitive. Like GC/MS, extra peaks in the NMR (C13 or proton) are not necessarily indicative of an incorrect identification. However, missing peaks or peaks at the wrong absorption region would be evidence that a substance was not cocaine. Be careful of the presence of paramagnetic impurities (unlikely), which may selectively shift

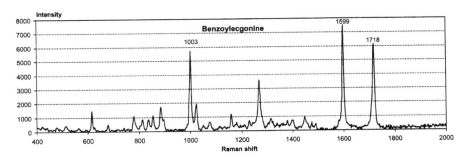

Figure 5.20

Raman spectrum of benzoylecgonine: The spectrum was taken, baseline zeroed, and the fluorescence removed. The spectra were taken on a Renishaw Ramascope. Note the similarity of the absorbances to cocaine HCl in Figure 5.19a.

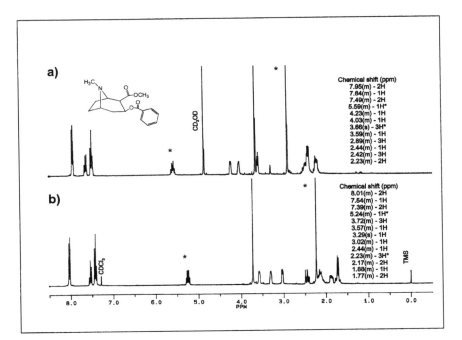

Figure 5.21

Proton NMR spectra of cocaine HCl and cocaine base: The spectra were obtained on a Bruker AC300. The cocaine HCl spectrum was taken in deuteromethanol (for solubility), and the cocaine base spectrum was taken in deuterochloroform. The slight shifts in absorptions may be due to differences in solvent effect. The peaks with an asterisk appear to be the most diagnostically useful to distinguish the two forms of cocaine.

certain NMR peaks or completely ruin the peak resolution. NMR can also be used to determine optical activity, especially when optically active, paramagnetic shift reagents are used. The proton spectra of cocaine hydrochloride and cocaine base are shown in Figure 5.21 and C13 spectra in Figure 5.22. The spectra were run in different solvents, so slight shifts in the absorbances were observed. The peaks with an asterisk appear to be the most diagnostically useful to distinguish the two forms of cocaine. Due to its sharp absorbance, the *N*-methyl absorbance in the proton spectra at 2.23 ppm for the freebase and 2.89 ppm for the hydrochloride would be the most useful.

Figure 5.22

C13 NMR spectra of cocaine HCl and cocaine base: The spectra were obtained on a Bruker AC300. The cocaine HCl spectra was taken in deuteromethanol (for solubility) and the cocaine base spectrum was taken in deuterochloroform. The slight shifts in absorptions may be due to differences in solvent effect. The peaks with an asterisk appear to be the most diagnostically useful to distinguish the two forms of cocaine.

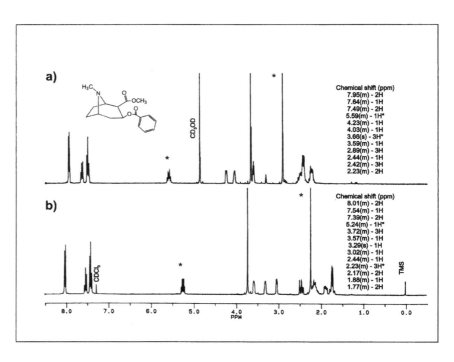

5.5 CONCLUSIONS

There is a large array of techniques available for the analysis and identification of cocaine. The most accepted approach is to employ two techniques that are complementary (just performing the same assay twice should never be acceptable). For low-cost, rapid analysis, color or crystal tests followed by TLC are often used. Alternatively, the preliminary tests may be followed by ion selective electrode analysis or immunoassy conformation. If available, the better (and more costly) analysis is to follow the preliminary screen (color or crystal tests, immunoassay, TLC, GC, or ion selective electrodes) with an instrumental confirmation. The more information that tests provide, the more assured the identification. Whatever the analyst chooses, he/she must be able to defend the choice in legal proceedings, because often careers and substantial costs are associated with the identification of an illicit substance.

REFERENCES

Allen, A.C., Cooper, D.A., Kiser, W.O., and Cottrell, R.C. (1981). The cocaine diastereoisomers. *J. Forensic Sci.* 26(1), 12–26.

Alliston, G.V., Bartlett, A.F.F., de Faubert Maunder, M.J., and Philips, G.F. (1972). An improved test for cocaine, methaqualone and methadone with a modified cobalt(II) thiocyanate reagent. *Analyst* 97, 263–265.

Alm, S., Jonson, S., Karlsson, H., and Sundholm, E.G. (1983). Simultaneous gas-chromatographic analysis of drugs of abuse on two fused-silica columns of different polarities. *J. Chromatogr.* 254(Jan), 179–186.

Armstrong, D.W., Han, S.M., and Han, Y.I. (1987). Separation of optical isomers of scopolamine, cocaine, homatropine, and atropine. *Anal. Biochem.* 167(2), 261–264.

Baker, P.B., and Gough, T.A. (1979). The rapid determination of cocaine and other local anesthetics using field tests and chromatography. *J. Forensic Sci.* 24(4), 847–855.

Campanella, L., Aiello, L., Colapicchioni, C., and Tomassetti, M. (1998). Lidocaine and benzalkonium analysis and titration in drugs using new ISFET devices. *J. Pharm. Biomed. Anal.* 18, 117–125.

Campanella, L., Colapicchioni, C., Tomassetti, M., Bianco, A., and Dezzi, S. (1995). A new ISFET device for cocaine analysis. *Sensors Actuators B* 24–25, 188–193.

Campbell, J.P., Wagner, R.L., and O'Connell, D.B. (1987). Solid-phase assay with visual readout. U.S. Patent 4,703,017, October 27.

Carroll, F.I., Lewin, A.H., Abraham, P., Parham, K., Boja, J.W., and Kuhar, M.J. (1991). Synthesis and ligand binding of cocaine isomers at the cocaine receptor. *J. Med. Chem.* 34(3), 883–886.

Carter, J.C., Brewer, W.E., and Angel, S.M. (2000). Raman spectroscopy for the in situ identification of cocaine and selected adulterants. *App. Spectrosc.* 54, 1876–1881.

Casale, J.F. (1987). A practical total synthesis of cocaine enantiomers. *Forensic Sci. Int.* 33(4), 275–298.

Casale, J.F. (1992). Methyl-esters of ecgonine—injection-port produced artifacts from cocaine base (crack) exhibits. *J. Forensic Sci.* 37(5), 1295–1310.

Casale, J.F., and Klein, R.F.X. (1993). Illicit production of cocaine. *Forensic Sci. Rev.* 5(2), 96–107.

Casale, J.F., and Waggoner, R.W. (1991). A chromatographic impurity signature profile analysis for cocaine using capillary gas chromatography. *J. Forensic Sci.* 36, 1312–1330.

Chan, M.L., Whetsell, C., and McChesne, J.D. (1974). Use of high-pressure liquid chromatography for separation of drugs of abuse. *J. Chromatogr. Sci.* 12(9), 512–516.

Chiarotti, M., and Fucci, N. (1990). HPLC analysis of cocaine diastereoisomers by chiral stationary phase. *Forensic Sci. Int.* 44(1), 37–41.

Clarke, E.G.C. (1969). *Isolation and Identification of Drugs in Pharmaceuticals, Body Fluids, and Postmortem Material.* Pharmaceutical Press, London.

Clarke, E.G.C. (1986). *Clarke's Isolation and Identification of Drugs in Pharmaceuticals, Body Fluids, and Postmortem Material.* Pharmaceutical Press, London.

Comparini, I.B., Centini, F., and Pariali, A. (1983). Simultaneous determination of narcotics, adulterants and diluents in street samples by means of gas chromatography with capillary columns. *J. Chromatogr.* 279(Nov), 609–613.

Comparini, I.B., Centini, F., and Pariali, A. (1984). High-resolution gas chromatography—simultaneous detection of narcotics, adulterants, and diluents in street samples. *J. High-Res. Chromatogr.* 7(3), 140–141.

Cooper, D.A., and Allen, A.C. (1984). Synthetic cocaine impurities. *J. Forensic Sci.* 29(4), 1045–1055.

Dandliker, W.B., and de Saussure, V.A. (1970). Fluorescence polarization in immunochemistry. *Immunochemistry* 7, 799.

Dandliker, W.B., and Feigen, G.A. (1961). Quantification of the antigen–antibody reaction by the polarization of fluorescence. *Biochem. Biophys. Res. Commun.* 5, 299.

Davidow, B., Li Petri, N., and Quame, B. (1968). A thin-layer chromatographic screening procedure for detecting drug abuse. *Am. J. Clin. Pathol.* 38(11), 714–719.

de Zeeuw, R.A., Hartstra, J., and Franke, J.P. (1994). Potential and pitfalls of chromatographic techniques and detection modes in substance identification for systematic toxicological analysis. *J. Chromatogr.* A 674(1–2), 3–13.

Ehleringer, J.R., Casale, J.F., Lott, M.J., and Ford, V.L. (2000). Tracing the geographical origin of cocaine. *Nature* 408, 311–312.

Elnemma, E.M., Hamada, M.A., and Hassan, S.S.M. (1992). Liquid and poly(vinyl chloride) matrix membrane electrodes for the selective determination of cocaine in illicit powders. *Talanta.* 39(10), 1329–1335.

Ensing, J.G., and de Zeeuw, R.A. (1991). Detection, isolation and identification of truxillines in illicit cocaine by means of thin-layer chromatography and mass spectrometry. *J. Forensic Sci.* 36(5), 1299–1311.

Eskes, D. (1978). Thin-layer chromatographic procedure for the differentiation of the optical isomers of cocaine. *J. Chromatogr.* 152, 589–591.

Fetterolf, D.D., and Yost, Y.A. (1984). *Int. J. Mass Spec. Ion Proc.* 62, 33–49.

Fulton, C.C. (1969). *Modern Microcrytal Tests for Drugs: The Identification of Organic Compounds by Microcrystalloscopic Chemistry.* Wiley, New York, pp. 300–301.

Grant, F.W., Martin, W.C., and Quackenbush, R.W. (1975). A simple sensitive specific field test for cocaine based on the recognition of the odor of methyl benzoate as a test product. *Bull Narc.* 27(2), 33–35.

Henson, M.C., Johnson, Z.B., and Piper, E.L. (1985). Quantitation of radioimmunoassay data through the use of an interactive computer program. *Instruments and Computers* 8, 8–12.

Hill, D.W., Kelley, T.R., and Langner, K.J. (1987). Computerized library search routine for comparing ultraviolet spectra of drugs separated by high-performance liquid chromatography. *Anal. Chem.* 59(2), 350–353.

Hussain, A. (1988). A simple method for the separation and identification of cocaine and lidocaine in a mixture. *Microgram* 21(6), 100–101.

Jukofsky, D., Verebey, K., and Mule, Joseph S. (1980). Qualitative differentiation between cocaine, lidocaine, and cocaine–lidocaine mixtures ("rock cocaine") using thin-layer chromatography. *J. Chromatogr.* 198, 534–535.

Julian, E.A., and Plein, E.M. (1983). Microcrystalline identification of drugs of abuse: stimulant street drugs. *J. Forensic Sci.* 28(4), 992–999.

Kaufman, M.S. (1990). Household bleach as a test for drugs. *Microgram* 23(4), 75–77.

Kidwell, D.A. (1993). Analysis of phencyclidine and cocaine in human hair by tandem mass spectrometry. *J. Forensic Sci.* 38, 272–284.

Kidwell, D.A., and Smith, F.P. (2000). Letter to editor. *J. Forensic Sci.* 45, 237–238.

Kidwell, D.A., and Riggs, L.A. (2004). Comparing two analytical methods: minimal standards in forensic toxicology derived from information theory. *Forensic Sci. Int.* 145(2–3), 85–96.

Kim, H.J., and Cerceo, E. (1976). Interference by sodium chloride with the EMIT method of analysis for drugs of abuse. *Clinical Chem.* 22, 1936.

Kovar, K.A., and Laudszun, M. (1989). *Chemistry and Reaction Mechanisms of Rapid Tests for Drugs of Abuse and Precursor Chemicals.* United Nations, Scientific and Technical Notes, SCITEC/6.

Leuvering, J.H.W. (1982). Metal sol particle immunoassay, U.S. Patent 4,313,734, February 2.

Lillsunde, P., and Korte, T. (1991). Comprehensive drug screening in urine using solid-phase extraction and combined TLC and GC/MS identification. *J. Anal. Toxicol.* 15, 71–81.

Logan, B.K., Nichols, H.S., and Stafford, D.T. (1989). A simple laboratory test for the determination of the chemical form of cocaine. *J. Forensic Sci.* 34(3), 678–681.

Lurie, I.S. (1998). Capillary electrophoresis of illicit drug seizures. *Forensic Sci. Int.* 92(2–3), 125–136.

Mannich, C. (1934). *Arch. Pharm.* 272, 323–359.

May, K. (2000). Assay devices. U.S. Patent 6,156,271, December 5.

Morales, R. (2000). The use of specific infared absorption bands to distinguish cocaine base and cocaine HCl when mixed with known adulterants or diluents. *Microgram* 33(9), 247–256.

Mura, P., Kintz, P., Papet, Y., Ruesch, G., and Piriou, A. (1999). Evaluation of six rapid tests for screening of cannabinoids in sweat, saliva, and urine. *Acta Clinica Belgica* 35–38, Suppl. 1.

O'Donnell, C.M., and Suffin, S.C. (1979). Fluorescent immunoassays. *Anal. Chem.* 51, 33A.

Perrin, F. (1926). Polarized fluorescence, influence of viscosity. *J. Phys. Radium* 7, 390.

Rosenstein, R.W. (1997). Solid-phase chromatographic immunoassay. U.S. Patent 5,591,645, January 7.

Rubenstein, K.E. (1978). New homogeneous assay methods for the determination of proteins. *Scand. J. Immunol.* 8, 57.

Rubenstein, K.E., Schneider, R.S., and Ullman, E.F. (1972). Homogeneous enzyme immunoassay: new immunochemical technique. *Biochem. Biophys. Res. Commun.* 47, 846.

Ruybal, R. (1982). Differentiation of d- and l-cocaine by microcrystalline test. *Microgram* 15(9), 160–161.

Samyn, N., and van Haeren, C. (2000). On-site testing of saliva and sweat with Drugwipe and determination of concentrations of drugs of abuse in saliva, plasma and urine of suspected users. *Int. J. Legal Med.* 113(3), 150–154.

Schlesinger, H.L. (1985). Topics in the chemistry of cocaine. *Bull. Narc.* 35(1), 63–78.

Scott, L.J. (1973). Specific field test for cocaine. *Microgram* 6(11), 179–181.

Skelley, D.S., Brown, L.P., and Besch, P.K. (1973). Radioimmunoassay. *Clin. Chem.* 19, 146.

Soini, E., and Hemmila, I. (1979). Fluoroimmunoassay: present status and key problems. *Clin. Chem.* 25, 353.

Sorgen, G.J. (1983). Identification of d- and l-Cocaine. *Microgram* 16(8), 126–131.

Stevens, H.M. (1986). *Color Tests in Clarke's Isolation and Identification of Drugs in Pharmaceuticals, Body Fluids, and Postmortem Material.* Pharmaceutical Press, London.

Tagliaro, F., Smith, F.P., Turrina, S., Equisetto, V., and Marigo, M. (1996). Complementary use of capillary zone electrophoresis and micellar electrokinetic capillary chromatography for mutual confirmation of results in forensic drug analysis. *J. Chromatogr. A* 735(1–2), 227–235.

Tandon, R. (1978). A new solvent system for the separation of cocaine from other alkaloids by thin-layer chromatography. *Microgram* 6(5), 82–87.

Travnikoff, B. (1983a). Screening test for cocaine. *Microgram* 16(4), 69–70.

Travnikoff, B. (1983b). Semiquantitative screening test for cocaine. *Anal. Chem.* 55, 795–796.

U.S. Department of Justice, Bureau of Narcotics and Dangerous Drugs. (1986). *Methods of Analysis: Alkaloids, Opiates, Marihuana, Barbiturates, and Miscellaneous Drugs.* U.S. Government Printing Office, Washington, DC.

U.S. Department of Justice, Office of Justice Programs, Bureau of Justice Statistics. (1994). In *United Nations, UNDCP, Rapid Testing Methods of Drugs of Abuse, Manual for Use by National Law Enforcement and Narcotics Laboratory Personnel.* U.N., New York.

United Nations, Division of Narcotic Drugs. (1986). *Recommended Methods for Testing Cocaine, Manual for Use by National Narcotic Laboratories.* U.N., New York.

United Nations, UNIDCP. (1994). *Rapid Testing Methods of Drugs of Abuse, Manual for Use by National Law Enforcement and Narcotics Laboratory Personnel.* U.N., New York.

Wallace, J.E., Hamilton, H.E., Schwertner, H., King, D.E., McNay, J.L., and Blum, K. (1975). Thin-layer chromatographic analysis of cocaine and benzoylecgonine in urine. *J. Chromatogr.* 114, 433–441.

Watanabe, K., Okada, K., Oda, H., and Katsu, T. (1997). Development of a portable cocaine-selective electrode. *Jpn. J. Toxicol. Environ. Health* 43, 17.

Wheals, B.B., and Jane, I. (1977). Analysis of drugs and their metabolites by high-performance liquid chromatography—review. *Analyst* 102, 625–644.

Yalow, R.S., and Berson, S.A. (1960). Immunoassay of endogenous plasma insulin. *J. Clin. Invest.* 39, 1157.

Young, J.L. (1931). The detection of cocaine in the presence of Novocain by means of cobalt thiocyanate. *Am. J. Pharm.* Dec., 709–710.

CHAPTER 6

OPIOIDS: METHODS OF FORENSIC ANALYSIS

M.J. Bogusz

King Faisal Specialist Hospital and Research Center,
Riyadh, Saudi Arabia

Contents

6.1 INTRODUCTION

This chapter reviews the use of separation methods for isolation, identification, and quantitative analysis of natural and synthetic opiates. Strictly speaking, the term *opiate* refers specifically to the products derived from the opium poppy. The review focuses on morphine derivatives and synthetic or semisynthetic opiates, showing agonistic action at opioid receptors OP_1 (δ), OP_2 (κ), or OP_3 (μ). The action of opiates on opioid receptors and the classification of receptors have been reviewed elsewhere (Dhawan et al., 1996). The present overview is limited to drugs of particular forensic significance and focuses on forensic analytical applications reported over the last decade and devoted mainly to biological samples. These applications are divided into sections:

- Preliminary methods for opioid detection in nonbiological and biological samples
- Isolation of opioids from various biological matrices
- Analysis of opium poppy constituents in plant material and in body fluids

Handbook of Forensic Drug Analysis
Frederick P. Smith, Editor

- Separation and detection of heroin, its congeners, and its specific metabolites in illicit drug preparations and in body fluids
- Analysis of morphine and other natural and synthetic opiates in body fluids and organs

In each section the relevant separation techniques (TLC, GC, HPLC, and CE), combined with various detection methods, are reviewed in turn.

6.2 PRELIMINARY METHODS FOR OPIATE DETECTION

Preliminary tests play a dual role in forensic toxicology. First, their use fulfills the main condition of forensic analysis, i.e., the application of two independent methods for positive results whenever possible. Second, the important economic and logistic factors should be considered. The purpose of these tests is to screen and exclude suspected samples, which certainly do not contain any opiates. This may filter a majority of negative samples and save the time and cost of analysis. Since the negative result of a preliminary test usually has decisive value, it should be absolutely reliable. In other words, there should be no room for false-negative results. Therefore, preliminary tests should show broad group specificity and possibly high sensitivity, whereas an absolute specificity is not required. An unequivocal identification and quantitation is usually done in the confirmatory step of analysis.

6.2.1 METHODS USED FOR STREET DRUGS

Preliminary testing for the presence of opiates, as well as other drugs of abuse, is performed mainly by law enforcement officers (police or custom officers, prison wardens) in field conditions. Therefore, the testing devices used for this purpose should be simple, robust, and sensitive, while the selectivity is not a particularly critical issue. The main task of these tests is to select suspicious samples or materials for possible further examination with confirmatory methods. Usually, well-known color reactions with various reagents are applied here.

Narcopouch® (ODV Inc., Paris, ME) is a battery of color tests for the tentative detection of opiates, amphetamines, cocaine, barbiturates, cannabinoids, and LSD in street samples. The detection principle is based on color reactions with known reagents, such as Marquis, Meyer's, Mecke, Ehrlich's, fast blue B, and Koppanyi. The whole procedure is performed in a plastic pouch under visual inspection. The Herosol® field kit (Mistral Detection Ltd., Jerusalem, Israel) consists of a spray reagent and special test paper. The suspected surface (e.g., skin) is wiped with the paper, which is then sprayed with Herosol. A violet color indicates the presence of heroin. A similar heroin test, Detect Now™, is supplied by Test Medical Symptoms@Home, Inc., and is marketed via the Internet as a simple test for parents who like to check their children for drug use. The NIK® narcotic field test (Public Safety Inc., Armor Holding, Jacksonville, FL) consists of individual ampoule tests for the main groups of drugs of abuse, among them opiates/amphetamines, and for heroin/opium. Drug Wipe and Drug Wipe II (Securetec AG, Germany) are immunochemical tests designed for the detection of drugs of abuse on various surfaces, e.g., luggage, passports, and currency, but also on skin or tongue. Therefore, these tests may be used for the detection of drugs in sweat or saliva. The detection limit for opiates is 25 ng of morphine equivalent. With the portable reader, a colorimetric quantitation may be performed.

6.2.2 METHODS USED FOR BIOLOGICAL FLUIDS

Preliminary methods used for biological fluids may be divided according to different criteria. From the technical point of view, one clearly would divide these methods into onsite (point-of-care) and laboratory tests. These two groups of tests are discussed next. However, preliminary tests may be used not only for forensic or preventive purposes, e.g., in employee screening, but also as a diagnostic procedure in suspected acute poisoning. This different purpose is also associated with a different strategy. In onsite tests applied in a hospital emergency ward, the confirmation analysis sometimes is not of primary importance. For instance, in clinical toxicology, in the case of suspected heroin overdose, after a positive result of a preliminary opiate test it is clear that the physician must immediately apply an opiate antagonist, such as naloxone, instead of waiting for the results of a confirmatory analysis. This practice is not limited to health professionals; the distribution of naloxone for administration in addicts' homes by their companions or family members is a novel approach being tested in the United States, Germany, and the United Kingdom (Sporer, 2003). The same strategy is valid in the case of positive results for a benzodiazepine test, indicating acute poisoning, and suggesting the use of the antagonist flumazenil.

6.2.2.1 Onsite Tests

The use and development of onsite tests capable of analyzing available body fluids for drugs of abuse has been stimulated by the general exposure to abused substances and by the requirements of modern society. There is a multitude of socially critical situations that demand full sobriety and unaffected psychomotor skills of a given individual. Therefore, onsite tests are demanded and widely used among very different social groups, such as automobile drivers, incarcerated criminals, the military, athletes, employees of the oil industry, among others. A particular value of the onsite test is in the testing of mobile groups, located in some remote areas. Additionally, it is very important to get a non-invasive sampling. For this reason, the testing of saliva or sweat instead of urine or blood became particularly attractive. It should be added that onsite tests might also be valuable in monitoring some therapeutic drugs, e.g., anticoagulants. For these reasons, such tests carry an alternative name: *point-of-care tests*. An excellent review of onsite drug testing, comprising all aspects of this analysis, was done in a recent book edited by Jenkins and Goldberger (2002). Table 6.1 shows the features of the most popular onsite testing devices used for opiate detection. All of them are based on the immunoassay principle; also, all of them are capable of detecting the whole panel of drugs of abuse: amphetamines, benzodiazepines, cannabinoids, cocaine, and opiates.

Crouch et al. (2002) performed a field evaluation of five onsite drug-testing devices: AccuSign, Rapid Drug Screen, TesT-Cup-5, TesTstik, and Triage. Urine samples were collected at two police agencies: in Houston, TX, and Nassau County, NY. Four hundred samples were tested at each site from November 1998 to November 1999. The cutoff for opiates was 300 ng/mL urine. All samples positive in onsite tests were confirmed with GC-MS (for morphine and codeine) and with LC-MS (for hydrocodone and hydromorphone). Only one false-negative result was observed. The false-positive rate was below 0.25% for all devices (one to two samples for each device). In conclusion, it was stated that onsite drug-testing devices are useful in DUI investigations, due to a very low rate of false-negative and false-positive results. Gronholm and Lillsunde (2001) evaluated eight various onsite devices for urine and oral fluid assay of opiates, cocaine, and amphetamines. In the case of opiates, the accuracy ranged from 94% to 98% for both matrices. Multicenter evaluation of the immunochromatographic onsite test Frontline® for drugs in urine was published by Wennig et al. (1998). In the case of opiates, the sensitivity and speci-

Table 6.1

Onsite tests used for opiate detection

Name	Manufacturer	Calibrator	Cutoff (ng/mL)	Matrix
Cozart RapiScan	www.cozart.co.uk	Morphine	10	Saliva
ONTRAK TesTcup	www.rochediagnostics.com	Morphine	300	Urine
ONTRAK TesTStik	www.rochediagnostics.com	Morphine	300	Urine
Syva RapidTest	www.dadebehring.com	Morphine	300	Urine
Triage DOA	www.biosite.com	Morphine	300	Urine
Rapid Drug Screen	www.bioscaninc.com	Morphine	300	Urine
AccuSign	www.pbmc.com	Morphine	300	Urine

ficity were above 99% for all centers involved. Buchan et al. (1998) evaluated accuracy and specificity of four onsite kits for urine testing. Opiates were detected in 100% by all kits.

A new ORALscreen System, an onsite kit for the analysis of drugs in oral fluid, consists of an oral fluid–collection device and immunoassay detection device. This system, evaluated by Barrett et al. (2001), showed very good agreement with laboratory-based urine-screening test results for 2–3 days following drug use.

6.2.2.2 Laboratory Tests

Preliminary laboratory tests for opiate detection are also based on the immunoassay principle, as is it in the case of onsite tests. Beside opiates, they usually comprise the whole battery of tests, such as amphetamines, cocaine, benzodiazepines, barbiturates, cannabinoids, and methadone, among others. Laboratory tests are used in situations when the number of examined samples is quite high, e.g., in drug screening of employees or the military. Each laboratory system used for drug screening consists of three main components that influence its reliability and efficiency:

- Antibodies used in the immunoassay—their sensitivity and selectivity
- The detection system applied—its robustness, susceptibility to matrix effects, and sensitivity
- The analyzer used for the test—its capability, speed, ease of operation, fool-proof construction, and applicability for forensic analysis

Regarding opiate immunoassay, the selectivity of all available tests is similar. All react with a broad range of opiates: morphine and its glucuronides, codeine, and semisynthetic opiates, such as dihydrocodeine and hydrocodone. One manufacturer (Microgenics, Fremont, CA) recently developed a CEDIA® 6-AM assay that was claimed to react selectively for 6-monoacetylmorphine (the primary metabolite of heroin). However, in the study of George and Parmar (2002), who analyzed 1100 urine specimens with the CEDIA 6-MAM, in 21 out of 282 positive specimens (7%), the presence of 6-MAM was not confirmed, using GC-MS. In all these samples, morphine was found in concentrations ranging from 410 to 2010 µg/L. The authors stressed that each positive result in this assay must be confirmed with a method that is more specific.

The detection systems most frequently used in drugs-of-abuse screening are based on enzyme-mediated immunoassay reactions, such as the enzyme-mediated immunoassay technique (EMIT), cloned enzyme donor immuno-assay (CEDIA), and enzyme-linked immunosorbent assay (ELISA). Other systems are based on a physical detection principle, e.g., fluorescence polarization immunoassay (FPIA) and kinetic interaction of microparticles in solution (KIMS). Radioimmunoassay (RIA), used broadly in the previous decade, is now being replaced by nonradioactive procedures and gradually disappearing in forensic laboratories. Each available system has its advantages and drawbacks.

Enzyme-mediated immunoassays, the most common screening methods used for detection of drugs of abuse, were developed in various versions, utilizing glucose-6-phospho-dehydrogenase and peroxidase as indicator enzymes. The methods can easily be automated and may also be adapted for the direct analysis of other biological fluids, e.g., serum and CSF. Since enzyme immunoassays are based on biochemical reaction, the calibration curve is usually less stable (for some weeks) than in methods based on physicochemical reactions, such as FPIA and KIMS (for some months). FPIA is a robust method of detection that is broadly used for urine screening and may be applied for serum or blood after protein precipitation (Bogusz et al., 1990; Maier et al., 1992; Keller et al., 2000). KIMS depends on the measurement of the optical absorbance of the sample, caused by the drug–microparticle–antibody aggregates. It was reported as a viable alternative to EMIT or FPIA assays.

In the choice of the analyzer for immunoassays, the following factors should be taken into consideration:

- The type of drug-testing system available for the specific instrument, since the test manufacturers usually collaborate with specific manufacturers of analytical systems
- The general applicability of the analyzer for forensic purposes (low susceptibility to matrix effects, possibility that the sample and reagent will cool, bar code identification)
- The throughput of the instrument, which should be adequate to the daily load of samples

Several authors have made systematic comparison of various laboratory screening systems in real-life conditions. Cone et al. (1992) compared the analytical sensitivity, specificity, and accuracy of FPIA, EMIT, and RIA for opiate detection in urine. In all cases, the apparent sensitivities of assays were higher than the cutoff required by government organizations. However, the pattern of sensitivity and selectivity of each assay was different. Armbruster et al. (1993) compared the performance of analyzers based on different detection principles, e.g., EMIT, KIMS, FPIA, and radioimmunoassay, for drugs-of-abuse screening. In the case of opiates, EMIT gave 3% nonconfirmed positive results, whereas other tests gave no such results. In the study of Smith et al. (2000), the influence of new U.S. legislation, changing the urine screening and confirmation cutoff concentrations from 300 to 2000 µg/L, was tested. Four commercial enzyme immunoassays using an old 300-µg/L cutoff and two immunoassays using a new 2000-µg/L cutoff were compared. The study was done on 920 urine samples taken from 11 volunteers receiving various IV or inhalatory doses of heroin. The specificity and sensitivity of assays were different, but morphine was detectable in urine for at least 12 h after heroin administration. A broad-scale study was conducted by Cone et al. (2002) in order to establish cutoff concentrations of drugs of abuse in oral fluid for workplace testing. The Intercept immunoassay, followed by GC-MS-MS, was applied. Intercept™ is a laboratory-based system where oral fluid samples are collected onsite with an adsorbent device and then analyzed in the laboratory. Out of 77,218 oral fluid specimens, 3908 (5.06%) were positive for various drugs. In the case of opiates, a very high prevalence of 6-MAM confirmations (66.7%) was observed, suggesting a high usefulness of oral-fluid testing. Cheever et al. (1999) compared the selectivity of two enzyme immunoassays, FPIA and KIMS, and two ELISAs for the cross-reactivity of l-alpha-acetylmethadol (LAAM) and methadol (a common metabolite of LAAM and methadone) in methadone immunoassay. Both LAAM and methadol showed high cross-reactivity with most immunoassays, indicating the need of chromatographic confirmation of results.

ELISA assay was applied not only for urine but also for postmortem blood and tissues. In the study of K. Moore et al. (1999), postmortem blood and tissue homogenates were screened for morphine, opiate class, and other eight classes of drugs using ELISA. The results were compared with RIA and verified with GC-MS. Morphine assay was very specific for free morphine but less sensitive than class opiate screening. The latter assay was recommended for screening postmortem specimens as an adequate alternative to RIA. Kemp et al. (2002) evaluated a commercial ELISA for opiate/benzodiazepine screening of postmortem blood. Blood samples were diluted 1:5 to facilitate pipetting, and no matrix effects were found. Ninety positive and 40 negative specimens were subjected to verification with GC-MS. The optimal cutoff for opiates was found to be between 20 and 50 µg/L morphine equivalents. At the cutoff of 20 µg/L, the sensitivity was 95% and the specificity 92% versus GC-MS.

Several studies were performed to check and compare the selectivity of various immunoassays used for opiate detection. Kerrigan and Phillips (2001) compared the analytical performance of two ELISA tests for detection of opiates and five other drugs of abuse in blood and urine. Of the 855 casework samples examined with both tests, there were 15 discordant results for opiates. The number of false positives was one and three for both assays, respectively. Detection limits for morphine in whole blood ranged from 1 to 3 µg/L. Schütz et al. (2002) studied whether therapeutic use of this apomorphine might interfere with the results of CEDIA and FPIA immunoassays for opiates. No false-positive results were observed using recommended cutoff values or urine. Apomorphine (Ixense) is widely used in the treatment of erectile disorders.

The broad use of drug testing and the grave consequences of positive results for the person involved created a tendency to "beat the test." This may be done by dilution of urine through excessive drinking, by replacement of an authentic urine sample with a "clean" one, or by adulteration of urine with household chemicals or commercially available preparations. Nowadays, there is a multitude of manufacturers offering various kits and reagents that may be added to urine to avoid the detection of drugs, both in preliminary and confirmatory phase. As a countermeasure to adulteration, the following can be applied: measuring of temperature, specific gravity, pH, and creatinine content of urine, as well as special chemical tests for detection of chemical adulterants. Cody et al. (2001a, 2001b) examined the influence of a "stealth" adulterant on the detectability of morphine and codeine in urine samples. "Stealth" consists of peroxidase and peroxide and is advertised as being undetectable by adulteration tests. It was demonstrated that samples with a low concentration of morphine and codeine (2.5 mg/L urine) rendered negative, both in immunochemical and GC-MS examination, while typical urine parameters remained unchanged. At higher opiate concentrations, however, immunoassays and GC-MS gave positive results despite adulteration. Microgenics developed a special assay named "sample check" that detects any possible interference with CEDIA assays caused by sample adulteration. This assay replaced a complex panel of adulteration assays offered by some other manufacturers or by Microgenics itself.

6.3 ISOLATION OF OPIATES FROM BIOSAMPLES

6.3.1 SOLVENT EXTRACTION

Solvent extraction has been widely used for the isolation of opioids from nonbiological, plant, and human samples for decades. Therefore, only new developments for this technique will be discussed. A Norwegian research team (Rasmussen et al., 2000; Ugland et al., 2000) established liquid-phase microextraction (LPME) and applied this procedure to the isolation of opioid methadone (Ho et al., 2002a, 2002b). The principle of LMPE is to extract 1–4 mL of liquid sample with a very small volume of solvent (15–25 μL). The solvent was immobilized on the hollow fiber and then immersed in the container with the sample and vibrated for 50 min. The collected solvent was then injected into GC without concentration. LPME was compared with conventional solvent extraction and appeared to be very successful for the isolation of hydrophobic analytes. In the case of more polar compounds, solvent extraction was superior. In addition, protein binding of some drugs, e.g., methadone and pethidine, affected the extraction efficiency of LPME. However, the efficiency of LMPE has been greatly enhanced by the addition of methanol to plasma samples.

6.3.2 SOLID-PHASE EXTRACTION

Solid-phase column extraction (SPE) methods have been used very often for opiate isolation from biological material. In this section, only those studies will be reviewed that dealt directly with the assessment of SPE as an isolation method in toxicology or with the comparison of various SPE materials. Usually, the studies involved were not limited only to opiates, but included other drugs of forensic or clinical toxicological interest. Solid-phase extraction may be regarded as a particular kind of column chromatography. Therefore, the optimization of extraction conditions, taking into account all three interacting factors, i.e., analyte, sorbent, and eluent, has been the subject of various studies (Marko et al., 1992; Soltes, 1992; Gelencser et al., 1994). At first, SPE cartridges filled with various reverse-phase packing (C_1, C_8, and C_{18}) or cation exchange material were applied, and the forensic applications, especially for tissues, have been reviewed (Scheurer and Moore, 1992). Among various packing materials available, C_{18} appeared most popular in toxicological applications, which was obviously caused by the wide acceptance of this phase in analytical HPLC. In the late 1980s, mixed-phase cartridges, containing reverse-phase and cation exchange sorbents, were commercially introduced. Standard procedures for the isolation of various drugs of forensic relevance from urine have been developed and supplied by the manufacturers. A comprehensive review of SPE methods was published by Thurman and Mills (1998). Solid-phase extraction in disk format was introduced by D.L. King et al. (1989). This technique consumed about 10–20 times less solvent than the classical column cartridge extraction. Trends in the development of disk-format SPE have been reviewed by Blevins and Hall (1998). Disk-format SPE has been applied for the isolation of opiates by Degel (1996). De Zeeuw et al. (2000) tested the efficiency of SPE in disk format for broad-spectrum isolation of drugs from urine. Urine was spiked with a selection of acidic, neutral, and basic drugs and subjected to SPE on disk cartridges. Acidic and neutral drugs were then eluted with ethyl acetate/acetone, followed by basic drugs eluted with ammoniated ethyl acetate. All drugs were detected with GC-FID. The disk procedure allowed 60% reduction of elution volumes and processing time in comparison with standard SPE.

6.3.3 REVERSE-PHASE SOLID-PHASE EXTRACTION

The first SPE (Sep-Pak C_{18}) methods for the isolation of morphine and its metabolites (normorphine, morphine glucuronides) from serum and urine were published by Svensson (1986) and Svensson et al. (1982). Bouquillon et al. (1992) applied C_{18} cartridges to the isolation of morphine and hydromorphone from plasma. The drugs and internal standard (naltrexone) were separated by HPLC on a Spherisorb C_8 column with coulometric detection. The limits of quantification (LOQ) of 1.2 ng/mL for morphine and 2.5 ng/mL for hydromorphone were achieved. The authors stressed the high recovery and good quality of extracts. The applicability of C_8, PTFE-based extraction disks (Empore™) to the isolation of various acidic and basic drugs (including codeine) from urine was tested by Ensing et al. (1992). The sample capacity for untreated urine, measured with radioactive drugs, was at least 25 mL, and up to 250 µg of drugs were retained on the disk. The recovery of codeine averaged 76% using methanol elution. Soares et al. (1992) performed a comparative study of SPE with C_{18} cartridges, Extrelut columns, and liquid–liquid extraction for morphine isolation from urine. The drug was determined by HPLC with UV detection at 212 nm. The best results were obtained with liquid–liquid extraction combined with Extrelut purification. Urine extracts obtained with C_{18} cartridges showed very high matrix interference under the applied conditions and were not suitable for analysis. Another comparative study of different commercially available SPE cartridges, among them six C_{18}, two C_8, and one C_1 column, was done by Papadoyannis et al. (1993). Serum and urine samples were spiked with morphine to concentrations from 443 to 7090 ng/mL and with codeine to concentrations from 500 to 8000 ng/mL. One-tenth-milliliter aliquots were then vortexed with 0.2 mL ACN and centrifuged. The supernatants were applied to buffered (pH 9.2) SPE cartridges, rinsed with water, and eluted with 2 mL methanol. The reconstituted residues were examined by HPLC on an Adsorbosphere ODS column in MeOH-ACN-0.1 M ammonium acetate (40:25:35). A UV detector set at 241 nm was used, and a limit of detection (LOD) (on column) of 2 ng for morphine and 1 ng for codeine was found. The extraction recoveries showed a very large variability of tested cartridges. For instance, morphine recoveries from plasma varied from 23.2% to 108.5% and those of codeine from 17.2% to 87.0%. In the next paper (Theodoridis, 1995) the same research group compared the applicability of various commercially available SPE cartridges (five C_{18} and two C_8) for systematic toxicological analysis. As model substances, morphine, codeine, 6-MAM, diamorphine, nalorphine, cocaine, and BE were selected. The same extraction procedure as reported in the previous study was applied. Reconstituted extracts were subjected to HPLC-DAD analysis, in which the mobile phase consisted of MeOH-

ACN-1.2% ammonium acetate (40:15:45). Again, very large differences in extraction recoveries were observed, which, according to the authors, were caused by different chromatographic characteristics of the particular SPE columns. The authors stated that there should be no judgment of a "bad" or "good" cartridge, because some materials are particularly suitable for specific applications or compounds. On the other hand, the whole extraction process should be very carefully optimized. The study of the reusability of SPE cartridges (fivefold extraction of spiked plasma and urine samples) demonstrated slow but steady loss of recovery after each consecutive extraction. Therefore, the authors did not recommend reusing the SPE columns. The carryover phenomenon, which may occur with a reused column, was not tested. Degel (1996) compared several new methods of solid-phase extraction in respect to their applicability to clinical toxicological analysis. Several SPE methods were tested: classical column extraction, disk extraction with C_{18} and mixed phase, and solid-phase microextraction (SPME) with polydimethylsiloxane fibers. Codeine, dihydrocodeine, and methadone were included among various acidic and basic drugs tested. Disk extraction and SPME performed very well for dedicated applications; the main advantages were low solvent consumption and simple procedure. On the basis of the reexamination of different SPE procedures using different sorbents, Geier et al. (1996) developed a method for the isolation of morphine, 6-MAM, DHC, and codeine from plasma and whole blood. Plasma extracts examined by GC-MS showed no interfering peaks. The LODs were below 5 µg/L for all compounds involved.

6.3.3.1 Mixed-Phase SPE

Mixed-phase (reverse-phase cation exchange) SPE Bond Elut Certify™ cartridges were used for the isolation of morphine, codeine, hydrocodone, hydromorphone, and oxycodone from urine after β-glucuronidase hydrolysis (Huang et al., 1992). The drugs were determined by EI-GC-MS (full scan) using nalorphine as internal standard. The recovery of all drugs but hydromorphone was independent of the pH of the urine and exceeded 80%. The extracts yielded low GC-MS background, which permitted full-scan identification at levels ranging from 10 to 50 µg/L. X.H. Chen et al. (1993) applied Bond Elut Certify™ columns to the extraction of morphine from whole blood. Several methods of sample pretreatment were tested: precipitation with zinc sulfate–methanol, with acetonitrile, and with methanol and sonication for 15 min with subsequent dilution and centrifugation. The last method ensured the best recovery (over 70%). For this study, ^{3}H-morphine was used as test substance, and the recovery was measured by comparing the radioactivity of samples. The authors observed that a low pH value (3.3) during sample application and column washing followed by alkaline elution (methanol–ammonia) were crucial for high recoveries and pure extracts. The extracts were analyzed by HPLC with electrochemical detection. The SPE method described earlier was extended to the isolation of various acidic, neutral, and basic drugs from whole blood (Zweipfenning et al., 1994). After application of the diluted blood sample on the Certify™ column and rinsing, a two-step elution was performed. The acidic-neutral fraction was eluted with acetone–chloroform, and the basic fraction was eluted with ethyl acetate–ammonia. Codeine, morphine, 6-acetyl-morphine, and nalorphine were tested together with nine other drugs. Capillary GC-NPD was used and the drugs were separated on an Ultra-1 column in a temperature program from 100 to 280°C at 5°C/min. Among the opiates tested, codeine showed satisfactory and stable recoveries (over 80%) in the basic fraction. On the other hand, for morphine at a concentration of 500 ng/mL the recovery of 171.3% (RSD 66.0%) was observed, and at the concentration of 250 μg/L the recovery was 56.3% (RSD 26.8%). At lower levels (100 and 50 μg/L), morphine was not detectable. The recoveries of 6-MAM varied from 57.6% at the concentration of 500 μg/L through 26.4% at 250 ng/mL to 90.7% at the level of 50 μg/L. At each concentration level, a high variability of recoveries has been observed. Since GC-NPD was not suitable for low morphine concentrations, the recoveries of this drug were additionally calculated over the concentration range from 5 to 500 μg/L blood using GC-MS (SIM), after derivatization with BSTFA. Drug recoveries ranging from 74.8% to 95.4% were found, at acceptable variability (RSD about 11%). The GC-MS measurements were limited only to these extracts, which showed satisfactory ion chromatograms of qualifier ions; the authors did not state how many samples fulfilled this requirement. This study demonstrated that SPE with mixed-phase columns might be applied to the selective extraction of acidic/neutral and basic drugs. About more polar opiates, however, such as morphine and 6-MAM, low or very variable recoveries were observed. Bogusz et al. (1996) examined four commercially available types of mixed-phase SPE cartridges in order to compare the chromatographic efficiencies and chromatographic purity of extracts. Morphine, codeine, and 6-MAM, used as test compounds, were isolated from blood or serum and determined by HPLC with amperometric detection and by GC-MS (ion trap). All extracts were chromatographically pure in both detection methods applied. A distinct variability in extraction recoveries was observed not only among various products, but also among various batches of the same brand. The morphometric analysis of particles showed a symmetrical distribution of particles for only one brand of cartridges. A large fraction of very fine particles was observed. Only in one case were the morphometric findings generally concordant with the data available from the manufacturer; in two cases the observed data varied considerably from expected values; and in one case no information was available at all. This study showed there is need and room for improvement in the quality of SPE cartridges. Weinmann et al. (1998) developed a method for the simultaneous isolation of morphine, codeine, benzoylecgonine, and amphetamine from 0.1 mL serum, using Chromabond Drug mixed-phase columns (Macherey & Nagel, Düren, Germany). Extracted drugs were determined by GC-MS (SIM) after derivatization with PFPA. The LOQ was 1 µg/L for morphine, codeine, and BE and 5 µg/L for amphetamine.

6.3.4 SOLID-PHASE MICROEXTRACTION

Solid-phase fiber microextraction (SPME) was introduced by the Pawliszyn research team in the 1990s (Lord and Pawliszyn, 2000) as a universal, solvent-free isolation technique. However, SPME is particularly suitable for volatile and thermally stable compounds. In the case of opiates, this technique was used for isolation of methadone and its metabolites (Sporkert and Pragst, 2000; Bermejo et al., 2000; dos Santos Lucas et al., 2000) and methadone with pethidine (Myung et al., 1999). Staerk and Kulpmann (2000) applied headspace SPME at high temperature (200°C) combined with simultaneous derivatization to the isolation of drugs of abuse from urine. In full-scan GC-MS, the LODs for opiates and methadone were 100 and 200 µg/L, respectively. In serum, the drugs were detectable in therapeutic range when SIM-GC-MS was applied.

6.3.5 SUPERCRITICAL FLUID EXTRACTION

Supercritical fluid extraction (SFE), together with supercritical fluid chromatography (SFC), was introduced on a broad scale in the 1980s in the separation sciences. It was hoped that the physicochemical properties of supercritical fluids might bring a new quality to the isolation of forensically relevant compounds. However, these hopes most probably will never be fulfilled. According to the bitter statement of Georges Guiochon: "Unlike Cinderella, SFC was invited three times to the ball, never made it, and probably won't dance" (Guiochon, 1999). Nevertheless, there some niche applications of SFE for opiate analysis, particularly in hair, have been published. Cirimele et al. (1995) extracted morphine, 6-MAM, and codeine from hair using SFE with supercritical CO_2 modified with methanol–TEA–water. Recoveries of 53–96% were reported. Brewer et al. (2001) applied SFE in CO_2 modified with 10% methanol to the isolation of morphine, codeine, and benzoylecgonine from human hair. The procedure was faster and gave higher recoveries than the conventional acid hydrolysis. GC-MS was applied for detection.

A Scottish research group (D.L. Allen et al., 1999; Scott and Oliver, 1999) applied SFE to the isolation of morphine and 6-MAM from blood and vitreous humor, reporting clean extracts. Staub (1997) and Radcliffe et al. (2000)

reviewed applications of SFE and SFC in forensic samples, comprising also some opioids.

6.4 *PAPAVER SOMNIFERUM* AS A SOURCE OF OPIATES

6.4.1 *INVESTIGATION OF THE PLANT MATERIAL*

The studies concerning the composition and alkaloid content in the *Papaver* plant and in poppy seeds are important not only to the pharmaceutical industry, but are also for its forensic relevance, since plant material has often been used for illegal, home-baked morphine preparations. Among the magnitude of publications concerning the *Papaver* plant, only some were selected on the basis of their forensic relevance.

6.4.1.1 Thin-Layer Chromatography

Circular multilayer–overpressured layer chromatography (ML-OPLC), followed by HPLC-UV, was used for the determination of morphine and thebaine content in poppy capsules (Fater et al., 1997). On the basis of the analytical results, new plant populations were formed, one with a high morphine content (ca. 20 mg/g) and the other with a high thebaine content (ca. 16 mg/g). Popa et al. (1998) described a two-method approach for determination of morphine and codeine in poppy seeds. The drugs were isolated from poppy capsules with solvent or solid-phase extraction and subjected to TLC-UV densitometric examination at 275 nm in ethyl acetate:toluene:methanol:ammonia (68:18:10:5 v/v), followed by GC-MS analysis after acetylation.

6.4.1.2 Gas Chromatography

Paul et al. (1996) inspected which alkaloids might be used as differentiating factors between heroin and poppy seed consumption. Two sorts of seeds, originating from India and the Netherlands, respectively, were subjected to alkaline liquid/liquid extraction and back-extraction. A portion of the extracts was acetylated with acetic anhydride/pyridine. Both acetylated and underivatized extracts were analyzed by GC-MS on a DB-5 column in a three-step temperature program from 180°C through 270°C to 320°C. A time-scheduled SIM was applied. Morphine, codeine, thebaine, papaverine, and noscapine were identified in the extracts (Figure 6.1).

Besides poppy seed extracts, Mexican and southwest Asian heroin samples were analyzed, which contained heroin, 6-MAM, 6-acetylcodeine, and papaverine but not thebaine and noscapine. The authors postulated the detection of urinary noscapine, papaverine, or thebaine in order to differentiate poppy seed consumption from illicit heroin use. It must be mentioned, however, that noscapine may occur in illicit heroin when a particular production process is

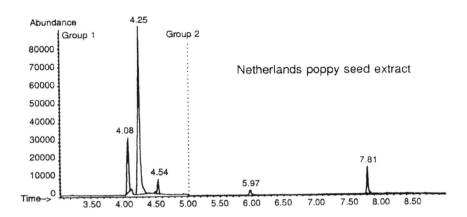

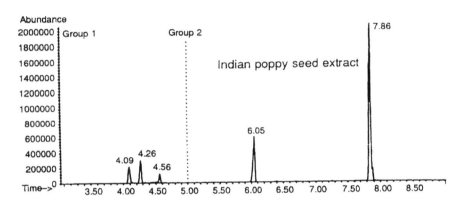

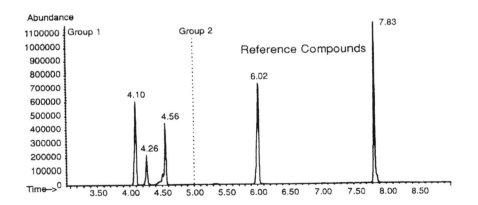

Figure 6.1

Selected ion chromatogram of opium alkaloids derived from various seeds of Papaver somniferum. *The following retention times (in minutes) of compounds are given: codeine, 4.10; morphine, 4.26; thebaine, 4.56; papaverine, 6.02; and narcotine, 7.83. (From Paul et al. (1996) with permission of G. Thieme Verlag.)*

applied. For example, Huizer (1988) analyzed 220 illicit heroin samples that contained 13–21% noscapine per sample.

6.4.1.3 Liquid Chromatography

Supercritical fluid chromatography with carbon dioxide on packed amino-propyl-bonded or straight silica columns has been applied to the separation of opium alkaloids extracted from poppy straw (Janicot et al., 1988). Methanol, water, and triethylamine were used as modifiers. The alkaloids were separated within 2–10 min and detected by DAD. The same group successfully applied near-critical extraction of morphine, codeine, and thebaine from poppy straw in a carbon dioxide–methanol–water mixture (Janicot et al., 1990). Carbon dioxide acted as an agent transporting the extraction solvent (methanol–water mixture) into the plant tissue. Five principal opium alkaloids (morphine, codeine, thebaine, noscapine, and papaverine), three minor alkaloids (laudanosine, cryptopine, and narceine), meconium acid, as well as some unidentified constituents were separated in gum opium extracts using HPLC with UV detection at 280 nm (Ayyangar and Bhide, 1988). Satisfactory separation was achieved in methanol–triethylammonium phosphate buffer (pH 3.2) gradient. Krenn et al. (1998) examined poppy straw and opium. The samples were pulverized and sonicated in 2.5% acetic acid. The filtered extract was adjusted to pH 9.0 and reextracted with dichlormethane–isopropanol using Extrelut columns. The reconstituted residue was subjected to HPLC examination using a C_{18} column and UV detection (280 nm). The method was used to investigate the alkaloid content of 24 samples of gum opium and 80 samples of poppy straw of different origin (Figure 6.2).

6.4.1.4 Capillary Electrophoresis

Crude morphine preparations, poppy straw extracts, and opium containing morphine, codeine, thebaine, papaverine, noscapine, narceine, oripavine, cryptopine, and salutaridine were examined by micellar electrokinetic capillary chromatography (MEKC) with UV detection at 254 nm (Trenerry et al., 1995). The drugs were separated on an uncoated fused silica capillary in less than 10 min. The results of quantitation were in good agreement with those obtained with HPLC.

6.4.2 MORPHINE AND OTHER OPIATES IN BODY FLUIDS AFTER INGESTION OF POPPY SEEDS

Poppy seeds are commonly used in traditional cakes and pastries, mainly in central Europe. These seeds may contain considerable amounts of morphine or codeine. It was therefore of forensic importance to assess, whether and to

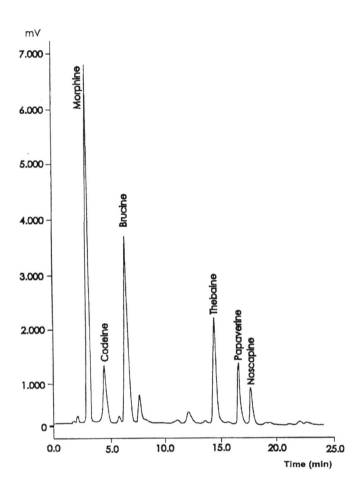

Figure 6.2
HPLC chromatogram of an extract of gum opium with brucine as internal standard. (From Krenn et al. (1998) with permission of Vieweg Verlag.)

what extent the intake of poppy seed–containing products is associated with any measurable elimination of psychoactive opiates. Since the alleged ingestion of poppy seed cake is often being used as an explanation in the case of positive opiates in urine, it is important to differentiate between opiates originating from poppy seeds and from illicit heroin.

Bjerver et al. (1982) published probably the first report on urine opiate excretion after poppy seed pastry ingestion. Morphine concentrations of 0.4 mg/L urine have been measured. Fritschi and Prescott (1985) determined the morphine content in 12 sorts of poppy seeds originating from eight countries and found 4–200 mg/kg. Five subjects were given poppy seed cake, resulting in the intake of 2.5–3.7 mg morphine per person. Peak morphine concentration in urine was observed 3–5 h after intake and ranged from 0.7 to 1.9 mg/L. About 30% of ingested morphine dose were found in urine. Total morphine in urine was determined by GC with FID, NPD, and MS detectors after acid hydrolysis. An attempt to isolate narcotoline as an alkaloid specific for poppy seeds was not successful. According to the authors, the differentiation between heroin and poppy seed intake was possible only when 6-MAM or heroin in urine was identified. Morphine and codeine were determined in the urine of a volunteer who ingested three poppy seed bagels (containing 5 g of seeds) from a commercial bakery (Struempler, 1987). Urine excretion of morphine and codeine, measured in hydrolyzed urine samples by GC-MS after acetylation, lasted 25 h for morphine and 22 h for codeine. Peak concentrations of morphine (2.797 mg/L) and codeine (0.214 mg/L) have been noted 3 h after ingestion. Zebelman et al. (1987) prepared poppy seed cookies from commercially available poppy seed filling, following the recipe on the label. Urine samples were obtained before and 2 h after the consumption of the cookies by five volunteers. Four persons ate two cookies and one ate three. Morphine levels, measured by GC-MS after derivatization with TFA, ranged from 722 µg/L to 979 µg/L in subjects who ate two cookies and 1481 µg/L in urine of person who ate three pieces. The authors concluded that food containing poppy seeds should be avoided by those persons subjected to drug testing. ElSohly et al. (1990) performed a systematic study on urine opiate elimination after poppy seed ingestion. Two males and two females ingested one, two, or three poppy seed rolls, each containing 2 g of Australian seeds (108 µg morphine/g seed) in three protocols. In the next experiment, one subject ingested a poppy seed cake containing 15 g seed obtained from a bakery and containing 169 µg morphine/g. GC-MS analysis of urine samples was done after enzymatic hydrolysis, liquid–liquid extraction, and derivatization with BSTFA. Relevant amounts of opiates were found after the ingestion of three poppy seed rolls; the highest morphine concentrations (298–954 µg/L urine) were found 3–8 h after ingestion. After the ingestion of poppy seed cake containing 15 g seeds, the peak morphine concentration amounted to 2010 µg/L urine and the peak codeine was 78 µg/L urine. On the basis of this study and literature data, the authors formulated the following conditions for ruling out poppy seed ingestion as the sole source of morphine and codeine in urine:

- Codeine levels exceeding 300 µg/L urine
- Morphine/codeine ratio of less than 2
- High levels of morphine (>1000 µg/L urine) with no codeine detected
- Morphine levels more than 5000 µg/L urine

These criteria were reevaluated by Selavka (1991), who investigated urinary morphine and codeine excretion up to 72 h after controlled ingestion of seven different poppy seed products (available in the Pacific Rim area). The drugs were isolated from acid-hydrolyzed urine and determined by GC-MS after silylation. Two of the differentiating criteria formulated by ElSohly et al. (1990), i.e., morphine level above 5000 μg/L and codeine above 300 μg/L, were not confirmed. Thirteen percent of the urine samples collected in the first 24 h after ingestion of poppy seed streusel showed morphine concentrations higher than 5000 μg/L. In addition, a significant number of these specimens contained codeine in concentrations higher than 300 μg/L. On the other hand, no specimen had a morphine/codeine ratio lower than 2. Therefore, this differentiating criterion of ElSohly was confirmed. In the study of Meneely (1992), poppy seed cakes were baked from three different brands of seeds and given to seven volunteers, who ingested an amount corresponding to 25 g of a given brand of seeds each. Morphine in urine was quantified by GC-MS up to 12 h after intake. The highest morphine levels, observed between 2 and 6 h after consumption, ranged from 2248 μg/L to 8940 μg/L. Despite positive analytical results, no symptoms of opiate impairment were observed. In a Dutch study (Pelders and Ros, 1996), seven sorts of poppy seeds available in the Netherlands were analyzed for the amount of morphine and codeine present. A large variability in alkaloid contents was observed; morphine contents ranged from 2 to 251 μg/kg, codeine contents from 0.5 to 57.1 μg/kg. Four grams of each sort, corresponding to one to two bagels, were given individually to seven volunteers with 1-week intervals. Urine samples were then collected over 24 h, and morphine and codeine were determined by GC-MS. Opiate excretions with urine were proportional to their concentration in the seeds. The alkaloid levels, corrected for urine creatinine, showed large interindividual variability. To inspect the intraindividual variability, 4 g of Spanish seeds, with the highest morphine content, were ingested by one volunteer with a 1-week interval. A distinct scatter of results was observed. Casella et al. (1997) investigated the applicability of thebaine as a marker of poppy seed ingestion. Since thebaine is heat- and acid-labile, a new SPE method was developed for the isolation of opiates from urine without hydrolysis and derivatization. Urine samples taken from nine subjects after ingestion of muffins containing poppy seeds were extracted and analyzed by GC-MS (ion trap) on thebaine, codeine, and morphine. Thebaine was found in all morphine-positive urine samples up to 12 h after ingestion of the muffins. Meadway et al. (1998) determined morphine and codeine content in several specimens of poppy seeds using GC-MS. In cooked seeds the concentration of morphine ranged from 0.1 to 11.9 μg/g, that of codeine from 0.2 to 0.7 μg/g. Urine samples taken from four subjects after the intake of poppy seed rolls and cakes were analyzed for opiates (morphine, codeine, normorphine, thebaine, and 6-MAM). Surprisingly large concentrations of morphine (15–832 μg/L) and codeine (1.5–47.9 μg/L) were observed. Thebaine was found only in 10 out of 27 urine samples. This suggested that the absence of thebaine couldn't rule out the intake of poppy seeds.

The "poppy seed dilemma" also became relevant in high-performance sports, since morphine is included on the IOC list of banned substances at a level exceeding 1 mg/L urine. Thevis et al. (2003) analyzed eight commercially available samples of baking mixtures with poppy seeds for the presence of morphine using GC-MS. One selected batch was used for baking a typical cake, which was given to nine volunteers. The morphine concentration in urine was, in many samples, higher than 1 mg/L and reached 10 mg/L. The authors confirmed the warning concerning the use of poppy seed–containing products by athletes. Not only poppy seeds, but also several herbal teas, present on the market, may be a source of morphine, since they contain part from the plant *Papaver somniferum*. Therefore, it was important to verify whether the consumption of such beverages might lead to the elimination of morphine at relevant concentrations. Van Thuyne et al. (2003) applied two sorts of herbal tea containing *Papaveris fructus* to five male volunteers. Morphine was detected in the urine of all volunteers after consumption of two 120-mL cups of tea. Maximum morphine concentrations were 4.3 and 7.4 mg/L, respectively. Therefore, the athletes should be warned against the use of herbal teas containing parts of poppy plants as well against the use of food products containing poppy seeds. The problem of morphine excretion after ingestion of poppy seeds is relevant also in animal sport. Kollias-Baker and Sams (2002) applied 1-, 5-, and 10-g doses of poppy seeds to four horses and analyzed their plasma and urine for morphine. Morphine was detectable in plasma for at least 4 h and in urine for up to 24 h after administration of poppy seeds. No behavioral changes were noted among the animals.

6.5 HEROIN AND ASSOCIATED ILLICIT OPIATE FORMULATIONS

6.5.1 INVESTIGATION OF ILLICIT PREPARATIONS (STREET DRUGS): PROFILING

6.5.1.1 Thin-Layer Chromatography

Nair et al. (1986) assessed the separating power of 35 TLC systems reported in the literature for opiate analysis. The developing system consisting of chloroform–*n*-hexane–triethylamine (9:9:4) was capable of separating eight opiates and five potential adulterants, with an LOD of 0.1 µg. Several TLC systems were studied and applied practically by Huizer (1988). The best results were

Compound	Rf	Compound	Rf
Dipyrone	00	Caffeine	38
Piracetam	01	6-MAM	39
Acetylsalicylic acid	01	Strychnine	44
Phenolphtaleine	02	Papaverine	55
Nicotinamine	04	Heroin	58
Paracetamol	05	Acetylcodeine	61
Phenobarbital	05	Aminophenazone	64
Morphine	07	Quinine ethylcarbonate	66
Barbital	11	Noscapine	70
Acetylprocaine	18	Lidocaine	71
Quinine	20	Methaqualone	73
Phenacetin	22	Acetylthebaol	75
Phenazone	31	Cocaine	80
Codeine	33	N-Phenyl-2-naphtylamine	84
Procaine	35		

Table 6.2

TLC Rf-values of heroin and some impurities and adulterants in toluene–diethylamine (85:15) developing system

Source: Huizer (1988).

obtained with systems: chloroform–cyclohexane–diethylamine (8:10:3) and toluene–diethylamine (85:15) (Table 6.2).

6.5.1.2 Gas Chromatography

Sperling (1991) developed a GC-FID method for the determination of illicit heroin constituents using a DB-1 capillary column and a temperature program from 200°C to 280°C. The separation achieved was much better than with packed-column GC. In another GC-FID method (Barnfield et al., 1988), illicit heroin samples were dissolved in *N,N*-dimethylformamide-ethanol and subjected to capillary GC-FID using a programmed temperature run (230–290°C). Apart from the opiates, a number of adulterants were identified that are useful for the profiling of a particular sample.

The sample pretreatment used in the aforementioned paper was criticized by Neumann (1990). He advocated derivatization of the heroin sample with MSTFA before GC-FID analysis. This procedure prevented various possible analytical problems, such as transacetylation, adsorption, and different responses for salt and base. Heroin chromatograms published by Neumann showed very good separation of all compounds, particularly in the first segment, where—in contrast to chromatograms published by Barnfield—the interference of the solvent peak was practically excluded.

Neumann (1994) also presented data concerning adulterants (e.g., caffeine, paracetamol, procaine, phenobarbital) most frequently encountered in illicit heroin from 1986 to 1992. Some changing trends in the use of adulterants have been observed. The analysis of these compounds, done with capillary GC with column switching, gave additional identification parameters. For profiling, several multidimensional statistical methods were used, such as principal component analysis and hierarchical cluster analysis. Kaa (1994) described changes in illicit heroin content in Denmark during the period from 1981 to 1992. The predominance of heroin base was observed in the last reported years. The profiles of adulterants changed from caffeine and procaine in the early 1980s through phenobarbital and methaqualone in the late '80s to paracetamol with caffeine in the '90s. The trends observed were in agreement with those described by Neumann (1994). 6-MAM in illicit drugs may originate not only from heroin as its deacetylation product, but also from partially acetylated morphine. Therefore, illicit drug samples that contain only 6-MAM without traces of heroin cannot be classified as illicit heroin (Sibley, 1996). L.A. King (1997) stressed that the measurement of heroin content as a mere indicator of sample potency gives unreliable information due to the possible presence of other opium alkaloids or pharmacologically active adulterants. Australian authors (Myors et al., 2001) assessed various GC parameters useful for the profiling of southeast Asian heroin. From the library of 649 impurities detected with GC-MS, 18 parameters were selected, which were applied to the identification of the origin of the samples. The European approach to heroin impurity profiling was presented by Stromberg et al. (2000), who established a gas chromatographic profiling system, harmonized for laboratories in Sweden, Germany, and the Netherlands. Sixteen chromatographic parameters were used for the identification of southwest Asian heroin, which is prevalent on the European drug market. The study demonstrated high interlaboratory variability in parameters, limiting the usefulness of a common database. The best option is still the use of one's own database for identification.

Brenneisen and Hasler (2002) determined the pyrolysis products of heroin, which are generated after heating of street heroin for inhalation ("chasing the dragon"). Heroin samples were heated on aluminum foil at 250–400°C and analyzed by GC-MS. Seventy-two pyrolysis products were detected, and half of these could be identified.

Besides opium alkaloids and adulterants, volatiles occluded in heroin preparations may be helpful in sample recognition. Cartier et al. (1997) identified traces of 16 different solvents in 41 illicit heroin samples, using solid-phase adsorption and headspace GC-FID on a DB-1 column (with subsequent GC-MS confirmation). Illicit cocaine samples were also investigated. The analysis of solvents provided a simple and independent means for the identification of sample origin.

6.5.1.3 Liquid Chromatography

In a series of papers, Lurie et al. (Lurie and Carr, 1986; Lurie and McGuiness, 1987; Hays and Lurie, 1991) developed HPLC methods for the analysis of unadulterated and adulterated heroin samples. ODS columns and DAD–multiwavelength detection (at 210, 228, and 240 nm) were used. The addition of sodium dodecylsulfate as an ion-pairing agent to the mobile phase allowed the separation of all relevant components of street heroin. Johnston and King (1998) applied multivariate statistical analysis of the composition of seized heroin to predicting the country of origin. The following components, determined by HPLC, were taken into consideration: heroin, 6-MAM, acetylcodeine, noscapine, papaverine, caffeine, methaqualone, paracetamol, and phenobarbital. The method was checked on 505 samples from Turkey, Pakistan, India, and southeast Asia and allowed the correct classification of about 83% of cases. Dams et al. (2002a, 2002b) applied sonic spray LC-MS (ion trap) to the profiling of street heroin samples. Chromatographic separation was performed on monolithic silica column (Chromolith Performance 100×4.6 mm) in gradient elution in acetonitrile–water at a flow of 5 mL/min. A postcolumn split of 1/20 was applied; the analysis time was 5 min. The protonated molecular ions of seven constituents of street heroin (morphine, codeine, 6-MAM, heroin, acetylcodeine, papaverine, noscapine, and levallorphan, used as internal standard) were monitored (Figure 6.3). The limits of SSI-MS detection ranged from 0.25 to 1 ng on-column.

6.5.1.4 Capillary Electrophoresis

The applications of various CE-based assays in forensic analysis, including illicit heroin, were reviewed by Tagliaro and Smith (1996) and by Heeren and Thormann (1997). Lurie et al. (1995) used MEKC for the separation of acidic and neutral impurities of illicit heroin. The substances were detected with DAD and laser-induced fluorescence. The latter method was used for phenanthrene-like compounds and appeared 500 times more sensitive for acetylthebaol. The applications of MEKC to the analysis of illicit drug seizures were reviewed by Lurie (1996, 1997) and by Tagliaro et al. (1996). Concerning illicit heroin and opium, MEKC appeared particularly amenable, combining high separation power similar to that of capillary GC with undemanding sample preparation similar to what is needed for HPLC. Both DAD and fluorescence detectors may be used. Lurie et al. (2001) applied capillary electrochromatography with laser-induced fluorescence to the analysis of heroin impurities. The method resolved a much higher number of peaks than gradient HPLC or MEKC. The samples of different geographical origin gave distinguishable chromatograms.

Figure 6.3

Selected ion chromatograms (LC-ESI-MS of an authentic heroin street sample. (From Dams et al. (2002a) with permission of the American Chemical Society.)

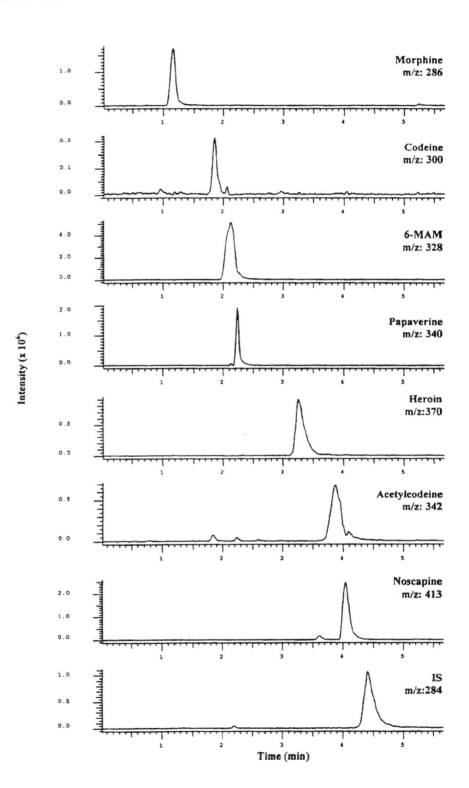

6.5.1.5 Multimethod Approach

Huizer (1988) identified illicit heroin samples using TLC, HPLC, and GC. In his study, the author went systematically through all steps from opium through crude and purified morphine to heroin and discussed the applicability of the chromatographic methods used. The procedures used for the illicit isolation of morphine from opium (the lime method and the ammonia method) may be recognized on the basis of percentage compositions of crude morphine. Also, during the acetylation step, various characteristic impurities may be formed. Straight-phase HPLC of illicit heroin ensured general information concerning the composition of the sample. On the other hand, capillary GC-FID of silylated heroin samples according to Neumann and Gloger (1982) allowed them to demonstrate distinct differences between each production batch of illicit heroin—even ones originating from the same production unit (Figure 6.4).

Chiarotti et al. (1991) presented a multimethod approach for the comparative analysis of illicit heroin samples. At first the volatile compounds were determined by headspace GC on Porapak Q column. Then the opiates and adulterants were analyzed using TLC on silica gel using *n*-hexane–dichloromethane–methanol (0.75% diethylamine) (72:20:5) as developing system and GC-MS (ion trap) on OV 101 capillary column using a

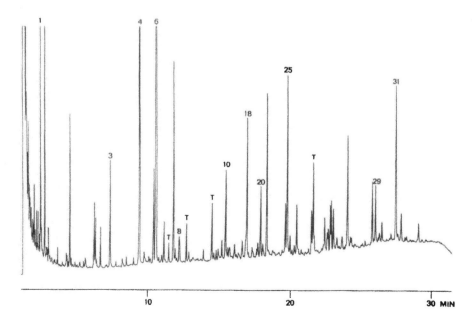

Figure 6.4

Capillary GC profile of a southwest Asian heroin sample treated according to the method of Neumann and Gloger (1982). (From Huizer (1988) with permission of the author.)

temperature program from 60 to 280°C. The sugar diluents (glucose, fructose, saccharose, maltose, and lactose) were analyzed by HPLC on a Supelcosil-LC-R-urea column in ACN-H_2O (75:25). Finally, the methanolic solutions of illicit drugs were analyzed on trace metals (Fe and Zn) content by atomic absorption spectroscopy. A combination of HPLC-DAD and GC-NPD has been used for the analysis of illicit heroin and cocaine samples (Hernandez et al., 1992). The alkaloids and adulterants were identified through retention parameters and UV spectra. On the base of comparative analysis of 40 illicit samples, the authors came to the conclusion that the proposed method is a good alternative to GC-MS analysis. Another multimethod approach was proposed by French authors (Besacier et al., 1997), who performed illicit heroin analysis in three steps. In the first step, all major and minor heroin constituents were identified and quantified using programmed-temperature GC-FID on a DB-1 column. In this step, heroin, 3-MAM, 6-MAM, acetylcodeine, papaverine, noscapine, as well as adulterants (e.g., paracetamol, caffeine) were determined. The ratios of morphine/acetylcodeine, morphine/papaverine, and noscapine/papaverine were calculated and subjected to principal component analysis. In the second step, the GC-FID analysis of impurities was done, based on the method of A.C. Allen et al. (1984). In the third and last step the isotope ratios $^{13}C/^{12}C$ were measured using a GC-isotope ratio mass spectrometer. This procedure, according to the authors, ensured batch identification of a given sample with a high degree of certainty. Turkish authors (Bora et al., 2002) measured levels of 10 elements in 44 illicit heroin samples originating from southeast Anatolia. Inductively coupled plasma–atomic emission spectrometry has been applied to the measurement of Al, Ba, Ca, Cu, Fe, Mg, Mn, and Zn and atomic absorption spectrometry for Cd and Pb. Observed profiles were useful for determining the source and trafficking routes of heroin.

Kala and Lechowicz (1997) analyzed Polish substitutes for heroin, so-called "kompot" and "makiwara," which are produced from macerated poppy straw or capsules subjected to extraction and acetylation. The composition of 20 samples of "kompot," investigated by HPLC-DAD and GC-MS (ion trap), showed very large variations between batches. As main constituents, morphine (1.2–49.7 g/L), codeine (0–4.4 mg/L), and acetylcodeine (0–12.5 g/L) were found. 3-MAM, 6-MAM, and heroin usually occurred in lower concentrations. The ratios between particular alkaloids were stable within the same batch. For computerized identification of "kompot" batches, the concentrations of morphine, 3-MAM, 6-MAM, heroin, codeine, acetylcodeine, and narceine were compared. Dams et al. (2001) reviewed the methods used in the last decade for batch-to-batch comparison or identification of origin of illicit heroin. Impurity profiling, including identification and quantitation of minor components, appeared particularly important.

6.5.2 HEROIN METABOLITES IN BIOLOGICAL MATRICES

Heroin is usually self-administered intravenously. In the last decade, however, a growing preference of other routes of administration has been observed, such as smoking and intranasal administration ("snorting"). This has been caused by several factors, including the fear of HIV, the possibility of administration of heroin without leaving external marks on the body, and the decrease in the price of street heroin. Irrespective of the administration route, heroin is rapidly deacetylated to 6-monoacetylmorphine (6-MAM). The half-life of heroin in blood after intravenous injection was estimated at 2–8 min (Umans et al., 1982; Inturrisi et al., 1984), after smoking at 3–5 min (Jenkins et al., 1994), after intranasal or intramuscular administration at 5–6 min (Cone et al., 1993; Skopp et al., 1997). 6-MAM is deacetylated at a somewhat slower rate than morphine; the half-life after intravenous administration was 6–38 min and 5, 11, and 12 min after smoking, intranasal administration, and intramuscular administration, respectively. The half-life of morphine was estimated at ca. 30 min. after heroin smoking and at 60–180 min after administration by other routes. Figure 6.5 shows the main steps of heroin biotransformation.

The pharmacokinetics of heroin indicate that the parent drug may be detectable in the body only under experimental conditions, when the blood sample is taken almost immediately after administration, or in the case of a very massive heroin overdose (e.g., in the "body packer syndrome"). 6-MAM, a specific heroin metabolite, may be detected in the blood of living subjects pretty soon after heroin intake. On the other hand, some unchanged 6-MAM (about 0.5% of the heroin dose) and some heroin is eliminated with the urine and may be detected for several hours (Cone et al., 1991). 6-MAM is the only known specific metabolite of heroin.

6.5.2.1 Urine

6.5.2.1.1 Gas Chromatography

The GC-MS determination of 6-MAM in urine as specific heroin metabolite was introduced in forensic toxicological practice by Fehn and Megges (1985). These authors isolated 6-MAM with SPE C_{18} cartridges and determined with GC-MS after PFPA derivatization. An LOD of 2 µg/L was found. In 33 of 47 examined morphine-positive urine samples 6-MAM was detected, the concentrations ranging from 4 to 10,000 µg/L. Paul et al. (1989) isolated 6-MAM from urine with alkaline liquid/liquid extraction, followed by SPE or a second organic solvent purification. The extracts were derivatized with propionic anhydride and examined by GC-MS (SIM). In 16 examined urine samples, the 6-MAM concentrations varied from 2 to 332 µg/L. The authors reported difficulties with solid-phase extraction on CN cartridges. An improvement in 6-MAM

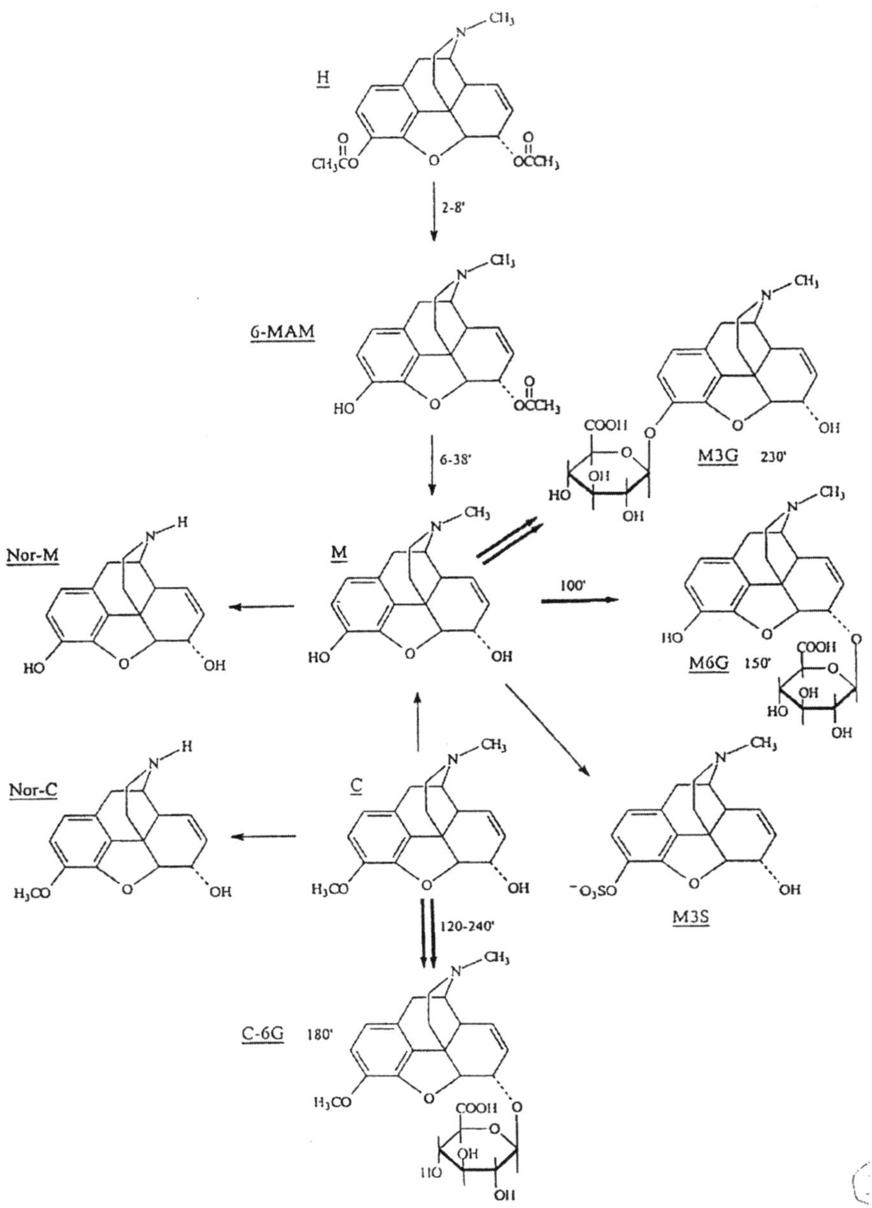

Figure 6.5

*Metabolic pathways of
heroin and codeine. (From
Bogusz (2000b) with
permission of Elsevier
Science.)*

Figure 6.5

Metabolic pathways of heroin and codeine. (From Bogusz (2000b) with permission of Elsevier Science.)

isolation from urine was reported by Romberg and Brown (1990), who used alkaline solvent extraction instead of SPE on CN columns. Much better purity of extracts was observed. Fuller and Anderson (1992) applied a mixed-phase Bond-Elut Certify SPE column to the isolation of 6-MAM, morphine, and codeine from urine. The extracts were derivatized with TFA and analyzed by GC-MS. The chromatograms showed no interfering peaks. The stability of 6-

MAM in urine samples was studied. A rapid GC-MS method was developed for the determination of morphine, 6-MAM, normorphine, codeine, norcodeine, and DHC in urine (Meadway et al., 2002). The method was applied to the analysis of 321 urine specimens from heroin abusers. The concentrations ranged for 6-MAM between 0.103 and 246.312 mg/L, for morphine between 0.129 and 193.600 mg/L, and for codeine between 0.103 and 519.000 mg/L. Higher concentrations of 6-MAM were observed in older subjects, indicating opiate tolerance.

In recent years, the differentiation between the intake of pure DAM and illicit heroin became relevant since introducing heroin prescription programs in some countries, such as Switzerland, Great Britain, Germany, and the Netherlands. One of the basic requirements of these programs is that the participants not use any illicit drugs, particularly illicit heroin. In illicit heroin not only DAM is present, but also several other opiates, such as 6-MAM, acetylcodeine, codeine, papaverine, noscapine, as well as various adulterants. It must be stressed that only acetylcodeine (AC) may be regarded as a specific marker of illicit heroin. AC is produced from codeine during acetylation of opium. Its content in illicit heroin ranges from 2 to 7% (Soine, 1986). A method for simultaneous determination of acetylcodeine, 6-MAM, morphine, codeine, and norcodeine by GC-MS was described by O'Neal and Poklis (1997). An LOQ of 1 µg/L for AC was achieved. AC was stable in urine at acidic and alkaline pH in refrigerator. The examination of 69 morphine/codeine-positive urine samples revealed AC in six cases, whereas 6-MAM was detected in 13 cases. The concentrations of AC were much lower than those of 6-MAM. In a second paper (1998), O'Neal and Poklis analyzed 100 morphine-positive urines and found AC in 37 samples at concentrations ranging from 2 to 290 µg/L (median, 11 µg/L). 6-MAM was also present in these samples at concentrations ranging from 49 to 12,600 µg/L (median, 740 µg/L). Moreover, 6-MAM was detectable in 36 other urine specimens. Codeine—a possible metabolite of AC—was found in all urine samples. The authors concluded that 6-MAM was a much more sensitive marker of illicit heroin use than AC. On the other hand, AC may play a very important role as a special indicator of illicit street heroin use. Staub et al. (2001) also used GC-MS and detected AC in over 85% and 6-MAM in over 94% of 71 urine samples obtained from illegal heroin consumers.

Urine samples taken from 532 participants of a heroin maintenance program in the United Kingdom were subjected to GC-MS analysis for putative markers of street heroin abuse (Mc-Lachlan-Troup et al., 2001). Among morphine-positive samples, 61% were positive for at least one of codeine, meconine, and putative papaverine and noscapine metabolites. The detection of urinary noscapine and papaverine metabolites was recommended as an indication of street heroin abuse, instead of pharmaceutical diamorphine.

Brenneisen et al. (2002) studied the pharmacokinetics of acetylcodeine-administered IV in healthy volunteers in order to use this compound as a marker of street heroin use. Peak urine concentration appeared at 2 h; the detection window in urine was 8 h. SPE, followed by GC-MS, was applied to the determination of acetylcodeine and its metabolite codeine in urine. In selected cases, papaverine and noscapine were also measured. In a study of 105 participants of a heroin maintenance program, 15 urine samples were positive for acetylcodeine and 8 for acetylcodeine, papaverine, and noscapine.

6.5.2.1.2 Liquid Chromatography

Derks et al. (1986) developed an HPLC method for the determination of 6-MAM in urine samples of drug addicts receiving daily injectable morphine under controlled conditions. Urine specimens were extracted on Extrelut columns in alkaline conditions. An automatic precolumn derivatization with potassium hexacyanoferrate (III) and fluorescence detection was applied. HPLC with electrochemical detection has been used for 6-MAM determination in urine samples. In a study of Hanisch and von Meyer (1993), the drug was extracted with C_{18} cartridges. The extraction procedure ensured very clean extracts; the LOD was 2 μg/L.

Gerostamoulos et al. (1993) applied combined electrochemical and UV detection for the simultaneous determination of 6-MAM, morphine, and codeine in urine samples, extracted with an alkaline chloroform/isopropanol mixture. Electrochemical detection performed better for 6-MAM and morphine, whereas UV detection was more sensitive for codeine. An LOD of 40 μg/L for 6-MAM was stated.

Usually, heroin metabolites are being separated on reverse-phase columns. Low and Taylor (1995) used a normal-phase HPLC (Hypersil column 2-mm ID) for the analysis of 6-MAM, heroin, morphine, codeine, DHC, and pholcodine in urine extracts. UV detection at 280 nm was applied, and the LODs varied from 4 to 20 μg/L.

Bogusz et al. (2001) determined putative street heroin markers in 25 morphine-positive urine samples in order to differentiate between the administration of illicit heroin and prescription diamorphine. LC-APCI-MS (positive ions) after solid-phase extraction was applied (Figures 6.6 and 6.7). Codeine-6-glucuronide was found in all samples, codeine in 24, noscapine in 22, 6-MAM in 16, papaverine in 14, DAM in 12, and AC in 4.

Katagi et al. (2001) developed an automatic method for determination of heroin and its metabolites monoacetylmorphine (6-MAM) and morphine as well as acetylcodeine, codeine, and dihydrocodeine in urine. Urine samples were applied on trapping cation exchange column and washed with ammonium

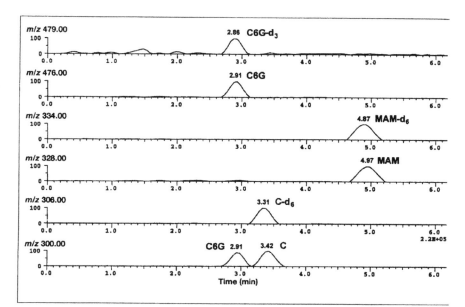

Figure 6.6

LC-APCI-MS ion chromatogram of urine extract from a heroin consumer showing the presence of codeine, codeine-6-glucuronide, and 6-MAM. (From Bogusz et al. (2001) by permission of Preston Publications.)

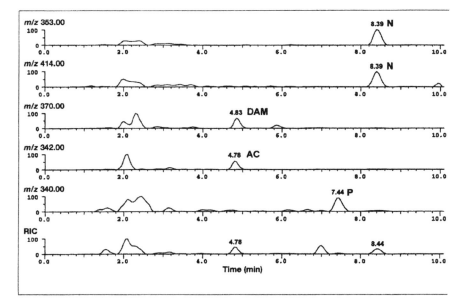

Figure 6.7

LC-APCI-MS ion chromatogram of urine extract from a heroin consumer showing the presence of acetylcodeine, diacetylmorphine, papaverine, and noscapine. (From Bogusz et al. (2001) by permission of Preston Publications.)

Figure 6.8

HPLC-DAD (upper) and HPLC-Fl (lower) chromatograms of the opiate mixture. (From Dams et al. (2002b) with permission of Elsevier Science.)

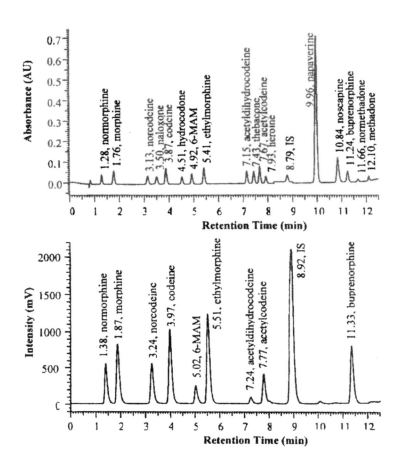

acetate; after column switching, the drugs were eluted and separated on analytical cation exchange column in ACN–ammonium acetate (70:30). The detection was done with ESI-MS in full scan or SIM mode. Protonated quasi-molecular ions or acetonitrile adducts were monitored. The LODs ranged from 2 to 30 μg/L in full-scan mode and from 0.1 to 3 μg/L in SIM. An HPLC method for the simultaneous determination of 17 opium alkaloids in urine and blood was published by Dams et al. (2002b). The drugs were isolated with cation exchange SPE, separated on a "high-speed" phenyl column (53 × 7 mm) within 12 min, and detected with DAD and fluorescence detectors (Figure 6.8). LODs in the range 2.5–9.7 μg/L were observed.

6.5.2.1.3 Capillary Electrophoresis

Taylor et al. (1996) described a method for the separation of heroin, 6-MAM, morphine, codeine, DHC, and pholcodine (pure drugs). The method was then applied to the determination of pholcodine, DHC, and morphine in urine extracts. LODs of 10 µg/L were reported. W.S. Wu and Tsai (1999) applied CZE to the determination of morphine and M3G in urine with minimal sample pretreatment. Urine specimens were only filtrated, acidified to pH 2–3, and centrifuged. The LODs were 0.2 mg/L and 0.5 mg/L for morphine ad M3G, respectively, using UV detection. The same research group (Tsai et al., 2000) developed a CZE method for the detection of morphine in urine using MS (IT) detection. An LOD of 10 µg/L was achieved.

6.5.2.2 Blood

6.5.2.2.1 Gas Chromatography

6-MAM in blood samples has usually been determined simultaneously with other substances that appear after heroin abuse, such as morphine and codeine. Schuberth and Schuberth (1989) published a GC-MS method for the determination of 6-MAM, morphine, and codeine in blood. The blood samples were precipitated with methanol, and the drugs were extracted with SPE C_{18} cartridges and derivatized with PFPA. The method was applied to forensic samples; in six cases of fatal heroin overdose, 6-MAM concentrations of 1.6–6.1 µg/L blood were found. The method of Schuberth was slightly modified by Musshoff and Daldrup (1993) by using acetonitrile for blood precipitation and changing the cartridge-washing procedure. Blood samples were also subjected to acid hydrolysis in order to measure total amounts of opiates. High-purity extracts were reported; the LOD was below 1 µg/L. Cone and Darwin (1992) reviewed the GC-MS methods for opiates, cocaine, and metabolites, including also 6-MAM. Wasels and Belleville (1994) presented an overview of GC-MS procedures for the identification of 6-MAM, morphine, and codeine. Several derivatization methods were reviewed: acetylation, propionylation, acylation (TFA, PFPA, HFBA), and silylation. Wang et al. (1994) published a method for the simultaneous determination of heroin and its metabolites 6-MAM, morphine, and normorphine as well as cocaine and its metabolites in hair, plasma, saliva, and urine. The drugs were extracted from biosamples with Clean Screen SPE cartridges and derivatized with BSTFA/TMCS before GC-MS (SIM) analysis. The LODs for heroin and 6-MAM were 1 µg/L saliva or urine. Heroin, 6-MAM, and morphine levels were monitored in saliva after experimental administration of intranasal heroin. Goldberger et al. (1994) developed a GC-MS method for the determination of heroin, 6-MAM, and morphine in body fluids and organs of 21 victims of heroin overdose. The samples were extracted with SPE cartridges and partially derivatized with MBTFA (for 6-MAM and morphine). Heroin was determined without derivatization. 6-MAM was detected in all 21 urine samples and in 14 blood samples. Heroin was not detected in blood and was present in

17 urine samples. The authors used the concentration ratios of drugs for the evaluation of the rapidity of death. Moeller and Mueller (1995) determined 6-MAM in serum, urine, and hair of heroin users by GC-MS. Solid-phase extraction with C18 cartridges was applied; the extracted drug was derivatized with PFPA before analysis. Twenty-five urine samples were examined, which showed positive immunochemical reaction on opiates. In 19 urine samples 6-MAM was detected, the concentration ranging from 1 to 9950 µg/L. In five serum samples 6-MAM levels of 2–9 µg/L were observed. Guillot et al. (1997) developed a GC-MS method for the determination of heroin, 6-MAM, and morphine in postmortem blood, urine, and vitreous humor. The drugs were isolated with alkaline solvent extraction and subjected to propionylation in the presence of 4-dimethylaminopyridine. Baseline separation was observed. The quantitation limits were 2 µg/L for morphine and 6-MAM and 5 µg/L for heroin. GC-MS-EI with trimethylsilylation and HPLC with electrochemical detection were applied in a case of fatal oral heroin poisoning. The concentrations of heroin, 6-MAM, and morphine in blood were 109, 168, and 1140 µg/L, respectively (Rop et al., 1997). Gas chromatographic methods for determination of heroin, its metabolites, and associated compounds in body fluids are summarized in Table 6.3.

6.5.2.2.2 *Liquid Chromatography*

HPLC methods used for opiate agonists since 1999 were reviewed by Bogusz (2000a, 2000b) and Pichini et al. (1999a). An advent of LC-MS brought very important progress in the determination of opiates and its metabolites in biological fluids. LC-MS is the only analytical technique that allows the specific detection of parent opiates and all polar metabolites without derivatization and without acidic or enzymatic cleavage.

An LC-TSP-MS-MS method for the determination of heroin and its metabolites (6-MAM, morphine, M3G, M6G) as well as for codeine and acetylcodeine has been developed by Polettini et al. (1995). A very simple sample preparation was applied: Blood was precipitated with methanol and centrifuged, whereas urine was only filtered before injection into LC-MS. Gradient elution in methanol–ammonium acetate was used. The limits of detection varied from 10 to 50 µg/L. Zuccaro et al. (1997) developed an LC-ESI-MS method for the simultaneous determination of heroin, 6-MAM, morphine, morphine 3-glucuronide (M3G), and morphine-6-glucuronide (M6G) in serum. The drugs were extracted with SPE C_2 cartridges and separated on a straight-phase silica column in a methanol–ACN–formic acid mobile phase. The authors used a silica column in order to separate all substances in one run under isocratic conditions. The LOD for heroin was 0.5 µg/L, for 6-MAM 4 µg/L. The method was applied to the pharmacokinetic study on heroin-treated mice. Bogusz et al.

Table 6.3

Gas chromatographic methods for heroin, 6-MAM, morphine, codeine, and metabolites

Drug	Sample	Isolation	Derivatization	Column, Conditions	Detection	LOD (μg/L)	Ref.
6-MAM	Urine	SPE C$_{18}$	PFPA	OV-1, 230°	EI-MS (SIM)	2	Fehn and Megges (1985)
6-MAM	Urine	SPE or I/I	Propionylation	DB 5, 130–250°	EI-MS (SIM)	0.8	Paul et al. (1989)
6-MAM	Urine	I/I alkaline	Propionylation	RSL 200, 146–246°	EI-MS (SIM)	n.s.	Romberg and Brown (1990)
6-MAM	Urine	SPE Certify	TFA	HP-1, 150–300°	EI-MS (SIM)	n.s.	Fuller and Anderson (1992)
AC, 6-MAM, M, C, NC	Urine	SPE	Propionylation	HP-1, 170–280°	EI-MS (SIM)	0.5	O' Neal et al. (1997)
6-MAM, M, C	Blood	SPE C$_{18}$	PFPA	DB 5, 150–256°	EI-MS (SIM)	0.5	Schuberth and Schuberth (1989)
6-MAM, M, C, DHC	Blood	SPE C$_{18}$	PFPA	OV 1, 150–220°	EI-MS (SIM)	1	Musshoff and Daldrup (1993)
heroin, 6-MAM	Serum, saliva, urine, hair	SPE	BSTFA/TMCS	HP 1, 70–250°	EI-MS (SIM)	1	Wang et al. (1994)
heroin, 6-MAM, M	Body fluids, organs	SPE	MBTFA	Rtx-5, 150–290°	EI-MS (SIM)	1	Golberger et al. (1994)
6-MAM	Serum, urine hair	SPE C$_{18}$	PFPA	n.s.	EI-MS (SIM)	n.s.	Moeller and Moeller (1995)
M, C	Urine	I/I pH 9	acetylation	DB-5, 240°C	EI-MS (SIM)	2 ng on col.	Paul et al. (1985)
M	Blood	I/I pH 9	PFPA	DB-5, 100–300°C	EI-MS-MS	1	Phillips et al. (1989)
M, C	Blood	SPE C$_{18}$	PFPA	CP-Sil5, 200–300°C	NCI-MS (SIM)	2–5	Schmitt et al. (1990)
M, C, NM	Plasma	I/I pH 9.5	HBFA	HP-1, 100–257°C	NCI-MS (SIM)	1 pg on col.	Watson et al. (1995)
M	Plasma	I/I pH 9	PFPA	HP-5MS, 150–250°C	EI-MS (SIM)	0.2	Fryirs et al. (1997)

M = morphine, C = codeine, AC = acetylcodeine, NC = norcodeine, NM = normorphine, DHC = dihydrocodeine, n.s. = not stated, on col. = on-column.

(1997a) used LC-APCI-MS for the determination of heroin metabolites (6-MAM, M3G, M6G, and morphine) in the blood, cerebrospinal fluid, vitreous humor, and urine of heroin victims. The drugs were extracted with C$_{18}$ cartridges using only volatile chemicals; the LOD for 6-MAM was 0.5 μg/L. In a follow-up study, Bogusz et al. (1997b) extended the LC-APCI-MS method to the determination of 6-MAM, M3G, M6G, morphine, codeine, and C6G, using

Figure 6.9

LC-APCI-MS chromatogram of morphine and its glucuronides extracted from the serum of a heroin consumer. (From Bogusz (2000a) with permission of Elsevier Science.)

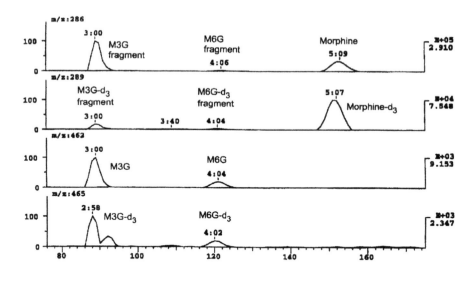

Figure 6.10

LC-APCI-MS chromatogram of codeine, codeine-6-glucuronide, and 6-MAM extracted from the serum of a heroin consumer. (From Bogusz (2000a) with permission of Elsevier Science.)

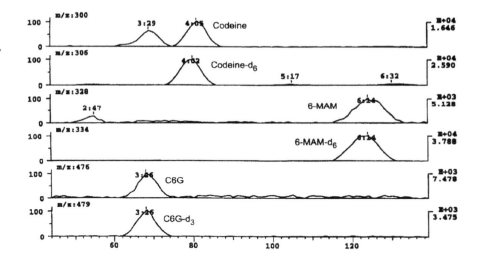

deuterated internal standards for each compound. The detection limits ranged from 0.5 to 2.5 µg/L. This procedure has been applied to routine casework (Bogusz, 2000a, 2000b) (Figures 6.9 and 6.10).

In recent years, several methods for the determination of morphine, codeine, and the corresponding glucuronides were published. The methods are generally based on solid-phase extraction and ESI-MS or ESI-MS/MS detection and are summarized in the Table 6.4.

Table 6.4

Liquid chromatographic methods for heroin, 6-MAM, morphine, codeine, and metabolites

Drug	Sample	Isolation	Column, Elution Conditions	Detection	LOD (µg/mL)	Ref.
6-MAM	Urine	Extrelut	ODS, ACN-H_2O-TEA,	Fl	1	Derks et al. (1986)
6-MAM	Urine	SPE C18	C8, ACN-MeOH-KH_2PO_4	EC	2	Hanisch and v. Meyer (1993)
6-MAM, M, C	Urine	l/l	Phenyl, ACN-NaH_2PO_4	EC + UV	40	Gerostamoulos et al. (1993)
Heroin, 6-MAM, M, C, Pholcodine	Urine	SPE BondElut	Silica, CH_2Cl_2-pentane-MeOH	UV	4–20	Low and Taylor (1995)
6-MAM, M	Blood	l/l	Silica, hexane-2PropOH-NH_3	Fl	10–25	Barrett et al. (1991)
6-MAM, M, C, M3G, M6G, AC	Blood, urine	filtration	Zorbax TMS, MeOH-H_2O-CH_3COONH_4	TSP-MS-MS	10–50	Pollettini et al. (1995)
Heroin, 6-MAM, M, M3G, M6G, C	Serum	SPE C_2	Silica, ACN-MeOH-H_2O-HCOOH	ESI-MS	0.5–4	Zuccarro et al. (1997)
Heroin, 6-MAM, M, M3G, M6G, C, C6G	Plasma	SPE C_{18}	ODS, ACN-H_2O-H_3PO_4	DAD	25	Bourquin et al. (1997)
M, M3G, M6G, 6-MAM, C, C6G	Serum, urine	SPE	C18, ACN-$HCOONH_4$ isocr.	APCI-Q, SIM	0.1–10	Bogusz et al. (1997)
M, M3G, M6G, NM	Plasma, urine	SPE C_{18}	ODS, ACN-phosphate buffer pH 2.1	EC + UV 210 nm	0.3	Svensson (1986)
M, M3G, M6G, NM	Plasma	SPE C_{18}	ODS, ACN-phosphate buffer pH 2.1	Fl + EC	1–5	Joel et al. (1988)
M, M3G, M6G	Plasma	SPE C_2	Phenyl, MeOH-phosphate buffer pH 4.0	Fl + EC	1–10	Rothsteyn and Weingarten (1996)
M, M3G, M6G	Plasma	SPE C_{18}	ODS, ACN-phosphate buffer pH 2.1	UV 210 nm	4–50	Milne et al. (1991)
M, M3G, M6G, NM	Plasma	SPE C_8	ODS, ACN-phosphate buffer pH 2.1	Fl	10–40	Glare et al. (1991)
M, M3G, M6G	Plasma	SPE C_8	ODS, ACN-H_3PO_4	Fl	5–10	Hartley et al. (1993)
M, M3G, M6G	Plasma	SPE C_2	RP, MeOH-H_2O	ESI-MS	10–100	Pacifici et al. (1995)
M, M3G, M6G	Plasma	SPE C_{18}	ODS, ACN-HCOOH	ESI-MS	0.8–5	Tyrefors et al. (1996)
M, M3G, M6G	Plasma	SPE	Silica, ACN-HCOOH isocr.	ESI-QQQ, MRM	0.5–1.0	Naidong et al. (1999)
M, 6-MAM, C, NorCod, Pholcodine	Plasma, urine	L/l	C8, ACN-$HCOONH_4$ isocr.	ESI-Q, SIM	10	Katagi et al. (2001)
M, M3G, M6G, NorM	Serum, urine	SPE	C18, ACN-HCOOH grad.	ESI-QQQ, MRM	0.3–2.5	Schanzle et al. (1999)
M, M3G, M6G, 6-MAM, Cod, C6G	Serum	SPE	C18, ACN-$HCOONH_4$ grad.	ESI-Q, SIM	0.5–5.0	Dienes-Nagy et al. (1999)
M, M3G, M6G	Serum	SPE	C18, ACN-$HCOONH_4$ isocr.	ESI-QQQ, MRM	1.0–5.0	Blanchet et al. (1999)
M, M3G, M6G	Plasma	SPE	C18, ACN-HCOOH isocr.	ESI-QQQ, MRM	0.25–0.5	Slawson et al. (1999)

M = morphine; M3G = morphine-3-glucuronide; M6G = morphine-6-glucuronide; C = codeine; C6G = codeine-6-glucuronide; Fl = fluorescence detection; EC = electrochemical detection.

Determination of free morphine and its glucuronides in body fluids may be helpful in the interpretation of a given case from the forensic and clinical points of view. A high free-morphine fraction generally indicates acute poisoning in a very early stage, particularly in a person who did not take heroin or morphine chronically. In addition, the differentiation between pharmacologically active M6G and inactive M3G is of practical importance for the interpretation of the severity of poisoning.

Cailleux et al. (1999) extracted opiate agonists (morphine, 6-MAM, codeine, norcodeine, pholcodine, codethyline) as well as nalorphine and cocaine and its metabolites (benzoylecgonine, ecgonine methyl ester, cocaethylene, and anhydromethylecgonine) from blood, plasma, or urine with chloroform/isopropanol (95:5) at pH 9. The drugs were separated on an octyl column in ACN–ammonium formate–formic acid. Protonated molecular ions and one fragment for each substance were monitored using ESI-MS/MS. The quantitation was done using deuterated internal standards. The limits of quantitation were 10 µg/L for opiates and 5 µg/L for cocaines and were higher than these after solid-phase extraction.

6.5.2.3 Alternative Matrices

The use of biological samples other than body fluids may bring several advantages in forensic analysis for drugs of abuse and also for opiates. The analysis of hair may expand the detection window to months after the exposure, while the analysis of sweat or oral fluid has an advantage of noninvasive collection. Therefore, these samples can be collected by police officers, not just by medical personnel. A review of the application of unconventional samples and alternative matrices was done by Kintz and Samyn (2000), who covered such materials as hair, oral fluid, sweat, and meconium.

Pichini et al. (1999b) developed an HPLC method with UV detection at 254 nm for the determination of heroin, 6-MAM, morphine, and codeine in human hair. Hair specimens were hydrolyzed with 0.1 M HCl and extracted with SPE cartridges. HPLC was done in ACN-phosphate buffer at pH 2.1. The LODs for 6-MAM, morphine, and codeine were 0.5 ng/mg hair, for heroin 5 ng/g. Samyn et al. (2002) performed a feasibility study on alternative samples in real-life conditions. Oral fluid, sweat wipes, blood, and urine samples were obtained from 180 drivers in Belgium who failed the field sobriety test at a police check. Mostly cannabinoids, amphetamines, and cocaine were detected; the number of opiate positives was lower. The sampling of sweat appeared simpler in field conditions than that of saliva.

6.5.3 MORPHINE AS HEROIN METABOLITE OR THERAPEUTIC DRUG

6.5.3.1 Morphine and Its Metabolites in Biosamples Taken from Living Subjects—Patients and Drug Addicts

6.5.3.1.1 Thin-Layer Chromatography

Thin-layer chromatography (TLC) is still used as a simple and inexpensive method for opiate detection in urine samples. Wolff et al. (1990) applied a horizontal TLC method for the detecting of opiates, cocaine, and amphetamines in urine after SPE C_{18} extraction. An LOD of 1 mg/L urine was reported. Dietzen et al. (1995) described the derivatization of opiates in urine extracts with acetic anhydride and methoxyamine. Using this procedure it was possible to differentiate between morphine, 6-MAM, codeine, dihydrocodeine, hydromorphone, oxycodone, and oxymorphone. Urine extraction and TLC was performed with the commercially available Toxi-Lab system. Vecerkova (1997) published a TLC method for the detection of morphine, 6-MAM, and codeine in urine extracts. Jain et al. (1996) used TLC with densitometry for free and total morphine assay in urine extracts. The method was applied in heroin addicts receiving intramuscular morphine; the limit of detection was 0.5 mg/L.

6.5.3.1.2 Gas Chromatography

GC-MS was recommended as a confirmation method for opiate identification in urine drug screening (de la Torre et al., 1997). The need to handle large numbers of urine samples in the shortest possible time brought several logistical and analytical problems. The main concern was focused on sample pretreatment procedures, such as the optimization of urine hydrolysis and the optimization of derivatization of opiates.

Effective hydrolysis of opiate conjugates is critical for all further steps of opiate determination with GC-MS. In the study of Zezulak et al. (1993), urine samples were subjected to enzymatic hydrolysis and solid-phase extraction for the isolation of total morphine, codeine, and 6-MAM. The drugs were analyzed by GC-MS after propionylation. An enzyme of bacterial origin (ß-glucuronidase from *E.coli*, E.C.3.2.1.31) was used. The authors stressed the diversity of commercially available ß-glucuronidase preparations, which may originate from snail (*Helix pomatia*), beef liver, limpets (*Patella vulgata*), or bacteria. Each enzyme preparation shows different specific activity and pH optimum. This dictated the need for a strict definition of the enzyme used in any practical analytical procedure. Lin et al. (1994) evaluated the performance of procedures used for total morphine and codeine measurements in urine. Three acid hydrolysis and four enzymatic hydrolysis methods were compared, and all urine samples were extracted with Bond Elut Certify SPE cartridges. Morphine and codeine were measured by GC-FID and GC-MS-ITD. The results were compared with those obtained with HPLC. Acid hydrolysis with 6.5 M HCl and the addition of bisulfite appeared the method of choice.

Several studies were devoted to the assessment of various derivatization procedures. Chromatographic behavior, stability, and specificity of derivatives were subjected to particular scrutiny. Paul et al. (1985) developed a GC-MS procedure for the determination of total morphine and codeine in urine. The following derivatization reagents were tried: acetic acid anhydride, trifluoroacetyl anhydride (TFA), pentafluoropropionyl anhydride (PFPA), and heptafluorobutyryl anhydride (HFBA). Acetylated compounds were most stable at room temperature, but this derivatization method prevented the detection of 6-MAM in urine. B.H. Chen et al. (1990) compared the GC-MS-EI mass spectra of HFBA, PFPA, TFA, acetyl, and trimethylsilyl (BSTFA/TMS) derivatives of morphine, codeine, and nalorphine. The TMS and acetyl derivatives showed the most stable mass spectra for SIM quantitation of morphine or codeine against nalorphine (internal standard). Grinstead (1991) studied the stability, chromatographic properties, and possible interferences of PFPA and acetic anhydride derivatives of morphine and codeine. Acetic acid anhydride produced stable derivatives, but morphine couldn't be distinguished from 6-MAM and diacetylated hydromorphone could interfere with morphine. PFPA derivatives appeared more selective and were stable enough for use in GC-MS confirmation assays. Wasels and Belleville (1994) reviewed the GC-MS procedures used for the identification of 6-MAM, morphine, and codeine. All relevant steps were scrutinized in this review, such as extraction, hydrolysis of conjugates, and derivatization methods. It was concluded that SPE had the advantage of decreasing the background noise and gradually replacing solvent extraction. The possibility of confounding morphine and codeine with hydromorphone and hydrocodone was studied by Fenton et al. (1994). Chemical reduction with sodium borohydride with subsequent trimethylsilylation resulted in better separations of the compounds and improved the quantitation of morphine in the presence of hydromorphone. Brooks and Smiths (1996) applied mild acetylation of urine samples in aqueous conditions with subsequent solvent extraction. Under these conditions, only morphine and hydromorphone were converted to their respective 3-monoacetates, and virtually no interference of hydrocodone and hydromorphone with codeine and morphine was observed. Broussard et al. (1997) prevented the interference of keto-opiates (hydromorphone, oxymorphone, hydrocodone, and oxycodone) with morphine and codeine determinations by the addition of hydroxylamine before silylation to form oxime derivatives. The keto-opiates could then be separated from morphine and codeine. Two aspects of opiates quantitation with GC-MS were evaluated by Rettinger et al. (1998): the quality of the most common derivatization procedures (TMS, TFA and PFPA) and the contributions to deuterated internal standards from unlabeled drugs. PFPA derivatives of morphine, codeine, hydromorphone, hydrocodone, and oxycodone showed the best resolution. The use of higher-labeled standards (D6 instead of D3) improved quantitation at the low and high ends of the curve due to the diminished contribution of labeled compounds to the target drug ions, and vice versa. Bogusz (1997) raised the problem of a contribution of nondeuterated morphine to D3-labeled standard and postulated the use of highly deuterated compounds as internal standards for LC-API-MS. The determination of morphine in blood has different purposes than that in urine. The concentration of free drug in blood or plasma may give an important clue concerning the acute influence at a given time. Therefore, the chromatographic methods applied for blood are usually devoted to the determination of both free and conjugated fractions of drug. Phillips et al. (1989) applied GC-EI-MS-MS for determination of free morphine in blood. The drug was extracted with ethyl acetate at pH 9.0 and derivatized with PFPA. The possible interference of codeine and 6-MAM was studied. An LOD of 1 µg/L was observed for morphine. Attempts to use chemical ionization, both in positive and negative ion modes, revealed some practical difficulties. Schmitt et al. (1990) developed a GC-CI-MS (negative and positive ions) method for the determination of PFPA derivatives of free morphine and codeine in blood samples. NCI appeared more sensitive and was applied in forensic practice. Cone and Darwin (1992) reviewed the GC-MS methods for the simultaneous determination of morphine and related opiates, including heroin, 6-MAM, and codeine, among others, in biological fluids. A growing number of methods for the simultaneous determination of various drugs and metabolites were observed. This was facilitated by the development of multipurpose SPE columns, allowing the isolation of multiple analytes of different chemical structures and different polarities. The same research team (Wang et al., 1994) published a GC-MS method for the simultaneous measurement of heroin and its metabolites and cocaine and metabolites in biosamples. The main focus of this assay was on hair analysis; however, the SPE method used also performed very well for plasma, urine, and saliva. Watson et al. (1995) described a GC-MS method for the determination of free and total morphine, codeine, and normorphine in plasma. Unconjugated drugs were isolated with alkaline liquid/liquid extraction and subjected to derivatization with HFBA before GC-MS-NCI determination. For enzymatic hydrolysis, several sources of enzyme were tested; the *E. coli* glucuronidase was the most effective. The LOD was estimated at 0.25 µg/L. The method was applied to morphine monitoring in children receiving drug via subcutaneous infusion. Fryirs et al. (1997a, 1997b) published a GC-MS method suitable for pharmacokinetic studies of free morphine. The drug was isolated from plasma with organic solvent and derivatized with PFPA. GC-MS-EI analysis was performed in the SIM mode using only one ion for morphine and one for the internal standard (nalorphine). The LOD was 0.2 µg/L. The importance of a proper derivatization procedure was stressed. In the study of Leis et al. (2000), morphine was extracted from plasma with ethyl acetate and analyzed by SIM-GC-MS (negative ions) after derivatization with heptafluorobutyric anhydride. An LOD 0.78 µg/L was reported. The method was applied for pharmacokinetic profiling of morphine.

6.5.3.1.3 Liquid Chromatography

The application of HPLC methods to the analysis of morphine and its metabolites was stimulated by two main factors. On one hand, the role of M6G as an active morphine metabolite (Osborne et al., 1990) was recognized. Moreover, it was demonstrated that the M6G receptor might be a major site of heroin action (Rossi et al., 1996). On the other hand, Svensson (1986) developed a suitable procedure for the isolation and determination of morphine and its glucuronides in biofluids. This method was based on solid-phase extraction with C_{18} cartridges and subsequent HPLC separation with UV or electrochemical (coulometric) detection. In the earlier phase, the problem of the different detectability of morphine glucuronides was solved by using HPLC with coulometric detection (for morphine and M6G) (Barberi-Heyob et al., 1991; Mason et al., 1991; Portenoy et al., 1991), fluorescence detection (for M3G) followed by coulometric detection (for assay of the morphine and M6G), (Joel et al., 1988; Rothsteyn and Weingarten, 1996). Glare et al. (1991) and Hartley et al. (1993) used fluorescence detection for all analytes.

The introduction of LC-API-MS in analytical toxicology brought new possibilities for the determination of morphine metabolites and rendered all previous methods obsolete. These techniques are discussed also in Section 6.5.2. Pacifici et al. (1995) used electrospray LC-MS for the determination of morphine, M3G, and M6G in plasma samples of patients receiving morphine and of heroin addicts. Codeine and naltrexone were used as internal standards; the limits of quantitation ranged from 10 µg/L (for morphine) to 100 µg/L (for M3G). Tyrefors et al. (1996) determined morphine, M3G, and M6G in human serum with ESI-LC-MS. The authors preferred quantitation through external standardization. Bogusz et al. (1997a, 1997b, 1998; Bogusz, 2000a, 2000b) applied LC-APCI-MS to the determination of morphine, M3G, M6G, as well as other opiates, for analysis of blood and urine samples. Isotope dilution has been applied for quantitation.

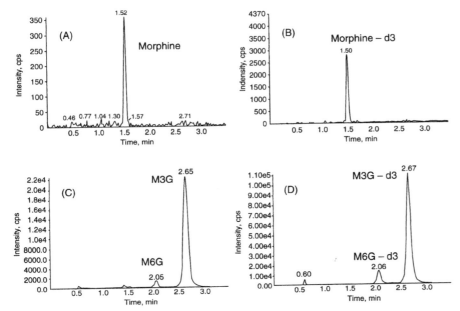

Figure 6.11

LC-ESI-MS-MS of morphine and morphine glucuronides extracted from serum. Transitions monitored: morphine, 286 > 152; morphine-d3, 289 > 152; M3G and M6G, 482 > 286; M3G-d3 and M6G-d3, 465 > 289. (From Shou et al. (2002) with permission of Elsevier Science.)

Zheng et al. (1998) used an ESI-LC-MS-MS system for the determination of morphine and glucuronides isolated from plasma samples from rats. Using plasma samples of 100 μL, detection limits of 3.8–12 μg/L were achieved. Shou et al. (2002) applied LC-ESI-MS-MS to the rapid, high-throughput analysis of morphine, M3G, and M6G in plasma. The compounds were isolated with automatic SPE in 96-well plate format and separated on a silica column. Chromatographic run time was 3.5 min; the LODs ranged from 0.5 to 10 μg/L. It should be noted that the elution order was inverted in comparison with reverse-phase chromatography (Figure 6.11).

6.5.3.2 Morphine and Its Metabolites in Autopsy Material after Heroin Overdose

The purposes of morphine determination in forensic autopsy samples are quite different from those in living subjects. The following points may be mentioned here.

- The main task is to demonstrate whether the measured concentration of drug can explain the fatal outcome.
- It is important to differentiate between heroin, morphine, and codeine intake.

- Analytical results may give some clues concerning the rapidity of death after heroin administration.

It must be added that heroin victims usually abuse several other drugs, e.g., cocaine, benzodiazepines, and methadone.

All the aforementioned points dictate the need to apply a particular analytical strategy, i.e., the use of a method that is universal with regard to the kind of biosample and the substances detected. Usually, not only morphine but also codeine, 6-MAM, acetylcodeine, morphine, and codeine glucuronides should be determined, as well as other nonopiate drugs. The methods that fulfill these requirements are reviewed in Section 6.5.2. Mass spectrometric detection coupled with GC or HPLC appeared most versatile. Less specific methods were also used for autopsy material. Lee and Lee (1991) described two GC methods for the quantitation of morphine and codeine in autopsy blood and bile. The samples were extracted with an organic solvent mixture and then subjected alternatively to derivatization with BSTFA with subsequent NP detection, or with HFBA followed by electron capture detection. Both methods assured LODs of 40 µg/L for morphine and 10 µg/L for codeine. In an HPLC procedure (Crump et al., 1994), morphine and codeine were isolated from postmortem blood and bile with alkaline solvent extraction after enzymatic hydrolysis. The drugs were separated on a phenyl column and detected with UV and fluorescence detectors. The detection limits in blood were 100 µg/L for morphine and 60 µg/L for codeine. The identification of the compounds was based on their relative retention times and ratios of fluorescence to UV peak heights. Aderjan et al. (1995) applied the method of Glare et al. (1991) to the determination of morphine and its glucuronides in autopsy blood samples taken from heroin victims. The molecular ratios were helpful for the differentiation between rapid and protracted death. A similar observation was made by Bogusz et al. (1997a, 1997b; Bogusz, 2000a, 2000b, 2000), who used LC-APCI-MS for the determination of morphine and its glucuronides in autopsy blood.

A particular application of opiate analysis is the determination of drugs in carnivorous fly larvae, infesting the decayed corpse. Goff et al. (1991) demonstrated the presence of morphine in the larvae of the flesh fly feeding on tissues of rabbit injected previously with heroin. Interesting was that the larvae feeding on these tissues developed more rapidly than those feeding on tissues from controls. Introna et al. (1990) observed a positive radioimmunoassay reaction on opiates in fly larvae fed on opiate-positive liver specimens. Kintz et al. (1994a, 1994b) determined morphine and codeine in the blood and bile of a putrefied cadaver and the fly larvae found on the corpse. The larvae were washed, homogenized in saline, and subjected to solvent extraction after enzymatic hydrolysis with β-glucuronidase. The extract was derivatized with BSTFA/TMCS and examined with GC-MS (ion trap). The following morphine concentrations were found (μg/L or μg/kg): in blood 168, in bile 357, in larvae 90. The codeine concentrations were: 37, 88, and 12, respectively. French authors (Hedouin et al., 1999, 2001; Bourel et al., 2001a, 2001b) performed systematic experimental studies on the usefulness of the necrophagous larvae *Coleoptera* and *Diptera* for the postmortem diagnosis of opiate poisoning. Rabbits were given morphine in dosages corresponding to human overdose and sacrificed. Eggs of flies were planted in the eyes, nostrils, and mouth of carcasses, and the larvae were analyzed for morphine in various developmental stages. Radioimmunoassay and immunohistochemistry were applied as detection methods. Morphine was detected in all larvae; however, the correlation between the dosage and the morphine levels was not found.

6.6 OTHER OPIATE AGONISTS

6.6.1 CODEINE AND DIHYDROCODEINE

In this section, only the studies devoted solely to codeine, dihydrocodeine, (DHC) and their metabolites will be reviewed. It must be noted that several authors have developed methods for the simultaneous determination of codeine and its metabolites together with other opiates, particularly morphine. The latter studies are reviewed in Sections 6.4 and 6.5, devoted to opiates and heroin.

DHC is a semisynthetic opiate that was used at first as an analgesic and antitussive drug. In the late 1980s DHC was used extensively in Germany in the treatment of heroin addicts; as a consequence, a number of fatal poisonings were observed (Skopp et al., 1998). As with all opiates, DHC possesses a primary addiction potential and may be abused (Balikova and Maresova, 1998). DHC in the human body undergoes *N*-demethylation to nor-DHC and *O*-demethylation to very toxic dihydromorphine (DHM). All these drugs are being conjugated to appropriate glucuronides (Aderjan and Skopp, 1998) (Fig. 6.12).

6.6.1.1 Gas Chromatography

Seno et al. (1995) determined underivatized codeine and DHC in plasma and urine using GC with surface ionization detection (SID) after SPE extraction. Dimemorfan was used as IS. The comparison of chromatograms with those obtained by GC-NPD demonstrated that SID was about 10 times more sensitive and that the matrix peaks in blank extracts were distinctly smaller. The LOD was estimated at 2.5 μg/L for both drugs. Hofmann et al. (1995) studied the

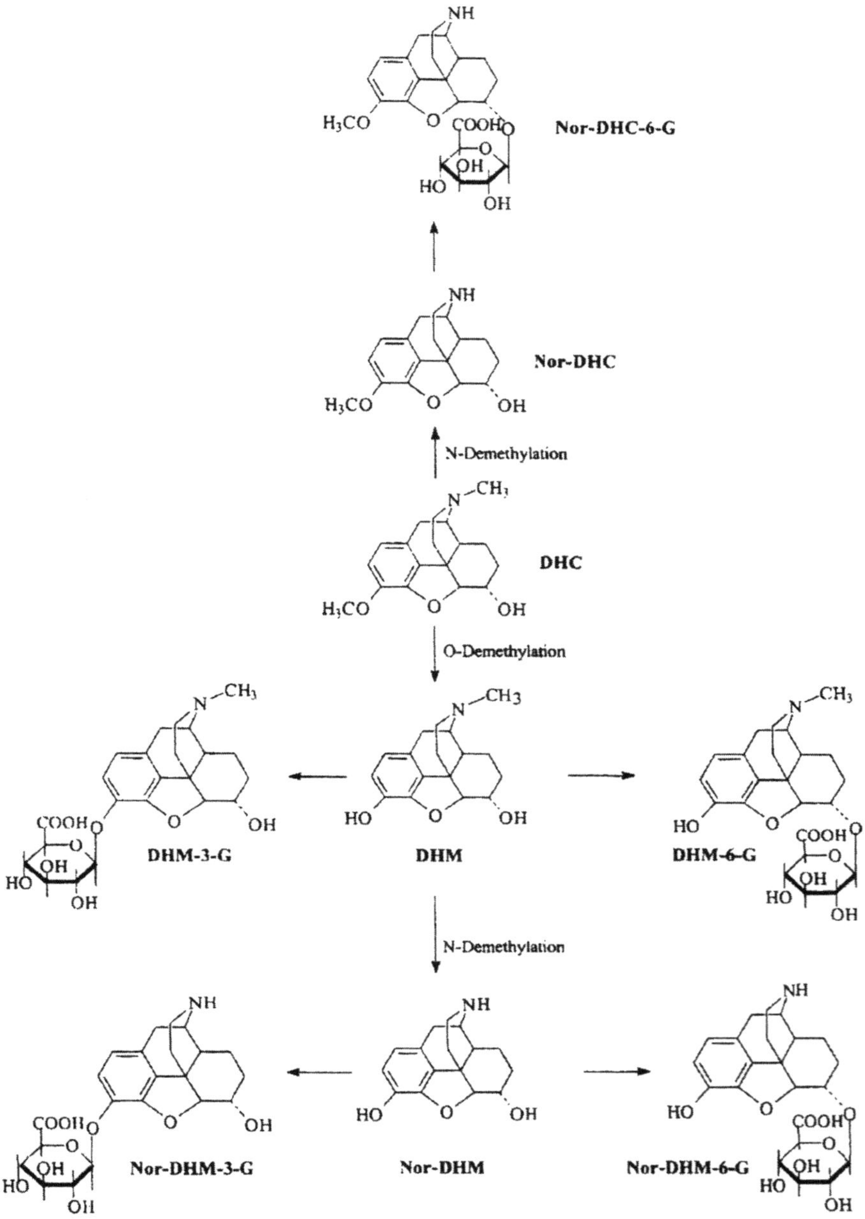

Figure 6.12
Metabolic pathways of dihydrocodeine. (From Bogusz (2000a) with permission of Elsevier Science.)

pharmacokinetics of dihydrocodeine. DHC and DHM were extracted from serum with dichlormethane–isopropanol at pH 9.6 and determined by NCI-GC-MS-MS after derivatization with PFPA. Codeine and morphine were used as internal standards. The limits of quantitation were $2\mu g/L$ for DHC and $0.04\mu g/L$ for DHM, respectively. The method allowed following drug concentrations up to 25 h after a single DHC dose of 60 mg. In fatal mixed intoxication with ethanol (1.25 g/L) and codeine, a blood concentration of 22.1 mg/L was found using GC-MS (Kintz and Tracqui, 1991). The distribution of drug in organs was also studied. Sachs et al. (1993), who examined hair samples of heroin abusers, frequently observed the presence of DHC. GC-MS after derivatization with HFBA was applied, with an absolute detection limit of 30 pg. Wilkins et al. (1995) determined codeine and morphine as codeine metabolites in human hair by PCI-GC-MS. The limits of detection for both drugs were 10 pg on-column. This allowed detecting codeine in hair for at least 8 weeks after a single oral dose of 120 mg. The same group analyzed codeine and morphine in rat hair after long-term, chronic application of codeine, using an ion-trap GC-MS (Gygi et al., 1995). The kinetics of drug incorporation into hair was followed. The excretion of DHC metabolites in urine was studied by Balikova et al. (2001), who applied GC/MS after solid-phase extraction and cleavage of conjugates.

6.6.1.2 *Liquid Chromatography*

Codeine and its metabolites norcodeine, morphine, normorphine as well as their corresponding glucuronides (C6G, M3G, M6G) were determined in plasma and urine samples by HPLC with electrochemical (coulometric) detection, using different oxidizing potentials for particular groups of compounds (Verwey-van Wissen et al., 1991). Drugs were isolated with SPE C_{18} cartridges. The method was applied to pharmacokinetic studies. Mohammed et al. (1993) extracted codeine from plasma with hexane–dichlormethane (2:1) at pH 8.0. After re-extraction and back-extraction the sample was analyzed by HPLC with fluorimetric detection (λ_{ex} 285 nm, λ_{em} 345 nm). The limit of detection was 5 $\mu g/L$. Svensson et al. (1995) isolated codeine and its metabolites (norcodeine, C6G, norcodeine-6-G, M3G, M6G, morphine, and normorphine) from serum or urine with SPE C_{18} cartridges and determined then by HPLC with electrochemical and UV (214 nm) detection. The LODs ranged from $0.14\mu g/L$ (for morphine) to $6\mu g/L$ (for codeine).

A similar method for the determination of codeine and its seven aforementioned metabolites was published by He et al. (1998). The limits of detection for codeine, C6G, norcodeine, norcodeine-6-G, and M3G, measured with UV, were 20 nmol/L. For M6G, normorphine, and morphine, monitored by electrochemical detection, a detection limit of 3 nmol/L was achieved. Lafolie

Figure 6.13

LC-APCI-MS chromatogram of urine extract after administration of 10 mg dihydrocodeine orally. DHC, dihydrocodeine; DHM, dihydromorphine; G, glucuronide. (From Bogusz (2000a) with permission of Elsevier Science.)

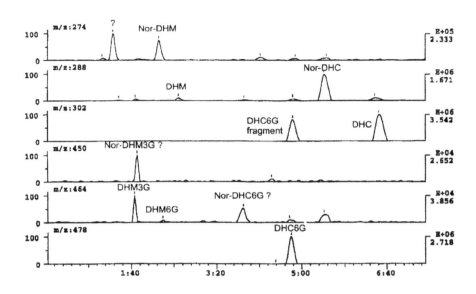

et al. (1996) determined codeine and metabolites (C6G, M3G, M6G, morphine) in plasma of 13 volunteers after experimental intake of 25 and 50 mg of codeine. HPLC with electrochemical and UV detection was applied. In urine, morphine, codeine, and norcodeine were determined by GC-MS. Large interindividual variability of peak concentrations of analytes was observed and the need for careful interpretation of results was stressed.

DHC metabolites (DHM and nordihydrocodeine), formed in liver microsomal incubates, were determined by HPLC with UV detection after alkaline solvent extraction (Kirkwood et al., 1997). The distribution of DHC and its metabolites (DHM, DHM-3-G, nor-DHC, and DHC-6-G) in various blood vessels and organs was examined in fatal dihydrocodeine intoxication (Skopp et al., 1998). HPLC with fluorescence detection was applied. In blood samples the following concentrations were found (mg/L): DHC ranged from 1.86 to 2.69, DHM from 0.100 to 0.206, DHM-3-G from 418 to 658, Nor-DHC from 0.170 to 0.295, and DHC-6-G from 1.12 to 1.85 mg/L. The authors stressed the role of DHM as an active, toxic metabolite of DHC. Bogusz (2000a) identified metabolites of DHC: Nor-DHC, DHM, DHC-6-G, DHM-3-G, DHM-6-G, Nor-DHM-3-G, in the extract of 1 mL urine after administration of 10 mg DHC orally. LC-APCI-MS was used (Fig. 6.13).

6.6.1.3 Capillary Electrophoresis

Hufschmid et al. (1996) determined urinary DHC and DHM by MEKC. The purpose of this study was to investigate the genetic polymorphism of

O-demethylation of DHC through urinary DHC/DHM ratios. Though this metabolic ratio did not give unequivocal results, the method applied appeared valuable for metabolic studies. In this study, both urine extracts and nonpretreated urine samples were analyzed. Wey et al. (2000) presented a CE-MS (IT) procedure for the determination of codeine, DHC, and their glucuronides. The metabolites were detected in urine samples after oral administration of 7 mg codeine or 25 mg DHC.

6.6.2 BUPRENORPHINE

Buprenorphine (BP), an oripavine derivative, was obtained from thebaine and displays partial agonist and antagonist opioid activity (Walsh et al., 1995). The drug was initially used as a potent analgesic (marketed under the commercial names Temgesic and Buprenex); further studies demonstrated the applicability of BP for treatment of heroin addiction (Amass et al., 2000). A monograph on the application of BP in therapy of opiate addiction was edited recently by Kintz and Marquet (2002). In this volume, an overview of therapeutical applications of buprenorphine as well as of analytical methods for drug monitoring is presented. Unfortunately, sublingual buprenorphine tablets prescribed for addiction therapy are used intravenously by heroin addicts (Vidal-Trecan et al., 2003).

6.6.2.1 Thin-Layer Chromatography

In the study of Alemany et al. (1996), BP was extracted from urine by a C_{18} SPE cartridge and derivatized with dansyl chloride. After unidimensional separation on HPTLC silica plates using two consecutive developing systems, the drug and its dealkylated metabolite were detected by fluorimetry. An LOD of 2 µg/L was achieved using fluorescence densitometry.

6.6.2.2 Gas Chromatography

Everhard et al. (1997) modified a GC-ECD method of BP determination developed initially by Cone et al. (1985). The drawback of an extensive sample pretreatment procedure was—according to the authors—counterbalanced by the use of a low-cost instrument—in comparison with GC-MS or LC-MS. The method was used for pharmacokinetic studies, and the bioavailability parameters are given. The stability of buprenorphine and morphine was assessed in spiked blood samples (Hadidi and Oliver, 1998). The drugs were determined with GC-MS (SIM) after silylation. Both drugs remained unchanged at −20°C, morphine was very stable at 4°C and 25°C (90% after 12 months' storage), BP was stable at 4°C and 25°C (80% and 70% after 12 months' storage). Kuhlman et al. (1996a) developed an NCI-MS-MS method for pharmacokinetic applications. BP and its internal standard (BP-D$_4$), as well as norbuprenorphine (NBP) and its IS (norcodeine) were derivatized with HFBA. For BP and BP-D$_4$, the molecular anions were selected as precursor ions for MS-MS. For HFBA-derivatized NBP and norcodeine, the molecular anions were too weak and the fragment ions were selected as precursors. The sensitivity for NBP was about 10 times higher than for BP due to the formation of a di-derivative by the former substance. The authors stressed the high quality of solid-phase extraction in comparison with liquid–liquid extraction. The method was consecutively applied to pharmacokinetics studies via intravenous, sublingual, and buccal routes of BP administration (Kuhlman et al., 1996b). Buprenorphine, due to its analgesic and euphorizing properties, may be abused as a doping substance in sport. Lisi et al. (1997) developed a GC-MS method for the detection of BP and its active metabolite, NBP, in urine after therapeutic doses. Urine samples were hydrolyzed with β-glucuronidase and subjected to extractive alkylation with hexane–iodomethane. The methyl derivatives of BP and NBP were determined by GC-MS (SIM), using BP-D$_4$ as IS. The conditions of hydrolysis were mild enough to prevent the formation of cyclic artifacts of BP and NBP, observed at low pH by Cone et al. (1984). BP and NBP were easily detected in urine taken 42.5 h after a sublingual dose of 0.2 mg Temgesic.

6.6.2.3 Liquid Chromatography

Debrabandere et al. (1992) published the first HPLC method with electrochemical detection for the detection of BP and NBP in urine samples. A three-step alkaline toluene extraction was applied, and the drugs were separated on a Lichrosorb-CN column with a mobile phase of ACN-phosphate buffer pH 4.0 (13:87), containing 1-heptane sulfonic acid and tetrabutylammonium sulfate. Detection limits of 0.2 μg/L for BP and 0.15 μg/L for NBP were reported. This method was applied to hair analysis by Kintz (1993) and Kintz et al. (1994a, 1994b). BP and NBP were separated on a Lichrosorb-CN column and coulometric detection was applied (first electrode at 0.15 V, second electrode at 0.50 V). The method was successfully applied to the examination of hair samples taken from BP addicts and from heroin abusers treated with BP. The authors also tried LC-MS (ESI and PBI), using instruments of an earlier generation. In a particle beam interface the buprenorphine molecule was thermally destroyed to many small fragments, and the sensitivity of an old electrospray interface was not high enough to detect drug in hair extract. In 1997, several LC-MS methods for the determination of BP and NBP were published. The main advantage in comparison with GC-MS was simpler sample pretreatment due to the omission of the derivatization step. Hoja et al. (1997)

determined BP and NBP in whole blood by LC-ESI-MS (single quadrupole) after β-glucuronidase hydrolysis, acetone precipitation, and Extrelut (toluene–ether) extraction. The LOQ was 0.1 ng/mL for both analytes. Tracqui et al. (1997) applied LC-ESI-MS to the determination of BP and NBP in blood, urine, and hair samples. A simple solvent extraction with a chloroform–isopropanol–heptane mixture at pH 8.4 was applied. The mass spectra of BP, NBP, and IS (BP-D$_4$) exhibited only protonated molecular peaks. The sensitivity was comparable with that of other ESI-MS methods. Moody et al. (1997) developed an LC-ESI-MS-MS method for BP determination in plasma and compared it with an existing GC-PCI-MS method. The LC-MS-MS method appeared more sensitive (LOQ 0.1 ng/mL) than GC-MS (LOQ 0.5 ng/mL) and allowed the authors to demonstrate the presence of drug up to 96 h after administration. The sensitivity was suitable for pharmacokinetic studies. The mass spectrum of BP observed by Hoja et al. (1997) was very similar to the spectrum observed in ESI-MS-MS by Moody et al. (1997), showing the protonated molecular ion as base peak ion and small fragments at m/z 414 and 396, respectively. According to Moody et al. (1997), the (M+H)$^+$ ion of BP remained stable up to a collision energy of 20 V; at higher energies it was shattered to many product ions of low intensity. In contrast to these observations, Bogusz et al. (1998), using the LC-APCI-MS technique, observed profound fragmentation of BP already at a collision energy of 10 V, with a base ion at m/z 450 and smaller ions at m/z 468 (protonated quasi-molecular) and 418, respectively (Fig. 6.14). In a later study, Moody et al. (2002) applied the LC-ESI-MS-MS procedure to the determination of buprenorphine and its active metabolite, norbuprenorphine, in human plasma. The transitions m/z 468 to 396 for buprenorphine and m/z 414 to 101 for norbuprenorphine were monitored, and an LOQ of 0.1 μg/L was achieved for both compounds.

Gaulier et al. (2000) reported a suicidal poisoning of 25-year-old male heroin addict from a high dose of buprenorphine. BU and NBU were determined in body fluids and organs with LC-ESI-MS after deproteinization and SPE. In gastric content, only BU was found, in a concentration of 899 mg/L. The following concentrations were found in selected matrices: in blood BU 3.3 mg/L, NBU 0.4 mg/L; in bile BU 2035 mg/L, NBU 536 mg/L; in brain BU 6.4 mg/L, NBU 3.9 mg/L. Besides BU and NBU, high concentrations of 7-aminoflunitrazepam were found in blood (1.2 mg/L), urine (4.9 mg/L), and gastric content (28.6 mg/L). Polettini and Huestis (2001) developed an LC-ESI-MS-MS method for determination of buprenorphine and its metabolites: norbuprenorphine and buprenorphine glucuronide in human plasma. SPE extraction with C18 cartridges and gradient elution was applied. For buprenorphine and norbuprenorphine as well as for deuterated analogs used as internal stan-

Figure 6.14

Mass spectra of buprenorphine obtained with LVC-ESI-MS-MS (upper), LC-ESI-MS (middle), and LC-APCI-MS (lower). (From Bogusz (2000b) with permission of Elsevier Science.)

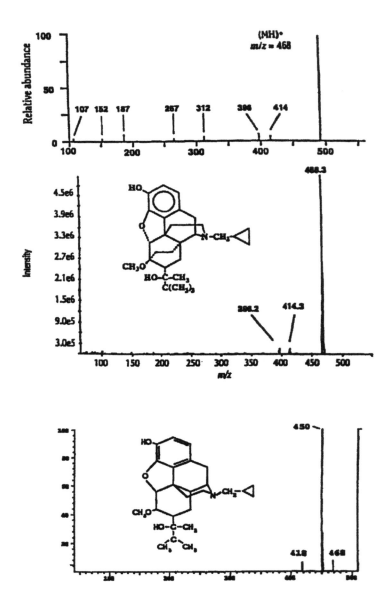

dards, the protonated quasi-molecular ions were monitored for buprenorphine glucuronide protonated quasi-molecular ion and buprenorphine aglycone. The LOQ was 0.1 μg/L for all compounds. On the basis of the transition m/z 590 → 414, norbuprenorphine glucuronide was also tentatively detected. The reference standard of this compound was not available. The authors stated that the useful fragmentation of buprenorphine molecule was not possible; after

Table 6.5

Gas chromatographic methods for synthetic opioids

Drug	Sample	Isolation	Derivatization	Column, Conditions	Detection	LOD (µg/L)	Ref.
BP	Blood	Extrelut + SCX	Silylation	CPSil-5, 180–300°	PCI-MS (SIM)	1 pg on column	Hadidi and Oliver (1998)
BP	Plasma	l/l pH 10.5	PFPA	DB-1, 160–310°	PCI-MS (SIM)	0.5 LOQ	Moody et al. (1997)
BP	Plasma	l/l pH 9.1	HFBA	HP 1, 150–325°	ECD	0.1 BP	Everhard et al. (1997)
BP, NBP	Plasma	SPE	HFBA	DB-5, 125–300°	NCI-MS-MS	0.15 BP 0.016 NBP	Kuhlman et al. (1996b)
BP, NBP	Urine	l/l alkaline	Methylation	HP 2, 247–310°	EI-MS (SIM)	0.2 both	Lisi et al. (1996)
Meth	Plasma, urine, CSF	l/l pH	—	SE-52	NPD	0.5 LOQ	Schmidt et al. (1993)
Meth, EDDP	Urine	l/l alkaline	—	DB-5, 190°	EI-MS (SIM)	50	Baugh et al. (1991)
Meth, EDDP, EMDP	Hair	l/l alkaline	—	DB-5, 80–280°	PCI-MS-ITD	0.5 ng/mg	Wilkins et al. (1996)
Meth, EDDP, EMDP	Plasma, urine, liver	SPE	—	HP-1, 80–280°	PCI-MS (SIM)	10	Alburges et al. (1996)
Tramadol	Blood	l/l pH 9	—	EC-5, 80–295°	EI-MS (SIM)	10	Goeringer et al. (1997)
Tramadol	Plasma	SPE C18	—	HP-5	EI-MS (SIM)	1	Merslavic and Zupancic-Kraj (1997)

BP = buprenorphine; NBP = norbuprenorphine; Meth = methadone; EDDP = 2-ethylidene-1,5,dimethyl-3,3-diphenylpyrrolidine; EMMP = 2-ethyl-5-methyl-3,3-diphenyl-pyrroline.

increasing the fragmentation energy, this compound dissipated to very small particles. Tables 6.5 and 6.6 show selected gas and liquid chromatographic methods applied to synthetic opiates.

6.6.3 METHADONE

Methadone, a morphine substitute synthesized in Germany during World War II, initially found limited application due to its very long elimination half-life and subsequent accumulation (Baselt, 2000). These properties drew the attention of Dole, who first applied methadone as a heroin substitute in the therapy of addicts (Dole, 1995). In the last 20 years, due to the international proliferation of methadone maintenance programs, this drug became the most widely

Table 6.6

Liquid chromatographic methods for synthetic opioids

Drug	Sample	Isolation	Column, elution Conditions	Detection	LOD (μg/ml)	Ref.
BP	Blood	SPE	C18, ACN-NH$_4$COOH	APCI-MS (SIM)	0.5	Bogusz et al. (1998)
BP	Plasma	l/l pH 10.5	C8, H$_2$O-MeOH-ACN-HCOOH	ESI-MS-MS	0.1 LOQ	Moody et al. (1997)
BP, NBP	Blood	Extrelut pH 9	C18, ACN-NH$_4$COOH	ESI-MS (SIM)	0.1 LOQ BP, NBP	Hoja et al. (1997)
BP, NBP	Blood, urine, hair	l/l pH 8.4	C18, ACN-NH$_4$COOH	ESI-MS (SIM)	0.1 BP, 0.05 NBP	Tracqui et al. (1997)
BP, NBP	Hair	l/l pH 8.5	CN, ACN–phosphate buffer	EC, ESI	0.02 ng/mg BP, 0.01 NBP	Kintz et al. (1994)
BP	Hair	l/l pH 8.5	CN, ACN–phosphate buffer	EC	0.02 ng/mg BP, 0.01 ng/mg NBP	Kintz (1993)
BP, NBP	Plasma	SPE	C18, ACN–phosphate buffer	EC	25 BP, 5 NBP	188
BP, BUG, NBUG	Plasma	SPE	C18, ACN-HCOONH$_4$ grad.	ESI-QQQ, MRM	0.1	Polettini and Huestis (2001)
Meth, EDDP	Urine, meconium	l/l pH 9	C18, ACN–phosphate buffer + TEA	DAD 204 nm	76 M, 127 EDDP	Stolk et al. (1997)
R/S-Meth, R/S-EDDP	Hair	SPE C18	Chiral-AGP, PropOH-NH$_4$COOH	ESI-MS (SIM)	0.2 M, 0.1 EDDP	Kintz et al. (1997)
R/S-Meth	Serum	SPE mixed	Chiral-AGP	UV 205 nm		Rudaz and Veuthey (1996)
Meth	Blood	SPE certify	C18, MeOH-NH$_4$COOH	TSP-MS-MS	50 pg on-col.	Verweij et al. (1995)
R/S-Meth	Serum	l/l	Chiral-AGP + CN, ACN–phosphate buffer	UV 200 nm	1.5 LOQ	Kristensen et al. (1994)
R/S-Meth	Plasma	l/l	Chiral-AGP	UV 215 mm	2.5 LOQ	Schmidt et al. (1992)
Meth, EDDP	Plasma	SPE C18	C18, ACN–phosphoric acid + DEA	UV 210 nm	0.25 ng	Pierce et al. (1992)
R/S-Meth	Plasma	l/l	Chiral-AGP	UV 212 nm		Beck et al. (1991)
(+)/(–)-Tramadol	Plasma	SPE C2	Chiralcel OD-R, ACN–phosphate buffer	Fluorimetry	0.5	Ceccato et al. (1997)
Fentanyl	Plasma	SPE 96	Silica, ACN-TFA isocr.	ESI-QQQ, MRM	0.05	Shou et al. (2001)
HYM, DHM, H3G, other metabolites	Plasma (rat)	SPE	C18, ACN-HCOONH$_4$ isocr.	ESI-QQQ, MRM	2–5	Zheng et al. (2002)
Ketobemidone, Nor-K	Urine	SPE	C8, ACN-HCOOH grad.	ESI-Q, SIM	25	Breindahl and Andreasen (1999)

BP = buprenorphine; NBP = norbuprenorphine; Meth = methadone; EDDP = 2-ethylidene-1,5,dimethyl-3,3-diphenylpyrrolidine; EC = electrochemical detection; BUG = buprenorphine glucuronide; HYC = hydrocodone; HYM = hydromorphone; DHM = dihydromorphine; H3G = hydromorphone-3-glucuronide; Nor-K = nor-ketobemidone; Q = single-stage quadrupole; QQQ = triple-stage quadrupole; SIM = selected ion monitoring; MRM = multiple reaction monitoring; ACN = acetonitrile; TFA = trifluoroacetic acid.

used opioid agonist (Newman, 1995). This dictated the need for methadone monitoring in body fluids, in order to control the compliance and to prevent the toxicity. It must be stressed that the wide availability of methadone was associated with its illicit use and with a growing number of drug-associated death cases, particularly among treated heroin addicts (La Harpe and Fryc, 1995; Heinemann et al., 1998).

6.6.3.1 Immunoassays

The immunoassays for methadone are discussed generally in Section 6.2.2, concerning all opioids. These tests are always included in a standard preliminary screening package for urine testing on drugs of abuse. Recent years brought some new developments concerning methadone and its metabolites, which should be discussed separately.

Methadone exists in two enantiomeric forms of different activity. Chikhi-Chorfi et al. (2001) developed antibodies selective for (R)-methadone (levomethadone) and for racemic (R-S)-methadone. Both antibodies showed low (0.5%) cross-reactivity with EDDP metabolite and no cross-reactivity with other opioids. An ELISA procedure has been developed for the determination of both forms of methadone in the serum of opiate addicts under maintenance treatment.

Standard methadone immunoassays do not cross-react with a prevalent metabolite, EDDP. This may be seen as a drawback, since some drug addicts who are supposed to ingest methadone spike the urine sample taken for control analysis. In such samples, high levels of methadone are detected, but not EDDP metabolite. Microgenics Corp. developed a selective CEDIA® EDDP assay. This assay was tested by George et al. (2000), who screened 1381 urine specimens, in parallel with a standard methadone EMIT immunoassay. Thirty-nine percent of samples were positive by the methadone assay, and 46% were positive for EDDP. In seven cases, only high methadone concentrations were found, with negative results for EDDP. These urine specimens originated most probably from "spikers," i.e., subjects who added methadone to urine.

L-Alpha-acetylmethadol (LAAM) was recently approved as a substitute for methadone. This drug, as well as methadol—a common metabolite of LAAM and methadone—showed very high cross-reactivity with all methadone immunoassays, including ELISA, KIMS, FPIA, and RIA (Cheever et al., 1999).

Various methadone immunoassays were applied to alternative samples. A Cozart RapiScan test was developed for the detection of methadone in saliva. The results obtained with this assay were confirmed with GC-MS (L. Moore et al., 2001; De Giovanni et al., 2002). ElSohly et al. (2001) used EMIT urine immunoassay for detection of methadone in 50 meconium samples and confronted the results with GC-MS. All EMIT results were negative. GC-MS analysis showed four samples to contain low concentrations of methadone and high concentrations of EDDP. The authors suggest using immunoassays directed at EDDP (e.g., EDDP-CEDIA) for the detection of prenatal exposure to methadone.

6.6.3.2 Gas Chromatography

Kintz et al. (1990) described a GC method for methadone and its metabolite 2-ethylidene-1,5,dimethyl-3,3-diphenylpyrrolidine (EDDP). The drugs were determined in biological fluids by GC-NPD after liquid/liquid extraction. A method for the simultaneous GC-MS assay of methadone and EDDP in urine was published by Baugh et al. (1991). The method was capable of processing a large number of urine samples, with an LOD of 50 μg/L. Schmidt et al. (1993) developed a GC assay using dextropropoxyphene as internal standard. Methadone was isolated from plasma, cerebrospinal fluid, and urine with liquid/liquid extraction. A quantification limit of 0.5 μg/L was claimed. Alburges et al. (1996) used GC-PCI-MS for the determination of methadone, EDDP, and 2-ethyl-5-methyl-3,3-diphenyl-pyrroline (EMDP). The substances were isolated from human plasma, urine, and liver microsomes by SPE. The protonated molecular ions of drugs and their trideuterated analogs, used as internal standards, were monitored. An LOQ of 10 μg/L was stated. The method was applied to the determination of methadone in the body fluids of 33 patients under methadone treatment. Methadone was found in all plasma samples and EDDP in 15 plasma samples, whereas EMDP was not present in plasma but was detectable in small concentrations in some urine samples. Methadone and its metabolites were stable in plasma and in urine at room temperature for at least 1 week. A GC-MS method for quantitation of methadone, EDDP, and EMDP in hair samples, via application of positive chemical ionization and ion trap detection, was published by Wilkins et al. (1996). Cooper and Oliver (1998) optimized a mixed-mode SPE column extraction for the isolation of methadone, EDDP, and EMPP from whole blood. Clean extracts and high recoveries were reported using GC-MS-SIM as detection technique. The detection limits for all substances were 5 μg/L. In a study of Myung et al. (1999), methadone and pethidine (meperidine) were isolated from urine with SPME and detected with a GC-NPD system. The LODs were below 1 ng/mL urine for both drugs.

Sporkert and Pragst (2000) isolated methadone, EDDP, and EMDP from human hair using automatic headspace–SPME combined with GC-MS (SIM). Hair pieces were digested in 1 M NaOH before extraction. The LODs were 0.03 ng/mg and 0.05 ng/mg for methadone and metabolites, respectively. The method was applied to the analysis of hair samples of 26 drug fatalities, and in 19 cases positive results were observed. Lachenmeier et al. (2003) isolated methadone from hair with headspace solid-phase dynamic extraction with subsequent determination with GC-MS-MS. The method was faster than conventional methods of hair analysis and more robust than SPME.

Methadone and EDDP were determined in human saliva using SPME and GC-MS (Dos Santos Lucas et al., 2000). The LODs were 40 ng/mL and 8 ng/mL for methadone and EDDP, respectively. The same research group applied SPME-GC-MS to the analysis of methadone and EDDP in plasma (Bermejo et al., 2000). The comparison with solvent extraction showed a shorter procedure time and better recovery for SPME.

6.6.3.3 Liquid Chromatography

Pierce et al. (1992) isolated methadone and its two metabolites from rat plasma by solid-phase extraction on C_{18} columns. The separation was achieved on a C_{18} column with subsequent UV detection. A method for determination of methadone and EDDP in meconium by HPLC-DAD was applied to the assessment of intrauterine exposure of neonates from methadone-using mothers (Stolk et al., 1997). Verweij et al. (1995) used thermospray LC-MS-MS for the determination of methadone and other analgesics in whole blood after solid-phase extraction (Certify™). The detection limit (on-column) was 1 ng for full-scan analysis and 50 pg for the product ion analysis.

Methadone contains a chiral carbon atom and exists in two enantiomeric forms: (S)-(+)methadone and the 25–50 times more potent (R)-(−)methadone, known also as levomethadone. In the methadone maintenance therapy of heroin addicts, both levomethadone and the racemic form are applied. It is of pharmacokinetic importance to separate the methadone enantiomers; hence, several stereoselective HPLC methods were developed for this purpose. Beck et al. (1991) published a chiral analysis of methadone in plasma using a Chiral-AGP column and UV detection. The method was applied to drug monitoring in maintenance therapy with racemic methadone. Differences in bioavailability and elimination of the two forms were observed. Similar methods were published by Schmidt et al. (1992) and by Norris et al. (1994). Kristensen et al. (1994) applied serially coupled columns (CN and Chiral-AGP) for the separation of methadone enantiomers. Rudaz and Veuthey (1996) isolated methadone enantiomers using mixed-mode solid-phase extraction columns or disks. The extract was subjected to HPLC separation on a Chiral-AGP column and to UV detection. The method, applied to drug monitoring and postmortem analyses, showed large variability in the proportion of active (R)-enantiomer, ranging from 37% to 67% in a group of heroin addicts receiving racemic drug. HPLC with UV detection was used for the separation of methadone and EDPP enantiomers in urine samples obtained from methadone maintenance patients as well as from patients with chronic pain (Angelo et al., 1999). The drugs were

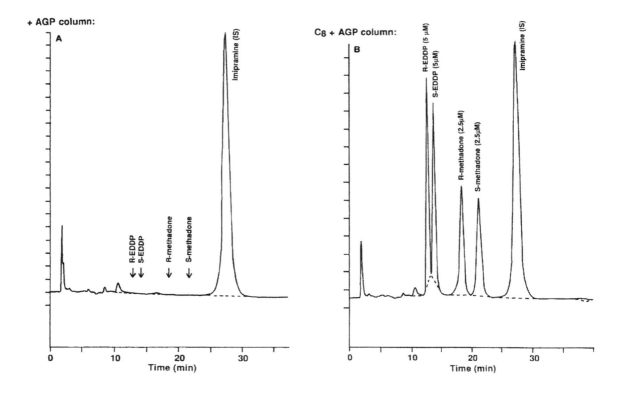

Figure 6.15

HPLC chromatograms of human urine extracts. A = blank urine; B = urine spiked with methadone and metabolite EDDP. (From Angelo et al. (1999) with permission of Elsevier Science.)

separated on an RP8 column coupled serially with a chiral AGP column. This combination improved the separation and prolonged the lifetime of the chiral column. The LOD was 9 μg/L (Fig. 6.15).

The first LC-ESI-MS method for the enantioselective separation of methadone and EDDP was published by Kintz et al. (1997). Deuterated analogs of all compounds involved were applied to quantification. The method was applied to the analysis of hair samples originating from subjects receiving racemic drug. Both enantiomers were detected, and the data collected suggested the predominance of the R-enantiomer in hair, which was in contrast to previous observations concerning serum (Beck et al., 1991; Kristensen et al., 1994). Ortelli et al. (2000) applied LC-MS to the enantioselective determination of methadone in saliva and serum. The method was applied to the analysis of samples taken from heroin addicts participating in a methadone maintenance program. The results of total methadone determination showed poor correlation between saliva and serum, while the enantiomeric ratios of drug correlated very well. Dale et al. (2002) studied the pharmacokinetics of methadone in healthy volunteers after nasal application, in comparison with the IV and oral routes. LC-MS was applied to the analysis of methadone and EDDP. After nasal administration, the onset of symptoms was much faster than after oral intake, with a similar duration. Nasal route may be an alternative to the oral one; however, the subjects reported a burning sensation after administration.

6.6.3.4 Capillary Electrophoresis

Molteni et al. (1994) investigated the possibility of methadone determination in urine with CE. The drug and its metabolite could easily be determined by cationic capillary zone electrophoresis; the application of MEKC was not successful. Direct injection of urine samples sometimes led to false-negative results. Therefore, solid-phase extraction of samples was recommended, and an LOQ of 20 µg/L was achieved. Thormann et al. (1998) developed two CE methods for the detection of methadone and EDDP in urine: an electrokinetic capillary-based immunoassay as a screening procedure, and a combination of CE with ESI-MS-MS for confirmation.

6.6.4 TRAMADOL

Tramadol is a centrally acting analgesic introduced in the late 1970s as a weak µ-opioid receptor agonist. Most reports concerning the forensic aspects of tramadol toxicity appeared in the 1990s, when the drug found its way to the drug abuse scene.

6.6.4.1 Gas Chromatography

Merslavic et al. (1997) published a GC-MS method for tramadol determination in plasma, using SPE on C_{18} cartridges. The method was applied to pharmacokinetic studies. Goeringer et al. (1997) determined tramadol and its metabolites N-desmethyltramadol (NDT) and O-desmethyltramadol (ODT) in blood from drug-related deaths (12 cases) and drug-impaired drivers (3 cases). GC-MS after butyl chloride extraction at pH 9 was applied. It was observed that variable amounts of an artifact of NDT were sometimes formed in the injection port of the GC. In all tramadol-related death cases and in all samples from living subjects a number of other relevant drugs were found, particularly tricyclic antidepressants and opiates. These compounds may interact with the metabolism and pharmacological activity of tramadol and its active metabolite ODT. Drug concentrations in 12 autopsy blood samples ranged from 0.03 to 22.59 mg/L for tramadol, from 0.02 to 1.84 mg/L for ODT and from 0.01 to 2.08 mg/L for NDT. In blood samples taken from impaired drivers tramadol concentrations ranged from 0.07 to 0.29 mg/L those of ODT from 0.05 to 0.11 mg/L, and of NDT from 0.03 to 0.09 mg/L. Therapeutic tramadol concentrations were between 0.23 to 0.77 mg/L. This study showed that every case of suspected tramadol intoxication must be very carefully scrutinized in regard to the role of other coexisting substances. In a monointoxication with tramadol, a concentration of 13 mg/L was found. GC-MS method was used, but the details were not given. Also, ODT was identified but not quantified (Lusthof and Zweipfenning, 1998). Levine et al. (1997) reported four cases in which tramadol was found, but death was attributed to other causes, like coronary disease, drowning, or gunshot wound. Tramadol, NDT, and ODT were extracted with *n*-butyl chloride in alkaline conditions and identified by GC-EI-MS. Quantitative determination of tramadol was performed with GC-NPD in body fluids and organs and the distribution data were presented. The authors stressed that urine is the specimen of choice for identifying of tramadol use. In contrast to the finding of Sticht et al. (1997) no evidence of sequestration of drug in liver or kidney was found, which was consistent with the reported volume of distribution of 3 L/kg.

6.6.4.2 Liquid Chromatography

Sticht et al. (1997) described the distribution of tramadol in a drug-associated death case. To a female patient with symptoms of generalized sepsis, 400 mg tramadol and 2.5 g metamizole were administered together on two occasions, with an interval of 20 h. The patient died 5 h after the second dose. The following tramadol concentrations were found postmortem (mg/kg): in peripheral blood 5.6, in heart blood 15.1, in heart muscle 14.9, in brain 14.7, in lung 23.2, in liver 20.0. Tramadol was determined by HPLC on octyl column, the metabolites were not analyzed. The patient was treated in an intensive care unit, and septic shock was established as the cause of death, despite the high drug concentrations. Nobilis et al. (1996) developed an HPLC method with fluorescence detection for a pharmacokinetic study of two commercial tramadol preparations. The drug was extracted with *t*-butylmethylether in alkaline conditions and separated on an RP-18 column. The limit of quantitation was 17 µg/L. Tramadol possesses two stereogenic centers and normally is used in therapy as the racemate of the *trans*-isomer, which is more active than the *cis*-isomer. Also, the (+)-*trans*-tramadol is about 10-fold more potent than the (−)-*trans*-tramadol (Frankus et al., 1978). Interindividual differences of the enantiomeric ratios of tramadol, NDT, and ODT in urine were studied by Elsing and Blaschke (1993) using Chiralpak AD and Chiralcel OD columns. Ceccato et al. (1997) developed an HPLC method for the determination of the enantiomers of *trans*-tramadol and its O-desmethylated metabolite in plasma, using automatic SPE extraction and chiral liquid chromatography with UV (220 nm) and fluorometric detection. The influence of SPE sorbent, elution conditions, and type of chiral column on the detectability of the substances was studied. The optimized method allowed achieving a 100% recovery and an LOD of 0.5 ng/mL for both enantiomers.

6.6.5 KETO-OPIOIDS

Semisynthetic 6-keto-opioids (hydrocodone, hydromorphone, oxycodone, and oxymorphone) are widely used as analgesics and antitussive drugs. These compounds also achieved popularity as abused drugs in some countries (Vecerkova, 1992). Most reports concerning 6-keto-opiates coped with the problems of chromatographic differentiation of these drugs from morphine and codeine. These papers, in which TLC (Dietzen et al., 1995) or GC (Fenton et al., 1994; Brooks and Smiths, 1996; Broussard et al., 1997) procedures are used, are discussed in Section?, devoted to morphine analysis. Cone and Darwin in their review of opiate analysis (1992) also discussed the application of GC-MS methods to keto-opiates. A gas chromatographic method for oxycodone assay was developed by Kapil et al. (1992). The drug and internal standard (hydrocodone) were extracted from plasma with toluene–isopropanol and quantified with a nitrogen detector. An LOQ of 1.8 μg/L was reported. C.M. Moore et al. (1995) reported the detection of hydrocodone in meconium samples in two cases. The drug was isolated with methyl-t-butyl ether in alkaline conditions, trimethylsilylated, and analyzed with GC-MS (SIM). In one case, hydromorphone (hydrocodone metabolite) and codeine were also found. Bouquillon et al. (1992) developed an HPLC method for the simultaneous determination of hydromorphone and morphine in plasma. A coulometric detection was used. The limits of quantitation (2.5 ng/mL for hydromorphone and 1.2 ng/mL for morphine) were sufficient for pharmacokinetic studies. Wright et al. (1998) synthesized hydromorphone-3-glucuronide (H3G) from hydromorphone using rat liver microsomes. The crude product was purified with semipreparative HPLC with UV detection. H3G evoked in rats similar behavioral effects as morphine or morphine-3-glucuronide or normorphine-3-glucuronide. In the Czech Republic, an illicit hydrocodone preparation called "brown" has been abused for 20 years. Besides hydrocodone, "brown" contains codeine as the precursor and dihydrocodeine as the by-product. Balikova and Maresova (1998) described a case of fatal overdose of "brown" together with ethylmorphine and morphine. The drugs were determined in autopsy blood with an ion trap GC-MS after solid-phase extraction. The following concentrations of unconjugated drugs were found: hydrocodone 15.9 mg/L, hydromorphone 11.88 mg/L, ethylmorphine 15.60 mg/L, morphine 12.15 mg/L, dihydrocodeine 2.26 mg/L, codeine 0.5 mg/L, and norcodeine 0.14 mg/L. Spiller (2003) analyzed 88 cases of oxycodone- and hydrocodone-associated death cases. The drugs were determined with GC. Twenty-four deaths were

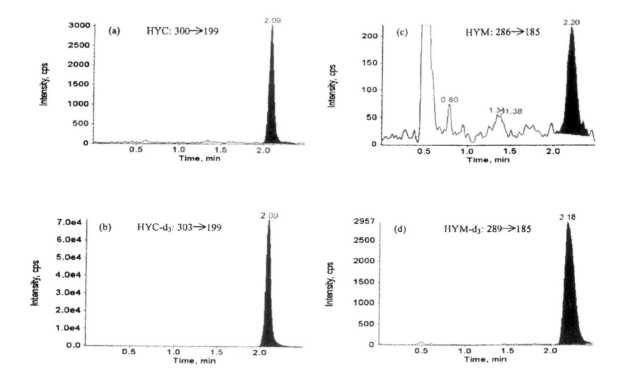

Figure 6.16

LC-ESI-MS-MS of hydrocodone (HYC) and hydromorphone (HYM) extracted from serum and the concentration level of 0.3 ng/mL. Transitions monitored are shown on the figure. (From Y.L. Chen et al. (2002) with permission of Elsevier Science.)

attributed to oxycodone alone. The mean and median oxycodone blood concentrations were 1.23 mg/L and 0.43 mg/L, respectively. In 17 fatal cases of hydrocodone intoxication, the mean and median postmortem blood concentrations were 0.53 mg/L and 0.40 mg/L, respectively. Jones et al. (2002) determined codeine, morphine, hydrocodone, hydromorphone, 6-acetylmorphine, and oxycodone in the hair and oral fluid of addicts by GC-MS after derivatization with methoxyamine. The use of this derivatization reagent prevented the formation of multiple derivative forms that may originate from the keto- or enol-form of keto-opioids, as observed for silyl derivatives. Y.L. Chen et al. (2002) published LC-ESI-MS-MS procedures for the determination of hydrocodone and hydromorphone in plasma. The drugs and deuterated analogs were extracted with solvent and separated from glucuronides using 50-mm × 2-mm silica column and mobile phase consisting of ACN–water–formic acid (80:20:1). The LOQ was 0.1 μg/L (Fig. 6.16).

Wey and Thormann (2002) determined oxycodone and its metabolites oxymorphone and noroxymorphone in urine with CE-MS (IT) and CE-UV. The existence of glucuronidated second-phase metabolites was postulated.

6.6.6 FENTANYL AND RELATED DRUGS (SUFENTANIL, ALFENTANIL, REMIFENTANIL)

Fentanyl and other structural analogs are very potent, specific μ-receptor agonists of synthetic origin. Besides its therapeutical application as an analgesic, fentanyl appeared on the 1970s in the illicit-drug market. Ohta et al. (1999) discriminated fentanyl and its 24 analogs using GC, GC-MS, and condensed-phase IR. The methyl- or fluoroderivatives of fentanyl, sold as "superheroin" or "China white" turned out to be particularly dangerous, and several reports concerning drug-associated death cases were published (Baselt, 2000). Beside immunochemical assays, fentanyl was usually determined by gas chromatography. Watts and Caplan (1988) used dual-column gas chromatography with nitrogen-sensitive and mass spectrometric detectors for the determination of fentanyl in whole blood. Two capillary columns of different polarity (5% and 50% phenyl methyl silicone) were used. Several related substances (sufentanil, carfentanil, lofentanil, and alfentanil) were also examined. The limit of detection for the nitrogen detector was found to be 0.1 μg/L and for MS detection to be 0.05 μg/L. Esposito and Winek (1991) used also GC-MS-EI for the identification of 3-methylfentanyl in street samples. Szeitz et al. (1996) developed a GC-MS assay of fentanyl suitable for pharmacokinetic studies of transdermally administered drug in a postoperative swine. Sufentanil was used as an internal standard. Quantitation in the SIM mode was possible down to 0.05 μg/L. A similar method was described by Fryirs et al. (1997), who determined fentanyl with GC-MS (SIM) in plasma. A limit of detection of 0.02 μg/L was observed. Fentanyl and sufentanil were determined in hair specimens of tumor patients receiving these drugs percutaneously or intravenously. The assay was performed with GC-PCI-MS-MS (Sachs et al., 1996). A postmortem distribution of fentanyl after its application in the form of a transdermal patch (Duragesic) was studied by Anderson and Muto (2000). Fentanyl was extracted with butyl chloride in alkaline conditions and determined by GC-MS. The distribution of fentanyl in heart and femoral blood, urine, vitreous humor, bile, and organs was given. Shou et al. (2001) determined fentanyl in plasma using automated 96-well solid-phase extraction, straight-phase chromatography, and ESI-MS-MS. The LOQ was 0.05 μg/L plasma, based on a 0.25-mL sample volume. Sufentanil is so far the most potent synthetic opioid used in therapy. An LC-ESI-MS-MS method for therapeutic drug monitoring of sufentanil has been published (Martens-Lobenhoffer, 2002). The drug was extracted from serum with toluene–isopropanol (10:1) and separated on an ODS column. An LOQ of 10 ng/L was achieved. The stability of sufentanil in human plasma under various storage conditions was studied by Dufresne et al. (2001). The drug was extracted with Oasis MCX columns and determined with GC-MS. A significant decrease was observed after 1 h in plasma stored at 4°C.

Alfentanil is an intravenous narcotic analgesic with a short duration of action. The concentrations of this drug were measured in plasma and tissues of experimental animals by GC-MS in a pharmacokinetic study (Edwards et al., 2002).

Another member of the fentanyl group, remifentanil, is an analgesic that has considerable abuse potential in racing horses. Lehner et al. (2000) studied the metabolism of remifentanil after IV administration of 5 mg of this drug to horse. A major metabolite of remifentanil was identified.

6.6.7 KETOBEMIDONE

Ketobemidone is a synthetic opioid agonist and narcotic analgesic that is frequently abused, particularly in Scandinavian countries. Breindahl and Andreasen (1999) developed an LC-ESI-MS method for the determination of ketobemidone and its demethylated metabolite in urine. Mixed-bed SPE cartridges were used for isolation, with a recovery over 90%. Protonated quasi-molecular ions for both substances as well as three fragments for ketobemidone were monitored. The LOD was 25 µg/L. Sunstrom et al. (2001) applied ESI-MS-MS to the determination of ketobemidone, its five phase I metabolites, as well as glucuronides of ketobemidone and norketobemidone in human urine. The same group used ESI-qTOF-MS besides LC-MS-MS for the determination of the glucuronides of ketobemidone, nor-, and hydroxymethoxyketobemidone in urine (Sundstrom et al., 2002). The accuracy of the mass measurement was better than 2 ppm.

6.6.8 BUTORPHANOL, DEXTROMETORPHAN

Andraus and Siquera (1997) determined butorphanol in the urine of race-horses with ELISA immunoassay kits followed by GC-MS. After IM application of 8 mg Torbugesic to a horse, the detection window in urine was up to 104 h with ELISA and up to 24 h with GC-MS. Y.J. Wu et al. (2003) described a GC method for the determination of dextrometorphan and its metabolite dextrorphan in human urine. The drugs were subjected to solvent extraction and detected with GC/FID on an HP-1 (17-m × 0.22-mm) column. The method was used for phenotyping a Chinese population.

6.7 SUMMARY

Immunoassays are the most important techniques used for preliminary testing on opiate agonists. The trend toward the use of noninvasive sampling, i.e., saliva or sweat, is observed. Onsite tests, used by law enforcement officers, are gaining more and more popularity. Thin-layer chromatography is still in use for the preliminary detection of opiates in plant material, street drugs, and urine. The method has the advantage of simplicity, speed, and low cost and is therefore preferred in modestly equipped laboratories. Positive results, however, always need a confirmative analysis with mass spectrometric detection.

Solid-phase extraction is gradually replacing solvent extraction procedures for the isolation of opiate agonists and their metabolites from biological samples. The advantages of this workup technique include broader polarity spectrum of isolated substances and rather pure extracts. So far, solid-phase extraction is used mainly in column format; the use of disk or 96-well plate formats will probably be enhanced in the future.

For identification of unknown opiates of low or middle polarity, gas chromatography coupled with a full-scan electron impact mass spectrometry is a most important tool. This method usually has been used for confirmation of the results of presumptive immunochemical tests. Unequivocal identification and quantitative analysis of defined opiates may be performed by gas or liquid chromatography, both separation methods being coupled to a mass spectrometer in selected ion monitoring mode, using electron impact or chemical ionization. The last decade brought a breakthrough in the development of atmospheric pressure ionization mass chromatography. This technique, in both the electrospray and atmospheric pressure chemical ionization modes, may be coupled to a liquid chromatograph and has shown distinct advantages over GC-MS with regard to the spectrum of detectable drugs and the simplicity of sample preparation. Therefore, solving the identity of target opiates and the consecutive quantitation will in the future most probably be performed only with LC-MS.

Other detection modes used with gas chromatography (nitrogen-selective or electron capture detection) or with liquid chromatography (diode array detection, electrochemical or fluorimetric detection) are still being (and will continue to be) successfully used for dedicated purposes in opiate analysis. The advantages of these techniques include lower cost and sometimes very high sensitivity. Due to their lower selectivity, these methods are particularly valuable for the analysis of less complicated matrices, such as illicit-drug specimens or pharmaceutical preparations. Capillary electrophoresis, in combination with UV (DAD) or MS-detection, is still in the development stage and has room for improvement. This separation technique combines the most important features of gas and liquid chromatography; it offers separation efficiency comparable to that of capillary GC and is applicable to polar and thermally unstable compounds that may be analyzed with HPLC. It is possible that this technique will play a crucial role in toxicological analysis in the near future.

ABBREVIATIONS

6-MAM: 6-acetylmorphine
ACN: acetonitrile
APCI: atmospheric pressure chemical ionization
BE: benzoylecgonine
BSTFA: bis-(trimethylsilyltrifluoroacetamide)
CE: capillary electrophoresis
CE-MS: capillary electrophoresis–mass spectrometry
CI: chemical ionization
CID: collision-induced dissociation
CSF: cerebrospinal fluid
CZE: capillary zone electrophoresis
DAD: diode array detector
DEA: diethylamine
DHC: dihydrocodeine
DMOA: dimethyloctylamine
EDDP: 2-ethylidene-1,5-dimethyl-3,3-diphenylpyrrolidine
EI: electron impact ionization
ESI: electrospray ionization
FAB: fast atom bombardment
G6PDH: glucose-6-phosphodehydrogenase
GC: gas chromatography
HFBA: hexafluorobutyric acid

HPLC: high-pressure liquid chromatography
ITD: ion trap detection
LC-MS: liquid chromatography–mass spectrometry
LOD: limit of detection
LOQ: limit of quantitation
M3G: morphine-3-glucuronide
M6G: morphine-6-glucuronide
MEKC: micellar electrokinetic capillary chromatography
MeOH: methanol
NCI: negative chemical ionization
NPD: nitrogen–phosphorus detection
PBI: particle beam ionization
PCI: positive chemical ionization
PFPA: pentafluoropropionyl anhydride
POD: peroxidase
RP: reverse phase
SFE: supercritical fluid extraction
SIM: selected ion monitoring
SPE: solid phase extraction
TEA: triethyleneamine
TLC: thin-layer chromatography
TMCS: trimethyl-chlorosilane
TSP: thermospray ionization

REFERENCES

Aderjan, R., and Skopp, G. (1998). *Ther. Drug. Monit.* 20, 561–569.

Aderjan, R., Hofmann, S., Schmitt, G., and Skopp, G. (1995). *J. Anal. Toxicol.* 19, 163–168.

Alburges, M.E., Huang, W., Foltz, R.L., and Moody, D.E. (1996). *J. Anal. Toxicol.* 20, 362–368.

Alemany, G., Gamundi, A., Rossello, C., and Nicolau, M.C. (1996). *Biomed. Chromatogr.* 10, 146–147.

Allen, A.C., Cooper, J.M., Moore, J.M., Gloger, M., and Neumann, H. (1984). *Anal. Chem.* 56, 2940–2947.

Allen, D.L, Scott, K.S., and Oliver, J.S. (1999). *J. Anal. Toxicol.* 23, 16–18.

Amass, L., Kamien, J.B., and Mikulich, S.K. (2000). *Drug Alcohol Depend.* 58, 143–152.

Anderson, D.T., and Muto, J.J. (2000). *J. Anal. Toxicol.* 24, 627–634.

Andraus, M.H., and Siquera, M.E. (1997). *J. Chromatogr. B* 704, 143–150.

Angelo, H.R., Beck N., and Kristensen, K. (1999). *J. Chromatogr. B* 724, 35–40.

Armbruster, D.A., Scharzhoff, R.H., Hubster, E.C., and Liserio, M.K. (1993). *Clin. Chem.* 39, 2137–2146.

Ayyangar, N.R., and Bhide, S.R. (1988). *J. Chromatogr.* 436, 455–465.

Balikova, M., and Maresova, V. (1998). *Forensic Sci. Int.* 94, 201–209.

Balikova, M., Maresova, V., and Habrdova, V. (2001). *J. Chromatogr. B* 752, 179–186.

Barberi-Heyob, M., Merlin, J.R., Krakowski, I., Kettani, C., Collin, E., and Poulain, P. (1991). *Bull. Cancer* 78, 1063–1070.

Barnfield, C., Burns, S., Byrom, D.L., and Kemmenoe, A.V. (1988). *Forensic Sci. Int.* 39, 107–117.

Barrett, C., Good, C., and Moore, C. (2001). *Forensic Sci. Int.* 122, 163–166.

Baselt, R.C. (2000). *Disposition of Toxic Drugs and Chemicals in Man*, 5th ed. Chemical Toxicology Institute, Foster City, CA, pp. 353–356.

Baugh, L.D., Liu, R.H., and Walia, A.S. (1991). *J. Forensic Sci.* 36, 548–555.

Beck, O., Boreus, L.O., Lafolie, P., and Jacobson, G. (1991). *J. Chromatogr.* 570, 198–202.

Bermejo, A.M., Seara, R., dos Santos Lucas, A.C., Tabernero, M.J., Fernandez, P., and Marsili, R. (2000). *J. Anal. Toxicol.* 24, 66–69.

Besacier, F., Chaudron-Thozet, H., Rousseau-Tsangaris, M., Girard, J., and Lamotte, A. (1997). *Forensic Sci. Int.* 85, 113–125.

Bjerver, K, Johnsson, J., and Schuberth, J. (1982). *J. Pharm. Pharmacol.* 34, 798–801.

Blanchet, M., Bru G., Guerret M., Bromet-Petit, M., and Bromet, N. (1999). *J. Chromatogr. A* 854, 93–108.

Blevins, D.D., and Hall, D.O. (1998). *LC-GC Int.* (Suppl.) September, 17.

Bogusz, M.J. (1997). *J. Anal. Toxicol.* 21, 246–247.

Bogusz, M.J. (2000a). *J. Chromatogr. B* 748, 3–19.

Bogusz, M.J. (2000b). Opioid agonists. In *Forensic Science Handbook of Analytical Separations*, Vol. 2 (ed. Bogusz, M.J.). Elsevier Science, Amsterdam, pp. 3–65.

Bogusz, M., Aderjan, R., Schmitt, G., Nadler, E., and Neureither, B. (1990). *Forensic Sci. Int.* 48, 27–37.

Bogusz, M.J., Maier, R.D., Schiwy-Bochat, K.H., and Kohls, U. (1996). *J. Chromatogr. B* 683, 177–188.

Bogusz, M.J., Maier, R.D., and Driessen, S. (1997a). *J. Anal. Toxicol.* 21, 346–355.

Bogusz, M.J., Maier, R.D., Erkens, M., and Driessen, S. (1997b). *J. Chromatogr. B* 703, 115–127.

Bogusz, M.J., Maier, R.D., Krüger, K.D., and Kohls, U. (1998). *J. Anal. Toxicol.* 22, 549–558.

Bogusz, M.J., Maier, R.D., Erkens, M., and Kohls, U. (2001). *J. Anal. Toxicol.* 25, 431–438.

Bora, T., Merdivan, M., and Hamamci, C. (2002). *J. Forensic Sci.* 47, 959–963.

Bouquillon, A.I., Freeman, D., and Moulin, D.E. (1992). *J. Chromatogr.* 577, 354–357.

Bourel, F., Fleurisse, L., Hedouin, V., Cailliez, J.C., Creusy, C., Gosset, D., and Goff, M.L. (2001a). *J. Forensic Sci.* 46, 596–599.

Bourel, F., Tournel, G., Hedouin, V., Goff, M.L., and Gosset, D. (2001b). *J. Forensic Sci.* 46, 600–603.

Breindahl, T., and Andreasen, K. (1999). *J. Chromatogr. B* 736, 103–113.

Brenneisen, R., and Hasler, F. (2002). *J. Forensic Sci.* 47, 885–888.

Brenneisen, R., Hasler, F., and Wursch, D. (2002). *J. Anal. Toxicol.* 26, 561–566.

Brewer, W.E., Galipo, R.C., Sellers, K.W., and Morgan, S.L. (2001). *Anal. Chem.* 73, 2371–2376.

Brooks, K.E., and Smiths, N.B. (1996). *J. Anal. Toxicol.* 20, 269–270.

Broussard, L.A., Presley, L.C., Pittman, T., Clouette, R., and Wimbish, G.H. (1997). *Clin. Chem.* 43, 1029–1033.

Buchan, B., Walsh, J.M., and Leaverton, P.E. (1998). *J. Forensic Sci.* 43, 395–399.

Cailleux, A., Le, Bouil, A., Auger, B., Bonsergent, G., Turcant, A., and Allain, P. (1999). *J. Anal. Toxicol.* 23, 620–624.

Cartier, J., Gueniat, O., and Cole, M.D. (1997). *Sci. Justice* 37, 175.

Casella, G., Wu, A.H.B., Shaw, B.R., and Hill, D.W. (1997). *J. Anal. Toxicol.* 21, 376–383.

Ceccato, A., Chiap, P., Hubert, Ph., and Crommen, J. (1997). *J. Chromatogr. B* 698, 161.

Cheever, M.L., Armendariz, G.A., and Moody, D.E. (1999). *J. Anal. Toxicol.* 23, 500–506.

Chen, B.H., Taylor, E.H., and Pappas, A.A. (1990). *J. Anal. Toxicol.* 14, 12–17.

Chen, X.H., Hommerson, A.L.C., Zweipfenning, P.G.M., Franke, J.P., Harmen-Boverhof, C.W., Ensing, K., and de Zeeuw, R.A. (1993). *J. Forensic Sci.* 38, 668–676.

Chen, Y.L., Hanson, G.D., Jiang, X., and Naidong, W. (2002). *J. Chromatogr. B* 769, 55–64.

Chiarotti, M., Fucci, N., and Furnari, C. (1991). *Forensic Sci. Int.* 50, 47–55.

Chikhi-Chorfi, N., Galons, H., Pham-Huy, C., Thevenin, M., Warnet, J.M., and Claude, J.R. (2001). *Chirality* 13, 187–192.

Cirimele, V., Kintz, P., Majdelani, R., and Maugin, P. (1995). *J. Chromatogr.* B673, 173–181.

Cody, J.T., and Valtier, S. (2001a). *J. Anal. Toxicol.* 25, 466–470.

Cody, J.T., Valtier, S., and Kuhlman, J. (2001b). *J. Anal. Toxicol.* 25, 572–575.

Cone, E.J., and Darwin, W.D. (1992). *J. Chromatogr.* 580, 43–61.

Cone, E.J., Gorodetzky, C.W., Darwin, W.D., and Bunchwald, W.F. (1984). *J. Pharm. Sci.* 73, 243.

Cone, E.J., Gorodetzky, C.W., Yousefnejad, D., and Darwin, W.D. (1985). *J. Chromatogr.* 335, 291–230.

Cone, E.J., Welch, P., Mitchell, J.M., and Paul, B.D. (1991). *J. Anal. Toxicol.* 15, 1–7.

Cone, E.J., Dickerson, S., Paul, B.D., and Mitchell, J.M. (1992). *J. Anal. Toxicol.* 16, 72–78.

Cone, E.J., Holicky, B.A., Grant, T.M., Darwin, W.D., and Goldberger, B.A. (1993). *J. Anal. Toxicol.* 17, 327–337.

Cone, E.J., Presley, L., Lehrer, M., Seiter, W., Smith, M., Kardos, K.W., Fritch, D., Salamone, S., and Niedbala, R.S. (2002). *J. Anal. Toxicol.* 26, 541–546.

Cooper, G.A.A., and Oliver, J.S. (1998). *J. Anal. Toxicol.* 22, 389–392.

Crouch, D.J., Hersch, R.K., Cook, R.F., Frank, J.F., and Walsh, J.M. (2002). *J. Anal. Toxicol.* 26, 493–439.

Crump, K.L., McIntyre, I., and Drummer, O.H. (1994). *J. Anal. Toxicol.* 18, 208–212.

Dale, O., Hoffer, C., Sheffels, P., and Kharasch, E.D. (2002). *Clin. Pharmacol. Ther.* 72, 536–545.

Dams, R., Benijst, T., Lambert, W.E., Massart, D.L., and De Leenheer, A.P. (2001). *Forensic Sci. Int.* 123, 81–88.

Dams, R., Benijst, T., Gunther, W., Lambert, W., and De Leenheer, A.P. (2002a). *Anal. Chem.* 74, 3206–3212.

Dams, R., Benijst, T., Lambert, W.E., and De Leenheer, A.P. (2002b). *J. Chromatogr.* B 773, 53–61.

De Giovanni, N., Fucci, N., Chiarotti, M., and Scarlata, S. (2002). *J. Chromatogr.* B 773, 1–6.

De la Torre, R., Segura, J., de Zeeuw, R., and Williams, J. (1997). *Ann. Clin. Biochem.* 34, 339–344.

De Zeeuw, R.A., Wijsbeek, J., and Franke, J.P. (2000). *J. Anal. Toxicol.* 24, 97–101.

Debrabandere, L., Van, Boven, M., and Daenens, P. (1992). *J. Forensic Sci.* 37, 82–89.

Degel, F. (1996). *Clin. Biochem.* 29, 529–540.

Derks, H.J., Van Twillert, K., Pereboom-De Fauw, D.P., Zomer, G., and Loeber, J.G. (1986). *J. Chromatogr.* 370, 173–178.

Dhawan, B.N., Cesselin, F., Raghubir, R., Reisine, T., Bradley, P.B., Porthogese, P.S., and Hamon, M. (1996). *Pharmacol. Rev.* 48, 567–592.

Dienes-Nagy, A., Rivier, L., Giroud, G., Augsburger, M., and Mangin, P. (1999). *J. Chromatogr. A* 854, 109–118.

Dietzen, D.J., Koening, J., and Turk, J. (1995). *J. Anal. Toxicol.* 19, 299–303.

Dole, V.P. (1995). In *Drug Addiction and Related Clinical Problems* (ed. A. Tagliamonte and L. Maremmani). Springer Verlag, New York, pp. 45–63.

Dos Santos Lucas, A.C., Bermejo, A., Fernandez, P., and Tabernero, M.J. (2000). *J. Anal. Toxicol.* 24, 93–96.

Dufresne, C., Favetta, P., Paradis, C., and Boulieu, R. (2001). *Ther. Drug Monit.* 23, 550–552.

Edwards, S.R., Minto, C.F., and Mather, L.E. (2002). *Br. J. Anesth.* 88, 94–100.

Elsing, B., and Blaschke, G. (1993). *J. Chromatogr.* 612, 223–230.

ElSohly, H.N., ElSohly, M.A., and Stanford, D.F. (1990). *J. Anal. Toxicol.* 14, 308–310.

ElSohly, M., Feng, S., and Murphy, T.P. (2001). *J. Anal. Toxicol.* 25, 40–44.

Ensing, K., Franke, J.P., Temmink, A., Chen, X.H., and de Zeeuw, R.A. (1992). *J. Forensic Sci.* 37, 460–466.

Esposito, F.M., and Winek, C.L. (1991). *J. Forensic Sci.* 26, 86.

Everhard, E.T., Cheung, P., Schwonek, P., Zabel, K., Tisdale, E.C., Jacob, P., Mendelson, J., and Jones, R.T. (1997). *Clin. Chem.* 43, 2292.

Fater, Z., Samu, Z., Szatmary, M., and Nyiredy, S. (1997). *Acta Pharm. Hung.* 67, 211–219.

Fehn, J., and Megges, G. (1985). *J. Anal. Toxicol.* 9, 134–138.

Fenton, J., Mummert, J., and Childers, M. (1994). *J. Anal. Toxicol.* 18, 159.

Frankus, E., Friderichs, E., Kim, S.M., and Osterloh, G. (1978). *Arzneim. Forsch.* 28, 114.

Fritschi, G., and Prescott, Jr., W.R. (1985). *Forensic Sci. Int.* 27, 111–117.

Fryirs, B., Dawson, M., and Mather, L.E. (1997a). *J. Chromatogr. B* 693, 51–57.

Fryirs, B., Woodhouse, A., Huang, J.L., Dawson, M., and Mather, L.E. (1997b). *J. Chromatogr. B* 688, 79–85.

Fuller, D.C., and Anderson, W.H. (1992). *J. Anal. Toxicol.* 16, 315–318.

Gaulier, J.M., Marquet, P., Lacassie, E., Dupuy, J.L., and Lachatre, G. (2000). *J. Forensic Sci.* 45, 226–228.

Geier, A., Bergemann, D., and von Meyer, L. (1996). *Int. J. Legal Med.* 109, 80–83.

Gelencser, A., Kiss, G., Krivacsy, Z., Varga-Puchony, Z., and Hlavay, J. (1995). *J. Chromatogr. A* 693, 217–226.

George, S., and Parmar, S. (2002). *J. Anal. Toxicol.* 26, 233–235.

George, S., Parmar, S., Meadway, C., and Braithwaite, R.A. (2000). *Ann. Clin. Biochem.* 37, 350–354.

Gerostamoulos, J., Crump, K., McIntyre, I., and Drummer, O.H. (1993). *J. Chromatogr.* 617, 152–156.

Glare, P.A., Walsh, T.D., and Pippenger, C.E. (1991). *Ther. Drug Monit.* 13, 226–232.

Goeringer, K.E., Logan, B.K., and Christian, G.D. (1997). *J. Anal. Toxicol.* 21, 529.

Goff, M.L., Brown, W.A., Hewadikaram, K.A., and Omori, A.I. (1991). *J. Forensic Sci.* 36, 537–542.

Goldberger, B.A., Cone, E.J., Grant, T.M., Caplan, Y.H., Levine, B.S., and Smialek, J.E. (1994). *J. Anal. Toxicol.* 18, 22–28.

Grinstead, G.F. (1991). *J. Anal. Toxicol.* 15, 293–298.

Gronholm, M., and Lillsunde, P. (2001). *Forensic Sci. Int.* 121, 37–46.

Guillot, J.G., Lefebvre, M., and Weber, J.P. (1997). *J. Anal. Toxicol.* 21, 127.

Guiochon, G. (1999). *Int. Lab.* 29, 13C–14C.

Gygi, S.P., Wilkins, D.G., and Rollins, D.E. (1995). *J. Anal. Toxicol.* 19, 387–391.

Hadidi, K.A., and Oliver, J.S. (1998) *Int. J. Leg. Med.* 111, 165–167.

Hanisch, H., and v. Meyer, L. (1993). *J. Anal. Toxicol.* 17, 48–50.

Hartley, C.E., Green, M., Quinn, M., and Levene, M.I. (1993). *Biomed. Chromatogr.* 7, 34–37.

Hays, P.A., and Lurie, I.S. (1991). *J. Liquid Chromatogr.* 14, 3513.

He, H., Shay, S.D., Caraco, Y., Wood, M., and Wood, A.J. (1998). *J. Chromatogr. B* 708, 185–193.

Hedouin, V., Bourel, B., Martin-Bouyer, L., Becart, A., Tournel, G., Devaux, M., and Gosset, D. (1999). *J. Forensic Sci.* 44, 351–353.

Hedouin, V., Bourel, B., Becart, A., Tournel, G., Devaux, M., Goff, M.L., and Gosset, D. (2001). *J. Forensic Sci.* 46, 12–14.

Heeren, F.V., and Thormann, W. (1997). *Electrophoresis* 18, 2415–2426.

Heinemann, A., Ribbat, J., Püschel, K., Iwersen, S., and Schmoldt, A. (1998). *Rechtsmedizin* 8, 55–60.

Hernandez, A.F., Pla, A., Moliz, J., Gil, F., Gonzalvo, M.C., and Villanueva, E. (1992). *J. Forensic Sci.* 37, 1276–1282.

Ho, T.S., Pedersen-Bjergaard, S., and Rasmussen, K.E. (2002a). *J. Chromatogr. A* 963, 3–17.

Ho, T.S., Pedersen-Bjergaard, S., and Rasmussen, K.E. (2002b). *Analyst* 127, 608–613.

Hofmann, U., Fromm, M.F., Sohnson, S., and Mikus, G. (1995). *J. Chromatogr. B* 663, 59–65.

Hoja, H., Marquet, P., Verneuil, B., Lofti, H., Dupuy, J.L., and Lachatre, G. (1997). *J. Anal. Toxicol.* 21, 160–165.

Huang, W., Andollo, W., and Hearn, W.L. (1992). *J. Anal. Toxicol.* 16, 307.

Hufschmid, E., Theurillat, R., Wilder-Smith, C.H., and Thormann, W. (1996). *J. Chromatogr. B* 678, 43–51.

Huizer, H. (1988). *Analytical Studies on Illicit Heroin*, Ph.D. dissertation, University of Leiden, The Netherlands.

Introna, F., Lo Dico, C., Caplan, Y.H., and Smialek, J.E. (1990). *J. Forensic. Sci.* 35, 118–122.

Inturrisi, C.E., Bax, M.B., Foley, K.M., Schutz, K., Shin, S.U., and Houde, R.W. (1984). *New Engl. J. Med.* 310, 1213–1217.

Jain, R., Ray, R., Tripathi, B.M., and Singh, C. (1996). *Indian J. Pharmacol.* 28, 220–223.

Janicot, J.L., Caude, M., and Rosset, R. (1988). *J. Chromatogr.* 437, 351–364.

Janicot, J.L., Caude, M., Rosset, R., and Veuthey, J.L. (1990). *J. Chromatogr.* 505, 247–256.

Jenkins, A.J., and Goldberger, B.A., eds. (2002). *On-Site Drug Testing*. Humana Press, Totowa, NJ.

Jenkins, A.J., Keenan, R.M., Heningfield, J.E., and Cone, E.J. (1994). *J. Anal. Toxicol.* 18, 317–330.

Joel, P., Osborne, R.J., and Slevin, M.L. (1988). *J. Chromatogr.* 430, 394–399.

Johnston, A., and King, L.A. (1998). *Forensic Sci. Int.* 95, 47–55.

Jones, J., Tomlinson, K., and Moore, C. (2002). *J. Anal. Toxicol.* 26, 171–175.

Kaa, E. (1994). *Forensic Sci. Int.* 64, 171–179.

Kala, M., and Lechowicz, W. (1997). In: Proceedings of the XXXV TIAFT Meeting, Centre of Behavioural and Forensic Toxicology, University of Padua, Italy, pp. 521–535.

Kapil, R.P., Padovani, P.K., King, S.Y., and Lam, G.N. (1992). *J. Chromatogr.* 577, 283–293.

Katagi, M., Nishikawa, M., Tatsuno, M., Miki, A., and Tsushihashi, H. (2001). *J. Chromatogr. B* 751, 177–185.

Keller, T., Schneider, A., Dirnhofer, R., Jungo, R., and Meyer, W. (2000). *Med. Sci. Law* 40, 258–262.

Kemp, P., Sneed, G., Kupiec, T., and Spiehler, V. (2002). *J. Anal. Toxicol.* 26, 504–512.

Kerrigan, S., and Phillips, WH. (2001). *Clin. Chem.* 47, 540–547.

King, D.L., Gabor, M.J., Martel, P.A., and O'Donnell, C.M. (1989). *Clin. Chem.* 35, 163–166.

King, L.A. (1997). *Forensic Sci. Int.* 85, 135–147.

Kintz, P. (1993). *J. Anal. Toxicol.* 17, 443–444.

Kintz, P., and Marquet, P., eds. (2002). *Buprenorphine Therapy of Opiate Addiction*. Humana Press, Totowa, NJ.

Kintz, P., and Samyn, N. (2000). Unconventional samples and alternative matrices. In *Forensic Science Handbook of Analytical Separations*, Vol. 2 (ed. M.J. Bogusz). Elsevier Science, Amsterdam, pp. 459–488.

Kintz, P., Mangin, P., Lugniert, A.A., and Chaumont, A.J. (1990). *J. Toxicol. Clin. Exp.* 10, 15–20.

Kintz, P., Cirimele, V., Edel, Y., Jamey, C., and Mangin, P. (1994a). *J. Forensic Sci.* 39, 1497–1503.

Kintz, P., Tracqui, A., and Mangin, P. (1994b). *J. Forensic Sci. Soc.* 34, 95–97.

Kintz, P., Tracqui, A., and Mangin, P. (1991). *Int. J. Leg. Med.* 104, 177.

Lafolie, P., Beck, O., Lin, Z., Albertioni, F., and Boreus, L. (1996). *J. Anal. Toxicol.* 20, 541.

Kintz, P., Eser, H.P., Tracqui, A., Moeller, M., Cirimele, V., and Mangin, P. (1997). *J. Forensic Sci.* 42, 291–295.

Kirkwood, L.C., Nation, R.L., and Somogyi, A.A. (1997). *J. Chromatogr. B* 701, 129–134.

Kollias-Baker, C., and Sams, R. (2002). *J. Anal. Toxicol.* 26, 81–86.

Krenn, L., Glantschnig, S., and Sorgner, U. (1998). *Chromatographia* 47, 21–24.

Kristensen, K., Angelo, H.R., and Blemmer, T. (1994). *J. Chromatogr. A* 666, 283–287.

Kuhlman, J.J., Magluilo, Jr., J., Cone, E.J., and Levine, B. (1996a). *J. Anal. Toxicol.* 20, 229–235.

Kuhlman, J.J., Lalani, S., Magluilo, J., Levine, B., Darwin, W.D., Johnson, R.E, and Cone, E.J. (1996b). *J. Anal. Toxicol.* 20, 369–378.

La Harpe, R., and Fryc, O. (1995). *Arch. Kriminol.* 196, 24–29.

Lachenmeier, D.W., Kroener, L., Musshoff, F., and Madea, B. (2003). *Rapid Commun. Mass Spectrom.* 17, 472–478.

Lee, H.M., and Lee, C.W. (1991). *J. Anal. Toxicol.* 15, 182–187.

Lehner, A.F., Almeida, P., Jacobs, J., Harkins, J.D., Karpiesiuk, W., Woods, W.E., Dirikolu, L., Bosken, J.M., Carter, W.G., Boyles, J., Holtz, C., Heller, T., Nattrass, C., Fisher, M., and Tobin, T. (2000). *J. Anal. Toxicol.* 24, 309–315.

Leis, H.J., Fauler, G., Raspotnig, G., and Windischhofer, W. (2000). *J. Chromatogr. B* 744, 113–119.

Levine, B., Ramcharitar, V., and Smialek, J.E. (1997). *For. Sci. Int.* 86, 43–48.

Lin, Z., Lafolie, P., and Beck, O. (1994). *J. Anal. Toxicol.* 18, 129–133.

Lisi., A.M., Kazlauskas, R., and Trout, G.J. (1997). *J. Chromatogr B* 692, 67–77.

Lord, H., and Pawliszyn, J. (2000). *J. Chromatogr. A* 885, 153–193.

Low, A.S., and Taylor, R.B. (1995). *J. Chromatogr. B* 663, 225–233.

Lurie, I.S. (1996). *Int. Lab.* March, 21–29.

Lurie, I.S. (1997). *J. Chromatogr. A* 780, 265–284.

Lurie, I.S., and Carr, S.M. (1986). *J. Liquid Chromatogr.* 9, 2485–2499.

Lurie, I.S., and McGuiness, K. (1987). *J. Liquid Chromatogr.* 10, 2189–2197.

Lurie, I.S., Chan, K.C., Spratley, T.K., Casale, J.F., and Issaq, H.J. (1995). *J. Chromatogr. B* 669, 3–13.

Lurie, I.S., Anex, D.S., Fintschenko, Y., and Choi, W.Y. (2001). *J. Chromatogr. A* 924, 421–427.

Lusthof, K.J., and Zweipfenning, P.G.M. (1998). *J. Anal. Toxicol.* 22, 260.

Maier, R.D., Erkens, M., Hoenen, H., and Bogusz, M. (1992). *Int. J. Legal Med.* 105, 115–119.

Marko, V., Soltes, L., and Radova, K. (1990). *J. Chromatogr. Sci.* 28, 403–406.

Martens-Lobenhoffer, J. (2002). *J. Chromatogr. B.* 769, 227–233.

Mason, J.L., Ashmore, S.P., and Aitkenhead, A.R. (1991). *J. Chromatogr. B* 570, 191–197.

McLachlan-Troup, N., Taylor, G.W., and Trathen, B.C. (2001). *Addict. Biol.* 6, 223–231.

Meadway, C., George, S., and Braithwaite, R. (1998). *Forensic Sci. Int.* 96, 29–38.

Meadway, C., George, S., and Braithwaite, R. (2002). *Forensic Sci. Int.* 127, 136–141.

Meneely, K.D. (1992). *J. Forensic Sci.* 37, 1158–1162.

Merslavic, M., and Zupancic-Kraj, L. (1997). *J. Chromatogr. B* 693, 222.

Moeller, M.R., and Mueller, C. (1995). *Forensic Sci. Int.* 70, 125–133.

Mohammed, S.S., Butschkau, M., and Derendorf, H. (1993). *J. Liquid Chromatogr.* 16, 2325–2334.

Molteni, S., Caslavska, J., Allemann, D., and Thormann, W. (1994). *J. Chromatogr. B* 658, 355–367.

Moody, D.E., Laycock, J.D., Spanbauer, A.C., Crouch, D.J., Foltz, R.L., Josephs, J.L., Amass, L., and Bickel, W.K. (1997). *J. Anal. Toxicol.* 21, 406–414.

Moody, D.E., Slawson, M.H., Strain, E.C., Laycock, J.D., Spanbauer, A.C., and Foltz, R.L. (2002). *Anal. Biochem.* 306, 31–39.

Moore, C.M., Deitermann, D., Lewis, D., and Leikin, J. (1995). *J. Anal. Toxicol.* 10, 514.

Moore, K., Werner, C., Zannelli, R.M., Levine, B., and Smith, M.L. (1999). *Forensic Sci. Int.* 106, 93–102.

Moore, L., Wicks, J., Spiehler, V., and Holgate, R. (2001). *J. Anal. Toxicol.* 25, 520–524.

Musshoff, F., and Daldrup, T. (1993). *Int. J. Leg. Med.* 106, 107.

Myors, R.B., Crisp, P.T., Skopec, S.V., and Wells, R.J. (2001). *Analyst* 126, 679–689.

Myung, S.W., Kim, S., Park, J.H., Kim, M., Lee, J.C., and Kim, T.J. (1999). *Analyst* 124, 1283–1286.

Nair, N.K., Navaratnam, V., and Rajananda, V. (1986). *J. Chromatogr.* 366, 363–372.

Neumann, H. (1990). *Forensic Sci. Int.* 44, 85–87.

Neumann, H. (1994). *Forensic Sci. Int.* 69, 7–13.

Neumann, H., and Gloger, M. (1982). *Chromatographia* 16, 261–266.

Newman, R.G. (1995). In *Drug Addiction and Related Clinical Problems* (ed. A. Tagliamonte and L. Maremmani). Springer Verlag, New York, pp. 109–136.

Nobilis, M., Pastera, J., Anzenbacher, P., Svoboda, D., Kopecky, J., and Perlik, F. (1996). *J. Chromatogr. B* 681, 177–183.

Norris, R.L., Ravenscroft, P.J., and Pond, S.M. (1994). *J. Chromatogr. B* 661, 346–350.

O'Neal, C.L., and Poklis, A. (1997). *J. Anal. Toxicol.* 21, 427–432.

O'Neal, C.L., and Poklis, A. (1998). *Forensic Sci. Int.* 95, 1–10.

Ohta, H., Suzuki, S., and Ogasawara, K. (1999). *J. Anal. Toxicol.* 23, 280–285.

Ortelli, D., Rudaz, S., Chevalley, A.F., Deglon, J.J., Balant, L., and Veuthey, J.L. (2000). *J. Chromatogr. A* 871, 163–172.

Osborne, R.J., Joel, S.P., Trew, D., and Slevin, M.L. (1990). *Clin. Pharmacol. Ther.* 47, 12–19.

Pacifici, R., Pichini, S., Altieri, I., Caronna, A., Passa, A.R., and Zuccaro, P. (1995). *J. Chromatogr. B* 664, 329–334.

Papadoyannis, I., Zotou, A., Samanidou, V., Theodoridis, G., and Zougrou, F. (1993). *J. Liquid Chromatogr.* 16, 3017–3040.

Paul, B.D., Mell, L.D., Mitchell, J.M., Irving, J., and Novak, A.J. (1985). *J. Anal. Toxicol.* 9, 222–226.

Paul, B.D., Mitchell, J.M., Mell, L.D., and Irving, J. (1989). *J. Anal. Toxicol.* 13, 2–7.

Paul, B.D., Dreka, C., Knight, E.S., and Smith, M.L. (1996). *Planta Med.* 62, 544–547.

Pelders, M.G., and Ros, J.J.W. (1996). *J. Forensic Sci.* 41, 209–212.

Phillips, W.H., Ota, K., and Wade, N.A. (1989). *J. Anal. Toxicol.* 13, 268.

Pichini, S., Altieri, I., Pellegrini, M., Zuccaro, P., and Pacifici, R. (1999a). *Mass Spectrom. Rev.* 18, 119–130.

Pichini, S., Altieri, I., Pellegrini, M., Pacifdici, R., and Zuccaro, P. (1999b). *J. Liq. Chrom. Rel. Technol.* 22, 873–874.

Pierce, T.L., Murray, A.G.W., and Hope, W. (1992). *J. Chromatogr. Sci.* 30, 443–447.

Polettini, A., and Huestis, M.A. (2001). *J. Chromatogr. B* 754, 447–459.

Polettini, A., Groppi, A., and Montagna, M. (1995). In *Advances in Forensic Sciences*, Vol. 5 (ed. B. Jacob and W. Bonte). Verlag Dr. Köster, Berlin, pp. 197–207.

Popa, D.S., Oprean, R., Curea, E., and Preda, N. (1998). *J. Pharm. Biomed. Anal.* 18, 645–650.

Portenoy, R.K., Khan, E., Layman, M., Lapin, J., Malkin, M.G., Foley, K.M., Thaler, H.T., Cerbone, D.J., and Inturrisi, C.E. (1991). *Neurology* 41, 1457–1461.

Radcliffe, C., Maguire, K., and Lockwood, B. (2000). *J. Biochem. Biophys. Methods* 43, 261–272.

Rasmussen, K.E., Pedersen-Bjergaard, S., Krogh, M., Ugland H.G., and Grønhaug, T. (2000). *J. Chromatogr. A* 873, 3–11.

Rettinger, M.M., Jones, C.J., Re, M.A., Rettinger, J.B., and Zisman, A.S. (1998). Presented at the SOFT-TIAFT Meeting, Albuquerque, NM.

Romberg, R.W., and Brown, V.E. (1990). *J. Anal. Toxicol.* 14, 58–59.

Rop, P.P., Fornaris, M., Salmon, T., Burle, J., and Bresson, M. (1997). *J. Anal. Toxicol.* 21, 232–235.

Rossi, G.C., Brown, G.P., Leventhal, L., Yang, K., and Pasternak, G.W. (1996). *Neuroscience Lett.* 216, 1–4.

Rothsteyn, Y., and Weingarten, B. (1996). *Ther. Drug Monit.* 18, 179–188.

Rudaz, S., and Veuthey, J.L. (1996). *J. Pharm. Biomed. Anal.* 14, 1271–1279.

Sachs, H., Denk, R., and Raff, I. (1993). *Int. J. Legal Med.* 105, 247–250.

Sachs, H., Uhls, M., Hege-Scheuing, G., and Schneider, E. (1996). *Int. J. Leg. Med.* 109, 213–215.

Samyn, N., De, Boeck, G., and Verstraete, A. (2002). *J. Forensic Sci.* 47, 1380–1387.

Schanzle, G., Li, S., Mikus, G., and Hofmann, U. (1999). *J. Chromatogr. B* 721, 55–65.

Scheurer, J., and Moore, C.M. (1992). *J. Anal. Toxicol.* 16, 264–269.

Schmidt, N., Brune, K., and Geisslinger, G. (1992). *J. Chromatogr.* 583, 195–200.

Schmidt, N., Sittl, R., Brune, K., and Geisslinger, G. (1993). *Pharm. Res.* 10, 441–444.

Schmitt, G., Bogusz, M., Aderjan, R., and Meyer, C. (1990). *Z. Rechtsmed.* 103, 513–521.

Schuberth, J., and Schuberth, J. (1989). *J. Chromatogr.* 490, 444–449.

Schütz, H., Erdmann, F., Risse, M., and Weiler, G. (2002). *Arzneimittelforschung* 52, 716–719.

Scott, K.S., and Oliver, J.S. (1999). *Med. Sci. Law.* 39, 77–81.

Selavka, C.M. (1991). *J. Forensic Sci.* 36, 685–696.

Seno, H., Hattori, H., Kurono, S., Yamada, T., Kumazawa, T., Ishii, A., and Suzuki, O. (1995). *J. Chromatogr. B* 673, 189–195.

Shou, W.Z., Jiang, X., Beato, B.D., and Naidong, W. (2001). *Rapid Commun. Mass Spectrom.* 15, 466–476.

Shou, W.Z., Pelzer, M., Addison, T., Jiang, X., and Naidong, W. (2002). *J. Pharm. Biomed. Anal.* 27, 143–152.

Sibley, A. (1996). *Forensic Sci. Int.* 77, 159–167.

Skopp, G., Ganssmann, B., Cone, E.J., and Aderjan, R. (1997). *J. Anal. Toxicol.* 21, 105–111.

Skopp, G., Klinder, K., Potsch, L., Zimmer, G., Lutz, R., Aderjan, R., and Mattern, R. (1998). *Forensic Sci. Int.* 95, 99–107.

Slawson, M.H., Crouch, D.J., Andrenyak, D.M., Rollins, D.E., Lu, J.K., and Bailey, P.L. (1999). *J. Anal. Toxicol.* 23, 468–473.

Smith, M.L., Shimomura, E.T., Summers, J., Paul, B.D., Nichols, D., Shippee, R., Jenkins, A.J., Darwin, W.D., and Cone, E.J. (2000). *J. Anal. Toxicol.* 24, 522–529.

Soares, M.E., Seabra, V., de Lourdes, A., and Bastos, M. (1992). *J. Liq. Chromatogr.* 15, 1533–1541.

Soine, W.H. (1986). *Med. Res. Rev.* 6, 41–74.

Soltes, L. (1992). *Biomed. Chromatogr.* 6, 43–49.

Sperling, A. (1991). *J. Chromatogr.* 538, 269–275.

Spiller, H.A. (2003). *J. Forensic Sci.* 48(2). Online: www.astm.org.

Sporer, K.A. (2003). *Brit. Med. J.* 326, 442–444.

Sporkert, F., and Pragst, F. (2000). *J. Chromatogr. B* 746, 255–264.

Staerk, U., and Kulpmann, W.R. (2000). *J. Chromatogr. B* 745, 399–411.

Staub, C. (1997). *Forensic Sci. Int.* 84, 295–304.

Staub, C., Marset, M., Mino, A., and Mangin, P. (2001). *Clin. Chem.* 47, 301–307.

Sticht, G., Schmidt, P., and Käferstein, H. (1997). *Rechtsmedizin* 7, 127.

Stolk, L.M., Coenradie, S.M., Smit, B.J., and van As, H.L. (1997). *J. Anal. Toxicol.* 21, 154–159.

Stromberg, L., Lundberg, L., Neumann, H., Bobon, B., Huizer, H., and van der Stelt, N.W. (2000). *Forensic Sci. Int.* 114, 67–88.

Struempler, R.E. (1987). *J. Anal. Toxicol.* 11, 97–99.

Sundstrom, I., Bondesson, U., and Hedeland, M. (2001). *J. Chromatogr. B* 763, 121–131.

Sundstrom, I., Hedeland, M., Bondesson, U., and Andren, P.E. (2002). *J. Mass Spectrom.* 37, 414–420.

Svensson, J.O. (1986). *J. Chromatogr.* 375, 174–178.

Svensson, J.O., Rane, A., Säwe, J., and Sjöqvist, F. (1982). *J. Chromatogr.* 230, 427.

Svensson, J.O., Yue, Q.Y., and Säwe, J. (1995). *J. Chromatogr. B* 674, 49–55.

Szeitz, A., Riggs, K.W., and Harvey-Clark, C. (1996). *J. Chromatogr. B* 675, 33.

Tagliaro, F., and Smith, F.P. (1996). *Trends Anal. Chem.* 15, 513–525.

Tagliaro, F., Turina, S., and Smith, F.P. (1996). *Forensic Sci. Int.* 77, 211–229.

Taylor, R.B., Low, A.S., and Reid, R.G. (1996). *J. Chromatogr. B* 675, 213–223.

Theodoridis, G., Papadoyannis, I., Tsoukali-Papadopoulou, H., and Vasilikiotis, G. (1995). *J. Liquid Chromatogr.* 18, 1973–1995.

Thevis, M., Opfermann, G., and Schänzer, W. (2003). *J. Anal. Toxicol.* 27, 53–56.

Thormann, W., Lanz, M., Caslavska, J., Siegenthaler, P., and Portmann, R. (1998). *Electrophoresis* 19, 57–65.

Thurman, E.M., and Mills, M.S. (1998). *Solid-Phase Extraction: Principles and Practice.* Wiley, New York.

Tracqui, A., Kintz, P., and Mangin, P. (1997). *J. Forensic Sci.* 42, 111–114.

Trenerry, V.C., Wells, R.J., and Robertson, J. (1995). *J. Chromatogr. A* 718, 217–225.

Tsai, J.L., Wu, W.S., and Lee, H.H. (2000). *Electrophoresis* 21, 1580–1586.

Tyrefors, N., Hyllbrant, B., Ekman, L., Johansson, M., and Langström, B. (1996). *J. Chromatogr. A* 729, 279–285.

Ugland, H.G., Krogh, M., and Rasmussen, K.E. (2000). *J. Chromatogr. A* 749, 85–92.

Umans, J.G., Chiu, T.S.K., Lipman, R.A., Schulz, M.F., Shin, S.U., and Inturrisi, C.E. (1982). *J. Chromatogr.* 233, 213–225.

Van Thuyne, W., Van Eenoo, P., and Delbeke, F.T. (2003). *J. Chromatogr. B* 785, 254–251.

Vecerkova, J. (1992). *Criminalistics* 25, 216–219.

Vecerkova, J. (1997). *Soud. Lek.* 42, 32–38.

Verveij, A.M.A., Hordijk, M.L., and Lipman, P.J. (1995). *J. Anal. Toxicol.* 19, 65–68.

Verwey-van, Wissen, C.P., Koopman-Kimenai, P.M., and Vree, T.B. (1991). *J. Chromatogr.* 570, 309.

Vidal-Trecan, G., Vareson, I., Nabet, N., and Boisonnas, A. (2003). *Drug Alcohol Depend.* 69, 175–181.

Walker, J.A., Kroeger, S.T., Lurie, I.S., Marchie, H.L., and Newby, N. (1995). *J. Forensic Sci.* 40, 6–9.

Walsh, S.L., Preston, K.L., Bigelow, G.E., and Stitzer, M.L. (1995). *J. Pharmacol. Exp. Ther.* 274, 361–372.

Wang, W.L., Darwin, W.D., and Cone, E.J. (1994). *J. Chromatogr. B* 660, 279–290.

Wasels, R., and Bellevile, F. (1994). *J. Chromatogr. A* 674, 225–234.

Watson, D.G., Su, Q., Midley, J.M., Doyle, E., and Morton, N.S. (1995). *J. Pharm. Biomed. Anal.* 13, 27–32.

Watts, V., and Caplan, Y. (1988). *J. Anal. Toxicol.* 12, 246–254.

Weinmann, W., Renz, M., Pelz, C., Brauchle, P., Vogt, S., and Pollak, S. (1998). *Blutalkohol* 35, 195–203.

Wennig, R., Moeller, M., Haguenoer, J.M., Marocchi, A., Zoppi, F., Smith, B.L., de la Torre, R., Carstensen, C.A., Goerlach-Graw, A., Schaeffler, J., and Leibberger, R. (1998). *J. Anal. Toxicol.* 22, 148–155.

Wey, A.B., and Thormann, W. (2002). *J. Chromatogr. B* 770, 191–205.

Wey, A.B., Caslavska, J., and Thormann, W. (2000). *J. Chromatogr. A* 895, 133–145.

Wilkins, D., Rollins, D.E., Seaman, J., Haughey, H., Krueger, G., and Foltz, R.L. (1995). *J. Anal. Toxicol.* 19, 269–274.

Wilkins, D.G., Nasagawa, P.R., Gygi, S.P., Foltz, R.L., and Rollins, D.E. (1996). *J. Anal. Toxicol.* 20, 355–361.

Wolff, K., Sanderson, M.J., and Hay, A.W. (1990). *Ann. Clin. Biochem.* 27, 482–488.

Wright, A.W., Nocente, M.L., and Smith. (1998). *Life Sci.* 63, 401–411.

Wu, W.S., and Tsai, J.L. (1999). *Biomed. Chromatogr.* 13, 216–219.

Wu, Y.J., Cheng, Y.Y., Zeng, C.S., and Ma, M.M. (2003). *J. Chromatogr. B* 784, 219–224.

Zebelman, A.B., Troyer, B.L., Randall, G.L., and Batjer, J.D. (1987). *J. Anal. Toxicol.* 11, 131–132.

Zezulak, M., Snyder, J.J., and Needleman, S.B. (1993). *J. Forensic Sci.* 38, 1275–1285.

Zheng, M., McErlane, K.M., and Ong, M.C. (1988). *J. Pharmaceut. Biomed. Anal.* 16, 971–980.

Zuccaro, P., Ricciarello, R., Pichini, S., Pacifici, R., Altieri, I., Pellegrini, M., and D'Ascenzo, G. (1997). *J. Anal. Toxicol.* 21, 268–277.

Zweipfenning, P.G.M., Wilderink, A.H.C.M., Horsthuis, P., Franke, J.P., and de Zeeuw, R.A. (1994). *J. Chromatogr. A* 674, 87–95.

CHAPTER 7

AMPHETAMINES: METHODS OF FORENSIC ANALYSIS

John T. Cody

Interservice Physician Assistant Program, Ft. Sam Houston, Texas

Contents

7.1 INTRODUCTION

This chapter describes the common methods used in the forensic analysis of amphetamines. For purposes of this chapter, the term *amphetamines* refers to amphetamine, methamphetamine, and their commonly encountered methylenedioxy derivatives. Although many other compounds can be categorized as amphetamines, the former represent the most important and commonly encountered. Other related compounds are generally analyzed in the same manner because of their similar chemical composition, but specific descriptions of the analyses of these drugs are not included except for a few examples of related compounds that pose particular problems of interest in the community.

Amphetamines are powerful central nervous system (CNS) stimulants that first came into use in the early 1900s. Amphetamine and methamphetamine, the two most commonly encountered of these drugs, have an asymmetric center and thus exist as one of two possible enantiomers. The enantiomers have quite different pharmacological properties, and determination of the enantiomeric form of the drugs is often an important consideration. The structures of amphetamine and methamphetamine enantiomers are shown in Figure 7.1.

Handbook of Forensic Drug Analysis
Frederick P. Smith, Editor

Figure 7.1

Structures of amphetamine and methamphetamine enantiomers

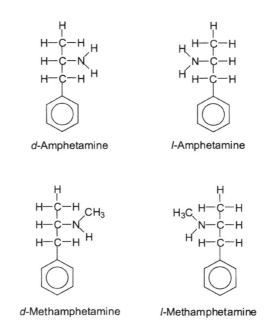

d-Amphetamine

l-Amphetamine

d-Methamphetamine

l-Methamphetamine

Substitutions have been made to amphetamine and methamphetamine for a variety of reasons. Many modifications were made to these drugs in attempts to maintain anorexic activity while limiting undesirable side effects. Others have been made to enhance the stimulatory activity or to avoid legal restrictions on the production and use of the drugs. These include 2-methoxyamphetamine, 4-hydroxymethamphetamine, 4-methoxyamphetamine, 4-methylthio-amphetamine, 2,5-dimethoxyamphetamine (DMA), 4-bromo-2,5-dimethoxy-amphetamine (DOB), 4-bromo-2,5-dimethoxyphenethylamine, 3,4,5-trimethoxyamphetamine (TMA), 4-ethyl-2,5-dimethoxyamphetamine (DOE), and 4-methyl-2,5-dimethoxyamphetamine (DOM, STP). These drugs have been abused in the past at one time or another and surface periodically in the illicit-drug market. In addition, new versions occasionally arise, as demonstrated by the recent identification of N-ethyl-4-methoxyamphetamine in a urine sample (Marson et al., 2000) and 2-chloro-4,5-methylenedioxymethylamphetamine in a seizure of illicit MDMA tablets (Lewis et al., 2000). (See Figure 7.2 for the structures of these compounds.)

A related group of drugs includes the methylenedioxy analogs of amphetamine and methamphetamine. These include the phenylisopropyl analogs N,N-dimethyl-3,4-methylenedioxyamphetamine, N-hydroxy-3,4- methylenedioxyamphetamine (N-OH-MDA), 3,4-methylenedioxyamphetamine (MDA), 3,4-methylenedioxymethamphetamine (MDMA), and 3,4-methylenedioxyeth-

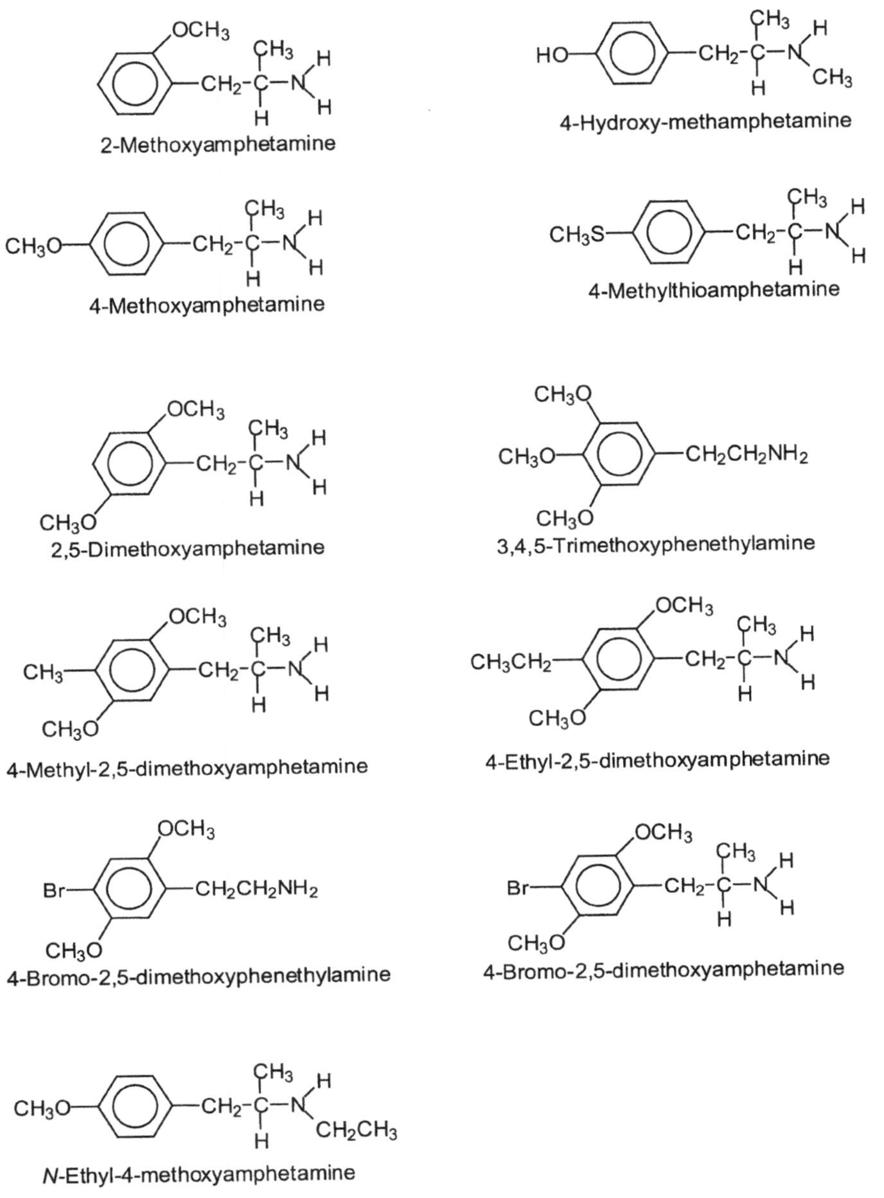

Figure 7.2
Structures of amphetamine-related compounds

2-Methoxyamphetamine

4-Hydroxy-methamphetamine

4-Methoxyamphetamine

4-Methylthioamphetamine

2,5-Dimethoxyamphetamine

3,4,5-Trimethoxyphenethylamine

4-Methyl-2,5-dimethoxyamphetamine

4-Ethyl-2,5-dimethoxyamphetamine

4-Bromo-2,5-dimethoxyphenethylamine

4-Bromo-2,5-dimethoxyamphetamine

N-Ethyl-4-methoxyamphetamine

ylamphetamine (MDEA). In addition to these, several compounds derived from the four-carbon analogs are also seen in the illicit market. These include benzodioxazolylbutanamine (BDB) and *N*-methyl-benzodioxazolylbutanamine (MBDB). The first of these methylenedioxy derivatives to enter the market was MDA. Although popular, it had some undesirable side effects, and its

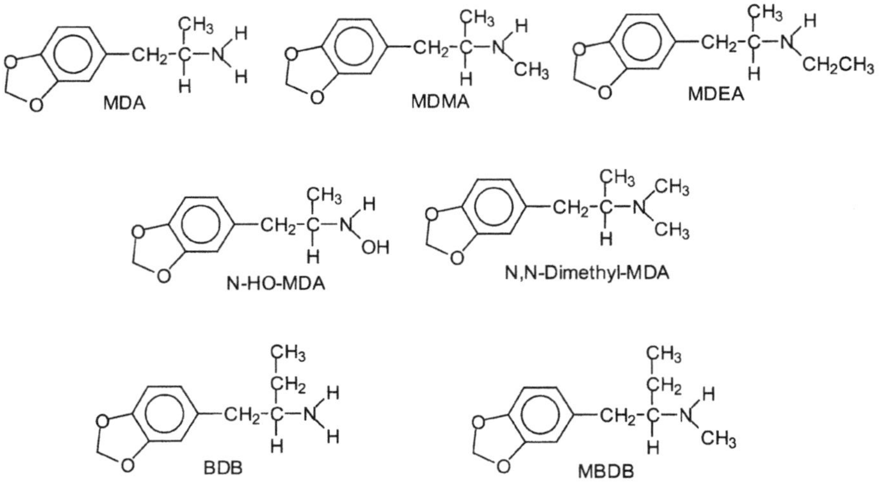

Figure 7.3

Structures of these methylenedioxy compounds: 3,4-methylenedioxyamphetamine (MDA), 3,4-methylehedioxymethamphetamine (MDMA), 3,4-methylenedioxyethylamphetamine (MDEA), N-hydroxy-3,4-methylenedioxyamphetamine (N-HO-MDA), N-dimethyl-3,4-methylenedioxyamphetamine (N,N-dimethyl-MDA), benzodioxazolylbutanamine (BDB), N-methylbenzodioxazolylbutanamine (MBDB)

appearance was soon followed by the development of MDMA, which had the desirable effects without some of the troublesome side effects. MDMA was used experimentally by some psychotherapists as an adjunct to treatment. Although there are still those who would argue that MDMA is a valuable tool for this purpose, it, together with its analogs MDA and MDEA, are Schedule I controlled substances. Structures of these methylenedioxy compounds are shown in Figure 7.3.

Another group of compounds related to the amphetamines is actually metabolized by the body to methamphetamine and/or amphetamine. This group of "precursor" drugs includes amphetaminil, benzphetamine, clobenzorex, deprenyl (selegiline), dimethylamphetamine, ethylamphetamine, famprofazone, fencamine, fenethylline, fenproporex, furfenorex, mefenorex, mesocarb, and prenylamine. See Figure 7.4 for the structures of these compounds. The fact these compounds are metabolized to methamphetamine and/or amphetamine has a significant role in the interpretation of the origin of the drugs when detected in biological samples. A discussion of some of these drugs and evaluation of their involvement in amphetamine-positive samples is given later in this chapter.

A wide variety of methods for the analysis of amphetamines have been described, many of which were developed decades ago, yet they form the basis for most procedures used today. Recently developed methods are targeted primarily at taking advantage of more automation, alternative matrices (hair, meconium, sweat, vitreous humor, saliva, etc.), or procedures that enjoy the sensitivity of newer analytical instruments and techniques. This chapter details references primarily from the 1990s, with the exception of descriptions of ana-

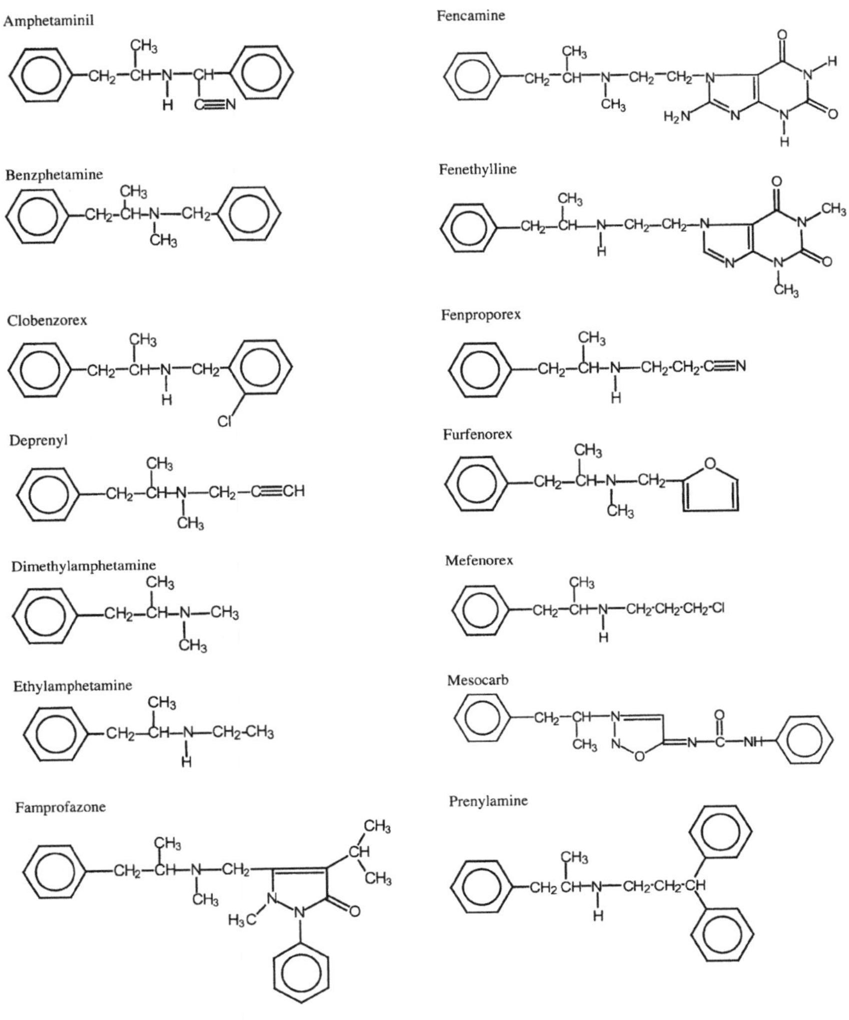

Figure 7.4

Structures of methamphetamine and/or amphetamine-precursor drugs

lytically sound procedures that serve as the basis of many of the currently used procedures.

7.2 DETECTION

Detection of amphetamines is often a complicated task made difficult by the very simplicity of the compounds. Their chemical structure and characteristics are similar to many other naturally occurring biological materials. This similarity offers many opportunities for problems and interference from these closely related compounds.

7.3 QUALITATIVE METHODS OF ANALYSIS

Analysis of the amphetamines, particularly in the forensic environment, is conducted in a two-stage approach. Typically this involves the use of two tests that differ in the fundamental underlying scientific principle. One of the two is commonly a *screening* test that is relatively easy to conduct and highly automated, while the other, usually only conducted on those samples that test positive by the first test, is commonly referred to as a *confirmation* test. In some cases, such as regulated workplace drug testing, the confirmation testing method is defined with regard to the instrumental analysis used.

This section of the chapter discusses methods that are qualitative or "semiquantitative." The term *semiquantitative* refers to procedures that are conducted in a manner to give a quantitative result but, due to the nature of the assay (such as cross-reactivity of an immunoassay) where the result is not considered definitive. Immunoassays are commonly run either in a purely qualitative mode, identifying the presence or absence of an analyte, or, using a calibration curve, in a manner that produces a "quantitative" result. Other methodologies are also sometimes used for qualitative analysis, even though they are capable of highly accurate quantitative analysis. For example, samples are sometimes analyzed by mass spectrometry to positively identify the compound present using techniques such as comparison to library spectra and relative retention indices. These procedures are designed for a comprehensive analysis of the sample for the presence of a large number of drugs and metabolites. Such assays are sometimes referred to as the *general unknown analysis* or *systematic toxicological analysis*. Several examples of such comprehensive assays have been described by several groups (Lho et al., 1990a, 1990b; Maurer, 1992; Solans et al., 1995). One such comprehensive procedure for the analysis of approximately 100 drugs and drug metabolites is described by Solans et al. (1995). The procedure used 2.5-mL samples of urine to which was added deuterated codeine and deuterated MDEA as internal standards. The pH was adjusted by addition of 1 mL of 1.1 M acetate buffer (pH 5.2), and the samples were then hydrolyzed using beta-glucuronidase and arylsulfatase at 55°C for 2 hours. After cooling to room temperature, the hydrolyzed samples were extracted using Bond Elute Certify solid-phase extraction columns. Extracts were derivatized using *N*-methyl-*N*-trimethylsilyl-trifluoroacetamide (MSTFA) and *N*-methyl-bis-trifluoroacetamide (MBTFA) followed by GC-MS analysis. Separation was accomplished using a 5% phenyl methyl silicone column (HP-5, 12.5 m × 0.2-mm i.d.) at temperatures of 100–290°C at 20°C per minute, with a 4-minute final time. The mass spectrometer was operated in the scan mode from m/z 50–600. The procedure was deemed sensitive enough to identify drugs and metabolites for 24 hours after administration when taken at normal therapeutic doses, with the exception of the β-agonists which required selected ion monitoring to provide the necessary sensitivity. Maurer (1992) summarized procedures for systematic toxicological analysis and describes an example method involving analysis of urine samples by refluxing samples with 30% HCl for 15 minutes to hydrolyze conjugates followed by addition of base to obtain a pH of 8–9. Extraction was accomplished with dichloromethane:isopropanol:ethyl acetate (1:1:3 v/v/v) and derivatization with acetic anhydride:pyridine (3:2 v/v) at 60°C for 30 minutes. Separation using cross-linked methylsilicone (12 m × 0.2-mm i.d.) at temperatures of 100–310°C at 30°C per minute. Full-scan mass spectra were obtained for identification of compounds (Maurer et al., 1997). Integrated computer programs allow for the automated extraction of ion chromatograms for the identification of related groups of drugs and metabolites.

The description of mass spectral analysis will be given later in the chapter in the sections dealing with GC/MS and LC/MS. There are a number of methods developed for the qualitative identification of a variety of drugs in samples. These methods are often used, with the simple addition of an internal standard, as a quantitative procedure. As a result, the discussion of these procedures will be included in the GC and LC sections of this chapter, though they are often used for qualitative analysis only.

7.3.1 IMMUNOASSAYS

Immunoassay tests are widely used in the analysis of amphetamines. These tests are relatively inexpensive and easily automated, making them ideal for screening large numbers of samples. The goal of any assay is to be as specific as it can be to eliminate false positives. In the case of the amphetamines this is a particularly challenging task because the chemical simplicity of these compounds makes it difficult to produce an antibody that will identify all samples that contain the amphetamines but not cross-react with other related compounds. With the amphetamines, being too specific is a problem. For example, many assays that cross-react well with amphetamine cross-react more or less well with methamphetamine. The *d-* and *l-*enantiomers of the two drugs also interact with the antibody at different rates.

Manufacturers of immunoassays used in the forensic setting are continually striving to improve their products and thus their competitive edge. As a result, changes to their assays are routinely made if there is an opportunity to increase the specificity or sensitivity of their assay. A major factor associated with the amphetamines is the cross-reactivity with small biomolecules that cause a response in the assay and can lead samples to give a positive response when amphetamines are not present. Because of the similarity of the amphetamines to many other commonly encountered biomolecules, eliminating cross-reactivity is a difficult task. The specificity to amphetamine, for example, typically decreases the reactivity to methamphetamine. Likewise, targeting the *d*-enantiomer often leads to diminished reactivity with the *l*-enantiomer. Each immunoassay is targeted to (calibrated against) one of the analytes of interest. It is important to know the target compound in evaluating an assay. Also, the cross-reactivity of substances to the reagents changes. As a result, this chapter will not delineate the details of the cross-reactivities of the current assays but will rather refer the reader to the current package insert for the respective assay to see what the sensitivity and specificity is regarding that assay.

In the last decade there have been a number of reports regarding immunoassays in the literature. For the most part, these studies have described the use of the assays with samples such as blood, tissue, and meconium (Bogusz et al., 1990; Asselin and Leslie, 1992; Simonick and Watts, 1992; Franssen et al., 1994; Moriya et al., 1994; Lewis et al., 1995; Meyer et al., 1997; Collison et al., 1998; Spiehler et al., 1998; ElSohly et al., 1999; Moore, K.A., et al., 1999; Loor et al., 2002), the effects of interference and adulteration on the assays (Kelly, K.L., 1990; Poklis et al., 1991; D'Nicuola et al., 1992; Olsen et al., 1992; Jones et al., 1993; Colbert, 1994b; Sloop et al., 1995; Kaufman et al., 1996; Tsai et al., 1998; Skopp et al., 1999), and devices using immunoassay technology that can be used onsite to test samples (Rohrich et al., 1994; Moriya and Hashimoto, 1996; Brown et al., 1997; Buchan et al., 1998; Ros et al., 1998; Spiehler et al., 1998; Samyn, Viaene, et al., 1999; Beck et al., 2000; Felscher and Schulz, 2000; Peace et al., 2000; Samyn and van Haeren, 2000; Leino et al., 2001; Yang and Lewandrowski, 2001; Mastrovitch et al., 2002; Peace et al., 2002; Peace and Tarnai, 2002; Yacoubian et al., 2002). In addition, several reports have described new technologies, such as implementation of microtiter plate assays in drugs-of-abuse testing and the combination of immunoassay with capillary electrophoresis (Aoki et al., 1990; Mongkolsirichaikul et al., 1993; Choi, M.J., et al., 1994; Dzantiev et al., 1994; Perez-Bendito et al., 1994; Choi, J., and Choi, 1998a, 1998b; Ramseier et al., 1998; Kimura et al., 1999b; Shindelman et al., 1999; Kupiec et al., 2002). Several fine reviews of immunoassay methodology and its utility and potential limitations have also been published (Suttijitpaisal and Ratanabanangkoon, 1992; Colbert, 1994a; Jirovsky et al., 1998; Jenkins and Goldberger, 2002).

Since immunoassays are typically used to screen large numbers of samples to rapidly assess the presence of a variety of drugs, followed by a more costly and time-consuming confirmation procedure, keeping the number of samples that do not confirm because the drug of interest is not present is a primary concern. In addition to evaluation of various compounds or their metabolites that might lead to a positive immunoassay result, minimizing positive results from the *l*-enantiomer of methamphetamine is desirable because, in the United

States, the presence of *l*-methamphetamine in a sample is considered to be indicative of use of a Vicks inhaler. The inhaler contains leumetamfetamine (*l*-methamphetamine) and can lead to positive results by both immunoassays and GC-MS confirmation. Several studies have evaluated the performance of immunoassays to the enantiomers. Most illicit methamphetamine in the United States is the *d*-enantiomer; however, racemic methamphetamine is also encountered, and an assay that does not cross-react well with *l*-methamphetamine would give a deceptively low result when compared to the actual concentration of methamphetamine in the sample.

In a study of the stereoselectivity and clinical consequence of the EMIT monoclonal and polyclonal assays, Poklis et al. (1993a) showed the monoclonal assay to be highly selective for the *d*-enantiomers of amphetamine and methamphetamine. Evaluating 16 urine specimens collected following excessive use of nasal inhalers (thus containing only the *l*-enantiomers), just one of these samples gave a positive result. Five hundred clinical urine specimens were analyzed by both assays, and only five of 131 amphetamine-positive samples were negative by the monoclonal assay that were positive by the polyclonal assay. In those five samples, the methamphetamine concentrations were all below 1000 ng/mL. The same group conducted another study evaluating the EMIT II amphetamine/methamphetamine assay with samples from seven subjects using Vicks inhalers and found that none of the urine samples collected were positive (Poklis et al., 1993b). Poklis and Moore (1995) conducted another study evaluating the Vicks inhaler and the reactivity of the TDxADx/FLx amphetamine/methamphetamine II fluorescence polarization immunoassay (Abbott Diagnostic) to the enantiomers of amphetamine and methamphetamine in urine. The authors showed there was a good correlation between the results of the immunoassay with those from GC-MS analysis following the administration of *d*-amphetamine. However, there was no correlation between results following the administration of racemic methamphetamine. Two urine samples from a subject using twice the recommended dose did test positive with the assay calibrated at 300 ng/mL but not when calibrated at 1000 ng/mL. These two samples were shown to contain 1560 and 1530 ng/mL methamphetamine by GC-MS.

Most immunoassays were developed to analyze urine samples, since they make up the bulk of samples analyzed for drugs of abuse. While this fact remains true, there are situations where laboratories have large numbers of other biological samples that must be tested. To address this, several studies have reported the use of immunoassays to test blood and/or tissue samples. Bogusz et al. (1990) used FPIA and EMIT-dau immunoassays for the determination of six drug classes in 1 mL of pre- or postmortem blood after acetone precipitation. While the assays performed reasonably well with most of the drugs, the performance with amphetamines was deemed by the authors to be unacceptable. An evaluation of the Abbott TDx assay for screening hemolyzed whole blood for *d*-methamphetamine was reported to provide reliable results when compared to RIA and GC-MS assays for methamphetamine controls and eight positive specimens from forensic cases (Simonick and Watts, 1992). This method mixed 200 µL of blood with zinc sulfate (1:1) to remove the proteins and then tested 50 µL of supernatant. In an evaluation of a microtiter plate immunoassay for analysis of blood samples for drugs of abuse, it was shown that the sensitivity and specificity of the assay for amphetamines (calibrated against methamphetamine) were better than those found using coated-tube or double-antibody radioimmunoassays (Spiehler et al., 1998). Because analysis of blood and tissue samples, by the nature of the concentrations encountered, may be better suited by using a different cutoff than is used for urine samples, a study was conducted to assess the optimum concentrations to use with blood (Collison et al., 1998). The evaluation included assessment of a number of cutoff concentrations and the corresponding specificity and sensitivity using double-antibody and coated-tube radioimmunoassays as compared to confirmation results from GC or GC-MS analysis. Results showed sensitivity and specificity of, respectively, 93% and 86% for amphetamines, with a cutoff based on 25 ng/mL methamphetamine using the coated-tube assay and 83% and 89% with the double-antibody assay at a cutoff of 50 ng/mL of methamphetamine. Another study evaluating immunoassay response to amphetamine and related compounds was conducted by Felscher and Schulz (2000). The authors compared the response of the Triage system with FPIA analysis of urine samples containing amphetamine, methamphetamine, MDMA, MDA, MDE, MBDB (*N*-methyl-1-(3,4-methylenedioxyphenyl)-2-butanamine), BDB (3,4-(methylenedioxyphenyl)-2-butanamine), PMA (4-methoxyamphetamine), DOM (2,5-dimethyloxy-4-methylamphetamine), DOB (4-bromo-2,5-dimethyloxyamphetamine), amphetaminil, pholedrine, fenfluramine, and amfepramone. MDA, MDMA, MDEA, and BDB reacted with the FPIA and Triage assays at reasonable concentrations of analyte. Detection limits of FPIA were less than 500 ng/mL for the analytes except MBDB, PMA, DOM, DOB, and amfepramone. The Triage system required three to sixfold higher concentrations to produce a threshold response compared to FPIA, with the exception of *l*-amphetamine which required a 25 fold excess to respond and both by DOM and DOB which gave no response even at 100 times threshold levels when tested with the Triage.

Several other studies evaluated the use of immunoassays with blood and/or tissue samples, including an enzyme-linked immunosorbent assay (ELISA) for nine drug classes, including amphetamines, that showed the results of this assay to be comparable to those found with double-antibody radioimmunoassay (Moore, K.A., et al., 1999). Another study evaluated a modification of the EMIT assay to increase sensitivity and decrease costs in the analysis of hemolyzed whole blood (Asselin and Leslie, 1992). This study showed that the urine amphetamine assay worked well with methanol extracts of blood samples without need for extensive sample cleanup or concentration. Another ELISA assay was evaluated for the analysis of post-mortem samples to allow rapid screening of samples for amphetamines (Kupiec, T., et al., 2002). Postmortem blood samples from drug and non-drug related deaths (including some that involved decomposition) were analyzed using the Neogen Amphetamine Ultra and methamphetamine/MDMA microtiter plate ELISA assays. The authors reported no significant matrix effects when using whole blood in these assays. They used a 1:5 dilution to facilitate pipetting of the samples. The assays were adjusted to use a cutoff of 50 ng/mL methamphetamine equivalents for the methamphetamine/MDMA assay and 100 ng/mL amphetamine equivalents for the amphetamine assay. Comparing positive results from these assays to GC-MS confirmation showed a sensitivity of 93.6% ± 3.5% and specificity of 77.6% ± 4.5% for the methamphetamine/MDMA assay and the amphetamine assay showed 95.7% ± 3.0% and 72.9% ± 5.2% for sensitivity and specificity respectively.

Prenatal exposure to drugs poses serious potential problems to the fetus, and testing strategies have included analysis of maternal urine and blood as well as analysis of neonatal urine, hair, and meconium. Urine has limitations due to the relatively short time drugs can be detected, and hair is often minimal or even absent on the newborn, although a report of analysis of hair from newborns has been described (Kintz and Mangin, 1993). Due to these limitations, meconium has become an important sample since it represents material from the fetus that reflects months of exposure rather than merely days. A number of chromatographically based assays have been described for the analysis of meconium samples and are discussed elsewhere in this chapter. Screening numerous samples by these methods, however, is time consuming and expensive using conventional chromatographic techniques; thus immunoassays were evaluated to ascertain their viability to detect the presence of drugs in this sample matrix. Several studies have reported success in this endeavor, including a study by Moriya et al. (1994), who describe a reliable and sensitive screening procedure for amphetamines, cocaine metabolites, opiates, and phencyclidine in meconium. Drugs were extracted with chloroform:isopropanol (3:1 v/v) and screened by enzyme-multiplied immunoassay. The limit of detection by this method was 730 ng/g for d-methamphetamine. ElSohly et al. (1999) described immunoassay and GC-MS procedures for the analysis of drugs in meconium. The immunoassay cutoff was administratively set at 200 ng/g for the amphetamines, although the authors noted that lower levels could be detected using the EMIT-ETS system. Although there were no immunoassay false negatives detected, the GC-MS confirmation rate for the immunoassay positive specimens was reported to be low for the amphetamines. Another evaluation of meconium involved analysis of 1175 samples from a neonatal intensive care unit by fluorescence polarization immunoassay (FPIA— Abbott Diagnostics) and GC-MS. The study tested the samples for cocaine, cocaethylene, marijuana metabolite, and amphetamine, with particular interest in the concordance of results from multiple births. In this study, none of the multiple births were positive for amphetamine, but the results for those drugs that were positive and all negative results were consistent (Lewis et al., 1995). Immunoassay of meconium with HPLC confirmation was described by another group (Franssen et al., 1994).

With the increase in the use of methylenedioxyamphetamines, several studies describe the cross-reactivity of these drugs. An evaluation of the methylenedioxy analogs, together with a variety of other illicit amphetamine analogs, using the amphetamine/methamphetamine II and amphetamine class fluorescence polarization immunoassays (Abbott Diagnostic) has been described (Cody and Schwarzhoff, 1993). The same reagents were also used by another group, which looked at 34 samples that tested positive for amphetamines by radioimmunoassay and had been confirmed to contain MDMA and MDA by GC-MS. All of the samples tested positive with both FPIA reagents (Kunsman et al., 1996). Results showed the two reagents gave comparable ability to identify the analogs in urine samples. Ensslin et al. (1996) used fluorescence polarization immunoassay for analysis of urine samples following administration of MDEA to a single subject. The amphetamine/methamphetamine II reagents gave positive results for 33–62 hours postadministration, and all were confirmed to contain the drug by GC-MS. Evaluation of a cloned enzyme donor immunoassay (CEDIA) assay designed for the analysis of a variety of amphetamines was conducted by Loor et al. (2002). Their study revealed the assay had significant cross-reactivities with amphetamines and minimal cross-reactivity with the undesirable, structurally related over-the-counter medications. The assay showed essentially 100% cross-reactivity with amphetamine and methamphetamine. It also gave the following results for related analytes of interest: 67.2% for d,l-amphetamine, 58.4% for d,l-methamphetamine, 113% for MDA, 199% for MDMA, 207% for MDEA, 123% for MBDB, 72% for BDB, 24% for PMA, and 100% for PMMA. In addition to these studies, readers are referred to package inserts for cross-reactivity data for the methylenedioxy analogs with specific assays. At the time of this writing, several manufacturers were working on the development of assays specific to MDMA. If implemented, there will be a consistent screening methodology and applicable cutoff level applied across assays for this increasingly popular drug.

A number of devices have recently been developed for onsite detection of drugs of abuse without the need to send the sample to a laboratory for analysis. This process involves use of a small amount of urine sample and gives a qualitative result in a very short time. Several studies have discussed the use and performance of these devices (Rohrich et al., 1994; Moriya and Hashimoto, 1996; Brown et al., 1997; Ros et al., 1998; Spiehler et al., 1998; Beck et al., 2000; Samyn and van Haeren, 2000). In most cases, the devices were reported to provide reasonably accurate results, but since they all represent only a single test, confirmation of all positive results is recommended. Ros et al. (1998) evaluated the Abu-Sign drugs-of-abuse slide tests compared to laboratory-based FPIA and GC-MS. The authors concluded the device, compared with FPIA, showed a high sensitivity (46% vs. 87%) but a low specificity (95% vs. 51%). They concluded the Abu-Sign slide test may be of value in toxicological screening but, because of the low interindividual agreement, was unsuitable for situations in which a reliable test result is desired. Another device, the Bionike one-step tests for the detection of drugs of abuse in urine, was evaluated for its ability to screen for various drugs, including the amphetamines. Amphetamine results correlated well with EMIT dau results when compared with GC-MS confirmation (Brown et al., 1997). Evaluation of the Triage device for the analysis of seven classes of drugs was carried out by Moriya and Hashimoto (1996). Hemolyzed blood was mixed with sulfosalicylic acid and the supernatant neutralized with ammonium acetate then screened using Triage. No false positives were observed with any of the drugs evaluated except for the amphetamines. Analysis of nine hemolyzed blood samples and three turbid urine samples from autopsy cases suspected of drug use gave five positives for amphetamines. Of those five, four were negative on GC confirmation tests. The authors determined all four of those samples contained large amounts of phenethylamine as a consequence of postmortem putrefaction. Closer examination showed that concentrations of over 5000 ng/mL of phenethylamine gave positive results with this test. Another report of postmortem samples analyzed with Triage tested 100 urine samples and found the confirmation rate for amphetamines by GC-MS to be 82%, substantially lower than the rates seen for the other drugs evaluated. Examination of 11 of those samples that did not contain amphetamines showed tyramine to be present at high concentrations. Tyramine, another product of postmortem putrefaction, gave positive results using Triage at concentrations over 5000 ng/mL (Rohrich et al., 1994). The Triage device was also evaluated in the emergency clinical setting and compared with EMIT and GC-MS results (Wu et al., 1993). The study evaluated 606 positive and 325 negative samples. For negative samples, the agreement ranged from 95% to 100% between the methods. For the amphetamines, 19 out of 27 samples positive by EMIT but negative with Triage contained combined amphetamine and methamphetamine concentrations of less than 1000 ng/mL by GC-MS (Wu et al., 1993). In another evaluation of onsite testing devices, Mastrovitch et al. (2002) compared results from the OnTrak device to those of the Triage system which was lab based in their setting. Results indicated 99% agreement for amphetamine samples between the two methods. The authors also evaluated time and cost of testing, both factors deemed important to the authors in the emergency department setting.

Four different onsite testing devices were evaluated to assess their accuracy in the determination of illicit-drug-use prevalence in drivers. The devices used were Abu-Sign, OnTrak and TesTcup (Roche Diagnostics Systems) and Triage (Biosite Diagnostics). Only the Triage and Abu-Sign devices were used to test for amphetamines, and neither gave any false negatives for amphetamines (when compared to laboratory-based immunoassay and GC-MS analysis). Both devices properly identified the one true positive (of 303 samples), but the Triage identified seven samples as positive that did not confirm, and the Abu-Sign identified two as positive that also did not confirm. This study summarized the sensitivity, specificity, and positive and negative predictive values for each of the devices for THC metabolite, cocaine metabolite, and opiates but not the other drugs, because those were the drugs in common for all devices and the number of positives for amphetamines was too small to base a valid conclusion. Beck et al. (2000) evaluated the Frontline immunochromatographic onsite device for amphetamine and methamphetamine using 658 clinical and forensic samples. The device demonstrated a sensitivity of 93% and a specificity of 98%. The authors noted close agreement between assays at concentrations less than 150 ng/mL and greater than 1000 ng/mL. Differences seen with concentrations between 300 and 1000 ng/mL were attributed, to some extent, to the enantiomeric specificity of the test to d-amphetamine. Onsite testing of saliva and sweat with Drugwipe was described by Samyn and van Haeren (2000). The onsite Drugwipe results were compared with the Drugwipe results for saliva obtained in the laboratory and GC-MS results of the corresponding saliva, plasma, and urine samples. The assay was shown to be sensitive enough to detect recent amphetamine abuse.

Serum and whole blood samples with no pretreatment were evaluated using cloned enzyme donor immunoassay (CEDIA) for the detection of amphetamines, benzoylecgonine, benzodiazepines, methadone, opiates, and THC metabolite (Iwersen-Bergmann and Schmoldt, 1999). The amphetamines assay was determined to be linear from 0 to 2500 ng/mL. A "cutoff" value was set at 20 ng/mL for the amphetamines. Within-run precision results ranged from 3.1% to 5.7%, and between-run precision was from 8.7% to 15.5% at concentrations of 500, 1000, and 2000 ng/mL of methamphetamine. The study evaluated immunoassay results from 500 original serum and whole-blood samples and compared them with GC-MS results. The assay performed well for most drugs; however, the authors reported that the amphetamine assay did not work without modification and that levels of less than 150 ng/mL of methamphetamine could not be detected. The authors suggested that modification of the procedure by increasing sample volume and precipitation of proteins might result in a viable assay.

In a study evaluating the Roche Abuscreen OnLine assays for drugs of abuse compared to the CEDIA assays at different laboratories, 149 samples tested for amphetamines gave the same two positive and 147 negative results with both assays. Analysis of samples above (750 ng/mL) and below (250 ng/mL) the 500-ng/mL cutoff showed within-run relative standard deviations of, respectively, 1.3% and 1.9% for the samples above and below the cutoff and 2.4% and 3.4% between-run relative standard deviations for the same samples. Based on these results, the authors concluded the OnLine assays compared well with CEDIA assays both within and between laboratories (Boettcher et al., 2000).

A fluoroimmunoassay procedure using a fluorescent europium chelate was used for the analysis of urine and hair samples to detect the presence of methamphetamine. Single-step and two-step methods were evaluated, and detection limits of 1 ng/mL and 1 pg/mL were achieved, which represented 10–1000 times the sensitivity of other immunoassays. The relative standard deviations of the methods were 2–8% at eight different concentrations across the linear range of the assay, and the method was shown to have a good correlation with conventional GC analysis (Kimura et al., 1999b).

Sweeney et al. (1998) described an enzyme-linked immunosorbent assay for the analysis of amphetamines in hair. The hair was washed with methanol and then extracted with hot methanol for 2 hours. Extracts were evaporated to dryness, reconstituted, and then analyzed. Relative standard deviations for this method were 3.3% and 10.5% for within-run and between-run precision, respectively. The optimum cutoff concentration was determined to be 300 pg/mg, with a detection limit of 60 pg/mg. Sensitivity and specificity of the method were reported as 83% and 92%, respectively. The assay was targeted to d-methamphetamine and showed cross-reactivity with d-amphetamine (30.8%), l-methamphetamine (7.4%), phentermine (4.3%), l-amphetamine (2.9%), and less than 1% for ephedrine, MDA, and MDMA, and no discernible activity to unrelated compounds.

Analysis of hair samples for a variety of drugs, including benzodiazepines, barbiturates, antidepressants, opiates, cocaine, amphetamine, and marijuana, using fluorescence polarization immunoassay (Abbott ADx) with confirmation with GC-MS was described by Kintz et al. (1992). The procedure included a wash with ethanol for 15 minutes at 37°C followed by treatment with sodium hydroxide at 100°C for 1 hour. Immunoassay was used to screen the samples, with GC-MS confirmation of all those that tested positive. No false positives were observed for amphetamines when using this technique. Analysis of hair samples

(10mg) for methamphetamine using enzyme multiplied immunoassay technique following extraction of the drug into 5M HCl/methanol (1:20, v/v). After solvent evaporation, the extract was dissolved in water (Miki et al., 2002). The analysis was completed with double-concentrated EMIT d.a.u. Amphetamine Class assay reagents. The "optimal" cutoff concentration of methamphetamine in hair was found to be 1.0ng/mg with a detection limit of 0.5ng/mg.

7.3.2 OTHER METHODS

Thin-layer chromatography (TLC) has been used for the analysis of drugs for many, many years. In recent years, its use has been superseded by techniques that give more conclusive results. Although it is possible to obtain some indication of the amount of drug (or metabolite) using TLC by imaging the size of the spot, density measurements, etc., it is generally used as a method for the qualitative identification of drugs and metabolites. In some laboratories, TLC is used to confirm the presence of a drug that is suspected by some other method (e.g., immunoassay). Although not as definitive as many other confirmation procedures, it can differentiate compounds that immunoassay cannot. It is also used in some laboratories as a screening method. Although it is far more labor intensive and time consuming than immunoassay screening using high-volume autoanalyzers, it can be used to identify drugs, or classes of drugs, for which there is no reliable immunoassay procedure available. Sensitivity is a serious limitation for TLC compared to most other techniques, with the normal levels of some drugs (e.g., LSD) far below the concentration necessary to be detected with this technique. Despite these limitations, it does provide a valuable tool for use in laboratories and, compared to most instrumental methods, is very inexpensive with regard to capital investment.

A method for the detection of a broad spectrum of drugs has been described using ChemElut extraction columns for isolation of the drugs from urine. Specimens were screened by thin-layer chromatography followed by confirmation with GC-MS (Lillsunde and Korte, 1991a). Although the system could identify over 300 different analytes, confirmation was required, and many analytes required additional chromatographic procedures for their identification.

The Toxi-Lab (ANSYS, Inc.) TLC system is a commonly used method. The system involves methods for the identification of over 300 different drugs and drug metabolites. Provided with the system are extraction tubes for the extraction of acidic or basic/neutral drugs and solvent and imaging procedures for the identification of analytes. The visualization process involves four sequential stages that allow for the identification of the drugs based on their migration from the origin (Rf) and color under the four conditions used for visualization. Although this general procedure is effective to isolate and identify hundreds of different drugs, the sympathomimetic amines are a problem for the system. Differentiation of amphetamine, methamphetamine, ephedrine, pseudo-ephedrine, phenylpropanolamine, and phentermine can be accomplished using specifically defined procedures for the differentiation of these compounds. The utility of this procedure has been evaluated in a number of studies and was found, in many cases, to provide useful information.

As part of an evaluation of an HPLC procedure (Talwar et al., 1999), samples that were positive for amphetamines by immunoassay were tested by the HPLC procedure and TLC (Toxi-Lab). There was complete agreement between HPLC and TLC for the immunoassay positive samples that contained amphetamine or methamphetamine of greater than 1000 ng/mL with both procedures properly identifying the analytes. Samples with concentrations between 500 and 1000 ng/mL, however, were not positive by TLC but were easily detected by HPLC. In addition to a number of clinical samples, this study evaluated several quality-control samples, one of which contained 5000 ng/mL of phenyl-propanolamine and 5000 ng/mL of ephedrine. This sample gave a positive result for amphetamine by TLC but not by HPLC. The procedure used in this study was the standard method, which, as described earlier, can be modified to properly separate the closely migrating sympathomimetic amines. Evaluation of urine and saliva samples using TLC following a single therapeutic dose of amphetamine showed the method was not sensitive enough to identify the presence of amphetamine in saliva, while it could be detected in urine for a short period of time (Vapaatalo et al., 1984).

Another commercially available TLC system is Drug-Skreen II (Eppendorf-Brinkman, Inc., Westbury, NY). This process involves alkaline extraction and separation on silica-coated plates using sequential spraying to visualize different drugs. In addition to these systems, there is a wide variety of other TLC procedures used by analysts to detect amphetamines. Tertiary amines (including dimethylamphetamine) were detected in a method developed by Kato and Ogamo (2001) who described a method for rapid development of coloration of the tertiary amines using a citric acid:acetic anhydride reagent following soaking the TLC plate in phosphoric acid:acetone solution to suppress color development. This technique allowed visualization of tertiary amines after 3 minutes. The variety of these procedures is beyond the scope of this chapter but can be found in the early literature on drug analysis.

Combination of TLC with other techniques does allow for much more sophisticated and definitive analysis of samples. High-performance thin-layer chromatography (HPTLC) in combination with Fourier transform infrared (FTIR) spectroscopy has been used for the analysis of 3,4-methylenedioxyethylamphetamine (MDEA) and several metabolites, including 4-hydroxy-3-methoxyamphetamine and 3,4-methylenedioxyamphetamine (MDA). The method allowed quantitative determination after a two-step automatic development procedure. The results compared favorably with an HPLC method with regard to quantitative accuracy and reliability. The linear range of the HPTLC method was 0.1–8.2 μg/mL, compared to 0.2–60.0 μg/mL for the HPLC method (Pisternick et al., 1997). Although these results demonstrate the utility of this method, the instrumentation required is not widely available in laboratories and shows no significant advantage to other, more common methods, such as GC- and LC-based methods.

7.4 QUANTITATIVE METHODS OF ANALYSIS

Quantitative analysis of amphetamines is accomplished primarily by gas or liquid chromatographic methods. The primary focus of this section of the chapter is to describe these procedures by a general discussion of principles associated with analyses such as hydrolysis, extraction, derivatization, separation, and detection. Depending on the procedure, all or only some of these fundamental steps are involved in the analysis of samples. Some general discussion will be given in this section to processes that apply to both chromatographic methods. The subsections of this chapter give specific details regarding individual techniques. In addition to gas and liquid chromatography, discussion of solid-phase microextraction and capillary electrophoresis is also included as part of this chapter. These procedures are becoming more important in the analysis of many compounds, including the amphetamines.

Specific detailed examples of analytical procedures are described later in this chapter, but a brief general discussion of some basic principles common to both gas and liquid chromatography procedures is given here. One of these is hydrolysis. Analysis of amphetamine, methamphetamine, MDA, MDMA, MDEA, and related compounds do not require hydrolysis, since these compounds are not conjugated by the body. Most of their metabolites, however, particularly those containing hydroxyl groups, are conjugated and therefore require hydrolysis prior to analysis by most analytical procedures. A variety of different methods of hydrolysis have been described, but virtually all fall into one of two different categories: acid or enzymatic. Acid hydrolysis is generally faster than enzymatic hydrolysis and more robust since there are fewer parameters that can have a negative influence on its ability to successfully free the metabolite from its conjugate. Enzyme hydrolysis most often yields a cleaner sample than is seen following acid hydrolysis. Amphetamines are sometimes analyzed as part of a broad screen to identify a variety of different drugs. These procedures commonly involve hydrolysis to release other analytes of interest that are normally conjugated and must be hydrolyzed prior to their analysis. Although, as mentioned earlier, amphetamines do not require hydrolysis, they are stable to normal hydrolytic conditions and do not suffer from commonly employed hydrolysis procedures.

Preparation of samples for analysis by gas or liquid chromatography typically involves extraction of the analyte from the sample matrix prior to analysis. Often the extraction procedures used for liquid chromatography are less extensive than those used for gas chromatography, but in many cases the extract prepared could be used with either analytical procedure. The most common methods are liquid–liquid and solid-phase extraction. Most procedures utilize one or the other of these two methods, although headspace, supercritical-fluid, and solid-phase microextraction are also used. In addition, direct analysis of samples without extraction from the biological matrix has been utilized in several procedures.

Liquid–liquid extraction is a widely used method for the extraction of amphetamines from biological samples. Amphetamines are basic drugs with pK values of approximately 10.0. Liquid–liquid extraction methods commonly employ an organic solvent to extract the drugs from their aqueous environment. Adjustment of sample pH to a value greater than the pK of amphetamine and methamphetamine is necessary to effect high recovery of these drugs by neutralizing the positive charge on the amine nitrogen, thus making the molecule less hydrophilic. Under these conditions both basic and neutral compounds are extracted into the organic solvent. Further purification is often employed to the initial extract by back-extracting the basic drugs into an aqueous solvent, thus effectively eliminating the neutral compounds by leaving them behind in the organic solvent, which is discarded. Typically, this is accomplished by acidification of the extract and extraction into an aqueous solvent. The basic drugs are again extracted from the aqueous layer by adding a base to increase the pH and extracting into an organic solvent.

Amphetamines are extracted from a wide variety of matrices, including urine, blood, plasma, serum, meconium, vitreous humor, saliva, hair, and various tissues. By far, urine samples make up the majority of assays conducted for the detection of amphetamines. Extraction from sources other than urine often involves additional preparative steps, such as elimination of protein. This is accomplished by a number of different methods, including salting out the protein, cold precipitation, and use of acetonitrile or some other agent to eliminate the proteins. Tissue samples are typically homogenized, followed by removal of the solid matter prior to extraction.

Although urine is the most common sample used in forensic analysis of biological samples for drugs of abuse, the most intensely investigated specimen over the last decade has been hair. Many methods have been developed and a good deal of fundamental research has been accomplished into the mechanism of deposition of amphetamines in hair (Kikura and Nakahara, 1995a, 1995b, 1997; Nakahara et al., 1995, 1998; Nakahara and Kikura, 1996, 1997; Kikura et al., 1997; Nakahara and Hanajiri, 2000; Stout et al., 2000) and investigations into external contamination and methods to eliminate or compensate for that situation. Other areas of active investigation include the impact of hair treatments (Takayama et al., 1999; Rohrich et al., 2000) and hair types (Paul and Smith, 1999) and their effect on drug concentrations. Several reviews have been published giving insightful summaries of hair analysis (Moeller et al., 1993a; Nakahara, 1995; Sachs and Kintz, 1998).

After such initial steps, most extraction procedures are essentially the same regardless of the initial matrix. Recent developments in solid-phase extraction columns allow extraction of blood and plasma samples with only simple dilution rather than more extensive preparative procedures. Similarly, some liquid–liquid extraction procedures require no special pretreatment and extract directly from the matrix. Extraction procedures used for amphetamines range from very simple to extensive. Despite these developments, most procedures call for some steps to be taken to remove substantial amounts of solid material prior to analysis. Improvements in solid-phase extraction procedures and materials has lead to significant increases in their application to the analysis of amphetamines. Many laboratories use the extraction procedures provided by manufacturers without modification.

Amphetamine-related compounds, such as ephedrine, pseudoephedrine, and phenylpropanolamine, are often encountered at high concentrations in urine sample. These alpha-hydroxy phenylisopropanolamines can cause significant interference with the analysis of the amphetamines. Targeted assays designed to identify the presence of specific drugs, such as amphetamine and methamphetamine, often must take steps to eliminate the interference caused by high concentrations of these drugs. Since these compounds are extracted using the same procedures designed to extract amphetamines, they can be responsible for interference in many assays if they are at high concentrations. In these cases, simple dilution is often not an acceptable alternative, since the analytes of interest will also be diluted and therefore may not be detected. The interference can be overcome using periodate to eliminate the hydroxy-containing compounds by chemically degrading the drugs. Several different methods describe periodate oxidation of these drugs to eliminate interference (ElSohly et al., 1992; Hornbeck et al., 1993; Paul et al., 1994; Valtier and Cody, 1999a). In fact, many assays routinely incorporate this step to eliminate the potential for interference with the associated requirement for reanalysis of the sample. A potential drawback of routine use of this technique is the fact that periodate treatment has been described as demethylating methamphetamine to amphetamine under some conditions. At pH 9.1 or higher, some demethylation of methamphetamine to amphetamine was shown to occur, but this demethylation was not observed at lower pH values. Since the periodate is effective at pH values above 5.2, the demethylation problem can be eliminated by using a pH between those two values (Paul et al., 1994).

Chromatographic analysis of amphetamines does not require derivatization. It is, however, commonly used, for a number of reasons. Derivatized amphetamines exhibit better chromatographic behavior than they do if not derivatized, when they have a tendency to demonstrate peak tailing. This is more pronounced in gas than liquid chromatography, but derivatized amphetamines typically demonstrate better peak shape with both chromatographic methods. Derivatization also alters the volatility of a compound, which is of particular importance for GC analysis of these compounds. The derivatized drugs are also more amenable to separation from other compounds because their retention times are generally longer than for their underivatized counterparts. Additionally, detection of the compounds can be greatly enhanced by using specific derivatives. Gas chromatography detectors, such as flame ionization (FID), readily respond to the amphetamines, as does a nitrogen–phosphorus detector (NPD), owing to the presence of the amine nitrogen, without derivatization. Derivatives can, however, be used to impart characteristics that are not native to the molecules (e.g., fluorescence) and can allow for selective manipulation of the compounds (e.g., enantiomer separation). Examples of this include addition of a derivative with strong electronegative characteristics, which then allows detection with electron capture detectors or the ready production of negative ions in electron capture negative ion chemical ionization mass spectrometry. These derivatives and detectors generally give greater sensitivity because the overall background levels are lower and fewer potentially interfering compounds exist when compared with the other, more universal detection techniques. Because amphetamine, methamphetamine, and their illicit analogs described earlier exist as enantiomers, derivatives can also be prepared to enable separation of the enantiomers' standard achiral stationary phases.

Amphetamines can be derivatized by a number of different chemical procedures, including silylation, acylation, and alkylation. Detailed descriptions of these derivatization reactions are not discussed in this chapter but are given in several books and review articles (Knapp, 1979, 1990; Halket and Blau, 1993; Baker et al., 1994). Derivatization of amphetamines is useful for qualitative and quantitative analysis of these drugs. In addition to the chromatographic improvements seen with derivatives of the amphetamines comes the increased mass useful in mass spectral analysis. The mass spectra of amphetamine and

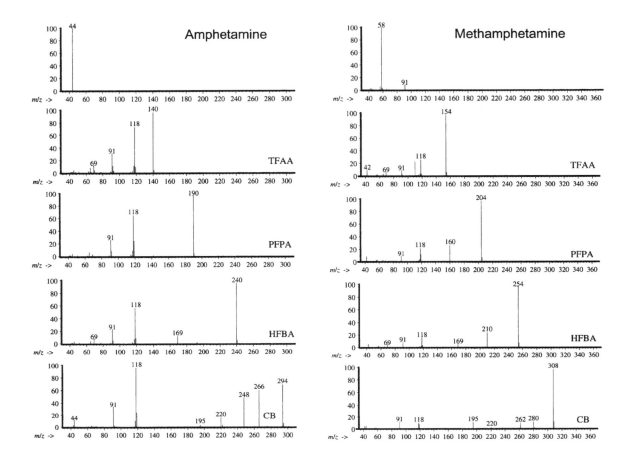

Figure 7.5

Mass spectra of underivatized and derivatized amphetamine and methamphetamine

methamphetamine are very simple. Using standard 70-eV electron ionization, the spectrum of amphetamine is dominated by an ion at m/z 44. There is virtually no molecular ion, nor, based on the tendency of the charge to reside on the nitrogen-containing fragment, is there an intense peak associated with the tropylium ion at m/z 91. Similarly, the electron ionization spectrum of methamphetamine is characterized by an ion at m/z 58. Derivatization of these compounds significantly increases the mass of the molecule and results in fragmentation, yielding several characteristic ions. As a result, the identification is much easier and more reliable, because the increased mass and number of fragments make the spectra more unique. See Figure 7.5 for the mass spectra of underivatized and derivatized amphetamine and methamphetamine.

The amphetamines have a single asymmetric center, which gives rise to two possible enantiomers. These enantiomeric forms have quite different pharmacological properties; however, they behave identically in normal analytical procedures, such as gas and liquid chromatography. Identification of which individual enantiomers are present in a sample can be important in the determination of source and the evaluation of the potential of illicit versus legitimate origin and use of the drug. Under ordinary chromatographic conditions, both enantiomers chromatograph as a single peak. To separate the enantiomers, two different approaches are used. One method, generally referred to as the *direct* method, involves columns that interact with each enantiomer differently, thereby effecting their separation. The other, and far more common, method is the use of a chiral derivatizing reagent. Chiral derivatization of the amphetamines converts the enantiomers to diastereomers that are separated using standard chromatographic columns. Gas and liquid chromatographic analysis of enantiomers by both direct and indirect methods are described in the corresponding GC and LC sections of this chapter.

Specific examples of commonly employed derivatization methods are described later in this chapter with respect to the analytical procedures for which they are used. For the most part, virtually all derivatives used for GC can be used with a mass spectrometer as the detector.

7.4.1 GAS CHROMATOGRAPHY AND GAS CHROMATOGRAPHY/MASS SPECTROMETRY

Gas chromatographic analysis of amphetamines has been described using a variety of different detectors, including flame ionization detection (FID), nitrogen–phosphorus detection (NPD), electron capture detection (ECD), and mass spectrometry (MS). Amphetamines can be analyzed without derivatization using any of these methods, including mass spectrometry. However, the drugs are often derivatized in order to improve chromatographic performance, because the amphetamines tend to demonstrate peak tailing unless derivatized. In mass spectrometry, there is the additional benefit of making the spectra of the amphetamines much more distinctive by increasing the mass and allowing for monitoring more ions than are possible with the underivatized compounds. (See Figure 7.5.)

A large number of publications have appeared describing the use of amphetamine and methamphetamine, their metabolites, or methylenedioxy analogs by GC and GC-MS. Methylenedioxy analogs generally require no substantial modification of procedures designed for amphetamine and methamphetamine, except to extend run times, monitor specific ions if using a mass spectrometer, etc., to analyze for those compounds. Likewise, the other amphetamine analogs mentioned earlier are generally extracted, derivatized, chromatographed, and detected by the same methods used for amphetamine and methamphetamine. As a result, this chapter will focus on procedures for the analysis of amphetamine, methamphetamine, and their commonly abused analogs.

This section describes various specific methods for the analysis of amphetamines using gas chromatography and a variety of common detectors. There are a number of different methods used in the preparation of derivatives. Some examples of derivatization procedures are described to illustrate basic techniques of derivatization. Use of perfluoronated acid anhydrides and silyl and acetyl derivatives has been reported by many investigators. Each of the reagents in common use provides usable results for both qualitative and quantitative analysis. Derivatization is commonly conducted at elevated temperatures, but that is not always the case. Some reagents are used at room temperature and can rapidly derivatize the compounds of interest, making their use attractive because of the time saved. One example of room-temperature derivatization of amphetamine and methamphetamine used 2,2,2-trichloroethyl chloroformate. Gas chromatography with electron and chemical ionization mass spectral analysis was evaluated, and the method proved comparable to results produced when using PFPA as the derivatizing reagent without the additional time and effort required to carry out the reaction at elevated temperatures (Dasgupta and Spies, 1998).

Derivatization has also been accomplished using microwave radiation to speed up the process. A procedure using microwave radiation to rapidly form trifluoroacetyl, pentafluoropropyl, heptafluorobutyryl, and perfluorooctanoyl derivatives of amphetamine, methamphetamine, and MDMA has been described (Thompson and Dasgupta, 1994). In this study, complete derivatization was accomplished in only 45 seconds, 1 minute, or 6 minutes for the tri-, penta-, and heptaperfluoroanhydrides, respectively, with overall acceptable results for all three analytes tested. However, microwave radiation was not successful in attempts to form the perfluorooctanoyl derivatives of methamphetamine or MDMA.

Typically, procedures used for the analysis of amphetamines are limited to looking for the compound(s) of interest. For example, the most commonly used procedures for amphetamine and methamphetamine are targeted only to these analytes. Both compounds have only one derivatizable group; therefore the derivatization is fairly straightforward. In cases where there are multiple derivatizable groups on the same molecule, derivatization can be accomplished either with a single derivatizing reagent or with mixed derivatization. An example of mixed derivatization is illustrated by a molecule that contains not only the amine group, but also another derivatizable group, such as a hydroxyl group. Examples of these molecules include ephedrine, pseudoephedrine, phenylpropanolamine, and hydroxy metabolites of amphetamine and methamphetamine. It is possible in these cases to derivatize both the amine nitrogen and the hydroxyl group with the same reagent or to use two different reagents, one derivatizing the amine and the other the hydroxyl. Typically, this process involves derivatization of the compounds with the first reagent, which reacts with the molecule, followed by use of a second derivatizing reagent, which preferentially reacts with one of the derivatizable groups but not the other. In this way, one group is derivatized with one reagent and the other group is derivatized with the second. This method is exemplified by a procedure described by Solans et al. (1995) in their comprehensive screening procedure for a variety of drugs and metabolites in urine. Sample extracts are selectively derivatized with N-methyl-N-trimethylsilyl-trifluoroacetamide (MSTFA), which forms the trimethylsilyl derivatives of hydroxyl, acidic, and phenolic groups, and N-methyl-bis-trifluoroacetamide (MBTFA), which forms the trifluoroacetamide derivatives of primary and secondary amines. The procedure used 100μL of MSTFA at 60°C for 5 minutes to form the trimethylsilyl derivative. After cooling, 20μL of MBTFA at 60°C for 5 minutes was used to form the trifluoroacetamide derivative. This technique has several useful applications. Since the difference in derivatives gives the compound different physical characteristics, it will chromatograph differently than when using a single reagent. In addition, this method can assist in the characterization of unknown compounds. For instance, if derivatization with one reagent gives a single peak at a specific GC retention time and derivatization of the same analyte with two different properly selected reagents gives a different retention time, it is an indication that the compound has two different derivatizable groups. Combination of this technique with mass spectral analysis can be a powerful tool in structure elucidation by assessing changes in fragment ions in light of the derivative(s) used.

Derivatization is typically accomplished by reconstituting the dried extract with a solvent containing a derivatizing reagent and then allowing the reaction to occur, usually at elevated temperatures, for a specific period of time. While effective, this method requires time for evaporation of the extract, reconstitution, and incubation to derivatize the analytes of interest. Derivation has also been accomplished using several other methods. Extractive derivatization of drugs is another method that has been successfully employed in a number of cases (Meatherall, 1995; Hara et al., 1997). As the name implies, this procedure combines extraction with derivatization, thus saving time. One such procedure described the extraction of amphetamine and methamphetamine from 200μL of urine into an organic solvent containing propylchloroformate. The amines react rapidly with the propylchloroformate, making them more soluble in the organic solvent, thus extracting them quickly in a single-step procedure. The study also evaluated the use of deuterated analogs and N-propylamphetamine as internal standards for quantitative analysis, both of which were shown to yield acceptable results. The method was linear to 10,000ng/mL and demonstrated limits of detection and quantitation of 50 and 5 ng/mL for amphetamine and methamphetamine, respectively, despite the small sample volume extracted.

Another method of derivatization involves coinjection of the drug and derivatizing reagent into the injection port of the GC. This process, commonly referred to as *on-column* derivatization, has been used with amphetamines for a number of years for both quantitative (Eiceman et al., 1984) and enantiomer (Fitzgerald et al., 1988) analysis. On-column derivatization is a misnomer since the derivation actually takes place in the injection port rather than on the column. It is a rapid technique and simple to accomplish. Typically, a small amount of the extract is drawn into a syringe, followed by drawing a comparable amount of the derivatizing reagent into the same syringe. The contents are then injected, and derivatization occurs very quickly in the high temperature of the injection port. One method using this technique employed trifluoroacetic anhydride injected together with the extract. While very rapid and effective, there are some drawbacks to the use of such a method. A complication of this procedure is that the reaction of the analyte with the derivatizing reagent, such as the anhydrides (the most commonly used derivatizing reagents for this purpose), produces the corresponding acid as a by-product of the reaction. This acid tends to degrade the liquid phase of the GC column and requires more routine maintenance and more frequent column replacement. Another method uses a derivatizing reagent that has been fixed on a support. This *solid-phase derivatization* has been described by a number of investigators (Bourque and Krull, 1991; Gao et al., 1991; Szulc and Krull, 1992).

A derivatization procedure employed by a number of investigators involves the use of acetic anhydride (Maurer, 1992, 1996; Ensslin et al., 1996; Kraemer et al., 1997; Maurer et al., 1997). The acetyl group is relatively small compared to many of the other derivatives used by laboratories. As with all derivatives, it improves the chromatographic behavior of the amphetamines and the resulting mass spectrum. A unique and characteristic mass spectrum is valuable in procedures using mass spectral analysis for identification and quantitation of the compounds. It helps to allow monitoring unique and characteristic ions for quantitative analysis, minimizing potential interference. In addition, for the qualitative analysis of unknown compounds, commercially available mass spectral libraries contain many spectra from acetyl derivatives, thus making identification of unknowns easier (Kraemer and Maurer, 1998).

Investigators have also successfully utilized other derivatizing reagents for the analysis of amphetamines, including trifluoroacetylation and trimethylsilylation (Solans et al., 1995), N-methyl-N-t-butyldimethylsilyl trifluoroacetamide (MTBSTFA) (Melgar and Kelly, 1993), pentafluorobenzolyl chloride (Shin and Donike, 1996), perfluorooctanoyl chloride (Gjerde et al., 1993), and carbethoxyhexafluorobutyryl chloride (CB) (Czarny and Hornbeck, 1989; Thurman et al., 1992). The mass spectra of the carbethoxyhexafluorobutyryl derivative show several major fragments that allow monitoring amphetamine without the need to use the ion at m/z 91, which is the most prone to interference due to the large number of molecules that give rise to this fragment ion. Caution must be used, however, to ensure the method accounts for the fact that the major ions typically monitored are the result of losses from the derivative itself and do not represent different fragments of the drug molecule.

Evaluation of a variety of derivatives and the use of deuterium-labeled internal standards has been reported in a number of publications. These publications demonstrate the need for careful consideration in the selection of internal standard and the effect different derivatizing reagents have on the selection of internal standards (Kennedy, 1999; Lin et al., 2000).

Procedures for the analysis of amphetamines range from very simple to far more complex. An example of a rapid procedure for the extraction of amphetamine and methamphetamine from blood was accomplished by adding base to alkalinize the sample, followed by addition of an internal standard and extraction into 2mL of cyclohexane by shaking the tubes for 10 minutes (Gjerde et al., 1993). Although a simple procedure, this method provided good linearity and low detection limits. Most procedures for the analysis of amphetamines are more extensive than this one. Most have been developed to improve recovery or eliminate interference. Several examples of GC procedures using various example extraction, derivatization, chromatographic, and detection methods are given later.

Amphetamine, methamphetamine, ephedrine, norephedrine, and related compounds have been analyzed using GC-NPD. This procedure produced good analytical results, but the authors noted it was important to remove excess derivatizing reagent (methyl chloroformate in their case) because the reagent caused rapid deterioration of the NPD (Jonsson et al., 1996). Pentafluorobenzylation was used with GC-NPD in a metabolic study of the monoamine oxidase inhibitor deprenyl (selegiline). The procedure analyzed for amphetamine, methamphetamine, and nordeprenyl from blood samples (Szebeni et al., 1995).

A description of a procedure using GC-NPD and GC-MS for the analysis of amphetamine and methamphetamine from urine, blood, and tissues has been described. Homogenized tissue was combined with 2mL of phosphoric acid and 10mL of saturated ammonium chloride solution, heated for 10 minutes, allowed to cool, and then filtered. At this point the tissue samples were treated the same as blood. Briefly, the remainder of the extraction involved pH adjustment to 9.0 with borate buffer and application to an Extrelut solid-phase extraction column. After 10 minutes, methylene chloride:isopropanol (9:1 v/v) was used as the elution solvent. The extracts were analyzed directly using GC-NPD or derivatized with pentafluoropropionic anhydride and hexafluoro-isopropanol for analysis by GC-MS. Ethylamphetamine and methylene-dioxypropylamphetamine (MDPA) were chosen as the internal standards since they are both chromatographically separated from the other analytes, thus allowing their use with either GC-NPD or GC-MS. This procedure proved to be viable for the identification of a number of different drugs, including amphet-amine, methamphetamine, MDA, MDMA, MDEA, and the *p*-methoxy deriva-tives of amphetamine and methamphetamine from postmortem blood, tissue, and urine (Tamayo-Lora et al., 1997). Another method using GC-NPD and GC-MS for screening large numbers of drugs from urine samples has been described (Lho et al., 1990b).

The methylenedioxy analogs MDA and MDMA were analyzed in a study described by Lillsunde et al. (1996). Samples were analyzed using both NPD and ECD. Quantitation was accomplished using MDEA as the internal standard for MDA and MDMA. The authors reasoned that MDEA use was not as fre-quently encountered as MDMA and that if it were found in a sample, MDMA could be used to quantitate the MDEA. This rationale seems reasonable; however, with the increasing use of both of these drugs and the fact they are sometimes encountered at the same time, care must be taken to ensure the drugs are properly identified and quantitated in such cases of mixed MDMA and MDEA use.

Electron capture detection (ECD) following liquid–liquid extraction and pentafluorobenzenesulfonylation of amphetamine and methamphetamine from urine and tissue was reported by Paetch et al. (1992). The method gave excellent sensitivity due to the highly electronegative nature of the perfluoro-nated derivative. The method was able to accurately quantitate concentrations from 1 to 50 ng/mL. Another method for the analysis of amphetamine using ECD has been described by Asghar et al. (2001). The authors used electron capture detection. The drug was extracted from plasma samples then deriva-tized with pentafluorobenzenesulfonyl chloride. The method gave a detection limit of <1 ng/mL and was linear from 1–100 ng/mL.

A procedure for the analysis of 12 different drugs, including amphetamine, methamphetamine, MDA, MDMA, and related compounds in seized material, blood, and urine has been described by Lillsunde and Korte (1991b). Sample extracts were derivatized with HFBA and analyzed using ECD, NPD, and GC-MS. Derivatization was carried out at room temperature by rapidly mixing the derivatizing reagent with the extract and then washing with a 10% solution of $NaHCO_3$ to eliminate the excess derivatizing reagent. The derivatization procedure worked well, but the chromatographic conditions used led several compounds to coelute from the column, thus limiting the use of ECD and NPD.

All of the compounds could be isolated and determined by their mass spectra, however, due to the selectivity of that technique.

Ortuno et al. (1999) reported a procedure using NPD for the analysis of MDMA and several metabolites (MDA, 4-hydroxy-3-methoxymethamphetamine, 4-hydroxy-3-methoxyamphetamine) in plasma and urine. The plasma samples were analyzed in splitless mode on a 5% phenyl-methylsilicone column (HP Ultra-2) with temperatures from 70°C for 2 minutes to 100°C at 30°C per minute and then to 200°C at 20°C per minute, and finally to 280°C at 25°C per minute. Urine extracts were analyzed using a temperature program from 100°C to 280°C at 15°C per minute. This assay used MBTFA as the derivatizing reagent and methylenedioxypropylamphetamine as the internal standard. The assay proved to have low ng/mL detection and quantitation limits. Taylor et al. (1989) described a method for the analysis of amphetamine and methamphetamine using propylamphetamine as the internal standard. The extraction was accomplished using a solid-phase method. Following evaporation of the extract, it was reconstituted in ethyl acetate and analyzed by GC-NPD. For MS analysis, HFBA was used to derivatize the extract. Recoveries from the extraction procedure were 78% and 87% for amphetamine and methamphetamine, respectively. The linear range was 50–7000 ng/mL for both drugs. Within-run and between-run precision was reported to be 6.7% and 8.9%, respectively, for amphetamine and 4.9% and 5.6%, respectively, for methamphetamine. These results are acceptable for most laboratory analyses but are higher than those typically seen with deuterium-labeled internal standards. However, the use of propylamphetamine, since it separates well from the other analytes, allows the option of using either NPD, GC-MS, or both. Other procedures involving NPD have also been reported using 4-chloroamphetamine (Poyhia et al., 1991; Lillsunde et al., 1996) as an internal standard.

The majority of recently described procedures using gas chromatography as the separation technique are coupled with a mass spectrometer. Because of improvements in the ease of use of the instruments and decreasing costs for this instrumentation, most laboratories now have mass spectrometry capabilities. Mass spectrometry is recognized as the "gold standard" for forensic analysis of drugs because this technique is generally considered to produce unequivocal results.

The unique ability of a mass spectrometer to monitor specific ions from different compounds even though they may coelute from the column allows use of stable isotope-labeled internal standard and the drug of interest. The similarity of the deuterated isotopomer to the drug provides, in almost every situation, superior accuracy and precision, as compared to other compounds serving as the internal standard. Not all deuterated internal standards provide acceptable results, however. A report describing the analysis of MDA, MDMA, and

MDEA evaluated the use of MDEA-d5 and MDEA-d6. For purposes of enantiomeric analysis of MDEA, both deuterated compounds were equally viable. However, when using heptafluorobutyryl derivatives for quantitative analysis, the MDEA-d5 had an ion in common with MDEA, limiting its utility in an assay involving ratios of several ions to confirm the identity of the drug (Hensley and Cody, 1999). Other investigators have evaluated internal standards and found most acceptable, although some were problematic, depending on the assay parameters (Ho et al., 1990; Valtier and Cody, 1995; Lin et al., 2000). The number of deuterium atoms on a candidate internal standard has also been shown to be important with LC-MS procedures (Bogusz, 1997).

Enzymatic hydrolysis of urine samples followed by solid-phase extraction and derivatization with propionic anhydride:pyridine was described for the analysis of a number of drugs, including amphetamine, methamphetamine, MDA, MDMA, MDEA, ephedrine, and pseudoephedrine (Galloway et al., 1998). GC-MS analysis included separation on an HP-5 capillary column with temperatures set to 85°C for 0.7 minutes to 285°C at 14°C per minute. The mass spectrometer was set to scan from m/z 40–500, which allowed detection of the amphetamines at 100 ng/mL.

A GC-MS method using PFPA derivatives of 1–4 mL urine samples monitoring ions at m/z 194, 123, 122 for amphetamine-d5; m/z 190, 118, 91 for amphetamine; m/z 208, 163, 120 for methamphetamine-d5; and m/z 204, 160, 118 for methamphetamine gave limits of detection of 1.7 ng/mL and a limit of quantitation of 27.5 ng/mL for both analytes using 4 mL of urine. Higher concentration samples could be readily measured by extracting from smaller volumes of urine to ensure sample results did not exceed the linear range of the assay (Valentine et al., 1995).

Dasgupta and Spies (1998) described a method for the analysis of amphetamine and methamphetamine by GC-MS. These authors compared the use of the derivatizing reagent 2,2,2-trichloroethyl chloroformate with N-propylamphetamine as the internal standard to results using PFPA as the derivatizing reagent. Chemical ionization mass spectral analysis showed strong M + 1 ions at m/z 310 and 312 and intense fragment ion peaks at m/z 274 and 276. Electron ionization, as expected, gave weaker molecular ion peaks, but did allow monitoring of three intense peaks at m/z 218, 220, and 222. The method showed a detection limit of 100 ng/mL in scan mode and was linear from 250 to 5000 ng/mL. At 1000 ng/mL, relative standard deviations of 4.8% and 3.6% (within-run) and 5.3% and 6.7% (between-run) were seen for amphetamine and methamphetamine, respectively.

Several other procedures describe the use of chemical ionization GC-MS analysis of amphetamines. Pellegrini et al. (2002) used positive ion chemical ionization using methanol as the reagent gas and monitored the molecular ions of amphetamine, methylamphetamine, MDA, MDMA, MDEA, and MBDB extracted from urine samples using a simple liquid–liquid method with no derivatization. The method allowed detection of the analytes at concentrations of 5–10ng/mL. Another method using positive ion chemical ionization was used by Oyler et al. (2002) to analyze samples from a controlled administration study of subjects administered 10 or 20mg doses of methamphetamine. Part of the evaluation of this study was determination of detection times of methamphetamine and the consequence of lowering cutoff concentrations to 250 (methamphetamine) and 100 (amphetamine). Doing so allowed confirmation of methamphetamine positives for up to 24 hours longer than with current cutoff criteria. Analysis of enantiomers using negative ion chemical ionization of l-heptafluorobutyrylprolyl chloride derivatives of amphetamine and methamphetamine extracted from 0.2mL of blood, plasma or serum has been described (Peters et al., 2002). This method allowed detection of low levels of drug (linear range 5–250ng/mL) from a small sample volume. Samples were extracted with mixed-mode–solid-phase extraction and with recoveries of 88.9% to 98.6%. Derivatized extracts were chromatographed through an HP-5MS column utilizing a 15-minute run.

Semi-automated extraction of amphetamine and methamphetamine from urine was investigated by Churley et al. (2002) using the Speedisk 48 Pressure Processor in combination with Cerex Polycrom Clin II solid-phase extraction columns. The authors reported the lower limit of their linear range to be 50 (methamphetamine) and 150ng/mL (amphetamine) with an upper limit of 10,000ng/mL for both analytes. The procedure resulted in average (mean) recovery of 500ng/mL samples of 96.4% and 95.7% for amphetamine and methamphetamine, respectively. Another method using the positive pressure manifold was described by Stout et al. (2002). This method was developed to determine amphetamine, methamphetamine, MDA, MDMA, and MDEA in urine samples. Limits of detection were 62.5ng/mL (amphetamine and MDEA), 15.6ng/mL (methamphetamine), and 31.3ng/mL (MDA and MDMA) with an upper limit of linearity of 5000ng/mL. Recoveries averaged 90% or more for each of the compounds from 2-mL aliquots of the urine samples.

In another interesting use of solid-phase extraction, a procedure was developed extracting drugs from small blood samples or dried blood stains. The investigators were able to analyze for the presence of morphine, codeine, cocaine, benzoylecgonine, methylecgonine, cocaethylene, THC, THC acid metabolite, 11-hydroxy-THC (11-OH-THC), amphetamine, methamphetamine, MDA, MDMA, and MBDB. Samples were extracted using solid-phase extraction columns with detection limits for the amphetamines of 1.62–4.10ng/50µL spot (Schutz et al., 2002).

Most procedures involve extraction, derivatization, and analysis steps that require as long as several hours to complete. Rapid analysis of samples in an emergency situation requires techniques developed for their simplicity and speed. One procedure for the analysis of sympathomimetic amines, including amphetamine, methamphetamine, their methylenedioxy analogs, several pro-drugs, and other related compounds, was described in the context of identification of the analytes in the emergency clinical toxicology setting (Valentine and Middleton, 2000). This procedure evaluated derivatization using trifluoroacetyl, pentafluoropropyl, and heptafluorobutyryl anhydrides. A 0.1-mL sample of urine was extracted using chloroform:isopropanol (9:1) after addition of deuterium-labeled amphetamine and methamphetamine as internal standards and adjustment of pH to 9.1 by addition of borate buffer. The extract was then centrifuged to separate the layers, and the organic phase evaporated under nitrogen after addition of 10% methanolic HCl to minimize evaporative losses. The extract was reconstituted in hexane:heptafluorobutyric anhydride (9:1) followed by injection into a GC-MS. On-column derivatization was accomplished at 260°C in the injection port. Of the derivatizing reagents evaluated, HFBA at 260°C gave the best results. Several of the analytes evaluated in this study did not derivatize (e.g., benzphetamine, deprenyl). For those compounds, 1 mL of sample was used with addition of deuterated diazepam as the internal standard. This simple extraction, derivatization, and analysis procedure took approximately 30 minutes to complete, thus making it a viable procedure for clinical toxicology purposes.

A procedure for analysis of amphetamine in plasma samples using GC-MS has been described (Pizarro et al., 1999). Using a single-step extraction of the drug with *t*-butyl methyl ether from 1 mL of plasma after addition of internal standard, 0.2 mL 0.4M NaOH, and 0.5 mL saturated NaCl solution. The organic phase was evaporated at 40°C under a stream of nitrogen after the addition of 20 µL of *N*-methylbis(trifluoroacetamide) (MBTFA) to minimize evaporative losses. Once dried, the extract was derivatized using 50 µL of MBTFA at 70°C for 20 minutes. The method gave limits of detection and quantitation of 0.43 and 1.42 ng/mL, respectively. The authors noted this method prevented evaporative losses without an additional preparative step, thus saving time for sample analysis.

Analysis of amphetamine, methamphetamine, MDA, MDMA, and MDEA in blood samples has been described by several investigators. One study described the analysis of 1-mL blood samples using 5 mL of diethyl ether to extract the drugs following addition of internal standards (the *d*-5 isotopomers of amphetamine, methamphetamine, MDA, MDMA, MDEA) and 0.5 mL of 1M NaOH. Following extraction, these investigators used isopropanol:HCl (99:1 v/v) to prevent volatilization of the amphetamines during drying, followed by derivatization with HFBA. After derivatization, the mixture was reconstituted in 400µL of hexane and 200µL of water and then vortex mixed and centrifuged and the aqueous phase discarded. Two hundred microliters of 4% ammonium hydroxide was then added, vortex mixed, and centrifuged and the organic phase was injected into the GC-MS. Recoveries of the drugs ranged from approximately 64% to 91%. The procedure gave detection limits of 1 ng/mL for amphetamine, 2 ng/mL for methamphetamine, 8 ng/mL for MDA, 1 ng/mL for MDMA, and 0.5 ng/mL for MDEA, which are lower than previously reported procedures for blood and plasma. Limits of quantitation for the analytes were 10 ng/mL for amphetamine, MDMA, and MDEA, 20 ng/mL for methamphetamine, and 50 ng/mL for MDA. The linear range was shown to be from the limits of quantitation to 1000 ng/mL for each analyte (Marquet et al., 1997).

Extraction of amphetamines from less commonly used biological matrices (sweat, hair, saliva, meconium, etc.), often referred to as *alternative matrices*, have been reported by a number of investigators. Examples of these procedures include several describing the use of sweat as the sample including a description of the analysis of amphetamine and methamphetamine extracted from filter paper or gauze used for the collection of sweat by Suzuki et al. (1989). The extracts were derivatized with trifluoroacetic anhydride and analyzed by GC-MS. Fay et al. (1996) described analysis of sweat using acetate buffer and methanol to elute the drugs from a patch used to collect the sample, followed by addition of sodium carbonate to increase the pH and then extraction with isoamyl alcohol:hexane. The sample was then back-extracted into acid followed by reextraction into 1-chlorobutane. The extracts were then derivatized with carbethoxyhexafluorobutyryl chloride (CB) and analyzed by GC-MS. A procedure has also been described for N-methyl-1-(3,4-methylenedioxyphenyl)-2-butanamine (MBDB) and 3,4-(methylenedioxyphenyl)-2-butanamine (BDB) in urine, saliva, and sweat specimens (Kintz, 1997). Drugs were eluted from sweat patches with methanol followed by GC-MS analysis. The study documented the excretion of drug and metabolite over several days following administration of 100 mg of MBDB. Sweat concentrations of both MBDB and BDB peaked at 36 hours, followed by a decline in their concentration. The concentration of MBDB was higher than BDB in all samples analyzed.

Analysis of drugs in saliva has been described by a number of investigators (Wan et al., 1978; Smith, 1981; Suzuki et al., 1989; Inoue and Seta, 1992; Kintz, 1997; Kidwell et al., 1998; Jenkins, 1999; Mancinelli et al., 1999; Samyn and van Haeren, 2000; Cone et al., 2002; Gentili et al., 2002; Samyn, De Boeck, and Verstraete, 2002; Samyn, De Boeck, Wood et al., 2002; Schepers et al., 2003) and summarized in several reviews (Kintz and Samyn, 1999; Samyn et al., 1999). In a study evaluating the prevalence rate of various drugs of abuse, Cone et al. (2002) evaluated the positive rate seen with saliva samples and compared the rates with those from urine drug testing. The authors concluded that the prevalence rates were similar for each of the drug classes [THC metabolite, opiates (morphine, codeine, and acetylmorphine) and PCP] with the exception of the amphetamines (amphetamine and methamphetamine) and cocaine metabolite. The saliva positive rate for amphetamines was 0.47 compared to general workforce data that showed a rate of 0.29. These data were based on the use of SAMHSA cutoffs for amphetamines in urine and a cutoff of 120ng/mL for the saliva samples based on the manufacturer's recommended cutoff level for saliva. Sample analysis was accomplished using an ELISA assay followed by liquid–liquid extraction, derivatization, and GC-MS-MS. The confirmation assay gave limits of quantitation of 30 and 12ng/mL for amphetamine and methamphetamine, respectively.

A GC-MS procedure for the identification of some of the more recent illicit amphetamine analogs N-methyl-1-(3,4-methylenedioxyphenyl)-2-butanamine (MBDB) and 3,4-(methylenedioxyphenyl)-2-butanamine (BDB) in urine, saliva, and sweat specimens has been described using deuterium-labeled MDEA as the internal standard (Kintz, 1997). Alkaline extraction with ethyl acetate of 1-mL aliquots of urine and saliva were derivatized with heptafluorobutyric anhydride prior to GC-MS analysis. The study documented the excretion of drug and metabolite over several days following administration of 100mg of MBDB. In all cases in all samples, MBDB was present in higher concentrations than BDB. Urine samples were positive for 36 hours, with peak concentration seen at 4 hours. Saliva samples were positive for the first 17 hours, with peak concentration seen at 2 hours. Evaluation of the ratio of amphetamine in plasma and saliva was investigated a number of years ago and shown to be 3.3 times higher in saliva than in plasma (Wan et al., 1978).

Analysis of meconium samples for the presence of amphetamines has been described using homogenization with HCl and liquid–liquid extraction of that supernatant with heptane:methylene chloride:ethylene dichloride:isopropanol (50:17:17:16 v/v/v/v). GC-MS analysis of the derivatized extract gave a detection limit of 1ng/g (Nakamura et al., 1992). Other methods for the analysis of amphetamines have been described and reviewed elsewhere (Franssen et al., 1994; Moriya et al., 1994; Lewis et al., 1995; Moore, C., et al., 1998; Strano-Rossi, 1999). Amphetamine and methamphetamine were extracted from the bone marrow of skeletonized remains using liquid–liquid extraction followed by solid-phase extraction (Kojima et al., 1986). The nature of the material required the combination of liquid–liquid and solid-phase extraction to adequately recover and clean up the sample extract. Following extraction, the trifluoroacetyl derivatives were analyzed by chemical ionization mass spectrometry.

Plasma methamphetamine levels were compared to saliva following 10 and 20mg oral doses of d-methamphetamine. Samples were analyzed by GC-MS following solid phase extraction and collected with 20μL of MTBSTFA + 1% TBDMCS to minimize evaporation during the evaporation of solvent. Derivatization was accomplished with BSTFA + 1% TMCS and analysis on an HP 5973 mass spectrometer. Saliva was collected using three different methods: stimulation with citric acid candy, a Salivette with citric acid, and a neutral Salivette. Results indicated the maximum concentrations were seen with the neutral method for both the 10 and 20mg doses. The authors concluded that there was too much variability between the plasma and saliva concentrations to make saliva a viable substitute for plasma. The authors also noted that, despite its ease of collection and diminished susceptibility of adulteration, saliva had a substantially shorter window of detection when compared to urine samples (Schepers et al., 2003). In a study of 180 drivers who failed field sobriety tests, saliva and sweat samples were compared to plasma findings. Saliva proved to have a positive predictive value of 98%, while sweat showed a positive predictive value of approximately 90%. Values were slightly lower for cocaine and cannabis using saliva, while sweat was comparable for cocaine and amphetamines but lower for cocaine (Samyn, De Boeck, and Verstraete, 2002). In another study using plasma, oral fluid and sweat, Samyn and coworkers (2002) evaluated the levels of MDMA for 5 hours following administration of a 75-mg dose of the drug. The authors found substantial intra- and intersubject variability with saliva; values ranged from 50 to 6982ng/mL MDMA. Saliva concentrations generally exceeded those in plasma, while sweat wipes averaged only 25ng/wipe. Samples were analyzed by LC-MS-MS procedure that required the use of only a 50-μL sample. Another method using LC-MS-MS analysis of saliva for the identification of amphetamines (amphetamine, methamphetamine, MDA, MDMA, and MDEA), as well as opiates (morphine and codeine), cocaine, and benzoylecgonine has been described. The method used 200μL of sample and mixed-mode–solid-phase extraction. The authors employed a gradient of 6% to 67.6% methanol with 10mM ammonium formate (pH 5.0) added to the mobile phase. Electrospray ionization with analysis using a quadrupole-time-of-flight mass spectrometer was used. The limit of detection ranged from 0.22–1.07ng/mL and the limit of quantitation was 2ng/mL for the amphetamines. The authors described an interference from the device used to collect the saliva that caused suppression of ionization and could not be eliminated by extraction. The device was eliminated from the study and saliva samples were collected directly into a tube (Mortier et al., 2002).

Analysis of hair for a variety of drugs and their metabolites, including the amphetamines, has been described in a number of publications. Although hair offers some potentially significant advantages over biological fluids in determining exposure to drugs, the potential for external contamination is a concern raised regarding the analysis of hair samples. This concern raises the question of whether detected drug(s) are from use of the drug or are the result of external contamination of the hair by the drug. Analysis of metabolites rather than the parent drug can help address this concern. In most cases, however, metabolites are much less likely to be incorporated into hair than are the parent drugs. Analysis of drugs in hair generally involves decontamination, some method to break down the hair (hydrolysis, homogenization, etc.), extraction, derivatization, and analysis. Hydrolysis is accomplished using acid, base, or enzymes. Although each of these three hydrolytic methods works, a study that compared these techniques reported alkaline hydrolysis to provide the best recovery (Kintz and Cirimele, 1997).

A reasonably large number of publications have appeared in recent history describing the analysis of amphetamine, methamphetamine, MDA, MDMA, and MDEA in hair using a variety of different analytical techniques (Nagai et al., 1988, 1989; Suzuki et al., 1989; Nakahara et al., 1990, 1991, 1993; Kintz et al., 1992, 1995; Moriya et al., 1992; Kintz and Mangin, 1993; Moeller et al., 1993b; Cirimele et al., 1995; Kikura and Nakahara, 1995b, 1997; Kikura et al., 1997; Miki et al., 1997, 2002; Nakahara and Kikura, 1997; Rohrich and Kauert, 1997; Rothe et al., 1997; Scarcella et al., 1997; Takayama et al., 1997; Uhl, 1997, 2000; Keller et al., 1998; Koide et al., 1998; Sweeney et al., 1998; Tagliaro et al., 1998a, 1998b, 1999; Al-Dirbashi et al., 1999a, 1999b, 2000a; Kimura et al., 1999a; Allen and Oliver, 2000; Cooper et al., 2000; Gaillard et al., 2000; Quintela et al., 2000; Sporkert and Pragst, 2000; Stout et al., 2000; Lachenmeier et al., 2003), along with several reviews (Moeller, 1992, 1996; Moeller et al., 1993a; Nakahara, 1995; Sachs and Kintz, 1998; Brettell et al., 1999; Kintz and Samyn, 1999). Several other papers describe the biology behind the incorporation of drugs in hair and use of the information in a forensic environment (Kikura and Nakahara, 1995a; Nakahara et al., 1995, 1997, 1998; Nakahara and Kikura, 1996; Takayama et al., 1999; Kelly, R.C., et al., 2000; Nakahara and Hanajiri, 2000; Rohrich et al., 2000). The significant number of publications, particularly of new procedures, is indicative of the rapid growth in this area.

Nakahara et al. (1997) evaluated the use of the hair root in determination of acute methamphetamine poisoning. After administration of methamphetamine to five rats, hair was plucked out and washed with detergent and then extracted with methanol:5M HCl (20:1 v/v) at room temperature for 14 hours. Extracts were then evaporated and derivatized with pentafluoropropionic anhydride and analyzed by GC-MS. The study revealed that washing the sample caused a four- to fivefold reduction in the concentration of the drug compared to unwashed samples, thought by the authors to be because the drugs were not yet immobilized in this early stage. The ratio of amphetamine to methamphetamine in the samples was shown to plateau after death, while before death the ratio increased over time. This information suggests the ratio of methamphetamine to its metabolite amphetamine is a viable probe for methamphetamine poisoning.

A GC-MS method for the analysis of amphetamine, methamphetamine, methylenedioxyamphetamine, methylenedioxymethamphetamine, methylenedioxyethylamphetamine, and N-methyl-1-(1,3-benzodioxol-5-yl)-2-butylamine (MBDB) in hair was described by Rothe et al. (1997). Samples were obtained from subjects with a self-reported history of amphetamine or ecstasy use. Samples were digested with 1M NaOH and then extracted with C-18 Bond Elute solid-phase extraction columns. Dried extracts were derivatized with pentafluoropropionic anhydride and quantitated based on deuterium-labeled isotopomers of amphetamine, methamphetamine, MDA, and MDMA. Concentrations seen in the samples were in the following ranges: 0.1–4.8 ng/mg for amphetamine, 0.05–0.89 ng/mg for MDA, 0.1–8.3 ng/mg for MDMA, 0.12–15 ng/mg for MDE, and 0.21–1.3 ng/mg for MBDB. Methamphetamine was not detected in any of the samples tested.

An interesting evaluation of hair samples taken from individuals with subsequent comparison of self-reported use of amphetamines versus laboratory findings was described by Cooper et al. (2000). Approximately 10 mg of hair was ground to a fine powder then treated with β-glucuronidase/aryl sulfatase followed by solid-phase extraction. Extracts were derivatized with pentafluoropropionic anhydride and analyzed by GC-MS for amphetamine, methamphetamine, MDA, MDMA, and MDEA. Of 139 segments analyzed, 77 (52.5%) were positive for at least one of the five amphetamines tested. The authors found no correlation between the reported number of "ecstasy" tablets consumed and the drug levels detected in hair.

In an evaluation of samples taken from athletes during a sporting event for the presence of amphetamines, corticosteroids, and anabolic steroids, Gaillard et al. (2000) collected hair and urine samples to determine drug use. Analysis of amphetamines in hair was accomplished by taking 50 mg of hair and digesting it in 1M NaOH. The digest was then extracted with ethyl acetate, derivatized with trifluoroacetic anhydride, and then analyzed by GC-MS using positive ion chemical ionization. Thirty individuals were sampled, and both hair and urine samples were tested. Ten of 19 hair samples were shown to be positive for amphetamine, while only 6 of 30 urine samples were positive, demonstrating the advantage of hair analysis for detecting drug use for periods longer than revealed by urine testing. Another procedure for the analysis of amphetamine, methamphetamine, MDA, and MDMA in hair involved washing with dichloromethane and warm water followed by alkaline hydrolysis. After liquid–liquid extraction, the extracts were derivatized with pentafluoropropionic anhydride/pentafluoropropanol. Using a 50-mg hair sample, the limits of detection were 0.05 ng/mg for amphetamine, methamphetamine, and MDA and 0.1 ng/mg for MDEA (Kintz et al., 1995).

Comparison of two different derivatizing reagents for the GC-MS analysis of hair samples for amphetamine, methamphetamine, MDA, and MDMA showed that propionic acid anhydride produced more stable derivatives than did trifluoroacetic acid anhydride. The limit of detection for all drugs was approximately 0.01 ng/mg when using 50–100 mg of hair with both derivatives. The authors noted, however, that the trifluoroacetyl derivatives produced more specific mass spectral analysis (Rohrich and Kauert, 1997). Another method for the analysis of hair samples for the presence of MDA, MDMA, and MDEA was conducted using supercritical fluid extraction followed by GC-MS analysis, with mephentermine used as the internal standard (Allen and Oliver, 2000). The authors concluded that this extraction procedure produced accurate and reliable results when evaluating both authentic and spiked hair samples.

A method has been described for analysis of amphetamine and methamphetamine in hair, nails, sweat, and saliva (Suzuki et al., 1989). External contamination was washed from hair and nail samples with water and methanol. The samples were then hydrolyzed with 0.6 M HCl, followed by alkalinization of the sample and extraction with chloroform:isopropanol (3:1 v/v). Sweat and saliva samples were extracted using methanol. The extracts were then derivatized and analyzed by GC-MS. Hair, nail, and sweat samples were all shown to contain both amphetamine and methamphetamine, but only methamphetamine was detected in the saliva.

Uhl described the analysis of hair samples for drugs of abuse using tandem mass spectrometry. GC-MS-MS analysis of hair to determine the presence of drugs such as amphetamine, methamphetamine, MDA, MDMA, MDE, MBDB, methadone and metabolite, THC and THC acid metabolite, cocaine, benzoylecgonine, cocaethylene, dihydrocodeine, codeine, heroin, 6-monoacetylmorphine, morphine, and acetylcodeine is detailed in terms of its utility in the forensic analysis of samples (Uhl, 1997, 2000). Ion mobility spectrometry has been utilized for the analysis of amphetamines in hair by several investigators. Miki et al. (1997) described a semiquantitative method for the analysis of methamphetamine in hair using this method. Hair samples were digested in 5M NaOH (methanol–water, 4:1, v/v) and quantitated using dibenzylamine as the internal standard. Two milligrams of hair was determined sufficient to allow four independent measurements, and the method had a limit of detection of 0.5 ng/mg. Analysis of MDMA and MDEA in hair samples has also been described using ion mobility spectrometry. This method developed for rapid screening of hair samples used trihexylamine as the internal standard (Kikura et al., 2000).

Chiral GC columns are designed to separate enantiomers without the need for chiral derivatization. Although effective, these columns have several drawbacks. Typically, chiral columns are more expensive than the corresponding achiral columns. Additionally, chiral columns tend to degrade more readily than achiral columns at the high temperatures typically encountered in GC procedures and thus must be replaced more frequently. In addition, since they have a specific purpose, they are typically dedicated and not used for general analysis.

Separation of the enantiomers of amphetamines is an important analytical technique that can be very useful in the interpretation of laboratory results. Assessment of enantiomeric composition of the drug used, time since administration, origin of the drug, etc., are all parameters that can be elucidated by knowing the enantiomer composition of the drug in the biological sample. Enantiomer analysis has been described by a number of investigators. One method used the derivatizing reagent (−)-methyl chloroformate (Hughes et al., 1991). Methamphetamine enantiomers were not separated to baseline, and the enantiomers of amphetamine were not separated effectively at all. Although the method provided good quantitative results, its utility was limited by the inability to separate the enantiomers effectively.

The most common chiral derivatizing reagent used with the amphetamines is *N*-trifluoroacetyl-*l*-prolyl chloride (*l*-TPC). *l*-TPC was the first readily available and successful chiral reagent used with the amphetamines and is currently available from a number of different commercial suppliers. For many years, it was the only commercially available chiral reagent, which is in no small part responsible for its widespread use. Related derivatives using the same prolyl imine but increasingly longer perfluoronated side chains have become available, including pentafluoropropionyl-*l*-prolyl chloride (*l*-PPC) and heptafluorobutyryl-*l*-prolyl chloride (*l*-HPC). All three of these reagents have been used with success in a number of laboratories. Derivatization of amphetamines with *l*-TPC can be carried out at room temperature for 15 minutes (Hensley and Cody, 1999), although some investigators carry out the reaction at high temperatures (85–90°C) for 10 minutes (Cooke, 1994). See Figure 7.6 for an example of enantiomeric separation of amphetamine and related compounds using this reagent. *l*-TPC derivatives of amphetamine and methamphetamine can also be formed by coinjection of the drug extract and derivatizing reagent (Fitzgerald et al., 1988). Three microliters of urine extract was drawn into a 10-microliter syringe, followed by 3 microliters of *l*-TPC reagent, and the contents were injected into the injection port at 250°C. The enantiomeric forms of the amphetamine and methamphetamine were readily separated using this method.

A procedure for the analysis of MDMA and its metabolites MDA, 4-hydroxy-3-methoxymethamphetamine, and 4-hydroxy-3-methoxyamphetamine enan-

Figure 7.6

Enantiomeric separation of amphetamine and related compounds. l-*Amphetamine (peak 1),* d-*amphetamine (peak 2),* l-*methamphetamine (peak 3),* d-*methamphetamine (peak 4),* l-*MDA (peak 5),* d-*MDA (peak 6),* l-*MDMA (peak 7),* d-*MDMA (peak 8),* l-*MDEA (peak 9),* d-*MDEA (peak 10)*

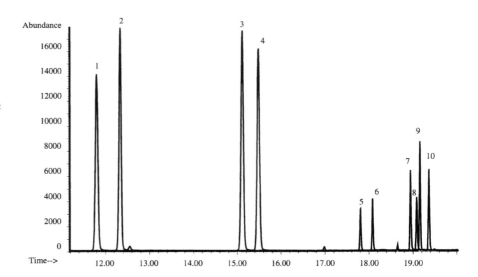

tiomers has been reported using positive ion chemical ionization on a GC coupled to an ion trap mass spectrometer (De Boer et al., 1997). The study also reported the presence of *N*-hydroxy-3,4-methylenedioxymethamphetamine and discussed the possibility of its being a metabolite of MDMA. The procedure evaluated trifluoroacetyl-*l*-prolyl chloride (*l*-TPC), pentafluoropropionyl-*l*-prolyl chloride (*l*-PPC) and heptafluorobutyryl-*l*-prolyl chloride (*l*-HPC) as chiral derivatizing reagents. The authors selected the *l*-HPC of the three because it gave them better chromatographic resolution and shorter retention times as well as the ability to carry out the reaction in aqueous solution. The hydroxy groups were derivatized following the derivatization of the amine group with the *l*-HBC using *N*-methylbis(trifluoroacetamide) (MBTFA) and *N*-methyl-*N*-trimethylsilyltrifluoroacetamide (MSTFA). The MSTFA gave the trimethylsilyl derivative, and the MBTFA yielded the trifluoroacetyl derivative. The authors noted that the trimethylsilyl derivative gave better reproducibility and higher signal than the trifluoroacetyl derivative. Evaluation of electron ionization versus positive ion chemical ionization using isobutane as the reagent gas was also made as part of this study. Because chemical ionization gave greater high-mass information while still maintaining some fragmentation, thus allowing structure elucidation, it was selected as the method of choice.

GC-MS analysis of the enantiomers of amphetamine, methamphetamine, MDA, MDMA, and MDEA using the *l*-TPC derivatives was evaluated using several different GC columns at varying concentrations and proportions of each enantiomer (Hensley and Cody, 1999). Since this procedure was designed to determine the enantiomeric composition of previously identified amphetamine-positive samples, only a single ion was monitored for each analyte. The ions monitored were m/z 237 for amphetamine and MDA, m/z 241 for amphetamine-D5 and MDA-D5, m/z 251 for methamphetamine and MDMA, m/z 255 for methamphetamine-D5 and MDMA-D5, m/z 265 for MDEA, and m/z 270 for MDEA-D5. The method could be used to separate and identify the enantiomers of each of the drug concentrations ranging from 5 to 10,000 ng/mL and enantiomer proportions from 0 to 100% of each enantiomer were tested and gave satisfactory results. All peaks were separated using the DB-1 column, but the d-enantiomers of MDMA and MDEA were not completely resolved using the DB-17. The authors noted that this was not a problem, since the mass spectrometer could selectively monitor the ions for each of these analytes and provide accurate results despite the fact that the peaks overlapped.

Fallon et al. (1999) analyzed urine and plasma samples collected following administration of MDMA (40 mg) to research subjects. Extracts of urine samples were derivatized with $(-)$-α-methoxy-α-(trifluoromethyl)phenylacetyl chloride (MTPA) and analyzed by GC-NPD using a DB-17 column with a temperature program of 50°C for 2 minutes to 250°C at 25°C per minute and then to 290°C at 2°C per minute. Plasma samples were similarly extracted and derivatized and then separated on a DB-1 equivalent (HP ultra 1) column at 100°C for 3 minutes to 285°C at 15°C per minute and held for 5 minutes and analyzed by mass spectrometry. Ions monitored were m/z 119, 139, 162, 189 for amphetamine, m/z 260, 135, 162, 189, 260 for MDA, and m/z 135, 162, 189, 260 for MDMA. Evaluation of the assay at three different concentrations and four different enantiomer ratios showed it produced accurate results at all levels tested. Several other investigators have used chiral prolyl derivatives successfully for enantiomer separation (Matin et al., 1977; Fitzgerald et al., 1989; Hegadoren et al., 1993; Lim et al., 1993; Moore, K.A., et al., 1996c).

The enantiomers of MDMA and its metabolites MDA, 4-hydroxy-3-methoxymethamphetamine (HMMA), and 4-hydroxy-3-methoxyamphetamine (HMA) has been described for plasma and urine samples (Pizarro et al., 2003). The authors used a two step derivatization process with MTPA as the first reagent which derivatized both the amine and —OH groups and serves as the chiral reagent. The derivative was cleaved from the —OH groups using ammonium hydroxide followed by derivatization with hexamethyldisilazane. The authors noted that use of triethylamine was to neutralize the HCl formed during the initial derivatization reaction provided quantitative derivatization resulting in substantial improvement in sensitivity of the method.

Compared to liquid–liquid and solid-phase extraction, solid-phase microextraction (SPME) is a relatively recent entrant into the preparation of samples for the analysis of amphetamines. SPME is a procedure that does not employ solvents, thus combining several steps in the normal process of sample extraction. This innovation allows for the extraction of analytes from biological matrices without the requirement for multistep extraction procedures, with their associated solvent cost and disposal issues, as well as personnel requirements to conduct the extraction. Simple analysis of amphetamines taken from the headspace of a sample has been described by several investigators (Martinez and Gimenez, 1983; Tsuchihashi et al., 1989). These techniques, while effective, were limited because the technique had no ability to concentrate the analytes. SPME, however, does concentrate analytes on the fiber, which allows for significantly lower detection limits.

After initial introduction and description of SPME as a technique (Arthur and Pawliszyn, 1990), several papers described its application to the analysis of amphetamine, methamphetamine, and related compounds (Yashiki et al., 1994, 1995; Centini et al., 1996; Ishii et al., 1996; Koide et al., 1996; Nagasawa et al., 1996; Ugland et al., 1997; Junting et al., 1998; Jurado et al., 2000; Kataoka et al., 2000; Namera et al., 2000; Song et al., 2000; Sporkert and Pragst, 2000; Gentili et al., 2002; Huang et al., 2002). SPME utilizes a fused-silica fiber coated with a sorbent material such as polydimethylsiloxane or polyacrylate. The fibers are exposed to the drugs of interest either by exposure to the headspace above a heated liquid sample or by direct immersion of the fiber into the liquid sample. The headspace method is based on the principle of sampling the vapor layer above a liquid sample that has been heated in a closed container. Many volatile compounds, including the amphetamines, are equilibrated into that space and are detected by sampling of the headspace using one of a number of analytical techniques, most commonly GC or GC-MS. Alternatively, the fiber is immersed directly into the sample itself, thus allowing binding of the compound, whether or not it is volatile at the temperature used in the procedure. Immersion has the shortcoming of binding any compound in the sample that will chemically interact with the fiber. If a compound is volatile, the headspace method allows selective binding only to those compounds that are in the vapor phase, thus limiting potential interference from nonvolatile compounds. SPME has been utilized in the analysis of amphetamines using both the headspace method (Yashiki et al., 1995; Centini et al., 1996; Nagasawa et al., 1996; Jurado et al., 2000; Namera et al., 2000; Song et al., 2000; Sporkert and Pragst, 2000) and direct immersion techniques (Ishii et al., 1996; Koide et al., 1996; Ugland et al., 1997; Kataoka et al., 2000). After sufficient time to allow the analytes of interest to bind to the fiber, it is either inserted into the injection port of a gas chromatograph and thermally desorbed to release the drugs or washed with mobile phase of a liquid chromatograph to afford chromatographic separation.

A method for the analysis of 21 amphetamine-related drugs, including amphetamine, methamphetamine, MDA, MDMA, MDEA, DOM, DOB, benzphetamine, clobenzorex, fenproporex, and mefenorex along with several other related compounds, using SPME followed by GC-MS analysis has been described (Battu et al., 1998). This method gave detection limits of 1–50 ng/mL, depending on the analyte, with a linear range from the detection limit to 500 ng/mL when analyzing for all underivatized analytes. The linear range was increased up to 2000 ng/mL when specific analytes were targeted. The reproducibility of this method was quite variable from one analyte to another, with relative standard deviations ranging from 1.33% for benzphetamine to 27.98% for MDA. Quantitation was based on comparison with deuterated analogs of methamphetamine, MDMA, and MDEA. The parameters described were based on analysis of control samples containing all 21 analytes and three internal standards. Several showed poor performance, most likely due to saturation of the fiber because of the amount of material in the samples. Limiting the number of analytes in the sample, a situation closer to what would be expected in actual unknown samples, improved the linear range and reproducibility of the method.

Another procedure for the analysis of amphetamine, methamphetamine, methylenedioxyamphetamine, and methylenedioxymethamphetamine involved heating 1 mL of urine to 75°C for 30 minutes followed by exposing the fiber to the headspace for 15 minutes. The method was evaluated with samples from 100 to 2000 ng/mL of each analyte and showed the method to be a viable alternative to more traditional techniques of extraction and derivatization (Centini et al., 1996). Another method using headspace SPME followed by analysis with GC flame ionization detection and GC-MS using chemical ionization has been described. The SPME fiber was exposed to the headspace of urine samples heated at 80°C for 5 minutes. This procedure yielded a linear range of 200–100,000 ng/mL. The detection limit was 100 ng/mL using deuterated methamphetamine as the internal standard, reportedly 20 times more sensitive than headspace alone without the concentrating power of SPME (Yashiki et al., 1995). Another method for SPME from urine involved addition of deuterated amphetamine as the internal standard followed by heating the sample for 10 minutes at 100°C, after which the fiber was inserted into the headspace of the vial for an additional 10 minutes (Jurado et al., 2000). The drugs were then derivatized by inserting the fiber into another vial containing trifluoroacetic anhydride at 60°C for 20 minutes followed by desorption in the injection port of the GC-MS system for 5 minutes. Quantitation limits using this method were 10 ng/mL for amphetamine and methamphetamine and 20 ng/mL for methylenedioxyamphetamine and methylenedioxymethamphetamine. The linear range for all four compounds was from 50 to 1000 ng/mL. The authors also evaluated direct immersion of the fiber into the urine sample. This gave comparable results to those seen with the headspace method; however, there were more compounds extracted using the immersion technique, opening that procedure to the potential for more interference. This method gave recoveries for all four drugs of interest of at least 71%. The elevated temperature used (100°C) with the urine sample in the SPME process was determined to be necessary for high recovery of the methylenedioxy analogs. Amphetamine and methamphetamine showed high recovery from urine at a much lower temperature (70°C).

Another method using SPME for analysis of amphetamine, methamphetamine, MDA, MDMA, and MDEA described the analysis of the underivatized drugs as well as results following derivatization with propylchloroformate or butylchloroformate (Ugland et al., 1999). Urine samples were placed into an autosampler vial, followed by addition of methoxyphenamine as the internal standard. Derivatization was accomplished by addition of derivatizing reagent to the sample, and SPME was accomplished by immersion of the fiber into the sample for 16 minutes. Results of these analyses showed that propylchloroformate completely derivatized the analytes under the conditions used, while the derivatization of MDA and MDEA was incomplete using the butylchloroformate. Using the propylchloroformate derivative, the detection limit ($S:N = 3:1$) was determined to be 5ng/mL for methamphetamine, MDMA, and MDEA and 15ng/mL for amphetamine and MDA. Linear ranges for all drugs were from 100 to 10,000ng/mL. Samples were analyzed by GC with NPD and mass spectrometry in both the electron ionization and chemical ionization modes. Chemical ionization was suggested as an option to compensate for the relatively low abundance of molecular ion in the electron ionization spectrum and the potential for interference and perhaps even the misidentification of a compound as a result. Another group, using immersion SPME, evaluated the analysis of amphetamine and methamphetamine from urine following addition of methoxyphenamine as an internal standard (Ugland et al., 1997). These authors evaluated the derivatization of the drugs with methylchloroformate, propylchloroformate, and butylchloroformate and showed that 2, 4, or 16μL of these reagents, respectively, were sufficient to completely derivatize the drugs within 1 minute. Analysis of the derivatives on a methylsilicone GC column (HP-1, 12m × 0.2-mm i.d.) showed that the retention times, as expected, increased with the increasing size of the derivatizing reagent. Amphetamine and methamphetamine were successfully separated from each other and from potentially interfering endogenous compounds when derivatized with the propylchloroformate and butylchloroformate but not with methylchloroformate. These authors also reported the detection limit ($S:N = 3:1$) for both drugs to be 50ng/mL. Quantitative analysis of amphetamine and methamphetamine with the propylchloroformate and butylchloroformate derivatives showed the amphetamine results to be more variable than was seen with methamphetamine, regardless of the derivative used. This was assumed to be reflective of the greater variability in extraction of amphetamine from the sample rather than an association with the derivative or derivatization process. A headspace SPME method is described for the analysis of a variety of drugs, including many lipophilic basic drugs such as nicotine, amphetamine derivatives, local anesthetics, phencyclidine, ketamine, methadone, diphenhydramine, tramadol, tricyclic antidepressants, and phenothiazines has been described for use with hair samples (Sporkert and Pragst, 2000). This method used 4% sodium hydroxide with excess sodium sulfate and a suitable internal standard as a one-step method for the measurement of these drugs. Detection limits were between 0.05 and 1.0 ng/mg with this method.

Several other methods have been described for the isolation of amphetamine and methamphetamine from whole blood. One of these methods employed a polydimethylsiloxane fiber in the headspace above the 0.5-mL sample of whole blood at 80°C for a period of 5 minutes. This showed a limit of detection of 10 ng/mL and a linear range from 10 to 200 ng/mL (Nagasawa et al., 1996). Another headspace SPME method for isolation of amphetamine, methamphetamine, and fenfluramine from 0.5 g of blood involved heating the sample to 70°C following addition of deuterated methamphetamine as the internal standard. The fiber was inserted into the headspace for 15 minutes to allow adsorption of the drugs. The derivatizing reagent, heptafluorobutyric anhydride, was then injected into the injection port, followed by insertion of the SPME fiber. This procedure allowed simultaneous desorption and derivatization of the analytes in the injection port (Namera et al., 2000). Another SPME method for analysis of amphetamine and methamphetamine involved vaporphase derivatization with heptafluorobutyric anhydride using a device holding six μL of 20% heptafluorobutyric anhydride in ethyl acetate (Song et al., 2000). This procedure used serum samples (3 mL) that were first diluted 1:3 with water and buffer, followed by exposure of the fiber for 40 minutes. GC-MS analysis was accomplished in both electron ionization and positive ion chemical ionization modes. Detection limits ($S{:}N = 3{:}1$) using deuterated methamphetamine as the internal standard were 0.6 and 0.4 ng/mL for amphetamine and methamphetamine, respectively, when analyzed underivatized and 0.08 and 0.05 ng/mL, respectively, when derivatized. The linear range for this procedure was reported to be 0.5–200 ng/mL. SPME of amphetamine and methamphetamine has also been reported from hair (Koide et al., 1996). Following base hydrolysis of the hair, the SPME fiber was immersed directly into the sample. The method showed linearity from 4 to 200 ng/mg. Gentili et al. (2002) described a headspace solid-phase microextraction GC-MS procedure for the analysis of MDA, MDMA, MDEA, and MBDB in hair samples. The method gave limits of detection of 0.7 ng/mg and limits of quantitation of 1.90 ng/mg for each of the analytes. The authors also suggested the procedure would be viable for the screening of samples for other substances (amphetamine, methamphetamine, ketamine, ephedrine, nicotine, phencyclidine, methadone) in hair and other biological matrices such as saliva, urine, and blood.

Although the technique requires little analyst intervention, the time for analysis of each sample would limit current methods in high-volume laboratories. Advances in this methodology and related technology and automation in the future promise to enhance the utility of SPME as an analytical tool. Several other procedures have been reported for the SPME of amphetamines (Yashiki et al., 1995; Centini et al., 1996; Ishii et al., 1996; Benko et al., 1998).

A related technique called solid-phase dynamic extraction (SPDE) addresses some of the issues raised regarding SPME. Automated headspace solid-phase dynamic extraction is a solventless extraction method utilizing a hollow needle with an internal coating of polydimethylsiloxane which is used to extract and pre-concentrate the analytes of interest. In this case, the headspace is passed through the needle by repeated aspirate/dispense cycles, thus allowing the adsorption of analytes onto the stationary phase rather than just passive exposure of the sorbent to the headspace as with SPME. As a result, analyte adsorption occurs more rapidly, thus saving time in the overall process. Following adsorption, the needle is then placed into the injection port where it was rapidly heated to desorb the derivatized analytes from the needle. Lachenmeier et al. (2003) described the use of this procedure for the analysis of methadone, the trimethylsilyl derivatives of cannabinoids and the trifluoroacetyl derivatives of amphetamines (amphetamine, methamphetamine, MDA, MDMA, MDEA, MBDB, and BDB) using GC-MS-MS. The authors reported the method to be linear from 0.1–20ng/mg with limits of detection ranging from 6 to 52pg/mg for each of the analytes. The signal-to-noise ratio gain by using MS-MS ranged 8–35 times more than obtained from single stage MS. SPDE was also reported for the analysis of amphetamine, methamphetamine, MDA, MDMA, MDEA, MBDB, and BDB in hair samples using GC-MS (Musshoff et al., 2002). In their procedure, the analytes were derivatized by placing the needle into the headspace of a second vial containing N-methyl-bis(trifluoroacetamide) after the analytes were sorbed onto the needle. The authors reported the method was linear from 0.1–20ng/mg with limits of detection ranging from 0.03–0.19ng/mg for each of the analytes.

6.4.2 LIQUID CHROMATOGRAPHY/MASS SPECTROMETRY

The analysis of amphetamines using GC and GC-MS is far more common in the United States than use of liquid chromatographic methods. Recently, the use of liquid chromatography has expanded dramatically, particularly with the advent of less expensive instrumentation and easy-to-use computers. Interfaces that allow ionization of column effluent at atmospheric pressure have also opened the possibility of widespread use of mass spectrometry as a detector with liquid chromatographic systems. Analysis of amphetamines using liquid chromatography refers here to high-performance liquid chromatography (HPLC), an analytical tool used for analysis of many compounds, ranging from small molecules such as the amphetamines to large biomolecules such as intact proteins and nucleic acids. HPLC methods employ a wide variety of detectors, each using different chemical principles imparting varying degrees of specificity. Among the detectors commonly used with HPLC are ultraviolet (UV) at single or multiple wavelengths, photodiode array (PDA), fluorescence, electrochemical (EC) and mass spectrometers (MS) using several different ionization techniques. Each of these detectors has its advantages and limitations.

Although a number of methods have been described for the analysis of amphetamines by HPLC without derivatization, amphetamines are not strong UV absorbers and have no native fluorescence. They are also not strongly electronegative and therefore do not lend themselves to electrochemical detection. As a result, these detectors are of limited use. Despite these limitations, a number of successful procedures have been described on the analysis of amphetamines using HPLC without derivatization (Garrett et al., 1991; Hartley et al., 1993; Michel et al., 1993; Helmlin et al., 1996; Katagi et al., 1996; Bogusz et al., 1997; Li et al., 1997). Although these are viable methods, because of low absorbances, detection of low concentrations is often difficult. Derviatization does enhance the chromatographic behavior of the amphetamines, although they typically demonstrate better chromatographic behavior in HPLC than they do on GC. In addition, sensitivity can also be greatly increased when using a derivatizing reagent. Amphetamines exhibit their own, albeit weak, UV absorbance that can be used for their detection. Derivatives are available, however, that impart stronger UV absorbance, thus increasing the signal, which increases the ability to detect the compounds. Other derivatives can be used to impart fluorescent or electrochemical characteristics that provide a strong signal with the appropriate detector.

A method has been described for the analysis of MDA, MDMA, MDEA, and N-methyl-benzodioxazolylbutanamine (MBDB) from urine, serum, saliva, and powdered samples using HPLC with fluorescence detection (Mancinelli et al., 1999). The method did not employ extraction of the analytes from the sample. Instead, the samples (100 μL) were diluted with 900 μL "reagent 1" (Cat. No. ECT-LC0050; Bracco, Milan, Italy) and vortex mixed, and 50 μL were injected into the HPLC. Samples with drug concentrations of less than 50 ng/mL were analyzed without dilution. The analytical column (LiChrocart-LiCrospher 100 RP-18; 250 × 4 mm; Merck) was protected by a guard column (LiChrocart-

LiCrospher 100 RP-18; 4×4 mm), which was changed every 30 injections when using undiluted samples and every 50 injections when using diluted samples. Fluorescence detection was accomplished at an excitation wavelength of 290 nm, and emission was monitored at 320 nm. Detection limits were 10 ng/mL using sample dilution and 2 ng/mL without dilution. The method was shown to be linear to 10,000 ng/mL using standard solutions but only to 1000 ng/mL in biological matrices. Because there was no extraction, recovery of the method was excellent, with the lowest reported as 97%. The relative standard deviations were 5% and 8%, respectively, for within-run and between-run for all analytes. Solid tablets were analyzed for MBDB by first pulverizing the tablets and adding the powder to 1 mL of methanol. An aliquot of this was diluted with water to 10^{-6} and injected into the HPLC. Quantitation was accomplished by comparing peak areas of unknowns against three-point calibration curves made at 250, 500, and 1000 ng/mL in water, urine, serum, and saliva. Related compounds, 4-bromo-2,5-dimethoxyamphetamine, 4-bromo-2,5-dimethoxy-β-phenethylamine, and 2,5-dimethoxy-4-methylamphetamine, were not tested by this method since these drugs do not exhibit native fluorescence and are therefore undetectable. Another procedure for the analysis of amphetamine and methamphetamine using HPLC with fluorescence detection has been described (Al-Dirbashi et al., 2000b). This procedure improved on a method previously described by the same authors (Al-Dirbashi et al., 1998b) by scaling the procedure down to use a semi-micro HPLC column (250×1.5-mm i.d.; Capsell Pak C18 UG 120 S5; Shiseido) for quantitation and a Chiralcel OD-RH column (150×2-mm i.d.; Diacel) for analysis of amphetamine and methamphetamine enantiomers.

Another method using fluorescence detection of MDMA and MDEA and their metabolites 3-hydroxy-4-methoxymethylamphetamine (HMMA) and 3-hydroxy-4-methoxyethylamphetamine (HMEA) was used to study enantioselective metabolism. The procedure described the analysis from blood, urine, and brain following solid-phase extraction of the samples. Samples were hydrolyzed with β-glucuronidase/arylsulfatase and protein precipitated using 1 mL of polyethylene glycol (PEG 6000). Because of the use of fluorescence detection, internal standards that gave a different retention time from the analyte of interest were required. In this case, *N*-propyl-3,4-methylenedioxyphenethylamine and *N*-ethyl-3,4-methylenedioxybenzylamine were used as internal standards. The mobile phase was 20 mM phosphate buffer, 50 mM sodium EDTA, and 8% methanol (MDMA) or 7% isopropanol (MDEA) at a flow rate of 0.7 mL/minute. Fluorescence was measured with an emission wavelength of 322 nm and extinction wavelength of 286 nm (Meyer, A. et al., 2002).

Another HPLC method for the identification of amphetamines, including amphetamine, methamphetamine, MDA, MDMA, MDEA, ephedrine, and phenylpropanolamine, used dimethylamine as internal standard (Talwar et al., 1999). This procedure employed precolumn derivatization with sodium napthaquinone-4-sulphonate. Detection of the compounds was based on monitoring in the UV at 260nm and in the visible at 450nm. Each of the analytes absorbed at both wavelengths and each exhibited a different ratio between the two absorbances, thus adding confidence to the identification of the compounds of interest. Quantitation was accomplished with the internal standard method using the absorbance at 450nm. While the absorbance at 260 was twice the intensity as was seen at 450nm, it was deemed to be less specific. Detection limits using 450-nm absorbances were 90ng/mL for methamphetamine, 105ng/mL for amphetamine, 120ng/mL for MDMA, and MDEA, and 135ng/mL for MDA. Quantitation limits were 210ng/mL for methamphetamine, 230ng/mL for amphetamine, 250ng/mL for MDMA, 270ng/mL for MDEA, and 330ng/mL for MDA. The limit of quantitation was defined as the concentration of analyte that gave a signal-to-noise ratio of 10. Identification of the drugs was based on the ratio of absorbances as compared to the average ratio obtained from analysis of controls containing the drugs at known concentrations. The criteria for identification of a compound required the ratio of an unknown sample be within two standard deviations of the ratio of the controls. The authors noted this method to be more specific and sensitive than thin-layer chromatography as a confirmation method for immunoassay positive samples. The viability of the assay is, however, dependent on the level of sensitivity of the assay. Using a cutoff concentration of 500ng/mL, assuming the need for control samples at lower concentrations, the method is adequate. At lower concentrations, however, the method may not have adequate sensitivity using the 450-nm wavelength.

Santagati et al. (2002) described an HPLC method for the analysis of amphetamine and 4-hydroxynorephedrine. The method used electrochemical detection of the 2,5-dihydroxybenzaldehyde derivatives of the analytes on a borohydride exchange resin. The analysis was performed on a 5-micron Hypersil ODS RP-18, 15CM reversed phase column, using a methanol-sodium phosphate buffer (50mM, pH 5.5) (30:70 v/v) containing triethylamine (0.5% v/v) mobile phase with the electrode set to an oxidation potential of +0.6V. The assay proved linear from 10–40nm/mL.

A method describing the analysis of amphetamine, methamphetamine, MDA, MDMA, MDEA, and eight other sympathomimetic amines by HPLC utilized UV at 250nm, photodiode array, and atmospheric pressure chemical ionization (APCI) for detection of the analytes (Bogusz et al., 1997). The method produced viable results with each of the detection techniques, although the detection limits were substantially lower using selected ion monitoring APCI, which gave limits of detection of 1ng/mL for methamphetamine, MDMA, and MDEA and 5ng/mL for amphetamine and MDA, compared to levels ranging from 50 to 100ng/mL using single-wavelength UV and 10–30ng/mL with PDA.

Fitzgerald et al. (1999) described use of a REMEDi HS (Bio-Rad Diagnostics) coupled with an ion trap mass spectrometer using an electrospray interface. The ion trap had the capability of MS-MS analysis. The REMEDi has the advantage of having a series of columns built, which allows injection of samples directly into the system. Seventeen different basic drugs were evaluated using this system without any evidence of interference. The method was used for qualitative analysis, with the exception of benzoylecgonine, which was evaluated quantitatively. Another study used the REMEDi system to analyze amphetamine and related compounds (Felscher and Schulz, 2000). This study compared the results of the analysis of amphetamine, methamphetamine, MDMA, MDA, MDE, MBDB (N-methyl-1-(3,4-methylenedioxyphenyl)-2-butanamine), BDB (3,4-(methylenedioxyphenyl)-2-butanamine), PMA (4-methoxyamphetamine), DOM (2,5-dimethyloxy-4-methylamphetamine), DOB (4-bromo-2,5-dimethyloxyamphetamine), amphetaminil, pholedrine, fenfluramine, and amfepramone. The REMEDi assay gave detection limits of 100ng/mL for all except d,l-methamphetamine (500ng/mL), MDMA and BDB (300ng/mL), and fenfluramine (200ng/mL). These are contrasted to substantially higher levels required for the Triage and, for most analytes, the FPIA assays. Another method using tandem mass spectrometry for the analysis of drugs from urine and serum was described by Weinmann and Svoboda (1998). The procedure used solid phase extraction of the samples and direct injection of the extract into the LC-MS without a column to separate the analytes. MS-MS capability was used to isolate parent ions of the drugs of interest and their deuterated analogues. After isolation of the ions at a single m/z the ions were collisionally dissociated to produce product ions to provide increased confidence in the identification. This process is very selective and sensitive with applicability to a wide variety of analytes. Eliminating the chromatography significantly decreases the analysis time. Another method using tandem mass spectrometry for the analysis of drugs from urine and serum was described by Weinmann and Svoboda (1998). The procedure used solid-phase extraction of the samples and direct injection of the extract into the LC-MS without a column to separate the analytes. MS-MS capability was used to isolate parent ions of the drugs of interest and their deuterated analogs. After isolation of the ions at a single m/z, the ions were collisionally dissociated to produce product ions to provide increased confidence in the identification. This process is very selective and sensitive, with applicability to a wide variety of analytes. Eliminating the chromatography significantly decreases the analysis time.

Analysis of amphetamines in hair using liquid chromatography has been described by a number of investigators. One method used HPLC with fluorescence detection to assay segmented hair for amphetamine and methamphetamine. The hair samples were extracted into acidified methanol and derivatized with 4-(4,5-diphenyl-1*H*-imidazol-2-yl)benzoyl chloride. Chromatography was accomplished using TRIS buffer (pH 7.0):methanol (30:70 v/v) through a C-18 column (250 × 4.5-mm i.d.) at 35°C and fluorescence detection using an excitation wavelength of 330nm and an emission wavelength of 440nm. The method had detection limits ($S:N = 3:1$) of 51.4 and 74.6pg/mg of hair for amphetamine and methamphetamine, respectively (Al-Dirbashi et al., 1999a). HPLC with fluorescence detection was used in another procedure for the analysis of MDA, MDMA, and MDEA in hair (Tagliaro et al., 1999). Hair samples (100mg) were incubated overnight in 1ml of 0.25M HCl at 45°C. After extraction, the dried extract was reconstituted in 500μL of 0.05M phosphate buffer (pH 5.2) and injected into a poly(styrene-divinylbenzene) column (250 × 4.6-mm i.d.) and chromatographed with a mobile phase of 0.1M potassium phosphate (pH 3):acetonitrile (82:18 v/v). Fluorometric detection was accomplished with an excitation wavelength of 285nm and emission at 320nm. Total run time was approximately 30 minutes. The limit of detection ($S:N = 5:1$) was less than 1ng/mL, allowing a cutoff of 0.1ng/mg in the hair. Relative standard deviations were 1–3% at low concentrations but decreased to 0.52–0.88% at concentrations of 10–100ng/mL. Potential interference was evaluated using nearly 100 samples, and none was detected in any of the samples.

Amphetamine and methamphetamine were detected in hair by an HPLC method using chemiluminescence detection (Takayama et al., 1997). The method described the use of a single human hair sample that was washed with water and methanol, cut into pieces and extracted with ultrasonication in a methanol and hydrochloric acid solution for 1 hour, and then allowed to stand at room temperature overnight. After evaporation, 0.1mL of carbonate buffer and 0.1mL of dansyl chloride solution were added and the solution heated at 45°C for 1 hour, followed by injection into the HPLC. The postcolumn reagents bis(2,4,6-trichlorophenyl)oxalate and hydrogen peroxide were used for detection. The detection limit was approximately 2pg/20μL injected and about 20pg in a single hair sample, which represents lower levels than seen with GC-MS analysis.

A method to analyze the methylenedioxy analogs MDA, MDMA, and MDEA in blood, serum, urine, and vitreous humor using HPLC with fluorescence detection of the underivatized compounds has been described. The method also used liquid chromatography–quadrupole orthogonal acceleration time-of-flight mass spectrometry–mass spectrometry to analyze the samples. The authors synthesized an MDMA analog, methylenedioxymethylpropylamphetamine (MDMPA), to use as an internal standard. This compound was selected because it was chromatographically separated from the other analytes, a requirement for use with fluorescence detection. Another important factor in its selection was its unique structure. The authors noted that poorly conducted illicit synthesis of the methylenedioxy analogs might produce the monopropyl, monobutyl, dimethyl, or diethyl forms of MDA, thus making their use as an internal standard potentially problematic. Deuterated isotopomers could be used for quantitative analysis using mass spectral analysis but not with fluorescence detection. The procedure involved extraction of 250 µL of sample by addition of 1 mL of water and internal standard and pH adjustment to 9.5 with carbonate buffer. Hexane:ethyl acetate (7:3 v/v) was used to extract the drugs, and the organic phase was evaporated after addition of 50 µL of methanolic HCl to prevent evaporative losses. The dried extract was reconstituted in mobile phase (100 µL for blood, serum, and vitreous humor, 250 µL for urine) and injected into the liquid chromatograph. Detection was accomplished using fluorescence and mass spectral analysis. The procedure used a gradient elution through a Hypercil BDS C-18 column (100×2.1 mm; Alltech), giving retention times of 13.1–17.1 for the drugs and internal standard. The methylenedioxy amphetamines have natural fluorescence, which was monitored with excitation at 288 nm and emission at 324 nm. Electrospray ionization mass spectral analysis showed $M + H^+$ ions at 180.1, 194.1, 208.1, and 236.1 for MDA, MDMA, MDEA, and MDMPA, respectively. Collisionally induced product ion spectra showed a single fragment ion at m/z 163.1 in each of these spectra. The assay was linear over the range of 2–1000 ng/mL for blood, serum, and vitreous humor and 0.1–5.0 µg/mL for urine. Relative standard deviations across the linear range for all analytes ranged from 2.5% to 19%, with the greatest variability seen at 2 ng/mL with blood, serum, and vitreous humor. Higher drug concentrations showed much lower variability. The detection limits for the assay were 0.8 ng/mL for each of the analytes in blood, serum, and vitreous humor and 2.5 ng/mL in urine. The quantitation limit was defined as the lowest concentration on the calibration curves (2 ng/mL for each of the analytes with blood, serum, and vitreous humor and 0.1 µg/mL in urine).

Chiral analysis of amphetamines using liquid chromatography has been described by a number of investigators. Various derivatives have been used for the analysis, including precolumn derivatization using Marfey's reagent (1-fluoro-2,4-dinitrophenyl-5-l-aniline amide) with fluorescence detection (Foster et al., 1998). Results using this derivative were compared with (−)-1-(9-fluorenyl)ethyl chloroformate (FLEC) and both were determined to produce comparable results. Other procedures utilizing derivatized amphetamines include (−)-α-methoxy-α-(trifluoromethyl)phenylacetyl chloride (MTPA) (Miller et al., 1984; Shin and Donike, 1996; Fallon et al., 1999), R-(+)-1-phenylethylisocyanate (PEIC), 2,3,4-tri-O-acetyl-α-d-arabinopyranosyl isothiocyanate (AITC) (Miller et al., 1984), 2,3,4,6-tetra-O-acetyl-β-d-glucopyranosyl isothiocyanate (GITC) (Miller et al., 1984; Noggle and Clark, 1986), 4-nitrophenylsulfonyl-l-prolyl chloride (NPSP) (Barksdale and Clark, 1985), (−)-1-(9-fluorenyl)ethyl chloroformate (FLEC) (Bourque and Krull, 1994; Hutchaleelaha et al., 1994; La Croix et al., 1994; Sukbuntherng et al., 1995; Herraez-Hernandez et al., 1996; Foster et al., 1998), 4-(4,5-diphenyl-1H-imidazol-2-yl)benzoyl chloride (DIB-Cl) (Al-Dirbashi et al., 1998a, 1998b, 1999a, 1999b, 2000a), and fluorenylmethyl-chloroformate-l-prolyl chloride (FMOC) (Gao and Krull, 1989). Enantiomeric separation has also been accomplished by using o-phthaldialdehyde and an optically active thiol (Spahn-Langguth et al., 1992; Desai and Gal, 1993). Three different derivatives (1,2-naphthoquinone-4-sulfonate, o-phthaldialdehyde, and 9-fluorenylmethyl chloroformate) were evaluated using precolumn derivatization and column switching. The derivatization was accomplished in a precolumn packed with unmodified ODS stationary phase into which the derivatives were injected, followed by separation of the derivatized analytes on an analytical column (Herraez-Hernandez et al., 1996).

The chiral derivative 4-(4,5-diphenyl-1H-imidazol-2-yl)benzoyl chloride (DIB-Cl) was used for the separation of enantiomers of amphetamine, methamphetamine, and 4-hydroxymethamphetamine. The extract was derivatized for 10 minutes at room temperature, followed by chromatography through an ODS column and fluorescence detection with excitation at 330nm and emission at 440nm. The detection capability of the assay was at least comparable to, and in some cases better than, most published procedures, owing to the strong fluorescent properties of this derivative. The same investigators evaluated a chiral column (Chiralcel OD-R) to separate the enantiomers but found it to be inferior to derivatization because it was not able to separate the d-enantiomers of amphetamine and methamphetamine (Al-Dirbashi et al., 1998a, 1998b).

Enantiomer analysis of amphetamine, methamphetamine, and p-hydroxymethamphetamine using both HPLC and LC-MS has been described. The procedure used solid-phase extraction of urine samples followed by chromatography on a beta-cyclodextrin phenylcarbamate-bonded silica column. The mobile phase used for HPLC analysis was acetonitrile:methanol:50mM potassium phosphate buffer (10:30:60 v/v/v) at a flow rate of 1mL per minute. Detection limits were 50ng/mL for d-amphetamine, l-amphetamine, and d-methamphetamine enantiomers and 100ng/mL for l-methamphetamine. The linear range of the assay was 200–20,000ng/mL, with relative standard deviations of less than 2.5% at 2000ng/mL for each analyte. The mobile phase used for thermospray LC-MS analysis was acetonitrile:methanol:100mM ammonium acetate (10:30:60 v/v/v). The detection limits for this assay were 10–20ng/mL using full-scan mode and 0.5–1ng/mL using selected ion monitoring, substantially more sensitive than the HPLC method (Katagi et al., 1996).

The advent of LC/MS/MS with its ability to handle samples with a minimum of processing before analysis was described as an alternative for immunoassay screening. Although immunoassays are relatively rapid and inexpensive, they require different reagents for each drug class and the availability for some drug classes is limited and often within a class, no differentiation of the specific analytes can be made. One study evaluated the use of LC/MS/MS for the screening of samples for amphetamines. The procedure was compared with the Roche Online Amphetamines immunoassay with GC/MS confirmation. The LC/MS/MS procedure was able to identify nearly four times as many samples as containing MDMA and MDA as was the immunoassay, leading the authors to suggest the procedure could be used as an alternative to immunoassays in drugs-of-abuse screening (Nordgren and Beck, 2003).

Several studies have described the use of HPLC to analyze the enantiomers of amphetamine and methamphetamine in hair samples. One group (Nagai et al., 1988) described the separation of amphetamine and methamphetamine enantiomers at various concentrations and enantiomer proportions and with different column conditions. The authors reported that chromatography at 40°C produced optimal separation of the analytes. The relative standard deviations seen using this method were less than 4% (1000ng of *d,l*-methamphetamine and *d,l*-amphetamine added to five hair samples). Analysis of several authentic hair samples from drug users by these investigators revealed only the *d*-enantiomer was present. More recently, another group (Al-Dirbashi et al., 1999b) used HPLC with fluorescence detection after derivatization with 4-(4,5-diphenyl-1*H*-imidazol-2-yl)-benzoyl chloride for enantiomer determination of amphetamine, methamphetamine, and the metabolite 4-hydroxymethamphetamine in hair and urine samples. The HPLC method was compared with an established GC-NPD method and showed reasonably good correlation ($r = 0.901$). Another study described the analysis of amphetamine and methamphetamine from samples of a single hair, including separation of the drug enantiomers (Al-Dirbashi et al., 2000a). The procedure described for quantitative analysis involved extraction of the drugs into 5% trifluoroacetic acid in methanol followed by derivatization with 4-(4,5-diphenyl-1*H*-imidazol-2-yl)-benzoyl chloride to impart strong fluorescence properties.

Chromatography was with a C-18 column (250 × 1.5-mm i.d.) and was able to easily resolve the compounds from each other and potential interference. Enantiomer separation was accomplished using an OD-RH column (150 × 2-mm i.d.), which readily separated the drug enantiomers from each other.

Within-run and between-run relative standard deviations for both methods were less than 9%. Detection limits ($S:N = 3:1$) were in the range of 1.0–4.7 fmol/5 µL injection for both methods; however, the achiral method was the more sensitive of the two. These low detection limits allowed accurate analysis of only a single strand of hair. These authors reported analysis of enantiomers from samples obtained from abusers and found all to contain only the *d*-enantiomer.

Direct enantiomer separation has been reported by a number of investigators. Aboul-Enein and Serignese described a direct, isocratic method, the enantiomeric resolution of cathinone, amphetamine, norephedrine, and norphenylephrine on an S-18-crown-6-ether chiral stationary phase (Aboul-Enein and Serignese, 1997). Use of chiralcel OB and chiralcel OJ columns in series was used by Nagai and Kamiyama (1991) for the enantiomeric separation of amphetamine, methamphetamine, and hydroxy metabolites of samples of the drug confiscated on the street and from the urine of users. Using the combination of l-TPC and a chiral column (N-3,5-(dinitrobenzoyl)phenylglycine) to separate the enantiomers of amphetamine and methamphetamine proved unsuccessful, in that the *d*- and *l*-enantiomers of methamphetamine were not completely separated by this method (Hayes et al., 1987). Another method for the analysis of enantiomers of amphetamine and methamphetamine in hair samples of abusers of confiscated drug material used two chiral columns (Chiralcel OB and Chiralcel OJ) connected in series. The drugs were extracted and their acetyl derivatives chromatographed at 50°C using hexane:isopropanol (9:1, v/v) as the mobile phase, with monitoring at 220 nm. Other direct separation methods have also been described (Nagai and Kamiyama, 1990; Nagai et al., 1995; Makino et al., 1999).

Polarimetry has also been used to study the stereoselective disposition of MDA, MDMA, and MDEA. In this case, HPLC with UV detection was used to identify the analytes, and polarimetry was used to discern the optically active forms of these drugs by monitoring the rotation of light (Matsushima et al., 1998a). This simple method requires only the availability of the detector, since the optical activity of the compounds is an inherent chemical property and requires no special column or derivatization.

Although most solid-phase microextraction (SPME) procedures are used to prepare samples for GC analysis, a procedure for the analysis of amphetamine, methamphetamine, and their methylenedioxy analogs MDA, MDMA and MDEA using SPME followed by LC-MS analysis has been described (Kataoka et al., 2000). This procedure used the direct immersion of the open tubular fiber into the sample, with 15 cycles of drawing 15 µL of the sample matrix into the capillary followed by ejection of the sample. Desorption of the analytes in this case was accomplished by the mobile phase. This method resulted in linear ranges of 2–100 ng/mL for each of the analytes and recoveries of greater than 81%, allowing detection limits ($S:N = 3:1$) ranging from 0.38 to 0.82 ng/mL using electrospray mass spectral analysis. Methamphetamine was used as the prototype basic drug in an examination of SPME and its application to gas chromatography, capillary electrophoresis, and HPLC (Rasmussen et al., 2000). These investigators found that a two-phase system worked well for preparation of samples for GC analysis and a three-phase system worked well with capillary electrophoresis and HPLC with detection limits ($S:N = 2:1$) of 2 ng/mL of plasma using GC, 3 ng/mL using capillary electrophoresis, and 700 pg/mL with HPLC. Detectors used in this study were NPD for the GC, UV at 200 nm, and fluorescence (excitation 249 nm; emission 302 nm) detection for the HPLC.

Capillary electrophoresis as a separation technique has grown significantly over the past few years, particularly in the area of forensic toxicology. One of the first uses of capillary electrophoresis in the analysis of drugs of forensic interest was described not long ago (Weinbeger and Lurie, 1991). Capillary electrophoresis uses either electrophoretic or electrokinetic separation or both. Some advantages of capillary electrophoresis include analysis of analytes from various matrices, with relatively little sample preparation and often no requirement for derivatization, a feature in common with liquid chromatography. Capillary zone electrophoresis (CZE) and micellar electrokinetic capillary chromatography (MECC) are the two most commonly used methods of capillary electrophoresis. Critical evaluation of fundamental parameters such as pH, stirring, temperature, addition of salts, and selection of sorbents has led to significant improvements of this technique over the past several years. A significant advantage of capillary electrophoresis is its simplicity and low sample volume requirements. Because of the small size of the capillary, typically 20–100 μM i.d., and 20–100 cm in length, only small amounts of sample are needed. Consequently, sample volumes of less than 0.1 mL are common. As a consequence, in the forensic environment where sample volume can be a significant limitation, this technique offers some advantages. Analysis time is the drawback of this technique as is the difficulty of combining this technique with mass spectrometry. Advances in nanospray interfaces and sample stacking techniques should make this a mainstream analytical tool. Several reviews of the technique and its application have been published (Lloyd, 1996; Bojarski and Aboul-Enein, 1997; Leveque et al., 1997; Tagliaro et al., 1997; von Heeren and Thormann, 1997; Brunner and DiPiro, 1998; Shihabi, 1998; Thormann and Caslavska, 1998; Thormann et al., 1998, 1999; Manetto et al., 2000; Zaugg and Thormann, 2000).

Detection of amphetamine, methamphetamine, 2-phenethylamine, 4-hydroxyamphetamine, and 4-hydroxymethamphetamine in urine using 1-

phenethylamine as the internal standard has been described using both CZE and MECC (Kuroda et al., 1998). These authors employed both UV and fluorescence detection. Using UV, the detection limits were in the low femtomole-per-injection range when using a 50-μL sample. Detection limits in the low to mid-attomole-per-injection range was obtained using laser-induced fluorescence detection. Since amphetamines do not exhibit native fluorescence, derivatization with 4-fluoro-7-nitro-2,1,3-benzoxadiazole (NBD-F) was used to facilitate fluorescence detection.

Amphetamine, methamphetamine, MDA, MDMA, and methadone and its metabolite were analyzed from urine samples using capillary electrophoresis with multiple-wavelength (rapid scanning from 195 to 320 nm) detection. Amphetamine, methamphetamine, MDA, and MDMA could be detected at microgram-per-milliliter concentrations by directly injecting the urine sample. Using a simple liquid–liquid extraction procedure, detection limits between 100 and 200 ng/mL were achieved. Electrospray ionization (ESI) mass spectral analysis was also described in this study. The ESI-MS procedure used a 70-cm capillary, which was longer than the 60 cm (55.4 cm to the detector) for the UV detection; differences in buffer, injection procedure, and applied voltage resulted in shorted analysis time, with all analytes eluting in less than 3.6 minutes. The selectivity of mass spectrometry allowed this rapid analysis even though not all peaks were baseline separated. Identification of the analytes was made by monitoring their $M + H^+$ ions, which allowed selective identification of peaks even when not chromatographically separated. Further confirmation of the identity of the analytes was accomplished by evaluation of the product ion spectra of these analytes, significantly adding to the confidence of identification. Amphetamine was monitored by the transition from m/z 136.1 to m/z 119.1, methamphetamine from m/z 150.1 to m/z 119.1, MDA from m/z 180.1 to m/z 163.1, and MDMA from m/z 194.1 to m/z 163.1 (Ramseier et al., 2000).

Chinaka et al. (2000) described a capillary electrophoresis method for the analysis of amphetamine, methamphetamine, dimethylamphetamine, ephedrine, norephedrine, methylephedrine, MDA, MDMA, and MDEA enantiomers in urine using a mixture of beta-cyclodextrin and heptakis(2,6-di-O-methyl)-beta-cyclodextrin added to the electrolyte. Detection limits for all enantiomers were 100 ng/mL and linear ranges for ephedrine and methamphetamine were 0.2–500 μg/mL. Another capillary electrophoresis method for the analysis of enantiomers of MDMA, its metabolites MDA, and HMMA has been described using (2-hydroxy)propyl-beta-cyclodextrin at 10 and 50 mM in 50 mM phosphate buffer (pH 2.5) to separate the enantiomers. The method was linear from 125–2000, 50–1000, and 125–1500 ng/mL for each enantiomer of MDMA, MDA, and HMMA, respectively (Pizarro et al., 2002).

The use of capillary electrophoresis for the analysis of hair samples is also gaining momentum, and several investigators have published procedures for a variety of drugs, including the amphetamines. A review of hair analysis, including a discussion of capillary electrophoresis applications, has been published and noted this technique to hold significant promise (Tagliaro et al., 1997). Hair analysis using RIA, HPLC, and capillary electrophoresis for evaluation of chronic exposure to heroin, cocaine, or MDMA has been described. Using a field-amplified sample stacking described earlier by this group (Tagliaro et al., 1998b), the authors obtained head-column concentration factors of over 100. This gave sufficient sensitivity to allow use of capillary electrophoresis with UV detection (Tagliaro et al., 2000). The use of capillary zone electrophoresis with field-amplified sample stacking was described by Tagliaro et al. as a method for the analysis of hair samples for the presence of morphine, cocaine, and MDMA (Tagliaro et al., 1998b). Electrophoresis was accomplished using a 100mM phosphate running buffer (pH 2.5) with an applied potential of 10kV at 20°C. Detection was by monitoring UV absorption at 200nm or between 190 and 400nm. Dried hair extracts were reconstituted in 0.1mM formic acid, the injection end of the capillary was then dipped in water for five seconds, a plug of 0.1mM phosphoric acid was loaded by applying 0.5psi for 10 seconds, and the sample was electrokinetically injected at 10kV for 10 seconds. Using this technique, the limit of detection ($S:N = 5:1$) for MDMA was 2ng/ml.

Chiral analysis of amphetamines can also be accomplished using capillary electrophoresis. An example of chiral analysis of the enantiomers of amphetamine, methamphetamine, MDA, MDMA, MDEA, and ephedrine using beta-cyclodextrin as the chiral agent has been described. In this case, an uncoated capillary (45cm × 50-μm i.d.) was used at a potential of 10kV with pH 2.5 phosphate buffer. Detection of the drugs was accomplished by monitoring at 200nm or by scanning from 190 to 400nm. This procedure proved successful for analysis of urine with a simple liquid–liquid extraction. Analysis of hair samples was also accomplished but required field-amplified sample stacking to obtain the sensitivity necessary to detect the levels of MDA, MDMA and MDEA typically seen in the hair of abusers (Tagliaro et al., 1998a). Another method described the chiral separation of amphetamine, methamphetamine, ephedrine, pseudoephedrine, norephedrine, and norpseudoephedrine using capillary electrophoresis and found it to be better than a standard HPLC procedure (Lurie, 1992). This method provided baseline separation for each of the drugs studied, with the exception of (−)-ephedrine and (+)-pseudoephedrine.

(2-Hydroxypropyl)-β-cyclodextrin was used as the chiral selector to separate the enantiomers of amphetamine, methamphetamine, and MDMA as well as methadone and its metabolites (Ramseier et al., 1999). Following a simple extraction procedure, sample extracts were analyzed by capillary electrophoresis with UV determination at either a single (200nm) or multiple wavelengths (195 and 320nm). Achiral analysis was accomplished using the same method without addition of the chiral selector. This procedure was used to assist in differentiation of the use of methamphetamine from that of a Vicks inhaler or an anti-Parkinson drug (deprenyl) based on the enantiomeric characteristics of the analytes.

Scarcella et al. (1997) described the chiral analysis of amphetamine, methamphetamine, and ephedrine using β-cyclodextrin in urine and hair samples. Various experimental conditions, such as the type and concentration of cyclodextrin, voltage, temperature, buffer concentration, and pH were evaluated. The authors determined that the optimal conditions were obtained using a bare fused-silica capillary (40cm × 50 microns i.d.), 150mM phosphate buffer (pH = 2.5), 15mM β-cyclodextrin at 10kV with the temperature set at 17.5°C. Detection was accomplished using UV absorption at 200nm. Under these conditions, amphetamine, methamphetamine, and ephedrine were easily separated, with baseline resolution of the respective enantiomers. Sensitivity was reported to be better than 300ng/mL. Other methods for the chiral analysis of amphetamines using capillary electrophoresis have been described by a number of investigators (Guttman, 1995; Sevcik et al., 1996; Lanz et al., 1997; Scarcella et al., 1997; Varesio et al., 1997; Lurie et al., 1998).

7.5 COMPARATIVE ANALYSIS AND PROFILING

Identification of the source of amphetamine and/or methamphetamine can be a difficult task. There is much, however, that can be determined by evaluation of the drug and its metabolites, potential precursors, and impurities. Pharmaceutical amphetamine and methamphetamine are high-purity drugs that can often be separated from illicitly produced drugs that typically are not purified to the high degree seen in the legitimate pharmaceutical industry. In addition, depending on the reaction pathway used in the manufacturer of the drug, characteristic profiles of precursors and reaction by-products can be used to determine if the material is consistent with legitimate manufacture. Profiling of contaminants found in the illicit preparation of methamphetamine as a means of identification of the source of the drug as not being from a legitimate source has been reported and is described later in this chapter. The profiling of drugs seized by law enforcement has long been used to associate illicit material with the synthetic mechanism, precursors used, matching material to a single "lab" or even batch of material. Analysis of some of these impurities and their metabolites has also been used to investigate that identification of illicit material in biological samples.

Analytical data from the analysis of biological samples can provide a great deal of information useful to the interpretation of the source of the drug, not only from looking at an impurity from illicit synthesis, as mentioned earlier, but also to differentiating several potential sources of the drugs. From the most fundamental evaluation of a sample that contained methamphetamine and amphetamine, it can unequivocally be said that the findings were not the result of the administration of amphetamine, for there is no methylation of amphetamine to methamphetamine in the body. Similarly, there is no racemization of the amphetamines. Therefore the presence of *d*-enantiomer in a biological sample could not have come from administration of the *l*-enantiomer. It is often not possible with these simple facts to determine if the use was from a legitimate medical source. It is, however, sometimes possible to exclude a legitimate source, depending on the circumstances. As an example, the presence of *d*-methamphetamine in a sample alleged to be the result of Vicks inhaler use would demonstrate the allegation to be false because the Vicks inhaler contains only the *l*-enantiomer. Oftentimes, unfortunately, results are not so easily interpreted. There are, however, substantial scientific data to evaluate results from the analysis of biological samples to assist in determining if the source of the drug in the biological samples was from use of a legitimate medical produce or not. One of the challenges in this interpretation is the fact that, in addition to prescription forms of amphetamine and methamphetamine, methamphetamine is found in the Vicks inhaler distributed in the United States. In addition, a number of other drugs are metabolized by the body to methamphetamine and/or amphetamine. While it is not possible to easily differentiate all of the drugs from other sources, it is possible to differentiate some of them with relative ease. This section of the chapter illustrates the use of analytical data to differentiate the source of drug material and help assess its origin.

7.5.1 ILLICIT MATERIAL

The process of examination of solid drug material can provide important information. Both strategic and tactical information can be gained from examination of the compounds found in the material in addition to the drug itself. From determination of the synthetic origin of the drug to assessment of whether or not two or more samples (exhibits) came from the identical source (i.e., same laboratory, same batch, etc.), this information can be invaluable to law enforcement activities in both prevention and prosecution. Drugs of pharmaceutical origin have a high degree of purity and well-defined additives used in the production of the dosage form (pill, capsule, etc.). Drugs of illicit origin are commonly encountered and analyzed using a process referred to as *profiling* to identify and characterize the materials found in the exhibit. The analysis identifies precursors, intermediates, impurities, and reaction by-products that provide useful information regarding the synthetic route and origin of the drug. Different synthetic routes are used by illicit chemists for a variety of reasons, including the starting materials available and equipment available for the synthesis. Each synthetic scheme gives rise to characteristic profiles that help to define the route and, to some extent, the reaction parameters used in the synthesis. Identification of route-specific markers can specifically identify the synthetic method used. To date, the synthetic routes of amphetamine and related drugs have been studied and described by various investigators. Although a well-established technique to find links between confiscated drugs, the actual process of comparison of the profiles can be a time-consuming task when comparing a large number of profiles. Application of computer capabilities to this task makes such comparisons manageable and far less laborious (Jonson and Stromberg, 1993).

Analysis of seized-drug material has been described by a number of investigators. The profiling of amphetamine using the Leuckart method was initially described in a report by Stromberg et al. (1983). Since that time, many other descriptions of illicit synthetic methods have been reported, including details of the compounds found that can be used to uniquely identify the source. Various methods have been used to profile the illicit material, including thin-layer chromatography, gas chromatography with various detectors, and several spectrographic methods. In addition, direct visual examination of the material using optical crystallographic and microcrystalline nature of these compounds is commonly used. In order to identify small differences between minor constituents or differences in the proportion of specific by-products, more sophisticated methods must be employed. In many cases, the material is simply dissolved in a suitable solvent and analyzed by one of a number of instrumental methods. Some minor constituents, however, require isolation of the constituents from the sample and concentration to accurately assess their presence and amount.

A simple profiling procedure for the identification of illicit amphetamine powders using direct injection of the dissolved material into an HPLC showed the process to be viable and rapid, with analytical results available within 30 minutes (Lambrechts et al., 1986). The illicit material was dissolved in acetonitrile:citrate buffer (pH 3.0) (2:8 v/v) and injected with on-line enrichment using a C-8 extraction column (15 mm × 3.2-mm i.d.) and column switching. After washing the column with water, acetonitrile:0.2 M butylamine in water (pH 8.0) was used to elute the impurities from the extraction column onto a C-18 analytical column (Spheri 5; 100 mm × 4.6-mm i.d.). Compounds were monitored using UV at 220 and 254 nm. This method allowed determination of the presence and amounts of amphetamine, N-formylamphetamine,

4-methyl-5phenylpurimidine, *N,N*-di-(β-phenylisopropyl)formamide, *N,N*-di-(β-phenylisopropyl)amine, and *N,N*-di-(β-phenylisopropyl)methylamine. Quantitation was accomplished via comparison of peak height ratios, and relative standard deviations seen with the method were less than 4% for the measured compounds.

Often the solid material encountered is not the pure drug but rather a combination of the drug and a diluent. Common materials used for this purpose include various sugars and caffeine. One procedure for the analysis of confiscated drug derivatized the amphetamine with acetic anhydride, which served to enhance the chromatographic peak shape and mass spectrum. Using UV detection, the authors also noted that monitoring at 260nm gave greater sensitivity and more selectivity than the 220nm commonly used for amphetamine. They also reported that the typical additives did not negatively affect the derivatization of amphetamine under the conditions described. Results from this procedure were compared to those obtained from a reverse-phase ion-pairing HPLC method following acidic aqueous extraction of amphetamine from the powered material and showed no statistical difference (Veress, 2000). Derivatization was accomplished in an autosampler vial with 1mL acetonitrile, 40μL of triethylamine, and 10μL of acetic anhydride. The triethylamine was used to eliminate the adverse effect of the acetic acid on the column. The authors used acetonitrile:tetrahydrofuran:0.1% triethylamine in water (15:15:70v/v/v). It was noted that the 0.1% triethylamine in water was not required for the analysis of amphetamine, but analysis of other drugs, including MDMA, MDEA, cocaine, LSD, and heroin, could be carried out successfully under the same conditions.

Evaluation of the synthesis of amphetamine, 4-methoxyamphetamine and 4-methylthioamphetamine used headspace and immersion solid-phase microextraction (SPME) to identify specific markers of the Leuckart reaction mechanism. Examination of reaction products showed the presence of 4-methyl-5-arylpyrimidines and 4-arylpyrimidines. Synthesis of amphetamine resulted in the identification of 4-benzylpyrimidine and 4-methyl-5-phenylpyrimidine. Following the synthesis of 4-methoxyamphetamine, 4-(4-methoxybenzyl)pyrimidine and 4-methyl-5-(4-methoxyphenyl)pyrimidine were identified in the reaction mixture. In each case, the 4-methyl-5-arylpyrimidines were found in a ratio of 5:1 to the 4-arylpyrimidines. Examination of tablets containing 4-methylthioamphetamine did not reveal the presence of 4-(4-methylthiobenzyl)pyrimidine or 4-methyl-5-(4-methylthiophenyl)pyrimidine, indicating its synthesis was not through the Leuckart reaction. Use of SPME showed excellent response to the compounds of interest without the problem of large peaks from the drug or other excipients, making identification of the low-concentration markers much easier as compared to that seen with liquid extractions. The GC-MS analysis showed relatively clean chromatograms and, with the conditions described, easy identification of the marker compounds (Kirkbride et al., 2001).

A systematic approach to the profiling of illicit amphetamine was described using an automated system for characterization of the components. The analytical procedure used was gas chromatography with flame ionization detection. The study emphasized the chromatographic retention parameters, preprocessing of data using normalization and quantitation, and the effect of drying on the analysis. This study showed that infrared drying of samples could considerably decrease the time required for analysis. Quantitation based on normalized peak areas was found to be more accurate as compared to using an internal standard. Use of an automated peak-selection algorithm allowed for rapid and consistent recognition of the peaks found in samples, which, when combined with the parameters described, allowed for rapid and consistent automated profiling of illicit amphetamine samples (Pikkarainen, 1996). Another study utilizing gas chromatography for profiling illicit tablets was conducted by Palhol et al. (2002). This study examined seized MDMA tablets and characterized approximately 30 different compounds including not only the drugs but their precursors, intermediates, and by-products as well. Samples were extracted with methylene chloride and analyzed by GC.

Methamphetamine is illicitly synthesized in a number of different ways. Basically, its synthesis begins with an achiral precursor such as phenyl-2-propanone or by reduction of its corresponding alpha-hydroxy precursor, such as ephedrine or pseudoephedrine. The product from the achiral precursor phenyl-2-propanone yields racemic methamphetamine. The enantiomeric composition of methamphetamine from ephedrine and pseudoephedrine is dependent on the chiral nature of the starting material (e.g., *l*-ephedrine gives rise to *d*-methamphetamine). The most common synthetic mechanism used in the United States is the hydriodic acid/red phosphorus reduction of ephedrine or pseudoephedrine to methamphetamine. Other common, though less used, methods include the so-called dry reduction method using hydriodic acid/red phosphorus with very little water, hypophosphorus acid reduction, sodium-ammonium reduction, and mercury aluminum amalgam reduction. Each of these methods generates a characteristic set of compounds that can be used to identify the synthetic route.

A procedure for profiling impurities from the hydriodic acid/red phosphorous reduction method for synthesis of illicit methamphetamine has been detailed using HPLC with photodiode array, UV and fluorescence detection, and capillary electrochromatography with laser-induced fluorescence detection (Lurie et al., 2000). The major impurities 1,3-dimethyl-2-phenylnaphthalene and 1-benzyl-3-methylnaphthalene were characterized, along with several other structurally related trace-level impurities. The authors noted that fluorescence detection gave as much as a 60-fold increase in sensitivity when compared with UV detection. The method employed a rapidly scanning fluorescence detection system that dynamically adjusted excitation and emission wavelengths. Based on the information gained from the resulting contour plots, it was possible to optimize the excitation and emission wavelengths to increase sensitivity and to decrease interference with the measurements. Capillary electrochromatography provided superior chromatographic results when compared with the HPLC method. The combination of the separation efficiency of capillary electrophoresis with the selectivity of HPLC makes this an attractive technique. Laser-induced fluorescence detection provided easy detection of the compounds even at low nanogram-per-milliliter concentrations.

Another study evaluating impurities commonly found in illicit methamphetamine samples, including their enantiomeric properties, has been described using capillary electrophoresis (Lurie et al., 1998). In this study, 10 anionic chiral selectors were evaluated to assess their ability to separate six chiral phenethylamines and three achiral impurities in samples. Assays were carried out with untreated capillaries at pH 8 using 25mM chiral surfactant or 10mM charged cyclodextrin. Sulfated(XIII)-β-cyclodextrin had the best overall enantiomeric selectivity, and all 15 solutes related to methamphetamine are simultaneously separated using sulfobutyl(VII)-ether-β-cyclodextrin. Several other investigators used capillary electrophoresis to analyze the composition of ceased illicit material. Huang et al. (2003) evaluated several electrophoretic parameters, including the concentration of beta-cyclodextrin and the amount of organic solvents required for the separation to analyze the enantiomers of MDMA in tablets. The authors also used the procedure for the analysis of MDMA and MDA in urine samples. Cheng and coworkers (2002) used beta-cyclodextrin to separate the enantiomers of ephedrine, pseudoephedrine, and methamphetamine by capillary electrophoresis. The authors evaluated the effects of the buffer pH, phosphate concentration, beta-cyclodextrin concentration, voltage, and temperature on the peak resolution. They found the combination of 15mM beta-cyclodextrin, 300mM NaH_2PO_4 (pH 2.5) using an uncoated capillary (64.5cm × 50 micron), at 20kV and with the temperature controlled at 30°C. Detection at 200nm measured by a diode array detector allowed highly reproducible migration times in a single analytical run. Capillary zone electrophoresis was also used for the analysis of amphetamine, methamphetamine, MDA, MDMA, MDEA, MBDB in illicit samples. The authors reported using a buffer 0.1M phosphoric acid adjusted to pH 3.0 with triethanolamine. The triethanolamine adsorbed to the capillary wall causing the electroosmotic flow to reverse, thus giving peaks that demonstrated good symmetry, high efficiency, and reproducible migration times. Detection was accomplished using a diode array detector scanning from 190–350nm. The procedure proved to allow detection of the compounds in an eight-minute run without suffering interference from adulterants commonly found in illicit powders (Piette and Parmentier, 2002). Lurie et al. (2001) described a procedure for the analysis of methamphetamine, amphetamine, MDA, MDMA, MDEA, and cocaine using capillary electrophoresis in illicit samples. The method used a 32cm × 50 micron capillary with a commercially available buffer kit and diode array detection. Dynamic coating of the capillary surface gave a relatively high and stable electroosmotic flow. The authors used a 75mM phosphate buffer at pH 2.5 as the background electrolyte resulting in baseline separation of all analytes and internal standard in a run of less than five minutes. No interference was seen with any of the commonly encountered substances found in illicit samples. They also reported the system allowed screening of basic, acidic, and neutral adulterants in drug seizures using an automated UV library search for identification.

K.A. Moore, et al. (1996a) identified α-benzyl-N-methylphenethylamine (BNMPA) as an impurity of illicitly synthesized methamphetamine and noted that it, like most impurities in illicit samples, has not been studied in vivo and that limited information exists concerning their pharmacology/toxicology. Evaluation of the compound's metabolism and excretion was undertaken and demonstrated that BNMPA could be detected in the urine of users (Moore, K.A., and Poklis, 1995; Moore, K.A., et al., 1995a, 1996b). The authors determined that since impurities can be characteristic of a particular synthetic method, their presence in seized samples or their detection in biological samples can be used to monitor sales of precursor chemicals, group seized compounds to common sources of illicit production, or provide links between manufacturers, dealers, and users. Monitoring of BNMPA in confiscated material or BNMPA and its metabolites in biological samples was shown to be a viable tool (Moore, K.A., and Poklis, 1995).

An extensive review of impurities in illicit preparations of MDA and MDMA described characteristic compounds found following several synthetic routes, including reductive amination, Leuckart reaction, and both the nitropropene and bromopropane methods (Verweij, 1992). This author summarizes the data from the electron ionization mass spectral analysis of the various reaction impurities, allowing identification of the route of synthesis as well as "signature" analysis of samples enabling the identification of the origin of the drugs. Another group recently evaluated extraction conditions for the chemical profiling of MDMA tablets (Gimeno et al., 2003). The study revealed, of five solvents studied, the optimum results were obtained with diethyl ether from a solution buffered to pH 11.5. The study also showed that mixing the sample for at least 10 minutes was important, but found no difference in stopping the evaporation process just before dryness than after the sample had completely dried.

One nondestructive method for the analysis for amphetamines is Raman spectroscopy. Use of Raman spectroscopy to identify drugs and other components found in illicit materials has previously been hampered by the cost of the instrumentation and the complexity of its use. Recently instruments using far-red excitation have been introduced. This longer wavelength eliminates the interference from many different compounds that luminesce when excited by shorter wavelengths. Rapid analysis of amphetamine, MDA, MDMA, MBDB, and 4-bromo-2,5-dimethoxyphenethylamine has been described using excitation at 745 nm (far-red) (Bell et al., 2000b). This study was able to identify not only the drug present but also materials added to the drug. Using relatively simple substraction routines, elimination of spectra from components of tablets such as sorbitol, lactose, and cellulose made comparison to drug standards a relatively simple task. In addition, spectral differences between varying degrees of hydration were also characterized. This research group further studied the utility of Raman spectroscopy in the profiling of ecstasy tablets (Bell et al., 2000a). In this case, the seized tablets were analyzed by GC-MS and shown to contain MDMA. Raman spectroscopy showed vibrational bands associated with the drug and excipient materials used in the tablets. Comparing the band heights allowed for ratio determination of the compounds. Comparison of drug excipient ratio and degree of hydration was used to characterize the batches of drugs and allowed identification of the source. The ability to analyze up to 50 samples per hour was also a positive factor for the use of this methodology. The importance of evaluating a large number of samples from a single seizure was demonstrated when it was found that samples differed from each other in ways that were not easily determined by other methods.

Following derivatization with 5-nitrobarbituric acid, the optical crystallographic and microcrystalline nature of nine different amphetamine-related compounds has been described (Julian, 1990). These visual methods are commonly used for the identification of the drug either initially or as confirmation of another analytical procedure. Because these are visual physical methods, they are limited to major components and do not lend themselves well to identification of minor reaction products.

In an evaluation of the enantiomer analysis of methamphetamine and amphetamine in urine samples, a number of different confiscated-drug materials was also analyzed. The analysis was accomplished by HPLC using a combination of UV detection at 220 nm for identification of the drug and quantitative analysis at 450 nm using an optical rotation detector following separation on a Chiralcel OB-H column (25 cm × 4.5 mm i.d.) at 50°C. Interestingly, these investigators found two of the five confiscated samples contained only the *d*-enantiomer. Two others contained both enantiomers, one 98% and the other approximately 4% *l*-enantiomer. The fifth sample contained only *l*-methamphetamine. Since *l*-methamphetamine has only a fraction of the central nervous system activity of the *d*-enantiomer, it is seldom abused. Sources of *l*-methamphetamine in the United States include the Vicks inhaler and the metabolism of the precursor drug deprenyl. Since this study was conducted in Japan, where neither of these sources is available, it appears the *l*-methamphetamine was specifically for illicit use (Nagai et al., 2000).

7.5.2 BIOLOGICAL SAMPLES

Comparative analysis and profiling in terms of biological samples is a different process than is used for illicit materials. There has been some work done to evaluate the possibility of using biological samples to identify synthetic reaction precursors and products to help establish the source of the illicit drug. This is, however, not a widely used technique. More commonly, the evaluation of biological samples is best described as determination of the origin of the drug or interpretation of such parameters as how much drug was used, when, and how often. In this case, the source of the drug is usually limited to evaluation of whether or not the drug was from a licit or illicit source, not which illicit source (i.e., specific clandestine laboratory).

Some determination of illicit versus licit drug use can be based on a simple analytical procedure. Determination of the enantiomeric form of the drug can provide clear evidence in some cases. For example, if methamphetamine were used and there was a question of whether or not it was the prescription form of the drug, finding the *l*-enantiomer in the sample would not be consistent with the use of the prescription form of methamphetamine (Desoxyn) that is the *d*-enantiomer only. Likewise the presence of *d*-methamphetamine would demonstrate that the methamphetamine present was not the result of using a Vicks inhaler (an over-the-counter product that contains 50 mg of *l*-methamphetamine, which is exempted for control).

Identification of pyrolysis products of smoked methamphetamine was undertaken to allow the detection of markers associated with this route of administration (Lee et al., 1999). Pyrolysis products of smoked methamphetamine were extracted by placing a C-8 column in line with a pump that drew in the smoke. Both mainstream and sidestream smoke were collected for this study. The column was eluted with 3 mL of methanol, and the eluent was brought to dryness and then reconstituted in a small amount of methanol. The extract was analyzed using a high-resolution double-focusing GC-MS-MS instrument. The pyrolysis of dimethylamphetamine was studied by GC-MS, headspace GC-MS, and LC-MS using electrospray ionization (Sato, Hida, and Nagase, 2001). This study showed that amphetamine and methamphetamine were produced by demethylation at 358°C and 386°C.

Analysis of urine samples to evaluate the potential presence of impurities associated with illicitly manufactured methamphetamine was described by Moore et al. (Moore, K.A., and Poklis, 1995; Moore, K.A., et al., 1995a, 1995b, 1996b). The compound of interest, α-benzyl-N-methylphenethylamine (BNMPA), was identified as an impurity of illicit methamphetamine synthesis. Investigation was carried out to determine if BNMPA could be identified in urine samples following administration of the drug. A procedure was developed to identify the presence of the compound and probable metabolites (Moore, K.A., et al., 1995b). Urine samples were hydrolyzed using β-glucuronidase or acid hydrolysis followed by liquid–liquid extraction and derivatization with heptafluorobutyric anhydride. GC-MS analysis of BNMPA, N-demethyl-α-benzyl-N-methylphenethylamine, 1,3-diphenyl-2-propanone, and 1,3-diphenyl-2-propanol gave limits of detection of 2.5 ng/mL and limits of quantitation of 25 ng/mL for all four compounds. The procedure was linear from 25 to 500 ng/mL. Analysis of urine samples collected following ingestion of 5 mg of BNMPA by a single volunteer showed the drug and its N-demethyl metabolites were found at 2–4 hours postingestion. 1,3-Diphenyl-2-propanone concentration peaked at 2 hours postingestion. Other metabolites were detected for up to 21 hours postingestion. Analysis of 80 urine specimens collected at drug rehabilitation programs that were previously shown to be positive for methamphetamine was completed using this method. Two of those urine specimens contained detectable amounts of BNMPA and/or its metabolites. One contained detectable (greater than the limit of detection but less than the limit of quantitation) amounts of N-demethyl-BNMPA and 1,3-diphenyl-2-propanone as well as 0.04 μg/mL p-hydroxy-N-demethyl-BNMPA. The other sample contained detectable amounts of BNMPA, p-hydroxy-BNMPA, and p-hydroxy-N-demethyl-BNMPA and measurable amounts (μg/mL) of N-demethyl-BNMPA (Moore, K.A., et al., 1996b). Samples taken from a mixed drug fatality showed the presence of p-hydroxy-BNMPA in urine (Moore, K.A., and Poklis, 1995). Based on the results of these studies, the authors suggest that the detection of the impurity and/or its metabolites is indicative of ingestion of the compound within the previous 24 hours (Moore, K.A., et al., 1995a).

Another potential source for methamphetamine and/or amphetamine in biological samples is the precursor drugs. *Precursor* in this case refers to compounds that are metabolically converted to methamphetamine and/or amphetamine by the body. These drugs have been described and reviewed in several publications (Cody, 1993, 1995, 2002; Kraemer and Maurer, 1998, 2002). Many of these drugs are available by prescription, in which case a valid medical prescription would help to confirm, although it must be remembered that prescription drugs are often abused. Some of these drugs, depending on the country, are available over the counter. Drugs that are metabolic precursors to amphetamine or methamphetamine include: Amphetaminil (Remberg et al., 1972; Honecker, 1975), benzphetamine (Beckett et al., 1967; Marsel et al., 1972; Budd and Jain, 1978; Brooks et al., 1982; Niwaguchi et al., 1982; Inoue et al., 1983; Akintonwa, 1986; Inoue and Suzuki, 1986; Kikura and Nakahara, 1995b; Nakahara, 1995; Nakahara et al., 1995, 1998; Spatzenegger and Jaeger, 1995; Herraez-Hernandez et al., 1996; Nakahara and Kikura, 1996; Cloyd, 1997; Shiiyama et al., 1997; Cody and Valtier, 1998; Fujinami et al., 1998a, 1998b; Teter, 1999; Sato, Mitsui, and Nagase, 2001), clobenzorex (Glasson et al., 1971; Tarver, 1994; Nakahara and Kikura, 1996; Maurer et al., 1997; Baden et al., 1999; Cody and Valtier, 1999, 2001; Valtier and Cody, 1999a, 1999b, 2000), deprenyl (selegiline)(Reynolds, et al., 1978b; Robinson, 1985; Kalasz et al., 1990, 1999; Maurer and Kraemer, 1992; Shin and Park, 1993; Heinonen et al., 1994, 1997; Kikura and Nakahara, 1995a; Nakahara, 1995; Nakahara et al., 1995; Romberg et al., 1995; Szebeni et al., 1995; Barrett et al., 1996; Lajtha et al., 1996; Sevcik et al., 1996; Rohatagi et al., 1997; Shin, 1997a; Kupiec, T.C. and Chaturvedi, 1999, Reynolds et al., 1978; Philips, 1981; Elsworth et al., 1982; Karoum et al., 1982; Heinonen et al., 1989; Meeker and Reynolds, 1990; Reimer et al., 1993; Lengyel et al., 1997; Mascher et al., 1997; Tarjanyi et al., 1998; Hasegawa et al., 1999; Melega et al., 1999; Pichini et al., 1999; Szoko et al., 1999; Bach et al., 2000; Laine et al., 2000; Sato et al., 2002), dimethylamphetamine (Beckett et al., 1967; Beckett and Al-Sarraj, 1972; Blume, 1981; Inoue and Suzuki, 1987; Takahashi et al., 1987; Witkin et al., 1990; Myung et al., 1998; Nakahara et al., 1998; Katagi et al., 2000, Sato et al., 2002), ethylamphetamine (Beckett et al., 1967, 1969, 1972; Beckett and Shenoy, 1973; Williams et al., 1973; Beckett and Haya, 1977, 1978; Delbeke and Debackere, 1986; Makino et al., 1989; Nagai et al., 1995, 1997; Matsushima et al., 1998b; Yamada et al., 1998; Bach et al., 1999), famprofazone (Mrongovius et al., 1984; Neugebauer, 1984; Oh et al., 1992; Shin and Park, 1993; Shin et al., 1994, 1997, 1998; Yoo et al., 1994; Cody, 1996; Neugebauer et al., 1997; Shin, 1997b; Musshoff and Kraemer, 1998), fencamine (Mallol et al., 1974), fenethylline (Ellison et al., 1970; Iffland, 1982; Goenechea and Brzezinka, 1984; Kristen et al., 1986; Nickel et al., 1986; Rucker et al., 1988; Yoshimura et al., 1988; Kikura and Nakahara, 1997; Yamada et al., 1998), fenproporex (Berry et al., 1971; Beckett et al., 1972; Tognoni et al., 1972; Sznelwar, 1975; Nazarali et al., 1983; Nakahara, 1995; Cody and Valtier, 1996; Cody et al., 1999; Kraemer et al., 2000; Bell, R.R. et al., 2001), furfenorex (Beckett et al., 1967; Boissier et al., 1968; Marsel et al., 1972; Inoue and Suzuki, 1986; Inoue et al., 1986; Nakahara and Kikura, 1996), mefenorex (Blum, 1969; Williams et al., 1973; Nazarali et al., 1983; Engel et al., 1986; Rendic et al., 1994; Nakahara, 1995; Kraemer et al., 1997), mesocarb (Polgar et al., 1979; Seredenin and Rybina, 1985; Ventura et al., 1993; Pyo et al., 1996), and prenylamine (Palm et al., 1969; Dengler et al., 1970; Remberg et al., 1977; Gietl et al., 1988, 1989, 1990; Paar et al., 1990; Nakahara and Kikura, 1996; Kraemer et al., 2003).

Several of these drugs are available directly in the United States or in adjoining countries (i.e., Mexico) or over the counter. Several of these drugs are discussed in this section of the chapter to illustrate the interpretation of laboratory data with regard to the involvement of these drugs as the source of a positive result for amphetamines. The drugs described are selected because of their likelihood of being encountered in the United States. Two of these drugs are available by prescription in the United States. Benzphetamine (Didrex) is a diet pill used for weight loss, and selegiline (Deprenyl) is an anti-Parkinson drug. Several others that are encountered include clobenzorex (Asenlix) and fenproporex (Fenisec). Although not distributed in the United States, they are available by prescription in Mexico. Clobenzorex has been documented to be one of the most common legal drugs brought back into the United States by persons visiting Mexico (McKeithan and Shepherd, 1996; Garza and Landeck, 1999). Clobenzorex is also available as an over-the-counter medication in Panama. Both clobenzorex and fenproporex are anorexic drugs used for weight loss, making them popular drugs. In addition to the availability of these drugs through "stone and mortar" pharmacies, access to ordering drugs over the Internet has made many of these drugs available to virtually anyone with access to the Internet.

Consideration of the interpretation of involvement of these precursor drugs in positive laboratory findings must be considered in the context of the drugs available on the legal and illicit markets. Methamphetamine is available by prescription in the United States for a number of clinical indications. The enantiomeric form of the drug is the d-enantiomer. Illicit synthesis of methamphetamine produces either d-methamphetamine or a mixture of d- and l-methamphetamine. The l-enantiomer can be synthesized and abused, but that is not common, since this enantiomer has far less central activity than the d-enantiomer. Prescription amphetamine in the United States is either the d-enantiomer or a mixture of both isomers. Illicit amphetamine is also found in these two forms as well.

Benzphetamine is metabolized by the body to amphetamine and methamphetamine (Beckett et al., 1967; Marsel et al., 1972; Budd and Jain, 1978; Niwaguchi et al., 1982; Inoue et al., 1983; Inoue and Suzuki, 1986; Kikura and Nakahara, 1995b; Swanson, 1996; Cody and Valtier, 1998; Fujinami et al., 1998b; Kraemer and Maurer, 1998). The drug is prescribed as an adjunct to a weight loss program (Silverstone, 1986, 1992; Bray, 1993; Anon., 2000) and is a scheduled drug due to its abuse potential. The amphetamine and methamphetamine produced by metabolism of benzphetamine are d-enantiomers

(Cody and Valtier, 1998). This eliminates samples containing all or some *l*-methamphetamine as being the consequence of benzphetamine use. While helpful, since most illicit methamphetamine in the United States is the *d*-enantiomer, enantiomeric composition alone does not allow differentiation from prescription or most illicit methamphetamine abuse. Examination of the proportion of amphetamine and methamphetamine can be a powerful tool in differentiation of source, however. The metabolic pathway for amphetamine and methamphetamine has been studied for many years (Beckett and Rowland, 1965a, 1965b, 1965c; Caldwell et al., 1972). Studies have established that pH and enantiomeric composition have striking effects on the metabolism and excretion of these drugs (Beckett and Rowland, 1964, 1965c; Beckett et al., 1965, 1969, 1972; Davis et al., 1971; Beckett and Shenoy, 1973; Beckett and Haya, 1978; Wan et al., 1978; Vree and Henderson, 1980). The *d*-enantiomers of amphetamine and methamphetamine are metabolized rapidly compared to the *l*-enantiomers; thus the ratio of *d*- to *l*-enantiomer changes over time. These facts are useful in the interpretation of laboratory results.

The concentration of methamphetamine and amphetamine found after administration of benzphetamine is low compared to peak levels seen with methamphetamine abuse. More useful, however, is the proportion of amphetamine to methamphetamine. After administration of methamphetamine, both methamphetamine and its metabolite amphetamine can be seen. The amount of amphetamine found, however, is substantially less than that of methamphetamine. The amphetamine-to-methamphetamine ratio from methamphetamine abuse would be expected to be 0.20 or less (Hornbeck and Czarny, 1993; Kim et al., 2000). Following benzphetamine administration, the amount of amphetamine commonly exceeds that of methamphetamine. Several studies have demonstrated the use of benzphetamine results in amphetamine concentrations exceeding that of methamphetamine, including 10 of 10 subjects in one study (Swanson, 1996), two of two (Kikura and Nakahara, 1995b), and eight of ten in a third study (Cody and Valtier, 1998). In the study where two subjects had methamphetamine concentrations greater than those of amphetamine, the ratio of the two drugs was far higher than seen with methamphetamine use, which is consistent with another study of a single subject that had amphetamine at a concentration less than that of methamphetamine but higher than expected (Budd and Jain, 1978). Overall concentrations seen even after multiple doses of benzphetamine gave peak concentrations of amphetamine and methamphetamine at $5.01\,\mu g/mL$ and $0.35\,\mu g/mL$, respectively (Kikura and Nakahara, 1995b).

In addition to the enantiomer data and the ratio of amphetamine to methamphetamine, benzphetamine use can be assessed by evaluation of the parent or unique metabolites of the drug. The parent drug has been detected in urine samples following administration in several studies, but only at low concentrations and for a short period of time (Beckett et al., 1967; Inoue and Suzuki, 1986; Kikura and Nakahara, 1995b; Cody and Valtier, 1998; Fujinami et al., 1998b). Several compounds have been identified including 4-hydroxybenzphetamine, 4-hydroxynorbenzphetamine (Inoue and Suzuki, 1986; Fujinami et al., 1998a, 1998b), 3-hydroxynorbenzphetamine, and 3-methoxy-4-hydroxynorbenzphetamine as unique metabolites of benzphetamine (Inoue and Suzuki, 1986). Following administration of 30mg per day for 5 days, norbenzphetamine was detected for up to 12 hours and the other metabolites were detected for longer periods (Fujinami et al., 1998b). Other investigators have utilized electrospray LC-MS to determine benzphetamine and its metabolites following administration of benzphetamine in the rat (Sato, Mitsui, and Nagase, 2001). The authors reported identification and quantitation of benzphetamine, 4-hydroxybenzphetamine, norbenzphetamine, 4-hydroxynorbenzphetamine, methamphetamine, and amphetamine using 1mL of urine. Their results suggest 4-hydroxybenzphetamine as a sensitive marker of benzphetamine use in the rat. Incorporation of benzphetamine and metabolites in hair has been studied and shows benzphetamine and norbenzphetamine were readily incorporated into hair, but the hydroxy metabolite incorporation was relatively low. The authors concluded from this study that hair analysis could be used to distinguish methamphetamine from use by analysis of the hair samples for benzphetamine and/or norbenzphetamine (Kikura and Nakahara, 1995b).

Deprenyl (Selegiline) is a monoamine oxidase inhibitor frequently used in conjunction with *l*-dopa in the treatment of Parkinson disease (Anon., 2000). It is a prescription drug available in the United States and is one of the few precursor compounds that is not a diet pill. From an interpretation standpoint, the single most telling characteristic point regarding the metabolism of deprenyl is that the product amphetamine and methamphetamine are the *l*-enantiomers. While it is possible for *l*-methamphetamine to be abused, the incidence is rare, due to the low activity of this enantiomer compared to the *d*-form of the drug. In the United States, the most common source of *l*-methamphetamine is the Vicks inhaler. Since that is an exempted product, results of the presence of this form of the drug are usually not reported. Deprenyl is metabolized to several metabolites, including desmethyldeprenyl, which is a unique metabolite, and its presence can help demonstrate the use of deprenyl. Several investigators have studied the metabolism of deprenyl to amphetamine and methamphetamine (Reynolds et al., 1978a; Elsworth et al., 1982; Liebowitz et al., 1985). Romberg et al. (1995) measured amphetamine and methamphetamine concentration of urine samples taken from patients taking deprenyl. Of the samples tested by immunoassay, only one screened positive for methamphetamine. GC-MS analysis showed concentrations of 1895 ng/mL and 4690 ng/mL of amphetamine and methamphetamine, respectively, in that sample. Other specimens showed amphetamine concentrations of 342–915 ng/mL and 829–2490 ng/mL for methamphetamine. Several other studies have also described the metabolism of deprenyl (Karoum et al., 1982; Reimer et al., 1993; Tarjanyi et al., 1998a, 1998b; Kim et al., 2000; Laine et al., 2000; Katagi et al., 2002; Slawson et al., 2002).

The ratio of amphetamine to methamphetamine can also be used in evaluation of deprenyl versus methamphetamine use. Studies evaluating the ratio of amphetamine and methamphetamine ranged from approximately 0.33 to 0.47 (Karoum et al., 1982; Reimer et al., 1993; Kim et al., 2000). These ratios are higher than expected following methamphetamine use (Hornbeck and Czarny, 1993; Kim et al., 2000). Kim et al. (2000) showed desmethyldeprenyl reached peak concentrations 0–3 hours postdose and could be detected for up to 9 hours. Amphetamine and methamphetamine reached peak concentrations 3–6 hours postdose and could be detected up to 12–24 hours. Another study reported amphetamine and methamphetamine could be detected for 96 hours after the last of five daily 15-mg doses of deprenyl (Kikura and Nakahara, 1995a). Deprenyl was detected up to 36 hours and desmethyldeprenyl for 72 hours. In a postmortem case involving deprenyl, femoral blood levels for amphetamine and methamphetamine were 70 and 170 ng/mL, respectively (Meeker and Reynolds, 1990).

Other investigators have examined the excretion of unique metabolites of deprenyl as well as amphetamine and methamphetamine. One study examined the deprenyl, desmethyldeprenyl, methamphetamine, and amphetamine in human plasma using atmospheric pressure chemical ionization LC-MS-MS. The assay showed a dynamic range of 0.1–20 ng/mL for deprenyl and desmethyldeprenyl and 0.2–20 ng/mL for methamphetamine and amphetamine. The limit of quantitation for the analytes were 0.1 ng/mL for deprenyl and desmethyldeprenyl, and 0.2 ng/mL for methamphetamine and amphetamine (Slawson et al., 2002). Another study evaluated the excretion of deprenyl, desmethyldeprenyl, deprenyl-*N*-oxide, methamphetamine, and amphetamine in urine using electrospray ionization LC-MS (Katagi et al., 2002). This study showed the amount of deprenyl-*N*-oxide excreted in the first 8–12 hours post administration was comparable to the amount of methamphetamine excreted. In the first 72 hours post dose, the amount of deprenyl-*N*-oxide was twice to nearly eight times greater than desmethyldeprenyl, demonstrating this to be a viable metabolite to monitor deprenyl versus methamphetamine use.

Hair analysis has been described for the differentiation of deprenyl versus methamphetamine use (Kikura and Nakahara, 1995a; Nakahara, 1995, 1999; Nakahara et al., 1995; Nakahara and Kikura, 1996). Deprenyl and desmethyldeprenyl were shown to have a low incorporation rate in hair compared to methamphetamine and amphetamine (Kikura and Nakahara, 1995a; Nakahara and Kikura, 1996). Evaluation of the drug and metabolite concentrations showed that methamphetamine was found at the highest concentration with decreasing levels of amphetamine and desmethyldeprenyl and only trace amounts of deprenyl in scalp hair (Kikura and Nakahara, 1995a).

Clobenzorex (Asenlix) is an anorexic drug used in the treatment of obesity (Schlesser, 1991; Parfitt, 1999). This drug is not sold in the United States; however, it is available in several countries. Clobenzorex is available over the counter in Panama and by prescription in Mexico. Obtaining a prescription for this drug is relatively easy for individuals (Valdez and Sifaneck, 1997). Amphetamine produced from the metabolism of clobenzorex has been shown to be the *d*-enantiomer only (Valtier and Cody, 1999a), important information for the correct interpretation of laboratory results. One study reported a peak concentration of amphetamine of 1365 ng/mL after administration of a 30-mg dose. In that study, only four samples were collected, the last at 7 hours post-dose, and it was that sample that contained the highest concentration of amphetamine (Tarver, 1994). In another study, administration of a single 30-mg dose to five subjects resulted in a peak urine amphetamine concentration of 2474 ng/mL. The parent drug was detected in some samples at low concentrations for up to 29 hours after administration. Of 22 amphetamine-positive (amphetamine concentrations equal to or greater than 500 ng/mL) samples found during that study, only half contained detectable levels of clobenzorex. Samples were positive for amphetamine for 7.5–46.5 hours after administration of the drug (Valtier and Cody, 1999a). Another study evaluating samples following multiple administration of the drug showed that as many as 75% of the samples positive for amphetamine did not contain detectable levels of parent drug (Baden et al., 1999). Peak amphetamine concentration reached as high as 4700 ng/mL and was detected in one subject for up to 53 hours after the last dose was administered. Although 4700 ng/mL is nearly 10 times the cutoff concentration for amphetamine, it is much lower than is commonly seen with abuse of amphetamine. The enantiomer composition is also helpful for interpretation, but it is most useful in excluding inconsistent results because both medicinal and illicit amphetamine may be encountered as the *d*-form of the drug.

Maurer et al. (1997) demonstrated the presence of seven metabolites following the administration of 60 mg of clobenzorex. Two different hydroxy metabolites of clobenzorex were identified, and one had detection times comparable to that of amphetamine. Later studies investigated the excretion profile of 4-hydroxyclobenzorex and showed that all samples that were positive for amphetamine contained detectable levels of this metabolite (Valtier and Cody,

2000; Cody and Valtier, 2001). Collectively, these studies show that the detection of 4-*HO*-clobenzorex can establish the involvement of clobenzorex. In an evaluation of the incorporation rates of various drugs in hair, Nakahara and Kikura (1996) showed clobenzorex to be typical of drugs containing a benzene or furan ring at the *N*-position as having a much higher incorporation rate than amphetamine or methamphetamine. In fact, the chlorine on the benzene ring led to greater incorporation than the ring by itself. Presence of a hydroxy group on the benzene ring, however, apparently decreased the incorporation rate, implying the hydroxy metabolites would be less likely to be incorporated.

Another drug used in the treatment of obesity is fenproporex (Harris, 1986; Schlesser, 1991; Parfitt, 1999; Halpern and Mancini, 2003). It is marketed in a number of countries including Mexico as a prescription drug where it is often obtained and brought back into the United States. It is also available in a number of other countries and over the Internet, making it readily available. Fenproporex metabolism has been studied by a number of different investigators (Beckett et al., 1972; Tognoni et al., 1972; Sznelwar, 1975; Cody, 1993, 1994, 1995; Cody and Valtier, 1996; Cody et al., 1999; Kraemer et al., 2000).

Peak concentrations of amphetamine following administration of a single 10-mg dose of fenproporex were seen at 5:50–20:20 hours at concentrations of up to 2099ng/mL. Fenproporex itself was measured at concentrations as high as 706ng/mL and was detected in all samples positive for amphetamine using a 500ng/mL cutoff (Cody and Valtier, 1996). The amphetamine produced from the metabolism of fenproporex was found to be made up of both *d*- and *l*-enantiomers. Following multiple doses of the drug (one capsule daily for seven days), the peak concentration of amphetamine reached 4150ng/mL and the parent was measured at levels as high as 3032ng/mL (Cody et al., 1999). In this study, urine samples were positive for amphetamine for approximately 40 hours following the last administered dose and, as seen with the single dose study, the parent was detectable in all positive samples. Enantiomer distribution of amphetamine was near 50% shortly after administration of the drug followed by a rise in the *d*-enantiomer for a short period of time after which there was a gradual increase in the proportion of *l*-enantiomer. This pattern repeated until administration of the drug was discontinued (Cody et al., 1999).

Metabolism of fenproporex produces a number of metabolites, including several unique to fenproporex, including two different isomers of hydroxyfenproporex, dihydroxyfenproporex, hydroxy-methoxy-fenproporex, desamino-oxo-fenproporex, desamino-oxo-hydroxyfenproporex, desamino-oxo-dihydroxyfenproporex, and desamino-oxo-hydroxy-methoxy-fenproporex (Kraemer et al., 2000). In this study, fenproporex was detected for up to 16 hours postdose, and one of the two isomers of hydroxyfenproporex could be detected for up to 28 hours. Amphetamine, however, was detected up to 60 hours postdose. Given this information it is reasonable to assume that using a cutoff of 500 ng/mL should yield samples that contain the parent drug. However, if the concentration of amphetamine present is below that, some samples will not contain the parent drug. Even using the metabolites as described by Kraemer et al. (2000) may result in samples that contain amphetamine but no unique metabolites.

Evaluating the incorporation of 32 amphetamine analogs into hair, investigators discovered that the presence of triple bonds on the N-substituent decreased the rate of incorporation. This was also shown to be true when a hydroxy group was present on the benzene ring. Together these characteristics of fenproporex and its metabolites lead to the finding of low rates of incorporation into hair (Nakahara and Kikura, 1996).

7.6 CONCLUSION

Amphetamines are a group of compounds with a variety of legitimate uses, but they have a high abuse potential. In addition to those amphetamines that have a legitimate use, there are a number of illicit amphetamines that have been abused over the years, and their abuse continues. Many of the illicit analogs, particularly the methylenedioxy compounds such as MDMA, are being abused at an increasing rate. In addition to the compounds that have been around for many years, newly developed compounds, such as methylthioamphetamine and N-ethyl-4-methoxyamphetamine are also being abused. These facts demonstrate the continuous need to be vigilant of the amphetamines and their applications, both licit and illicit. While the use and abuse patterns differ slightly throughout the world, one thing remains constant: Abuse of amphetamines is universal and those chemists and toxicologists who work in the area must constantly be aware of the state of the science in order to meet the ever-increasing challenges posed by these drugs.

Analysis of amphetamines can be accomplished using a variety of different analytical methods. The sheer number of different analytical procedures employing various hydrolysis, extraction, derivatization, and instrumental methods shows the diversity and complexity of analyzing for these drugs, whether in the form of the drug material itself or for the drug and/or its metabolites in biological matrices. Improvement of established procedures is a hallmark of this area, made interesting by the advances in instrumentation and automation as well as the challenges of evaluation of various nontraditional samples that will allow for significant advances in the near future. Collectively these circumstances make the amphetamines one of the most dynamic and intriguing drug classes with which to be involved.

REFERENCES

Aboul-Enein, H.Y., and Serignese, V. (1997). *Biomed. Chromatogr.* 11, 7–10.

Akintonwa, D.A.A. (1986). *J. Theor. Biol.* 120, 303–308.

Al-Dirbashi, O., Kuroda, N., Menichini, F., Noda, S., Minemoto, M., and Nakashima, K. (1998a). *Analyst* 123, 2333–2337.

Al-Dirbashi, O., Qvarnstrom, J., Irgum, K., and Nakashima, K. (1998b). *J. Chromatogr., B* 712, 105–112.

Al-Dirbashi, O., Kuroda, N., Inuduka, S., Menichini, F., and Nakashima, K. (1999a). *Analyst* 124, 493–497.

Al-Dirbashi, O., Wada, M., Kuroda, N., Inuduka, S., and Nakashima, K. (1999b). *Biomed. Chromatogr.* 13, 543–547.

Al-Dirbashi, O.Y., Kuroda, N., Wada, M., Takahashi, M., and Nakashima, K. (2000a). *Biomed. Chromatogr.* 14, 293–300.

Al-Dirbashi, O.Y., Wada, M., Kuroda, N., Takahashi, M., and Nakashima, K. (2000b). *J. Forensic Sci.* 45, 708–714.

Allen, D.L., and Oliver, J.S. (2000). *Forensic Sci. Int.* 107, 191–199.

Anon. (2000). *Physician's Desk Reference.* Medical Economics Company, Montvale, NJ.

Aoki, K., Hirose, Y., and Kuroiwa, Y. (1990). *Forensic Sci. Int.* 44, 245–255.

Arthur, C.L., and Pawliszyn, J. (1990). *Anal. Chem.* 62, 2145–2148.

Asghar, S.J., Baker, G.B., Rauw, G.A., and Silverstone, P.H. (2001). *J. Pharmacol. Toxicol. Methods* 46, 111–115.

Asselin, W.M., and Leslie, J.M. (1992). *J. Anal. Toxicol.* 16, 381–388.

Bach, M.V., Coutts, R.T., and Baker, G.B. (1999). *Xenobiotica* 29, 719–732.

Bach, M.V., Coutts, R.T., and Baker, G.B. (2000). *Xenobiotica* 30, 297–306.

Baden, K.L., Valtier, S., and Cody, J.T. (1999). *J. Anal. Toxicol.* 23, 511–517.

Baker, G.B., Coutts, R.T., and Holt, A. (1994). *J. Pharmacolog. Toxicolog. Methods* 31, 143–418.

Barksdale, J.M., and Clark, C.R. (1985). *J. Chromatogr. Sci.* 23, 176–180.

Barrett, J.S., Szego, P., Rohatagi, S., Morales, R.J., De Witt, K.E., Rajewski, G., and Ireland, J. (1996). *Pharm. Res.* 13, 1535–1540.

Battu, C., Marquet, P., Fauconnet, A.L., Lacassie, E., and Lachatre, G. (1998). *J. Chromatogr. Sci.* 36, 1–7.

Beck, O., Kraft, M., Moeller, M.R., Smith, B.L., Schneider, S., and Wennig, R. (2000). *Ann. Clin. Biochem.* 37, 199–204.

Beckett, A.H., and Al-Sarraj, S.M. (1972). *Biochem. J.* 130, 14P.

Beckett, A.H., and Haya, K. (1977). *J. Pharm. Pharmacol.* 29, 89–95.

Beckett, A.H., and Haya, K. (1978). *Xenobiotica* 8, 85–96.

Beckett, A.H., and Rowland, M. (1964). *Nature* 204, 1203–1204.

Beckett, A.H., and Rowland, M. (1965a). *J. Pharm. Pharmacol.* 17, 628–639.

Beckett, A.H., and Rowland, M. (1965b). *J. Pharm. Pharmacol.* 17, 109S–114S.

Beckett, A.H., and Rowland, M. (1965c). *Nature* 206, 1260–1261.

Beckett, A.H., and Shenoy, E.V.B. (1973). *J. Pharm. Pharmacol.* 25, 793–799.

Beckett, A.H., Rowland, M., and Turner, P. (1965). *Lancet* 1, 303.

Beckett, A.H., Tucker, G.T., and Moffat, A.C. (1967). *J. Pharm. Pharmacol.* 19, 273–294.

Beckett, A.H., Brookes, L.G., and Shenoy, E.V.B. (1969). *J. Pharm. Pharmacol.* 21, 151S–156S.

Beckett, A.H., Shenoy, E.V.B., and Salmon, J.A. (1972). *J. Pharm. Pharmacol.* 24, 194–202.

Bell, R.R., Crookham, S.B., Dunn, W.A., Grates, K.M., and Reiber, T.M. (2001). *J. Anal. Toxicol.* 25, 652–656.

Bell, S.E., Burns, D.T., Dennis, A.C., Matchett, L.J., and Speers, J.S. (2000a). *Analyst* 125, 1811–1815.

Bell, S.E., Burns, D.T., Dennis, A.C., and Speers, J.S. (2000b). *Analyst* 125, 541–544.

Benko, A., Dona, A., Kovacs, A., Maravelias, C., Mikone, H.Z., and Kerner, A. (1998). *Acta Pharmaceutica Hungarica* 68, 269–275.

Berry, M.J., Poyser, R.H., and Robertson, M.I. (1971). *J. Pharm. Pharmacol.* 23, 140–142.

Blum, J.E. (1969). *Arzneim.-Forsch.* 19, 748–755.

Blume, H. (1981). *Arzneim.-Forsch.* 31, 805–809.

Boettcher, M., Haenseler, E., Hoke, C., Nichols, J., Raab, D., and Domke, I. (2000). *Clinica y Laboratorio* 46, 49–52.

Bogusz, M.J. (1997). *J. Anal. Toxicol.* 21, 246–247.

Bogusz, M., Aderjan, R., Schmitt, G., Nadler, E., and Neureither, B. (1990). *Forensic Sci. Int.* 48, 27–37.

Bogusz, M.J., Kala, M., and Maier, R.D. (1997). *J. Anal. Toxicol.* 21, 59–69.

Boissier, J.R., Hirtz, J., Dumont, C., and Gerardin, A. (1968). *Ann. Pharm. Fr.* 26, 215–226.

Bojarski, J., and Aboul-Enein, H.Y. (1997). *Electrophoresis* 18, 965–969.

Bourque, A.J., and Krull, I.S. (1991). *J. Chromatogr.* 537, 123–152.

Bourque, A.J., and Krull, I.S. (1994). *Biomed. Chromatogr.* 8, 53–62.

Bray, G.A. (1993). *Ann. Intern. Med.* 119, 707–713.

Brettell, T.A., Inman, K., Rudin, N., and Saferstein, R. (1999). *Anal. Chem.* 71, 235R–255R.

Brooks, J.P., Phillips, M., Stafford, D.T., and Bell, J.S. (1982). *Am. J. Forensic Med. Pathol.* 3, 245–247.

Brown, E.R., Jarvie, D.R., and Simpson, D. (1997). *Ann. Clin. Biochem.* 34, 74–80.

Brunner, L.J., and DiPiro, J.T. (1998). *Electrophoresis* 19, 2848–2855.

Buchan, B.J., Walsh, J.M., and Leaverton, P.E. (1998). *J. Forensic Sci.* 43, 395–399.

Budd, R.D., and Jain, N.C. (1978). *J. Anal. Toxicol.* 2, 241.

Caldwell, J., Dring, L.G., and Williams, R.T. (1972). *Biochem. J.* 129, 11–22.

Centini, F., Masti, A., and Barni Comparini, I. (1996). *Forensic Sci. Int.* 83, 161–166.

Cheng, W.C., Lee, W.M., Chan, M.F., Tsui, P., and Dao, K.L. (2002). *J. Forensic Sci.* 47, 1248–1252.

Chinaka, S., Tanaka, S., Takayama, N., Komai, K., Ohshima, T., and Ueda, K. (2000). *J. Chromatogr. B, Biomed. Sci. Appl.* 749, 111–118.

Choi, J., Kim, C., and Choi, M.J. (1998a). *Electrophoresis* 19, 2950–2955.

Choi, J., Kim, C., and Choi, M.J. (1998b). *J. Chromatogr., B* 705, 277–282.

Choi, M.J., Gorovits, B.M., Choi, J., Song, E.Y., Nam, K.S., and Park, J. (1994). *Biol. Pharm. Bull.* 17, 875–880.

Churley, M., Robandt, P.V., Kuhnle, J.A., Lyons, T.P., and Bruins, M.R. (2002). *J. Anal. Toxicol.* 26, 347–354.

Cirimele, V., Kintz, P., and Mangin, P. (1995). *Arch. Toxicol.* 70, 68–69.

Cloyd, M.L. (1997). *J. Occup. Environ. Med.* 39, 1135.

Cody, J.T. (1993). *Forensic Sci. Rev.* 5, 109–127.

Cody, J.T. (1994). *Forensic Sci. Rev.* 6, 81–96.

Cody, J.T. (1995). In *Handbook of Workplace Drug Testing* (ed. R.H. Liu and B.A. Goldberger). AACC Press, Washington, DC, pp. 239–288.

Cody, J.T. (1996). *Forensic Sci. Int.* 80, 189–199.

Cody, J.T. (2002). *J. Occup. Environ. Med.* 44, 435–450.

Cody, J.T., and Schwarzhoff, R. (1993). *J. Anal. Toxicol.* 17, 26–30.

Cody, J.T., and Valtier, S. (1996). *J. Anal. Toxicol.* 20, 425–431.

Cody, J.T., and Valtier, S. (1998). *J. Anal. Toxicol.* 22, 299–309.

Cody, J.T., and Valtier, S. (1999). *J. Anal. Toxicol.* 23, 603–608.

Cody, J.T., and Valtier, S. (2001). *J. Anal. Toxicol.* 25(3), 158–165.

Cody, J.T., Valtier, S., and Stillman, S. (1999). *J. Anal. Toxicol.* 23, 187–194.

Colbert, D.L. (1994a). *Br. J. Biomed. Sci.* 51, 136–146.

Colbert, D.L. (1994b). *Clin. Chem.* 40, 948–949.

Collison, I.B., Spiehler, V.R., Guluzian, S., and Sedgwick, P.R. (1998). *J. Forensic Sci.* 43, 390–394.

Cone, E.J., Presley, L., Lehrer, M., Seiter, W., Smith, M., Kardos, K.W., Fritch, D., Salamone, S., and Niedbala, R.S. (2002). *J. Anal. Toxicol.* 26, 541–546.

Cooke, B.J.A. (1994). *J. Anal. Toxicol.* 18, 49–51.

Cooper, G.A., Allen, D.L., Scott, K.S., Oliver, J.S., Ditton, J., and Smith, I.D. (2000). *J. Forensic Sci.* 45, 400–406.

Czarny, R.J., and Hornbeck, C.L. (1989). *J. Anal. Toxicol.* 13, 257–261.

Dasgupta, A., and Spies, J. (1998). *Am. J. Clin. Pathol.* 109, 527–532.

Davis, J.M., Kopin, I.J., Lemberger, L., and Axelrod, J. (1971). *Ann. N.Y. Acad. Sci.* 179, 493–501.

De Boer, D., Tan, L.P., Gorter, P., Van de Wal, R.M.A., Kettenes-van den Bosch, J.J., De Bruijn, E.A., and Maes, R.A.A. (1997). *J. Mass Spectrom.* 32, 1236–1246.

Delbeke, F.T., and Debackere, M. (1986). *Arzneim.-Forsch.* 36, 1413–1416.

Dengler, H.J., Eichelbaum, M., and Schomerus, M. (1970). In *Clinico-Pharmacological and Therapeutic Aspects of Prenylamine* (ed. U.S. von Euler, C. Bartorelli, A. Berreta, H.J. Dengler, and A. Giotti). Casa Editrice, Mila, pp. 26–45.

Desai, D.M., and Gal, J. (1993). *J. Chromatogr.* 629, 215–228.

D'Nicuola, J., Jones, R., Levine, B., and Smith, M.L. (1992). *J. Anal. Toxicol.* 16, 211–213.

Dzantiev, B.B., Choi, M.J., Park, J., Choi, J., Romanenko, O.G., Zherdev, A.V., Eremin, S.A., and Izumrudov, V.A. (1994). *Immunol. Lett.* 41, 205–211.

Eiceman, G.A., Leasure, C.S., and Selim, S.L. (1984). *J. Chromatogr. Sci.* 22, 509–513.

Ellison, T., Levy, L., Bolger, J., and Okun, R. (1970). *European J. Pharmacol.* 13, 123–128.

ElSohly, M.A., Stanford, D.F., Sherman, D., Shah, H., Bernot, D., and Turner, C.E. (1992). *J. Anal. Toxicol.* 16, 109–111.

ElSohly, M.A., Stanford, D.F., Murphy, T.P., Lester, B.M., Wright, L.L., Smeriglio, V.L., Verter, J., Bauer, C.R., Shankaran, S., Bada, H.S., and Walls, H.C. (1999). *J. Anal. Toxicol.* 23, 436–445.

Elsworth, J.D., Sandler, M., Lees, A.J., Ward, C., and Stern, G.M. (1982). *J. Neural Transmission* 54, 105–110.

Engel, J., Kristen, G., Schaefer, A., and von Schlichtegroll, A. (1986). *Drug Alcohol Depend.* 17, 229–234.

Ensslin, H.K., Kovar, K.A., and Maurer, H.H. (1996). *J. Chromatogr., B* 683, 189–197.

Fallon, J.K., Kicman, A.T., Henry, J.A., Milligan, P.J., Cowand, D.A., and Hutt, A.J. (1999). *Clin. Chem.* 45, 1058–1069.

Fay, J., Fogerson, R., Schoendorfer, D., Niedbala, R.S., and Spiehler, V. (1996). *J. Anal. Toxicol.* 20, 398–403.

Felscher, D., and Schulz, K. (2000). *J. Forensic Sci.* 45, 1327–1331.

Fitzgerald, R.L., Ramos, J.M., Jr., Bogema, S.C., and Poklis, A. (1988). *J. Anal. Toxicol.* 12, 255–259.

Fitzgerald, R.L., Blanke, R.V., Glennon, R.A. and Y., MY, Rosecrans, J.A., and Poklis, A. (1989). *J. Chromatogr.* 490, 59–69.

Fitzgerald, R.L., Rivera, J.D., and Herold, D.A. (1999). *Clin. Chem.* 45, 1224–1234.

Foster, B.S., Gilbert, D.D., Hutchaleelaha, A., and Mayersohn, M. (1998). *J. Anal. Toxicol.* 22, 265–269.

Franssen, R.M., Stolk, L.M., van den Brand, W., and Smit, B.J. (1994). *J. Anal. Toxicol.* 18, 294–295.

Fujinami, A., Miyazawa, T., and Kobayashi, Y. (1998a). *Ann. Clin. Biochem.* 35, 775–779.

Fujinami, A., Miyazawa, T., Tagawa, N., and Kobayashi, Y. (1998b). *Biol. Pharm. Bull.* 21, 1207–1210.

Gaillard, Y., Vayssette, F., and Pepin, G. (2000). *Forensic Sci. Int.* 107, 361–379.

Galloway, J.H., Ashford, M., Marsh, I.D., Holden, M., and Forrest, A.R. (1998). *J. Clin. Pathol.* 51, 326–329.

Gao, C.X., and Krull, I.S. (1989). *J. Pharmaceut. Biomed. Anal.* 7, 1183–1198.

Gao, C.X., Schmalzing, D., and Krull, I.S. (1991). *Biomed. Chromatogr.* 5, 23–31.

Garrett, E.R., Seyda, K., and Marroum, P. (1991). *Acta. Pharm. Nord.* 3, 9–14.

Garza, C., and Landeck, M. (1999). *Proc. Southwest Rev. Int. Business Res.* 20.

Gentili, S., Torresi, A., Marsili, R., Chiarotti, M., and Macchia, T. (2002). *J. Chromatogr. B, Anal. Technol. Biomed. Life Sci.* 780, 183.

Gietl, Y., Spahn, H., and Mutschler, E. (1988). *J. Chromatogr.* 426, 304–314.

Gietl, Y., Spahn, H., and Mutschler, E. (1989). *Arzneim.-Forsch.* 39, 853–856.

Gietl, Y., Spahn, H., Knauf, H., and Mutschler, E. (1990). *Eur. J. Clin. Pharmacol.* 38, 587–593.

Gimeno, P., Besacier, F., and Chaudron-Thozet, H. (2003). *Forensic Sci. Int.* 132, 182–194.

Gjerde, H., Hasvold, I., Pettersen, G., and Christophersen, A.S. (1993). *J. Anal. Toxicol.* 17, 65–68.

Glasson, B., Benakis, A., and Thomasset, M. (1971). *Arzneim.-Forsch.* 21, 1985–1992.

Goenechea, S., and Brzezinka, H. (1984). *Arch. Kriminol.* 173, 97–102.

Guttman, A. (1995). *Electrophoresis* 16, 1900–1905.

Halket, J.M., and Blau, K., eds. (1993). *Handbook for Derivatives for Chromatography.* Wiley, New York.

Halpern, A., and Mancini, M.C. (2003). *Obes. Rev.* 4, 25–42.

Hara, K., Kashimura, S., Hieda, Y., and Kageura, M. (1997). *J. Anal. Toxicol.* 21, 54–58.

Harris, L.S. (1986). *Drug Alcohol Depend.* 17, 107–118.

Hartley, R., Green, M., Quinn, M., and Levene, M.I. (1993). *Arch. Disease Childhood* 69, 55–58.

Hasegawa, M., Matsubara, K., Fukushima, S., Maseda, C., Uezono, T., and Kimura, K. (1999). Forensic Science International 101(2): 95–106.

Hayes, S.M., Liu, R.H., Tsang, W.S., Legendre, M.G., Berni, R.J., Pillion, D.J., Barnes, S., and Ho, M.H. (1987). *J. Chromatogr.* 398, 239–246.

Hegadoren, K.M., Baker, G.B., and Coutts, R.T. (1993). *Res. Commun. Subs. Abuse* 14, 67–80.

Heinonen, E.H., Anttila, M.I., and Lammintausta, R.A. (1994). *Clin. Pharmacol. Ther.* 56, 742–749.

Heinonen, E.H., Anttila, M.I., Karnani, H.L., Nyman, L.M., Vuorinen, J.A., Pyykko, K.A., and Lammintausta, R.A. (1997). *J. Clin. Pharmacol.* 37, 602–609.

Heinonen, E.H., Myllyla, V., Sotaniemi, K., Lamintausta, R., Salonen, J.S., Anttila, M., Savijarvi, M., Kotila, M., and Rinne, U.K. (1989). Acta Neurologica Scandinavica – Supplementum 126: 93–99.

Helmlin, H.J., Bracher, K., Bourquin, D., Vonlanthen, D., and Brenneisen, R. (1996). *J. Anal. Toxicol.* 20, 432–440.

Hensley, D., and Cody, J.T. (1999). *J. Anal. Toxicol.* 23, 518–523.

Herraez-Hernandez, R., Campins-Falco, P., and Sevillano-Cabeza, A. (1996). *Anal. Chem.* 68, 734–739.

Herraez-Hernandez, R., Campins-Falco, P., and Verdu-Andres, J. (2002). *J. Biochem. Biophys. Methods* 54, 147–167.

Ho, Y.-S., Liu, R.H., Nichols, A.W., and Kumar, S.D. (1990). *J. Forensic Sci.* 35, 123–132.

Honecker, H. (1975). *Int. J. Clin. Pharmacol. Biopharm.* 12, 121–128.

Hornbeck, C.L., and Czarny, R.J. (1993). *J. Anal. Toxicol.* 17, 23–25.

Hornbeck, C.L., Carrig, J.E., and Czarny, R.J. (1993). *J. Anal. Toxicol.* 17, 257–263.

Huang, M.K., Liu, C., and Huang, S.D. (2002). *Analyst* 127, 1203–1206.

Huang, Y.S., Liu, J.T., Lin, L.C., and Lin, C.H. (2003). *Electrophoresis* 24, 1097–1104.

Hughes, R.O., Bronner, W.E., and Smith, M.L. (1991). *J. Anal. Toxicol.* 15, 256–259.

Hutchaleelaha, A., Walters, A., Chow, H.H., and Mayersohn, M. (1994). *J. Chromatogr., B* 658, 103–112.

Iffland, R. (1982). *Arch. Kriminol.* 169, 81–88.

Inoue, T., and Seta, S. (1992). *Forensic Sci. Rev.* 4, 89–108.

Inoue, T., and Suzuki, S. (1986). *Xenobiotica* 16, 691–698.

Inoue, T., and Suzuki, S. (1987). *Xenobiotica* 17, 965–971.

Inoue, T., Suzuki, S., and Niwaguchi, T. (1983). *Xenobiotica* 13, 241–249.

Inoue, T., Yasuda, T., Suzuki, S., Kishi, T., and Niwaguchi, T. (1986). *Xenobiotica* 16, 109–121.

Ishii, A., Seno, H., Kumazawa, T., Nishikawa, M., Watanabe, K., Hattori, H., and Suzuki, O. (1996). *Jpn. J. Forensic Toxicol.* 14, 228–232.

Iwersen-Bergmann, S., and Schmoldt, A. (1999). *J. Anal. Toxicol.* 23, 247–256.

Jenkins, A.J. (1999). In *Principles of Forensic Toxicology* (ed. B. Levine). AACC Press, Washington, DC, pp. 31–45.

Jenkins, A.J., and Goldberger, B.A., Eds. (2002). *On-Site Drug Testing.* Humana Press, Totowa, NJ.

Jirovsky, D., Lemr, K., Sevcik, J., Smysl, B., and Stransky, Z. (1998). *Forensic Sci. Int.* 96, 61–70.

Jones, R., Klette, K., Kuhlman, J.J., Levine, B., Smith, M.L., Watson, C.V., and Selavka, C.M. (1993). *Clin. Chem.* 39, 699–700.

Jonson, C.S.L., and Stromberg, L. (1993). *J. Forensic Sci.* 38, 1472–1477.

Jonsson, J., Kronstrand, R., and Hatanpaa, M. (1996). *J. Forensic Sci.* 41, 148–151.

Julian, E.A. (1990). *J. Forensic Sci.* 35, 821–830.

Junting, L., Peng, C., and Suzuki, O. (1998). *Forensic Sci. Int.* 97, 93–100.

Jurado, C., Gimenez, M.P., Soriano, T., Menendez, M., and Repetto, M. (2000). *J. Anal. Toxicol.* 24, 11–16.

Kalasz, H., Kerecsen, L., Knoll, J., and Pucsok, J. (1990). *J. Chromatogr.* 499, 589–599.

Kalasz, H., Bartok, T., Szoko, E., Haberle, D., Kiss, J.P., Hennings, E.C., Magyar, K., and Furst, S. (1999). *Cur. Med. Chem.* 6, 271–278.

Karoum, F., Chuang, L.W., Eisler, T., Calne, D.B., Liebowitz, M.R., Quitkin, F.M., Klein, D.F., and Wyatt, R.J. (1982). *Neurology* 32, 503–509.

Katagi, M., Nishioka, H., Nakajima, K., Tsuchihashi, H., Fujima, H., Wada, H., Nakamura, K., and Makino, K. (1996). *J. Chromatogr., B* 676, 35–43.

Katagi, M., Tatsuno, M., Miki, A., Nishikawa, M., and Tsuchihashi, H. (2000). *J. Anal. Toxicol.* 24, 354–358.

Katagi, M., Tatsuno, M., Tsutsumi, H., Miki, A., Kamata, T., Nishioka, H., Nakajima, K., Nishikawa, M., and Tsuchihashi, H. (2002). *Xenobiotica* 32, 823–831.

Kataoka, H., Lord, H.L., and Pawliszyn, J. (2000). *J. Anal. Toxicol.* 24, 257–265.

Kato, N., and Ogamo, A. (2001). *Sci. Justice* 41, 239–244.

Kaufman, M.S., Hubbs, L.M., and Melander, K. (1996). *Clin. Chem.* 42, 1720–1721.

Keller, T., Miki, A., Regenscheit, P., Dirnhofer, R., Schneider, A., and Tsuchihashi, H. (1998). *Forensic Sci. Int.* 94, 55–63.

Kelly, K.L. (1990). *Clin. Chem.* 36, 1391–1392.

Kelly, R.C., Mieczkowski, T., Sweeney, S.A., and Bourland, J.A. (2000). *Forensic Sci. Int.* 107, 63–86.

Kennedy, R. (1999). In *Proceedings of the 1998 Joint SOFT/TIAFT International Meeting* (ed. V. Spiehler). SOFT/TIAFT, Newport Beach, CA, pp. 14–18.

Kidwell, D.A., Holland, J.C., and Athanaselis, S. (1998). *J. Chromatogr., B* 713, 111–135.

Kikura, R., and Nakahara, Y. (1995a). *Biol. Pharm. Bull.* 18, 267–272.

Kikura, R., and Nakahara, Y. (1995b). *Biol. Pharm. Bull.* 18, 1694–1699.

Kikura, R., and Nakahara, Y. (1997). *J. Anal. Toxicol.* 21, 291–296.

Kikura, R., Nakahara, Y., Mieczkowski, T., and Tagliaro, F. (1997). *Forensic Sci. Int.* 84, 165–177.

Kikura, R., Nakahara, Y., and Kojima, S. (2000). *J. Chromatogr., B* 741, 163–173.

Kim, E.M., Chung, H.S., Lee, K.J., and Kim, H.J. (2000). *J. Anal. Toxicol.* 24, 239–244.

Kimura, H., Mukaida, M., and Mori, A. (1999a). *J. Anal. Toxicol.* 23, 577–580.

Kimura, H., Yuan, J., Wang, G., Matsumoto, K., and Mukaida, M. (1999b). *J. Anal. Toxicol.* 23, 11–16.

Kintz, P. (1997). *J. Anal. Toxicol.* 21, 570–575.

Kintz, P., and Cirimele, V. (1997). *Forensic Sci. Int.* 84, 151–156.

Kintz, P., and Mangin, P. (1993). *J. Forens. Sci. Soc.* 33, 139–142.

Kintz, P., and Samyn, N. (1999). *J. Chromatogr., B* 733, 137–143.

Kintz, P., Ludes, B., and Mangin, P. (1992). *J. Forensic Sci.* 37, 328–331.

Kintz, P., Cirimele, V., Tracqui, A., and Mangin, P. (1995). *J. Chromatogr., B* 670, 162–166.

Kirkbride, K.P., Ward, A.D., Jenkins, N.F., Klass, G., and Coumbaros, J.C. (2001). *Forensic Sci. Int.* 115, 53–67.

Knapp, D.R. (1979). *Handbook of Analytical Derivatization Reactions.* Wiley, New York.

Knapp, D.R. (1990). *Methods Enzymol.* 193, 314–329.

Koide, I., Yokoyama, A., Noguchi, O., Okada, K., and Oda, H. (1996). *Jpn. J. Forensic Toxicol.* 14, 142–143.

Koide, I., Noguchi, O., Okada, K., Yokoyama, A., Oda, H., Yamamoto, S., and Kataoka, H. (1998). *J. Chromatogr., B* 707, 99–104.

Kojima, T., Okamoto, I., Miyazaki, T., Chikasue, F., Yashiki, M., and Nakamura, K. (1986). *Forensic Sci. Int.* 31, 93–102.

Kraemer, T., and Maurer, H.H. (1998). *J. Chromatogr., B* 713, 163–187.

Kraemer, T., and Maurer, H.H. (2002). *Ther. Drug Monit.* 24, 277–289.

Kraemer, T., Vernaleken, I., and Maurer, H.H. (1997). *J. Chromatogr., B* 702, 93–102.

Kraemer, T., Theis, G.A., Weber, A.A., and Maurer, H.H. (2000). *J. Chromatogr., B* 738, 107–118.

Kraemer, T., Roditis, S.K., Peters, F.T., and Maurer, H.H. (2003). *J. Anal. Toxicol.* 27, 68–73.

Kristen, G., Schaefer, A., and von Schlichtegroll, A. (1986). *Drug Alcohol Depend.* 17, 259–271.

Kunsman, G.W., Levine, B., Kuhlman, J.J., Jones, R.L., Hughes, R.O., Fujiyama, C.I., and Smith, M.L. (1996). *J. Anal. Toxicol.* 20, 517–521.

Kupiec, T.C., and Chaturvedi, A.K. (1999). *J. Forensic Sci.* 44, 222–226.

Kupiec, T., DeCicco, L., Spiehler, V., Sneed, G., and Kemp, P. (2002). *J. Anal. Toxicol.* 26, 513–518.

Kuroda, N., Nomura, R., al-Dirbashi, O., Akiyama, S., and Nakashima, K. (1998). *J. Chromatogr.* 798, 325–334.

La Croix, R., Pianezzola, E., and Strolin Benedetti, M. (1994). *J. Chromatogr.*, *B* 656, 251–258.

Lachenmeier, D.W., Kroener, L., Musshoff, F., and Madea, B. (2003). *Rapid Commun. Mass Spectrom.* 17, 472–478.

Laine, K., Anttila, M., Huupponen, R., Maki-Ikola, O., and Heinonen, E. (2000). *Clin. Neuropharmacol.* 23, 22–27.

Lajtha, A., Sershen, H., Cooper, T., Hashim, A., and Gaal, J. (1996). *Neurochem. Res.* 21, 1155–1160.

Lambrechts, M., Tonnesen, F., and Rasmussen, K.E. (1986). *J. Chromatogr.* 369, 365–377.

Lanz, M., Brenneisen, R., and Thormann, W. (1997). *Electrophoresis* 18, 1035–1043.

Lee, M.-R., Jeng, J., Hsiang, W.-S., and Hwang, B.-H. (1999). *J. Anal. Toxicol.* 23, 41–45.

Leino, A., Saarimies, J., Gronholm, M., and Lillsunde, P. (2001). *Scand. J. Clin. Lab. Invest.* 61, 325–331.

Lengyel, J., Magyar, K., Hollosi, I., Bartok, T., Bathori, M., Kalasz, H., and Furst, S. (1997). Journal of Chromatography A 762(1–2): 321–326.

Leveque, D., Gailion-Renault, C., Monteil, H., and Jehl, F. (1997). *J. Chromatogr.*, *B* 697, 67–75.

Lewis, D., Moore, C., Leikin, J.B., and Kechavarz, L. (1995). *Veterinary Human Toxicol.* 37, 318–319.

Lewis, R.J., Reed, D., Service, A.G., and Langford, A.M. (2000). *J. Forensic Sci.* 45, 1119–1125.

Lho, D.-S., Hong, J.-K., Paek, H.-K., Lee, J.-A., and Park, J. (1990a). *J. Anal. Toxicol.* 14, 77–83.

Lho, D.S., Shin, H.S., Kang, B.K., and Park, J. (1990b). *J. Anal. Toxicol.* 14, 73–76.

Li, N.Y., Li, Y., and Sellers, E.M. (1997). *Eur. J. Drug Metab. Pharmacokinet.* 22, 427–432.

Liebowitz, M.R., Karoum, F., Quitkin, F.M., Davies, S.O., Schwartz, D., Levitt, M., and Linnoila, M. (1985). *Biol. Psychiatry* 20, 558–565.

Lillsunde, P., and Korte, T. (1991a). *J. Anal. Toxicol.* 15, 71–81.

Lillsunde, P., and Korte, T. (1991b). *Forensic Sci. Int.* 49, 205–213.

Lillsunde, P., Michelson, L., Forsstrom, T., Korte, T., Schultz, E., Ariniemi, K., Portman, M., Sihvonen, M.L., and Seppala, T. (1996). *Forensic Sci. Int.* 77, 191–210.

Lim, H.K., Su, Z., and Foltz, R.L. (1993). *Bio. Mass Spectrom.* 22, 403–411.

Lin, D.L., Chang, W.T., Kuo, T.L., and Liu, R.H. (2000). *J. Anal. Toxicol.* 24, 275–280.

Lloyd, D.K. (1996). *J. Chromatogr.* 735, 29–42.

Loor, R., Lingenfelter, C., Wason, P.P., Tang, K., and Davoudzadeh, D. (2002). *J. Anal. Toxicol.* 26, 267–273.

Lurie, I.S. (1992). *J. Chromatogr.* 605, 269–275.

Lurie, I.S., Odeneal, N.G., II, McKibben, T.D., and Casale, J.F. (1998). *Electrophoresis* 19, 2918–2925.

Lurie, I.S., Bailey, C.G., Anex, D.S., Bethea, M.J., McKibben, T.D., and Casale, J.F. (2000). *J. Chromatogr.* 870, 53–68.

Lurie, I.S., Bethea, M.J., McKibben, T.D., Hays, P.A., Pellegrini, P., Sahai, R., Garcia, A.D., and Weinberger, R. (2001). *J. Forensic Sci.* 46, 1025–1032.

Makino, Y., Higuchi, T., Ohta, S., and Hirobe, M. (1989). *Forensic Sci. Int.* 41, 83–91.

Makino, Y., Suzuki, A., Ogawa, T., and Shirota, O. (1999). *J. Chromatogr., B* 29, 97–101.

Mallol, J., Pitarch, L., Coronas, R., and Pons, A., Jr. (1974). *Arzneim.-Forsch.* 24, 1301–1304.

Mancinelli, R., Gentili, S., Guiducci, M.S., and Macchia, T. (1999). *J. Chromatogr., B* 735, 243–253.

Manetto, G., Crivellente, F., and Tagliaro, F. (2000). *Ther. Drug Monit.* 22, 84–88.

Marquet, P., Lacassie, E., Battu, C., Faubert, H., and Lachatre, G. (1997). *J. Chromatogr., B* 700, 77–82.

Marsel, J., Doring, G., Remberg, G., and Spiteller, G. (1972). *Z. Rechtsmed.* 70, 245–250.

Marson, C., Schneider, S., Meys, F., and Wennig, R. (2000). *J. Anal. Toxicol.* 24, 17–21.

Martinez, D., and Gimenez, M.P. (1983). *Human Toxicol.* 2, 391–393.

Mascher, H.J., Kikuta, C., Millendorfer, A., Schiel, H., and Ludwig, G. (1997). International Journal of Clinical Pharmacology and Therapeutics 35(1): 9–13.

Mastrovitch, T.A., Bithoney, W.G., DeBari, V.A., and Nina, A.G. (2002). *Ann. Clin. Lab. Sci.* 32, 383–386.

Matin, S.B., Wan, S.H., and Knight, J.B. (1977). *Biomed. Mass Spectrom.* 4, 118–121.

Matsushima, K., Nagai, T., and Kamiyama, S. (1998a). *J. Anal. Toxicol.* 22, 33–39.

Matsushima, K., Nagai, T., Kanaya, H., Kato, Y., Takahashi, M., and Kamiyama, S. (1998b). *Nippon Hoigaku Zasshi* 52, 19–26.

Maurer, H.H. (1992). *J. Chromatogr.* 580, 3–41.

Maurer, H.H. (1996). *Ther. Drug Monit.* 18, 465–470.

Maurer, H.H., and Kraemer, T. (1992). *Arch. Toxicol.* 66, 675–678.

Maurer, H.H., Kraemer, T., Ledvinka, O., Schmitt, C.J., and Weber, A.A. (1997). *J. Chromatogr., B* 689, 81–89.

McKeithan, E.K., and Shepherd, M.D. (1996). *Clin. Ther.* 18, 1242–1251.

Meatherall, R. (1995). *J. Anal. Toxicol.* 19, 316–322.

Meeker, J.E., and Reynolds, P.C. (1990). *J. Anal. Toxicol.* 14, 330–331.

Melega, W.P., Cho, A.K., Schmitz, D., Kuczenski, R., and Segal, D.S. (1999). Journal of Pharmacology and Experimental Therapeutics 288(2): 752–758.

Melgar, R., and Kelly, R.C. (1993). *J. Anal. Toxicol.* 17, 399–402.

Meyer, A., Mayerhofer, A., Kovar, K.A., and Schmidt, W.J. (2002). *Neurosci. Lett.* 330, 193–197.

Meyer, E., Van Bocxlaer, J.F., Dirinck, I.M., Lambert, W.E., Thienpont, L., and De Leenheer, A.P. (1997). *J. Anal. Toxicol.* 21, 236–239.

Michel, R.E., Rege, A.B., and George, W.J. (1993). *J. Neurosci. Methods* 50, 61–66.

Miki, A., Katagi, M., and Tsuchihashi, H. (2002). *J. Anal. Toxicol.* 26, 274–279.

Miki, A., Keller, T., Regenscheit, P., Dirnhofer, R., Tatsuno, M., Katagi, M., Nishikawa, M., and Tsuchihashi, H. (1997). *J. Chromatogr., B* 692, 319–328.

Miller, K.J., Gal, J., and Ames, M.M. (1984). *J. Chromatogr.* 307, 335–342.

Moeller, M.R. (1992). *J. Chromatogr.* 580, 125–134.

Moeller, M.R. (1996). *Ther. Drug Monit.* 18, 444–449.

Moeller, M.R., Fey, P., and Sachs, H. (1993a). *Forensic Sci. Int.* 63, 43–53.

Moeller, M.R., Fey, P., and Wennig, R. (1993b). *Forensic Sci. Int.* 63, 185–206.

Mongkolsirichaikul, D., Tarnchompoo, B., and Ratanabanangkoon, K. (1993). *J. Immunol. Methods* 157, 189–195.

Moore, C., Negrusz, A., and Lewis, D. (1998). *J. Chromatogr., B* 713, 137–146.

Moore, K.A., and Poklis, A. (1995). *J. Anal. Toxicol.* 19, 549–553.

Moore, K.A., Lichtman, A.H., Poklis, A., and Borzelleca, J.F. (1995a). *Drug Alcohol Depend.* 39, 83–89.

Moore, K.A., Soine, W.H., and Poklis, A. (1995b). *J. Anal. Toxicol.* 19, 542–548.

Moore, K.A., Daniel, J.S., Fierro, M., Mozayani, A., and Poklis, A. (1996a). *J. Forensic Sci.* 41, 524–526.

Moore, K.A., Ismaiel, A., and Poklis, A. (1996b). *J. Anal. Toxicol.* 20, 89–92.

Moore, K.A., Mozayani, A., Fierro, M.F., and Poklis, A. (1996c). *Forensic Sci. Int.* 83, 111–119.

Moore, K.A., Werner, C., Zannelli, R.M., Levine, B., and Smith, M.L. (1999). *Forensic Sci. Int.* 106, 93–102.

Moriya, F., and Hashimoto, Y. (1996). *Nippon Hoigaku Zasshi* 50, 50–56.

Moriya, F., Miyaishi, S., and Ishizu, H. (1992). *Jpn. J. Alcohol Studies Drug Depend.* 27, 152–158.

Moriya, F., Chan, K.M., Noguchi, T.T., and Wu, P.Y. (1994). *J. Anal. Toxicol.* 18, 41–45.

Mortier, K.A., Maudens, K.E., Lambert, W.E., Clauwaert, K.M., Van Bocxlaer, J.F., Deforce, D.L., Van Peteghem, C.H., and De Leenheer, A.P. (2002). *J. Chromatogr. B, Anal. Technol. Biomed. Life Sci.* 779, 321–330.

Mrongovius, R., Neugebauer, M., and Rucker, G. (1984). *Eur. J. Med. Chem.* 19, 161–166.

Musshoff, F., and Kraemer, T. (1998). *Int. J. Legal. Med.* 111, 305–308.

Musshoff, F., Lachenmeier, D.W., Kroener, L., and Madea, B. (2002). *J. Chromatogr.* 958, 231–238.

Myung, S.W., Min, H.K., Kim, S., Kim, M., Cho, J.B., and Kim, T.J. (1998). *J. Chromatogr., B* 716, 359–365.

Nagai, T., and Kamiyama, S. (1990). *J. Chromatogr.* 525, 203–209.

Nagai, T., and Kamiyama, S. (1991). *J. Anal. Toxicol.* 15, 299–304.

Nagai, T., Kamiyama, S., and Nagai, T. (1988). *Z. Rechtsmed.* 101, 151–159.

Nagai, T., Sato, M., Nagai, T., Kamiyama, S., and Miura, Y. (1989). *Clin. Biochem.* 22, 439–442.

Nagai, T., Kamiyama, S., and Matsushima, K. (1995). *J. Anal. Toxicol.* 19, 225–228.

Nagai, T., Kanaya, H., Matsushima, K., and Kamiyama, S. (1997). *J. Anal. Toxicol.* 21, 112–115.

Nagai, T., Matsushima, K., Nagai, T., Yanagisawa, Y., Fujita, A., Kurosu, A., and Tokudome, S. (2000). *J. Anal. Toxicol.* 24, 140–145.

Nagasawa, N., Yashiki, M., Iwasaki, Y., Hara, K., and Kojima, T. (1996). *Forensic Sci. Int.* 78, 95–102.

Nakahara, Y. (1995). *Forensic Sci. Int.* 70, 135–153.

Nakahara, Y. (1999). *J. Chromatogr., B* 733, 161–180.

Nakahara, Y., and Hanajiri, R. (2000). *Life Sci.* 66, 563–574.

Nakahara, Y., and Kikura, R. (1996). *Arch. Toxicol.* 70, 841–849.

Nakahara, Y., and Kikura, R. (1997). *Biol. Pharm. Bull.* 20, 969–972.

Nakahara, Y., Takahashi, K., Takeda, Y., Konuma, K., Fukui, S., and Tokui, T. (1990). *Forensic Sci. Int.* 46, 243–254.

Nakahara, Y., Takahashi, K., Shimamine, M., and Takeda, Y. (1991). *J. Forensic Sci.* 36, 70–78.

Nakahara, Y., Takahashi, K., and Konuma, K. (1993). *Forensic Sci. Int.* 63, 109–119.

Nakahara, Y., Takahashi, K., and Kikura, R. (1995). *Biol. Pharm. Bull.* 18, 1223–1227.

Nakahara, Y., Kikura, R., Yasuhara, M., and Mukai, T. (1997). *Forensic Sci. Int.* 84, 157–164.

Nakahara, Y., Kikura, R., and Takahashi, K. (1998). *Life Sci.* 63, 883–893.

Nakamura, K.T., Ayau, E.L., Uyehara, C.F., Eisenhauer, C.L., Iwamoto, L.M., and Lewis, D.E. (1992). *Develop. Pharmacol. Ther.* 19, 183–190.

Namera, A., Yashiki, M., Liu, J., Okajima, K., Hara, K., Imamura, T., and Kojima, T. (2000). *Forensic Sci. Int.* 109, 215–223.

Nazarali, A.J., Baker, G.B., Coutts, R.T., and Pasutto, F.M. (1983). *Prog. Neuropsychopharmacol. Biol. Psychiatry* 7, 813–816.

Neugebauer, M. (1984). *J. Pharmaceut. Biomed. Anal.* 2, 53–60.

Neugebauer, M., Khedr, A., El-Rabbat, N., El-Kommos, M., and Saleh, G. (1997). *Biomed. Chromatogr.* 11, 356–361.

Nickel, B., Niebch, G., Peter, G., von Schlichtegroll, A., and Tibes, U. (1986). *Drug Alcohol Depend.* 17, 235–257.

Niwaguchi, T., Inoue, T., and Suzuki, S. (1982). *Xenobiotica* 12, 617–625.

Noggle, F.T., Jr., and Clark, C.R. (1986). *J. Forensic Sci.* 31, 732–742.

Nordgren, H.K., and Beck, O. (2003). *J. Anal. Toxicol.* 27, 15–19.

Oh, E.S., Hong, S.K., and Kang, G.I. (1992). *Xenobiotica* 22, 377–384.

Olsen, K.M., Gulliksen, M., and Christophersen, A.S. (1992). *Clin. Chem.* 38, 611–612.

Ortuno, J., Pizarro, N., Farre, M., Mas, M., Segura, J., Cami, J., Brenneisen, R., and de la Torre, R. (1999). *J. Chromatogr., B* 723, 221–232.

Oyler, J.M., Cone, E.J., Joseph, R.E., Jr., Moolchan, E.T., and Huestis, M.A. (2002). *Clin. Chem.* 48, 1703–1714.

Paar, W.D., Brockmeier, D., Hirzebruch, M., Schmidt, E.K., von Unruh, G.E., and Dengler, H.J. (1990). *Arzneim.-Forsch.* 40, 657–661.

Paetsch, P.R., Baker, G.B., Caffaro, L.E., Greenshaw, A.J., Rauw, G.A., and Coutts, R.T. (1992). *J. Chromatogr.* 573, 313–317.

Palhol, F., Boyer, S., Naulet, N., and Chabrillat, M. (2002). *Anal. Bioanal. Chem.* 374, 274–281.

Palm, D., Hansjoachim, F., and Grobecker, H. (1969). *Life Sci.* 8, 247–257.

Parfitt, K., ed. (1999). *Martindale: The Complete Drug Reference.* Pharmaceutical Press, Taunton, MA.

Paul, B.D., and Smith, M.L. (1999). *Forensic Sci. Rev.* 11, 157–174.

Paul, B.D., Past, M.R., McKinley, R.M., Foreman, J.D., McWhorter, L.K., and Snyder, J.J. (1994). *J. Anal. Toxicol.* 18, 331–336.

Peace, M.R., Poklis, J.L., Tarnai, L.D., and Poklis, A. (2002). *J. Anal. Toxicol.* 26, 500–503.

Peace, M.R., and Tarnai, L.D. (2002). *J. Anal. Toxicol.* 26, 464–470.

Peace, M.R., Tarnai, L.D., and Poklis, A. (2000). *J. Anal. Toxicol.* 24, 589–594.

Pellegrini, M., Rosati, F., Pacifici, R., Zuccaro, R., Romolo, F.S., and Lopez, A. (2002). *J. Chromatogr. B, Anal. Technol. Biomed. Life Sci.* 769, 243–251.

Perez-Bendito, D., Gomez-Hens, A., and Gaikwad, A. (1994). *Clin. Chem.* 40, 1489–1493.

Peters, F.T., Kraemer, T., and Maurer, H.H. (2002). *Clin. Chem.* 48, 1472–1485.

Philips, S.R. (1981). Journal of Pharmacy and Pharmacology 33(11): 739–741.

Pichini, S., Pacifici, R., Altieri, I., Pellegrini, M., and Zuccaro, P. (1999). *J. Anal. Toxicol.* 23, 343–348.

Piette, V., and Parmentier, F. (2002). *J. Chromatogr. A* 979, 345–352.

Pikkarainen, A.L. (1996). *Forensic Sci. Int.* 82, 141–152.

Pisternick, W., Kovar, K.A., and Ensslin, H. (1997). *J. Chromatogr., B* 688, 63–69.

Pizarro, N., Llebaria, A., Cano, S., Joglar, J., Farre, M., Segura, J., and de la Torre, R. (2003). *Rapid Commun. Mass Spectrom.* 17, 330–336.

Pizarro, N., Ortuno, J., Farre, M., Hernandez-Lopez, C., Pujadas, M., Llebaria, A., Joglar, J., Roset, P.N., Mas, M., Segura, J., Cami, J., and de la Torre, R. (2002). *J. Anal. Toxicol.* 26, 157–165.

Pizarro, N., Ortuno, J., Segura, J., Farre, M., Mas, M., Cami, J., and de la Torre, R. (1999). *J. Pharmaceut. Biomed. Anal.* 21, 739–747.

Poklis, A., and Moore, K.A. (1995). *J. Toxicol. Clin. Toxicol.* 33, 35–41.

Poklis, A., Hall, K.V., Still, J., and Binder, S.R. (1991). *J. Anal. Toxicol.* 15, 101–103.

Poklis, A., Hall, K.V., Eddleton, R.A., Fitzgerald, R.L., Saady, J.J., and Bogema, S.C. (1993a). *Forensic Sci. Int.* 59, 49–62.

Poklis, A., Jortani, S.A., Brown, C.S., and Crooks, C.R. (1993b). *J. Anal. Toxicol.* 17, 284–286.

Polgar, M., Vereczkey, L., Szporny, L., Czira, G., Tamás, J., Gács-Baitz, E., and Holly, S. (1979). *Xenobiotica* 9, 511–520.

Poyhia, R., Olkkola, K.T., Seppala, T., and Kalso, E. (1991). *Br. J. Clin. Pharmacol.* 32, 516–518.

Pyo, H., Park, S.-J., Park, J., Yoo, J.K., and Yoon, B. (1996). *J. Chromatogr., B* 687, 261–269.

Quintela, O., Bermejo, A.M., Tabernero, M.J., Strano-Rossi, S., Chiarotti, M., and Lucas, A.C.S. (2000). *Forensic Sci. Int.* 107, 273–279.

Ramseier, A., Caslavska, J., and Thormann, W. (1998). *Electrophoresis* 19, 2956–2966.

Ramseier, A., Caslavska, J., and Thormann, W. (1999). *Electrophoresis* 20, 2726–2738.

Ramseier, A., Siethoff, C., Caslavska, J., and Thormann, W. (2000). *Electrophoresis* 21, 380–387.

Rasmussen, K.E., Pedersen-Bjergaard, S., Krogh, M., Ugland, H.G., and Gronhaug, T. (2000). *J. Chromatogr., A* 873, 3–11.

Reimer, M.L.J., Mamer, O.A., Zavitsanos, A.P., Siddiqui, A.W., and Dadgar, D. (1993). *Bio. Mass Spectrom.* 22, 235–242.

Remberg, G., Marsel, J., Doring, G., and Spiteller, G. (1972). *Arch. Toxicol.* 29, 153–157.

Remberg, G., Eichelbaum, M., Spiteller, G., and Dengler, H.J. (1977). *Biomed. Mass Spectrom.* 4, 297–304.

Rendic, S., Slavica, M., and Medic-Saric, M. (1994). *Eur. J. Drug. Metab. Pharmacokinet.* 19, 107–117.

Reynolds, G.P., Elsworth, J.D., Blau, K., Sandler, M., Lees, A.J., and Stern, G.M. (1978a). *Br. J. Clin. Pharmacol.* 6, 542–544.

Reynolds, G.P., Riederer, P., Sandler, M., Jellinger, K., and Seemann, D. (1978b). *J. Neural Transmission* 43, 271–277.

Robinson, J.B. (1985). *Biochem. Pharmacol.* 34, 4105–4108.

Rohatagi, S., Barrett, J.S., DeWitt, K.E., Lessard, D., and Morales, R.J. (1997). *Biopharm. Drug Dispos.* 18, 665–680.

Rohrich, J., and Kauert, G. (1997). *Forensic Sci. Int.* 84, 179–188.

Rohrich, J., Schmidt, K., and Bratzke, H. (1994). *J. Anal. Toxicol.* 18, 407–414.

Rohrich, J., Zorntlein, S., Potsch, L., Skopp, G., and Becker, J. (2000). *Int. J. Legal. Med.* 113, 102–106.

Romberg, R.W., Needleman, S.B., Snyder, J.J., and Greedan, A. (1995). *J. Forensic Sci.* 40, 1100–1102.

Ros, J.J., Pelders, M.G., and Egberts, A.C. (1998). *J. Anal. Toxicol.* 22, 40–44.

Rothe, M., Pragst, F., Spiegel, K., Harrach, T., Fischer, K., and Kunkel, J. (1997). *Forensic Sci. Int.* 89, 111–128.

Rucker, G., Neugebauer, M., and Heiden, P.G. (1988). *Arzneim.-Forsch.* 38, 497–501.

Sachs, H., and Kintz, P. (1998). *J. Chromatogr., B* 713, 147–161.

Samyn, N., De Boeck, G., and Verstraete, A.G. (2002). *J. Forensic Sci.* 47, 1380–1387.

Samyn, N., De Boeck, G., Wood, M., Lamers, C.T.J., De Waard, D., Brookhuis, K.A., Verstraete, A.G., and Riedel, W.J. (2002). *Forensic Sci. Int.* 128, 90–97.

Samyn, N., and van Haeren, C. (2000). *Int. J. Legal. Med.* 113, 150–154.

Samyn, N., Verstraete, A., van Haeren, C., and Kintz, P. (1999). *Forensic Sci. Rev.* 11, 1–19.

Samyn, N., Viaene, B., and van Haeren, C. (1999). In *Proceedings of the 1998 Joint SOFT/TIAFT International Meeting* (ed. V. Spiehler). SOFT/TIAFT, Newport Beach, CA, pp. 168–178.

Santagati, N.A., Ferrara, G., Marrazzo, A., and Ronsisvalle, G. (2002). *J. Pharm. Biomed. Anal.* 30, 247–255.

Sato, M., Hida, M., and Nagase, H. (2001). *J. Anal. Toxicol.* 25, 304–309.

Sato, M., Hida, M., and Nagase, H. (2002). *Forensic Sci. Int.* 128, 146.

Sato, M., Mitsui, T., and Nagase, H. (2001). *J. Chromatogr. B, Biomed. Sci. Appl.* 751, 277–289.

Scarcella, D., Tagliaro, F., Turrina, S., Manetto, G., Nakahara, Y., Smith, F.P., and Marigo, M. (1997). *Forensic Sci. Int.* 89, 33–46.

Schepers, R.J., Oyler, J.M., Joseph, R.E., Jr., Cone, E.J., Moolchan, E.T., and Huestis, M.A. (2003). *Clin. Chem.* 49, 121–132.

Schlesser, J.L., ed. (1991). *Drugs Available Abroad—A Guide to Therapeutic Drugs Available and Approved Outside the U.S.* MEDEX Books, Detroit.

Schutz, H., Gotta, J.C., Erdmann, F., Risse, M., and Weiler, G. (2002). *Forensic Sci. Int.* 126, 191–196.

Seredenin, S.B., and Rybina, I.V. (1985). *Farmakol. Toksikol.* 48, 79–83.

Sevcik, J., Stransky, Z., Ingelse, B.A., and Lemr, K. (1996). *J. Pharm. Biomed. Anal.* 14, 1089–1094.

Shihabi, Z.K. (1998). *J. Chromatogr., A* 807, 27–36.

Shiiyama, S., Soejima-Ohkuma, T., Honda, S., Kumagai, Y., Cho, A.K., Yamada, H., Oguri, K., and Yoshimura, H. (1997). *Xenobiotica* 27, 379–387.

Shin, H.S. (1997a). *Drug Metab. Dispos.* 25, 657–662.

Shin, H.S. (1997b). *Chirality* 9, 52–58.

Shin, H.-S., and Donike, M. (1996). *Anal. Chem.* 68, 3015–3020.

Shin, H.-S., and Park, J. (1993). *Korean Biochem. J.* 26, 741–745.

Shin, H.S., Park, J.S., Park, P.B., and Yun, S.J. (1994). *J. Chromatogr., B* 661, 255–261.

Shindelman, J., Mahal, J., Pizzo, P., and Coty, W.A. (1999). *J. Anal. Toxicol.* 23, 506–510.

Silverstone, T. (1986). *Drug Alcohol Depend.* 17, 151–167.

Silverstone, T. (1992). *Drugs* 43, 820–836.

Simonick, T.F., and Watts, V.W. (1992). *J. Anal. Toxicol.* 16, 115–118.

Skopp, G., Potsch, L., Rohrich, J., Becker, J., and Mattern, R. (1999). In *Proceedings of the 1998 Joint SOFT/TIAFT International Meeting* (ed. V. Spiehler). SOFT/TIAFT, Newport Beach, CA, pp. 66–73.

Slawson, M.H., Taccogno, J.L., Foltz, R.L., and Moody, D.E. (2002). *J. Anal. Toxicol.* 26, 430–437.

Sloop, G., Hall, M., Simmons, G.T., and Robinson, C.A. (1995). *J. Anal. Toxicol.* 19, 554–556.

Smith, F.P. (1981). *Forensic Sci. Int.* 17, 225–228.

Solans, A., Carnicero, M., de la Torre, R., and Segura, J. (1995). *J. Anal. Toxicol.* 19, 104–114.

Song, Y.S., Hwang, B.H., and Chou, C.C. (2000). *J. Chromatogr., A* 896, 265–273.

Spahn-Langguth, H., Hahn, G., Mutschler, E., Mohrke, W., and Langguth, P. (1992). *J. Chromatogr.* 584, 229–237.

Spatzenegger, M., and Jaeger, W. (1995). *Drug Metab. Rev.* 27, 397–417.

Spiehler, V.R., Collison, I.B., Sedgwick, P.R., Perez, S.L., Le, S.D., and Farnin, D.A. (1998). *J. Anal. Toxicol.* 22, 573–579.

Sporkert, F., and Pragst, F. (2000). *Forensic Sci. Int.* 107, 129–148.

Stout, P.R., Claffey, D.J., and Ruth, J.A. (2000). *Drug Metab. Dispos.* 28, 286–291.

Stout, P.R., Horn, C.K., and Klette, K.L. (2002). *J. Anal. Toxicol.* 26, 253–261.

Strano-Rossi, S. (1999). *Drug Alcohol Depend.* 53, 257–271.

Stromberg, L., Bergkvist, H., and Edirisinghe, E.A. (1983). *J. Chromatogr.* 258, 65–72.

Sukbuntherng, J., Hutchaleelaha, A., Chow, H.H., and Mayersohn, M. (1995). *J. Anal. Toxicol.* 19, 139–147.

Suttijitpaisal, P., and Ratanabanangkoon, K. (1992). *Asian Pacific J. Allergy Immunol.* 10, 159–164.

Suzuki, S., Inoue, T., Hori, H., and Inayama, S. (1989). *J. Anal. Toxicol.* 13, 176–178.

Swanson, C.N.A., II. (1996). Didrex tablets—pharmacokinetics. Personal Communication; Pharmacia & Upjohn, Inc. Study.

Sweeney, S.A., Kelly, R.C., Bourland, J.A., Johnson, T., Brown, W.C., Lee, H., and Lewis, E. (1998). *J. Anal. Toxicol.* 22, 418–424.

Szebeni, G., Lengyel, J., Szekacs, G., Magyar, K., Gaal, J., and Szatmari, I. (1995). *Acta Physiol. Hung.* 83, 135–141.

Sznelwar, R.B. (1975). *Eur. J. Toxicol. Environmental Hygeine* 8, 5–13.

Szoko, E., Kalasz, H., and Magyar, K. (1999). *Neurobiology (Budapest)* 7, 247–254.

Szulc, M.E., and Krull, I.S. (1992). *Biomed. Chromatogr.* 6, 269–277.

Tagliaro, F., Smith, F.P., De Battisti, Z., Manetto, G., and Marigo, M. (1997). *J. Chromatogr. B* 689, 261–271.

Tagliaro, F., Manetto, G., Bellini, S., Scarcella, D., Smith, F.P., and Marigo, M. (1998a). *Electrophoresis* 19, 42–50.

Tagliaro, F., Manetto, G., Crivellente, F., Scarcella, D., and Marigo, M. (1998b). *Forensic Sci. Int.* 92, 201–211.

Tagliaro, F., De Battisti, Z., Groppi, A., Nakahara, Y., Scarcella, D., Valentini, R., and Marigo, M. (1999). *J. Chromatogr., B* 723, 195–202.

Tagliaro, F., Valentini, R., Manetto, G., Crivellente, F., Carli, G., and Marigo, M. (2000). *Forensic Sci. Int.* 107, 121–128.

Takahashi, K., Ishigami, A., Shimamine, M., Uchiyama, M., Ochiai, T., Sekita, K., Kawasaki, Y., Furuya, T., and Tobe, M. (1987). *Bull. Nat. Inst. Hyg. Sci.* 105, 1–6.

Takayama, N., Tanaka, S., and Hayakawa, K. (1997). *Biomed. Chromatogr.* 11, 25–28.

Takayama, N., Tanaka, S., Kizu, R., and Hayakawa, K. (1999). *Biomed. Chromatogr.* 13, 257–261.

Talwar, D., Watson, I.D., and Stewart, M.J. (1999). *J. Chromatogr., B* 735, 229–241.

Tamayo-Lora, C., Tena, T., and Rodriguez, A. (1997). *Forensic Sci. Int.* 85, 149–157.

Tarjanyi, Z.S., Kalasz, H., Hollosi, I., Bathori, M., Bartok, T., Lengyel, J., Maguar, K., and Furst, S. (1998a). *Eur. J. Drug. Metab. Pharmacokinet.* 23, 324–328.

Tarjanyi, Z., Kalasz, H., Szebeni, G., Hollosi, I., Bathori, M., and Furst, S. (1998b). *J. Pharmaceut. Biomed. Anal.* 17, 725–731.

Tarver, J.A. (1994). *J. Anal. Toxicol.* 18, 183.

Taylor, R.W., Le, S.D., Philip, S., and Jain, N.C. (1989). *J. Anal. Toxicol.* 13, 293–295.

Teter, D.F. (1999). *J. Occup. Environ. Med.* 41, 139.

Thompson, W.C., and Dasgupta, A. (1994). *Clin. Chem.* 40, 1703–1706.

Thormann, W., and Caslavska, J. (1998). *Electrophoresis* 19, 2691–2694.

Thormann, W., Aebi, Y., Lanz, M., and Caslavska, J. (1998). *Forensic Sci. Int.* 92, 157–183.

Thormann, W., Wey, A.B., Lurie, I.S., Gerber, H., Byland, C., Malik, N., Hochmeister, M., and Gehrig, C. (1999). *Electrophoresis* 20, 3203–3236.

Thurman, E.M., Pedersen, M.J., Stout, R.L., and Martin, T. (1992). *J. Anal. Toxicol.* 16, 19–27.

Tognoni, G., Morselli, P.L., and Garattini, S. (1972). *European J. Pharmacol.* 20, 125–126.

Tsai, S.C., ElSohly, M.A., Dubrovsky, T., Twarowska, B., Towt, J., and Salamone, S.J. (1998). *J. Anal. Toxicol.* 22, 474–480.

Tsuchihashi, H., Nakajima, K., Nishikawa, M., Shiomi, K., and Takahashi, S. (1989). *J. Chromatogr.* 467, 227–235.

Ugland, H.G., Krogh, M., and Rasmussen, K.E. (1997). *J. Chromatogr., B* 701, 29–38.

Ugland, H.G., Krogh, M., and Rasmussen, K.E. (1999). *J. Pharmaceut. Biomed. Anal.* 19, 463–475.

Uhl, M. (1997). *Forensic Sci. Int.* 84, 281–294.

Uhl, M. (2000). *Forensic Sci. Int.* 107, 169–179.

Valdez, A., and Sifaneck, S.J. (1997). *J. Drug Issues* 27, 879–897.

Valentine, J.L., and Middleton, R. (2000). *J. Anal. Toxicol.* 24, 211–222.

Valentine, J.L., Kearns, G.L., Sparks, C., Letzig, L.G., Valentine, C.R., Shappell, S.A., Neri, D.F., and Dejohn, C.A. (1995). *J. Anal. Toxicol.* 19, 581–590.

Valtier, S., and Cody, J.T. (1995). *J. Anal. Toxicol.* 19, 375–380.

Valtier, S., and Cody, J.T. (1999a). *J. Forensic Sci.* 44, 17–22.

Valtier, S., and Cody, J.T. (2000). *J. Anal. Toxicol.* 24, 606–613.

Vapaatalo, H., Karkainen, S., and Senius, K.E. (1984). *Int. J. Clin. Pharmacol. Res.* 4, 5–8.

Varesio, E., Gauvrit, J.Y., Longeray, R., Lanteri, P., and Veuthey, J.L. (1997). *Electrophoresis* 18, 931–937.

Ventura, R., Nadal, T., Alcalde, P., and Segura, J. (1993). *J. Chromatogr.* 647, 203–210.

Veress, T. (2000). *J. Forensic Sci.* 45, 161–166.

Verweij, A.M.A. (1992). *Forensic Sci. Rev.* 4, 125–136.

von Heeren, F., and Thormann, W. (1997). *Electrophoresis* 18, 2415–2426.

Vree, T.B., and Henderson, P.T. (1980). In *Amphetamines and Related Stimulants: Chemical, Biological, Clinical, and Sociological Aspects* (ed. J. Caldwell). CRC Press, Boca Raton, FL, pp. 47–68.

Wan, S.H., Matin, S.B., and Azarnoff, D.L. (1978). *Clin. Pharmacol. Ther.* 23, 585–590.

Weinbeger, R., and Lurie, I.S. (1991). *Anal. Chem.* 63, 823–827.

Weinmann, W., and Svoboda, M. (1998). *J. Anal. Toxicol.* 22, 319–328.

Williams, R.T., Caldwell, J., and Dring, L.G. (1973). In *Frontiers in Catecholamine Research* (ed. E. Usdin and S.H. Snyder). Pergamon Press, New York, pp. 927–932.

Witkin, J.M., Ricaurte, G.A., and Katz, J.L. (1990). *J. Pharmacol. Exp. Ther.* 253, 466–474.

Wu, A.H.B., Wong, S.S., Johnson, K.G., Callies, J., Shu, D.X., Dunn, W.E., and Wong, S.H.Y. (1993). *J. Anal. Toxicol.* 17, 241–245.

Yacoubian, G.S., Jr., Wish, E.D., and Choyka, J.D. (2002). *J. Psychoactive Drugs* 34, 325–329.

Yamada, H., Ikeda-Wada, S., and Oguri, K. (1998). *Biol. Pharm. Bull.* 21, 778–781.

Yang, J.M., and Lewandrowski, K.B. (2001). *Clinica Chimica Acta* 307, 27–32.

Yashiki, M., Miyazaki, T., and Kojima, T. (1994). *Jpn. J. Forensic Toxicol.* 12, 120–121.

Yashiki, M., Kojima, T., Miyazaki, T., Nagasawa, N., Iwasaki, Y., and Hara, K. (1995). *Forensic Sci. Int.* 76, 169–177.

Yoo, Y., Chung, H., and Choi, H. (1994). *J. Anal. Toxicol.* 18, 265–268.

Yoshimura, H., Yoshimitsu, T., Yamada, H., Koga, N., and Oguri, K. (1988). *Xenobiotica* 18, 929–940.

Zaugg, S., and Thormann, W. (2000). *J. Chromatogr., A* 875, 27–41.

CHAPTER 8

ILLICIT DRUG MANUFACTURE (WITH AN EMPHASIS ON CLANDESTINE METHAMPHETAMINE PRODUCTION): SYNTHETIC METHODS AND LAW ENFORCEMENT CONCERNS

Robert B. Palmer

Front Range Toxicology, Greeley, Colorado, Toxicology Associates, Denver, Colorado, Rocky Mountain Poison and Drug Center, Denver, Colorado

Contents

8.1 RANGE OF OPERATIONS IN CLANDESTINE LABORATORIES

The vast majority of illicit laboratories are involved in the production of methamphetamine. However, this is not the only activity known to occur in a clandestine lab. Many other drugs have been manufactured illegally, as have explosives and even chemical and biological warfare agents. The focus of this chapter is the illicit synthesis of drugs, specifically methamphetamine, so other substances, such as explosives and agents of chemical and biological terrorism, will not receive further mention. A brief list of some other illicitly synthesized drugs is presented in the first section of this chapter, prior to entering a much more detailed discussion of illegal methamphetamine synthesis. The following should not be construed as a comprehensive list of illicitly prepared drugs, nor are the lists of synthetic routes to any given substance exhaustive. The purpose of this section is to provide the forensic scientist with an idea of the diversity of illegal drug substances and the range of complexity of the illegal syntheses that have been attempted.

Drugs are produced in clandestine laboratories as a method for supplying drug abusers. As such, drugs devoid of abuse potential (e.g., antibiotics,

Handbook of Forensic Drug Analysis
Frederick P. Smith, Editor

over-the-counter analgesics) are generally not targets of interest to clandestine chemists. Synthetic routes used in the illicit preparation of opioids (heroin, methadone, meperidine, fentanyl derivatives), sedatives (gamma-hydroxybutyrate [GHB], phencyclidine [PCP], methaqualone), hallucinogens (lysergic acid diethylamide [LSD], dimethyltryptamine [DMT]), and non-methamphetamine stimulants (3,4-methylenedioxyamphetamine [MDA, Eve], 3,4-methylenedioxymethamphetamine [MDMA, Ecstasy, Adam], 4-methyl-aminorex [U4EUh]) are presented. It must, however, be reiterated that despite the diversity of pharmacological classes represented in this list, the preparation of methamphetamine and its congeners (e.g., MDMA) is by far the most significant problem.

8.1.1 ILLICIT MANUFACTURE OF OPIOIDS

Opium is essentially the raw sap isolated from the opium poppy (*Papaver somniferum*). The *Ebers Papyrus* mentioned opium as a medicinally significant agent in 1500 BC (Mann, 1995). Morphine, thebaine, and codeine are all components of opium. The concentrations of opiate alkaloids contained in opium vary considerably by growing region, but raw opium typically contains at least 10% morphine (Kalant, 1997). Though opium has been used as a therapeutic agent (e.g., laudanum, paregoric), more purified single-compound preparations are more commonly used in contemporary clinical practice.

As already stated, morphine is a natural product isolated from the opium poppy. Some of the opioid drugs are semisynthetic (i.e., prepared by chemical treatment of natural products as starting material). For example, treatment of the natural product morphine with palladium in hydrochloric acid provides the active semisynthetic opioid hydromorphone (Figure 8.1). Other opioids, including meperidine and fentanyl, do not require natural products as starting material and are completely man-made and therefore classified as fully synthetic opioids. Compounds that are isolated from the opium poppy and bind the opioid receptor are classified as *opiates*, while any compound (natural, semi-

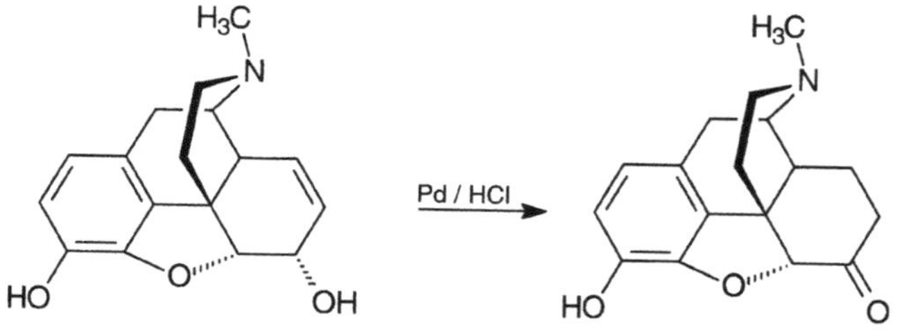

Figure 8.1

The chemical conversion of the natural product morphine to the semisynthetic opioid hydromorphone

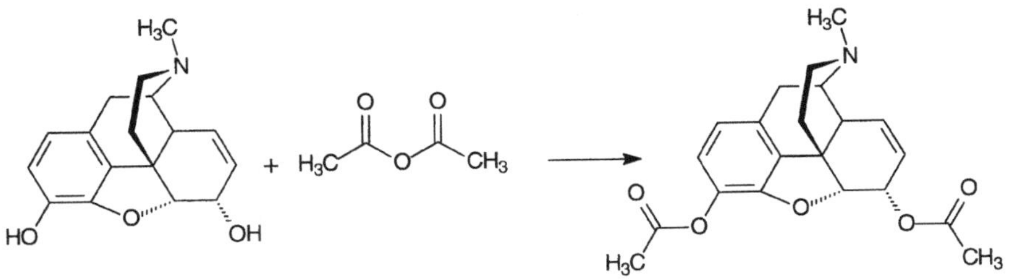

Figure 8.2
The synthesis of heroin from morphine

synthetic, or fully synthetic) that binds the same receptor is classified as an *opioid*. The most common illicitly synthesized opioid is the semisynthetic drug heroin (3,6-diacetylmorphine).

Heroin is a DEA schedule I drug that is prepared by the direct acetylation of morphine (Figure 8.2). Typically, this is accomplished by treatment of morphine with either acetic anhydride or acetyl chloride. The conversion can be performed either on bulk scale for preparation of heroin or distribution or on a single-dose basis immediately prior to use. In situations where imported heroin has become difficult for users to obtain, single-dose preparation, called *home baking*, has become popular (Sibley, 1996). "Home bake" cooks often use morphine provided by demethylation of codeine that has been extracted from pharmaceutical sources as a starting material. The use of raw opium as well as crushed tablets of regular and slow-release morphine sulfate have been reported as sources of morphine starting material for this process. The "home-bake" cook simply treats the morphine with a few milliliters of acetyl chloride over a small heat source, such as a lighter or alcohol lamp. One report indicates that the home-bake approach to heroin can result in significant amounts of monoacetylated product (6-monoacetylmorphine, 6-MAM) rather than the diacetylated heroin, which may make interpretation of postmortem toxicology results more complicated than usual (Sibley, 1996).

Not all illicitly prepared opioids are DEA schedule I. Many synthetic opioids, especially those of the phenylpiperidine class, also have clinical utility. This is due to their increased potency relative to morphine (e.g., fentanyl) as well as to lower-incidence side effects such as histamine release when compared to morphine (e.g., meperidine and fentanyl). As expected, these compounds have also found their way into the battery of drugs clandestine chemists have attempted to prepare.

Fentanyl is a fully synthetic opioid analgesic, available for clinical use in the United States since 1968. Its potency (roughly 100–300 times that of morphine) and short duration of action (usually less than 30 minutes) make it an excellent agent for surgical analgesia as well as for abuse (Buchanan and Brown,

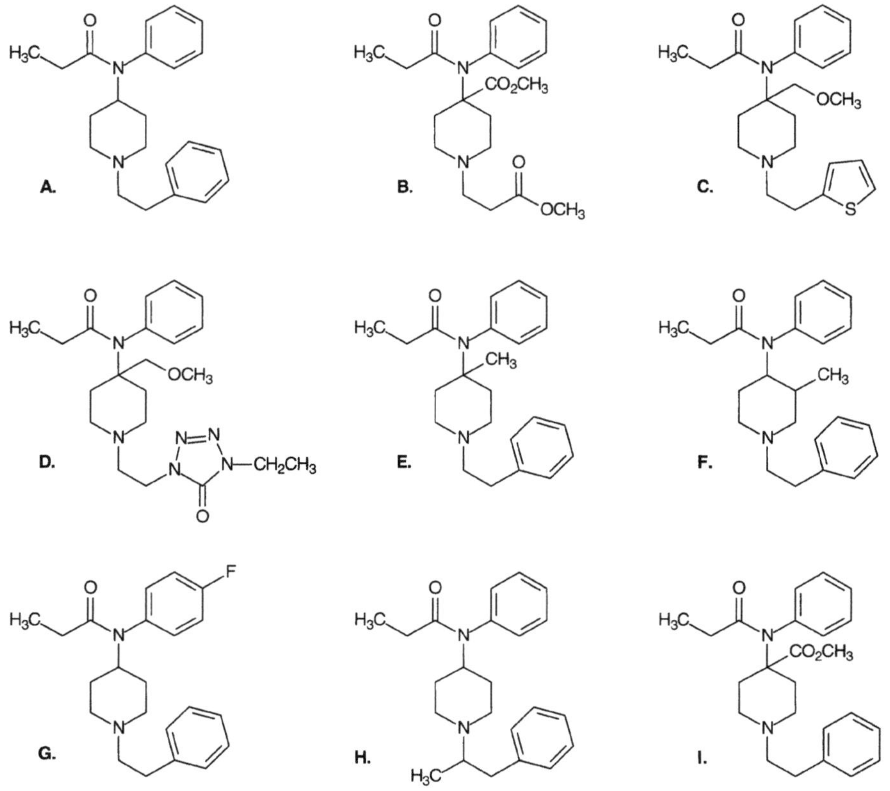

Figure 8.3

The chemical structures of several fentanyl derivatives. (A) fentanyl; (B) remifentanil; (C) sufentanil; (D) alfentanil; (E) 4-methylfentanyl; (F) 3-methylfentanyl; (G) para-fluorofentanyl; (H) α-methylfentanyl; (I) carfentanil

1988; Wax et al., 2003). A number of fentanyl derivatives are also used clinically, including alfentanyl (20–30 times the potency of morphine), sufentanyl (4500 times the potency of morphine), and remifentanil (220 times the potency of morphine) (Figure 8.3) (Wax et al., 2003). Carfentanyl is approximately 10,000 times more potent than morphine (Wax et al., 2003). Most often, carfentanyl (Wildnil) is used as an incapacitating agent for large wild animals, including elephants, rhinoceroses, polar bears, wood bison, and elk (Haigh et al., 1983; Wax et al., 2003). Carfentanyl is not approved for use in humans (Shaw et al., 1995). This drug was also implicated as a component of the "toxic gas," which likely also included an inhaled anesthetic such as halothane, released by Russian military special forces in the Moscow Dubrovka Theater Center occupied by Chechen rebel forces on October 26, 2002, where over 120 poisoning victims died (Wax et al., 2003).

At least nine fentanyl homologs have been reportedly used illicitly since the late 1970s (Buchanan and Brown, 1988). Some of these compounds are not used in medical practice and only appear in the illicit drug trade, including α-methylfentanyl and 3-methylfentanyl. Benzyl fentanyl has also been found in illicit-drug samples, though this compound is devoid of opioid activity and is likely present as a synthetic by-product or residual synthetic intermediate from the preparation of other fentanyl derivatives (Fritschi and Klein, 1995).

In the late 1970s and early 1980s, a decline in the availability of heroin in the United States fueled the illicit manufacture of derivatives of fentanyl (Buchanan and Brown, 1988). These compounds were most often α-methylfentanyl and 3-methylfentanyl mixed with an inactive adulterant to increase bulk and decrease drug concentration. Sometimes these fentanyl derivatives were sold as heroin, while at other times they went by street monikers such as "synthetic heroin" and "China white," which is the same term used for high-quality southeast Asian heroin (Buchanan and Brown, 1988). Illicit preparation and the use of fentanyl derivatives is blamed for at least 100 deaths along the west coast of the United States in 1986 (Henderson, 1988). However, with heroin once again readily available in the United States, it is presently unusual to encounter illicitly produced fentanyl analogs.

The synthesis of fentanyl is a multistep procedure that requires some familiarity with synthetic organic chemistry. However, at least for fentanyl itself, the reactions are typically run at room temperature, proceed in high yield, and require little purification beyond extraction and occasional recrystallization prior to the next step in the synthesis.

A common synthetic scheme for the illicit production of fentanyl begins with the preparation of the precursor, N-phenethylpiperidone (NPP) from the S_N^2 condensation of piperidone and 1-bromo-2-phenylethane (Figure 8.4). The NPP is then reacted with aniline over molecular sieves to form the imine, which can be reduced *in situ* with NaBH$_4$ to form 4-anilino-N-phenethylpiperidine (4-ANPP). Reaction of 4-ANPP with propinonyl chloride yields fentanyl, which is often then converted to the hydrochloride salt by bubbling HCl gas through a solution of the free base of the drug in an organic solvent and collecting the precipitate. The hydrochloride salt is often diluted ("cut") before sale and use with an inactive bulk solid such as lactose. Minor variations in reagents, reaction, and purification conditions can produce other fentanyl derivatives. For example, use of 1-phenyl-2-bromopropane in place of 1-bromo-2-phenylethane in the first step yields the α-methyl derivative of NPP. This compound is then used instead of NPP to prepare the potent α-methylfentanyl. Likewise, substitution of *para*-fluoroaniline for plain aniline results in the production of *para*-fluorofentanyl.

Though another phenylpiperidine derivative, meperidine, has been illicitly prepared, it was a botched synthesis of a derivative of this compound that captured the attention of the country in the early 1980s (Figure 8.5). In a widely publicized episode, a clandestine chemist in San Jose, California, attempted to

Figure 8.4
Synthetic scheme for the
preparation of fentanyl

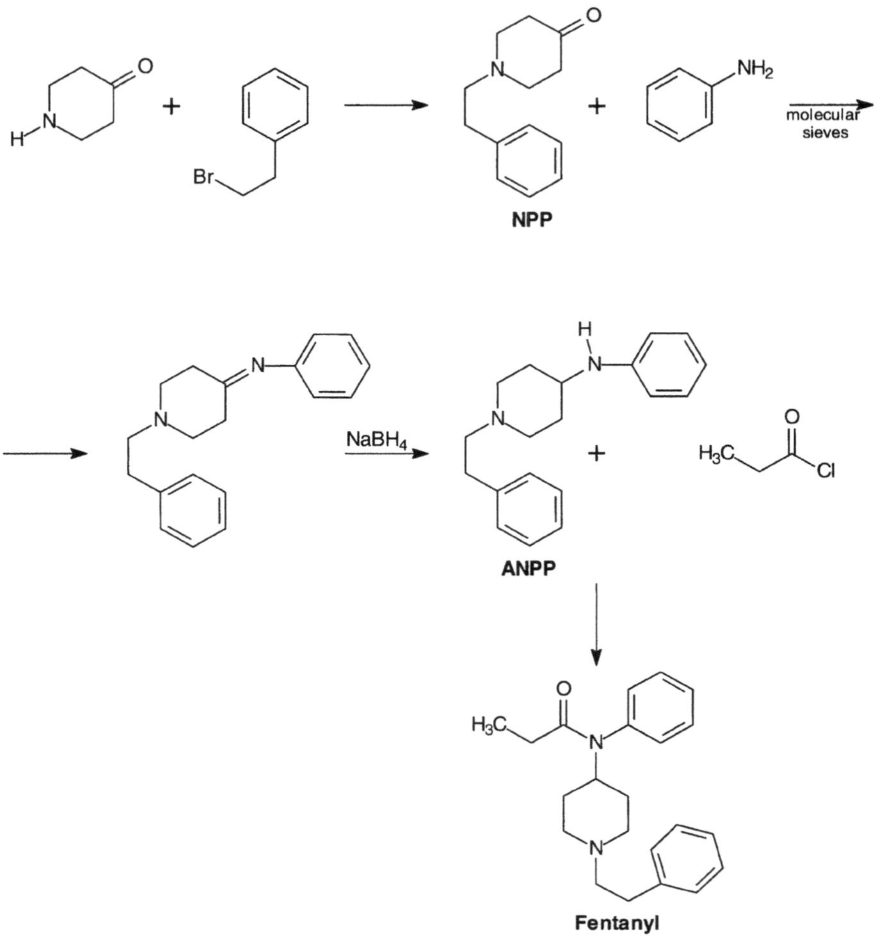

produce 1-methyl-4-phenyl-4-propionoxypiperidine (MPPP), a potent reverse ester of meperidine, which was sold as "new heroin" (Perrine, 1996). Analysis of this material at Stanford University revealed that it was composed of 96% inert material (street drug "cutting" agent), 3.2% 1-methyl-4-phenyl-1,2,5,6-tetrahydropyridine (MPTP), and only about 0.3% of the intended MPPP product (Langston et al., 1983a). Unfortunately, the MPTP contaminant is a potent neurotoxin. It has been suggested that MPTP was produced when either the incorrect esterification process was used or excess sulfuric acid was present and the reaction mixture was overheated (Perrine, 1996). The MPTP contamination of the drugs led to a reported "epidemic" of Parkinsonism within the Bay Area intravenous drug–using population (Langston et al., 1983). Other clandestine chemists have also inadvertently produced MPPP contaminated

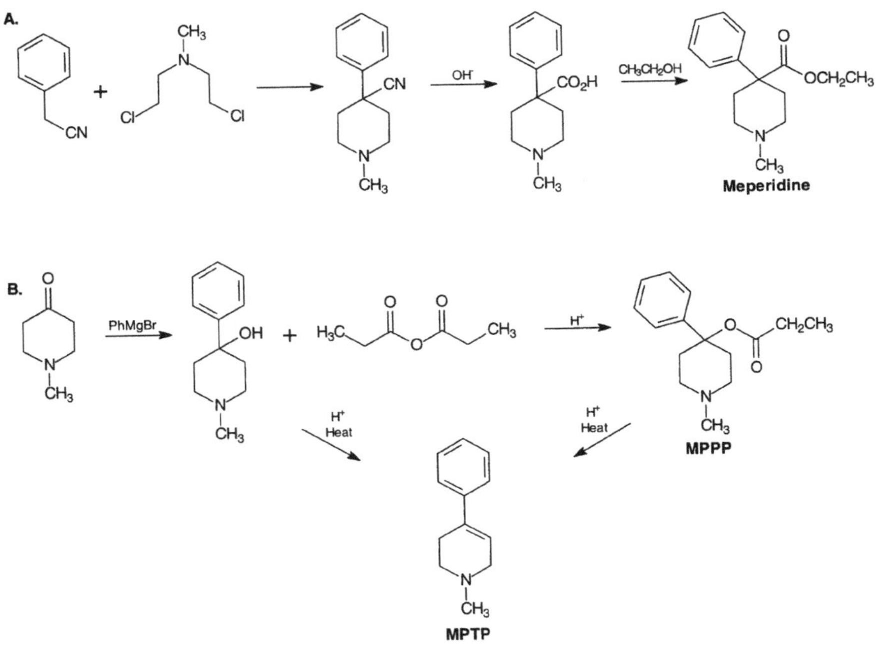

Figure 8.5
A. Synthetic route to meperidine; B. synthetic route to MPPP, indicating formation of MPTP with heat and acid

with MPTP, by at least two different synthetic routes (MMWR, 1984). Cases of MPTP-induced Parkinsonism have been reported not only in California but also in Maryland and Vancouver, British Columbia (MMWR, 1984).

It is estimated that hundreds of intravenous drug users may have developed some degree of Parkinsonism as a result of MPTP exposure. Seven severe cases were studied during the epidemic, and at least two deaths were attributed directly to MPTP, though this number dramatically underrepresents the actual number of deaths. There is utility for MPTP as a synthetic intermediate, and it is sold by some chemical companies for this purpose. However, at least three non-drug-abusing industrial chemists whose job it was to synthesize MPTP have reportedly developed symptoms of Parkinsonism (Langston and Ballard, 1983; Perrine, 1996).

The neurologic damage associated with MPTP poisoning is a result of the oxidative metabolic conversion of MPTP by monoamine oxidase B (MAO-B), which is widely distributed in the mammalian brain (Figure 8.6) (Langston et al., 1984; Perrine, 1996). This transformation produces the 1-methyl-4-pyridinium ion (MPP$^+$), which selectively destroys the zona compacta of the substantia nigra (Langston et al., 1983, 1984). Pretreatment with the drug selegiline or pargyline, both of which are specific MAO-B inhibitors, is protective against the neurologic damage caused by MPTP in some models (Langston et al., 1984; Buchanan and Brown, 1988; Perrine, 1996; Kupsch et al., 2001). So potent, predictable, and specific is the neurotoxicity of MPTP that it is now frequently used to induce Parkinsonism in experimental animal models of the condition.

Methadone (amidone) is commonly used to assist in the management of opiate addiction and also has clinical utility in the management of severe chronic pain. It is active at opioid receptors and has an analgesic potency approximately 1.5–4 times that of morphine (Perrine, 1996; Wax et al., 2003). Synthetic routes to methadone and its congeners have been reported in the chemical literature (Cusic, 1949; Cheney, 1949). One method used to synthetically prepare methadone begins with diphenylacetonitrile, which is reacted with the hydrochloride salt of 2-chloro-N,N-dimethylpropylamine under basic conditions in dimethylformamide (DMF) (Figure 8.7). Under these conditions,

Figure 8.6

The metabolism of MPTP to the neurotoxin MPP+

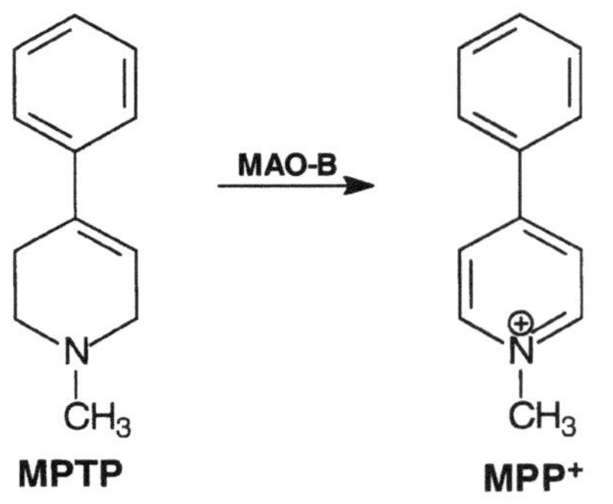

Figure 8.7

Synthetic scheme for the production of methadone

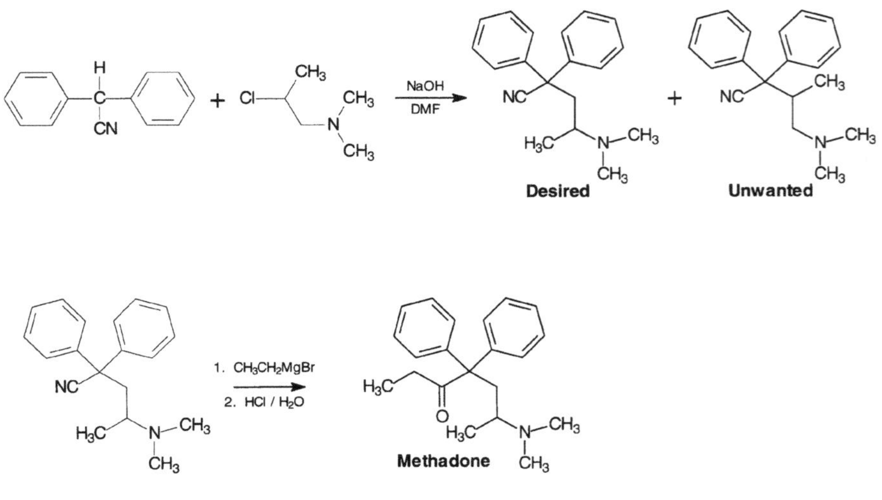

the amine cyclizes to form an intermediate aziridinium ion, which is attacked by the anion formed by the concomitant deprotonation of the diphenylacetonitrile. Since both carbons of the aziridinium ring are subject to nucleophilic attack, two isomeric nitriles are formed. The 2,2-diphenyl-4-dimethylaminovaleronitrile is the desired intermediate for the synthesis of methadone; the simultaneously formed 2,2-diphenyl-3-methyl-4-dimethylaminobutyronitrile is unwanted. The slight steric hindrance of one of the aziridinium ring carbons caused by the methyl group, along with the use of DMF as a solvent, produces a slight excess of the desired nitrile (Cusic, 1949). The desired nitrile can be isolated from the unwanted product through recrystallization from hexane. Reacting the 2,2-diphenyl-4-dimethylaminovaleronitrile with ethyl magnesium bromide (ethyl Grignard) yields an imine, which, when treated with aqueous acid, provides methadone. Despite the fact that this and other synthetic routes to methadone are known, illicitly used methadone is more likely to have been diverted from legitimate medical sources than synthesized in a clandestine laboratory.

Illicit attempts at the preparation of other opioids are also known. However, many of these procedures, such as the conversion of codeine to oxycodone, are more complicated and require specialized training, equipment, facilities, or reagents that are not easy for the clandestine chemist to acquire. That said, however, there is always a chance that a simple and efficient scheme for these conversions will be developed and put to use for the manufacture of street drugs.

8.1.2 ILLICIT MANUFACTURE OF SEDATIVES

Many abused agents are sedatives with anesthetic-like effects that may or may not give way to agitation in a dose-dependent fashion. Among these drugs are ketamine, phencyclidine (PCP), gamma hydroxybutyrate (GHB), methaqualone, and toluene (usually from huffing of spray paints or solvents). The most common drugs in this group that are illicitly prepared are the GABA agonist, GHB, the arylcyclohexylamine, PCP, and the quinazolinone, methaqualone.

Gamma hydroxybutyrate, the sodium salt of which is also known as sodium oxybate, is a GABA-active general anesthetic that has found widespread use in the illicit drug market. Use of GHB as an induction agent for general anesthesia has been common in Europe since the 1960s (Marnell, 1999). It is an inexpensive and readily available compound. Unfortunately, the precise dose needed is difficult to titrate, and patients in whom this drug is used have a propensity to display myoclonic jerking. These difficulties led to its being abandoned as an anesthesia induction agent in the United States. Nonetheless, sodium oxybate has recently gained FDA approval and is marketed as Xyrem® for the treatment of cataplexy associated with narcolepsy.

In the mid-1990s, GHB gained popularity as a drug of abuse. It was used principally by weightlifters, under claims that it would increase lean muscle mass while the user slept (Lee, 2002). The exact origin of these claims is unclear, though it is likely due to animal studies in which rats treated with GHB demonstrated a statistically significant (though likely not clinically significant) increase in growth hormone secretion. A more nefarious use of GHB is as a "date rape drug." Claims exist touting GHB as an aphrodisiac. There is a dose dependence on sexual stimulation effects versus sedation from the drug. With the difficulty in controlling the dose of GHB and its pronounced sedative effects, it is difficult to see any great utility for the drug as a true aphrodisiac. More commonly, its use in a sexual context is simply as a sedative for the facilitation of sexual assault. Derivatives of GHB, including gamma-butyrolactone (GBL), gamma-valerolactone (GVL), gamma-hydroxyvaleric acid (GHV), 1,4-butanediol diacetate (BDDA), *trans*-4-hydroxycrotonic acid (T-HCA), and 1,4-butandiol (BD), are also abused, for essentially the same reasons as GHB (Figure 8.8).

The synthesis of GHB is chemically very easy (Figure 8.9). Most often, simple saponification of the lactone, gamma-butyrolactone (GBL), is the selected synthetic route. The source of GBL is often floor-stripping products. The treatment of GBL with a strong base such as sodium or potassium hydroxide opens

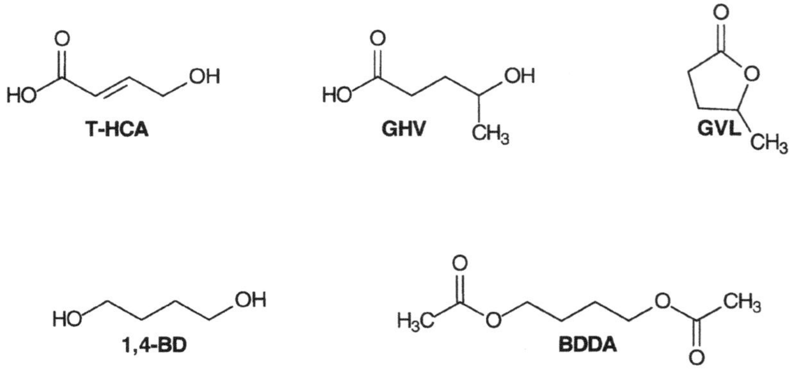

Figure 8.8

Chemical structures of several congeners of gamma-hydroxybutyrate (GHB). GABA = gamma aminobutyric acid; GHB = gamma hydroxybutyrate; GBL = gamma butyrolactone; T-HCA = trans-4-hydroxycrotonic acid; GHV = gamma hydroxyvaleric acid; GVL = gamma valerolactone; 1,4-BD = 1,4-butane diol; BDDA = 1,4-butane diol diacetate

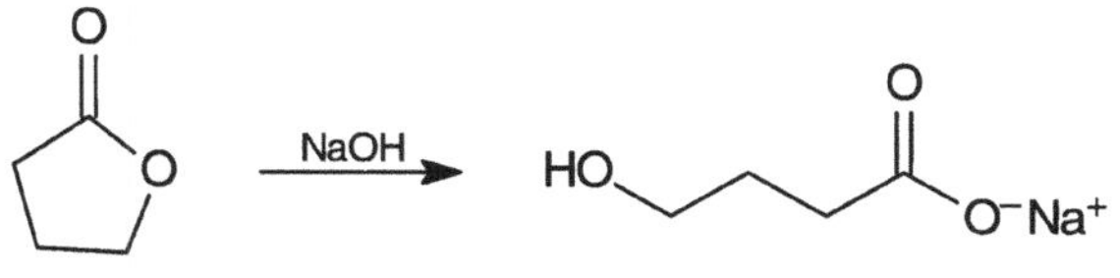

Figure 8.9
Synthetic scheme for the
preparation of the sodium
salt of GHB

the lactone ring and provides the corresponding salt of GHB in nearly quantitative yield. The pH of the solution must then be adjusted, to neutralize the excess base, and the salt collected. The compound is occasionally distributed as a solid, but more commonly it is dissolved in a small amount of water or other aqueous liquid. The route of administration is most often ingestion. Inadequate neutralization of excess base following saponification of GBL has resulted in caustic injury when the substance was swallowed (Dyer and Reed, 1997).

Phencyclidine (1-(1-phenylcyclohexyl)piperidine; PCP) is a psychoactive arylhexylamine investigated by Parke-Davis as a possible surgical adjuvant in humans (Shulgin and MacLean, 1976). Initial trials demonstrated that complete analgesia was achieved within minutes after intravenous administration of doses of approximately 20mg. However, doses of roughly four times this amount were needed for surgical anesthesia (Greifenstein et al., 1958; Shulgin and MacLean, 1976). At these higher doses, a significant state of excitation requiring barbiturate sedation for control was observed. Other untoward side effects of the drug, including trancelike ecstatic states, mania, dizziness, euphoria, visual distortions, and hallucinations, led to abandonment of this drug as a clinical agent in 1965. However, it is likely that word of these very effects also fostered the beginnings of the street use of this compound. Despite the clinical failure of phencyclidine, it is the lead compound for the development of a variety of derivatives, including ketamine, which is currently used in both human and veterinary anesthesia.

Illicit preparation of PCP has been commonplace since the late 1960s and early 1970s. Shulgin and MacLean (1976) reviewed illicit synthetic methods for PCP and several of its derivatives in 1976. They concluded that for an illicit synthesis of PCP or its congeners, at least one representative from each of the following five groups must be present in addition to the usual chemical accessories, such as drying agents and solvents: (1) an aliphatic amine (e.g., piperidine, ethylamine); (2) an aliphatic ketone (usually cyclohexanone); (3) an aromatic halide (e.g., bromobenzene, bromotoluene, bromothiophene); (4) a leaving group intermediate (e.g., potassium cyanide, hydrogen bromide, *p*-toluenesulfonic acid); and (5) a metal (e.g., magnesium, lithium). It must be noted, however, that working with many of these reagents in clandestine laboratory facilities as well as the drug itself may contribute to a potentially toxic environment.

One report of a hazardous situation associated with illicit preparation of PCP in open cooking pots was published in 1980 (Aniline et al., 1980). In this case, a 62-year-old woman occupied an apartment that, unbeknownst to her, was immediately above a working clandestine PCP lab in which the drug was prepared in open vats. She was evaluated in the hospital emergency department, where she reported that every Wednesday when she went into the lavatory in her apartment, the smell from the apartment below caused her to become dizzy and fall. Due to her past history of recurrent psychotic depressions superimposed on milder depressive illness, she was also evaluated by the psychiatry service at the hospital. An incidental analysis of her blood revealed a serum PCP concentration of 8 ng/mL. This finding, combined with a cited communication from the chief laboratory chemist at the Los Angeles County Sheriff's Department indicating that illicit PCP synthesis usually takes about a week to perform, led the authors to conclude that the patient's statement of experiencing symptoms on Wednesdays may have been completely rational.

The syntheses of PCP and its derivatives can be classified into three groups: those employing the nitrile compound 1-piperidinocyclohexane carbonitrile (PCC), those that depend on intermediate formation of an imine (Schiff's base), and those that use an enamine compound (Maddox et al., 1965; Shulgin and MacLean, 1976). The most frequent approach is the first (Figure 8.10). Facile removal of the nitrile moiety by an aryl Grignard reagent is easily accomplished, and a known reaction for a number of aryl Grignards.

Therefore, the illicit preparation of PCP and its derivatives begins with the preparation of the PCC starting material. This can be accomplished through the addition of cyclohexanone and KCN to an aqueous solution of piperidine HCl. Once the nitrile compound is synthesized, reaction with the selected aromatic Grignard is performed, followed by treatment with HBr or NH_4Cl to give PCP. Attempts to use phenyllithium rather than phenylmagnesium bromide were not successful because they resulted in addition to the nitrile rather than its displacement (Shulgin and MacLean, 1976).

Due to the great variability in the skill of those performing the synthesis of PCP, it is common to find unreacted PCC starting material in the final product (Buchanan and Brown, 1988; Shulgin and MacLean, 1976). In fact, concen-

Figure 8.10

Synthetic scheme for the preparation of phyencyclidine (PCP)

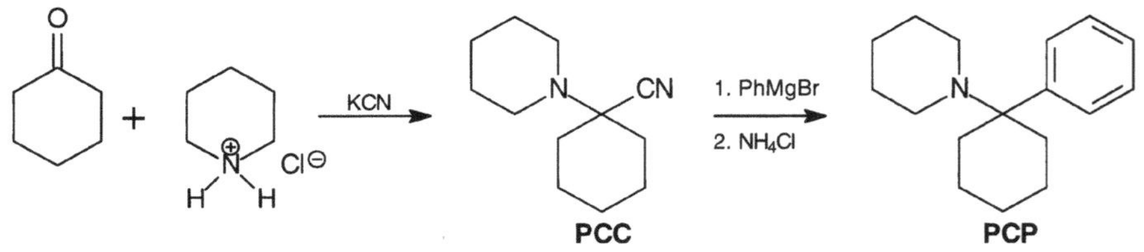

trations of PCC ranging from 10% to 70% of the bulk drug have been reported (Buchanan and Brown, 1988; Shulgin and MacLean, 1976). One concern about the use of PCP with high levels of PCC contamination was whether or not cyanide was released upon heating of the compound. It was suggested by Soine that smoking large amounts of drug contaminated with PCC might release enough cyanide to produce toxicity, but this has not been demonstrated experimentally (Soine et al., 1979). The pharmacology and toxicology of PCC have not been thoroughly studied.

By varying the reagents used slightly, a variety of PCP homologs can be prepared (Figure 8.11). For example, using ethylamine or pyrrolidine rather than piperidine as the aliphatic amine provides the N-ethyl PCP derivative (PCE) and the pyrrolidine PCP derivative (PHP), respectively. Substituting thiophene for phenyl in the final step creates TCP, the thiophene analog of PCP.

Laboratory evaluation of the pyrrolidine analog found this compound to be qualitatively and quantitatively similar to PCP when given to mice and primates (Kalir et al., 1969; Shulgin and MacLean, 1976). However, street-level users found that the compound caused a degree of sedation akin to that seen with barbiturates, and street use was largely abandoned (Shulgin and MacLean, 1976; Buchanan and Brown, 1988). The potencies of both PCE and TCP are greater than that of PCP, though the qualitative effects of TCP are similar to those of PCP (Shulgin and MacLean, 1976; Buchanan and Brown, 1988). Phenylcyclohexyl-4-methylpiperidine is synthesized when 4-methylpiperidine is used in place of piperidine. This compound was identified in a sample of

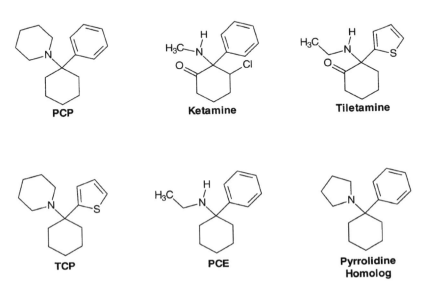

PCP   Ketamine   Tiletamine

TCP   PCE   Pyrrolidine
                               Homolog

Figure 8.11

Chemical structures of structural relatives of phencyclidine (PCP)

alleged PCP, and it was presumed that it was prepared in order to circumvent laws at the time that restricted the availability of piperidine but not 4-methylpiperidine (Shulgin and MacLean, 1976; Soine et al., 1982; Buchanan and Brown, 1988). Animal data indicate that the 4-methylpiperidine derivative is approximately 12% as potent as PCP but 1.4 times less toxic (Buchanan and Brown, 1988; Soine et al., 1982). In other words, the doses required to obtain psychotropic effects similar to those of PCP would more likely produce toxic effects.

In South Africa, the sedative methaqualone is a drug of choice for abuse and therefore for illicit manufacture (van Zyl, 2001). This drug was originally marketed in the mid-1960s in a nonbarbiturate nonaddictive sedative-hypnotic under the trade name "Quaalude." However, in reality, abuse of methaqualone gives rise to a barbiturate-like dependence (van Zyl, 2001). This effect became quickly apparent, and most member countries of the United Nations (UN) banned its sale and use. Since its removal from the legal pharmaceutical market, methaqualone and several structural relatives of the drug have been prepared in illicit laboratories (Angelos and Meyers, 1985; van Zyl, 2001). In South Africa, methaqualone is usually smoked in a "witpyp" (i.e., white pipe) mixed with *Cannabis* (van Zyl, 2001).

Numerous synthetic routes to methaqualone and other 2,3-disubstituted-4(3H)-quinazolinones have been reported (Kacker and Zaheer, 1951; Soliman and Soliman, 1979; Dal Cason et al., 1981; van Zyl, 2001). However, there are two primary routes used for illegal production, because both involve only simple one- or two-step reaction sequences that are easily adapted to the clandestine laboratory environment (Angelos and Meyers, 1985; van Zyl, 2001). The one-step method is performed by simply refluxing anthranilic anhydride with acetic acid or acetic anhydride and *o*-toluidine (Figure 8.12a). Polyphosphoric acid is often added to remove residual water, providing methaqualone in reasonable yield though likely in need of some form of purification. In the two-step method, *N*-acetylanthranilic acid is isolated after being produced by reacting anthranilic acid with acetic anhydride (Figure 8.12b). This acetamide intermediate is then condensed with *o*-toluidine in the presence of phosphorus trichloride to give methaqualone. Additional synthetic routes to methaqualone and related compounds have been reviewed (van Zyl, 2001).

8.1.3 ILLICIT MANUFACTURE OF HALLUCINOGENS

Hallucinogens alter the perception of the brain to external stimuli. Other terms used for this class of drugs include *pychotomimetics* and *psychedelics*. The 1970 Controlled Substance Act uses the term *hallucinogen* and places all compounds of this general description into DEA schedule I (Perine, 1996). That is, all of

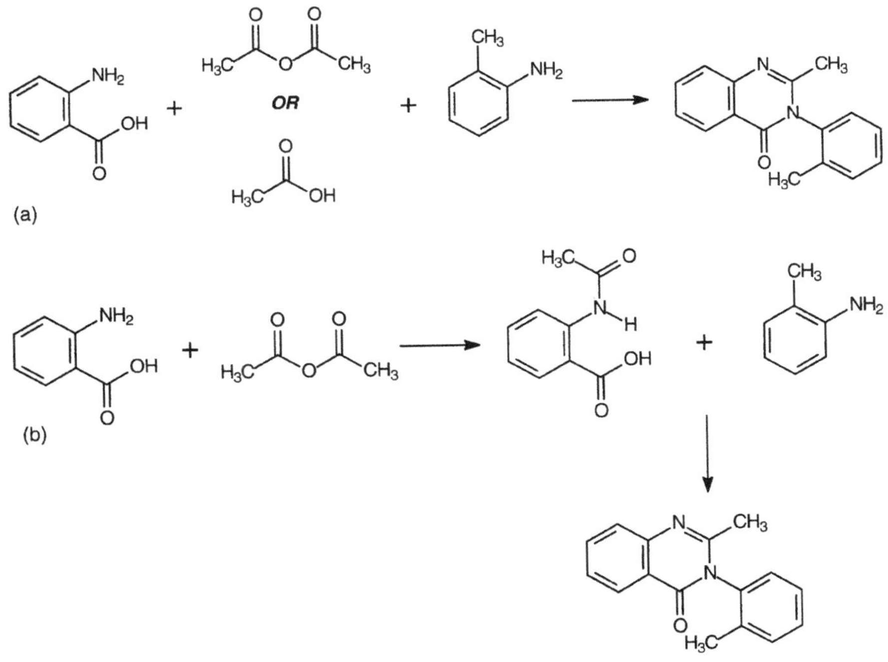

Figure 8.12

(a) One-step synthetic scheme for the preparation of methaqualone; (b) two-step synthetic scheme for the preparation of methaqualone

(a)

(b)

these agents have a high potential for abuse and lack accepted medical use or safety. Listed within this category are *Cannabis*, lysergic acid diethylamide (LSD) and its derivatives, psilocybine, mescaline, and a variety of tryptamine analogs, among many others. In truth, none of the compounds in this classification causes hallucinations (Perrine, 1996). The use of the different terms in referring to these compounds is largely semantic, in that many people have a positive association with the term *psychedelic*, but negative connotations are expressed when the term *hallucinogen* is used—even when both cases are making reference to the same compound. Though many of these compounds can cause bizarre behavior and conflicting accounts exist of "flashbacks," especially with LSD use, acute intoxication with hallucinogens rarely produces direct life-threatening effects. Deaths from LSD are typically due to trauma while the patient is experiencing altered perceptions as a result of drug intoxication (Ellenhorn and Barceloux, 1988).

Lysergic acid diethylamide (LSD), usually a semisynthetic hallucinogenic agent, has numerous street names, including "acid," "paper," "ticket," "stamps," and "blotter," among others (Figure 8.13). It is extremely potent, with effective doses measured in the tens of micrograms, and is well absorbed through the mucous membranes and gastrointestinal tract and percutaneously (Perrine, 1996; Marnell, 1999). It is, however, a heat-labile compound, so smoking is not

Figure 8.13

Some sources of ergotamine

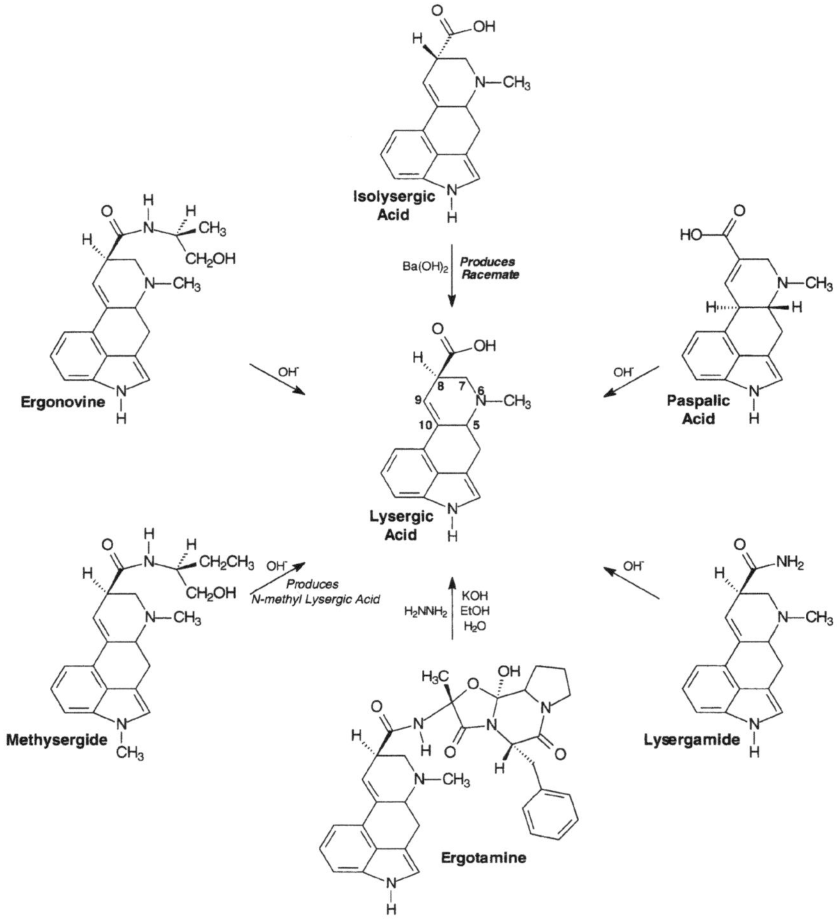

a viable method of delivery (Marnell, 1999). Most often, LSD is taken by placing a square of blotter paper (discussed later) on the tongue, allowing absorption of the drug through the mucosal surfaces of the mouth.

The usual starting material for the preparation of LSD is lysergic acid. Kornfeld and Woodward published the first successful synthesis of lysergic acid in 1956, starting from indole 3-propionic acid (Kornfeld et al., 1956). Several other researchers have reported different synthetic routes to lysergic acid. Rebek published a total synthesis of lysergic acid starting from its biosynthetic precursor, tryptophan, in 1984 (Rebek, Tai, and Shue, 1984). It must be noted that the total synthesis of lysergic acid is quite complicated. Therefore, it is much simpler and more economical to isolate lysergic acid from pharmaceutical or plant or fungal sources. Hydrolysis of the antimigraine medication ergotamine tartrate provides lysergic acid (Figure 8.13). Alternatively, ergonovine or methylergonivine, both of which are used medically to stimulate uterine contractions, could also be utilized (Figure 8.13). Chemical transformation of methysergide or dihydroergotamine could potentially yield lysergic acid, though this has not been reported in illicit laboratories (Figure 8.13) (Perrine, 1996). Methysergide, the N-methyl analog of methylergonovine, could be used to produce N-methyl LSD, which is approximately 10% as potent a hallucinogen as LSD (Perrine, 1996).

Ergotamine can also be isolated from natural sources, including the seeds of the Hawaiian woodrose, morning glory, and stipa robusta plants (Perrine, 1996; Shulgin and Shulgin, 1997; Marnell, 1999). Fungal cultures of *Claviceps paspali* produce abundant quantities of paspalic acid when raised under saprophytic conditions in fermenters (Perrine, 1996). Paspalic acid can be isomerized to the thermodynamically preferable lysergic acid by treatment with a base (Figure 8.13) (Perrine, 1996). The use of *C. pupurea* has also been suggested, though cultures of this fungus are reportedly difficult to raise except directly on grain growing in fields (Perrine, 1996). Other fungal cultures, including *Aspergillus clavatus*, are also possible sources of lysergic acid or its derivatives. Though morning glory plants are readily available and raising fungal cultures for lysergic acid production is not much more difficult than culturing yogurt, diversion of pharmaceutical ergotamine tartrate is probably the most economically feasible method for illicit production of LSD (Perrine, 1996; Marnell, 1999). Since ergotamine tartrate is tightly controlled in the United States, it is likely that much of the compound used in the illegal production of LSD is smuggled into the United States from foreign sources where fewer restrictions on its sale exist (Marnell, 1999).

Lysergic acid is produced by refluxing ergotamine tartrate with potassium hydroxide and hydrazine in a solvent of alcohol–water. It is estimated that in order to satisfy the annual use of pure LSD in the United States (approximately 11 pounds), 60 pounds of ergotamine tartrate is required (Marnell, 1999). Once the lysergic acid is prepared, one of four methods is probably used to convert it to LSD (Figure 8.14). First, the lysergic acid may be treated with lithium hydroxide to produce the lithium salt, which is reacted with sulfur trioxide, dimethylformamide, and diethylamine to produce LSD. The second possible method involves the reaction of lysergic acid with N,N-carbonyldiimidazole followed by treatment with diethylamine. The third method involves the reaction of lysergic acid with trifluoroacetic anhydride followed by subsequent reaction with diethylamine. Finally, the lysergic acid and diethylamine can be combined in chloroform and refluxed. After this, $POCl_3$ is added and the solution allowed to return to room temperature. It is suggested that the $POCl_3$ method is preferred today because it is the cleanest and most efficient method

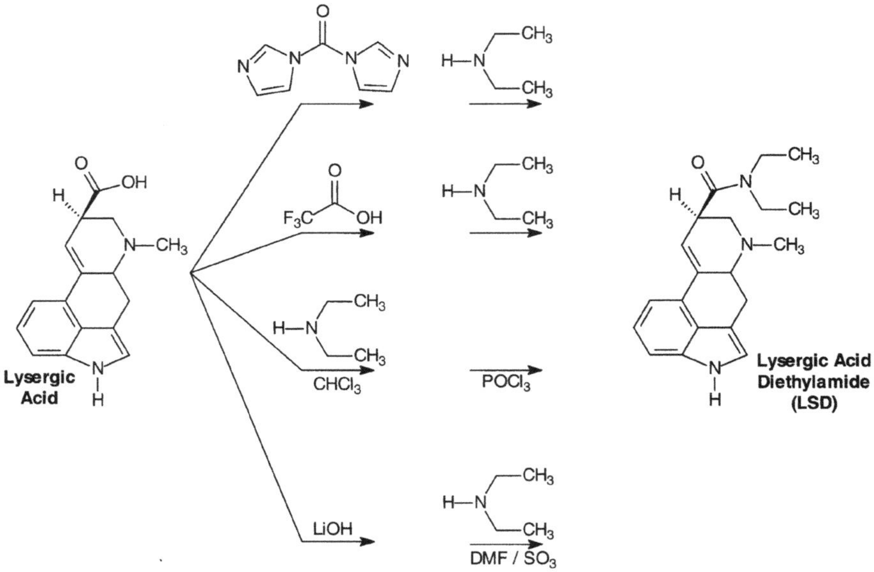

Figure 8.14

Four synthetic schemes for the conversion of ergotamine to lysergic acid diethylamide (LSD)

for producing a wide variety of lysergamide derivatives (Shulgin and Shulgin, 1997).

In all cases, the crude LSD must be purified prior to distribution and use (Marnell, 1999). This can be accomplished through a series of acid–base extractions, recrystallizations from benzene or methanol, preparation of the tartaric acid salt of LSD, or alumina column chromatography. A very pure dry LSD salt will reportedly emit flashes of white light when shaken in a dark room (Shulgin and Shulgin, 1997).

The most common form of distribution of LSD is on blotter paper. To prepare the blotters, the chemist dips blotter paper in an alcoholic solution of LSD. The blotter paper is perforated into squares for distribution (100 squares per sheet, with 10 sheets per book) (Marnell, 1999). The squares of blotter paper are often printed with a logo or design as a trademark of the distributor. A single square of blotter paper contains one dose of LSD (typically, 20–80 μg). Doses of LSD used in the 1960s and 1970s were frequently as high as 100–300 μg (Perrine, 1996; Marnell, 1999). The average lethal dose of LSD in a human is estimated to be between 0.2 and 1 mg/kg (Hoffer, 1965; Leiken et al., 1989). One report of an LSD-overdose death details a case of an individual injecting an estimated 320 mg of LSD intravenously (i.e., ~6400 times the typical oral dose) (Griggs, 1977). A bull elephant was reportedly killed with a single intramuscular injection of 300 mg of LSD, which was a dose of approximately 1 mg/kg (West et al., 1962).

There are two positions on LSD that are notoriously chemically unstable (Shulgin and Shulgin, 1997). These are the stereochemistry of the 8-carboxamide, which is rapidly epimerized to the inactive iso-lysergic acid diethylamide with exposure to pH above neutral, and the olefin between the 8-position and the aromatic ring, to which water and alcohol can readily add, especially in the presence of UV rays from sunlight. The product of water addition to the olefin, lumi-LSD, is also inactive in man. Chlorine, even the small amounts found in tap water, will rapidly degrade LSD (Shulgin and Shulgin, 1997). Because degradation of LSD is rapid upon exposure to light, blotter paper is impregnated with LSD shortly before distribution, and the impregnated blotter paper squares are kept tightly sealed, often in opaque photographic film canisters (Marnell, 1999). Other methods of distribution of LSD include placement on sugar cubes or toothpicks, as tablets and capsules, on thin gelatin squares, and in liquid form, though the blotter paper method is by far the most prevalent (Marnell, 1999).

Numerous other derivatives of lysergic acid exist, including ololiuqui, lysergic acid amide (lysergamide), ergonovine, and several alkylamide congeners (Figure 8.15). Investigations of the structure–activity relationships (SARs) of some of these compounds have been published (Hoffmann and Nichols, 1985; Perrine, 1996). However, these compounds are not common in the current U.S. illicit drug trade. As such, discussion of the synthetic methods and SARs of these drug substances is beyond the scope of the current chapter.

The syntheses of numerous tryptamine derivatives have been reported. The book *TIHKAL (Tryptamines I Have Known and Loved): The Continuation*, by the husband and wife team Alexander and Ann Shulgin (Shulgin and Shulgin, 1997), details the syntheses of over 50 such compounds. A number of tryptamine derivatives, including bufotenine and *N,N,*-dimethyl-5-methoxytryptamine, which are isolated from the venoms of two species of toads, have been subjected to some form of pharmacologic assessment (Perrine, 1996). However, probably the most prominent member of this group in terms of illicit synthesis and use is *N,N*-dimethyltryptamine (DMT).

Many hallucinogenic snuffs and drinks used by the indigenous peoples of the Amazon and the Caribbean contain DMT (Perrine, 1996). This observation, combined with the fact that the relatively simple structure of DMT is present in both LSD and psilocybin, led to the investigation of the intrinsic hallucinogenic properties of DMT during the 1950s (Perrine, 1996). Though DMT is inactive if taken orally, reportedly as a result of degradation by monoamine oxidase (MAO) in the gastrointestinal tract, DMT is active if insufflated or taken parenterally (Perrine, 1996). The reason hallucinogenic activity is maintained in cases of ingestion of DMT-containing drinks is hypothesized to be the result of inhibition of gastric MAO by harmaline alkaloids also present in the solu-

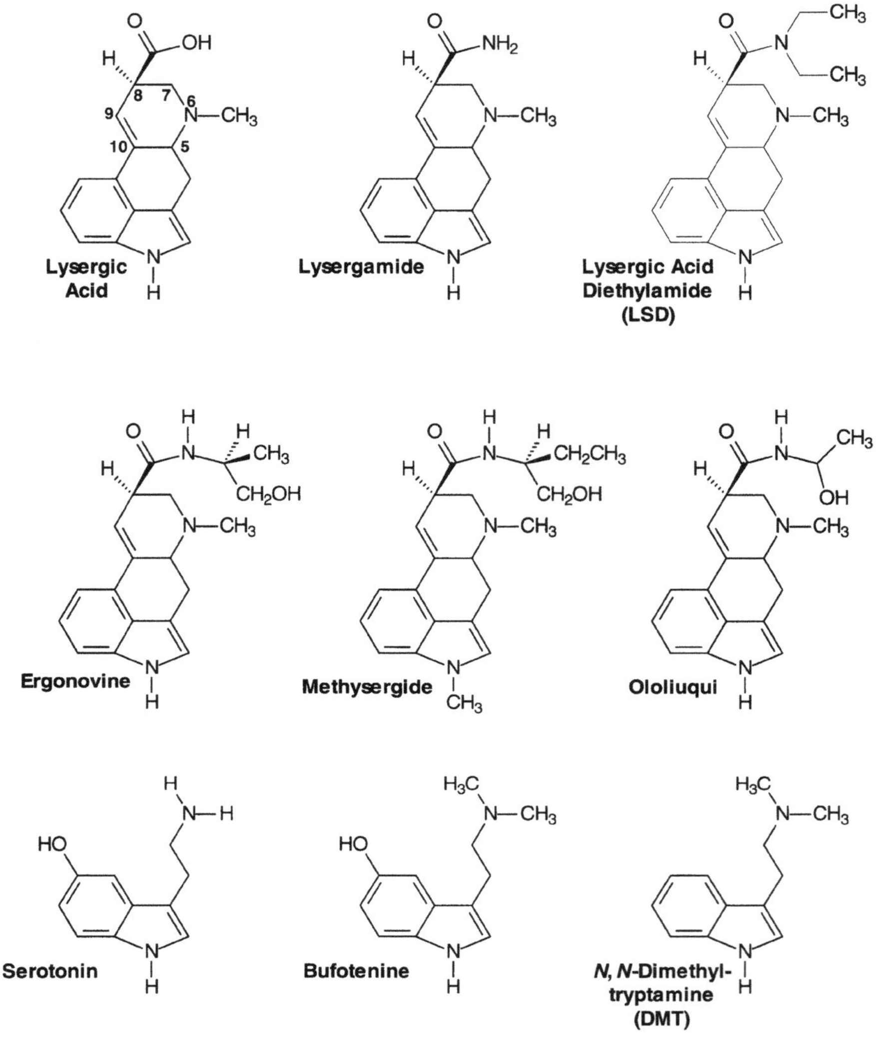

Figure 8.15

Chemical structures of compounds related to lysergic acid diethylamide (LSD)

tion (Figure 8.16) (Perrine, 1996). Intramuscular doses of 30mg DMT provided pharmacologic effects similar to those of LSD, though with an exceptionally rapid onset (within seconds of administration and peaking within 15 minutes) and short duration of action (complete resolution of effects within less than 1 hour (Perrine, 1996).

The brief duration of the psychedelic experience popularized the use of DMT in the 1960s, when it became known as "businessman's LSD." However, DMT also developed a reputation of causing "bad trips" (negative psychedelic

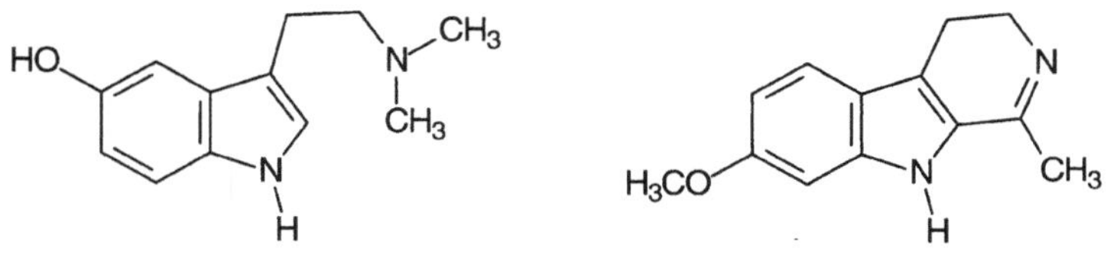

Figure 8.16

Chemical structures of N,N-dimethyltryptamine (DMT) (left) and the monoamine oxidase inhibitor, harmoline

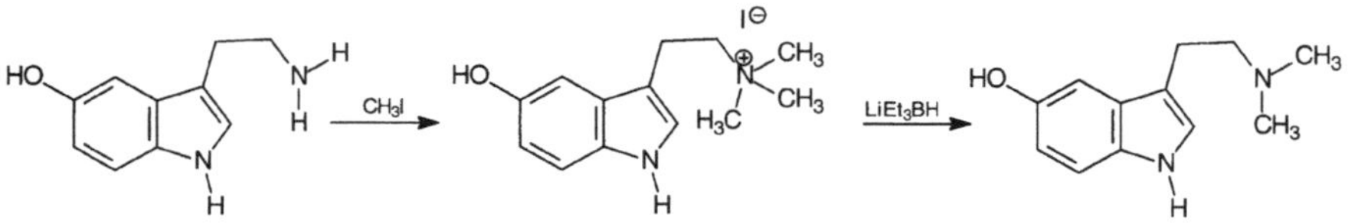

Figure 8.17

Synthetic scheme for the preparation of N,N-dimethyltryptamine (DMT) from tryptamine

experiences) and, as a result, has never attained the popularity of some other illicit hallucinogens. In recent years, however, a renewed interest has been shown in DMT. It is suggested that the basis for this resurgence in popularity is likely the result of legal issues. Specifically, though DMT is a DEA schedule I compound and its synthesis is illegal, possession of the plants that contain it is not regulated. Therefore, many of the DMT-containing plants are used for a "legal high" (Marnell, 1999).

The synthesis of DMT is not difficult, though apparatus for an inert atmosphere is required. Though DMT can be prepared from indole through a lengthy series of reactions, it is far simper to begin with tryptamine (Figure 8.17). Shulgin reports preparation of DMT by first obtaining the quaternary ammonium salt, *N,N,N*-trimethyltryptammonium iodide, by the treatment of tryptamine with excess methyl iodide (Shulgin and Shulgin, 1997). This salt is then demethylated with triethyllithium borohydride (LiEt$_3$BH) in tetrahydrofuran under an inert atmosphere. A combination of acid–base extractions and distillations is used to purify the product.

The subjective effects of a series of doses of DMT administered by a variety of routes (oral, smoking, intramuscular, and intravenous) were reported by Shulgin and Shulgin (1997). Depending upon dose and route, a range of experiences from pleasant to frightening was reported.

8.1.4 ILLICIT MANUFACTURE OF NONMETHAMPHETAMINE STIMULANTS

Though methamphetamine is the most common illegally synthesized stimulant, numerous other active phenethylamine derivatives have been illicitly prepared. Some of the more common illicitly prepared stimulants include 3,4-methylenedioxyamphetamine (MDA, Eve), 3,4-methylenedioxymethamphetamine (MDMA, ecstasy), 4-methylaminorex (U4EUh), and *p*-methoxymethamphetamine. Often, MDMA is classified as a hallucinogen at commonly used doses, and sympathomimetic effects appear with higher doses (Buchanan and Brown, 1988). However, due to the structural relationship of MDMA with the amphetamines, it is included in the stimulants section of this chapter.

The methylenedioxy derivatives of amphetamine and methamphetamine (MDA and MDMA, respectively) are frequently abused. At lower doses of MDMA, serotonergic effects, including feelings of empathy and, in some cases, hallucinations, predominate. With increasing doses, sympathomimetic effects similar to those seen with methamphetamine become apparent. Due to the similarity in the names of the compounds, some early reports confused MDMA with the neurotoxin MPTP, which was produced as a result of a botched meperidine analog synthesis (*vide infra*) (Baggott et al., 1999). In these cases, MDMA was reported to be responsible for the development of Parkinsonism. Though neurotoxicity associated with the use of MDMA has been reported, the toxic effects are vastly different from those attributed to MPTP (Schmidt et al., 1986; Buchanan and Brown, 1988).

Synthesis of the methylenedioxy compounds usually begins with either isosafrole or piperonal (Figure 8.18) (Shulgin and Shulgin, 1992). From these starting materials, the key intermediate, 3,4-methylenedioxyphenylacetone, can be prepared. To accomplish this goal, isosafrole is treated with 30% hydrogen peroxide and 80% formic acid in acetone for 16 hours at a modest temperature. Removal of the solvent and treatment of the deep red residue with acidified methanol over a steam bath followed by extraction from aqueous base and vacuum distillation provides 3,4-methylenedioxyphenylacetone as a pale yellow oil.

Figure 8.18

Two common synthetic schemes for the preparation of the key intermediate, 3,4-methylenedioxyphenyl-acetone

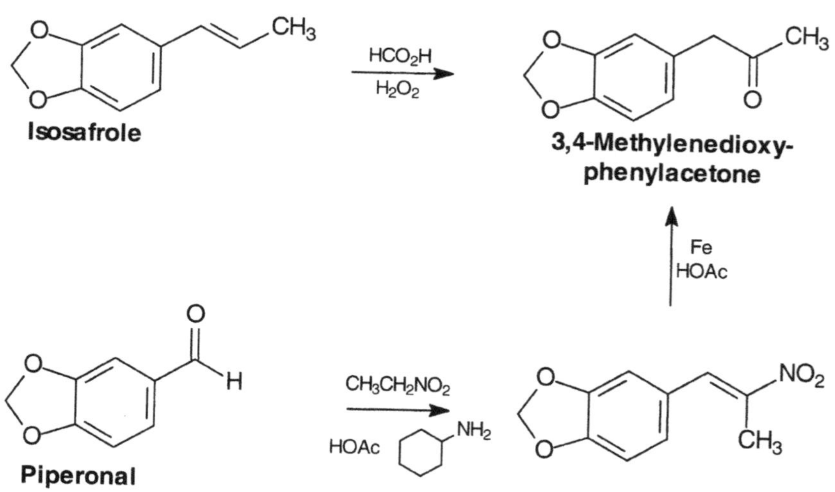

The same aromatic ketone can also be prepared from piperonal. In this scheme, piperonal is reacted with nitroethane in cyclohexylamine and glacial acetic acid, which gives 1-(3,4-methylenedioxyphenyl)-2-nitropropene. This intermediate is then treated in a solution of electrolytic iron in glacial acetic acid. When the reaction is complete, the mixture is diluted with water and extracted with methylene chloride. The organic layers are washed with base and concentrated, and the residue is vacuum distilled to give 3,4-methylenedioxyphenylacetone.

Once the 3,4-methylenedioxyphenylacetone is prepared, it can be used as a common starting material for both 3,4-methylenedioxyamphetamine (MDA, Eve) and 3,4-methylenedioxymethamphetamine (MDMA, ecstasy, Adam). To convert 3,4-methylenedioxyphenylacetone to MDA, the ketone is reacted with anhydrous ammonium acetate, forming an intermediate imine (Figure 8.19). The imine is then reduced, using an agent such as sodium cyanoborohydride, to give MDA as an oil. This oil is easily converted to the solid MDA hydrochloride salt using hydrogen chloride in anhydrous diethyl ether. An alternative synthetic route to MDA is the simple reduction of 1-(3,4-methylenedioxyphenyl)-2-nitropropene with a stronger reducing agent, such as lithium aluminum hydride (LAH), in an anhydrous solvent like tetrahydrofuran (THF). Acid–base extraction followed by treatment of the MDA oil with hydrogen chloride in anhydrous diethyl ether yields the solid MDA hydrochloride salt.

The more commonly abused methylenedioxy derivative of methamphetamine is 3,4-methylenedioxymethamphetamine (MDMA, ecstasy). This drug can also be prepared in a variety of ways. Most often, MDMA is synthesized either by N-methylation of MDA or through a series of transformations beginning with 3,4-methylenedioxyphenylacetone (Figure 8.20).

If MDA is selected as a precursor, the N-methylation is accomplished by the reaction of MDA with formic acid in benzene under dehydrating conditions (e.g., using a Dean–Stark trap). The resultant N-formyl-MDA is then reduced using LAH in anhydrous THF. Acid–base extraction, removal of the solvent,

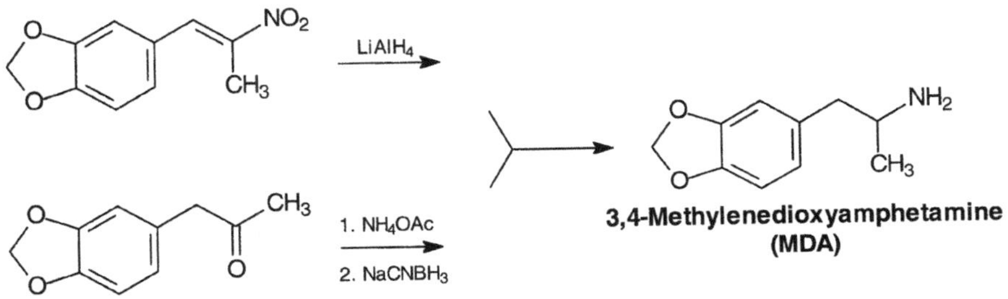

Figure 8.19

Two synthetic routes for the preparation of 3,4-methylenedioxyamphetamine (MDA)

3,4-Methylenedioxyamphetamine (MDA)

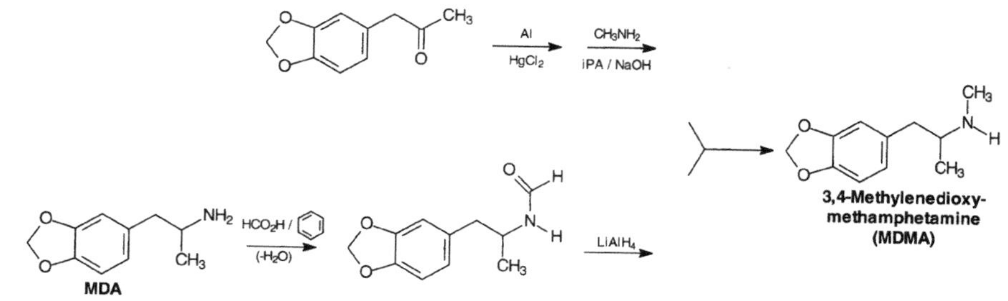

Figure 8.20

Two synthetic routes for the preparation of 3,4-methylenedioxymetham-phetamine (MDMA)

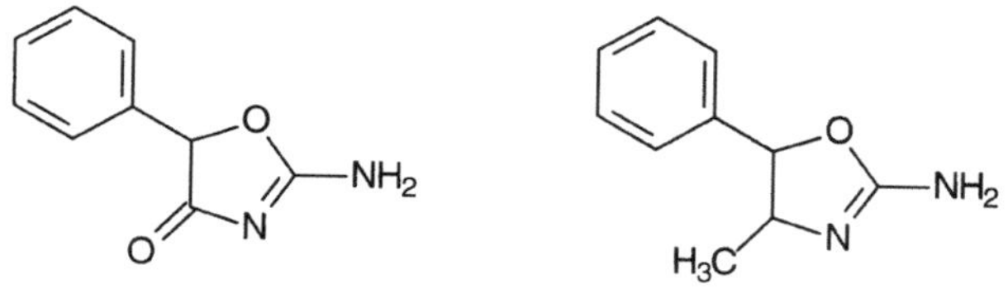

Figure 8.21

Chemical structures of pemoline (left) and 4-methylaminorex (U4EUh)

and distillation of the residue provides MDMA as an oil. This oil is converted to the solid hydrochloride salt by using hydrogen chloride in anhydrous diethyl ether.

Alternatively, MDMA can be prepared from 3,4-methylenedioxyphenylace-tone. In this scheme, an amalgam is formed from aluminum (usually small pieces of aluminum foil) and mercuric chloride in water. This reagent is then isolated and an aqueous solution of methylamine hydrochloride, isopropyl alcohol, sodium hydroxide, and 3,4-methylenedioxyphenylacetone is added with stirring. When the reaction is complete, it is extracted, purified, and converted to the salt as described earlier.

A group of related compounds have been purported to be cognition- and memory-enhancing drugs. The most common member of this class is the phenyl oxazoline, 4-methylaminorex (U4EUh, ice, intellex) is a structural relative of pemoline, a compound investigated in the 1960s as an appetite suppressant but later abandoned (Figure 8.21). At the typical doses preferred by recreational users of the drug (15–30mg as the free base), 4-methylaminorex reportedly causes increased awareness of the user's body, vivid imagery, and bizarre ideation along with moderate stimulant effects (Strassman and Qualls, 1994a, 1994b). Stimulant effects on heart rate, blood pressure, and body temperature, as well as blood levels of some circulating hormones, increased in a dose-dependent fashion (Strassman and Qualls, 1994a, 1994b).

4-Methylaminorex (U4EUh) is prepared by reacting phenylpropanolamine with cyanogen bromide (CNBr) and sodium acetate (Henderson et al., 1995). The synthesis of CNBr is accomplished by the slow addition of an aqueous solution of sodium cyanide on top of a stirred aqueous solution of bromine (Br₂) while the reaction temperature is kept near ambient (Figure 8.22). The CNBr

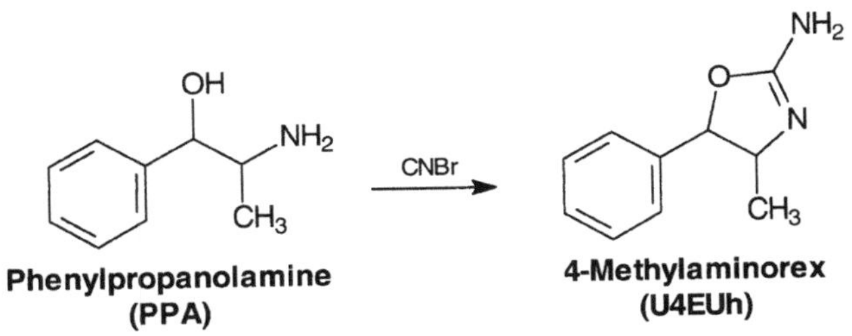

Figure 8.22

Synthetic scheme for the preparation of 4-methylaminorex (U4EUh) from phenylpropanolamine

is distilled from the reaction mixture and the product then distilled a second time from $CaCl_2$ to give the CNBr as a low-melting-point solid that is stored in the freezer. Sodium acetate is prepared by combining equimolar amounts of sodium hydroxide and glacial acetic acid and drying the resulting solid. Phenyl-propanolamine can be extracted from over-the-counter cold and appetite-suppressant medications using ethanol and water followed by ether extraction of an aqueous base solution of the drug, though this has become somewhat more difficult since the U.S. Food and Drug Administration recommended removal of phenylpropanolamine from the market in 2000 due to an apparent increase in hemorrhagic stroke associated with its use (FDA, 2000).

The preparation of 4-methylaminorex is then accomplished by combining the isolated phenylpropanolamine with sodium acetate in methanol at 0°C (Figure 8.22). Next, chilled CNBr in methanol is added and the reaction allowed to proceed at 0°C. The methanol is distilled away and the residue dissolved in water. The solid 4-methylaminorex base produced is precipitated by the addition of aqueous sodium carbonate. This solid is filtered, washed with ice cold water, and dried. The free base can then be recrystallized and the hydrochloride salt prepared in the usual fashion.

Though these compounds are well known to appear on the illicit drug market, their popularity is still significantly less than that of methamphetamine and MDMA. It is also known within the circles of clandestine chemists that the preparation and use of cyanogen bromide is dangerous, in that some popular Internet sites actually recommend that the preparation of cyanogen bromide be performed outside on a breezy day.

Numerous other illicitly prepared phenethylamine derivatives are known in the illegal drug market, including 4-methoxyamphetamine (*para*-methoxyamphetamine, PMA), 4-methylthioamphetamine (4-MTA), 4-methyl-2,5-dimethoxyamphetamine (DOM), 4-bromo-2,5-dimethoxyamphetamine (DOB), and many others (Figure 8.23). Though these compounds are illicitly prepared, their syntheses are somewhat more complicated than those for methamphetamine; therefore, their popularity seems to be correspondingly lower. Nonetheless, deaths attributed to abuse of illicitly manufactured DOB, PMA, and 4-MTA have been reported (Cimbura, 1974; Bohn, 1981; Winek et al., 1981; Elliott, 2000; Johansen et al., 2003).

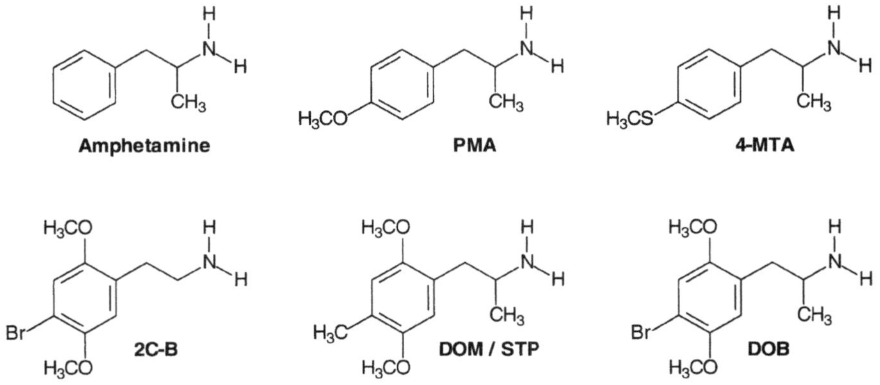

Figure 8.23

Chemical structures of some abused phenethylamine derivatives. PMA = 4-methoxyamphetamine (para-methoxyamphetamine); 4-MTA = 4-methylthioamphetamine, 2C-B = 4-bromo-2,5-dimethoxyphenethylamine; DOM = 4-methyl-2,5-dimethoxyamphetamine; DOB = 4-bromo-2,5-dimethoxyamphetamine

Amphetamine

PMA

4-MTA

2C-B

DOM / STP

DOB

Methamphetamine is by far the most prevalent of the drugs illicitly synthesized in clandestine laboratories. Numerous synthetic routes, both realistic and unrealistic, to produce methamphetamine have been reported. The remainder of this chapter will focus primarily on the clandestine production of methamphetamine. The forensic scientist must keep in mind, however, that a wide array of drugs has been and may be produced in clandestine laboratories, as is illustrated in the previous sections of this chapter.

8.2 MANUFACTURE OF METHAMPHETAMINE

8.2.1 ILLICIT MANUFACTURE OF METHAMPHETAMINE

8.2.1.1 Structure–Activity Relationships of Phenethylamines

The word *amphetamine* is an abbreviation for **alpha-methyl-phenethylamine** (Nichols, 1994). The class of CNS stimulant drugs to which amphetamine belongs is known as the phenethylamines. The basic structural motif of this group of drugs is composed of an aromatic ring ("phen," for phenyl) attached to a two-carbon chain ("ethyl") bearing a basic nitrogen at the distal end of the carbon chain ("amine") (Figure 8.24). One of the first phenethylamines (amphetamine) was prepared in 1887; shortly thereafter, in 1919, its *N*-methyl derivative, methamphetamine, was synthesized (Baselt, 2000).

Prior to discussing the various synthetic routes to methamphetamine, it is reasonable to closely examine the pharmacologic reasons why this compound and its derivatives are desired. Though primarily regarded as CNS stimulants, substitution of the fundamental phenethylamine nucleus can result in effects ranging from sedation to stimulation to hallucination induction (Nichols, 1994). The large number of derivatives that have been prepared containing the

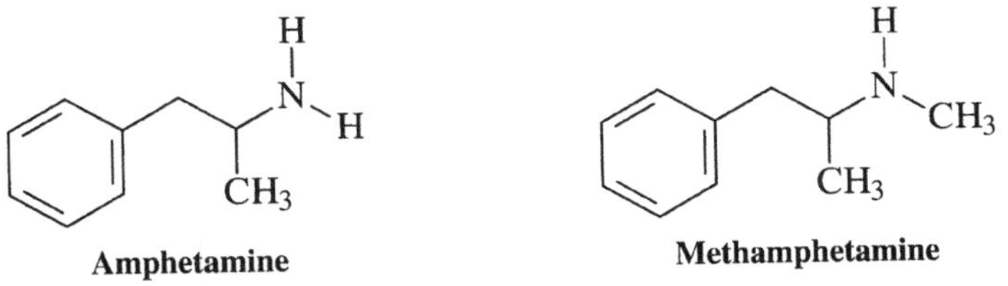

Figure 8.24

Structures of amphetamine and methamphetamine

Amphetamine

Methamphetamine

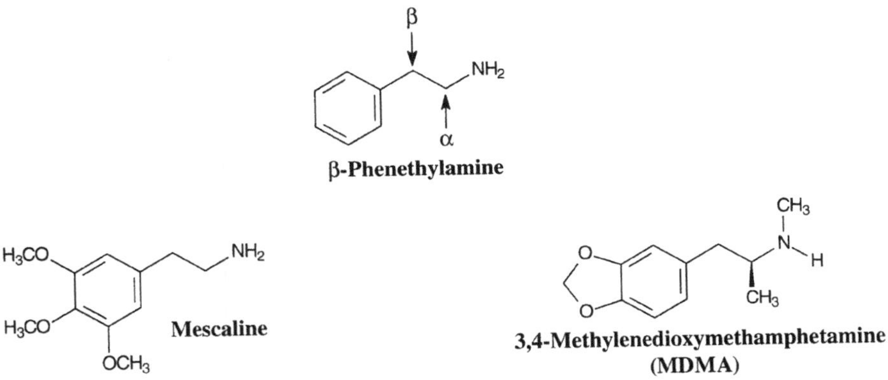

Figure 8.25

SARs of phenethylamines

β-Phenethylamine

Mescaline

3,4-Methylenedioxymethamphetamine (MDMA)

phenethylamine nucleus allowed detailed study of the structure–activity relationships (SARs) of this series of compounds (Nichols, 1994; Shulgin and Shulgin, 1992). Based on the results of the SAR investigations, some general inferences can be made about the pharmacologic effects of a given phenethylamine derivative from its chemical structure. It must be noted that this section is meant to provide the reader with a general treatment of the SAR features of this class of compounds, with specific reference to methamphetamine; it is not designed to be an all-inclusive review of the available studies.

Adrenergically active compounds are classed as either direct acting (those that bind directly to the adrenergic receptor) or indirect acting (those that induce release of neurotransmitters) (Hoffman and Lefkowitz, 1996). Catecholamines such as epinephrine and norepinephrine are direct-acting agents, while amphetamine and methamphetamine are primarily indirect-acting agents. The principal neurotransmitters affected by phenethylamine derivatives are norepinephrine, epinephrine, dopamine, and serotonin (Hoffman and Lefkowitz, 1996). The specific chemical structure of the agent has significant effects on which neurotransmitter is principally affected.

There are essentially four sites on the phenethylamine on which substitution will affect the overall pharmacology of the compound. These are: the amino nitrogen, the carbons of the "ethyl chain" α and β to the nitrogen, and the aromatic ring, as illustrated in Figure 8.25. Each of these sites is examined next.

Allowable substitution on the amino nitrogen is quite restrictive. A single methyl group approximately doubles potency, as seen when comparing methamphetamine to amphetamine (Nichols, 1994). However, when amphetamine is substituted with an ethyl or propyl group, activity of the substituted compounds drops to approximately one-half that of amphetamine (Van der Schoot et al., 1961). The central effects of amphetamine are diminished relative to methamphetamine, while amphetamine causes more pronounced peripheral actions than methamphetamine. Single alkyl *N*-substituents larger than methyl also cause a decrease in excitatory properties, though anorexiant effects are retained (Baselt, 2000). This observation has been exploited in the development of antiobesity agents, such as benzphetamine and diethylpropion, which have diminished abuse potential relative to the amphetamines. Disubstitution of the nitrogen to form a tertiary amine significantly reduces activity. For example, *N,N*-dimethylamphetamine has only about 20% of the activity of amphetamine (Nichols, 1994). It is noteworthy that *N,N*-dimethylamphetamine can be metabolically dealkylated to give the potent methamphetamine. Disubstitution of the nitrogen with alkyl groups larger than methyl frequently reduces activity to the point of abolition (Nichols, 1994).

Monosubstitution of the nitrogen on hallucinogenic (e.g., ring substituted compounds such as 4-bromo-2,5-dimethoxyamphetamine, DOB) amphetamine derivatives results in significant attenuation of hallucinogenic effects (Shulgin, 1981; Shulgin and Shulgin, 1992). Disubstitution or substitution with an alkyl group larger than methyl on the nitrogen or incorporation of the nitrogen into a heterocycle in these compounds eliminates hallucinogenic activity completely (Nichols, 1994; Wolters et al., 1974). Substitution with an *N*-methyl group does not significantly affect a given compound's ability to cause release of endogenous neuronal amines (Nichols, 1994).

Substitution of the carbon α to the nitrogen (henceforth referred to as the α-carbon) with a methyl group causes the agent to have central nervous system stimulant and anorexic effects (Glennon, 1989). Larger substituents at this position reduce stimulant and cardiovascular effects, but anorectic properties are retained (Battaglia and DeSouza, 1989; Glennon, 1989). The lack of significant central effects of compounds not substituted in the α-position (e.g., β-phenethylamine) is apparently due largely to their facile degradation by monoamine oxidase (MAO) (Nichols, 1994). The metabolic products of MAO do not penetrate the central nervous system (CNS) to an appreciable degree. Compounds with an α-methyl substituent (e.g., amphetamine) are poor substrates for MAO and therefore readily penetrate the CNS (Nichols, 1994). Increasing the length of the α-substituent to anything larger than a methyl group in amphetamine-like compounds results in a compound with a dramatically diminished ability to release dopamine. For example, though methamphetamine is approximately twice as potent as amphetamine, the α-ethyl analog of methamphetamine is only about one-tenth as potent when compared to amphetamine (Nichols, 1994). Interestingly, substitution of an ethyl moiety for a methyl group in serotonergic compounds such as MDMA results in compounds that largely retain their ability to release neuronal serotonin and actually increases serotonin selectivity, presumably through diminished effects at other neuronic sites; α-alkyl groups longer than ethyl are inactive (Nichols, 1986, 1994). Incorporation of the α-subtituent into a carbocyclic ring fused with the aromatic ring results in compounds somewhat less potent than amphetamine. Both the five-membered carbocyclic 2-aminoindan and the seven-membered ring derivatives are less potent than the six-membered 2-aminotetralin (Glennon et al., 1984a; Oberlender and Nichols, 1991). One study reported the 2-aminotetralin to be approximately 30% as potent as (+)-amphetamine (Glennon et al., 1984a), while another assessment indicated the potency of the same compound to be approximately one-eighth that of amphetamine (Oberlender and Nichols, 1991).

Branching at the α-carbon induces chirality in the phenethylamines. One must take great care to remember the conventions of organic chemistry when examining the different enantiomers. The absolute stereochemistry designations R- and S- can be assigned directly from a three-dimensional structure using Hughes–Ingold–Prelog priority assigments. The R- and S-designations are synonymous with D and L, respectively. However, the designations (+) and (−) and their respective synonyms, *d-* and *l-*, can only be assigned using experimental determination of plane polarized light rotation; these designations *cannot* be empirically assigned. Therefore, *d-/l-* is not interchangeable with D-/L-. When dealing with pharmacologic and forensic data of amphetamines, most investigators use the *d-/l-* or (+)/(−) designations for the isomers. This convention will be followed herein as well.

With specific respect to the absolute configuration of amphetamine, two isomers exist: S-(+), *dextro* (*d*) and R-(−), *levo* (*l*). The pharmacologic profiles of these two compounds are quite distinct. The alerting activity of the *levo*(−)-isomer is only about one-tenth that of the *dextro*(+)-isomer and about half the strength of a psychotomimetic (Isaacson, 1998). This stereospecificity is also apparent with methamphetamine. The *l*-isomer of methamphetamine (present in Vick's® inhalers and listed as "*l*-desoxyephedrine") is reported to possess greater peripheral sympathomimetic and less CNS stimulant activity than the *d*-isomer (Baselt, 2000) (Figure 8.26). Note that methamphetamine also has the *d*-(+) isomer with the S-absolute configuration and the *l*-(−) isomer with the R-absolute configuration. The greater CNS stimulation induced by *d*-methamphetamine has made it the preferred agent not only as an illicit stimulant but also as a therapeutically useful antiobesity agent.

Figure 8.26
Isomers of
methamphetamine

d-**Methamphetamine**   *l*-**Methamphetamine**

Several compounds oxidized at the β-carbon possess variable degrees of central activity (e.g., methcathinone, cathinone, ephedrine, and pseudoephedrine). Hydroxylation at the β-position, as in ephedrine and pseudoephedrine, does result in a less potent agent than the corresponding carbonyl agents, such as in methcathinone. For examples, cathinone is reported to have stimulant effects similar to those of amphetamine (Nichols, 1994). This is due largely to the diminished ability of the hydroxylated compound to cross the blood–brain barrier. For example, phenylpropanolamine has only about one one-hundredth the ability to cross the blood–brain barrier as its nonhydroxylated congener, amphetamine (Isaacson, 1998). Ephedrine has markedly greater central activity than pseudoephedrine due to the stereochemical difference in the β-hydroxyl. This is due primarily to the greater direct adrenergic action of ephedrine as compared to pseudoephedrine (Griffith and Johnson, 1995).

No substituent can be added to the phenyl ring with complete conservation of the simple catecholamine-releasing properties of amphetamine. Higgs and Glennon (1990) investigated substitution of *ortho*-, *meta*-, and *para*-methyl substituted amphetamine for (+)-amphetamines in a two-lever discrimination test using rats trained to distinguish (+)-amphetamine from saline. It was discovered that the *ortho*-methyl group was tolerated and provided complete substitution for (+)-amphetamine, but at doses 10-fold higher than for amphetamine. The *meta*- and *para*-substituted compounds produced only disruption in the rats at much higher doses. Halogenation of the aromatic ring with F, Cl, or Br reduces sympathomimetic action; however, other activities (e.g., serotonin-releasing ability) may be retained or increase (Johnson et al., 1990; Fuller, 1992). For example, *p*-chloroamphetamine is a potent neurotoxin that has been shown to destroy serotonergic neurons in experimental animals (Nichols, 1994; Fuller, 1978). Hydroxylation of the aromatic ring also leads to diminished central activity, presumably due to decreased blood–brain barrier penetration (Nichols, 1994).

Appending methoxy moieties to the phenyl ring, particularly in the 3,5-, the 2,5-, or the 3,4,5-positions leads to agents with somewhat diminished central activity but significant hallucinogenic effects (Nichols, 1994). The production of these hallucinogenic agents suggests a trophism for dopaminergic (D_2) receptors, though all hallucinogenic compounds have a high affinity for serotonin 5-HT_2 receptors (Glennon et al., 1984b; Titeler et al., 1988). However, it is known that ring-substituted compounds such as 3,4-methylenedioxymethamphetamine (MDMA) are weak hallucinogens but potent serotonin-releasing agents (Nichols, 1994). Monosubstitution at the *para*-position induces serotronin-releasing properties (Nichols, 1994). A single *meta*-trifluoromethyl group or a 3,4-disubstitution creates an agent that is relatively serotonin selective (Nichols, 1994). This serotonin selectivity is diminished if an *ortho*-alkoxy ring is added (Nichols, 1994).

A brief summary of these SAR properties is best demonstrated by example (Figure 8.25). Mescaline has a 3,4,5-trimethoxy substitution pattern on the phenyl ring without *N*-substitution, thereby imparting hallucinogenic properties. However, it lacks substitution on the α-carbon resulting in an agent with limited stimulant effects. On the other hand, 3,4-methylenedioxymethamphetamine (MDMA) is only a mild hallucinogen (due to the methyl group on the amino nitrogen) but possesses stimulant and anorexic effects due to the methyl group on the α-carbon. Examination of the structure of methamphetamine reveals an agent that should have both stimulant and anorexic properties, limited serotonin selectivity, and no hallucinogenic properties. All of these predictions hold true for methamphetamine.

8.2.1.2 Chemistry

Compounds other than methamphetamine are mentioned for illustrative purposes in the structure–activity relationship (SAR) section of this chapter; the following section, however, will focus entirely upon the synthetic chemistry used for illicit production of methamphetamine and its precursors. The synthesis of serotonergic and hallucinogenic amphetamine derivatives such as MDMA, MDA, and DOB tend to be somewhat more difficult. Therefore, these drugs tend to be less commonly prepared illegally, though this is changing. Other methods that could potentially be used for the synthesis of methamphetamine and its precursors clearly exist and are available to well-equipped legal research laboratories. However, these methods are not discussed herein due to the lack of their use by underground chemists. Further, there are many purported methods for simple and convenient home synthesis of methamphetamine available through books and the Internet. Some of these methods are chemically reasonable, while others are not. The author has made every attempt to be as comprehensive as possible in the discussion of chemically reasonable synthetic methods used by clandestine chemists. However, those methods judged by the author to have little basis in chemical fact or no reasonable chance to produce methamphetamine or its precursors are not discussed.

Illicit chemists do not publish their syntheses in scientific journals, though several books, such as *PIHKAL: A Chemical Love Story* by Shulgin and Shulgin, *Secrets of Methamphetamine Manufacture* by Uncle Fester, and *The Construction and Operation of Clandestine Drug Laboratories* by Jack B. Nimble are readily available (Shulgin and Shulgin, 1992; Fester, 1994; Nimble, 1994). The issue with many such books is that while much of the information may be essentially correct, there are also many technical misstatements and inaccuracies that are presented as fact. These points may be subtle but have crucial bearing on the outcome of the syntheses. The three books just listed were regularly used for reference in the preparation of this chapter.

The number of places where forensic scientists report the synthetic methods used by clandestine chemists is also relatively limited. Some of the more traditional sources used for this purpose are journals such as the *Journal of Clandestine Laboratory Investigating Chemists* and the *Journal of Forensic Sciences*. These journals were extensively used in the preparation of this chapter. Professional seminars on methods of illicit methamphetamine synthesis, such as that given by DEA senior forensic chemist Roger A. Ely at the American Academy of Forensic Sciences in February of 1998, were also used for information regarding some less common synthetic routes to methamphetamine and its precursors (Ely, 1998). The final sources of information for this chapter are professional communication between the author and other forensic scientists and law enforcement agents, as well as the author's own experience within the forensic community.

The illicit synthesis of methamphetamine is not difficult and requires little or no formal education in synthetic chemistry. The individuals making methamphetamine in clandestine laboratories are known as "cooks." The training, technical abilities, and facilities used by cooks vary tremendously. For example, in one case, a former physical chemistry professor from the state of Idaho was arrested for illegal methamphetamine production (Farnsworth, 2000). In a separate case, a man that has previously taught chemistry at the UCSF was indicted on drug charges when the company he owned was investigated for selling chemicals to manufacturers of methamphetamine (Harris, 1998). At the other end of the spectrum, several individuals have stated emphatically on the Internet and to law enforcement that methamphetamine can be extracted from chicken feed or prepared from gun-bluing salts (Ely, 1990; Massetti, 1996a; Anonymous, 1999). Both of these situations are chemically impossible. As a general rule, cooks have little formal education in synthetic organic chemistry (NNICC, 1998).

Methamphetamine cooks learn the synthetic procedures they use from a variety of sources, including word of mouth or apprenticeship with another cook, jailhouse conversation, a wide variety of books, the Internet, and, occasionally, the primary chemical literature. This, combined with generalized chemical ignorance and misinformation from the training sources, leads to hazardous conditions within the labs and relatively poor yields of methamphetamine, with concomitant production of numerous potentially dangerous synthetic by-products.

Multiple synthetic routes are employed by "cooks" in the illicit production of methamphetamine (Figure 8.27). Historically, the preparation of methamphetamine centered about derivatization of phenyl-2-propanone (P2P; phenylacetone). Specifically, P2P is condensed with methylamine to form the imine (Schiff base), which is then reduced to form the amine (methamphetamine). In more recent years, cooks have favored reduction of the benzyl hydroxyl of ephedrine or pseudoephedrine to form methamphetamine directly. A 1998 report by the National Narcotics Intelligence Consumers Committee (NNICC) stated that in 1997, only 1.6% of the labs seized by authorities used P2P methods of production (NNICC, 1998). The following section describes synthetic routes used for the illicit production of methamphetamine as well as its precursors, such as P2P and methylamine. This section is organized by first discussing the preparation of starting materials, followed by a discussion of routes used to convert these starting materials into methamphetamine.

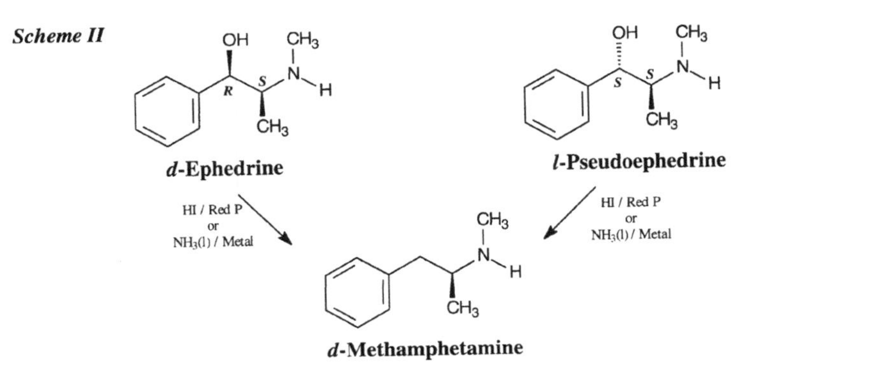

Figure 8.27
General syntheses of methamphetamine

8.2.1.2.1 Preparation of Phenyl-2-Propanone (P2P; Phenylacetone)

With the listing of P2P as a DEA schedule II compound in 1980 and its position on List I of the Special Surveillance List, access to this key precursor has become more difficult for the clandestine chemist. This has created a need for concealed sources of the compound. In response to this need, several illicit chemists have begun solely to produce P2P either for their own use or for sale to other illicit chemists, who then convert this precursor to methamphetamine. Though they vary in number of steps, yield, technical difficulty, and ease of acquisition of starting materials, each of the following methods has been used by clandestine chemists for the production of P2P suitable for subsequent conversion to methamphetamine.

One of the earliest routes of P2P preparation involved the reaction of phenylacetic acid (PAA) with acetic anhydride (Magidson and Garkusha, 1941; Fester, 1994) (Figure 8.28). In this reaction, refluxing PAA is combined with acetic anhydride in the presence of a pyridine catalyst and the reaction allowed to proceed for several hours. The pyridine, excess acetic anhydride, and acetic acid are then distilled away, leaving behind crude P2P. Simple acid and base extractions followed by careful vacuum distillation provide P2P suitable for subsequent conversion to methamphetamine.

Books such as *Secrets of Methamphetamine Manufacture* by Uncle Fester recommend reclamation of the excess pyridine after the reaction is complete (Fester, 1994). This is accomplished via careful fractional distillation of the residue following removal of the P2P. This text further recommends disposal of acetic anhydride distilled away from the pyridine by dumping it down the drain. Many clandestine chemists attempt to reuse or recycle chemicals and solvents. However, the recycling can also be taken to extremes, as is illustrated by a 1996 report in which several gallons of urine were located in a suspect's home. Investigators indicated that the suspect, a methamphetamine abuser, intended to extract the methamphetamine from the urine for reuse (T. Barnes, 1996a).

The "Uncle Fester" text mentions the use of sodium acetate as the catalyst instead of pyridine but states quite emphatically that this is an unacceptable catalyst (Fester, 1994). However, sodium acetate has been reported to be effective as a catalyst for this reaction by Russian investigators (Magidson and Garkusha, 1941). The key factor is that the sodium acetate must be absolutely

Figure 8.28

Synthesis of P2P from phenylacetic acid (PAA) and acetic anhydride

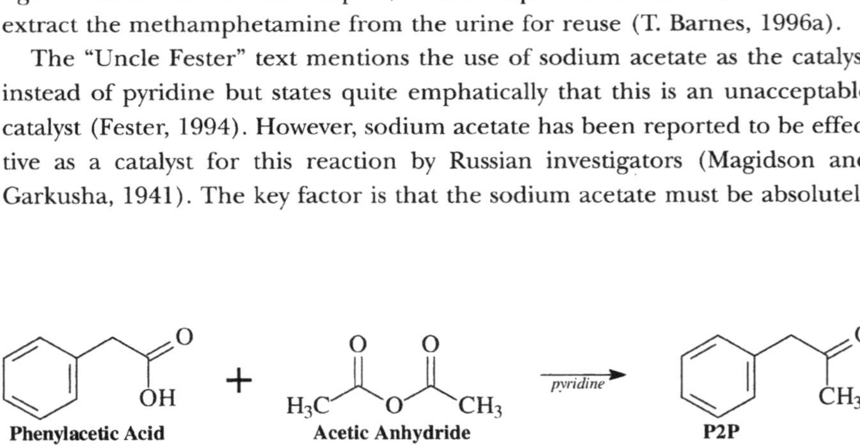

Phenylacetic Acid + **Acetic Anhydride** → (pyridine) **P2P**

anhydrous to avoid poisoning of the reaction. It is conceivable that the rigorously dry conditions are simply beyond the capabilities of the typical clandestine laboratory.

P2P production can also proceed through the use of phenylacetyl chloride, the acid chloride of PAA, which is made by reacting PAA with thionyl chloride (Fester, 1994) (Figure 8.29). For example, PAA is produced if phenylacetyl chloride is reacted under anhydrous conditions with a methyl anion source, such as methyllithium or methyl Grignard (CH₃MgCl). This reaction would also be successful using phenylacetaldehyde with methyl Grignard followed by an acidic workup.

In the absence of the acid chloride, two molar equivalents of methyllithium can be reacted with PAA to give P2P (Fester, 1994) (Figure 8.30). The first equivalent of methyl anion abstracts the acidic proton and bubbles off as methane, leaving behind the lithium salt of PAA. The methyl anion from the second equivalent of methyllithium attacks the carbonyl carbon, forming a covalent carbon–carbon bond with a dialkoxide. The lithium salts of the dialkoxides become geminal hydroxy groups during aqueous acid workup. Geminal diols (aka hydrates) are well known to undergo facile dehydration to form carbonyls, in this case P2P. This is a very effective synthetic method associated with high

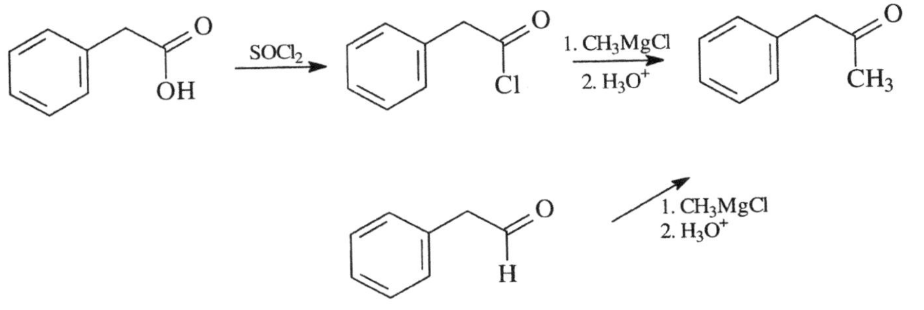

Figure 8.29

Synthesis of P2P from phenylacetic acid (PAA) via phenylacetyl chloride or phenylacetaldehyde and methyl Grignard

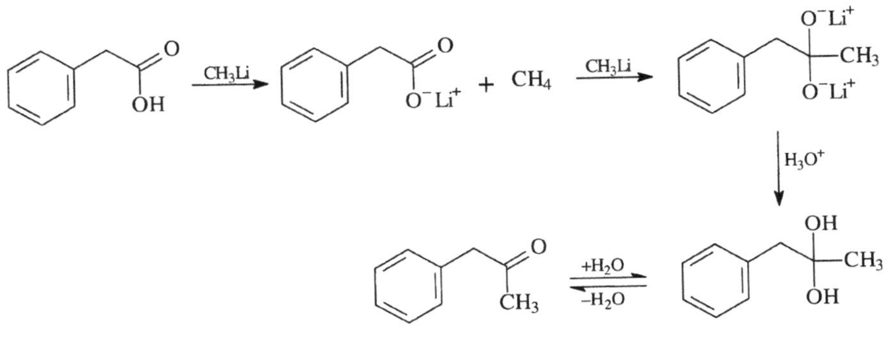

Figure 8.30

Synthesis of P2P from phenylacetic acid (PAA) and two equivalents of methyllithium

Figure 8.31

Synthesis of P2P from phenylacetic acid (PAA) and lead(II) acetate

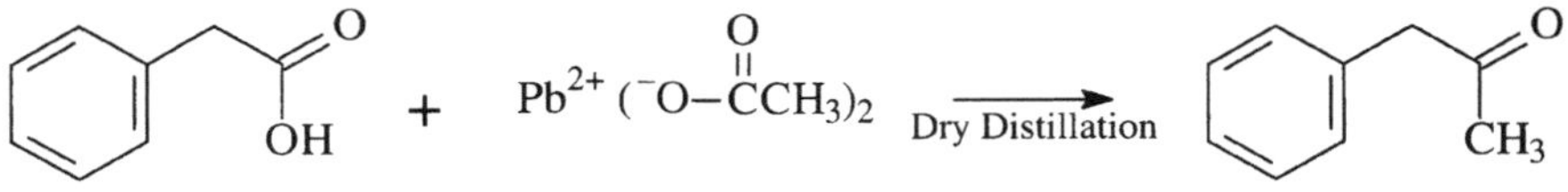

product yields. However, the high cost and explosive nature of organolithium reagents limit its utility in clandestine laboratories (Fester, 1994).

When PAA is reacted with lead(II) acetate under dry distillation conditions, P2P is produced (Tsutsumi, 1953) (Figure 8.31). In the late 1980s, methamphetamine abusers in Oregon presented with elevated lead levels (Alcott et al., 1987; MMWR, 1988; CDC 1990; Norton et al., 1996). Samples of illicit methamphetamine contaminated with lead(II) acetate were found (Alcott et al., 1987). Lead(II) acetate (aka "sugars of lead") has been known as a source of lead poisoning for centuries. Ancient Romans were known to use lead cooking pots that, when used with vinegar, gave foods a sweetened taste with the release of lead(II) acetate. It has been suggested that lead poisoning from this practice may have played a significant role in the downfall of the Roman Empire. As for the presence of lead(II) acetate in illicit methamphetamine in Oregon, it was initially thought it was present due to carryover from the P2P synthesis. However, it was later discovered that this was not the case; in fact, the lead(II) acetate had been used as an adulterating agent (Ely, 1998). It is unlikely that this adulteration was performed to sweeten the taste of the illicit methamphetamine. Further, the Oregon methamphetamine trade has certainly not suffered the same fate as the Roman Empire.

Production of P2P through these methods is dependent upon an adequate supply of PAA. The inclusion of PAA on List I of the Attorney General's Special Surveillance List has limited the use of this synthetic approach due to increasingly difficult access to the compound. However, it is also reasonably simple to synthesize PAA. Esters of PAA (i.e., toluic acid esters) are often used in the fragrance industry and are not controlled substances (Ely, 1998). Simply hydrolyzing these esters through heating with dilute acid or saponifying them by treatment with base gives PAA (Figure 8.32). Generally, the base method is preferred, for this reaction is less readily reversible than is the acid hydrolysis.

Illicit chemists have also used β-keto esters to prepare P2P (Fester, 1994) (Figure 8.33). According to "Uncle Fester," the chief advantage of this synthetic scheme is that it avoids the use of phenylacetic acid, making it less suspicious to authorities as to what the cook is doing with the chemicals he or she buys (Fester, 1994). A typical scheme involves reaction of ethylacetoacetate with bromobenzene to form the phenyl-β-ketoester intermediate. This compound is then subjected to acid-catalyzed ester hydrolysis and subsequent decarboxylation to form crude P2P. The product is purified by steam distillation. Even underground chemists acknowledge that the yields of P2P provided by this

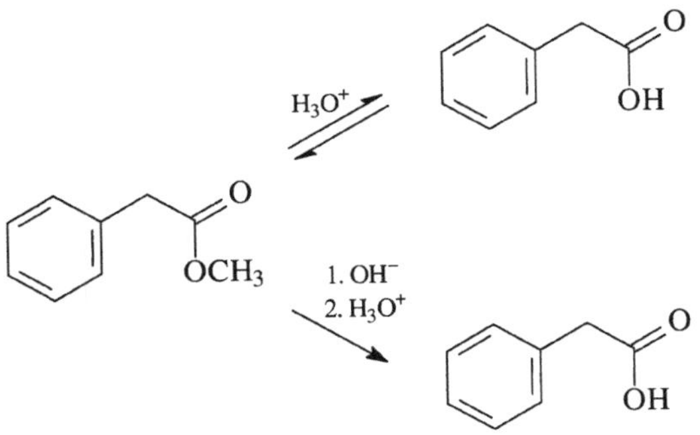

Figure 8.32

Acidic and basic hydrolysis of PAA esters used in the fragrance industry to give PAA

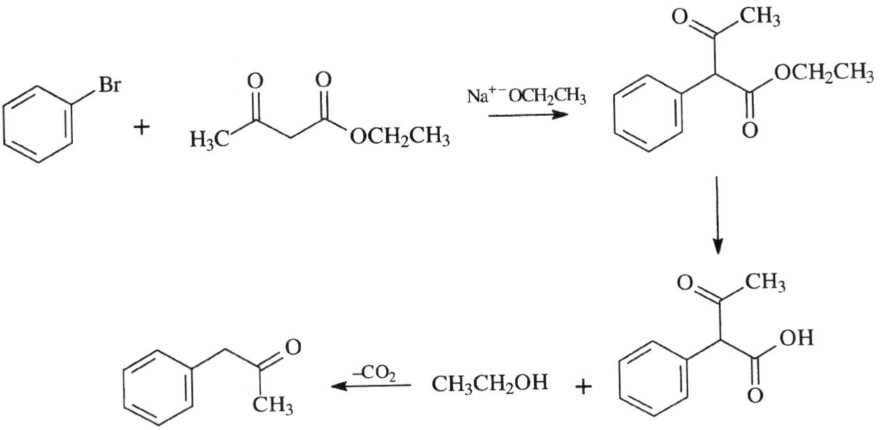

Figure 8.33

Synthesis of P2P from P2P β-ketoesters

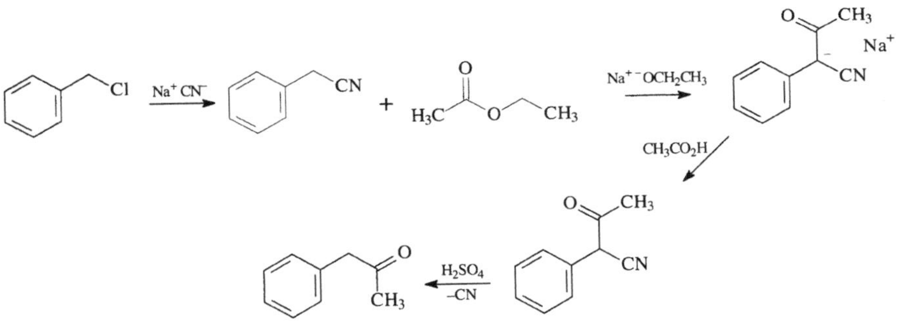

Figure 8.34

Synthesis of P2P from benzyl cyanide

method are low and that significant quantities of dimeric and polymeric by-products are produced (Fester, 1994). It is possible that this reaction proceeds via a benzyne intermediate, which may account for the dismal synthetic yield.

Yet another method of P2P production involves combining benzylcyanide and ethylacetate in the presence of sodium ethoxide (Julian and Oliver, 1943) (Figure 8.34). The benzyl cyanide is prepared from benzyl chloride and sodium cyanide (Adams and Thal, 1932). The benzylcyanide, ethylacetate, and sodium ethoxide mixture is refluxed to create the sodium salt of α-phenylacetonitrile intermediate. The salt is isolated and washed with ether and then treated with acetic acid to isolate the stable free base, α-phenylacetoacetonitrile. The freebase is subsequently treated with concentrated sulfuric acid to remove the nitrile, leaving behind the crude P2P. Organic extraction followed by simple steam distillation is then used to purify the P2P prior to its use in making methamphetamine. Alternatively, PAA can be produced from the benzyl cyanide intermediate through reflux in dilute sulfuric acid (Adams and Thal, 1932).

A standard synthetic transformation known as the Knoevenagel reaction has also been used to prepare P2P (Hass et al., 1950; Gairaud and Lappin, 1953; Fester, 1994). The classical description of the Knoevenagel reaction involves a methylene that is either mono- or disubstituted with electron-withdrawing groups (Mundy and Ellerd, 1988) (Figure 8.35). This methylene is treated with a base such as an amine to form a methylene carbanion that performs a nucleophilic attack on a carbonyl carbon. The intermediate oxyanion is protonated to form the tertiary alcohol, and then the second proton from the original methylene group is abstracted. The resultant carbanion collapses to form a double bond between the former methylene and former carbonyl carbons, with elimination of the hydroxy group as water.

In the production of P2P, a Knoevenagel condensation is performed between benzaldehyde and nitroethane in the presence of a basic catalyst (e.g., *n*-butylamine or ammonium acetate) (Hass et al., 1950; Gairaud and Lappin, 1953; Fester, 1994) (Figure 8.36). Though the Knoevenagel condensation product, 1-phenyl-2-nitropropene, is produced with either catalyst, the reaction times differ substantially. When *n*-butylamine is used, the reaction requires a reflux for 3–4 hours, followed by a period of several days of allowing the reaction to stand in the dark; in contrast, the same reaction using ammonium

Figure 8.35

General mechanism of the Knoevenagel condensation

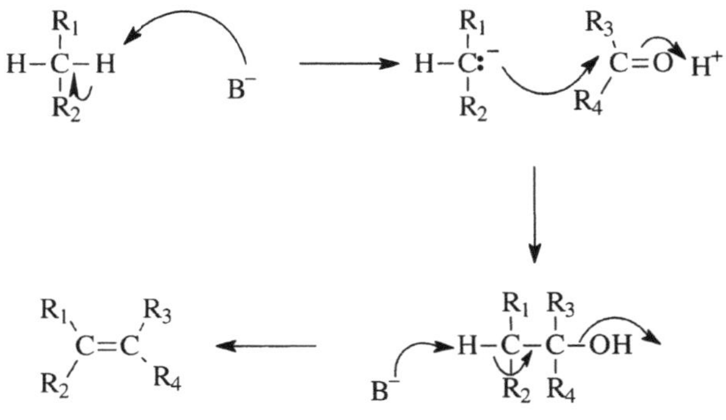

acetate as the catalyst requires only reflux for 2 hours followed by an acetic acid wash (Hass et al., 1950; Gairaud and Lappin, 1953). Once the nitropropene is created, it is reduced with iron, $FeCl_3$, and HCl to produce the P2P oxime. The oxime is subsequently hydrolyzed with water to yield P2P. The reactions are quite simple and not very sensitive to technique or conditions. One variation used in clandestine labs to increase the Knoevenagel condensation product yield uses a Dean–Stark trap, which removes water, thereby diminishing the back-reaction (Fester, 1994).

Clandestine chemists have also used the nitropropene intermediate in other ways. For example, direct reduction of the olefin and nitro group of 1-phenyl-2-nitropropene gives amphetamine (Fester, 1994) (Figure 8.36). This technique is suggested to be useful in the preparation of substituted phenyl compounds, such as 3,4-methylenedioxybenzaldehyde (i.e., piperonal), in order to make the hallucinogen 3,4-methylenedioxyamphetamine (MDA) (Fester, 1994).

In 1987, a patent by Nakai and Enomiya demonstrated that allylbenzene could be converted directly into P2P (Nakai and Enomiya, 1987). In this scheme, allylbenzene is reacted with two molar equivalents of methyl or ethyl nitrite to make 1-phenyl-2,2-dialkoxypropane. Aqueous hydrolysis of this ketal yields P2P (Figure 8.37). The original reaction conditions called for the rather expensive catalyst palladium chloride. The patent investigators discovered that by adding a small amount of cuprous chloride or trimethylamine to the reaction mixture, the required amount of palladium chloride could be dramatically reduced. It is noteworthy that though this makes the reaction overall less expensive to perform, there is a corresponding decrease in the yield of P2P.

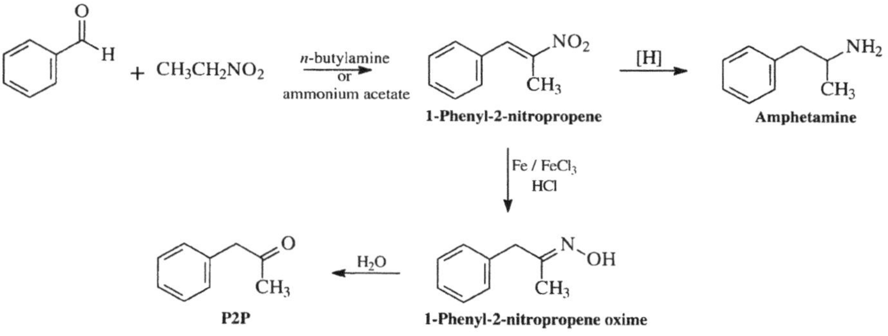

Figure 8.36

Knoevenagel condensation of benzaldehyde and nitroethane en route to P2P

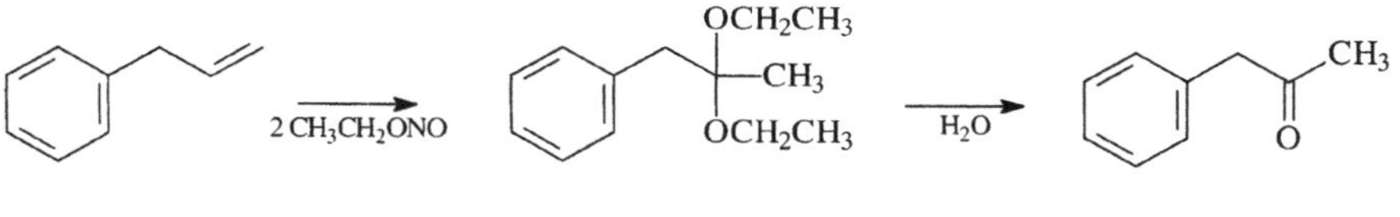

Figure 8.37

Preparation of P2P from allylbenzene using alkylnitrite reagent

Obviously, the foregoing reaction schemes are dependent upon ready access to allylbenzene. This compound is difficult to purchase directly but not difficult to make. Allylbenzene can be readily prepared from phenylcopper and allylbromide (Fester, 1994). First, phenyllithium is made by reacting bromobenzene with lithium metal in ether. The phenyllithium is then treated with cuprous bromide, and the phenylcopper reagent precipitates as a white powder. This powder is separated and reacted with allylbromide, quenched with water, and extracted to give allylbenzene (Figure 8.38). This is a fairly expensive reaction, and the lithium reagents require some technical skill for effective manipulation. A less expensive method for the preparation of allylbenzene is to make the phenyl Grignard reagent from bromobenzene and magnesium. The phenyl Grignard is then reacted with allylbromide, followed by aqueous quenching and organic extraction to give allylbenzene (Figure 8.38). It is noteworthy that bromobenzene is difficult to obtain because it is on the Special Surveillance List [it is also used in the illicit preparation of phencyclidine (PCP)]. In order to avoid the use of bromobenzene, a direct Friedel–Crafts alkylation between benzene and allylbromide with an $AlBr_3$ catalyst will also produce allylbenzene (Figure 8.38). Allylbenzene can undergo a Ritter reaction (a nitrile plus an alkene to give an amine) with acetonitrile to produce amphetamine directly (Figure 8.39).

Alkylnitrites such as methylnitrite, ethylnitrite, and *t*-butyl nitrite are required for the synthesis of P2P from allylbenzene using the Nakai method (Nakai and Enomiya, 1987). However, these compounds are difficult for a clandestine chemist to obtain without arousing suspicion due to their high abuse potential as "poppers." Chemically, alkylnitrites are simply nitrous acid esters of alkanes.

Figure 8.38

Preparation schemes for allylbenzene

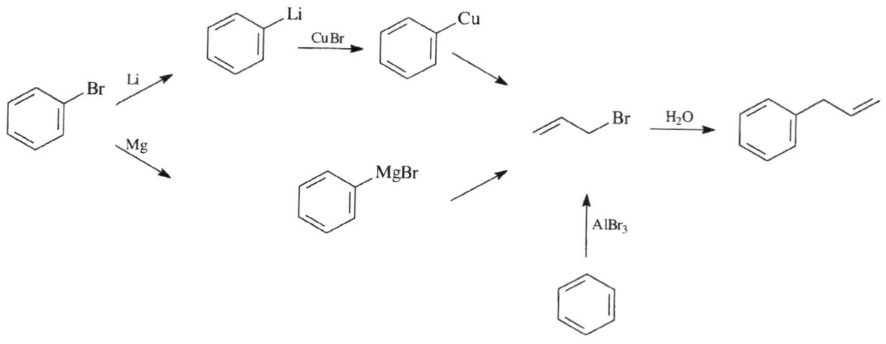

Figure 8.39

Ritter reaction of allylbenzene to form amphetamine

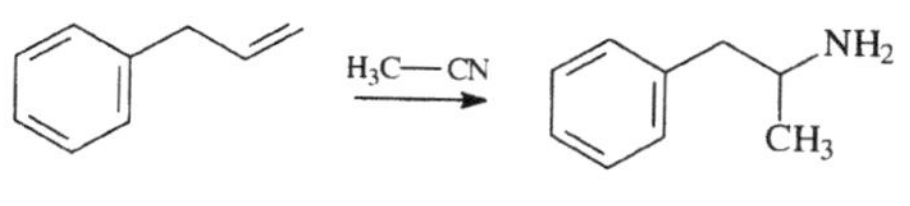

As such, they can be made fairly easily by reacting nitrous acid (generated from mixing sodium nitrite with excess sulfuric acid) with the corresponding alykl alcohol in the presence of an acid catalyst (Fester, 1994) (Figure 8.40). A wide variety of alkylnitrites can be prepared with minor procedural variations by substituting different alkyl alcohols.

P2P is also synthetically available through oxidative means (Fester, 1994). 1-Phenyl-2-propanol can be prepared through the reaction of benzyl Grignard (benzyl magnesium chloride) with acetaldehyde, followed by aqueous quenching and organic extraction. This alcohol is readily oxidized with acidic sodium dichromate ($Na_2Cr_2O_7/H_2SO_4$) to produce P2P (Figure 8.41).

A slightly more "exotic" reaction employed for P2P production involves the use of a tube furnace and a thorium oxide (ThO_2) catalyst (Herbst and Manske, 1943; Fester, 1994) (Figure 8.42). In this scheme, PAA and acetic acid are added dropwise through a tube furnace maintained at 430–450°C. Inside the furnace is a bed of thorium oxide, which acts as a catalyst for the methylation of PAA to form P2P. The exact chemical mechanism of this reaction is not well understood. Though the yield is fairly good, there are several disadvantages to P2P production via this method. First, the thorium oxide must be generated. This is done by first mixing aqueous solutions of thorium nitrate and sodium carbonate to produce a precipitate of thorium carbonate. The thorium carbonate is converted to thorium oxide by the heat of the tube furnace. Production of P2P is relatively slow, because the furnace system must be maintained at temperature for 12–18 hours prior to beginning the reaction. The reaction is also quite sensitive to the rate at which the reactants are added to the furnace, and the tube furnaces themselves are relatively expensive (Fester, 1994). Thorium is also somewhat difficult to obtain discretely, and thorium dust is a known pulmonary toxin (De Vuyst et al., 1990; Ely, 1998).

8.2.1.2.2 Preparation of Methylamine and its Synthetic Equivalents

As previously stated, P2P must be reacted with methylamine to make an intermediate imine, which is reduced to give methamphetamine. One of the limitations of this approach to methamphetamine production is the lack of a convenient source of methylamine. Methylamine gas can be purchased directly

Figure 8.40
Preparation of alkylnitrites

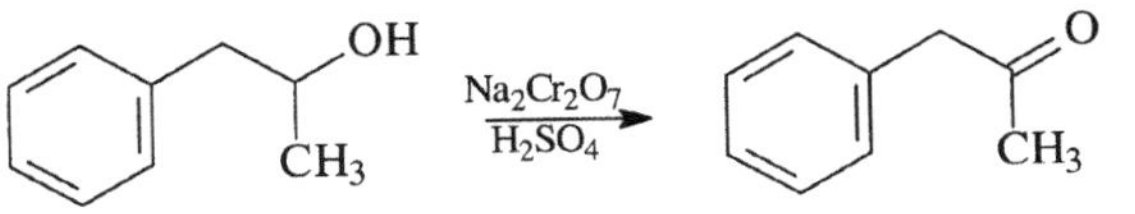

Figure 8.41
Oxidation of 1-phenyl-2-propanol to give P2P

from chemical suppliers. However, this is very difficult to do without attracting attention, because methylamine and its salts appear on List I of the Special Surveillance List. Furthermore, because it is a gas, methylamine is more difficult to work with than many of the other reagents used in illicit drug production. Though it is available as an aqueous solution, the presence of water in the initial condensation reaction perturbs the imine formation equilibrium by shifting it back toward starting materials, thereby diminishing yield. A variety of reaction schemes have been developed to effectively combat these problems. Some of these schemes use methylamine gas or aqueous solutions of the compound, while others use methylamine "synthons" (synthetic equivalents) to accomplish the reaction.

One method for making methylamine more amenable to easy manipulation is to create the hydrochloride salt (Fester, 1994). Methylamine hydrochloride is prepared by heating a mixture of aqueous formaldehyde and ammonium chloride; the residual water and the formic acid produced in the reaction are removed via vacuum distillation. This leaves behind solid methylamine hydrochloride (Figure 8.43). The solid is then purified by organic extractions and additional vacuum distillations. Methylamine gas for the reaction with P2P is generated *in situ* by heating the hydrochloride salt with sodium hydroxide. Alternatively, methylamine can be liberated from the hydrochloride with base and collected in a cold finger or flask immersed in a dry ice bath.

Clandestine chemists have also used a reductive approach to the generation of methylamine (Fester, 1994). Via this method, nitromethane "dragster fuel" is reduced using hydrogenation in the presence of a Raney nickel catalyst (Figure 8.44). This is easily done using a hydrogenation bomb fashioned from a champagne bottle (Fester, 1994) (Figure 8.45).

Another method to avoid the need for gaseous reactants in the clandestine laboratory is to use the methylamine synthon *N*-methylformamide instead of methylamine. In this reaction, methylamine and formic acid are combined to

Figure 8.42

Synthesis of P2P from phenylacetic acid (PAA) and acetic acid in a tube furnace with a thorium oxide catalyst

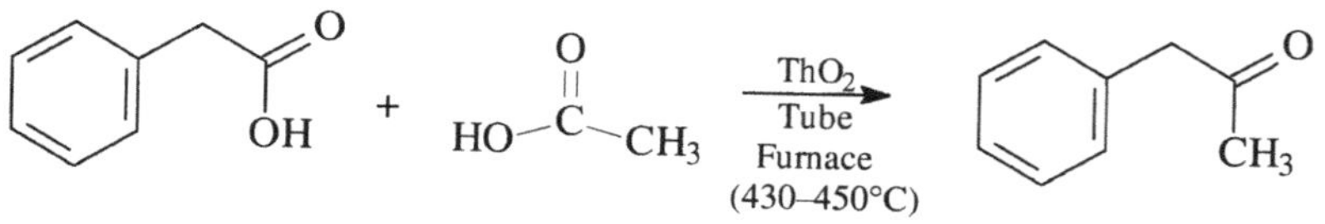

Figure 8.43

Preparation of methylammonium chloride from ammonium chloride and formaldehyde

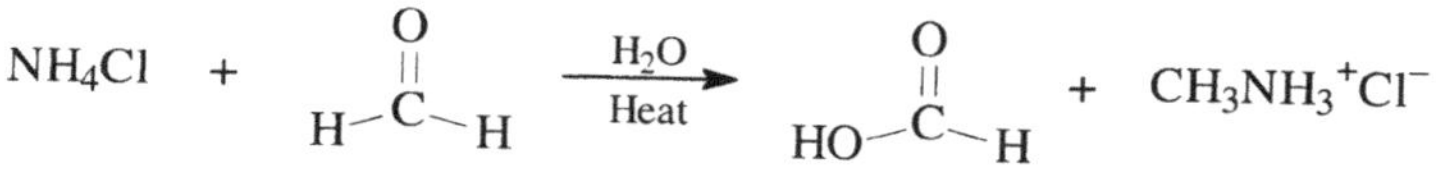

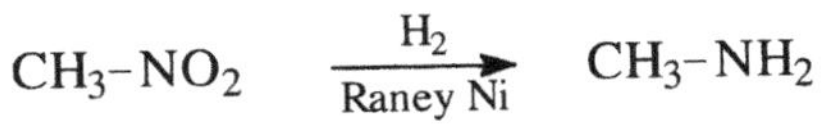

$$CH_3-NO_2 \xrightarrow[\text{Raney Ni}]{\text{H}_2} CH_3-NH_2$$

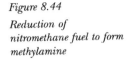

Figure 8.44

Reduction of nitromethane fuel to form methylamine

Figure 8.45

Champagne bottle hydrogenator schematic

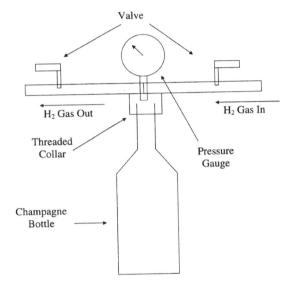

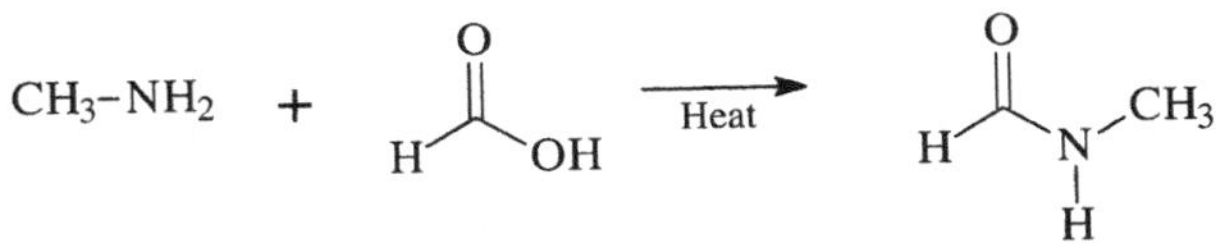

Figure 8.46

Formation of N-methylformamide from methylamine and formic acid

produce *N*-methylformamide (Figure 8.46). If an aqueous solution of methylamine is used, it is heated such that the methylamine gas is liberated from the water and piped over and bubbled through a bath of formic acid. If a cylinder of methylamine gas is used, it is bubbled directly through the formic acid (Figure 8.47). The *N*-methylformamide is then purified by distillation.

The Curtius rearrangement can also be used to generate methylamine (Fester, 1994). In this case, acetyl chloride is reacted with sodium azide. The resulting azido compound eliminates nitrogen gas and rearranges to a methyl isocyanate. In the presence of water, the methylisocyanate readily decarboxylates to form methylamine (Figure 8.48). An adaptation of this process involves the use of acetamide as a starting material. First, acetamide is exposed to bromine liquid, converting it to *N*-bromoacetamide. The *N*-brominated compound then undergoes a facile loss of HBr and Curtius-type rearrangement (specifically, a Hofmann rearrangement) to form methylisocyanate, which, as

Figure 8.47

Schematic of apparatus used to deliver methylamine gas from an aqueous solution into formic acid to make N-methylformamide

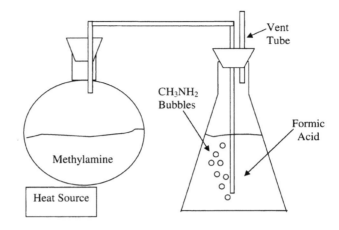

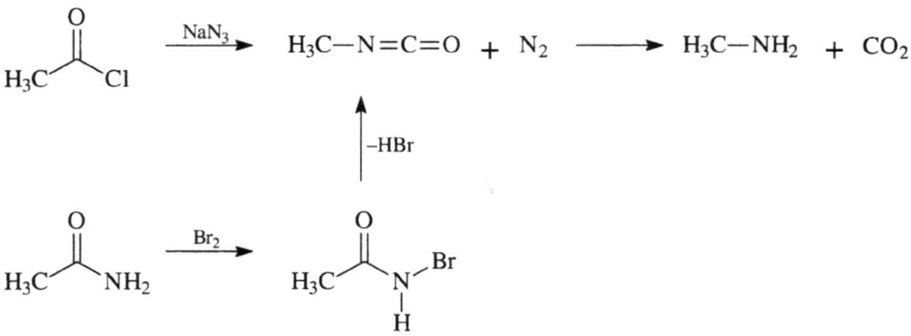

Figure 8.48

Preparation of methylamine from two versions of the Curtius rearrangement

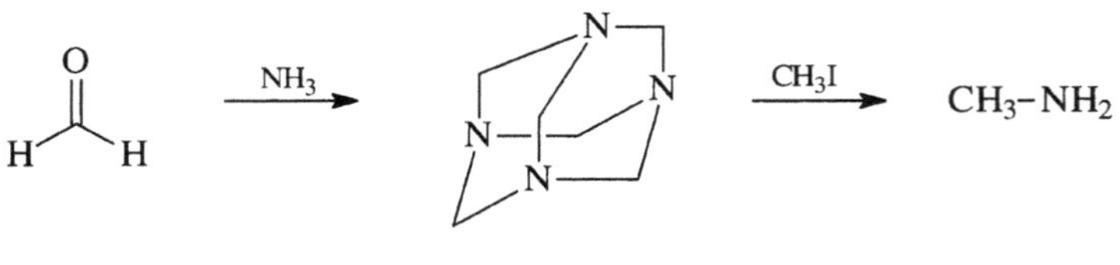

Figure 8.49

Preparation of methylamine from methenamine

described earlier, decarboxylates, yielding methylamine (Figure 8.48). It has also been suggested by at least one clandestine chemistry text that direct treatment of acetamide with Clorox bleach will yield methylamine (Fester, 1994).

Methylamine can also be produced through the reaction of methenamine (hexamethylene tetramine) with methyliodide (Fester, 1994). Hexenamine is readily prepared from ammonia and formaldehyde (Budavari, 1989) (Figure 8.49).

8.2.1.2.3 Preparation of Methamphetamine using Reductive Amination of P2P
A variety of production methods for methamphetamine use P2P as a starting material. Most of these methods involve preparation of the imine intermediate through condensation of the phenylacetone with methylamine or one of its syn-

thetic equivalents to form an imine intermediate. A variety of methods have been employed by clandestine chemists to perform both the initial condensation and the final reduction of the imine intermediate to methamphetamine.

One of the early reported methods of illicit reduction of the methylimine derivative of P2P to methamphetamine used aluminum amalgam (Laboratories Amido, 1964; Wassink et al., 1974; Fester, 1994) (Figure 8.50). In this reductive amination scheme, the imine intermediate reacts with aluminum grit and mercuric chloride to form methamphetamine. Aluminum grit was often difficult to obtain, so clandestine chemists simply shredded aluminum foil for this purpose. The original report of this synthetic method for legitimate purposes employed a 16-fold molar excess of methylamine (Wassink et al., 1974). Clandestine chemists, however, typically run the reaction with only a five- to six-fold molar excess of this reagent (Ely, 1998). The reaction is quite exothermic and has a reputation of shooting up the condenser. For this reason, the reaction was often run with the apparatus in a bathtub, ultimately giving rise to the term *bathtub dope* (Ely, 1998). Though reports of mercury-contaminated drug samples prepared using this method exist, elevated mercury levels in drug users were not found (Burton, 1991).

Another reductive amination technique is a derivative of the Leuckart–Wallach reaction. This is a series of reactions in which the Leuckart portion of the name makes reference to the use of a salt of a formamide to generate an amine and the Wallach portion refers to hydrogenolysis of the intermediate iminium with formic acid (Mundy and Ellerd, 1988) (Figure 8.51). In the most generic sense, the Leuckart–Wallach reaction series involves, first, the nucleophilic attack of an amine on a carbonyl carbon in the presence of formic acid, creating an intermediate iminium with the elimination of water. A second nucleophilic attack may take place between the nitrogen and carbonyl carbon of formic acid, with elimination of water to provide an *N*-formylated iminium product. The Wallach portion of the reaction series then takes place, and the *N*-formyl group is reductively removed with formic acid. In modifications of the Wallach reaction, the final reduction of the iminium can be performed by a

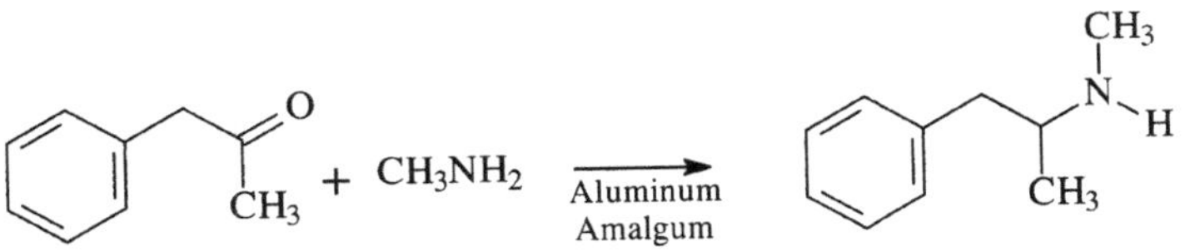

Figure 8.50

Aluminum amalgum condensation of P2P and methylamine to form methamphetamine

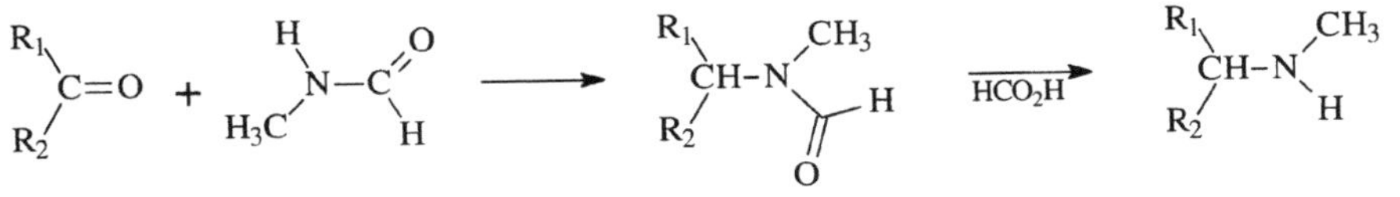

Figure 8.51

General scheme for Leuckart–Wallach reactions

variety of reducing agents, including sodium borohydride, sodium cyanoborohydride, and catalytic hydrogenation.

With specific respect to the synthesis of methamphetamine, P2P and methylamine are reacted with formic acid to produce the intermediate *N*-formylmethamphetamine (Crossley and Moore, 1944) (Figure 8.52). The *N*-formylated product is refluxed in dilute aqueous acid, where it readily decarboxylates to give methamphetamine. Prior to 1980, this was a very common method of methamphetamine production in the southeastern United States, including Texas and Arkansas (Ely, 1998).

Other methods exist for the preparation of methamphetamine from phenylacetone that do not involve the use of methylamine. One such method involves protecting group chemistry. The term *protecting group chemistry* refers to a technique used by organic chemists where functional groups such as carbonyls and amines are reversibly derivatized to protect them from reaction during transformations of other portions of the molecule (McKibben, 1997). This approach to synthetic transformations has also been applied to methamphetamine production. In a specific example, *N*-benzylation, a classic protection scheme for amines, was used to prepare methamphetamine (Skinner, 1993). In this scheme, P2P is reacted with *N*-benzylmethylamine to produce *N*-benzylmethamphetamine in good yield. The *N*-benzyl group is then quantitatively removed with a palladium/charcoal-catalyzed hydrogenolysis, yielding methamphetamine and toluene as the final products (Figure 8.53).

Figure 8.52

Methamphetamine from P2P via the Leuckart–Wallach reactions

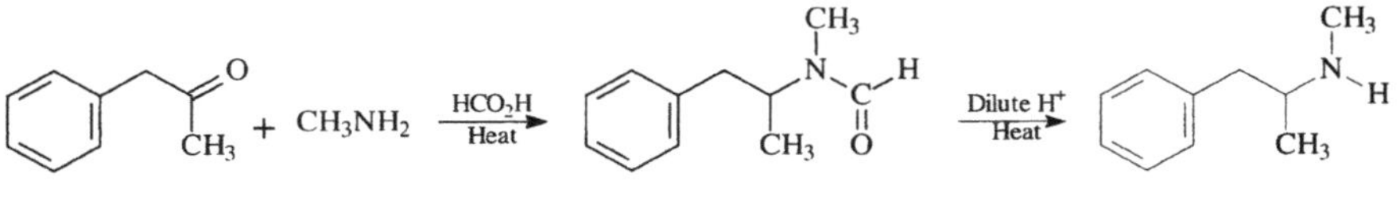

Figure 8.53

Preparation of methamphetamine from P2P using N-benzyl protecting-group chemistry

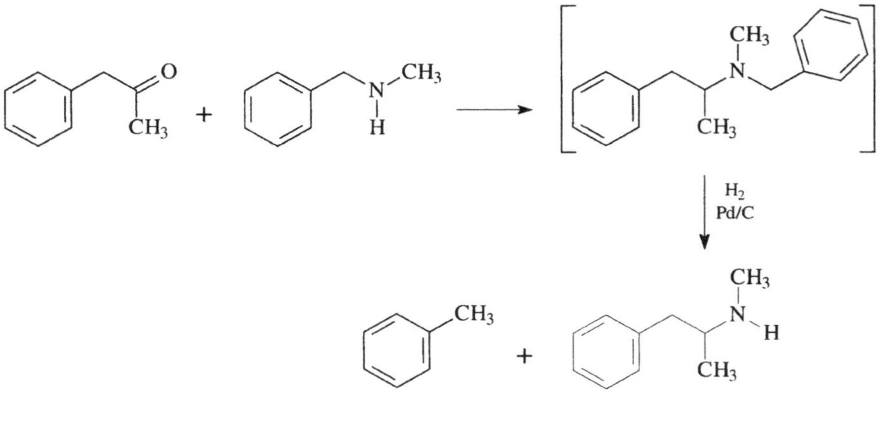

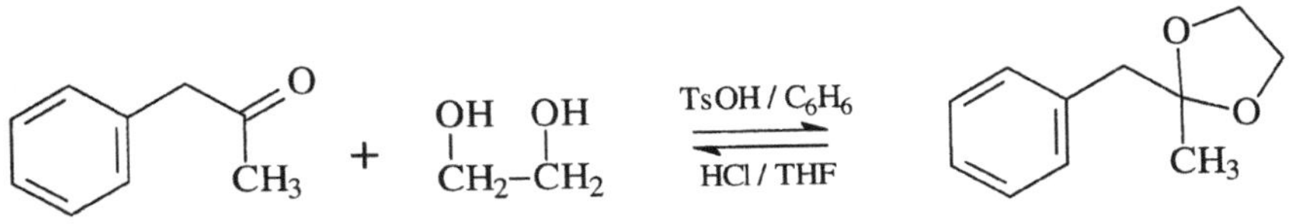

Figure 8.54
Ethylene glycol ketal of P2P

The use of protecting-group chemistry was also reported in a Dutch case in which the ethylene glycol ketal of P2P was found in samples seized in a clandestine laboratory (Poortman-van der Meer, 2000). The ethylene glycol ketal is easily prepared and removed (Figure 8.54). Synthetic organic chemists often use this group to protect carbonyl functionalities. It is not clear from the Dutch report whether the cooks were using the protecting group in an attempt to circumvent controlled-substance laws pertaining to P2P or whether the ketal simply represented an intermediate from an alternative, but undescribed, synthesis of P2P.

Though popular for many years, the use of synthetic methods involving P2P to produce methamphetamine has declined substantially. The impetus for this decline is multifactorial but includes reasons such as P2P is now a DEA schedule II compound and the detection of a "P2P lab" is quite easy, since P2P has a strong odor. The odor of P2P is exceptionally permeating and is very difficult to remove from the walls and carpets of the facility in which the cooking was performed as well as the clothing and skin of the cook. Consequently, identifying a P2P cook in a crowded bus or elevator is not difficult. Furthermore, ephedrine and pseudoephedrine (starting materials for reductive dehydroxylation methods) and the necessary reducing agents are inexpensive and readily available.

8.2.1.2.4 Preparation of Methamphetamine using Reduction of Ephedrine/Pseudoephedrine

P2P was scheduled by the DEA in 1980. By about 1990, the restrictions on access to P2P forced cooks to find an alternate source for illicit methamphetamine. The result of this search was a shift in methodology to the reductive removal of the benzylic (β) hydroxy group of ephedrine or pseudoephedrine. This remains the preferred synthetic approach to illicit methamphetamine today. Multiple ways exist to effect this synthetic transformation in a well-equipped synthetic organic laboratory. However, many of the methods that might be used by a trained organic chemist are difficult or impractical for illicit methamphetamine cooks and the primitive facilities in which they work.

It is possible to synthesize ephedrine and pseudoephedrine. However, with the ready availability of these compounds over the counter, this is rarely done. Rather, most clandestine chemists extract ephedrine or pseudoephedrine from over-the-counter stimulant/bronchodilator or decongestant pills, respectively. Most illicit chemists prefer the HCl salt to the sulfate salt of the compounds (Fester, 1994). The drug is removed from the tableting binders by grinding the tablets into a fine powder, adding water, and passing the mixture through a coffee filter. The salts of the drugs are more water-soluble than the binders and will pass through the filter, while the gummy binders will largely remain behind. The water is then evaporated and crystals of active drug are obtained. If colored coatings or binders contaminate the extracted drug, acetone or ethanol is added to the dried crystals and the solution is again filtered. In this case, the colored coatings dissolve in the solvent and pass through the filter, while the insoluble salt crystals are filtered off.

One of the early methods of conversion of ephedrine to methamphetamine involved the initial preparation of chloroephedrine (1-phenyl-1-chloro-2-methylaminopropane) (Emde, 1929; Ely, 1998; Fester, 1994) (Figure 8.55). A variety of reagents are known to replace hydroxy groups with chloride atoms. Among these, thionyl chloride ($SOCl_2$) and phosphorus pentachloride (PCl_5) are the most common. Phosphorus oxychloride ($POCl_3$) and phosphorus trichloride (PCl_3) can also be used. Alternatively, bromoephedrine can be prepared by treatment of ephedrine with phosphorus pentabromide or phosphorus tribromide. Though ephedrine is specifically mentioned earlier, pseudoephedrine is more frequently used. A 1998 NNICC report states that of the labs seized by authorities in 1997, 85% were using pseudoephedrine and 10% were using ephedrine (NNICC, 1998).

Once the benzyl halide compound is prepared, it is reductively dehalogenated to give methamphetamine (Figure 8.55). A wide array of reduction methods is available to effect this transformation. Some hydrogenation methods include the use of hydrogen gas on a platinum catalyst or hydrogen gas with acetic acid and a palladium catalyst containing a barium sulfate poisoning agent (Gero, 1951; Ely, 1998; Fester, 1994). Alternatively, calcium hydride with palladium and hydrochloric acid can be used (Ely, 1998). Other methods of catalytic reduction include the use of lithium aluminum hydride ($LiAlH_4$; LAH), which is reported to give good yields but is on the DEA Special Surveillance List. Others suggest that LAH is ineffective for this reduction (Ely, 2001). Zinc dust and Raney nickel can also be used for the reduction and are more readily available (Fester, 1994). However, the reduction does require large amounts of Raney nickel, if this method is selected (Fester, 1994).

Figure 8.55

Preparation of chloroephedrine/ chloropseudoephedrine

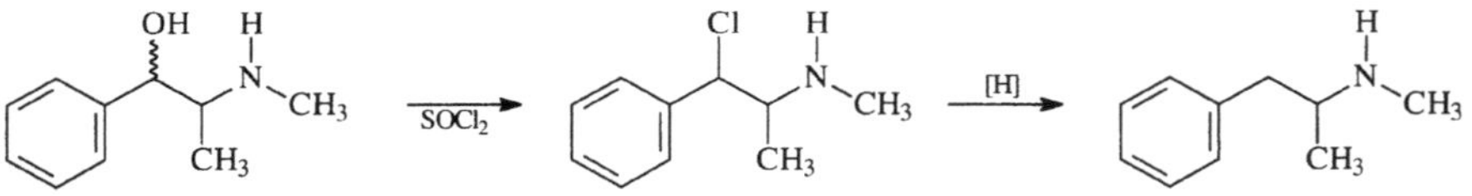

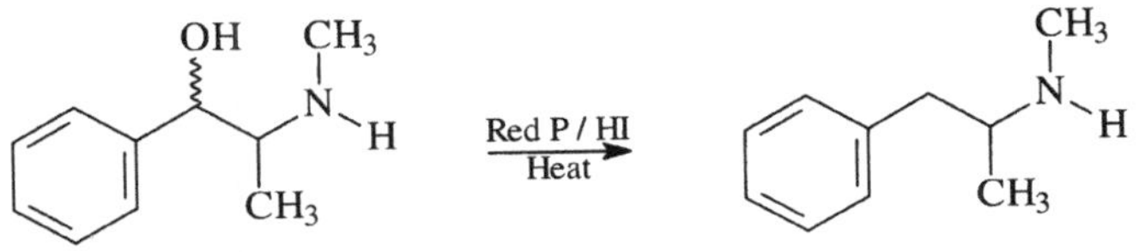

Figure 8.56

Red phosphorus/
hydriodic acid reduction
of ephedrine/
pseudoephedrine to form
methamphetamine

Perhaps the most common method of reductive methamphetamine production from ephedrine or pseudoephedrine employs red phosphorus and hydriodic acid (HI) (Kishi et al., 1983; Skinner, 1990; Fester, 1994; NNICC, 1998) (Figure 8.56). This reaction is very simple. The illicit chemist simply refluxes red phosphorus, iodine, and ephedrine or pseudoephedrine in water for 12–72 hours. At the completion of this time, the flask is cooled, more water added, and the mixture filtered through a coffee filter. The solid red phosphorus catalyst may be retained for future use. The solution is then made basic with sodium hydroxide and extracted with toluene. The final step is the precipitation and filtration of the hydrochloride salt of the finished methamphetamine. In this case, it is not necessary to prepare the benzyl halide derivative as a separate step. In fact, the benzyl iodo compound is generated *in situ* and then reduced to methamphetamine in the same reaction (Cantrell et al., 1988; Skinner, 1990). Of note is the fact that both red phosphorus and HI are listed on the Special Surveillance List. Therefore, the cook will often obtain these chemicals from more discrete or veiled sources.

Red phosphorus is commonly used and can be extracted from matchbook strikers or road flares. A report from Pocatello, ID, indicated that white phosphorus has also been used in the manufacture of methamphetamine (Cutler, 1998). The white phosphorus in this report was presumably acquired from one of the three large phosphorus plants in the Pocatello area. The HI is produced in the laboratory by combining the phosphorus and iodine (I_2) crystals. The iodine crystals are often purchased for water purification or from veterinary supply stores for use in treating thrush in horses. Other methods of producing HI include the use of hypophosphorous acid or hydrogen sulfide with I_2 and through the reaction of phosphoric acid with sodium iodide (Vallely, 1997a). Of particular note is the fact that the reduction of ephedrine or pseudoephedrine to methamphetamine has been reported to work without the use of red phosphorus when HI is generated from hypophosphorous acid and I_2 (Massetti, 1997). The reactions involved in these syntheses of HI are detailed in Figure 8.57.

Refluxing red phosphorus during the cooking of methamphetamine can produce phosphine (PH_3) gas. In order to contain this deadly gas as well as diminish the chemical odors produced by cooking methamphetamine, many of the reactions will be vented via a vacuum cleaner or clothes drier hose into

Figure 8.57

Preparation of HI

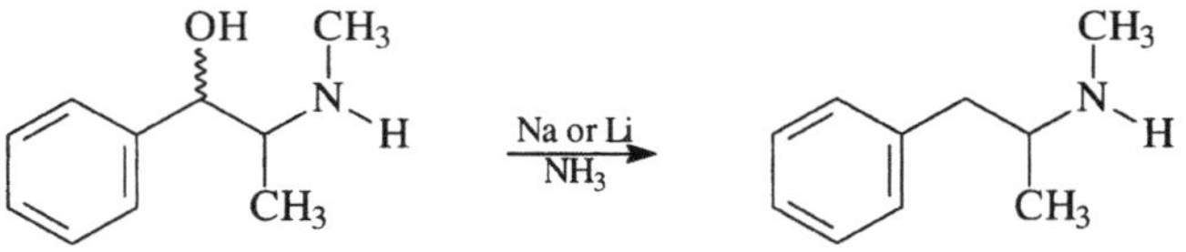

$$2P + 5I_2 + 8H_2O \longrightarrow 10HI + 2H_3PO_4$$

$$H_3PO_2 + 2I_2 + 2H_2O \longrightarrow 4HI + H_3PO_4$$

$$H_3PO_3 + I_2 + H_2O \longrightarrow 2HI + H_3PO_4$$

$$FeS + 2H^+ \longrightarrow H_2S + Fe^{++}$$

$$\downarrow I_2$$

$$2HI + S$$

Figure 8.58

"Nazi" method reduction of ephedrine/ pseudoephedrine to give methamphetamine

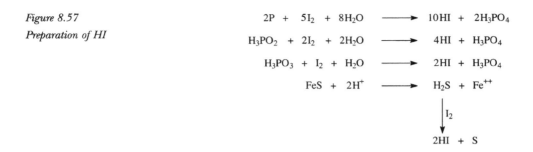

a bag of cat litter. The cat litter absorbs the odors and is believed to offer some containment of potentially hazardous gases such as PH_3 and CN. This bag, called the "vent bag" or "death bag," poses a potentially significant risk of toxic inhalation if opened by an unsuspecting person.

Another common method employed by clandestine chemists for reductive dehydroxylation of ephedrine or pseudoephedrine involves the use of an alkali metal such as lithium or sodium in the presence of liquid ammonia (Ely and McGrath, 1990) (Figure 8.58). The NNICC report indicates that only 18% of the labs seized in 1997 used the metal/ammonia reduction method (NNICC, 1998). Though currently somewhat less popular than the HI/red phosphorus method, the popularity of this approach is increasing. This is simply a modified Birch reduction of ephedrine or pseudoephedrine. As with the HI/red phosphorus method, this reduction can be performed directly on ephedrine or pseudoephedrine without first converting the starting material to its benzyl halide derivative. The Birch reduction proceeds via two separate single-electron transfers, followed by protonation of the resultant anion. The benzyl hydroxyl group is eliminated as water, leaving behind methamphetamine.

This reduction may be performed on the freebase or hydrochloride salt of the ephedrine or pseudoephedrine. The freebase is isolated by dissolving the hydrochloride salt in hot alcohol and adding NaOH until the hydrochloride is neutralized. The alcohol is distilled off of the reaction mixture and the freebase of the starting material is then vacuum-distilled away from the residual hydroxide. Alternatively, the base can be isolated with extraction into tetrahydrofuran. For the reduction, liquid ammonia is added to a container, such as a thermos bottle. The lithium or sodium metal is then added to the liquid ammonia to produce the characteristic brilliant blue "solvated electron" solution. The ephedrine or pseudoephedrine is then added, possibly as freebase in tetrahydrofuran (to aid in the solubility of the drug to the solution) or as a salt that becomes the freebase in the presence of the liquid ammonia. As the reduction proceeds, the deep blue color shifts to a brown-copper. The reaction typically goes to completion in approximately 10–15 minutes. Many illicit chemists simply wait for the ammonia to evaporate overnight and then treat the residue with either alcohol or very slowly with water to deactivate any excess unreacted metal (Fester, 1994). Isolation of the methamphetamine is then accomplished with a simple organic extraction.

Though it is a misnomer, this method of illicit methamphetamine production is often referred to as the "Nazi" method. Though phenethylamine-derived stimulants such as methcathinone were studied by Axis powers during WWII, this method of synthesis was not among those used (Ely, 1998). Lithium metal is typically obtained from batteries (Vallely, 1996). In fact, this very issue has led some stores to put lithium batteries behind the counter. Sodium metal can be purchased directly, though it does appear on the Special Surveillance List. Alternatively, sodium metal has been produced through the electrolysis of molten sodium hydroxide. Clearly, however, this is a very dangerous process. The ammonia is typically acquired from agrochemical sources (Ely, 1998). A 1999 report indicated that ethylenediamine is a viable reaction medium in place of ammonia (Barnes, 1999).

The Wolff–Kishner reduction has reportedly also been applied to the synthesis of methamphetamine from ephedrine or pseudoephedrine (Fester, 1994) (Figure 8.59). In the most generic description of this reduction, hydrazine reacts with a carbonyl to form an intermediate hydrazone, with the

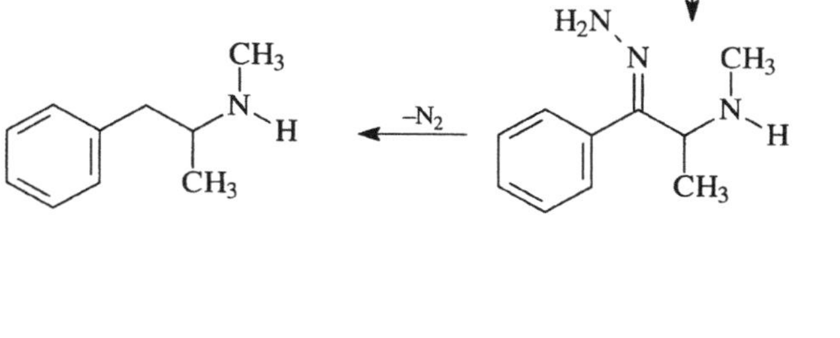

Figure 8.59

Possible route of Wolff–Kishner reduction when applied to the reduction of ephedrine or pseudoephedrine to form methamphetamine

elimination of water. The hydrazone then decomposes to release nitrogen gas, leaving behind the fully reduced methylene. With respect to the synthesis of methamphetamine, hydrazine and ephedrine or pseudoephedrine are combined with a strong base (NaOH or KOH) in hot diethylene glycol and refluxed and then distilled. The collected distillate is treated with aqueous KOH and extracted with toluene. Final purification of the methamphetamine freebase is effected using fractional distillation. The report further suggests the reason this reduction is effective in this circumstance is through a "masked carbonyl" in the ephedrine, accessible through tautomerism. This is, however, chemically impossible. If these conditions do reduce ephedrine to methamphetamine, an initial oxidation to methcathinone prior to the Wolff–Kishner reduction's being performed would be the most likely route. It is possible that there is some neighboring-group effect or other chemical process that takes place. Oxidation of α-hydroxy functions has been reported in hydrazine chemistry, as in the preparation of osazones (Smith and March, 2001). At present, however, the mechanism behind this reduction of ephedrine or pseudoephedrine to methamphetamine is unclear. Assuming this reduction is effective, it has the reported advantages of being relatively inexpensive and largely free of pungent odors. The disadvantages of this approach are that it requires the use of the freebase of the starting material, which are prepared as described earlier, and the fact that hydrazine is a known carcinogen (Toth, 2000).

As already mentioned, ephedrine and pseudoephedrine can be treated oxidatively rather than reductively. When the benzyl hydroxy group of ephedrine or pseudoephedrine is oxidized to form a ketone, the resultant compound is the stimulant methcathinone (Figure 8.60). This oxidation can be performed using a variety of oxidizing agents, including chromium trioxide, dichromate, and potassium permanganate. Dichromate has been found in illicit labs synthesizing methcathinone (Kemper, 1996).

Methamphetamine has also been prepared from phenylalanine using protecting-group chemistry (Repke et al., 1978) (Figure 8.61). The first step in this method is the reduction of R-(+)-phenylalanine to R-(+)-2-amino-3-phenylpropanol using lithium aluminum hydride (LAH, LiAlH₄). The amino moiety of the resultant amino alcohol is then protected using benzylchloroformate. Next, the hydroxy group is converted to the *p*-toluenesulfonate with

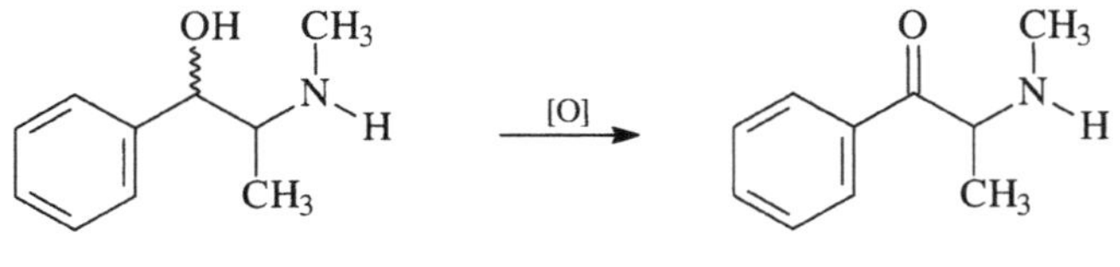

Figure 8.60

Oxidation of ephedrine or pseudoephedrine to form methcathinone

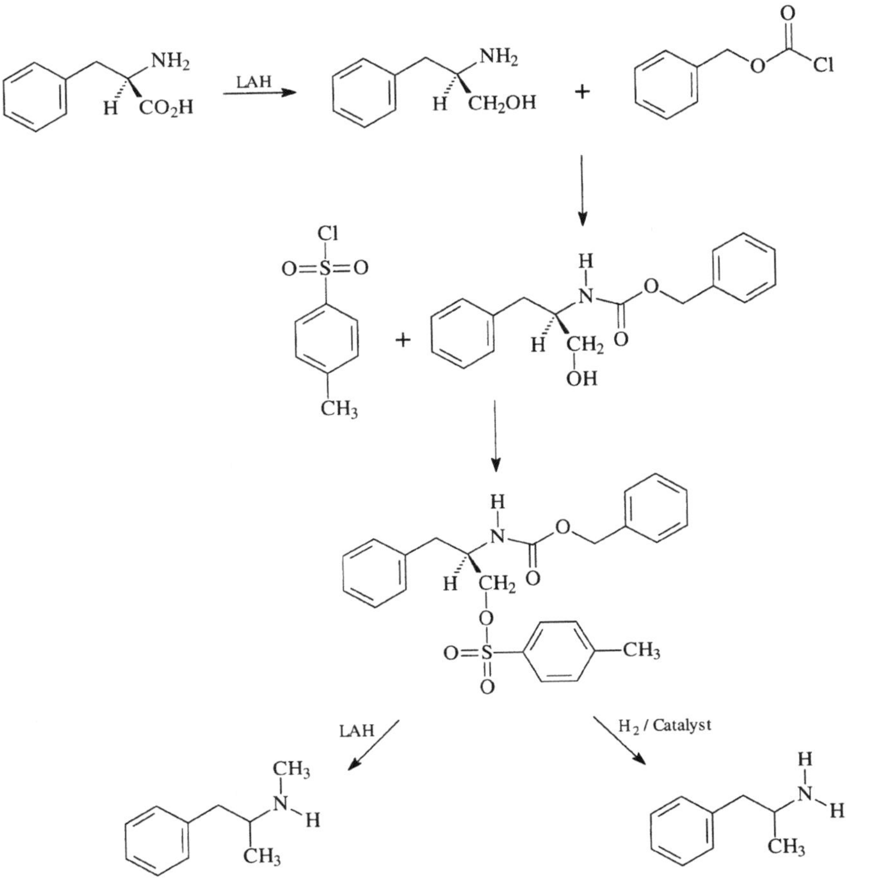

Figure 8.61

Synthesis of methamphetamine from phenylalanine using protecting-group chemistry

p-toluenesulfonyl chloride. The diderivatized compound is then subjected to a second reduction with LAH in tetrahydrofuran to remove the derivatizing groups and leave S-(+)-methamphetamine (i.e., *d*-methamphetamine). This method, though not difficult in a well-equipped organic chemistry laboratory, is somewhat challenging for clandestine chemists. It requires not only several steps but also inert atmosphere and rigorously dried solvents.

Clandestine chemists use a variety of organic solvents in the preparation of methamphetamine and its precursors. These solvents serve primarily as organic extractions of intermediates and products. Many of the organic solvents used are readily available from retail sources as common household chemicals. Coleman Fuel® is composed of naphtha (a mixture of hexanes and pentanes). Diethyl ether is easily obtained from starting fluid and methylene chloride from paint strippers. Freon 113 (trichlorotrifluoroethane) is listed on the Special Surveillance list because of its use in illicit drug production.

Figure 8.62

HCl gas generator for forming HCl salts of methamphetamine

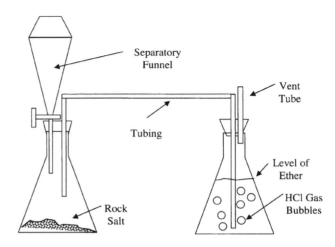

Dichlorofluoroethane has also been used in the manufacture of methamphetamine (Oulton, 1996). Solvents as common as cooking oil have been used to store sodium metal in clandestine laboratories.

Methamphetamine freebase is an oil. In order to easily distribute it as a solid, it must be converted to the hydrochloride salt. This is typically done by dissolving the oil in a dry organic solvent, such as diethyl ether, and bubbling HCl gas through the solution. The hydrochloride salt of the methamphetamine precipitates and is collected by filtration and dried. The HCl gas can be purchased directly in cylinders, though this is likely to arouse suspicion. Most often it is generated by combining sulfuric acid and NaCl rock salt in a homemade generator (Figure 8.62).

Ice is the street term for the smokable form of methamphetamine hydrochloride. The term *ice*, which comes from the appearance of the compound, was popularized by the media during the late 1980s, when this new dosage form was being used with increasing regularity in Hawaii. The same substance is also referred to as *crystal, crystal meth, shards, glass,* and *batu* (Filipino for "rock") (Miller and Hughes, 1994). Unlike many other salts, methamphetamine hydrochloride is sufficiently volatile that it can be smoked. Smoking the compound results in rapid systemic uptake and resultant effects similar to those seen with intravenous administration (Albertson et al., 1998). Ice is prepared by first rinsing the methamphetamine hydrochloride salt with hot acetone. The acetone-rinsed solid is then dissolved in hot ethanol to make a supersaturated solution (Anonymous, 1997). This solution is allowed to cool slowly, and the methamphetamine hydrochloride forms large, clear, solid crystals having the characteristic broken-glass or rock-candy appearance. This substance is almost exclusively the *d*-isomer of methamphetamine. This is a result of the *d*-isomer's being the primary constituent of the mixture prior to crystallization; the crystallization further increases the enantiomeric purity.

Illicit chemists have also been known to extract the active ingredient from Vick's® inhalers. This ingredient, listed on the label as *l*-desoxyephedrine, is just as correctly named *l*-methamphetamine (Figure 8.62). Obviously, this is the "wrong" (i.e., less pharmacologically active) enantiomer. Though some approaches to reversing the stereochemistry at the α-carbon have been reported on the Internet, these reactions are not very effective in clandestine labs and are rarely used for bulk methamphetamine production.

The accessibility of ephedrine and pseudoephedrine starting materials has become more limited due to legislative attempts to curb illicit methamphetamine manufacture. This situation has forced cooks to become ever more creative in their search for inexpensive, readily available sources of methamphetamine precursors that do not attract the attention of the authorities. To this end, at least one illicit cook has attempted to use the plant ephedra, also known as the Chinese herb Ma Huang, as a substitute for ephedrine or pseudoephedrine starting material in illicit methamphetamine synthesis (Andrews, 1995).

The stems and leaves of the ephedra plant do contain both *d*-pseudoephedrine and *l*-ephedrine along with many other alkaloids. Specific analysis of ephedra extracts demonstrates the presence of three primary sets of ephedra alkaloid pairs (Andrews, 1995) (Figure 8.63). The first pair, as mentioned earlier, is ephedrine and pseudoephedrine. The other two pairs are the *N*-demethylated pair norephedrine and norpseudoephedrine and the *N,N*-dimethylated pair, methylephedrine and methylpseudoephedrine.

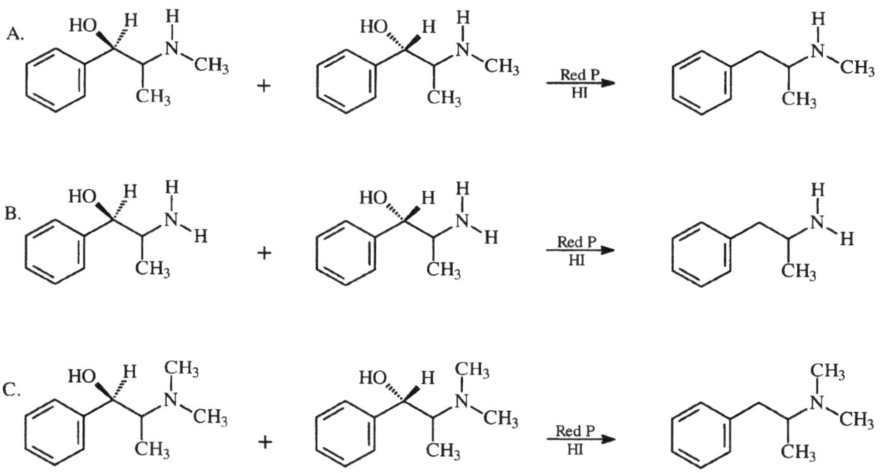

Figure 8.63

Alkaloid pairs and reduction products of ephedra extracts treated under red phosphorus/HI reduction conditions

Quantitatively, some ephedra tablets analyzed contain as much of the methamphetamine precursor compounds as a synthetic 25-mg ephedrine tablet (Andrews, 1995).

In a report by Andrews, the viability of using ephedra as a starting material for methamphetamine production was examined (Andrews, 1995). In this study, ground ephedra plant material was washed three times with methanol and the methanol washings collected and evaporated to a greenish brown tar. This tarry substance was treated with hydriodic acid and red phosphorus and refluxed for 5 hours. The solution was then filtered, made basic with NaOH, and extracted with Freon-113. The Freon-113 solution was dried over Na_2SO_4 and the hydrochloride salts of the products precipitated in the standard fashion. The reaction products were analyzed using gas chromatography with infrared and mass spectral detection methods.

Aliquots sampled throughout the progress of this reaction showed the presence of amphetamine and methamphetamine in addition to some well-known intermediate contaminants of methamphetamine synthesis, including phenyl-2-propanone and *trans*-1,2-dimethyl-3-phenylaziridine. Analysis of the final hydrochloride salt product, however, showed the presence of amphetamine, methamphetamine, and *N,N*-dimethylamphetamine. The largest peak in the chromatogram is that corresponding to methamphetamine, with the *N,N*-dimethylamphetamine peak being approximately half that size. The amphetamine peak in the same chromatogram is approximately one-tenth the height of the methamphetamine peak.

The methamphetamine produced was from the reduction of the ephedrine and pseudoephedrine in the plant material (Figure 8.63). The source of the *N,N*-dimethylamphetamine was reduction of the methylephedrine and methylpseudoephedrine. The amphetamine was produced when the norephedrine and norpseudoephedrine were reduced. The author points out that the relative distributions of the final products are dependent upon the relative concentrations of the various alkaloids in the ephedra raw material. It was concluded from this study that ephedra does provide a viable alternative for starting material for the illicit production of methamphetamine. Therefore, an increase in the use of ephedra as a precursor source would not be completely unexpected.

8.2.1.2.5 Stereochemistry in Illicit Methamphetamine Synthesis

With specific reference to the differential pharmacological profiles of the *d*- and *l*-isomers of methamphetamine, their synthetic derivations are important. The P2P method is not a stereospecific synthesis (Figure 8.64a). This is due to the trigonal planar geometry of the sp^2-hybridized imine carbon in the intermediate. The reduction of the imine intermediate to methamphetamine takes place with equal probability of hydride delivery from either the top or bottom

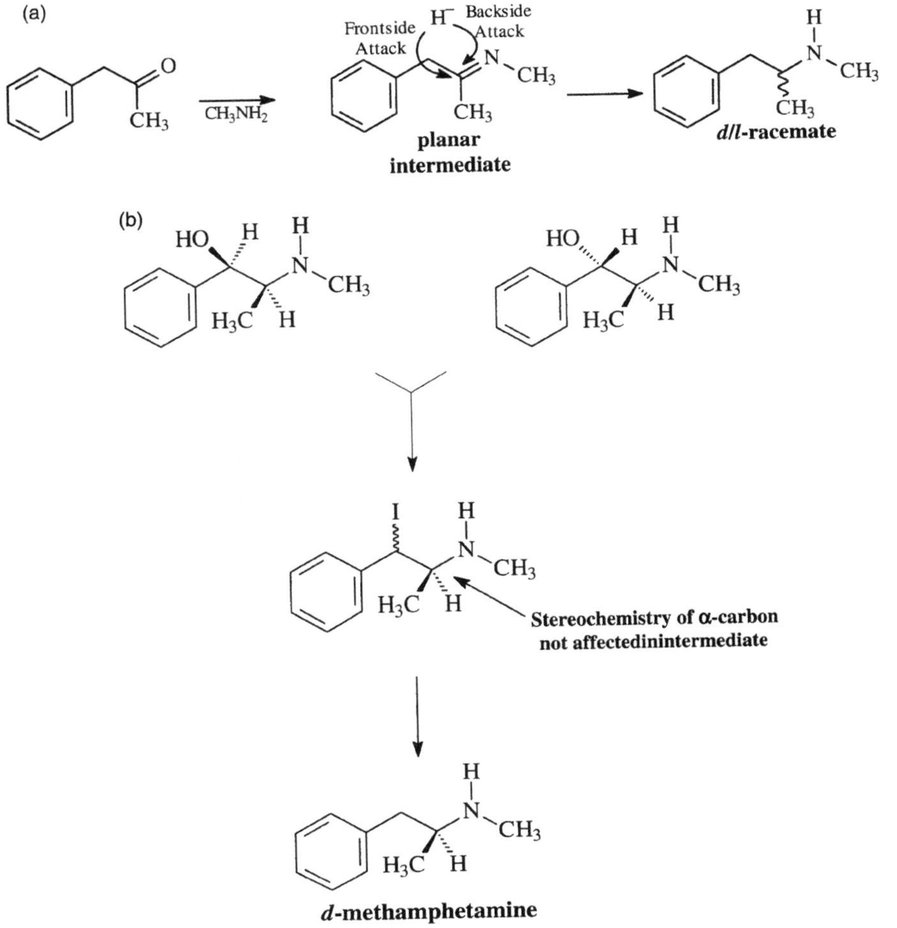

(a)

planar
intermediate

d/l-racemate

Figure 8.64

(a) Stereochemical basis
of P2P methods of
methamphetamine
synthesis; (b)
stereochemical basis
of ephedrine/
pseudoephedrine
reduction methods of
methamphetamine
synthesis

(b)

Stereochemistry of α-carbon
not affectedinintermediate

d-methamphetamine

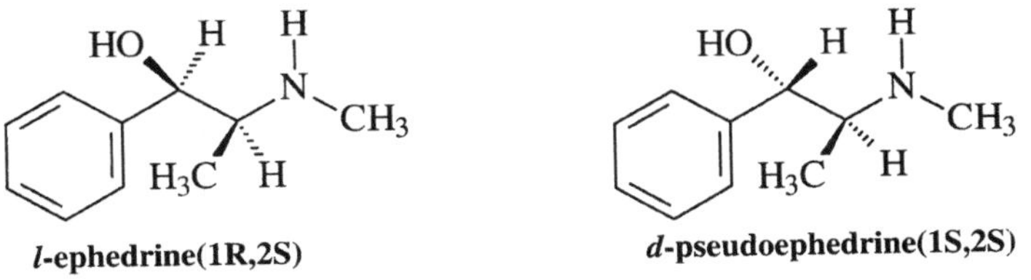

l-ephedrine(1R,2S)

d-pseudoephedrine(1S,2S)

Figure 8.65

Naturally occurring
diastereomers of ephedrine
and pseudoephedrine

face. Therefore, methamphetamine produced by this method is a racemate
(50:50 d:l mixture).

Naturally occurring and pharmaceutically used ephedrine is the l-isomer
(specifically, the 1R,2S diastereomer), while naturally occurring and pharmaceutically used pseudoephedrine is the d-isomer (specifically, the 1S,2S diastereomer) (Andrews, 1995) (Figure 8.65). Reduction of either l-ephedrine or

d-pseudoephedrine via the red phosphorus/HI or the "Nazi" method yields the more pharmacologically active *d*-methamphetamine—yet another reason cooks tend to favor these methods and starting materials (Figure 8.64b). Another way of stating this is that the reduction is stereospecific, so the (S) absolute configuration of the α-carbon in the precursor is retained in the product. The stereochemical retention in these methods of methamphetamine production is a result of the reduction involving only the β-hydroxyl moiety and not the α-carbon and the absences of a planar sp^2 intermediate.

8.2.1.2.6 Synthetic By-Products

Because of the impure starting materials, primitive facilities, chemical ignorance, and very nature of the reactions, even when methamphetamine is actually synthesized, a number of synthetic by-products are concomitantly produced (Soine, 1986; Tanaka et al., 1992, 1994). These by-products can be structurally quite diverse and may be present in highly variable amounts in samples of illicitly prepared methamphetamine. Several reports exist characterizing various by-products of the reactions (Cantrell et al., 1988; Skinner, 1990; Tanaka et al., 1992, 1994; Windahl et al., 1995). The presence of specific by-products provides some insight into the synthetic methodology that was employed by a given cook in the preparation of a given sample of an illicit drug.

When the Leuckart–Wallach reaction (i.e., P2P-methylamine condensation) is used for methamphetamine production, some specific by-products are created (Figure 8.66). *N*-Formylmethamphetamine has been positively identified in samples of illicit methamphetamine (Lambrechts and Rasmussen, 1984). The production of this compound is less a by-product than an intermediate whose presence is reflective of incomplete conversion of the final intermediate to methamphetamine. Nonetheless, the presence of *N*-formylmethamphetamine in illicit methamphetamine has been confirmed.

Figure 8.66
P2P method by-products

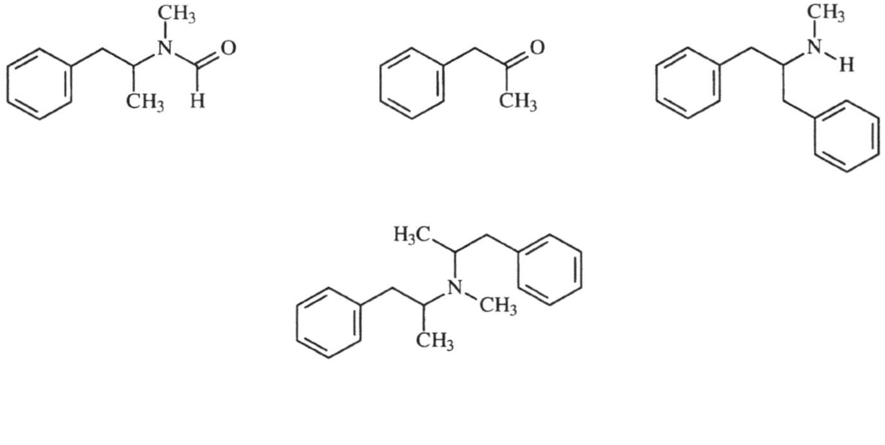

Additional synthetic impurities detected in samples of illicit methamphetamine prepared from P2P include unreacted starting materials, N,α,α'-trimethyldiphenethylamine, and α-benzyl-N-methylphenethylamine (Barron et al., 1974). The presence of N,α,α'-trimethyldiphenethylamine is a result of the reaction of the intermediate N-formylmethamphetamine with another equivalent of P2P in the presence of formic acid. A tertiary amine such as N,α,α'-trimethyldiphenethylamine is an expected side reaction product of a Leuckart-type synthesis (Smith and March, 2001). It is also possible that this same side reaction product can be formed in a mixture of P2P and methylamine that is catalytically hydrogenated in an attempt to form methamphetamine.

The genesis of α-benzyl-N-methylphenethylamine (BNMPA) actually begins earlier than the Leuckart reaction. In fact, in methamphetamine synthesized from P2P, the presence of BNMPA is the result of a by-product of P2P synthesis. When phenylacetic acid is in the presence of a dehydrating agent such as acetic acid or acetic anhydride, dibenzylketone is produced. Treatment of dibenzylketone with methylamine and formic acid followed by acid reflux as in the Leuckart–Wallach reaction provides BNMPA.

N,N-Di(β-phenethylisopropyl)methylamine, the N-desmethyl derivative of N,α,α'-trimethyldiphenethylamine, is also produced in the Leuckart reaction. An additional nine other minor side reaction products and impurities have been identified in illicit methamphetamine samples prepared from P2P (Kram and Kreugel, 1977).

Currently, the most common method employed for illicit methamphetamine synthesis is the reduction of ephedrine or pseudoephedrine with red phosphorus and hydriodic acid. Several of the by-products of this reaction have been identified and characterized.

As is apparent from Figure 8.67, many of the by-products of illicit MA synthesis by the red phosphorus/HI method can be categorized into three groups: (1) single-aromatic-ring compounds, (2) nitrogen-containing multiple-aromatic-ring compounds, and (3) non-nitrogenous substituted naphthalenes. These organic by-products are produced through a variety of reactions. The naphthalene derivatives are reported to be a result of Aldol condensation and dehydration of P2P in the presence of acid (Cantrell et al., 1988). The aziridines are a result of an intramolecular nucleophilic attack of the amino nitrogen on the iodinated benzyl carbon intermediate (Cantrell et al., 1988; Skinner, 1990). The two-ring nitrogenous compounds are the result of a variety of dimerization reactions (Windahl et al., 1995). It is noteworthy that P2P is also produced as a by-product in the reduction of ephedrine and pseudoephedrine with red phosphorus and hydriodic acid (Windahl et al., 1995; Skinner, 1990; Cantrell et al., 1988). Mechanisms for the formation of some by-products formed in

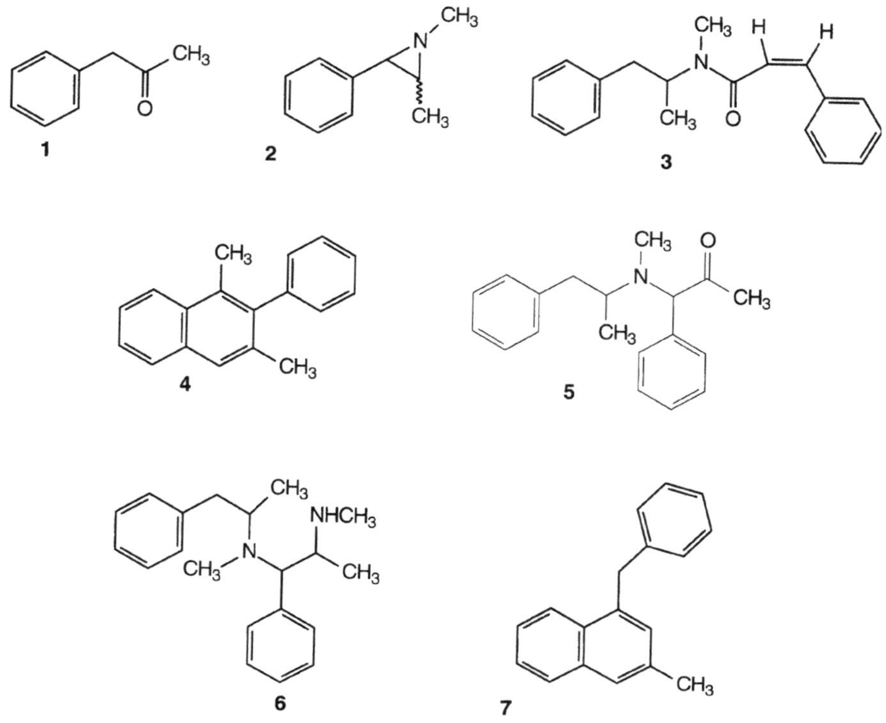

Figure 8.67

Red phosphorus/HI
method reaction
by-products

Figure 8.67

Red phosphorus/HI
method reaction
by-products

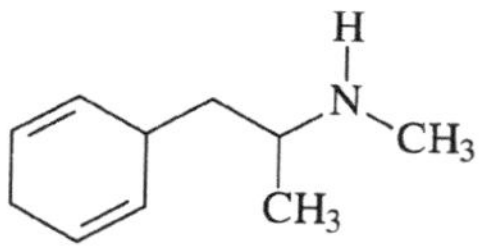

Figure 8.68

"Nazi" method (Birch
reduction) by-product

illicit methamphetamine production have been proposed but generally not studied in detail.

The Birch reduction method of methamphetamine production is associated primarily with one by-product (Valleley, 1997b; Ely, 1998) (Figure 8.68). This compound, (S)-1-(1,4-cyclohexadienyl)-2-methylaminopropane, commonly known as CMP, is the result of overreduction, which destroys the aromatic ring of the methamphetamine. Reduction of aromatic rings using the Birch reaction is well known (Mundy and Ellerd, 1988).

The reactions used to produce HI also produce by-products (Figure 8.69) (Ely, 1998). Some of the compounds inadvertently produced, the most notable of which is phosphine gas, can be lethal (Willers-Russo, 1996, 1999; Wheeler

$$3I_2 \; + \; 2P \quad \longrightarrow \quad 2PI_3$$

$$4H_3PO_3 \quad \xrightarrow{\text{Heat}} \quad 3H_3PO_4 \; + \; PH_3$$

$$2PI_3 \; + \; 6H_2O \quad \longrightarrow \quad 6HI \; + \; 2H_3PO_3$$

Figure 8.69

Generation of phosphine gas (PH₃) from the reactions of iodine and red phosphorus

and Griffin, 1997). A proposed molecular mechanism for the formation of phosphine in this reaction series is provided in Figure 8.69 (Willers-Russo, 1999).

Additional impurities that have been noted in samples of illicit methamphetamine include *N*-acetylmethamphetamine, α-phenylethylamine, and *N*-(2-hydroxyethyl)amphetamine hydrochloride (Meyer et al., 1995; Conn et al., 1996; Cyr et al., 1996). Other impurities in illicit-drug samples may be a result of "carryover" from the synthetic process. One Internet discussion group attempted to characterize various impurities based on the color of the finished product. This group stated that if the product is red, pseudoephedrine was used and the red tablet coating not adequately removed from the drug; if the product is orange, it is stated that ephedrine sulfate must have been used; if the product is green, copper or other metallic salts have been carried over into the product; and, if the product is purplish, iodine from the red phosphorus/HI reaction has been carried over into the product. Though these suggestions may not be rigorously accurate, color and color change have been significant issues in legal cases. Specifically, iodide salts may be white or colorless; but over time, as the iodide (I^-) decomposes to form iodine (I_2), the color of the substance turns first to orange and then to a reddish brown. This has led to questions of evidence tampering, though this was later proven not to be the case (Ely, 1998).

The decongestant pseudoephedrine is often available over the counter in cold-relief preparations. Often, it is in combination with cough suppressants such as dextromethorphan, analgesics such as acetaminophen, and antihistamines such as diphenhydramine. With the restrictions placed upon pseudoephedrine purchases, clandestine chemists have used such common cold-tablet preparations as starting materials for methamphetamine synthesis. Since clandestine chemists may not have the skill to effectively separate the compounds in mixtures, it is possible that the other drugs present in the cold-medication mixture may also be transformed under the reaction conditions. In a 1999 study of this situation, Oulton and Skinner (1999) describe an assessment of the extent to which seven common medications (chlorpheniramine, acetaminophen, dextromethorphan, doxylamine, diphenhydramine, guaifenesin, and triprolidine) present in cold tablets along with pseudoephedrine react under HI/red phosphorus reduction conditions. It was found that only chlopheniramine did not react under the reduction conditions. Reaction products for the other six compounds tested are described. Investigating forensic chemists may use this information in determining what method and starting materials cooks were attempting to use. Further, this information may be valuable to clinicians treating individuals intoxicated with the contaminated drugs.

Obviously, there is no consumer protection or standardization within the illicit drug market. In an examination of bulk drug substances sold as methamphetamine over 10 years, the Los Angeles Street Drug Identification Program found that 63% of the time the substances actually contained none of the drug (Klatt et al., 1986). Instead, substances sold as amphetamines contained caffeine, phenylpropanolamine, ephedrine, pseudoephedrine, lidocaine, or phencyclidine (Klatt et al., 1986; Rasmussen et al., 1989; Morgan, 1992; Lago and Kosten, 1994). Since illegal drugs are typically sold by weight, they are often "cut" with something else in order to increase bulk weight and simultaneously diminish actual drug content. Cutting agents (i.e., adulterants) may be inert substances, other drugs in an attempt to get a combined effect, or, occasionally, toxins in deliberate attempts to poison users. Dimethylsulfone has been detected as an adulterant in many samples of illicit methamphetamine hydrochloride powder as well as in "ice" (Chappell, 1996; Willers-Russo and Barley, 1996; Anonymous, 1996). It has been suggested that this compound is used as a cutting agent because it is a white crystalline solid difficult to distinguish macroscopically from methamphetamine hydrochloride. Other substances that have been identified as cutting agents include cornstarch, lactose, maltose, talc, quinine, and even strychnine (Chiang, 1998). Needless to say, substitution and cutting agents can significantly complicate the analytical and toxicological pictures of illicit drug abuse cases.

8.3 LAW ENFORCEMENT

8.3.1 HAZARDS IN CLANDESTINE LABORATORIES

As has been stated previously, though the focus of this chapter is illegal methamphetamine laboratories, clandestine laboratories producing a myriad of other substances have been found. The majority of hazards posed to law enforcement personnel in a clandestine lab are the same regardless of the specific agent or agents being produced and include to name a few, explosions; chemical and thermal burns; slip, trip, and fall hazards; electrical and water diversion; and chemical incompatibility.

However, there are also a few item-specific hazards unrelated to methamphetamine that deserve mention. Law enforcement personnel entering a lab where phencyclidine (PCP), lysergic acid diethylamide (LSD), or fentanyl derivatives may be in production are usually advised to wear level-A protection. This is because these compounds are all potent and can cause effects with small exposures and are well absorbed through the skin. Percutaneous absorption may be dramatically increased if a solvent with dermal-penetration-enhancing capabilities (e.g., dimethylsulfoxide, DMSO) is also contacted. Inhalation of these compounds may also present some risk, though this has not been adequately studied. Cyanogen bromide is used in the production of 4-methylaminorex (Henderson et al., 1995). Inhalation of this compound could represent a significant toxic exposure.

8.3.1.1 Chemical Hazards

Prior to 1980, illicit methamphetamine was prepared primarily by motorcycle gangs, such as the Hells Angels, the Gypsy Jokers, and the Nomads, using reductive amination reactions of phenylacetone (P2P) (Ely, 1998). At that time, P2P was not controlled. These early labs were fairly simple in their design and, chemically speaking, were relatively safe, with the only major chemical hazard being the explosive potential of diethyl ether (Ely, 1998). With the addition of P2P to the DEA schedule II list in 1980, the face of clandestine laboratories changed completely. Initially, the P2P reductive amination techniques were still used to make methamphetamine. However, now the cooks were forced to prepare their own P2P starting material, which also meant that chemicals not previously needed were now being used and that significant amounts of hazardous waste were being generated (Ely, 1998). Regulation of key chemicals has made access to them more difficult. However, with the increase in the number of labs, it seems apparent that these efforts have done little to actually curb the problem of illicit methamphetamine synthesis. It is likely that as long there is a continued and growing demand for methamphetamine, cooks will continue to look for simple, inexpensive, high-yield methods to produce the substance. This will involve increasingly more creative efforts on the part of the cooks at chemical synthesis and construction of lab facilities and apparatus. As an ultimate result, it has been suggested that clandestine methamphetamine labs are now significantly more dangerous than previously was the case (Ely, 1998).

Almost every illicit drug laboratory has mineral acids, such as HCl and H_2SO_4, and strong hydroxide bases, such as NaOH. These substances may cause serious contact burns. Other chemicals frequently used in clandestine methamphetamine synthesis are organic solvents, such as diethyl ether, acetone, and ethanol. Significant toxicity may result from inhalational exposure to these substances. Frequently, the acids and bases are improperly stored and may come in contact with one another. This can begin a reaction that generates sufficient heat to cause a fire or explosion within the laboratory. This would likely initiate a chain reaction and ignite volatile flammable solvents. Thermal burns and blast injuries may result from this situation.

The metal–ammonia reduction method has both inhalation and chemical burn hazards associated with it. Concentrated ammonia vapor is a severe pulmonary irritant and may cause intense difficulty in breathing or lung-tissue damage. Furthermore, liquid ammonia has a boiling point of $-33°C$, which can cause frostbite on contact. Skin contact with sodium or lithium metal can produce deep burns. Sodium or lithium metal may come in contact with atmospheric moisture or decontamination water, resulting in an explosive or corrosive hazard. Red phosphorus also poses a significant ignition hazard. This typically appears to be the result of friction or striking the phosphorus. Unfortunately, this has been reported during disposal of a 50-gallon metal drum containing red phosphorus as well as when a red phosphorus sample was being ground with a mortar and pestle for analysis (Massetti, 1996b; Quinn, 2000). Ignition of red phosphorus has also been reported when a sample from a clandestine lab was treated with concentrated nitric acid as part of the phosphate-ammonium molybdate crystal test for phosphorus (Christian, 1996).

Another dangerous situation associated with clandestine laboratories includes liquid or solid chemical spills. Containers may have cryptic markings understood only by the cook or may be completely unmarked or unlabeled. Containers are often corroded or damaged because they contain substances for which they are chemically inappropriate. For example, organic solvents may be stored in plastic soda bottles and mineral acids in metal gas cans. Organic solvents and other volatile compounds may also be kept in large buckets or uncapped containers, creating a potential explosion hazard and a toxic or oxygen-depleted atmosphere. Inhalation of other toxic gases, including H_2S and phosphine, has caused injury in investigators (Burgess, 2001) and deaths in occupants of clandestine laboratories (Willers-Russo, 1996, 1999; Anjaria and Evans, 1997; Wheeler and Griffin, 1997).

Many clandestine laboratories also contain improperly stored gas cylinders, which may become missiles if tipped over or explode if caught in or near a fire. Furthermore, cylinders may not be exactly what they appear to be at first glance. A report exists of a gas cylinder that had been opened and filled with a combination of NaCl rock salt and sulfuric acid. The cylinder was then recapped and used as an HCl gas generator (Johnston, 1999). Gas cylinders and tanks and, in particular, tanks of ammonia are a tremendous safety concern to those investigating and dismantling clandestine methamphetamine laboratories. This concern is so great that a report originally published by the Washington State Department of Ecology on the safe handling of 5-gallon pressurized tanks of ammonia was reprinted in a 1996 issue of the *Journal of Clandestine Laboratory Investigating Chemists* (Kummerlowe, 1996).

The risk of fire in clandestine laboratories is enormous (Stone, 1996; Hall, 1997; White, 1997). Numerous deaths, including those of three children, and tremendous property damages, including the burning of a hotel, were the result of clandestine-laboratory fires (T. Barnes, 1996b; Associated Press, 1997a, 1997b). Certainly these fires can be the result of out-of-control chemical reactions. Fire risk is also associated with smoking, exposed wiring, non-explosion-proof refrigerators, and the lack of spark-free switches and power tools frequently used in makeshift laboratories. If a fire does occur in a clandestine laboratory, traditional suppression methods may be ineffective or even increase the damage of the blaze. For example, if hydride reducing agents or phosphorus are present, these substances may react explosively with water from firefighters or cooks attempting to control the fire.

Chemicals that have nothing to do with the illicit manufacture of methamphetamine may also be encountered in a clandestine laboratory. For example, authorities located hydrofluoric acid (HF) in an illicit methamphetamine laboratory (Lazarus, 1997). The impetus for the presence of HF in a methamphetamine laboratory is not clear. Possible reasons include cooks attempting to use it for some part of the synthetic process, using it in the production of some other material, using it as a booby trap agent, simply thinking it might be valuable but not really knowing why or how, or even legitimate use as a glass-etching agent.

The chemical risks associated with clandestine laboratories do not simply cease with the dismantling of the lab and movement away from the lab site. Chemists must be continually vigilant in dealing with evidence collected from clandestine laboratories. Incidents illustrating this point include a violent reaction occurring while a flask was being entered into evidence and multiple reports of ignition of red phosphorus during disposal and analysis (Masetti, 1996b; Christian, 1996; Perkal and White, 1999).

8.3.1.2 Physical Hazards

A clandestine methamphetamine synthetic operation was discovered in a large pharmaceutical company (Lawrence, 1997). However, this represents a very unusual circumstance. Most clandestine laboratories are assembled in makeshift facilities without due regard for basic safety principles. This makes the chemical hazards in clandestine laboratories enormous. However, the risk does not end by solely addressing chemical hazards. Numerous physical hazards also exist for law enforcement personnel and the general public.

The structures containing the laboratories may themselves be dangerous. For example, in order to avoid detection, cooks may elect to operate illicit laboratories in abandoned or condemned buildings. Attempts to conceal chemical waste or to dissuade intruders from entering the facility may involve poorly excavated pits, further jeopardizing the structural integrity of the facility and adding to the falling hazard potential to entering personnel.

Another consideration that cannot be overlooked is the hazard of clandestine labs in vehicles. The cooks may simply be moving from one location to another and have a "boxed lab," or they may be in full operation in a vehicle with a power supply, such as a motor home. In either case, significant risk is associated with the circumstances. Although it has not been specifically studied, the probability of an accident would seem to be increased if the operator of a vehicle transporting a lab became impaired due to inhalation of the chemical vapors. It seems reasonable that this would potentially be compounded if the vehicle windows were rolled up to prevent others from smelling the chemicals and if the ambient temperature was high, elevating the temperature of the vehicle's interior. In the event of an auto accident involving a lab in transit, cooks, others involved in the accident, and responding emergency personnel may all suffer significant chemical or fire-related injuries. Additional concerns surround police officers who may attempt contact with the occupants of the vehicles on traffic stops.

Clandestine laboratories are usually cluttered, which creates numerous trip hazards. The floors may also be covered with chemical spills or residue that is slippery. Stacked boxes and trash can pose additional hazards if they fall on responding personnel or cause workers to bump their heads. Furthermore, visibility is frequently poor, because lighting in clandestine laboratories is often inadequate. This is not only a result of an effort to conceal the identity of the laboratory from people outside but also because electrical power sources may be diverted from lighting to run laboratory equipment, such as hot plates, heating mantles, and vacuum pumps. The diversion of electricity is not usually done according to standard electrical code. Circuits are frequently overloaded, and "jerry-rigged" wiring is often found. This sloppy electrical work not only heightens the possibility of fires inside the lab but also creates an electrical shock hazard for emergency responders. Laboratory equipment is also frequently homemade and, as a result, substandard. In one report, light bulbs with the receptacle end removed were being used as round-bottomed flasks in which synthetic reactions were being run (Giusto, 1996). Obviously, the propensity for this sort of "glassware" to break is much greater than with actual Pyrex laboratory glassware.

These situations are particularly dangerous for law enforcement and other emergency personnel, who may need to work very quickly to subdue a suspect or extricate an injured party. In a dark and cluttered lab, both entrance and emergency egress become quite difficult. The issue of confined space has been addressed by the Occupational Health and Safety Administration (OSHA) (Lazarus, 2000). Specific definitions of what constitutes a confined space have been published (Counts, 1997). Many clandestine laboratories easily fit more than one of the listed criteria for a dangerously confined space.

Protective clothing is a must for personnel investigating clandestine laboratories. Individuals not accustomed to working in full protective clothing and using self-contained breathing apparatus (SCBA) or respirators may suffer claustrophobic episodes. Furthermore, with the limited amount of space in the laboratories and the additional bulk of SCBA packs, the risk of inadvertently knocking over reactive or dangerous chemicals is heightened. This is particularly relevant if personnel are inexperienced or inadequately trained in the use of SCBA in confined spaces.

The combination of protective clothing with the physical demands of clandestine laboratory investigation also adds the dimension of heat stress to the list of risks to emergency personnel. Mild heat-related illness may be manifested by muscle cramps or nausea, while progression through heat exhaustion to heat stroke is a life-threatening emergency. Heat-related illnesses, which may be further complicated by chemical vapor inhalation, are also a concern for cooks working with heated reactions in poorly ventilated areas. The American Industrial Hygiene Association (AIHA) has well-established detailed guidelines for dealing with heat stress (Boyd, 1996). These guidelines, along with basic common sense, are largely applicable to personnel investigating and dismantling clandestine laboratories. Clearly, the best way to combat heat-related illness is to prevent its occurrence with proper technique and adequate training.

The effects of heat can be further compounded if the weather conditions are not only hot but also humid. However, these are not the only weather concerns when dealing with clandestine laboratories. Obviously, excessively high atmospheric temperatures may cause chemicals to react and possibly detonate. Very cold and wet conditions may cause responding personnel to become hypothermic. Humid, rainy, or snowy conditions may cause immediate dangers through ignition of hydride reducing agents or sodium or lithium metals exposed to the weather, as is often the case during laboratory dismantling and cleanup.

8.3.1.3 Toxicologic Hazards

Briefly, methamphetamine is a sympathomimetic amine whose mode of action is a result of its effects on neurotransmitters, such as dopamine, serotonin (5-

HT), and norepinephrine (Nichols, 1994). Methamphetamine also significantly alters brain concentrations of many neuropeptides (e.g., cholecystokinin (CKK) and neurotensin).

In acute high-dose methamphetamine intoxication, symptomology can include hyperthermia, agitated delirium, rhabdomyolysis, coagulopathies, acute renal failure, hypertension, and lethal cardiac dysrhythmias (e.g., ventricular tachycardia and ventricular fibrillation) as well as the clinical sequelae of each of these conditions (Chiang, 1998). Coronary vasospasm, myocardial infarction, and sudden death are also associated with methamphetamine abuse (Chiang, 1998). Cardiomyopathy induced by methamphetamine is well documented clinically and morphologically and has also been found in cases of acute and chronic methamphetamine abuse (He et al., 1996). Methamphetamine also causes significant central nervous system effects. Agitation, paranoid psychosis, seizures, bruxism, and choreoathetoid movements have all been reported with acute methamphetamine intoxication (Chiang, 1998). Chronic toxicity may result in permanent damage to both dopaminergic and serotonergic neurons (Nichols, 1994). Methamphetamine has also been established to be a developmental neurotoxin, which may have particular significance in pregnant users (Weissman and Caldecott-Hazard, 1995).

Of course, the toxicologic effects just listed are associated with pure methamphetamine. This does not provide a thorough toxicologic profile of the hazards within clandestine laboratories. Cooks, law enforcement personnel, and even the general public may be subjected to myriad toxic incidents from the laboratories. It is obviously difficult to clearly differentiate between chemical hazards and toxicologic hazards within a clandestine laboratory. For example, iodine, which is commonly used in the production of methamphetamine, is a thyrotoxin (Backer and Hollowell, 2000). Red phosphorus, though certainly a burn hazard, fortunately does not share the propensity to induce catastrophic liver damage of yellow phosphorus (Chiang, 1998).

Vapors from organic solvents can cause lung damage and hypoxia and increase myocardial irritability and sensitization to catecholamines (Bailey et al., 1997). The latter can cause catastrophic ventricular dysrhythmias. In one report, fumes off-gassing from a 2-liter flask in a clandestine laboratory are believed to have killed three persons (Massetti, 1996c). Lethal inhalation has also been attributed to phosphine and hydrogen sulfide gases in clandestine methamphetamine laboratories (Willers-Russo, 1996, 1999; Anjaria and Evans, 1997; Wheeler and Griffin, 1997). In one case, three persons were found dead in a house by sheriff's deputies. It is suspected that a red phosphorus/HI reduction caused production of phosphine gas, which overcame the victims (Willers-Russo, 1999). In 1999, two latent-print examiners from Los Angeles were taken to the hospital with sore throats and coughing after processing a reaction vessel from a clandestine laboratory (Gravitt, 1999). Both print examiners were experienced and clandestine-lab certified. Initial suspicion was for phosphine inhalation, but none was detected at the scene. They were examined and released, and the specific substance to which they were exposed was never identified.

The discussion of chemical hazards brings to question the safety of medical personnel involved in caring for those injured in clandestine laboratories. In general, the risks associated with the chemicals with which one would come in contact in the course of medical management of a victim from a clandestine methamphetamine lab accident are believed to be minimal. However, this area has not been exhaustively studied. Though the acute effects of many individual chemicals used in illicit methamphetamine manufacture are known from industrial use, no comprehensive risk assessment has been performed on cooks, law enforcement personnel, or subsequent residents of a space that formerly held a clandestine methamphetamine laboratory. The lay press is replete with anecdotal reports of individuals suffering ill health effects from living in a structure that once held a clandestine methamphetamine laboratory. However, to date, no peer-reviewed controlled scientific studies of subsequent residents of former labs have been published detailing specific medical consequences of these reported exposures.

Three key papers have been published examining the issues of protection for law enforcement and other first-response personnel. In 2000, the Centers for Disease Control and Prevention (CDC) published an account in the *Morbidity and Mortality Weekly Report* (MMWR) that examined the public health consequences among first responders dealing with emergent responses to illicit methamphetamine laboratories (MMWR, 2000). This report classified first responders as police and fire department personnel and EMT and hospital workers. The most common injuries reported were respiratory and eye irritation. The largest number of injuries was reported in police officers, because they were most often present in the laboratories during and immediately after a toxic release. Firefighters were the least often injured of on-site personnel, largely as a result of their wearing PPE in the form of self-contained breathing apparatus (SCBA) and firefighting bunker gear. It was surmised that standard uniforms worn by emergency medical technicians (EMTs), police officers, and hospital personnel provided little or no protection from chemical exposure. A total of seven injuries was reported in hospital personnel, with three workers complaining of nausea/vomiting and the other four of dizziness and unspecified CNS symptoms. It was suggested that the hospital workers may have become ill as a result of inadequate decontamination of patients prior to their arrival at the hospital. However, the possible involvement of psychosomatic and mass hysterical etiologies for these complaints was not addressed.

Few studies have examined the effects of exposure to personnel processing and dismantling clandestine laboratories. Burgess published two papers related to this topic. The first, from 1996, examined two study populations: (1) law enforcement chemists ($n = 46$) sent a survey through the Clandestine Laboratory Investigating Chemists' Association (CLIC) and (2) a group of Washington State clandestine laboratory investigators ($n = 13$) (Burgess et al., 1996). The study retrospectively examined approximately 2800 combined investigations. Reported symptoms experienced by the study subjects most often included headache, respiratory complaints, and skin and mucous membrane irritation. Total illness rates included 0.75–3.4% of responses, with most illnesses occurring during the processing phase of the investigation. No illnesses were reported during the entry phase. The authors concluded that response to an active lab (as opposed to a boxed lab or a lab not actively cooking) was associated with a 7- to 15-fold increase in developing some sort of illness.

The second paper by Burgess retrospectively examined HARP forms and medical records of 40 Bureau of Narcotics Enforcement (BNE) agents who investigated a total of 2030 clandestine laboratories between 1991 and 1998 (Burgess et al., 2002). The average amount of time to complete each of the investigative phases was recorded as: entry, 11 min; assessment, 34 min; processing, 194 min. Medical monitoring parameters recorded were measurements of white blood cell (WBC) and platelet counts, hemoglobin, measurement of the liver enzymes aspartate aminotransferase (AST) and alanine aminotransferase (ALT), and determination of the forced expiratory volume over one second (FEV_1), a general assessment of pulmonary function. Results of the evaluation showed an average annual decline in FEV_1 of 64 ± 138 mL/yr in clandestine-laboratory investigators. The authors concluded that use of respiratory protection was associated with a reduced rate of decline in FEV_1.

An additional word of caution is in order because clandestine labs are not used exclusively for the production of methamphetamine. Other possible clandestine laboratory uses include synthesis of other drugs, preparation of chemical warfare agents, and production of explosives. A 1999 report describes a clandestine laboratory that was serving a dual role, as a methamphetamine production facility and as a bomb factory (Walker and Doerr, 1999). Many other chemicals that have substantial associated dangers may be present. With this in mind, it is good practice to carefully and thoroughly to decontaminate all persons presenting with a history of having been in a clandestine laboratory environment.

The availability of allegedly reliable chemical information from not only print sources but also word of mouth and, more importantly, the Internet has caused a surge in the amount of information and misinformation to be readily available. Unfortunately, the accuracy of some of this information may be, at best, questionable. In truth, a number of the methods purported by clandestine chemists to be effective have absolutely no basis in scientific fact (Ely, 1990). This raises the obvious issue of how well the average cook, with limited chemical knowledge, can assess what will or will not actually produce the drug of interest. Clearly, the toxicologic implications are significant but ill defined when a cook uses inappropriate synthetic methods. In short, there is no telling what the cook may actually be preparing and, therefore, no telling what the drug user may actually be taking.

It is further possible that synthetic by-products may contribute either inherently or synergistically to the toxicity of a given batch of illicit methamphetamine, but very few studies have examined this possibility. Preliminary investigations have demonstrated significant neurotoxic effects when α-benzyl-N-methylphenethylamine (BNMPA) was studied in mice (Noggle et al., 1985; Moore et al., 1995). One study determined the LD_{50} and CD_{50} (convulsive dose 50) for BNMPA, MA, amphetamine, and the N-demethylated analog of BNMPA, α-benzylphenethylamine, in mice (Noggle et al., 1985). The results suggested that while the LD_{50} and CD_{50} of methamphetamine were very similar, BNMPA induced seizure activity at a dose only 70% of its LD_{50} (Noggle et al., 1985). A second study investigated the potential neurotoxic interaction of BNMPA with methamphetamine. The results, however, are somewhat ambiguous. At doses of greater than 30 mg/kg, BNMPA was associated with toxic effects on the central nervous system (CNS) of mice, as measured by stereotypy and "popcorn-like" hyperactivity, tonic-clonic convulsions, and death (Moore et al., 1995). Of note, however, is the additional observation that BNMPA neither alters locomotor activity nor affects methamphetamine-induced increases in spontaneous activity or convulsions. The investigators stated that these data suggest that BNMPA and methamphetamine produce their respective pharmacological effects through different mechanisms. No hypothesis was offered detailing the specific mechanism through which BNMPA is thought to exert its toxic effects. These studies are particularly significant in light of a report in which BNMPA and several of its metabolites were detected in the urine of human methamphetamine abusers (Moore et al., 1996).

Among some of the other compounds known to be by-products of illicit methamphetamine synthesis, aziridines are highly reactive alkylating agents also known to cause chemical pneumonia and noncardiogenic pulmonary edema in those exposed (Sanz and Prat, 1993). Substituted naphthalenes are known to elicit serious responses, including hemolysis and fever (Zuelzer and Apt, 1949). Clearly, additional comprehensive study is necessary to fully determine the extent of the toxic implications of synthetic by-products to the overall toxicity of illicitly prepared methamphetamine.

The presence of these impurities and a lack of adequate purification of the intermediates and final products may significantly complicate the toxicologic picture. Additional impurities, the toxicologic significance of which cannot be dismissed, are impurities that are carried over from the synthetic process (e.g., red phosphorus) and adulterants used to increase sample weight and bulk.

A concern whose importance cannot be overstated is the potential environmental impact of clandestine laboratories (NNICC, 1998). In a 1999 Bureau of Justice report, it was stated that in an illicit laboratory, each pound of methamphetamine that was produced generated 5–6 pounds of chemical waste (Gist, 1999). Obviously, cooks rarely practice proper hazardous waste disposal and are not subject to legal monitoring. Instead, chemical waste may be dumped in pits, on the ground, or directly into the sewer system. The environmental impact of the labs is no doubt significant, though this is a very difficult subject to fully study (Irvine and Chin, 1991). In July 1999, Donnie R. Marshall, the Acting Administrator of the DEA, testified before the U.S. Senate Judiciary Committee regarding the dangers associated with clandestine methamphetamine trafficking and production (Marshall, 1999a). In this address, Mr. Marshall, estimated the costs associated with the cleanup of a small clandestine lab to be approximately $3000, while costs to clean up a large lab could exceed $100,000. Clearly, these chemical waste cleanup costs from even a single clandestine laboratory of moderate size can be enough to bankrupt a small police or sheriff's department.

As previously mentioned, a number of the chemicals used in the illicit production of methamphetamine have pungent odors. Houses in which drugs were cooked may be so permeated with the chemical vapors that it has been suggested that it might be easier and less expensive to simply bulldoze such buildings and destroy the materials (The Press, 1997a). The concern that a house will be "toxic" to inhabitants or nearby residents because of the chemical vapor saturation of the walls and carpets after the lab was removed has also been expressed (The Press, 1997b). However, no reports exist of toxicologic medical maladies directly attributable to living in a house that formerly held an illicit methamphetamine lab.

Recently, an increased amount of attention has been focused on how best to care for children removed from methamphetamine labs. In 1998, Kolecki published one of the landmark reports dealing with the subject of children and illicit methamphetamine intoxication (Kolecki, 1998). This study was a retrospective review of the records of 18 children aged 13 years and younger that presented to the emergency department over a 9-year period and had a confirmed oral exposure to methamphetamine. Mass spectrometric confirmation of the result was required, and children with mixed ingestions or ingestions involving sympathomimetic agents other than methamphetamine were excluded. Recorded signs and symptoms present in the children included agitation, inconsolability, abdominal pain, vomiting, seizures, rhabdomyolysis, and hyperthermia. Five of the children had head CT scans, three had lumbar punctures, and three received *Centruroides sculpturatus* (scorpion) antivenom prior to the realization that the children were suffering methamphetamine intoxication. Of particular note, one child who received *Centruroides sculpturatus* antivenom experienced an anaphylactic reaction. This report goes on to illustrate that illicit methamphetamine intoxication must be kept on the differential diagnosis for patients with sympathomimetic signs and symptoms, even in the pediatric population. However, there are many potentially toxic compounds in a clandestine laboratory other than simply methamphetamine.

Active drug-endangered children (DEC) programs have been started in states, including California, Utah, and Colorado, in which clandestine labs are a major focus. Due to the lack of data regarding ill effects from chronic exposure to chemicals in clandestine laboratories and the fact that many of the children removed from these laboratories do not appear to be acutely ill, development of guidelines detailing which specific physical, psychological, and laboratory assessments should be performed has been a difficult process. However, it must be understood that a clandestine laboratory is an inherently dangerous environment, especially for children, and that there are many more concerns than toxic chemical exposure. A few examples of the many potential hazards for children in a clandestine laboratory include not having routine medical care, living in unsanitary conditions, being inadequately fed, and being at a dramatically increased risk for physical and sexual abuse. Clearly, with the myriad additional risks posed to children in clandestine laboratories, the assessment must go well beyond checking only for a positive amphetamine result on a urine drug screen. The development of DEC guidelines is ongoing, and many iterations of protocols will need to be made as more data become available.

The three most important means of protecting oneself from the hazards of a clandestine laboratory are limiting exposure, good intelligence information about the contents of the lab, and adequate training. Federal law mandates that all law enforcement officers complete a clandestine laboratory safety training program prior to entering a clandestine laboratory (Marshall, 1999a). However, the Occupational Safety and Health Administration (OSHA) generally does not provide the training. One of the best-known training programs for clandestine laboratory enforcement personnel is the DEA Clandestine Lab School in Quantico, Virginia. Students graduating from this program are issued several thousand dollars in specialized safety gear, including nomex fire-resistant level-III ballistic vests, nomex fire-resistant pants, jackets, and gloves, chemical-resistant boots, combat retention holsters, special flashlights, goggles, etc. (Marshall, 1999a). This gear is necessary in order to safely enter a clandestine laboratory. According to current law enforcement recommendations, all skin and clothing should be covered with some sort of suit (e.g., Tyvek) that is either disposable or able to withstand decontamination. Gloves and boots sealed at the seams with duct tape must be worn. Respiratory protection, afforded by either an air-purifying respirator (APR) or a SCBA, is required. OSHA-approved training is required for the proper use of these respiratory support devices (Conibear, 1997). The types of respirators used for a given application are also subject to certification by the National Institute for Occupational Safety and Health (NIOSH) (Conibear, 1997). Flowcharts are available for assistance in the selection of the most appropriate filter system. Variables included in the flowchart include duration of wear, desired filter efficiency, and the presence or absence of oil in the aerosol to be filtered. Further protection is provided by limiting time spent in the laboratory and adhering to EPA exposure limits.

Most law enforcement agencies will complete a Hazard Assessment and Recognition Plan (HARP) statement of some kind. This collection of forms, which many agencies design themselves, is typically started well before the lab site is actually approached. It contains not only information on the lab itself, but also specific contact numbers for fire, rescue, medivac helicopter, hospital emergency department, poison control, and the disposal company, to name a few. Officials from each of these agencies are contacted in advance and their names and telephone numbers recorded on the forms. Information specific to the raid itself is also included on the form. For example, raid team member assignments (e.g., entry, assessment, or processing) and vital signs before and after entry into the laboratory are also recorded. Any unusual happenings (e.g., fires, medical complaints) are also noted on the forms. At the completion of the raid, the site safety officer and case agent are required to sign and certify the HARP forms indicating all safety precautions were taken.

8.3.1.4 Tactical Hazards (Booby Traps)

Though it is obvious that home production of methamphetamine is illegal, the extent to which cooks will go to protect their operations is often less apparent. It is not unusual for cooks to install a variety of "booby traps" in a clandestine laboratory (T. Barnes, 1996c; A.F. Smith, 1996). Certainly, not every clandestine laboratory has booby traps installed, but a heightened sense of observance by personnel approaching a lab is warranted.

These devices are easily homemade using sources such as the *Anarchist Cookbook* (Powell, 1970). These devices have all of the attributes of tactical booby traps used for guerrilla warfare. They are surreptitiously placed devices with the sole purpose of indiscriminately injuring or killing whomever happens to activate them. Anecdotal reports from methamphetamine cooks indicate these devices are not targeting law enforcement officials but rather other cooks and drug users that might rob their operations. The obvious shortcoming of these statements is that the traps themselves are incapable of distinguishing between a competing cook, a police officer, and an unsuspecting neighbor, child, or pet.

Booby traps used in illicit methamphetamine labs include both chemical and blast-type devices. A fairly simple and common chemical trap is the positioning of a container of mineral acid immediately above a pan of sodium or potassium cyanide. The acid container is arranged such that the opening of a door or window will cause it to spill into the cyanide salt, releasing cyanide gas in the immediate vicinity of whomever opened the door or window.

Numerous explosive devices have been used as booby traps in clandestine laboratories. Commercial, military, and homemade explosives have been found at clandestine labs. These may be pressure-triggered land mine–type devices or guns or grenades in which the trigger mechanism has been equipped with a trip wire. These devices are usually hidden and attached to windows and doors or set about a perimeter outside the lab to keep trespassers from getting close to the actual site.

Most often, booby trap devices are placed on the most obvious routes of access (e.g., the front door or main pathway up to the building containing the lab). It is for this reason that many law enforcement agencies require detailed intelligence information regarding cook entrance and egress routes prior to serving warrants at clandestine-laboratory sites.

Obviously, safety hazards, regardless of type (chemical, physical, tactical, etc.) cannot be taken in isolation. All of these hazards are simultaneously present to varying degrees in clandestine laboratories. Training seminars are offered in all aspects of clandestine laboratory enforcement, including recognition and appropriate countermeasures for bombs and booby traps that might be encountered (A.F. Smith, 1996).

8.3.1.5 Medical Use of Methamphetamine and Blood Level Significance

Methamphetamine is a DEA schedule II drug. As such, it does have clinical utility in the management of certain medical conditions, such as narcolepsy, attention deficit–hyperactivity disorder (ADHD), and obesity (Chiang, 1998). However, the frequency of abuse far outweighs the drug's therapeutic utility. There are several licit medications that contain amphetamine derivatives or are metabolized to methamphetamine. At first glance it seems likely that diversion of methamphetamine from these legal sources would be a significant problem. However, this situation has not been observed. According to a report by the NNICC, "Clandestine production accounted for nearly all of the methamphetamine trafficked and abused in the United States in 1997" (Strange, 1998). This

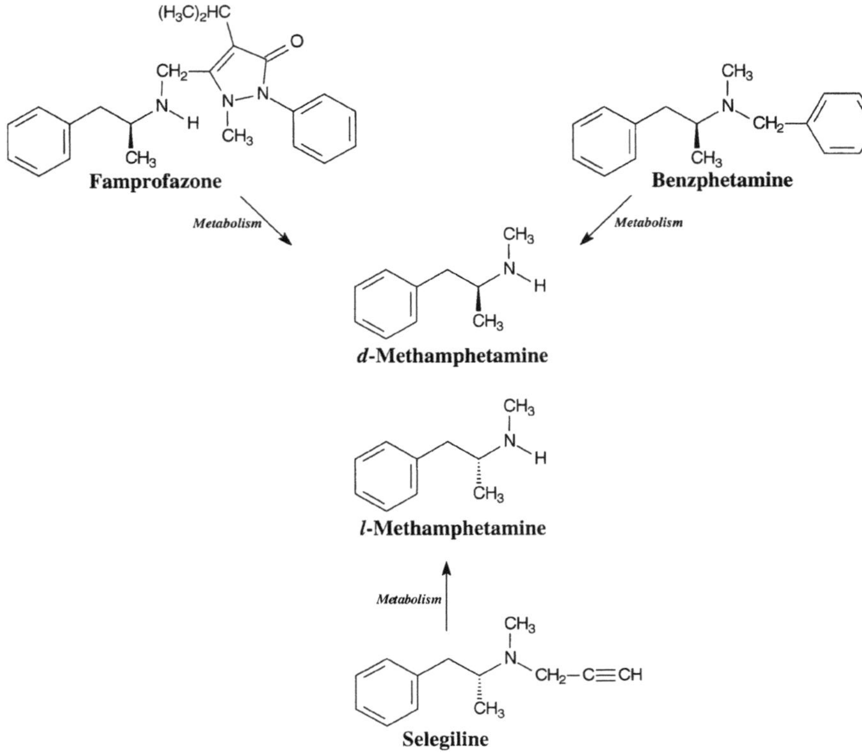

Figure 8.70

Metabolism of drugs to form optical isomers of methamphetamine

Famprofazone

Benzphetamine

d-Methamphetamine

l-Methamphetamine

Selegiline

is largely due to the strict control of the legally produced compounds as well as the ease of illicit production.

The presence of methamphetamine in the blood or urine of an individual does not provide absolute proof of illicit drug use. In addition to its own therapeutic use, both isomers of methamphetamine are produced metabolically from therapeutic medications (Figure 8.70). The *l*-isomer is also formed as a metabolite of the anti-Parkinson's drug selegiline (Baselt, 2000). The *d*-isomer of methamphetamine is a metabolite of the antiobesity agent benzphetamine and the European over-the-counter analgesic/antipyretic famprofazone (Baselt, 2000).

Clinical and forensic interpretation of concentrations of methamphetamine in blood is an area fraught with difficulty. As mentioned previously, several therapeutically used drugs produce methamphetamine metabolically. Even when metabolic production can be ruled out and only illicit methamphetamine is considered as a source, there are still difficult issues with respect to clinical or forensic interpretation of blood levels. There is no consistent link between measured concentration and level of intoxication or impairment with methamphetamine. In 1996, a group of 27 drivers arrested for erratic driving provided blood methamphetamine concentrations ranging from 0.05 to 2.6 mg/L (Logan, 1996). Similarly, deaths have been attributed to methamphetamine intoxication at levels well below those in individuals that have survived without deficit. In another study, also by Logan, postmortem blood concentrations were determined in 13 cases of deaths attributed to methamphetamine poisoning (Logan et al., 1998). Though the average blood methamphetamine concentration in this series was 0.96 mg/L, the range was 0.09–18 mg/L. By comparison, in a study that examined nine cases in which the decedent was a drug abuser who died as a result of traumatic injuries inflicted by violent means, Reynolds reported postmortem blood methamphetamine concentrations ranging from 1.4 to 13 mg/L (average = 5.1) (Reynolds and Weingarten, 1983). Interpretation of postmortem methamphetamine measurements is further complicated by postmortem redistribution. In a series of 20 deaths, postmortem heart : femoral blood concentration ratios ranged from 1.2 to 5.0 (average = 2.1) (Baselt, 2000).

8.3.2 LAW ENFORCEMENT APPROACHES TO CLANDESTINE LABORATORIES

Law enforcement concerns over chemical, toxicologic, environmental, tactical, logistical, and financial difficulties associated with clandestine methamphetamine laboratories have not gone unnoticed by governmental agencies. In April 1999, the U.S. Department of Justice Office of Justice Programs released a research report entitled "*Meth Matters: Report on Methamphetamine Users in Five Western Cities*" (Pennell et al., 1999). In this report, general and statistical data are presented regarding methamphetamine use in the American cities of Los Angeles, San Diego, San Jose, Phoenix, and Portland, OR. One of the principal conclusions of this report is: "Law enforcement agencies need resources and training to identify and contain meth labs. The dynamics of the meth market warrant different enforcement techniques than those used in open air drug markets." This report is widely cited by law enforcement agencies in requests for additional funding and training to combat clandestine laboratories.

The Bureau of Justice Assistance (BJA) has also produced fact sheets to help guide law enforcement agencies in the development of programs to effectively combat clandestine laboratories. Examples of such BJA fact sheets include *Multiagency Response to Clandestine Drug Laboratories* and *Strategic Approaches to*

Clandestine Drug Laboratory Enforcement (Gist, 1995, 1999). The Methamphetamine Interagency Task Force issued its final report in January 2000 (Travis and
Vereen, 2000). This report also offers detailed recommendations for law
enforcement agencies with respect to clandestine methamphetamine labs. All
of the listed documents, and many more, are readily available from governmental Web sites, and many law enforcement agencies are using the Internet
for exactly this sort of information.

The difficulties associated with acquisition of funding, large geographical
areas, training, and hazardous cleanup have led many law enforcement agencies to take a task force approach. Task forces are generally composed of
personnel from multiple agencies working collectively on the same issue. This
approach allows for the development of a single entity to combat the problem
without severely depleting the personnel or financial resources of any one
agency. Though it generally works well, there are still occasional jurisdictional,
funding, and workload disputes. Perhaps the largest financial issue surrounds
the question of who will bear the cost of hazardous materials cleanup once a
lab is dismantled. Though the federal government (i.e., the DEA) is often contacted in this regard, they, too, have limited resources, which are increasingly
taxed in light of the steady increase in the number of clandestine laboratories.
In short, there is no simple answer to the question of who will bear the cost.

Other, less direct law enforcement approaches to the methamphetamine
situation in the United States have involved legislative action. On October 3,
1996, President Bill Clinton signed into law a bill approved by both houses of
the 104th Congress. This bill bears the short title of the "Comprehensive
Methamphetamine Control Act of 1996." A second federal act was brought
before the 106th Congress and is known as the "Methamphetamine Anti-
Proliferation Act of 1999." Though the actual language of these pieces of legislation is complex, they have the purpose of directly legislating against illicit
methamphetamine production.

The U.S. Attorney General publishes the Special Surveillance List, which contains a list of "chemicals, products, materials or equipment used in the manufacture of controlled substances and listed chemicals" (Marshall, 1999b). There
was obvious concern about the impact these legislative maneuvers might have
on the livelihood of small businesses that legitimately deal in products that can
be used in the illegal manufacture of methamphetamine and other listed chemicals. However, provisions are contained within the legal language allowing for
legitimate commerce with minimal governmental intrusion.

The complete list consists of all chemicals listed in Title 21 of the Code of
Federal Regulations (CFR), Section 1310.02(a) and (b), as well as some addi-
tional chemicals and laboratory equipment listed by the DEA Diversion Control
Program. The chemicals listed in CFR Section 1310.02(a) are often referred to

as "List I chemicals," while those in Section 1310.02(b) are commonly called "List II chemicals." List II agents have legitimate uses, but are also involved in illicit drug production. Though illegal methamphetamine production is certainly a central target of the Special Surveillance List, chemicals used to make other illegal substances (e.g., PCP and LSD) are also included. These lists are reproduced in Table 8.1.

Table 8.1

U.S. Attorney General's Special Surveillance List of chemicals and equipment

CFR Section 1310.02(a)—List I
- Anthranilic acid, its esters and its salts
- Benzyl cyanide
- Ephedrine, its salts, optical isomers, and salts of optical isomers
- Ergonovine and its salts
- Ergotamine and its salts
- *N*-Acetylanthranilic acid, its esters, and its salts
- Norpseudoephedrine, its salts, optical isomers, and salts of optical isomers
- Phenylacetic acid, its esters, and its salts
- Phenylpropanolamine, its salts, optical isomers, and salts of optical isomers
- Piperidine and its salts
- Pseudoephedrine, its salts, optical isomers, and salts of optical isomers
- 3,4-Methylenedioxyphenyl-2-propanone
- Methylamine and its salts
- Ethylamine and its salts
- Propionic anhydride
- Isosafrole
- Safrole
- Piperonal
- *N*-Methylephedrine, its salts, optical isomers, and salts of optical isomers
- *N*-Methylpseudoephedrine, its salts, optical isomers, and salts of optical isomers
- Hydriodic acid
- Benzaldehyde
- Nitroethane

CFR Section 1310.02(b)—List II
- Acetic anhydride
- Acetone
- Benzyl chloride
- Ethyl ether
- Potassium permanganate
- 2-Butanone (or methyl ethyl ketone, or MEK)
- Toluene
- Hydrochloric acid
- Sulfuric acid
- Methyl isobutyl ketone (MIBK)

Additional Listed Chemicals
- Ammonia gas
- Ammonium formate
- Bromobenzene
- 1,1-Carbonyldiimidazole
- 1,1-Dichloro-1-fluoroethane (Freon 141B)
- Diethylamine and its salts
- 2,5-Dimethoxyphenethylamine and its salts
- Formamide
- Formic Acid
- Hypophophorous acid
- Lithium metal
- Lithium aluminum hydride
- Magnesium metal (turnings)
- Mercuric chloride
- *N*-Methylformamide
- Organomagnesium halides (Grignard reagents)
- Phenylethanolamine and its salts
- Phosphorus pentachloride
- Potassium dichromate
- Pyridine and its salts
- Red phosphorus
- Sodium dichromate
- Sodium metal
- Thionyl chloride
- *ortho*-Toluidine
- Trichloromonofluoromethane (Freon-11, Carrene-2)
- Trichlorotrifluoroethane (Freon 113)

Listed Equipment
- Hydrogenators
- Tableting machines
- Encapsulating machines
- 22-Liter heating mantles

8.4 CONCLUDING REMARKS

As consumer demand for methamphetamine continues to increase, so too does the number of synthetic approaches used to make the drug and its precursors. The labs in which these compounds are produced are fraught with chemical, physical, toxicologic, and tactical hazards. A thorough understanding of the chemical processes used to produce these compounds is key to the ability to safely investigate and dismantle the labs and prosecute and medically treat individuals that have been involved with illicit methamphetamine production.

REFERENCES

Adams, R., and Thal, A.F. (1932). Benzyl cyanide. *Org. Syn.* Coll. Vol. I, 107–109.

Albertson, T.E., Van Hoozen, B.E., and Allen, R.P. (1998). Amphetamines. In *Clinical Management of Poisoning and Drug Overdose*, 3rd ed. (ed. L.M. Haddad, M.W. Shannon, and J.F. Winchester). Saunders, Philadelphia.

Alcott, J.V., Barnhart, R.A., and Mooney, L.A. (1987). Acute lead poisoning in two users of illicit methamphetamine. *JAMA* 258, 510–511.

Andrews, K.M. (1995). Ephedra's role as a precursor in the clandestine manufacture of methamphetamine. *J. Forensic Sci.* 40, 551–560.

Angelos, S.A., and Meyers, J.A. (1985). The isolation and identification of precursors and reaction products in the clandestine manufacture of methaqualone and mecloqualone. *J. Forensic Sci.* 30, 1022–1047.

Aniline, O., Pitts, F.N., Allen, R.E., and Burgoyne, R. (1980). Incidental intoxication with phencyclidine. *J. Clin. Psychiatry* 41, 393–394.

Anjaria, M.B., and Evans, H.K. (1997). "Cook" fails chem 101: hydrogen sulfide fatality. *J. Clan. Lab. Invest. Chem.* 7(3), 5.

Anonymous. (1996). Dimethylsulfone identified in amphetamine and methamphetamine samples. *J. Clan. Lab. Invest. Chem.* 6(1), 12–13.

Anonymous. (1997). Methamphetamine recrystallization process described in alt.drugs.chemistry. *J. Clan. Lab. Invest. Chem.* 7(4), 3.

Anonymous. (1999). Bogus meth recipes being circulated: Gun bluing salts and chicken laying feed said to produce methamphetamine. *J. Clan. Lab. Invest. Chem.* 9(1), 5–6.

Associated Press. (1997a). Mom who cooked meth convicted of killing kids. *J. Clan. Lab. Invest. Chem.* 7(1), 3.

Associated Press. (1997b). Judge gives mother 45-to-life term for meth lab deaths of three children. *J. Clan. Lab. Invest. Chem.* 7(1), 3.

Backer, H., and Hollowell, J. (2000). Use of iodine for water disinfection: Iodine toxicity and maximum recommended dose. *Environ. Health Perspect.* 108, 679–684.

Baggott, M., Mendelson, J., and Jones, R. (1999). More about Parkinsonism after taking ecstasy. *NEJM* 341, 1400–1401.

Bailey, B., Loebstein, R., Lai, C., and McGuigan M.A. (1997). Two cases of chlorinated hydrocarbon–associated myocardial ischemia. *Vet. Human Toxicol.* 39, 298–301.

Barnes, T. (1996a). Suspects take recycling to extremes. *J. Clan. Lab. Invest. Chem.* 6(2), 7.

Barnes, T. (1996b). Lab fire burns down 122-unit motel. *J. Clan. Lab. Invest. Chem.* 6(2), 6.

Barnes, T. (1996c). Explosive device ready to go. *J. Clan. Lab. Invest. Chem.* 6(2), 6.

Barnes, M. (1999). Viability of ethylenediamine as a substitute for liquid ammonia. *J. Clan. Lab. Invest. Chem.* 9(4), 5–6.

Barron, R.P., Kruegel, A.V., Moore, J.M., et al. (1974). Identification of impurities in illicit methamphetamine samples. *J. AOAC* 57, 1147–1158.

Baselt, R.C. (2000). *Disposition of Toxic Drugs and Chemicals in Man*, 5th ed. Chemical Toxicology Institute, Foster City, CA.

Battaglia, G., and DeSouza, E.B. (1989). Pharmacologic profile of amphetamine derivatives at various brain recognition sites: Selective effects on serotonergic systems. *NIDA Res. Monogr.* 94, 240–258.

Bohn, G. (1981). Illegally manufactured 2,5-dimethoxy-4-bromoamphetamine in connection with fatal intoxication. *Toxichemistry* 14, 140–141.

Boyd, V. (1996). Dealing with heat stress: Basic precautions can prevent workers in hot environments from becoming victims of serious heat-related illness. *J. Clan. Lab. Invest. Chem.* 6(4), 18–19.

Buchanan, J.F., and Brown, C.R. (1988). "Designer drugs": A problem in clinical toxicology. *Med. Toxicol. Adverse. Drug Exp.* 3, 1–17.

Budavari, S. (1989). Entry 5879, Methenamine. In *The Merck Index: An Encyclopedia of Chemicals, Drugs and Biologicals*, 11th ed. Merck and Co., Rahway, NJ.

Burgess, J.L. (2001). Phosphine exposure from a methamphetamine laboratory investigation. *Clin. Tox.* 39, 165–168.

Burgess, J.L., Barnhart, S., and Checkoway, H. (1996). Investigating clandestine drug laboratories: Adverse medical effects in law enforcement personnel. *Am. J. Indust. Med.* 30, 488–494.

Burgess, J.L., Kovalchick, D.F., Siegel, E.M., et al. (2002). Medical surveillance of clandestine drug laboratory investigators. *J. Occup. Environ. Med.* 44, 184–189.

Burton, B.T. (1991). Heavy metal and organic contaminants associated with illicit methamphetamine production. *NIDA Res. Monogr.* 115, 47–59.

Cantrell, T.S., Boban, J., Johnson, L., et al. (1988). A study of impurities found in methamphetamine synthesized from ephedrine. *Forensic Sci. Int.* 39, 39–53.

CDC. (1990). From the centers for disease control. Lead poisoning associated with intravenous methamphetamine use—Oregon, 1988. *JAMA* 263, 797–798.

Chappell, J. (1996). Hawaii "ice" cut with dimethylsulfone. *J. Clan. Lab. Invest. Chem.* 6(3), 12.

Cheney, L.C. (1949). Ketimines and acylketimines related to amidone. *J. Am. Chem. Soc.* 71, 53.

Chiang, W.K. (1998). Amphetamines. In *Goldfrank's Toxicologic Emergencies*, 6th ed. (ed. L.R. Goldfrank, N.E. Flomenbaum, N.A. Lewin, et al.). Appleton and Lange, Stamford, CT, pp. 1091–1104.

Christian, D. (1996). Spontaneous ignition of red phosphorus samples. *J. Clan. Lab. Invest. Chem.* 6(2), 2.

Cimbura, G. (1974). PMA deaths in Ontario. *Can. Med. Assoc. J.* 110, 1263–1267.

Conibear, S.A. (1997). What NIOSH's new respirator certification regulation means for you. *J. Clan. Lab. Invest. Chem.* 7(1), 21–22.

Conn, C., Dawson, M., Baker, A.T., et al. (1996). Identification of *N*-acetylmethamphetamine in a sample of illicitly synthesized methamphetamine. *J. Forensic. Sci.* 41, 645–647.

Counts, J.W. (1997). When is a confined space not a confined space? *J. Clan. Lab. Invest. Chem.* 7(1), 19–20.

Crossley, F.S., and Moore, M.L. (1944). Studies on the Leuckart reaction. *J. Org. Chem.* 9, 529–536.

Cusic, J.W. (1949). An improvement on the process for making amidone. *J. Am. Chem. Soc.* 71, 3546.

Cutler, R. (1998). White phosphorus replacing red phosphorus in Idaho. *J. Clan. Lab. Invest. Chem.* 8(1), 3.

Cyr, T.D., Dawson, B.A., By, A.W., et al. (1996). Structural elucidation of unusual police exhibits. II. Identification and spectral characterization of *N*-(2-hydroxyethyl)amphetamine hydrochloride. *J. Forensic Sci.* 41, 608–611.

Dal Cason, T.A., Angelos, S.A., and Washingon, O. (1981). The identification of some chemical analogues and positional isomers of methaqualone. *J. Forensic Sci.* 26, 793–833.

DeVuyst, P., Dumortier, P., Ketelbant, P., et al. (1990). Lung fibrosis induced by thorotrast. *Thorax* 45, 899–901.

Dyer, J.E., and Reed, J.H. (1997). Alkali burns from illicit manufacture of GHB (abstract). *J. Tox. Clin. Tox.* 35, 553.

Ellenhorn, M.J., and Barceloux, D.G. (1988). *Medical Toxicology: Diagnosis and Treatment of Human Poisoning.* Elsevier, New York.

Elliott, S.P. (2000). Fatal poisoning with a new phenylethylamine: 4-Methylthioamphetamine (4-MTA). *J. Anal. Toxicol.* 24, 85–89.

Ely, R.A. (1990). An investigation of the extraction of methamphetamine from chicken feed and other myths. *J. Forensic Sci.* 30, 363–370.

Ely, R.A. (1998). *Methamphetamine Labs, Synthesis and Investigator Safety.* Presented at the American Academy of Forensic Sciences Annual Meeting, Seminar—Methamphetamine: Synthesis, pharmacology, analysis and toxicology. February 10, 1998.

Ely, R.A. (2001). Personal communication.

Ely, R.A., and McGrath, D.C. (1990). Lithium–ammonia reduction of ephedrine to methamphetamine: An unusual clandestine synthesis. *J. Forensic Sci.* 35(3), 720–723.

Emde, H. (1929). Diastereoisomerism. III. Chloro- and bromoephedrine. *Helv. Chim. Acta* 12, 384–399.

Farnsworth, R. (2000). Former Idaho chemistry professor suspected of synthesizing pseudoephedrine and ephedrine via benzaldehyde and nitroethane. *J. Clan. Lab. Invest. Chem.* 10(1), 8–10.

FDA. (2000). FDA Talk Paper: FDA issues public health warning on phenylpropanolamine. Rockville, M.D., U.S. Food and Drug Administration, U.S. Department of Health and Human Services.

Fester, U. (1994). *Secrets of Methamphetamine Manufacture,* 3rd ed. Loompanics Unlimited, Port Townsend, WA.

Fritschi, G., and Klein, B. (1995). Intermediate and by-products in the illegal production of fentanyl and fluorofentanyls and synthesis of acetyl homologues. *Arch. Kriminol.* 196, 149–155.

Fuller, R.W. (1978). Structure–activity relationships among the halogenated amphetamines. *Ann. N.Y. Acad. Sci.* 305:147–159.

Fuller, R.W. (1992). Effects of *p*-chloroamphetamine on brain serotonin neurons. *Neurochem. Res.* 17, 449–456.

Gairaud, C.B., and Lappin, G.R. (1953). The synthesis of ω-nitrostyrenes. *J. Org. Chem.* 18, 1–3.

Gero, A. (1951). Some reactions of 1-phenyl-1-chloro-2-methylaminopropane. I. Reaction with metals and with hydrogen. *J. Org. Chem.* 16, 1731–1735.

Gist, N.E. (1995). Multiagency response to clandestine drug laboratories. Bureau of Justice Assistance Fact Sheet, November 1995.

Gist, N.E. (1999). Strategic approaches to clandestine laboratory enforcement. Bureau of Justice Assistance Fact Sheet, September 1999.

Giusto, M. (1996). New source for round-bottom flasks. *J. Clan. Lab. Invest. Chem.* 6(2), 12.

Glennon, R.A. (1989). Stimulus properties of hallucinogenic phenalkylamines and related designer drugs: Formulation of structure–activity relationship. *NIDA Res. Monogr.* 94, 43–67.

Glennon, R.A., Young, R., Hauck, A.E., et al. (1984a). Structure–activity studies on amphetamine analogues using drug discrimination methodology. *Pharmacol. Biochem. Behav.* 21, 895–901.

Glennon, R.A., Titeler, M., and McKenney, J.D. (1984b). Evidence for 5-HT$_2$ involvement in the mechanism of action of hallucinogenic agents. *Life Sci.* 35, 2505–2511.

Gravitt, R. (1999). Unknown chemical exposure injures latent print examiners. *J. Clan. Lab. Invest. Chem.* 9(4), 3–5.

Greifenstein, F.E., DeVault, M., Yoshitake, J., and Gajewski, J. (1958). An appraisal of new anesthetic induction agents. *Curr. Res. Anaesth.* 37, 283.

Griffith, R.K., and Johnson, E.A. (1995). Adrenergic drugs. In *Principles of Medicinal Chemistry*, 4th ed. (ed. W.O. Foye, T.L. Lemke, and D.A. Williams). Williams and Wilkins, Baltimore, pp. 345–365.

Griggs, E., and Ward, M. (1977) LSD-toxicity: a suspected cause of death. *J Ky Med Assoc.* 75, 172–173.

Haigh, J.C., Lee, L.J., and Schweinsburg, R.E. (1983). Immobilization of polar bears with carfentanyl. *J. Wildlife Dis.* 19, 140–144.

Hall, J. (1997). Clan lab cook blown up, burned, bitten, broken down and booked. *J. Clan. Lab. Invest. Chem.* 7(4), 4.

Harris, S.A. (1998). Indicted chemist innocent, attorney says. *J. Clan. Lab. Invest. Chem.* 8(1), 7.

Hass, H.B., Susie, A.G., and Heider, R.L. (1950). Nitroalkane derivatives. *J. Org. Chem.* 15, 8–14.

He, S.-Y., Matoba, R., Fujitani, N., et al. (1996). Cardiac lesions associated with chronic administration of methamphetamine in rats. *Am. J. Forensic Med. Path.* 17, 155–162.

Henderson, G.L. (1988). Designer drugs: Past history and future prospects. *J. Forensic Sci.* 33, 569–575.

Henderson, G.L., Harkey, M.R., and Chueh, Y.T. (1995). Metabolism of 4-methylaminorex ("U4EUh") in the rat. *J. Anal. Toxicol.* 19, 563–570.

Herbst, R.M., and Manske, R.H. (1943). Methyl benzyl ketone from phenyl-acetic and acetic acids. *Org. Syn. Coll. Vol. II*, 389–391.

Higgs, R.A., and Glennon, R.A. (1990). Stimulus properties of ring-methyl amphetamine analogs. *Pharmacol. Biochem. Behav.* 37, 835–837.

Hoffer, A. (1965). D-Lysergic acid diethylamide (LSD): A review of its present status. *Clin. Pharmcol. Ther.* 6, 183–255.

Hoffman, B.B., and Lefkowitz, R.J. (1996). Catecholamines, sympathomimetic drugs and adrenergic receptor antagonists. In *Goodman and Gilman's, The*

Pharmacological Basis of Therapeutics, 9th ed. (ed. J.G. Hardman, L.E. Limbird, P.B. Molinoff, R.W. Ruddon, and A.G. Gilman. McGraw-Hill, New York, pp. 199–248.

Hoffmann, A.J., and Nichols, D.E. (1985). Synthesis and LSD-like discriminative stimulus properties in a series of N(6)-alkyl norlysergic acid N,N-diethylamide derivatives. *J. Med. Chem.* 28, 1252–1255.

Irvine, G.D., and Chin, L. (1991). The environmental impact and adverse health effects of the clandestine manufacture of methamphetamine. *NIDA Res. Monogr.* 115, 33–46.

Isaacson, E.I. (1998). Central nervous system stimulants. In *Wilson and Gisvold's Textbook of Organic Medicinal and Pharmaceutical Chemistry*, 10th ed. (ed. J.N. Delgado and W.A. Remers). Lippincott-Raven, Philadelphia, pp. 463–477.

Johansen, S.S., Hansen, A.C., Muller, I.B., Lundmose, J.B., and Franzmann, M.B. (2003). Three fatal cases of PMA and PMMA poisoning in Denmark. *J. Anal. Toxicol.* 27, 253–256.

Johnson, M.P., Huang, X., Oberlender, R., et al. (1990). Behavioral, biochemical and neurotoxicological actions of the α-ethyl homologue of p-chloroamphetamine. *Eur. J. Pharmacol.* 191, 1–10.

Johnston, B. (1999). Hydrogen chloride generators. *J. Clan. Lab. Invest. Chem.* 9(4), 5.

Julian, P.L., and Oliver, J.J. (1943). Methyl benzyl ketone from α-phenylacetoacetonitrile. *Org. Syn. Coll.* Vol. II, 391–392.

Kacker, I.K., and Zaheer, S.H. (1951). Potential analgesics. Part I. Synthesis of substituted 4-quinazolines. *J. Ind. Chem. Soc.* 28, 344–346.

Kalant, H. (1997). Opium revisited: A brief review of its nature, composition, nonmedical use and relative risks. *Addiction* 92, 267–277.

Kalir, A., Edery, H., Pelah, Z., Balderman, D., and Porath G. (1969). 1-Phenylcyclohexylamine derivatives. II. Synthesis and pharmacological activity. *J. Med. Chem.* 12, 473.

Kemper, N. (1996). Chromium trioxide in clandestine methcathinone laboratories. *J. Clan. Lab. Invest. Chem.* 6(2), 2.

Kishi, T., Inoue, T., Suzuki, S., et al. (1983). Analysis of impurities in methamphetamine. *Eisei Kagaku* 29, 400–406.

Klatt, E.C., Montgomery, S., Nemiki, T., et al. (1986). Misrepresentation of stimulant street drugs: A decade of experience in an analysis program. *J. Toxicol. Clin. Toxicol.* 24, 441–450.

Kolecki, P. (1998). Inadvertent methamphetamine poisoning in pediatric patients. *Pediatr. Emerg. Care* 14, 385–387.

Kornfeld, E.C., Fornefeld, E.J., Kline, G.B., Mann, M.J., Morrison, D.E., Jones, R.G., and Woodward, R.B. (1956). The total synthesis of lysergic acid. *J. Am. Chem. Soc.* 78, 3087–3114.

Kram, T.C., and Kruegel, A.V. (1977). Analysis of impurities in illicit methamphetamine exhibits. III. Determination of methamphetamine and methylamine adulterant by nuclear magnetic resonance spectroscopy. *J. Forensic. Sci.* 22, 40–52.

Kummerlowe, D. (1996). Initial considerations for handling 5-gallon pressurized tanks of ammonia gas associated with clandestine drug labs. *J. Clan. Lab. Invest. Chem.* 6(4), 23–35.

Kupsch, A., Sautter, J., Gotz, M.E., Breithaupt, W., Schwarz, J., Youdim, M.B., Riederer, P., Gerlach, M., and Oertel, W.H. (2001). Monoamine oxidase inhibition and MPTP-induced neurotoxicity in the nonhuman primate: Comparison of rasagiline (TVP 1012) with selegiline. *J. Neural Transm.* 108, 985–1009.

Laboratories Amido. (1964). Patent 2782M, September 7, 1964 (France). Chemical Abstracts 62:5228b; 1965.

Lago, J.A., and Kosten, T.R. (1994). Stimulant withdrawal. *Addiction* 89, 1477–1481.

Lambrechts, M., and Rasmussen, K.E. (1984). Leuckart-specific impurities in amphetamine and methamphetamine seized in Norway. *Bull. Narc.* 36, 47–57.

Langston, J.W., and Ballard, P.A. (1983a). Parkinson's disease in a chemist working with 1-methyl-1,2,5,6-tetrahydropyridine. *NEJM* 309, 310.

Langston, J.W., Ballard, P., Tetrud, J.W., and Irwin, I. (1983b). Chronic Parkinsonism in humans due to a product of meperidine-analog synthesis. *Science* 219, 979–980.

Langston, J.W., Irwin, I., Langston, E.B., and Forno, L.S. (1984). Pargyline prevents MPTP-induced Parkinsonism in primates. *Science* 225, 1480–1482.

Lawrence, E. (1997). Meth lab found in large pharmaceutical company. *J. Clan. Lab. Invest. Chem.* 7(4), 9.

Lazarus, B. (1997). Hydrofluoric acid exposure hazards: First aid and treatment. *J. Clan. Lab. Invest. Chem.* 7(4), 24–27.

Lazarus, B. (2000). OSHA training requirements for clandestine laboratory enforcement teams. *J. Clan. Lab. Invest. Chem.* 10(1), 19–23.

Lee, D.C. (2002). Sedative–hypnotic agents. In *Goldfrank's Toxicologic Emergencies*, 7th ed. (ed. L.R. Goldfrank, N.E. Flomenbaum, N.A. Lewin, M.A. Howland, R.S. Hoffman, and L.S. Nelson. McGraw-Hill Medical, New York, pp. 940–941.

Leikin, J.B., Krantz, A.J., Zell-Lanter, M., Barkin, R.L., and Hryhorczuk, D.O. (1989). Clinical features and management of intoxication due to hallucinogenic drugs. *Med. Toxicol. Adverse Drug Exp.* 4, 324–350.

Logan, B.K. (1996). Methamphetamine and driving impairment. *J. Forensic Sci.* 41, 457–464.

Logan, B.K., Fligner, C.L., and Haddix, T. (1998). Cause and manner of death in fatalities involving methamphetamine. *J. Forensic Sci.* 43, 28–34.

Maddox, V.H., Godefroi, E.F., and Parcell, R.F. (1965). The synthesis of phencyclidine and other 1-arylcyclohexylamines. *J. Med. Chem.* 12, 473.

Magidson, O.Y., and Garkusha, G.A. (1941). The synthesis of 2-phenylisopropylamine (phenamine). *J. General Chem. (USSR)* 11, 339–343.

Mann, J. (1995). *Murder, Magic and Medicine.* Oxford, England, Oxford University Press.

Marnell, T. (1999). *The Drug Identification Bible*, 4th ed. Amera-Chem, Grand Junction, CO.

Marshall, D.R. (1999a). DEA congressional testimony. Senate Judiciary Committee, U.S. Senate, July 28, 1999.

Marshall, D.R. (1999b). Special surveillance list of chemicals, products, materials and equipment used in the clandestine production of controlled substance or listed. DEA Advisory to the Public. May 3, 1999.

Massetti, J. (1996a). Chicken feed crank. *J. Clan. Lab. Invest. Chem.* 6(4), 13.

Massetti, J. (1996b). Ignition of red phosphorus reaction mixtures. *J. Clan. Lab. Invest. Chem.* 6(4), 13.

Massetti, J. (1996c). Fumes from a two-liter flask kill three. *J. Clan. Lab. Invest. Chem.* 6(4), 13.

Massetti, J. (1997). Hypophosphorus acid use increases at California clandestine methamphetamine labs. *J. Clan. Lab. Invest. Chem.* 7(3), 6.

McKibben, T. (1997). Protecting group chemistry. *J. Clan. Lab. Invest. Chem.* 7(4), 30–42.

Meyer, E., Van Bocxlaer, J., Lambert, W., et al. (1995). α-Phenylethylamine identified in judicial samples. *Forensic Sci. Int.* 76, 159–160.

Miller, M.A., and Hughes, A.L. (1994). Epidemiology of amphetamine use in the United States. In *Amphetamine and Its Analogs—Psychopharmacology, Toxicology and Abuse* (ed. A.K. Cho and D.S. Segal). Academic Press, San Diego, pp. 439–457.

MMWR. (1984). Street drug contaminant causing Parkinsonism. *Morb. Mortal. Wkly. Rep.* 33, 351–352.

MMWR. (1988). Lead poisoning associated with intravenous-methamphetamine use—Oregon, 1988. *Morb. Mortal. Wkly. Rep.* 38, 830–831.

MMWR. (2000). Public health consequences among first responders to emergency events associated with illicit methamphetamine laboratories—Selected states, 1996–1999. *Morb. Mortal. Wkly. Rep.* 49, 1021–1024.

Morgan, J.P. (1992). Amphetamine and methamphetamine during the 1990s. *Pediatr. Rev.* 13, 330–333.

Moore, K.A., Lichtman, A.H., Poklis, A., and Borzelleca, J.F. (1995). α-Benzyl-N-methylphenethylamine (BNMPA), an impurity of illicit methamphetamine synthesis: Pharmacological evaluation and interaction with methamphetamine. *Drug Alcohol Depend.* 39, 83–89.

Moore, K.A., Ismaiel, A., and Poklis, A. (1996). α-Benzyl-*N*-methylphenethylamine (BNMPA), an impurity of illicit methamphetamine synthesis: III. Detection of BNMPA and metabolites in urine of methamphetamine users. *J. Analyt. Toxicol.* 20, 89–92.

Mundy, B.P., and Ellerd, M.G. (1988). *Name Reactions and Reagents in Organic Synthesis.* Wiley, New York.

Nakai, M., and Enomiya, T. (1987). Process for preparing phenylacetones. US Patent No. 4,638,094, granted Jan. 20, 1987.

Nichols, D.E. (1986). Differences between the mechanism of action of MDMA, MBDB, and the classical hallucinogens: Identification of a new therapeutic class: Entactogens. *J. Psychoact. Drugs* 18, 305–313.

Nichols, D.E. (1994). Medicinal chemistry and structure–activity relationships. In *Amphetamine and Its Analogs—Psychopharmacology, Toxicology and Abuse* (ed. A.K. Cho and D.S. Segal). Academic Press, San Diego, pp. 3–41.

Nimble, J.B. (1994). *The Construction and Operation of Clandestine Drug Laboratories,* 2nd ed. Loompanics Unlimited, Port Townsend, WA.

NNICC. (1998). *National Narcotics Intelligence Consumers Committee (NNIC) Report 1997: The Supply of Illicit Drugs to the United States.* Washington, DC. Drug Enforcement Administration, pp. 61–72.

Noggle, F.T., Clark, C.R., Davenport, T.W., and Coker, S.T. (1985). Synthesis, identification and acute toxicity of α-benzylphenethylamine and α-benzyl-*N*-methylphenethylamine. Contaminants in clandestine preparation of amphetamine and methamphetamine. *J. Assoc. Off. Anal. Chem.* 68, 1213–1222.

Norton, R.L., Burton, B.T., and McGirr, J. (1996). Blood lead of intravenous drug users. *J. Toxicol. Clin. Toxicol.* 34, 425–430.

Oberlender, R., and Nichols, D.E. (1991). Structural variation and (+)-amphetamine-like discriminative stimulus properties. *Pharmacol. Biochem. Behav.* 38, 581–586.

Oulton, S. (1996). Dichlorofluoroethane in the clandestine manufacture of methamphetamine. *J. Clan. Lab. Invest. Chem.* 6(4), 16–17.

Oulton, S.R., and Skinner, H.F. (1999). Reaction of common cold tablet ingredients via hydriodic acid/red phosphorus. *J. Clan. Lab. Invest. Chem.* 9(4), 21–35.

Pennell, S., Ellett, J., Rienick, C., et al. (1999). Meth matters: Report on methamphetamine users in five western cities. National Institute of Justice, Washington, DC.

Perkal, M., and White, J. (1999). "Boxed lab" with a difference. *J. Clan. Lab. Invest. Chem.* 9(1), 7.

Perrine, D.M. (1996). *The Chemistry of Mind-Altering Drugs: History, Pharmacology and Cultural Context.* American Chemical Society, Washington, DC.

Poortman-van der Meer, A.J. (2000). P-2-P and MDP-2-P coverted to cyclic ketals: A new meaning to protective chemistry. *J. Clan. Lab. Invest. Chem.* 10(1), 17–18.

Powell, W. (1970). *The Anarchist Cookbook.* Lyle Stuart, New York.

Quinn, P. (2000). Chunky red phosphorus ignites during analysis. *J. Clan. Lab. Invest. Chem.* 10(1), 2.

Rasmussen, S., Cole, R., and Spiehler, V. (1989). Methamphetamine prevalence in sheriff's crime lab samples. *J. Anal. Toxicol.* 12, 263–267.

Rebek, J., Tai, D.F., and Shue, Y.-K. (1984). Synthesis of lysergic acid from tryptophan. *J. Am. Chem. Soc.* 6, 1813–1819.

Repke, D.B., Bates, D.K., and Ferguson, W.J. (1978). Synthesis of dextroamphetamine sulfate and methamphetamine hydrochloride from D-phenylalanine. *J. Pharm. Sci.* 67(8), 1167–1168.

Reynolds, P.C., and Weingarten, H. (1983). Presentation at the Quarterly Meeting of the California Association of Toxicologists, Yosemite National Park, CA, November 5, 1983.

Sanz, P., and Prat, A. (1993). Toxicity in textile air-brushing in Spain. *Lancet* 342(8865), 240.

Schmidt, C.J., Wu, L., and Lovenberg, W. (1986). Methylenedioxymethamphetamine: A potentially neurotoxic amphetamine analog. *Eur. J. Pharmacol.* 124, 165–178.

Shaw, M.L., Carpenter, J.W., and Leith, D.E. (1995). Complications with the use of carfentanyl citrate and xylazine hydrochloride to immobilize domestic horses. *J. Am. Vet. Med. Assoc.* 206, 833–836.

Shulgin, A.T. (1981). Hallucinogens. In *Burger's Medicinal Chemistry*, 4th ed., Part III (ed. M.E. Wolff). Wiley, New York, pp. 1109–1137.

Shulgin, A.T., and MacLean, D.E. (1976). Illicit synthesis of phencyclidine and several of its analogs. *Clin. Tox.* 9, 553–560.

Shulgin, A., and Shulgin, A. (1992). *PIHKAL (Phenethylamines I Have Known and Loved): A Chemical Love Story.* Transform Press, Berkeley, CA.

Shulgin, A., and Shulgin, A. (1997). *TIHKAL (Tryptamines I Have Known and Loved): The Continuation.* Transform Press, Berkeley, CA.

Sibley, J.A. (1996). Formation of O-6-acetylmorphine in the "homebake" preparation of heroin. *Forensic Sci. Int.* 77, 159–167.

Skinner, H.F. (1990). Methamphetamine synthesis via hydriodic acid/red phosphorus reduction of ephedrine. *Forensic Sci. Int.* 48, 123–134.

Skinner, H.F. (1993). Methamphetamine synthesis via reductive alkylation hydrogenolysis of phenyl-2-propanone with N-benzylmethylamine. *Forensic Sci. Int.* 60, 155–162.

Smith, A.F. (1996). Bombs and booby traps in clandestine labs. *J. Clan. Lab. Invest. Chem.* 6(4), 9.

Smith, M.B., and March, J. (2001). *Advanced Organic Chemistry: Reactions, Mechanisms and Structure*, 5th ed. Wiley, New York.

Soine, W.H. (1986). Clandestine drug synthesis. *Med. Res. Rev.* 6, 41–74.

Soine, W.H., Vincek, W.C., and Agee, D.T. (1979). Phencyclidine contaminant generates cyanide. *NEJM* 301, 438.

Soine, W.H., Balster, R.L., Berglund, K.E., Martin, C.D., and Agee, D.T. (1982). Identification of a new phencyclidine analog, 1-(1-phenylcyclohexyl)-4-methylpiperidine, as a drug of abuse. *J. Anal. Toxicol.* 6, 41–43.

Soliman, R., and Soliman, F.S.G. (1979). A facile synthesis of 2,3-disubstituted-4-oxo-3,4-dihydroquinazolines. *Synthesis* 803–804.

Stone, R. (1996). Flash fire injures two suspects in Las Vegas. *J. Clan. Lab. Invest. Chem.* 6(3), 14.

Strange, E.D. (1998). *The NNICC Report 1997: The Supply of Illicit Drugs to the United States.* National Narcotics Intelligence Consumers Committee (NNICC), Washington, DC, November 1998, pp. 61–72.

Strassman, R.J., and Qualls, C.R. (1994a). Dose–response study of *N,N*-dimethyltryptamine in humans. I. Neuroendocrine, autonomic and cardiovascular effects. *Arch. Gen. Psychiatry* 51, 85–97.

Strassman, R.J., and Qualls, C.R. (1994b). Dose–response study of *N,N*-dimethyltryptamine in humans. II. Subjective effects and preliminary results of a new rating scale. *Arch. Gen. Psychiatry* 51, 98–108.

Tanaka, K., Ohmori, T., and Inoue, T. (1992). Analysis of impurities in illicit methamphetamine. *Forensic Sci. Int.* 56, 157–165.

Tanaka, K., Ohmori, T., Inoue, T., et al. (1994). Impurity profiling analysis of illicit methamphetamine by capillary gas chromatography. *J. Forensic Sci.* 39, 500–511.

The Press (Christchurch, NZ). (1997a). Cleanup bill at drug house costs $21,000. *J. Clan. Lab. Invest. Chem.* 7(1), 7.

The Press (Christchurch, NZ). (1997b). Residents worry odour from house is toxic. *J. Clan. Lab. Invest. Chem.* 7(1), 6–7.

Titeler, M., Lyon, R.A., and Glennon, R.A. (1988). Radioligand-binding evidence implicates the brain 5-HT$_2$ receptor as a site of action for LSD and phenylisopropylamine hallucinogens. *Psychopharmacology* 94, 213–216.

Toth, B. (2000). A review of the natural occurrence, synthetic production and use of carcinogenic hydrazines and related chemicals. *In Vivo* 14, 299–319.

Travis, J., and Vereen, D.R. (2000). *Methamphetamine Interagency Task Force: Final Report.* Federal Advisory Committee, January 2000.

Tsutsumi, M. (1953). An illegal preparation of an amphetamine-like compound. *Sci. Crime Detection* (Japan) 6, 50–52.

Vallely, P. (1996). Lithium batteries used in lithium–ammonia methamphetamine labs. *J. Clan. Lab. Invest. Chem.* 6(1), 9–11.

Vallely, P. (1997a). Sodium iodide—phosphoric acid preparation of HI. *J. Clan. Lab. Invest. Chem.* 7(3), 10.

Vallely, P. (1997b). Birch product from methylamphetamine. *J. Clan. Lab. Invest. Chem.* 7(3), 7.

Van der Schoot, J.B., Ariens, E.J., Van Rossum, J.M., et al. (1961). Phenylisopropylamine derivatives, structure and action. *Arzneim. Forsch.* 9, 902–907.

van Zyl, E.F. (2001). A survey of reported syntheses of methaqualone and some positional and structural isomers. *Forensic Sci. Int.* 122, 142–149.

Walker, L., and Doerr, J. (1999). Meth lab and bomb factory seized near Watsonville, CA. *J. Clan. Lab. Invest. Chem.* 9(4), 3.

Wassink, B.H.G., Duijndam, A., and Jansen, A.C.A. (1974). A synthesis of amphetamine. *J. Chem. Educ.* 51, 671.

Wax, P.M., Becker, C.E., and Curry, S.C. (2003). Unexpected "gas" casualties in Moscow: A medical toxicology perspective. *Ann. Emerg. Med.* 41, 700–705.

Weissman, A.D., and Caldecott-Hazard, S. (1995). Developmental neurotoxicity to methamphetamines. *Clin. Exp. Pharm. Physiol.* 22, 372–374.

West, L., Pierce, C.M., and Thomas, W.D. (1962). Lysergic acid diethylamide: Its effects on a male Asiatic elephant. *Science* 138, 1100–1103.

White, M.J. (1997). Drug lab found in suburban house after fire in Melbourne, Australia. *J. Clan. Lab. Invest. Chem.* 7(4), 4–5.

Wheeler, T.M., and Griffin, L. (1997). Phosphine linked to two deaths at clandestine methamphetamine lab. *J. Clan. Lab. Invest. Chem.* 7(4), 8.

Willers-Russo, L.J. (1996). Phosphine gas deaths in Los Angeles County. *J. Clan. Lab. Invest. Chem.* 6(4), 11.

Willers-Russo, L.J. (1999). Three fatalities involving phosphine gas, produced as a result of methamphetamine manufacturing. *J. Forensic Sci.* 44, 647–652.

Willers-Russo, L.J., and Barley, E. (1996). Dimethylsulfone encountered in Los Angeles. *J. Clan. Lab. Invest. Chem.* 6(2), 11.

Windahl, K.L., McTigue, M.J., Pearson, J.R., et al. (1995). Investigation of the impurities found in methamphetamine synthesized from pseudoephedrine by reduction with hydriodic acid and red phosphorus. *Forensic Sci. Int.* 76, 97–114.

Winek, C.L., Collom, W.D., and Bricker, J.D. (1981). A death due to 4-bromo-2,5-dimethoxyamphetamine. *Clin. Tox.* 18, 267–271.

Wolters, R.J., Bei, A.J., and Tanner, N.S. (1974). Conformationally constrained analogs of mescaline. *J. Pharm. Sci.* 63, 1379–1382.

Zuelzer, W.W., and Apt, L. (1949). Acute hemolytic anemia due to naphthalene poisoning. *JAMA* 141, 185–190.

INDEX

Page numbers followed by "f" denote figures, and those followed by "t" denote tables

Lightning Source UK Ltd.
Milton Keynes UK
UKHW050355240519
343223UK00002B/28/P